Black
Protest

History, Documents,
and Analyses
1619 TO THE PRESENT
EDITED WITH INTRODUCTION AND COMMENTARY BY
JOANNE GRANT
SECOND EDITION, WITH NEW MATERIAL

They say that freedom is a constant struggle.
They say that freedom is a constant struggle.
Oh, Lord, we've struggled so long,
We must be free, we must be free.

FAWCETT PREMIER • NEW YORK

TO VICTOR

A Fawcett Premier Book
Published by Ballantine Books

ISBN 0-449-30044-7

Manufactured in the United States of America

First Fawcett Premier Edition: February 1968
First Ballantine Books Edition: December 1983
20

The Political Perspectives Series

Two generations ago historians in the United States were calling for a "New History" that would put the study of the past at the service of the present and future. The demand is now even more urgent.

This series of books is intended to fill this need. Under the overall title "Political Perspectives," a wide variety of books will be issued in inexpensive format. The series will include original works and anthologies, as well as reprints of important older books and monographs. The common theme will be the placing of contemporary political problems in their historical perspective.

Marvin E. Gettleman

Contents

PART IX. Black Liberation

Introduction

Little white child: "I'm English, Dutch and Irish. What are you?
Little Negro child: "Nothin'."

FOR THE GREATER part of the three centuries that Negroes
have been in the United States most have felt they were, indeed, nothing. In the late 1960's, however, it is conceivable
that a large number of Negro children might reply to that
question "What are you?" with "I'm black."

Despite the pervasiveness of the concept of nothingness,
worthlessness, inferiority, the Negro has continued to assert
his worth and attempt to validate his claim to human rights.
While it could not be argued that the majority of the country's black population at any time participated in the struggle
for freedom, for citizenship, for equality, for dignity, the
history of the black man's protest against enslavement, subor-
dination, cruelty, inhumanity began with his seizure in African ports and has not yet ended.

Africans drowned in the harbors when they leaped from
slave ships and attempted to return to shore, and to escape
bondage untold numbers committed suicide during the passage.

Harvey Wish has written of mutinies on slave ships:

The insurrection itself was a desperate struggle waged with the
courage of despair. Sometimes weapons would reach the slaves
through the female captives who were frequently given comparative freedom on the deck. Naturally, in the greater number of
cases the revolt was doomed to failure, and the retribution was
swift and terrible. Every refinement of torture was utilized by the
captain, and the ring leaders, at least, were killed. Captain Harding, for example, borrowed the methods of savagery by compelling the rebels to eat the heart and liver of a sailor who had
been killed, and hanged a woman leader by her thumbs, whipping
and slashing her with knives.[1]

[1] Harvey Wish, "American Slave Insurrections Before 1861," Journal
of Negro History, Vol. XXII, July 1937, p. 302. Wish cites Elizabeth
Donnan, ed., *Documents Illustrative of the Slave Trade to America*
(Washington, 1930-35), II, 266. The Wish article is excerpted on pp.
35-45 below.

The first known revolt by slaves in the United States is that of a group of 100 African slaves (probably the first on the U.S. mainland) brought by Lucas Vasquez de Ayllon in 1526. Three months after arrival Vasquez died, the slaves revolted and the Spanish survivors returned to Haiti.[2]

Since those early revolts the Negro has used many methods to protest—from petitions to Congress and appeals to Presidents to armed uprisings. In Revolutionary days it was fairly common for slaves to save enough money to purchase their freedom, and in several cases in the North to initiate court suits, some even winning compensation for work done as slaves. Negroes petitioned for manumission, were major supporters of and active participants in the abolitionist movement, sent petitions to Congress against the anti-manumission law and the Fugitive Slave Act and to legislatures against segregated transportation and education. Throughout, from acts of sabotage by slaves to the sit-ins of the 60's, the Negro has used passive resistance as one of his methods of protest.

Requests for aid from the Government have also persisted, while at the same time Negroes consistently have maintained a sense of unrelatedness to the nation. It is common among Negroes even today to speak of "they" government or "they" war. Just as there is common rejoicing over the nose-thumbing attitude of Rep. Adam Clayton Powell in his junkets to Europe and elsewhere, there is, too, a general, though often well-hidden enjoyment of American humiliations or defeats in the international political sphere.

This reflects the real dualism of the Negro-hyphen-American. He is a citizen, yet he is not. This is his country, yet not wholly. One need not search for patriotism in the Negro-American, yet he is outside of and alienated from much of American life. Here I speak of the masses of Negroes and not of the intellectual elite or the upward-striving middle class. Alienation, both from the mainstream of American life and from the Negro elite, is readily apparent among the mass-

[2] Daniel P. Mannix and Malcolm Cowley, *Black Cargoes: A History of the Atlantic Slave Trade, 1518-1865* (New York: Viking, 1962), p. 54. The authors say the incident took place at what may have later been the site of Jamestown, Va.; however, Herbert Aptheker in *American Negro Slave Revolts* (New York: Columbia University Press, 1943), p. 163, puts the probable location at or near the mouth of the Pedee River in South Carolina. Aptheker says the Negroes remained forming the first permanent settlement, other than Indians, in the United States.

es of poorer Negroes involved in today's civil rights struggles in the South and in the Northern ghettos. "The food that Ralph Bunche eats doesn't fill my stomach," the sentiment expressed by a Mississippi Negro woman, is widespread.

Yet Negro intellectuals, as all true intellectuals, are alienated from mass culture. Thus, the late James Weldon Johnson, Negro author and former NAACP leader, would write:

> There comes a time when the most persistent integrationist becomes an isolationist, when he curses the white world and consigns it to hell. This tendency toward isolation is strong because it springs from a deep-seated natural desire—a desire for respite from the unremitting gruelling struggle; for a place in which refuge might be taken.[3]

No greater proof of the Negro's feeling of separateness exists than the Black Nationalism of today and yesterday; the separatist urge which has ebbed and flowed through the years. One of the persistent threads in the history of the Negro movement has been a demand for a positive assertion of the Negro's blackness. C. Vann Woodward in an essay "The Search for Southern Identity" commented that while Alexis de Tocqueville in an important generalization about national character said that America was "born free,"

> There *are* Americans, after all, who were not 'born free.' They are also Southerners. They have yet to achieve articulate expression of their uniquely un-American experience. This is not surprising, since white Southerners have only recently found expression of the tragic potentials of their past in literature. The Negro has yet to do that. His first step will be an acknowledgement that he is also a Southerner as well as an American.[4]

However, the Negro is convinced that his uniquely un-American experience stems from his blackness, and that acknowledgement of this is the step which must first be secured. This concept has operated within the Negro protest movement in two ways and has led it in two directions simultaneously: wanting out and wanting in.

Wanting out has been expressed in several ways. Early in the 19th century free Negroes broke away from the established churches and organized independent Negro churches to escape prejudice, at least during worship, and in order

[3] In *Charles Silberman, Crisis in Black and White* (New York: Vintage Books, 1964), pp. 145-46.

[4] C. Vann Woodward, "The Search for Southern Identity," *The Burden of Southern History* (New York: Vintage Books, Random House, 1960), p. 22.

to run their own affairs. Self-expression in the churches paved the way for similar action in other fields. The first Negro newspaper, *Freedom's Journal,* established at this same time (1827) said in its first editorial: "We wish to plead our own cause. Too long have others spoken for us."

Negroes joined together in a National Convention movement which between the years 1830 and 1861 held 11 national Negro conventions dealing with such problems as the need for training schools for Negroes, discrimination in public accommodations and the struggle for political rights. Numerous state conventions were also held during this period. Connecticut alone held 20 or more.[5]

At the convention of 1843 Henry Highland Garnet, a leading emigrationist, delivered a call to rebellion which lacked one vote for adoption by the body. After extolling the leaders of slave insurrections, Garnet said:

Brethren, arise, arise! Strike for your lives and liberties. Now is the day and the hour. Let every slave throughout the land do this, and the days of slavery are numbered. You cannot be more oppressed than you have been—you cannot suffer greater cruelties than you have already. *Rather die* freemen than live to be slaves. Remember that you are FOUR MILLIONS! . . . In the name of God, we ask, are you men? Where is the blood of your fathers? Has it all run out of your veins? Awake, awake . . .
Let your motto be resistance! *resistance!* RESISTANCE![6]

Emigration, a manifestation of wanting out which Garnet later espoused, reached a high point in the antebellum period. Numerous plans to colonize in the Caribbean area, particularly Haiti, or in Africa were advanced by prominent Negro leaders, as well as by the American Colonization Society (whose purpose was to get rid of the problem of slavery by getting rid of the slaves). President Lincoln, who long endorsed the idea of colonization, promised government aid to colonization schemes in Central America in a meeting with several Negro leaders in 1862. He said: "There is an unwillingness on the part of our people, harsh as it may be, for you free colored people to remain with us. . . . It is better for us both, therefore, to be separated."[7]

While colonization appealed to a minority of Negroes, near-

[5] For more on the convention movement see Howard H. Bell, *A Survey of the Negro Convention Movement 1839-61* (Unpublished Ph.D. thesis, Northwestern, 1953).

[6] Herbert Aptheker, ed., *A Documentary History of the Negro People in the United States* (New York: Citadel Press, 1951), p. 232.

[7] James McPherson, *The Negro's Civil War* (New York: Pantheon Books, 1965), pp. 91-92.

ly every nationally known Negro leader expressed emigrationist inclinations. There was strong opposition, however, to such government-sponsored colonization plans. A meeting of Boston Negro leaders on April 28, 1862 adopted the following concise resolutions:

Resolved, That when we wish to leave the United States we can find and pay for that territory which shall suit us best.
Resolved, That when we are ready to leave, we shall be able to pay our own expenses of travel.
Resolved, That we don't want to go now.
Resolved, That if anybody else wants us to go, they must compel us.[8]

It is estimated, however, that about 50,000 Negroes did emigrate to Canada before the Civil War, and without doubt it was only the hope aroused by the imminence of the war that reduced the interest in colonization schemes.

During the 1920's interest in emigration was revived again by Marcus Garvey whose "back to Africa" movement claimed four million adherents. Garvey's main thrust, however, was building black economic power in the ghettos of the United States, another form of opting out of the majority society.

The appeal "wanting out" held for Negroes was evidenced again in the 1930's in the popularity of the "black nation" concept of the Communist Party and in modern-day Black Nationalism which in all its various forms seeks to wrest economic and political control of the ghettos from the white power structure.

The most militant elements in the current movement tend to want *out* in the sense that they have decided to end cooperation with the Liberal Establishment, both in government and outside it, and go it alone. Manifestations of this are the Lowndes County Freedom Party which sought to take control over an Alabama county by political action, and local groups in the North which have gained control of community boards of the Office of Economic Opportunity or who demand control of local school boards.

This development has come after a period during which there was extensive consultation between Negro protest leaders and Washington. No period before the current one has seen such widespread government attention to the Negro struggle.

The development of the current government interest can be traced to two factors: the Negro vote and the Negro pro-

[8] *Ibid.*, p. 91.

test of the 1960's. The importance of the Negro vote was clear by 1944, and its role in the balance of power has increased ever since. In the 1960 election, in which the margin of the Kennedy victory was narrow, the percentage of Negro votes for the Democratic ticket was high. In the Negro wards of Chicago it was 80 percent and in Philadelphia 82 percent. Harlem gave 77.7 percent of its vote to Kennedy. This, coupled with the strength and dynamism of the Negro movement of the 1960's, served notice to the federal government that once more the Negro's condition was a matter with which to reckon. The picture of hundreds of Negro youngsters singing, jammed in a stockade in Orangeburg, South Carolina, was flashed around the world putting the Negro in America, not only in the national spotlight, but in the international as well. America set about repairing its image.

Declaring that discrimination against Negroes was not only a legal or a legislative issue, but that it was a "moral issue," President John F. Kennedy in an address on June 11, 1963, said:

Today we are committed to a world wide struggle to promote and protect the rights of all who wish to be free. And when Americans are sent to Vietnam or West Berlin we do not ask for whites only.

It ought to be possible, therefore, for American students of any color to attend any public institution they select without having to be backed up by troops. It ought to be possible for American consumers of any color to receive equal service in places of public accommodation, such as hotels and restaurants, and theaters and retail stores without being forced to resort to demonstrations in the street.

And it ought to be possible for American citizens of any color to register and to vote in a free election without interference or fear of reprisal.[9]

Kennedy called on Congress "to make a commitment it has not fully made in this century to the proposition that race has no place in American life or law."

The commitment was not fully made, yet a strong Civil Rights Act barring discrimination in public accommodations was passed in 1964 and a Voting Rights Bill in 1965, in response to the pressure of the civil rights movement. The Justice Department participated in scores of voting rights suits, and dozens of consultations and formal conferences were held between Negro leaders and the President and other feder-

9 *Public Papers of the President of the United States, John F. Kennedy, III, January 1 to November 22, 1963* (Washington: U.S. Government Printing Office, 1964), pp. 468-471.

al officials. A measure of the intimacy is the fact that scores of young civil rights workers carried the home telephone number of the head of the Justice Department's Civil Rights Division and used it to report acts of violence at any hour of the day or night.

However, much of the flurry of activity by the federal government was aimed, in the words of President Kennedy, at getting the demonstrators out of the streets and into the courts. This, too, has been the aim of large sections of the movement.

What I have described as the most militant elements of the movement is by far not the largest organized grouping. That larger part of the movement, now, as always, has wanted in; it has sought to fight for Negro rights within the system and by its rules. The main thrust of the Negro protest has been to take a rightful place in American life, side by side with white Americans. The prevailing impetus has been the adoption of the majority society's goals, methods and system of values. The primary aim has been integration, and throughout the movement's history whites and blacks have worked together toward this end. There have been repeated appeals to the federal government through the years for equality, for integration of transportation, housing, schools. Throughout, the main fight—except for the periods of separatist ascendancy —has been for the Negro to be included in the mainstream of American politics and economics.

Sometimes both tendencies have motivated Negro leaders. Booker T. Washington, for example, preached separation of the races, but sought to train Negroes to be integrated into the economic life of the country. The ultimate aim of his progam was the procurement of equal rights for Negroes.

C. Eric Lincoln has asserted that "The 'nationalism' of the American Negro is not voluntary, prompted by a desire to set himself apart in order to preserve some cultural values. It is, rather, a defensive response to external forces—hostile forces which threaten his creative existence. It is a unity born of the wish not to conserve, but to escape a set of conditions." [10]

The question which faces the country now is whether the conditions can be alleviated to such an extent that the thrust to join the majority society will prevail over the thrust to leave it or to fight to change the system itself.

As Stokely Carmichael, then chairman of the Student Non-violent Coordinating Committee, expressed it: "Let me make one thing clear: I am not saying that the goal is for

[10] C. Eric Lincoln, *Black Muslims in America* (Boston: Beacon Press, 1961), p. 45.

Negroes and other persons to be allowed to join the middle-class mainstream of American society as we see it today. Aside from the fact that at least some Negroes don't want that, such inclusion is impossible under present circumstances. For a real end to exclusion in American society, that society would have to be so radically changed that the goal cannot really be defined as inclusion." [11]

There is much truth in Carmichael's contention. Reputable sociologists have pointed to economic deprivation as the cause of low educational achievement among Negroes, of lower life expectancy, of high crime rates. And there is no solution in sight. There simply is no room in the American economy, which has an increasing labor supply and increasing displacement of workers through automation, to raise the Negro's economic standard. Racism is at the root of this economic disparity. It has long been said that the Negro is the last hired and the first fired, and there is no indication that preferential treatment for Negroes in reparation for 300 years of exploitation will solve the problem. There is a fundamental block to such a solution. This is a white man's country and culture, and no matter how much it may absorb of the black man's creative contributions it refuses to accept the black man. Dr. Kenneth B. Clark describes the white reaction:

The 'white backlash' is a new name for an old phenomenon, white resistance to the acceptance of the Negro as a human being. As the Negro demands such status—as he develops more and more effective techniques to obtain it, and as these techniques come closer to success—the resistance to his demands rises in intensity and alarm. The forms it takes vary from the overt and barbaric murders and bombings to the more subtle innuendo of irritation and disparagement.[12]

Never having been stripped of his humanness despite all he has endured, the Negro has continued to follow the advice of Frederick Douglass:

. . . there shall be no peace to the wicked . . . this guilty national shall have no peace . . . we will do all that we can to *agitate!* AGITATE! AGITATE!!! [13]

[11] Stokely Carmichael, "Who Is Qualified?" *New Republic,* Jan. 8, 1966, p. 21.
[12] Kenneth B. Clark, *Dark Ghetto* (New York: Harper & Row, 1965), p. 17.
[13] Frederick Douglass, *Resolution of the National Convention of Colored People and Their Friends,* Troy, New York, 1847.

In this volume I have attempted to collect representative documents to record the history of the Negro protest movement together with statements of opinion and interpretative material to lay the historical setting for the study of the current movement. Since the current movement has gone through many changes from the time that the Negro workers of Montgomery, Alabama, decided to walk rather than ride segregated buses to their jobs, and since, too, the current movement is what concerns us most, I have given more space to more recent documents than to those of earlier periods.

Responsibility for any error of omission or commission is mine. I wish, without attempting to share that responsibility, to express my deep appreciation to Marvin Gettleman, the editor of the series of which this volume is one, for his aid and comfort and for the prompt dispatch to me of many valuable source materials. I also want to thank Prof. C. Vann Woodward, Prof. James McPherson, Dr. Herbert Aptheker, Prof. Tilden Edelstein, Prof. Eugene Genovese, Dr. John Henrik Clarke and Elizabeth Sutherland for kindly reading draft outlines of the book and suggesting items for inclusion. That some of these were not included does not necessarily indicate disagreement, only inability to stretch the book's covers further. My special thanks to librarians who have been particularly helpful, Mr. Ernest Kaiser of the Schomberg Collection of the New York Public Library and Mrs. Jean Norrington of the *National Guardian.* My deep thanks to my editor, Mrs. Pat Mancini, to Jonathan Miller for invaluable research assistance and to Ella J. Baker for the many source materials which she provided, for her wise counsel and for her careful reading of introductory pieces on the current movement.

New York, New York
June, 1967

The Preface to the 1974 edition appears on page 507.

PART I

Slavery and the Early Protests

INTRODUCTION

THE RECORD OF the United States vis-à-vis the Negro from the beginning has given a surface appearance of ambivalence. Policy seems to have followed the ups and downs of Negro attempts to gain freedom; throughout history the government has shown a limited response to the stimuli of signals of unrest. For the most part, it has been a policy of compromise. At times when the protest was strong and the goals of a protest movement radical, significant steps were taken, but this only when sufficient pressure had built up and tension had mounted to the seeming breaking point. The question of race has always been potentially explosive and the official approach has always been tentative.

In their earliest compromise the founding fathers changed the original draft of the Declaration of Independence to exclude mention of the Negro slave. And, even in this, its first step as a nation, the country found itself embroiled in a heart-searing contradiction. For, the Declaration itself, in the form which it finally took, was a great impetus to early protests against slavery. Its very doctrine of the natural rights of man was inconsistent with slavery. Many a patriot was torn by the contradiction implicit in the Colonies' revolt against the tyranny of Great Britain during which those who fought for their own freedom were yet enslavers of other men.

In the draft of the Declaration of Independence Thomas Jefferson had written:

He [King George III] has waged cruel war against human nature itself, violating its most sacred rights of life and liberty in the persons of a distant people who never offended him, captivating and carrying them into slavery in another hemisphere, or to incur miserable death in their transportation thither. This warfare, the opprobrium of *INFIDEL* powers, is the warfare of the CHRISTIAN king of Great Britain. Determined to keep open a market where MEN should be bought and sold, he has prostituted his negative for suppressing every legislative attempt to prohibit or to restrain this execrable commerce.

Jefferson said that a condemnation of slavery was omitted because South Carolina and Georgia wanted the importation of slaves, and, he said: "Our Northern brethren also, felt a little tender under these censures; for though their people had very few slaves themselves, yet they had been pretty considerable carriers of them to others."

Then the founding fathers progressed from merely striking out an anti-slavery statement to specifically accepting slavery in the Constitution which provided that Congressional representation was to be determined by the numbers of free persons residing in each state plus three-fifths of "all other Persons." Thus, the South had greater representation than was justified by the number of voters, and the existence of unfree persons officially became an accepted circumstance.

The country's leaders had varying attitudes toward slavery. Washington was against it and in favor of gradual abolition; Jefferson was anti-slavery, but he believed that the Negro was inferior and therefore should not remain in the country were slavery to be abolished. Jefferson put forth as a "suspicion only" in *Notes on Virginia* that "the blacks are inferior to the whites in the endowments both of body and mind" and said, "This unfortunate difference of color, and perhaps of faculty, is a powerful obstacle to the emancipation of these people." He added: "Among the Romans emancipation required but one effort. The slave, when made free, might mix with, without staining the blood of his master. But with us a second is necessary, unknown to history. When freed, he is to be removed beyond the reach of mixture." [1] Benjamin Franklin took an extremely vigorous anti-slavery position as did Alexander Hamilton, John Jay and John Adams. Patrick Henry was ambivalent. "I am drawn along by the general inconvenience of living without them [but] I will not, I cannot justify it," he said.

Although Negroes had fought in the Battle of Bunker Hill, in the early days of the war they were excluded from recruit-

[1] Thomas Jefferson, *Notes on the State of Virginia* (Boston: David Carlisle, 1801), pp. 212-14.

ment or enlistment in the Revolutionary Army. It was not until after the British called on slaves to join His Majesty's forces that the ban on recruitment was reversed. (At first, the ban was lifted only as regards free Negroes; later slaves were also enlisted.) By the end of the war only two states, Georgia and South Carolina, had not recruited slaves as soldiers.

In the end, Negroes became part of the Revolutionary Army, not only as orderlies or laborers, but they fought side by side with white soldiers. Most of the 5,000 Negroes who served fought in integrated regiments.

Many slaves gained freedom through service in the war, and, in addition, many escaped servitude by running away. The presence of British troops and the fact of war itself had an unsettling effect on slavery. Historian John Hope Franklin has pointed out that "Slaves ran away in large numbers even if they had no intention of reaching the British lines. Thomas Jefferson estimated that in 1778 alone more than 30,000 Virginia slaves ran away. Ramsay, the South Carolina historian, asserted that between 1775 and 1783 his state lost at least 25,000 Negroes. It has been estimated that during the war Georgia lost about 75 percent of her 15,000 slaves." [2]

There was widespread fear of insurrection even during this early period; and the fears continued until the Civil War ended. (Even after the Civil War fear was not stilled, for while rebellion was no longer to be expected, revenge was thought to be a possibility.) Apprehension was greatest in areas where the Negro population was most concentrated. In Maryland in April, 1775, a delegation visited Gov. Robert Eden to request arms and ammunition to put down any slave uprisings. Eden supplied arms to four counties. Two months later, in South Carolina, the Council of Safety issued warnings against "instigated insurrections by our Negroes." [3] Major-General Charles Lee wrote five letters during the month of April, 1776, while at Williamsburg, Virginia, concerned with keeping firm control over slaves.[4]

Much of the fear was in reaction to revolts in the West Indies. There are countless reports of white fear, especially in the Southern areas, of the actual export of revolution from Santo Domingo and Haiti. The Southern states were afraid to

[2] John Hope Franklin, *From Slavery to Freedom* (second ed., rev. and enlarged; New York: Alfred A. Knopf, 1956, 1967), p. 133.

[3] Benjamin Quarles, *The Negro in the American Revolution* (Chapel Hill: University of North Carolina Press, 1961), p. 14.

[4] Herbert Aptheker, *American Negro Slave Revolts* (New York: Columbia University Press, 1943), p. 21.

import slaves because of this, and in 1792 South Carolina prohibited Negroes "from Africa, the West India Islands, or other places beyond the sea" from entering for two years. In 1794 North Carolina prevented "further importation and bringing of slaves." [5]

John Rutledge of South Carolina said in Congress in a debate on anti-slave laws:

These horrid effects [the St. Domingo rebellion] have succeeded what was conceived once to be trifling. Most important consequences may be the result, although gentlemen little appreciate it. . . . There have been emissaries amongst us in the Southern States; they have begun their war upon us; an actual organization has commenced; we have had them meeting in their clubrooms and debating on that subject. . . . Sir, I do believe that persons have been sent from France to feel the pulse of this country, to know whether these [i.e., the Negroes] are the proper engines to make use of: these people have been talked to; they have been tampered with . . .[6]

There was also the fear that black revolts to the south would inspire home-grown rebellion. In virtually every plantation novel, a Southern literature justifying slavery, there is mention of the fear of insurrection. Indeed, while such fears were exaggerated, there was considerable basis in fact for their existence. Dr. Aptheker reports finding records of about 250 slave revolts and conspiracies.[7]

The record is far from complete, however. It is generally conceded that news of insurrections was often suppressed because of the fear that such reports would create panic, and might encourage the spread of revolts. Despite the relative scarcity of documentary materials on rebellions, enough evidence has been amassed to prove that considerable unrest did exist. In view of the knowledge we do possess concerning slave conditions and the protests against slavery, it is somewhat surprising that the legend of the happy, docile slave singing at his work under the benevolent eye of a kindly master should have persisted. The legend has been embroidered to describe the period of segregation which followed slavery.

[5] Franklin, op. cit., pp. 149-150.

[6] W. E. Burghardt Du Bois, The Suppression of the African Slave Trade to the United States of America, 1638-1870 (New York: Longmans, Green & Co., 1896), pp. 82–83. (From Annals of Congress, 6th Cong., 1st Session.)

[7] Aptheker, op. cit., p. 162. The author explains that the tests for insurrection or conspiracy he uses are: a minimum of ten slaves involved, freedom as the apparent aim and the contemporary references calling the event an uprising, plot, insurrection, or the equivalent. Also see Wish, "American Slave Insurrections Before 1861," p. 35 and Bauer and Bauer, "Day to Day Resistance to Slavery," p. 45 below.

But the tenacity with which Americans have held to the vision of content can be explained by the fact that slavery and the degradation of a people is a moral issue which it is preferable not to have to confront. The legend even has been deliberately nourished by some historiàns who have colored the picture of plantation life by painting out the more gruesome aspects. How else could the vision of the happy slave be squared with separation of wives from husbands, children from mothers, brother from brother? How with the floggings and other brutal treatment? [8] How with the auction block?

After the War for Independence was won, the slave-holding states enacted a series of laws designed to control the slaves and protect them, as property. These Black Codes codified general attitudes that had prevailed as a matter of common understanding among the slave-holders. Enforcement of these rules was stricter after their adoption as state laws, but there was variation in compliance from state to state and even, to some extent, from plantation to plantation. Slaves were forbidden to be parties to court suits and could not testify in court except against a slave or free Negro. A slave could make no contract, could not buy or sell, and could not hire out his labor.

Many of the laws were designed to provide safeguards against insurrection. Slaves were forbidden to gather even for religious services except in the presence of a white person; they were forbidden to have Negro preachers. They could not possess arms and were forbidden to receive, transmit or possess "incendiary" literature designed to incite insurrections. They were forbidden to leave the plantation without written permission and they could not strike a white person even in self-defense.

After an insurrection or plot to revolt especially stringent laws were passed. So after the Vesey conspiracy in Charleston, South Carolina adopted regulations providing for the imprisonment of Negro seamen who entered the city while their ship was in port. After the Nat Turner insurrection [9] in Virginia, Alabama provided that attempting to teach a Negro to read, write or spell was punishable by fines of $250 to $500. The effects of the insurrection were still being felt two years later. In 1833 Gov. Robert Y. Hayne of South Carolina told the state assembly: "A state of military preparation must always be with us a state of perfect domestic security. A period of profound peace and consequent apathy may expose us

8 See excerpts from *American Slavery As It Is,* p. 72 below.

9 The Vesey conspiracy is described on p. 42 below and the Turner insurrection on pp. 53-59.

to the danger of domestic insurrection." [10] The circulation of pamphlets tending to cause insurrections was made punishable by death.

Some white Americans then, as now, did not attempt to obscure the evils of the mistreatment of Negroes. Antislavery activity was already under way during the Revolutionary period, especially among religious groups. The Quakers were among the most active, their already troubled consciences prodded by a few radical individuals. Among these were Ralph Sandiford and Benjamin Lay [11] who were so outspoken against slave-holding by Quakers that they were both expelled from the Society of Friends. Disapproval of slavery in the early days manifested itself rather obliquely in the imposition of tariffs on slave importation, though the reason may well have been fear of the slaves more than hatred of slavery. Thomas Drake, expressing this view, wrote: "In the quiet decade after 1719, the Pennsylvania Assembly, troubled like the legislatures of the non-Quaker colonies by fears of slave revolts, or by a surplus of Negroes in the province, continued to experiment with the tariff on slaves." [12] After several years of adopting non-enforcible resolutions admonishing Friends against buying slaves, the Philadelphia Yearly Meeting finally voted in 1758 to disown members who bought or sold slaves. Drake comments: ". . . the zeal of the martyr-prophets ultimately worked to the advantage of their cause. Their church might deny and disown them. At the same time it began to take a more advanced position in regard to their testimony, if only to prove its Jeremiahs wrong." [13]

While such agitation against slavery continued, free Negroes in the North found increasing non-legal restraints against their freedom. In response to one such act of discrimination Negroes founded the first Negro organization, marking the first of many withdrawals from white society. Richard Allen and Absalom Jones, two Philadelphia Negro leaders, organized the Free African Society, a mutual-aid association to help the needy. The immediate spur to its creation was an incident at St. George Methodist Episcopal Church where Negroes had been accustomed to worship along with white

[10] Message of Governor Robert Y. Hayne to the Senate and House of Representatives of South Carolina (Columbia, Nov. 26, 1833). Quoted by Harvey Wish in "American Slave Insurrections Before 1861," which is excerpted on pp. 35-45 below.

[11] Excerpts from Lay's work, p. 32 below.

[12] Thomas E. Drake, Quakers and Slavery in America (New Haven: Yale University Press, 1950), p. 39.

[13] Ibid., p. 47.

Christians. One Sunday, church officials tried forcibly to remove Jones and Allen and other Negroes to the rear of the gallery as they were kneeling in prayer. The Negroes left the church and set about forming the African Society open to members of all denominations. Subsequently two Negro churches grew out of the Society: the Bethel African Methodist Episcopal Church in 1793, headed by Allen and the St. Thomas African Episcopal Church in 1794, headed by Jones.

1. EARLY DAYS IN AMERICA

*The Middle Passage**

DANIEL P. MANNIX AND MALCOLM COWLEY

As soon as an assortment of naked slaves was taken aboard a Guineaman, the men were shackled two by two, the right wrist and ankle of one to the left wrist and ankle of another. Then they were sent to the hold or, at the end of the eighteenth century, to the "house" that the sailors had built on deck. The women—usually regarded as fair prey for the sailors—and the children were allowed to wander by day almost anywhere on the vessel, though they spent the night between decks in other rooms than the men's. All the slaves were forced to sleep without covering on bare wooden floors, which were often constructed of unplaned boards. In a stormy passage the skin over their elbows might be worn away to the bare bones.

William Bosman says, writing in 1701, "You would really wonder to see how these slaves live on board; for though their number sometimes amounts to six or seven hundred, yet by careful management of our masters of ships"—the Dutch masters, that is—"they are so regulated that it seems incredible: And in this particular our nation exceeds all other Europeans; for as the French, Portuguese and English slave-ships are always foul and stinking; on the contrary ours are for the most part clean and neat." Slavers of every nation insisted

* From Daniel P. Mannix and Malcolm Cowley, *Black Cargoes, A History of the Atlantic Slave Trade,* pp. 104-7. Copyright © 1962 by Daniel Mannix. All Rights Reserved. Reprinted by permission of The Viking Press, Inc.

that their own vessels were the best in the trade. Thus, James Barbot, Jr., who sailed on an English ship to the Congo in 1700, was highly critical of the Portuguese. He admits that they made a great point of baptizing the slaves before taking them board, but then, "It is pitiful," he says, "to see how they crowd those poor wretches, six hundred and fifty or seven hundred in a ship, the men standing in the hold ty'd to stakes, the women between decks and those that are with child in the great cabin and the children in the steeridge which in that hot climate occasions an intolerable stench." This youngest Barbot adds, however, that the Portuguese provided the slaves with coarse thick mats, which were "softer for the poor wretches to lie upon than the bare decks . . . and it would be prudent to imitate the Portuguese in this point." The English never displayed that sort of prudence, and neither did they imitate the Dutch, who had special ships built for the trade, Barbot says, "very wide, lofty and airy betwixt decks, with gratings and scuttles . . . to let in more air. Some also have small ports . . . and that very much contributes to the preservation of those poor wretches who are so thick crowded together."

There were two schools of thought among the Guinea captains, called the "loose-packers" and the "tight-packers." The former argued that by giving the slaves a little more room, with better food and a certain amount of liberty, they reduced the mortality among them and received a better price for each slave in the West Indies. The tight-packers answered that although the loss of life might be greater on each of their voyages, so too were the net receipts from a larger cargo. If many of the survivors were weak and emaciated, as was often the case, they could be fattened up in a West Indian slave yard before being offered for sale. The argument between the two schools continued as long as the trade itself, but for many years after 1750 the tight-packers were in the ascendant. So great was the profit on each slave landed alive in the West Indies that hardly a captain refrained from loading his vessel to her utmost capacity. The hold of a slaving vessel was usually about five feet high. That seemed like waste space to the Guinea merchants, so they built a shelf or platform in the middle of it, extending six feet from each side of the vessel. When the bottom of the hold was completely covered with flesh, another row of slaves was packed on the platform. If there was as much as six feet of vertical space in the hold, a second platform might be installed above the first, sometimes leaving only twenty inches of headroom for the slaves; they could not sit upright during the whole voyage.

The Reverend John Newton writes from personal observation:

The cargo of a vessel of a hundred tons or a little more is calculated to purchase from 220 to 250 slaves. Their lodging rooms below the deck which are three (for the men, the boys and the women) besides a place for the sick, are sometimes more than five feet high and sometimes less; and this height is divided toward the middle for the slaves lie in two rows, one above the other, on each side of the ship, close to each other like books upon a shelf. I have known them so close that the shelf would not easily contain one more.

The poor creatures, thus cramped, are likewise in irons for the most part which makes it difficult for them to turn or move or attempt to rise or to lie down without hurting themselves or each other. Every morning, perhaps, more instances than one are found of the living and the dead fastened together.

Dr. Falconbridge stated in his Parliamentary testimony that "he made the most of the room," in stowing the slaves, "and wedged them in. They had not so much room as a man in his coffin either in the length or breadth. When he had to enter the slave deck, he took off his shoes to avoid crushing the slaves as he was forced to crawl over them." Taking off shoes on entering the hold seems to have been a widespread custom among surgeons. Falconbridge "had the marks on his feet where [the slaves] bit and pinched him."

In 1788 Captain Parrey of the Royal Navy was sent to measure such of the slave vessels as were then lying at Liverpool and to make a report to the House of Commons. He discovered that the captains of many slavers possessed a chart showing the dimensions of the ship's half deck, lower deck, hold, platforms, gunroom, orlop, and great cabin, in fact of every crevice into which slaves might be wedged. Miniature black figures were drawn on some of the charts to illustrate the most effective method of packing in the cargo.

On the *Brookes*, which Captain Parrey considered to be typical, every man was allowed a space six feet long by sixteen inches wide (and usually about two feet, seven inches high); every woman, a space five feet, ten inches long by sixteen inches wide; every boy, five feet by fourteen inches; every girl, four feet, six inches by twelve inches. The *Brookes* was a vessel of 320 tons. By the law of 1788 it was permitted to carry 454 slaves, and the chart, which later became famous, showed how and where 451 of them could be stowed away. Captain Parrey failed to see how the captain could find room for three more. Nevertheless, Parliament was told by reliable witnesses, including Dr. Thomas Trotter, formerly surgeon of the *Brookes*, that before the new law was passed she had carried 600 slaves on one voyage and 609 on another.

*   *   *

Quaker Resolution Against Slavery, 1652*

AT A GENERAL COURT held in Warwick the 18th. of May, 1652

Whereas their is a common course practiced among Englishmen, to buy negroes to that end that they may have them for service or as slaves forever; for the preventing of such practices among us, let it be ordered, that no black mankind or white being shall be forced, by covenant, bond, or otherwise, to serve any man or his assignees longer than ten years, or until they come to be twenty-four years of age, if they be taken in under fourteen, from the time of their coming within the liberties of this Colony—at the end or term of ten years, to set them free as the manner is with the English servants. And that man that will not let them go free, or shall sell them away elsewhere, to that end they may be enslaved to others for a longer time, he or they shall forfeit to the colony forty pounds.

Mennonites Protest Slavery, 1688†

This is to the monthly meeting held at Richard Worrell's:

These are the reasons why we are against the traffic of mens-body, as followeth: Is there any that would be done or handled at this manner? viz., to be sold or made a slave for all the time of his life? How fearful and faint-hearted are many at sea, when they see a strange vessel, being afraid it

---

* From *The Friend*, IV, Seventh Day; English Month, 1831, No. 46, p. 363. A copy of this resolution was sent to *The Friend* in 1831 by a 93-year-old New Englander named Moses Brown who wrote that "it shows the inhabitants of that day had a much better idea of liberty and the rights of man, than too many of their descendants now have." The effect of the resolution was to give Negroes the same status as white indentured servants.

† Resolution of Germantown Mennonites, April 18, 1688, in Samuel W. Pennypacker, "The Settlement of Germantown and the Causes which led to it," *The Pennsylvania Magazine of History and Biography*, IV, 1880, pp. 28-30.

should be a Turk, and they should be taken, and sold for slaves into Turkey. Now, what is *this* better done, than Turks do? Yea, rather it is worse for them, which say they are Christians; for we hear that the most part of such negers are brought hither against their will and consent, and that many of them are stolen. Now, though they are black, we cannot conceive there is more liberty to have them slaves, as it is to have other white ones. There is a saying, that we should do to all men like as we will be done ourselves; making no difference of what generation, descent, or colour they are. And those who steal or rob men, and those who buy or purchase them, are they not all alike? Here is liberty of conscience, which is right and reasonable; here ought to be likewise liberty of the body, except of evil-doers, which is another case. But to bring men hither, or to rob and sell them against their will, we stand against. In Europe there are many oppressed for conscience-sake; and here there are those oppressed which are of a black colour. And we who know that men must not commit adultery—some do commit adultery *in* others, separating wives from their husbands, and giving them to others: and some sell the children of these poor creatures to other men. Ah! do consider well this thing, you who do it, if you would be done at this manner—and if it is done according to Christianity! You surpass Holland and Germany in this thing. This makes an ill report in all those countries of Europe, where they hear of [it], that the Quakers do here handel men as they handel there the cattle. And for that reason some have no mind or inclination to come hither. And who shall maintain this your cause, or plead for it? Truly, we cannot do so, except you shall inform us better hereof, viz.: that Christians have liberty to practice these things. Pray, what thing in the world can be done worse towards us, than if men should rob or steal us away, and sell us for slaves to strange countries; separating husbands from their wives and children. Being now this is not done in the manner we would be done at; therefore, we contradict, and are against this traffic of men-body. And we who profess that it is not lawful to steal, must, likewise, avoid to purchase such things as are stolen, but rather help to stop this robbing and stealing, if possible. And such men ought to be delivered out of the hands of the robbers, and set free as in Europe. Then is Pennsylvania to have a good report, instead, it hath now a bad one, for this sake, in other countries; Especially whereas the Europeans are desirous to know in what manner *the Quakers* do rule in *their* province; and most of them do look upon us with an envious eye. But if this is done well, what shall we say is done evil?

If once these slaves (which they say are so wicked and stubborn men,) should join themselves—fight for their freedom, and handel their masters and mistresses, as they did handel them before; will these masters and mistresses take the sword at hand and war against these poor slaves, like, as we are able to believe, some will not refuse to do? Or, have these poor negers not as much right to fight for their freedom, as you have to keep them slaves?

Now consider well this thing, if it is good or bad. And in case you find it to be good to handel these blacks in that manner, we desire and require you hereby lovingly, that you may inform us herein, which at this time never was done, viz., that Christians have such a liberty to do so. To the end we shall be satisfied on this point, and satisfy likewise our good friends and acquaintances in our native country, to whom it is a terror, or fearful thing, that men should be handelled so in Pennsylvania.

This is from our meeting at Germantown, held ye 18th of the 2d month, 1688, to be delivered to the monthly meeting at Richard Worrell's.

> Garret Henderich,
> Derick op de Graeff,
> Francis Daniel Pastorius,
> Abram op de Graeff.

Slaves Petition for Freedom During Revolutionary War*

Boston, April 20th, 1773

SIR, THE EFFORTS made by the legislative of this province in their last sessions to free themselves from slavery, gave us, who are in that deplorable state, a high degree of satisfaction. We expect great things from men who have made such a noble stand against the designs of their *fellow-men* to enslave them. We cannot but wish and hope Sir, that you will have the same grand object, we mean civil and religious liberty, in view in our next session. The divine spirit of *freedom*, seems to fire every humane breast on this continent, except such as are bribed to assist in executing the execrable plan.

We are very sensible that it would be highly detrimental to

* Herbert Aptheker, ed. *A Documentary History of the Negro People in the United States* (New York: The Citadel Press, 1951), pp. 6-9. By permission.

our present masters, if we were allowed to demand all that of *right* belongs to us for past services; this we disclaim. Even the *Spaniards*, who have not those sublime ideas of freedom that English men have, are conscious that they have no right to all the services of their fellow-men, we mean the *Africans*, whom they have purchased with their money; therefore they allow them one day in a week to work for themselves, to enable them to earn money to purchase the residue of their time, which they have a right to demand in such portions as they are able to pay for (a due appraizement of their services being first made, which always stands at the purchase money). We do not pretend to dictate to you Sir, or to the Honorable Assembly, of which you are a member. We acknowledge our obligations to you for what you have already done, but as the people of this province seem to be actuated by the principles of equity and justice, we cannot but expect your house will again take our deplorable case into serious consideration, and give us that ample relief from, *as men,* we have a natural right to.

But since the wise and righteous governor of the universe, has permitted our fellow men to make us slaves, we bow in submission to him, and determine to behave in such a manner as that we may have reason to expect the divine approbation of, and assistance in, our peaceable and lawful attempts to gain our freedom.

We are willing to submit to such regulations and laws, as may be made relative to us, until we leave the province, which we determine to do as soon as we can, from our joynt labours procure money to transport ourselves to some part of the Coast of *Africa,* where we propose a settlement. We are very desirous that you should have instructions relative to us, from your town, therefore we pray you to communicate this letter to them, and ask this favor for us.

In behalf of our fellow slaves in this province, and by order of their Committee.
Peter Bestes, Sambo Freeman, Felix Holbrook, Chester Joie.

For the Representative of the town of Thompson.

To his Excellency Thomas Gage Esq. Captain General and Governor in Chief in and over this Province.
To the Honourable his Majestys Council and the Honourable House of Representatives in General Court assembled May 25, 1774
The Petition of a Grate Number of Blacks of this Prov-

ince who by divine permission are held in a state of Slavery within the bowels of a free and Christian Country

Humbly Shewing

That your Petitioners apprehind we have in common with all other men a naturel right to our freedoms without Being depriv'd of them by our fellow men as we are a freeborn Pepel and have never forfeited this Blessing by aney compact or agreement whatever. But we were unjustly dragged by the cruel hand of power from our dearest frinds and sum of us stolen from the bosoms of our tender Parents and from a Populous Pleasant and plentiful country and Brought hither to be made slaves for Life in a Christian land. Thus we are deprived of every thing that hath a tendency to make life even tolerable, the endearing ties of husband and wife we are strangers to for we are no longer man and wife than our masters or mistresses thinkes proper marred or onmarred. Our children are also taken from us by force and sent maney miles from us wear we seldom or ever see them again there to be made slaves of for Life which sumtimes is vere short by Reson of Being dragged from their mothers Breest Thus our Lives are imbittered to us on these accounts By our deplorable situation we are rendered incapable of shewing our obedience to Almighty God how can a slave perform the duties of a husband to a wife or parent to his child How can a husband leave master to work and cleave to his wife How can the wife submit themselves to there husbands in all things How can the child obey thear parents in all things. There is a great number of us sencear . . . members of the Church of Christ how can the master and the slave be said to fulfil that command Live in love let Brotherly Love contuner and abound Beare yea onenothers Bordenes How can the master be said to Beare my Borden when he Beares me down whith the Have chanes of slavery and operson against my will and how can we fulfill our parte of duty to him whilst in this condition and as we cannot searve our God as we ought whilst in this situation. Nither can we reap an equal benefet from the laws of the Land which doth not justifi but condemns Slavery or if there had bin aney Law to hold us in Bondage we are Humbely of the Opinion ther never was aney to inslave our children for life when Born in a free Countrey. We therfor Bage your Excellency and Honours will give this its deer weight and consideration and that you will accordingly cause an act of the legislative to be pessed that we may obtain our Natural right our freedoms and our children be set at lebety at the yeare of twenty one for whoues sekes more petequeley your Petitioners is in Duty ever to pray.

Petition Against Poll Tax[*]

To the honourable David Ramsay Esquire President of the Honourable Senate, and to the others the Honourable the Members of the same—

The Petition of John Morris William Morris and other Inhabitants of Camden District in behalf of themselves and others who come under the description of Free Negroes Mulattoes and Mustizoes—

Humbly Sheweth

That with submission your Petitioners beg leave to observe that they conceive their ancestors merited the Publick confidence and obtained the Title of a Free People by rendering some particular Services to their Country, which the Wisdom & goodness of Government thought just and right to notice and to reward their Fidelity with Emancipation, & other singular Privileges.

That before the War, and till very lately your Petitioners who were Freeholders or Tradesmen, paid a Tax only for their Lands, trades, and other Taxable property in common with others the Free White Citizens of the State, and in consequence of their paying the same, was Exempted from paying a Pole-Tax for any of their children while under their Jurisdiction.—

That in March 1789, an Ordinance was passed that a Tax of One fourth of a Dollar per head per Annum be Imposed upon all Negroes Mustizoes & Mulattoes: the same to commence in February 1791, and from thence continue for the space of Ten years.—

That by a Subsequent Act, Intitled an Act for raising Supplies for the year of our Lord One thousand seven hundred and ninety two, past the 21st day of December last past, your Petitioners besides paying a Tax for their Lands & other Taxable property are made liable & have accordingly paid the sum of Two Dollars per head for themselves—the same sum per head for their Wives—and the same sum per head for each of their Children above Sixteen Years of age, who are under their Jurisdiction:

That your Petitioners are generally a Poor needy People;

* Petition of free Negroes to the South Carolina legislature, 1793, 1794, in Herbert Aptheker, "South Carolina poll tax, 1737-1895," *Journal of Negro History*, XXXI (April, 1946), pp. 134-136. By permission.

have frequently large Families to maintain; and find it exceeding difficult and distressing to support the same, and
answer the large demands of the Publick; which appears to
them considerably more than double what was formerly Exacted from them; In consequence of which they conceive
their Situation in life but a small remove from Slavery; that
they are likely to suffer continued inconvenience & disadvan-
tages; and in the end to be reduced to poverty and want itself.—

In confidence therefore of the high Opinion we entertain
of your Honours Veracity, and readiness to redress every
Grievance which may appear really such, We do most humbly Pray, That Your Honours would condescend to take the
distressed Case of your Petitioners into your wise Consideration, and Vouchsafe to Grant them such relief as your Honours in your Wisdom shall see meet.—

And your Petitioners as in duty bound shall ever Pray &c

All Slave-keepers that Keep the Innocent
in Bondage; Apostates*

BENJAMIN LAY

MATTH. VII. 17. *Every good Tree bringeth good Fruit, but a
corrupt Tree bringeth evil fruit.* Is there any eviler Fruit in
the world than Slave-keeping? any thing more devilish? it is
of the very Nature of Hell itself, and is the Belly of Hell.

Verse 18: *A good Tree cannot bring forth* such cursed *evil
Fruit* as Slave-trading, if this Practice be the worst, the greatest Sin in the World (with what goes and grows with it) as it
is, to be sure. But if any should say that good Trees, good
odious, to be sure, and is very foul in Ministers especially.
Let them keep on their Sheeps Cloathing, and preach and
pray as long as they may, until their Tongues are weary, and
their Hearers Ears too; they'll preach more to Hell, I firmly

---

* *All Slave-Keepers that Keep the Innocent in Bondage, Apostates,*
Benjamin Lay (Philadelphia: Printed by the author, 1737), pp. 27-30,
61-2, 87, 91-93. Lay was among a small number of early eighteenth
century Quakers who took a radical position toward slave-holding. His
book excerpted here, was printed by Benjamin Franklin who prudently
kept his name off the title page as he had done with other anti-slavery
works.

believe, than they will to Heaven, while they continue in said Practice.

For Custom in Sin, hides, covers as it were, takes away the Guilt of Sin. Long Custom, the Conveniency of Slaves working for us, waiting and tending continually on us, beside the Washing, cleaning, scouring, cooking very nicely fine and curious, sewing, knitting, darning almost over at hand and command; and in other Places milling, churning, cheese-maling, and all the Drudgery in Dairy and Kitchin, within doors and without. And the proud, dainty, lazy Daughters sit with their Hands before 'em, like some of the worst idle Sort of Gentlewomen, and if they want a Trifle, rather than rise from their Seats, call the poor Slave from her drudgery to come and wait upon them. . . .

Now, dear Friends, behold a Mystery! These Ministers that be Slave-keepers, and are in such very great Repute, such eminent Preachers, given to Hospitality, charitable to the Poor, loving to their Neighbours, just in their Dealings, temperate in their Lives, visiting of the Sick, sympathising with the Afflicted in Body, or Mind, very religious seemingly, and extraordinary devout and demure, and in short strictly exact in all their Decorums, except Slave-keeping, these, these be the Men, and the Women too, for the Devil's purpose, and are the choicest Treasures the Devil can or has to bring out of his Lazaretto, to establish Slave-keeping. By these Satan works Wonders many ways. These are the very Men, or People of both Sexes, that come the nearest the Scribes and Pharisees of any People in the whole World, if not sincere: For the Scribes were exact and demure seemingly in their Appearance before Men, according to Christ's Account of them, and yet the worst Enemies the dear Lamb had, or that the Devil could procure for or against him. And I do surely believe that one such as these, now in this our Day, in this very Country, does more Service for the Devil, and Hurt in the Church, in Slave-keeping, than twenty Publicans and Harlots: For by their extraordinary conduct, in Hypocracy, smooth and plausible appearance, they draw into the snare almost insensibly, and so beguile unstable Souls . . .

I suppose the pure holy eternal Being, which made of one Blood all Nations of Men to dwell upon the face of the Earth, did not make others to be Slaves to us, any more than we to be so to them; if God has appointed the Bounds of their Habitation, what Man fearing God, dare to remove or receive them when they are removed?

How did many Dear Friends like to be banished from their Native Countries, from Wives, Children and Friends, although but for a few Years, both from *Old* and *New England* especially? are all these Things forgotten by us, and a thousand time more; are the Progeny in this Age, doing the Same Things themselves, which their Progenitors so greatly complained of, and justly too; but this Progeny have been and are acting a Thousand times worse, and more cruelly; for our dear and worthy Friends and Progenitors were Banished from *England* but for a few Years, and where they might and did Preach and help forward the Gospel of Christ; but the poor Slaves and their Progeny, have been Stolen, Banished, Tortured and Tormented, for ever more; to the great and unutterable hinderance of the Blessed Gospel of Preach and Salvation, for which our dear Progenitors, suffered so deeply by their Persecutors.

And now this is carried on, encouraged and done by them, that profess to be lead by the same pure Holy Spirit, as their Progenitors were. . . .

I have understood lately, that some have made their Wills when they were Sick, to set their Negroes free at such an Age, 30 or 40, after their Death; that will not salve the Sore, it is too deep and rotten, God will not be mocked so, nor Wise men neither; they rather think of the old Proverb, it may be.

When the Devil was Sick, the Devil a Monk would be,
But when the Devil was well, the Devil a Monk was he. . . .

Now Friends, you that are Slave-keepers, I pray and beseech ye, examine your own Hearts, and see and feel too, if you have not the same answer from Truth now within; while you Preach and exhort others to Equity, and to do Justice and love Mercy, and to walk humbly before the Lord and his People, and you yourselves live and act quite contrary, behave proudly, do unjustly and unmercifully, and live in and encourage the grossest Iniquity in the whole World. For I say, you are not beyond Gospel, Law, *Abraham,* Prophets, Patriarchs, to *Cain* the Murtherer, and beyond him too, to the Devil himself, beyond *Cain,* for he Murthered but one, that we know of, but you have many Thousands, and caused 'em to be so, and for ought I know many Hundreds of Thousands . . . What do you think of these things, you brave Gospel Ministers? that keep poor Slaves to Work for you to maintain you and yours in Pride, Pride and much Idleness or Laziness, and Fulness of Bread, the Sons of *Sodom:* How do these Things become your plain Dress, Demure Appearance, feigned Humility, all but Hypocrisy, which according to Truth's Testimony, must have the hottest Place in Hell; to keep those miserable Creatures at hard Labour continually, into their old Age, in Bondage and sore captivity, working out their Blood and Sweat, and Bowels, youthful strength and vigour, when you drop into your Graves, go to your Places ordained or appointed for you; so leave these poor unhappy Creatures in their worn-out old Age, to your proud, Dainty Lazy, Scornful, Tyrannical, and often beggerly Children, for them to Domineer and Tyrannize over, cursing them and you in your Graves, for working out their youthful Blood and strength for you, and then leave 'em to be a Plague to us; and then of the abuses, miseries and cruelties those miserable worn-out Slaves go through, no Tongue can express, starved with Hunger, perish with Cold, rot as they go, for want of every an Humane Creature; so that Dogs and Cats are much better taken care for, and yet some have the Confidence, or rather Impudence, to say their Slaves or Negroes live as well as themselves. I could almost wish such hardened, unthinking, Sinful devilish Lyars were put into their Places, at least for a time, in a very hard Service, that they might feel a little in themselves, of what they make so light of in other People . . .

2. SLAVE REVOLTS AND RESISTANCE

*American Slave Insurrections Before 1861**

HARVEY WISH

A GRAPHIC ILLUSTRATION of the cyclic fears of Negro uprisings during the 1830's is afforded by the remarks of several whites of Mississippi in 1859 to Frederick L. Olmsted:

Where I used to live (Alabama) I remember when I was a boy—must ha' been about twenty years ago—folks was dreadful frightened about the niggers. I remember they built pens in the woods where they could hide and Christmas time they went and got into the pens, fraid the niggers was risin'.[1]

The speaker's wife added her recollection to this comment:

* Harvey Wish, "American Slave Insurrections Before 1861," *Journal of Negro History*, XXII (July, 1937), pp. 229-320. Reprinted by permission.

[1] Frederick Law Olmsted, *A Journey in the Back Country* (New York, 1860), 203.

I remember the same time where we was in South Carolina, we had all our things put up in bags so we could tote 'em if we heard they was comin' our way.[2]

Slave outbreaks and plots appeared both North and South during the Colonial period. Sometimes the white indentured servants made common cause with the Negroes against their masters. This was the case in 1663 when a plot of white servants and Negroes was betrayed in Gloucester County, Virginia.[3] The eastern counties of Virginia, where the Negroes were rapidly outnumbering the whites, suffered from repeated scares in 1687, 1709, 1710, 1722, 1723, and 1730.[4] A patrol system was set up in 1726 in parts of the state and later extended. Attempts were made here as elsewhere to check the importation of slaves by high duties.

Two important slave plots, one a serious insurrection, disturbed the peace of New York City in 1712 and 1741. In revenge for ill-treatment by their masters, twenty-three Negroes rose on April 6, 1712, to slaughter the whites and killed nine before they were overwhelmed by a superior force. The retaliation showed an unusual barbarous strain on the part of the whites. Twenty-one Negroes were executed, some were burnt, others hanged, and one broken on the wheel.[5] In 1741 another plot was reported in New York involving both whites and blacks. A white, Hewson (or Hughson), was accused of providing the Negroes with weapons. He and his family were executed; likewise, a Catholic priest was hanged as an accomplice. Thirteen Negro leaders were burnt alive, eighteen hanged, and eighty transported.[6] Popular fears of further insurrections led the New York Assembly to impose a prohibitive tax on the importation of Negroes. This tax, however, was later rescinded by order of the British Commissioner for Trade and Plantations.[7]

[2] *Ibid.*

[3] Ulrich B. Phillips, *American Negro Slavery* (New York, 1918), 472.

[4] William P. Palmer, ed., *Calendar of Virginia State Papers* (Richmond, 1875), I (1652-1781), 129-130; also James Curtis Ballagh, *A History of Slavery in Virginia* (Baltimore, 1902), 79-80; also Coffin, *Principal Slave Insurrections*, 11.

[5] Letter of Governor Robert Hunter to the Lords of Trade in E. B. O'Callaghan, ed., *Documents Relative to the Colonial History of the State of New York* (Albany, 1855), V (1707-1733), 341-2.

[6] *Gentleman's Magazine*, XI (1741), 441.

[7] Elizabeth Donnan, ed., *Documents Illustrative of the Slave Trade to America* (Washington, 1930-35), III, 409. (Hereafter: *D.S.T.*) Joshua Coffin also reports plots and actual outbreaks in other slaveholding areas in the Northern Colonies. East Boston is said to have experienced a minor uprising in 1638. In 1723, a series of incendiary fires in Boston led the selectmen to suspect a slave plot and the militia was ordered to police the slaves. Another plot was reported in Burlington, Pennsylvania during 1734. Coffin, *Principal Slave Insurrections*, 10, 11, 12.

The situation in colonial South Carolina was worse than in her sister states. Long before rice and indigo had given way to King Cotton, the early development of the plantation system had yielded bumper crops of slave uprisings and plots. An insurrection, resulting in the deaths of three whites, is reported for May 6, 1720.[8] Ten years later an elaborate plot was discovered in St. John's Parish by a Negro servant of Major Cordes. This plan was aimed at Charleston, an attack that was to inaugurate a widespread war upon the planters. Under the pretense of conducting a "dancing bout" in the city and in St. Paul's Parish the Negroes gathered together ready to seize the available arms for the attack. At this point the militia descended upon the blacks and killed the greater number, leaving few to escape.[9]

Owing partly to Spanish intrigues the same decade in South Carolina witnessed many more uprisings. An outbreak is reported for November, 1738.[10] The following year, on September 9, the Stono uprising created panic throughout the southeast. About twenty Angola Negroes assembled at Stono under their captain, Tommy, and marched toward Spanish territory, beating drums and endeavoring to attract other slaves. Several whites were killed and a number of houses burnt or plundered. As the "army" paused in a field to dance and sing they were overtaken by the militia and cut down in a pitched battle.[11] The following year an insurrection broke out in Berkeley County.[12] Charleston was threatened repeatedly by slave plots.[13] These reports are confirmed officially in the petition of the South Carolina Assembly to the King on July 26, 1740. Among the grievances of 1739 the Assembly complained of:

. . . an insurrection of our slaves in which many of the Inhabitants were murdered in a barbarous and cruel manner; and that no sooner quelled than another projected in Charles Town, and a third lately in the very heart of the Settlements, but happily discovered in time enough to be prevented.[14]

8 Coffin, *Principal Slave Insurrections*, 11.

9 Edward Clifford Holland, *A Refutation of the Columnies Circulated Against the Southern and Western States Respecting the Institution and Existence of Slavery* (Charleston, 1822), 68-69, 81.

10 Ralph Betts Flander, *Plantation Slavery in Georgia* (Chapel Hill, 1933), 24.

11 *Gentleman's Magazine*, X (1740), 127-8.

12 See the Constable's bill in the *Magazine of American History*, XXV (1891), 85-6.

13 Edward McGrady, *The History of South Carolina Under the Royal Government (1719-1776)*, (New York, 1899), 5.

14 Appendix to Holland, *A Refutation of the Calumnies*, —, 71. Another plot of December 17, 1765, is mentioned in *D.S.T.*, IV, 415.

Repercussions of slave uprisings in South Carolina sometimes affected Georgia as well. This was particularly true in
1738.[15] In 1739 a plot was discovered in Prince George
County.[16] To many slaves St. Augustine on Spanish soil
seemed a welcome refuge from their masters.

Indications of many other insurrections in the American
Colonies may be inferred from the nature of early patrol
laws: The South Carolina law of 1704 for example contains
a reference in its preamble to recent uprisings in that
Colony.[17] In the British and French possessions to the south,
particularly in the West Indies, affairs were much worse and
put the planter of the North in constant fear of importing rebellious slaves and the contagion of revolt.

In considering the insurrections of the national period, it is
at once evident that abolitionist propaganda played a relatively minor role despite the charges of southern politicians
after 1831. The genealogy of revolt extends much further
back than the organized efforts of anti-slavery advocates. It is
true, however, that white men played an important role in
many Negro uprisings, frequently furnishing arms, and even
leadership, as well as inspiration.[18] The motives for such assistance varied from philanthropy to unadulterated self-interest. As might be expected, insurrections tended to occur
where King Cotton and his allies were most firmly en-
trenched and the great plantation system established.

Slave unrest seems to have been far greater in Virginia
rather than in the states of the Lower South. Conspiracies
like those of Gabriel in 1800 and Nat Turner in 1831 attained national notoriety. The Gabriel plot was developed in
the greatest secrecy upon the plantation of a harsh slave-mas-
ter, Thomas Prosser, several miles from Richmond. Under
the leadership of a young slave, Gabriel, and inspired by the
examples of San Domingo and the emancipation of the ancient Israelites from Egypt, some eleven hundred slaves had
taken an oath to fight for their liberty. Plans were drawn for
the seizure of an arsenal and several other strategic buildings

15 Flanders, *Plantation Slavery in Georgia*, 24; similarly, South Carolina's slave plots sometimes required the assistance of North Carolina
as in the scare of 1766. William L. Saunders, ed., *Colonial Records
of North Carolina* (Raleigh, 1890), VIII (1769-1771), 559.

16 Jeffrey R. Brackett, *The Negro in Maryland* (Baltimore, 1889),
93.

17 H. M. Henry, *The Police Control of the Slave in South Carolina*
(Vanderbilt University, 1914), 30.

18 One aspect of this subject is discussed in James Hugo Johnston's
article, "The Participation of White Men in Virginia Negro Insurrections," *Journal of Negro History*, XVI (1931), 158-167.

of Richmond which would precede a general slaughter of all
hostile whites. After the initial successes, it was expected that
fifty thousand Negroes would join the standard of revolt. Beyond this point, the arrangements were hazy.[19] A faithful
slave however exposed the plot and Governor James Monroe
took rapid measures to secure the cooperation of the local
authorities and the federal cavalry. Bloodshed was averted by
an unprecedented cloudburst on the day set for the conspiracy
and the utter demoralization of the undisciplined "army." . . .

Between Gabriel's abortive plot and the Nat Turner uprising, several more incidents occurred which disturbed the
sleep of Virginians. In January, 1802, Governor Monroe received word of a plot in Nottaway County. Several Negroes
suspected of participation were executed.[20] That same year
came disclosures of a projected slave uprising in Goochland
County aided by eight or ten white men.[21] Several plots were
reported in 1808 and 1809 necessitating almost continuous
patrol service.[22] The war of 1812 intensified the apprehen-
sions of servile revolt. Petitions for troops and arms came
during the summer of 1814 from Caroline County and
Lynchburg.[23] Regiments were called out during the war in
anticipation of insurrections along the tidewater area. During
the spring of 1816 confessions were wrung from slaves concerning an attack upon Fredericksburg and Richmond. The
inspiration for this enterprise was attributed to a white military officer, George Boxley. The latter claimed to be the recip-
ient of divine revelations and the instrument of "omnipo-
tence" although he denied any intention of leading an insurrection. His relatives declared that he was insane, but his
neighbors in a complaint to the governor showed serious mis-
givings on this point:

"On many occasions he has declared that the distinction
between the rich and the poor was too great; that offices were
given to wealth than to merit; and seemed to be an advocate
for a more leveling system of Government. For many years
he has avowed his disapprobation of the slavery of the
Negroes and wished they were free." [24]

[19] Details of the Gabriel Plot are in the *Calendar of Virginia State Papers*, X (1808-1835), 140-173, *et passim;* T. W. Higginson, "Gabriel's Defeat," *The Atlantic Monthly*, X (1862), 337-345; Robert R. Howison, *A History of Virginia* (Richmond, 1848), II, 390-3.

[20] Hamilton, ed., *Writings of James Monroe*, III, 328-9.

[21] James H. Johnston, "The Participation of White Men in Virginia Negro Insurrections," 161.

[22] *Calendar of Virginia State Papers*, X (1808-1835), 31, 62.

[23] *Ibid.*, 367, 388.

[24] *Calendar of Virginia State Papers*, X, 433-6.

Boxley was arrested but escaped. About thirty Negroes were sentenced to death or deportation in consequence.

The years preceding the Nat Turner insurrection brought further news of plots discovered. During the middle of July, 1829, the governor received requests for aid from the counties of Mathews, Gloucester, the Isle of Wight and adjacent counties.[25] The ease with which "confessions" were obtained under duress casts doubt upon the reality of such outbreaks, but the reports are indicative of the ever-present fear of attack.

Nat Turner's insurrection of August 21, 1831, at Southampton, seventy miles from Richmond, raised fears of a general servile war to their highest point. The contemporary accounts of the young slave, Nat, tend to overemphasize his leanings toward mysticism and under-state the background of unrest.[26]. . .

Rumors of slave plots continued to disturb Virginia up to the era of emancipation. During 1856, the state, in common with other slaveholding states, shared in the general feeling that a widespread conspiracy, set for December 25, was maturing. Requests for aid came to the Governor from the counties of Fauquier, King and Queen, Culpeper, and Rappahannock; and particularly from the towns of Lynchburg, Petersburg, and Gordonsville.[27] As for John Brown's visionary deed at Harper's Ferry in the autumn of 1859, the aftermath can be easily imagined. The spectre of a general insurrection again haunted the minds of the white citizenry and large patrols were kept in constant service to prevent Negro meetings of all types.[28]

Maryland and North Carolina, although more fortunate than their slave-ridden neighbor, did not escape unscathed. The news of Nat Turner and John Brown brought panic to

[25] Ibid., 567-9.

[26] Thomas Gray, ed., Nat Turner's Confession (Richmond, 1832); Samuel Warner, ed., The Authentic and Impartial Narrative of The Tragical Scene of the Twenty Second of August, 1831, New York, 1831 (A collection of accounts by eye witnesses); and William Sidney Drewry, Slave Insurrections in Virginia, 1830-1865 (Washington, 1900), passim. The immediate results of the Nat Turner affair are summarized in John W. Cromwell's "The Aftermath of Nat Turner's Insurrection," The Journal of Negro History, V (1920), 208-234.

[27] Calendar of Virginia State Papers, XI (1836-1869), 50. Other rumors of unrest during 1856 came from the towns of Williamsburgh and Alexandria, and from Montgomery County. See Laura A. White, "The South in the 1850's as seen by British Consuls," The Journal of Southern History, I (1935), 44.

[28] Brackett, The Negro in Maryland, 97-99.

the other states. In Maryland, baseless rumors of conspiracies, rather than actual outbreaks, seemed to be the rule. In 1845 a plot was "disclosed" in Charles County, Maryland, and a number of Negroes were subsequently sold out of the state.[29] Ten years later there was general excitement over alleged uprisings in Dorchester, Talbot and Prince George's Counties. Resolutions were adopted at the time by various citizens asking that slaveholders keep their servants at home.[30] The reaction to John Brown's raid of 1859 was more intense than had ever before been experienced over insurrections in Maryland. The newspapers for days were full of nothing else but the Harper's Ferry incident. Large patrols were called out everywhere and talk was general of a concerted uprising of all the slaves in Maryland and Virginia. A martial atmosphere prevailed.[31]

In 1802 an insurrection was reported in Bertie County, North Carolina, necessitating an elaborate patrol system.[32] A decade later, another outbreak in Rockingham County was narrowly averted;[33] and in 1816 further plots were discovered at Tarboro, New Bern, Camden and Hillsboro.[34] Several minor disturbances occurred in 1821 among the slaves of Bladen, Carteret, Jones, and Onslow Counties.[35] On October 6, 1831, a Georgia newspaper reported an extensive slave conspiracy in North Carolina with ramifications in the eastern counties of Duplin, Sampson, Wayne, New Hanover, Lenoir, Cumberland, and Bladen.[36]

[29] Brackett, *The Negro in Maryland*, 96.

[30] *Ibid.*, 97.

[31] *Ibid.*, 97-99.

[32] John Spencer Bassett, *Slavery in the State of North Carolina*, Johns Hopkins University Studies in Historical and Political Science, XVII (Baltimore, 1899), 332. The nature of North Carolina laws during 1777-1788 regarding insurrections indicates the keen fears entertained of slave uprisings. One preamble of 1777 begins ". . . Whereas the evil and pernicious practice of freeing slaves in this State, ought at this alarming and critical time to be guarded against by every friend and well-wisher to his country . . ." This idea is repeated in the insurrection laws of 1778 and 1788. Walter Clark, ed., *The State Records of North Carolina* (Goldsboro, N. C., 1905), XXIV (1777-1788). 14, 221, 964. The laws regulating manumission were made increasingly stringent for fear of creating a dangerous class of free Negroes.

[33] *Calendar of Virginia State Papers*, X (1808-1835), 120-2.

[34] A. H. Gordon, "The Struggle of the Negro Slaves for Physical Freedom," *Journal of Negro History*, XIII (1928), 22-35.

[35] Hugh T. Lefler, ed., *North Carolina History told by Contemporaries* (Chapel Hill, 1934), 265.

[36] Milledgeville (Georgia) *Federal Union*, October 6, 1831, quoted in *ibid.*; The repercussion of the Nat Turner insurrection at Murfreesboro, Hertford County, has been graphically described by an

Slave plots in South Carolina during the national period seem to have been abortive for the most part, but several of the projects could easily have been uprisings of the first magnitude. During November, 1797, slave trials in Charleston disclosed a plot to burn the city. Two Negroes were hanged and three deported.[37] The Camden plot of June, 1816, was a very serious affair and envisaged a concerted attempt to burn the town and massacre its inhabitants. A favorite slave reported the plot to his master, Colonel Chesnut, who thereupon informed Governor Williams. Six of the slave leaders were executed and patrol measures were strengthened.[38]

The outstanding threat of insurrection in the State was the Denmark Vesey plot of 1822. . . . The leader, Denmark, was a free Negro of Charleston, a native of St. Thomas in the West Indies, who had purchased his freedom in 1800 from the proceeds of a lottery prize and had since worked in the city as a carpenter. He desired to emulate the Negro leaders of St. Domingo and win the freedom of his people. Preaching that conditions had become intolerable for the slave, he urged a war against the slave-holder. A white man was to purchase guns and powder for his proposed army; Charleston was to be captured and burnt, the shipping of the town seized and all would sail away for the West Indies to freedom. Again a "faithful slave"—or spy—exposed the plot and severe reprisals were instituted. Thirty-five Negroes were executed and thirty-seven sold out of the state.

Because of the number of free Negroes involved, the Legislature passed an act preventing such persons from entering the state. To avoid, as far as possible, the contagion of abolitionist and kindred ideas, the purchase of slaves was forbidden from the West Indies, Mexico, South America, Europe, and the states north of Maryland. Slaves, who had resided in these forbidden areas, were likewise denied entrance into South Carolina. A Charleston editor, Benjamin Elliot, penned a sharp reply to the Northern accusations of cruelty, by pointing out that New York in the insurrection of 1741 had executed thirty-five and deported eighty-five. He demand-

---

eye witness. "It was court week and most of our men were twelve miles away at Winton. Fear was seen in every face, women pale and terror stricken, children crying for protection, men fearful and full of foreboding, but determined to be ready for the worst." Quoted from the Baltimore *Gazette*, November 16, 1831, by Stephen B. Weeks, "The Slave Insurrection in Virginia." *American Magazine of History*, XXV (1891), 456.

[37] H. M. Henry, *The Police Patrol of the Slave in South Carolina*, 150.

[38] Holland, *A Refutation of the Calumnies*, 75.

ed that the Federal Government act under its power to suppress insurrection. In July, 1829, another plot was reported in
Georgetown County and in 1831, the year of Nat Turner's
attack, one in Laurens County.

Georgia, like South Carolina, was able to avert the worst
consequences of repeated slave plots. One was reported in
Greene County in 1810,[39] a plan to destroy Atlanta came to
light in May, 1819,[40] during 1831, disquieting rumors came
from Milledgeville and Laurens County,[41] four years later, a
plot for a general uprising on the Coast was disclosed; [42] in
1851 another plot in Atlanta was reported; [43] and in 1860,
similar reports came from Crawford and Brooks Counties.[44]

Florida experienced an uprising in March, 1820, along
Talbot Island which was put down by a detachment of federal troops.[45] Another was reported in December, 1856, in
Jacksonville.[46] Alabama discovered a plot in January, 1837,
believed to have been instigated by a free Negro,
M'Donald.[47] Mississippi seems to have been the central area
of a widespread slave plot in July, 1835, threatening the entire Cotton Kingdom. Far-reaching plans of revolt had been
drawn up by a white, John A. Murrell, who enjoyed a reputation as a Negro kidnapper and land pirate. Ten or fifteen
Negroes and a number of whites were hanged for participation in the plot.[48]

Next to Virginia, Louisiana had the greatest difficulty
among the southern states in coping with repeated attempts at
insurrection. Governor Claiborne of the Mississippi Territory
received frequent letters concerning plots in various parts of

[39] Flanders, *Plantation Slavery in Georgia*, 274.

[40] *Niles Register*, XVI (1819), 213.

[41] Flanders, *Plantation Slavery in Georgia*, 274.

[42] *Niles Register*, XLIX (1935-6), 172.

[43] Flanders, *Plantation Slavery in Georgia*, 275. Georgia suffered in
common with the other southern states during the scare of 1856;
White, "The South in the 1850's as Seen by British Consuls," 43.

[44] Flanders, *Plantation Slavery in Georgia*, 275-6, 186. The abolitionists were accused of organizing the slave plots of the thirties and thereafter. One New England abolitionist, Kitchel, who opened a school for
Negroes in Tarversville, Twigg County, Georgia, in 1835, was driven
out of the community because he was said to have incited the slaves to
revolt. *Ibid.*, 275.

[45] Helen H. Catterall, ed., *Judicial Cases Concerning American Slavery and the Negro* (Washington, 1926), III, 327 (Hereafter: *J.C.N.*).

[46] James Stirling, *Letters from the Slave States* (London, 1857), 299.

[47] *J.C.N.*, III, 141. Alabama had two rumors of slave plots reported
in 1860; White, "The South in the 1850's as Seen by British Consuls,"
47.

[48] *Niles Register*, XLIX (1835-6), 119; also Elizur Wright, ed.,
Quarterly Anti-Slavery Magazine (New York, 1837), II, 104-11.

Louisiana. In 1804, New Orleans seems to have been threatened.[49] Several months later another alarm came from the plantations at Pointe Coupee.[50] In 1805, the attempt of a Frenchman to teach the doctrine of equality to slaves, led to general fears of an uprising.[51]

An actual outbreak occurred in January, 1811. Beginning from a plantation in the parish of St. John the Baptist, about thirty-six miles above New Orleans, a concerted slave uprising spread along the Mississippi. The Negroes formed disciplined companies to march upon New Orleans to the beating of drums. Their force, estimated to include from 180 to 500 persons, was defeated in a pitched battle with the troops.[52] According to one historian many of those executed were decapitated and their heads placed on poles along the river as an example to others.[53]

Another uprising took place in the same area in March, 1829, causing great alarm before it was suppressed. Two leaders were hanged.[54] Other plots were reported in 1835, 1837, 1840, 1841 and 1842.[55] An uprising occurred in August, 1856, at New Iberia.[56]

The situation in Tennessee, Kentucky, and Texas may be briefly summarized. In Tennessee, plots were disclosed during 1831, 1856, and 1857.[57] Kentucky, in December, 1856, hanged several ringleaders of an attempted insurrection at Hopkinsville, in which a white man was involved.[58] That same year, two Negroes were punished by being whipped to death in Texas for an alleged conspiracy at Columbus, Colorado County.[59]

Owing to the nature of such a study any claim to an ex-

[49] Dunbar, Rowland, ed., *Official Letter Book of W.C.C. Claiborne* (Jackson, 1917), II (1801-1816), 337-8.

[50] *Ibid.*, III (1804-1806), 6.

[51] *Ibid.*, 187.

[52] *Ibid.*, V (1809-1811), 93-142.

[53] Francois Xavier Martin, *The History of Louisiana* (New Orleans, 1829), II, 300-301. During the fall of the following year another plot was reported. *J.C.N.*, III, 449.

[54] *Niles Register*, XXVI (1829), 53.

[55] *Ibid.*, LIII (1937-8), 129; LX (1841), 368; LXIII (1842-3), 212.

[56] V. Alton Moody, *Slavery on the Louisiana Sugar Plantations* (Univ. of Michigan Press, 1924), 41; also Phillips, *American Negro Slavery*, 486. *J.C.N.*, III, 648.

[57] Caleb P. Patterson, *The Negro in Tennessee*, Univ. of Texas Bulletin No. 225 (Austin, February 1, 1922), 49; *J.C.N.*, II, 565-6; Stirling, *Letters from the Slave States*, 294.

[58] *J.C.N.*, 299.

[59] Frederick Law Olmsted, *A Journey Through Texas* (New York, 1857), 513-4; Stirling, *Letters from the Slave States*, 300.

haustive treatment would be mere pretense. An analysis of slave patrol history alone would suggest the existence of far more conspiracies and outbreaks than those already mentioned. It is clear however that *ante-bellum* society of the South suffered from a larger degree of domestic insecurity than the conventional view would indicate. No doubt many Negroes made the required adjustments to slavery, but the romantic picture of careless abandon and contentment fails to be convincing. The struggle of the Negro for his liberty, beginning with those dark days on the slaveship, was far from sporadic in nature, but an ever-recurrent battle waged everywhere with desperate courage against the bonds of his master.

Day to Day Resistance to Slavery*

RAYMOND A. BAUER AND ALICE H. BAUER

THE NEGROES WERE well aware that the work they did benefited only the master. "The slaves work and the planter gets the benefit of it." [1] "The conversation among the slaves was that they worked hard and got no benefit, that the masters got it all." [2] It is thus not surprising that one finds many recurring comments that a slave did not do half a good day's work in a day . . .

. . . Just how much of this was due to indifference and how much due to deliberate slowing up is hard to determine. . . .

There is, indeed, a strong possibility that this behavior was a form of indirect aggression. While such an hypothesis cannot be demonstrated on the basis of the available contemporary data, it is supported by Dollard's interpretation of similar behavior which he found in Southern towns.

If the reader has ever seen Stepin Fetchit in the movies, he can picture this type of character. Fetchit always plays the part of a well-accommodated lower-class Negro, whining, vacillating, shambling, stupid, and moved by very simple cravings. There is probably an element of resistance to white society in the shambling,

* Excerpts from R. A. Bauer and A. H. Bauer, "Day to Day Resistance to Slavery," *Journal of Negro History*, XXVII (Oct., 1942), pp. 388-419. Reprinted by permission.

[1] Wm. Brown, an escaped slave; in: Benjamin Drew, *The Refugee*, Boston, 1856, p. 281.

[2] Thomas Hedgebeth, a free Negro, in: Benjamin Drew, *The Refugee*, Boston, 1856, p. 276.

sullenly slow pace of the Negro; it is the gesture of a man who is forced to work for ends not his own and who expresses his reluctance to perform under these circumstances.[3] . . .

The few statements on this point we have by ex-slaves seem to indicate that the slaves as a group made a general policy of not letting the master get the upper hand.

I had become large and strong; and had begun to take pride in the fact that I could do as much hard work as some of the older men. There is much rivalry among slaves, at times, as to which can do the most work, and masters generally seek to promote such rivalry. But some of us were too wise to race with each other very long. Such racing, we had the sagacity to see, was not likely to pay. We had times out for measuring each other's strength, but we knew too much to keep up the competition so long as to produce an extraordinary day's work. We knew that if, by extraordinary exertion, a large quantity of work was done in one day, the fact, becoming known to the master, might lead him to require the same amount every day. This thought was enough to bring us to a dead halt whenever so much excited for the race.[4]

Writer after writer, describing incidents in which slaves were compelled to assist in punishing other slaves, states that they did so with the greatest of reluctance.

The hands stood still;—they knew Randall—and they knew him also take a powerful man, and were afraid to grapple with him. As soon as Cook had ordered the men to seize him, Randall turned to them, and said—"Boys, you all know me; you know that I can handle any three of you, and the man that lays hands on me shall die. This white man can't whip me himself, and therefore he has called you to help him." The overseer was unable to prevail upon them to seize and secure Randall, and finally ordered them all to go to their work together.[5]

In some cases it was noted that the slave resisting punishment took pains not to treat his fellows with any more than the absolute minimum of violence.

With such demonstrations of solidarity among the slaves it is not surprising to find a slave telling of how he and his fellows "captured" the institution of the driver. The slave Solomon Northrup was such a driver. His task was to whip the other slaves in order to make them work.

[3] Dollard, John, *Caste & Class in a Southern Town,* (New Haven, 1937), p. 257.

[4] Douglass, Frederick, *Life and Times of Frederick Douglass,* p. 261.

[5] Brown, W. W., *Life of Williams Welles Brown, A Fugitive Slave* (Boston, 1848), p. 18. See also Williams, James, *Narratives of James Williams* (Boston, 1838), pp. 56, 62, 65.

"Practice makes perfect," truly; and during eight years' experience as a driver I learned to handle the whip with marvelous dexterity and precision, throwing the lash within a hair's breadth of the back, the ear, the nose without, however, touching either of them. If Epps was observed at a distance, or we had reason to apprehend he was sneaking somewhere in the vicinity, I would commence plying the lash vigorously, when, according to arrangement, they would squirm and screech as if in agony, although not one of them had in fact been grazed. Patsey would take occasion, if he made his appearance presently, to mumble in his hearing some complaints that Platt was whipping them the whole time, and Uncle Abraham, with an appearance of honesty peculiar to himself would declare roundly I had just whipped them worse than General Jackson whipped the enemy at New Orleans.[6] . . .

The amount of slowing up of labor by the slaves must, in the aggregate, have caused a tremendous financial loss to plantation owners. The only way we have of estimating it quantitatively is through comparison of the work done in different plantations and under different systems of labor. The statement is frequently made that production on a plantation varied more than 100% from time to time. Comparison in the output of slaves in different parts of the South also showed variations of over 100%. Most significant is the improvement in output obtained under the task, whereby the slaves were given a specific task to fulfill for their day's work, any time left over being their own. Olmsted gives us our best information on this point:

These tasks certainly would not be considered excessively hard by a northern laborer; and, in point of fact, the more industrious and active hands finished them often by two o'clock. I saw one or two leaving the field soon after one o'clock, several about two; and between three and four, I met a dozen women and several men coming home to their cabins, having finished their day's work.

Under this "Organization of Labor" most of the slaves work rapidly and well. In nearly all ordinary work, custom has settled the extent of the task, and it is difficult to increase it. The driver who marks it out, has to remain on the ground until it is finished, and has no interest in overmeasuring it; and if it should be systematically increased very much, there is danger of a general stampede to the swamp, a danger the slave can always hold before his master's cupidity.[7] . . .

The slaves were well aware of their economic value, and used it to good advantage. The skilled laborers among the

[7] Olmsted, F. L., *A Journey in the Seaboard Slave States* (New York, 1863), pp. 192, 193.

[6] Northrup, Solomon, *Twelve Years a Slave*, 1853, pp. 226, 227.

slaves knew their worth, and frequently rebelled against unsatisfactory work situations. Slaves who were hired out would run away from the masters who had hired them, and then either return home, or remain in hiding until they felt like returning to work. . . .

Even the threat of a whipping did not deter such slaves from running off for a time when they were displeased. The quotation from Olmsted below is typical of a constantly recurring pattern of statements:

"The manager told me that the people often ran away after they have been whipped or something else had happened to make them angry. They hide in the swamp and come into the cabins at night to get food. They seldom remain away more than a fortnight and when they come in they are whipped." [8]

Some of the resistance took on the aspects of organized strikes:

"Occasionally, however, a squad would strike in a body as a protest against severities. An episode of this sort was recounted in a letter of a Georgia overseer to his absent employer: 'Sir: I write you a few lines in order to let you know that six of your hands has left the plantation—every man but Jack. They displeased me with their work and I give some of them a few lashes, Tom with the rest. On Wednesday morning they were missing. I think they are lying out until they can see you or your Uncle Jack.' The slaves could not negotiate directly at such a time, but while they lay in the woods they might make overtures to the overseer through slaves on a neighboring plantation as to terms upon which they would return to work, or they might await their master's posthaste arrival and appeal to him for a redress of grievances. Humble as their demeanor might be, their power of renewing the pressure by repeating their act could not be ignored." [9] . . .

The indifference of the slaves to the welfare of the masters extended itself to a complete contempt for property values. The slaves were so careless with tools that they were equipped with special tools, and more clumsy than ordinary ones. . . .

Not only tools but live stock suffered from the mistreatment by the slaves. Olmsted found not only the "nigger hoe" [a particularly heavy, strong hoe] but even discovered that mules were substituted for horses because horses could not stand up under the treatment of the slaves. . . .

[8] Olmsted, F. L., *A Journey in the Back Country* (New York, 1863), p. 79.

[9] Phillips, U. B., *American Negro Slavery*, pp. 303, 304.

Redpath verifies Olmsted's statement—by telling how he saw slaves treat stock. It is important to note that Redpath was a strong abolitionist and most sympathetic toward the slaves.

He rode the near horse, and held a heavy cowhide in his hand, with which from time to time he lashed the leaders, as barbarous drivers lash oxen when at work. Whenever we came to a hill, especially if it was very steep, he dismounted, lashed the horses with all his strength, varying his performances by picking up stones, none of them smaller than half a brick, and throwing them with all his force, at the horses' legs. He seldom missed.
The wagon was laden with two tons of plaster in sacks.
This is a fair specimen of the style in which Negroes treat stock.[10] . . .

In the Sea Islands off the coast of Georgia, Kemble reported that the slaves started immense fires, destroying large sections of woods through carelessness or maliciousness.

The "field hands" make fires to cook their midday food wherever they happen to be working, and sometimes through their careless neglect, but sometimes, too, undoubtedly on purpose, the woods are set fire to by these means. One benefit they consider . . . is the destruction of the dreaded rattlesnakes.

. . . not only did the Negro slaves refuse to work, and not only did they destroy property, but they even made it impossible for planters to introduce new work techniques by feigning clumsiness. They prevented the introduction of the plow in this way on many plantations.[11] . . .

Malingering was a well-known phenomenon throughout the slave states.[12] The purpose of feigning illness was generally to avoid work, although occasionally a slave who was being sold would feign a disability either to avoid being sold to an undesirable master, or to lower his purchase price so as

[10] Redpath, James, *The Roving Editor: or, Talks with Slaves in the Southern States* (New York, 1859), p. 241.

[11] Olmsted, F. L., *A Journey in the Seaboard States*, p. 145.

[12] Since this paper was written a significant contribution has appeared which throws a new light on the subject of slave illness. (Felice Swados, "Negro Health on the Ante Bellum Plantations," *Bulletin of the History of Medicine*, vol. x, no. 3, October, 1941.) Though Swados demonstrated that the rate of actual sickness among the Negroes was very high, she leaves some doubt as to what proportion of sickness was feigned. For instance, in a footnote (p. 472) she refers to Sydnor's compilations of the records of sickness on several plantations as indications of the extent of actual sickness, even going so far as to note that on one plantation most of the sickness occurred during the picking season. Sydnor, himself, indicates that he believes that these records demonstrate that a great deal of the sickness was feigned.

to obtain revenge on a former master. The women occasionally pretended to be pregnant, because pregnant women were given lighter work assignments and were allowed extra rations of food.

In a situation such as this in which physical disability was an advantage, one would expect much malingering. One might also expect to find functional mental disorders, hysterical disorders which would get one out of work. . . .

Of the extent to which illness was feigned there can, however, be little doubt. Some of the feigning was quite obvious, and one might wonder why such flagrant abuses were tolerated. The important thing to remember is that a slave was an important economic investment. Most slave owners sooner or later found out that it was more profitable to give the slave the benefit of the doubt. A sick slave driven to work might very well die. . . .

Fortunately in this field we have some quantitative estimates which enable us to appreciate fully the extent of these practices. Sydnor has digested the records of sickness on various plantations. From the Wheeles plantation records he found that of 1,429 working days 179 were lost on account of sickness, a ratio of almost one in seven. On the Bowles' plantation, in one year 159½ days were missed on account of sickness but only five days were on Sundays. This is a recurrent pattern, everybody sick on Saturday, and scarcely anybody sick on Sunday. On the Leigh plantation, where thirty persons were working there were 398 days of sickness. In examining this record Sydnor discovered that the rate of sickness was greatest at the times of the year when there was the most work to be done.[13] Olmsted says that he never visited a plantation on which twenty Negroes were employed where he did not find one or more not at work on some trivial pretext.[14] . . .

An outstanding example of malingering is given by Smedes, a writer who insisted so emphatically on the devotion of the slaves to their masters.

The cook's husband, who for years had looked on himself as nearly blind, and therefore unable to do more than work about her, and put her wood on the fire, sometimes cutting a stick or two, made no less than eighteen good crops for himself when the war was over. He was one of the best farmers in the country.[15]

13 Sydnor, C. S., *Slavery in Mississippi* (New York, 1933), pp. 45ff.
14 Olmsted, F. L., *A Journey in the Seaboard Slave States*, p. 187.
15 Smedes, S., *Memorials of a Southern Planter* (Baltimore, 1887), p. 80.

The most effective means of retaliation against an unpopular master which the slave had at his command was by feigning disability on the auction block. How often this was done we do not know, but Phillips accepts it as a recognized pattern.

Those on the block often times praised their own strength and talents, for it was a matter of pride to fetch high prices. On the other hand if a slave should bear a grudge against his seller, or should hope to be bought only by someone who would expect but light service he might pretend a disability though he had it not.[16] . . .

The strength of Negro resistance to slavery becomes apparent in the extent to which the slaves mutilated themselves in their efforts to escape work. A girl on Lewis' plantation who had been injured tied pack thread around her wounds when they started to heal and then rubbed dirt in them. In her anxiety to avoid work she gave herself a very serious infection.[17] But this action was mild compared to that of others.

General Leslie Coombs, of Lexington, owned a man named Ennis, a house carpenter. He had bargained with a slave-trader to take him and carry him down the river. Ennis was determined not to go. He took a broadaxe and cut one hand off, then contrived to lift the axe, with his arm pressing it to his body, and let it fall upon the other, cutting off the ends of the fingers.[18]
"But some on 'em would rather be shot then be took, sir," he added simply.
A farmer living near a swamp confirmed this account, and said he knew of three or four being shot on one day.[19]

Planters had much trouble with slaves fresh from Africa, the new slaves committing suicide in great numbers. Ebo Landing in the Sea Islands was the site of the mass suicide of Ebo slaves who simply walked in a body into the ocean and drowned themselves. A planter writing on the handling of slaves mentions the difficulty of adjusting the Africans to slavery. He advocates mixing them in with seasoned slaves.

It too often happens that poor masters, who have no other slaves or are too greedy, require hard labor of these fresh negroes, exhaust them quickly, lose them by sickness and more often by

[16] Phillips, U. B., *American Negro Slavery*, p. 199.
[17] Clarke, Lewis, *Narratives of the Sufferings of Lewis and Milton Clarke* (Boston, 1846), p. 168.
[18] *Ibid.*, p. 125.
[19] Olmsted, F. L., *A Journey in the Seaboard Slave States*, p. 160.

grief. Often they hasten their own death; some wound themselves, others stifle themselves by drawing in the tongue so as to close the breathing passage, others take poison, or flee and perish of misery and hunger.[20]

Several cases, where it was certain that parents killed their children to keep them from slavery, have been described. . . .

Of all the cases of slave rendition, the saddest and probably the most circulated at the time was that of Margaret Garner. Winter was the best time for flight across the Ohio River, for when it was frozen over the difficulties of crossing were fewer. Simeon Garner, with his wife Margaret and two children, fled from slavery in Kentucky during the cold winter of 1856 and, after crossing the frozen stream at night, made their ways to the house of a free Negro in Cincinnati.

Quickly tracing the fugitive Negroes to their hideout in Cincinnati, the armed pursuers, after some resistance, broke down the door and entered the house. There they found Margaret, the mother, who, preferring death to slavery for her children, had striven to take their lives, and one child lay dead on the floor. The case was immediately brought into court, where despite the efforts made by sympathetic whites, rendition was ordered. On their return to slavery, Margaret in despair attempted to drown herself and child by jumping into the river but even the deliverance of death was denied her, for she was recovered and soon thereafter sold to a trader who took her to the cotton fields of the Far South.[21]

Not only were slaves known to take the lives of their masters or overseers, but they were now and then charged with the murder of their own children, sometimes to prevent them from growing up in bondage. In Covington a father and mother, shut up in a slave baracoon and doomed to the southern market, "when there was no eye to pity them and no arm to save," did by mutual agreement "send the souls of their children to Heaven rather than have them descend to the hell of slavery," and then both parents committed suicide.[22]

"Take off your shoes, Sylva," said Mrs. A., "and let this gentleman see your feet."

"I don't want to," said Sylva.

"But I want you to," said her mistress.

"I don't care if you do," replied Sylva sullenly.

"You must," said the mistress firmly.

The fear of punishment impelled her to remove the shoes. Four toes on one foot, and two on the other were wanting! "There!" said the mistress, "my husband, who learned the blacksmith's trade for the purpose of teaching it to the slaves, to increase their

[20] Phillips, U. B., *Plantation and Frontier Documents*, II, p. 31.

[21] Coleman, J. W., *Slavery Times in Kentucky* (Chapel Hill, 1940), p. 208.

[22] *Ibid.*, p. 269.

market value, has, with his own hands, pounded off and wrung off all those toes, when insane with passion. And it was only last week that he thought Sylva was saucy to me, and he gave her thirty lashes with the horse whip. She was so old that I could not bear to see it, and I left the house.

"Sylva says," Mrs. A. continued, "that she has been the mother of thirteen children, every one of whom she has destroyed with her own hands, in their infancy, rather than have them suffer slavery!" 23

*Nat Turner's Insurrection**

Near the southeastern border of Virginia, in Southampton County, there is a neighborhood known as "The Cross Keys." It lies fifteen miles from Jerusalem, the county-town or "court-house," seventy miles from Norfolk, and about as far from Richmond. It is some ten or fifteen miles from Murfreesboro' in North Carolina and about twenty-five from the Great Dismal Swamp. Up to Sunday, the twenty-first of August, 1831, there was nothing to distinguish it from any other rural, lethargic, slipshod Virginia neighborhood, with the due allotment of mansion-houses and log-huts, tobacco-fields and "old-fields," horses, dogs, negroes, "poor white folks," so called, and other white folks, poor without being called so. One of these last was Joseph Travis, who had recently married the widow of one Putnam Moore, and had unfortunately wedded to himself her negroes also.

In the woods on the plantation of Joseph Travis, upon the Sunday just named, six slaves met at noon for what is called in the Northern States a picnic and in the Southern a barbecue. The bill of fare was to be simple: one brought a pig, and another some brandy, giving to the meeting an aspect so cheaply convivial that no one would have imagined it to be the final consummation of a conspiracy which had been for six months in preparation. In this plot four of the men had been already initiated,—Henry, Hark or Hercules, Nelson, and Sam. Two others were novices, Will and Jack by name. The party had remained together from twelve to three o'clock, when a seventh man joined them,—a short, stout, powerfully built person, of dark mulatto complexion and

23 Parson, C. G., *Inside View of Slavery* (Boston, 1853), p. 212.

* Excerpts from Thomas Wentworth Higginson, "Nat Turner's Insurrection," *Atlantic Monthly*, VIII (August, 1861), pp. 173-87. This article was published anonymously.

strongly-marked African features, but with a face full of expression and resolution. This was Nat Turner.

He was at this time nearly thirty-one years old, having been born on the second of October, 1800. He had belonged originally to Benjamin Turner,—whence his last name, slaves having usually no patronymic,—had then been transferred to Putnam Moore, and then to his present owner. He had, by his own account, felt himself singled out from childhood for some great work; and he had some peculiar marks on his person, which, joined to his great mental precocity, were enough to occasion, among his youthful companions, a superstitious faith in his gifts and destiny. He had great mechanical ingenuity also, experimentalized very early in making paper, gunpowder, pottery, and in other arts which in later life he was found thoroughly to understand. His moral faculties were very strong, so that white witnesses admitted that he had never been known to swear an oath, to drink a drop of spirits, or to commit a theft. And in general, so marked were his early peculiarities, that people said "he had too much sense to be raised, and if he was, he would never be of any use as a slave." This impression of personal destiny grew with his growth;—he fasted, prayed, preached, read the Bible, heard voices when he walked behind his plough, and communicated his revelations to the awe-struck slaves. They told him in return, that, "if they had his sense, they would not serve any master in the world." . . .

Whatever Nat Turner's experiences of slavery might have been, it is certain that his plans were not suddenly adopted, but that he had brooded over them for years. To this day there are traditions among the Virginia slaves of the keen devices of "Prophet Nat." If he was caught with lime and lamp-black in hand, conning over a half-finished county-map on the barn-door, he was always "planning what to do, if he were blind," or "studying how to get to Mr. Francis's house." . . .

The religious hallucinations narrated in his Confession seem to have been as genuine as the average of such things, and are very well expressed. It reads quite like Jacob Behmen. He saw white spirits and black spirits contending in the skies, the sun was darkened, the thunder rolled. . . .

When he came, therefore, to the barbecue on the appointed Sunday, and found not these four only, but two others, his first question to the intruders was, How they came thither. To this Will answered manfully, that his life was worth no more than the others, and "his liberty was as dear to him." This admitted him to confidence, and as Jack was known to be entirely under Hark's influence, the strangers were no bar to their discussion. Eleven hours they remained there, in anxious consultation: one can imagine those terrible dusky faces, beneath the funereal woods, and amid the flickering of pine-knot torches, preparing that stern revenge whose shuddering echoes should ring through the land so long. Two things were at last decided: to begin their work that night, and to begin it with a massacre so swift and irresistible as to create in a few days more terror than many battles, and so spare the need of future bloodshed. "It was agreed that we should commence at home on that night, and, until we had armed and equipped ourselves and gained sufficient force, neither age nor sex was to be spared: which was invariably adhered to."

John Brown invaded Virginia with nineteen men, and with the avowed resolution to take no life but in self-defence. Nat Turner attacked Virginia from within, with six men, and with the determination to spare no life until his power was established. John Brown intended to pass rapidly through Virginia, and then retreat to the mountains. Nat Turner intended to "conquer Southampton County as the white men did in the Revolution, and then retreat, if necessary, to the Dismal Swamp." Each plan was deliberately matured; each was in its way practicable; but each was defeated by a single false step, as will soon appear.

We must pass over the details of horror, as they occurred during the next twenty-four hours. Swift and stealthy as Indians, the black men passed from house to house,—not pausing, not hesitating, as their terrible work went on. In one thing they were humaner than Indians or than white men fighting against Indians,—there was no gratuitous outrage beyond the death-blow itself, no insult, no mutilation; but in every house they entered, that blow fell on man, woman, and child,—nothing that had a white skin was spared. From every house they took arms and ammunition, and from a few, money; on every plantation they found recruits: those dusky slaves, so obsequious to their master the day before, so prompt to sing and dance before his Northern visitors, were all swift to transform themselves into fiends of retribution now; show them sword or musket and they grasped it, though it were an heirloom from Washington himself. The troop increased from house to house,—first to fifteen, then to forty, then to sixty. Some were armed with muskets, some with axes, some with scythes; some came on their masters' horses. As the numbers increased, they could be divided, and the awful work was carried on more rapidly still. The plan then was for an advanced guard of horsemen to approach each house at a gallop, and surround it till the others came up. Meanwhile what agonies of terror must have taken place within, shared alike by innocent and guilty! what memories of wrongs inflicted on those dusky creatures, by some, —what innocent participation, by others, in the penance! The outbreak lasted for but forty-eight hours; but during that period fifty-five whites were slain, without the loss of a single slave.

One fear was needless, which to many a husband and father must have intensified the last struggle. These negroes had been systematically brutalized from childhood; they had been allowed no legalized or permanent marriage; they had beheld around them an habitual licentiousness, such as can scarcely exist except in a Slave State; some of them had seen their wives and sisters habitually polluted by the husbands and the brothers of these fair white women who were now absolutely in their power. Yet I have looked through the Virginia newspapers of that time in vain for one charge of an indecent outrage on a woman against these triumphant and terrible slaves. Wherever they went, there went death, and that was all. Compare this with ordinary wars; compare it with the annals of the French Revolution. . . .

When the number of adherents had increased to fifty or sixty, Nat Turner judged it time to strike at the county-seat, Jerusalem. Thither a few white fugitives had already fled, and couriers might thence be despatched for aid to Richmond and Petersburg, unless promptly intercepted. Besides, he could there find arms, ammunition, and money; though they had already obtained, it is dubiously reported, from eight hundred to one thousand dollars. On the way it was necessary to pass the plantation of Mr. Parker, three miles from Jerusalem. Some of the men wished to stop here and enlist some of their friends. Nat Turner objected, as the delay might prove dangerous; he yielded at last, and it proved fatal.

He remained at the gate with six or eight men; thirty or forty went to the house, half a mile distant. They remained too long, and he went alone to hasten them. During his absence a party of eighteen white men came up suddenly, dispersing the small guard left at the gate; and when the main body of slaves emerged from the house, they encountered, for the first time, their armed masters. The blacks halted, the whites advanced cautiously within a hundred yards and fired a volley; on its being returned, they broke into disorder, and hurriedly retreated, leaving some wounded on the ground. The retreating whites were pursued, and were saved only by falling in with another band of fresh men from Jerusalem, with whose aid they turned upon the slaves, who in their turn fell into confusion. Turner, Hark, and about twenty men on horseback retreated in some order; the rest were scattered. The leader still planned to reach Jerusalem by a private way, thus evading pursuit; but at last decided to stop for the night, in the hope of enlisting additional recruits.

During the night the number increased again to forty, and they encamped on Major Ridley's plantation. An alarm took place during the darkness,—whether real or imaginary does not appear,—and the men became scattered again. Proceeding to make fresh enlistments with the daylight, they were resisted at Dr. Blunt's house, where his slaves, under his orders, fired upon them, and this, with a later attack from a party of white men near Captain Harris's, so broke up the whole force that they never reunited. The few who remained together agreed to separate for a few hours to see if anything could be done to revive the insurrection, and meet again that evening at their original rendezvous. But they never reached it.

Sadly came Nat Turner at nightfall into those gloomy woods where forty-eight hours before he had revealed the details of his terrible plot to his companions. At the outset all his plans had succeeded; everything was as he predicted: the slaves had come readily at his call, the masters had proved perfectly defenseless. Had he not been persuaded to pause at Parker's plantation, he would have been master before now of the arms and ammunition at Jerusalem; and with these to aid, and the Dismal Swamp for a refuge, he might have sustained himself indefinitely against his pursuers.

Now the blood was shed, the risk was incurred, his friends were killed or captured, and all for what? Lasting memories of terror, to be sure, for his oppressors; but on the other hand, hopeless failure for the insurrection, and certain death for him. . . .

There he waited two weary days and two melancholy nights,—long enough to satisfy himself that no one would rejoin him, and that the insurrection had hopelessly failed. The determined, desperate spirits who had shared his plans were scattered forever, and longer delay would be destruction for him also. He found a spot which he judged safe, dug a hole under a pile of fence-rails in a field, and lay there for six weeks, only leaving it for a few moments at midnight to obtain water from a neighboring spring. Food he had previously provided, without discovery, from a house near by. . . .

Worn out by confinement in his little cave, Nat Turner grew more adventurous, and began to move about stealthily by night, afraid to speak to any human being, but hoping to obtain some information that might aid his escape. Returning regularly to his retreat before daybreak, he might have continued this mode of life until pursuit had ceased, had not a dog succeeded where men had failed. The creature accidentally smelt out the provisions hid in the cave, and finally led thither his masters, two negroes, one of whom was named Nelson. On discovering the terrible fugitive, they fled precipitately, when he hastened to retreat in an opposite direction. This was on October 15th, and from this moment the neighborhood was all alive with excitement, and five or six hundred men undertook the pursuit.

It shows a more than Indian adroitness in Nat Turner to have escaped capture any longer. The cave, the arms, the provisions were found; and lying among them the notched stick of this miserable Robinson Crusoe, marked with five weary weeks and six days. But the man was gone. For ten days more he concealed himself among the wheat-stacks on Mr. Francis's plantation, and during this time was reduced almost to despair. Once he decided to surrender himself, and walked by night within two miles of Jerusalem before his purpose failed him. Three times he tried to get out of that neighborhood, but in vain: travelling by day was, of course, out of the question, and by night he found it impossible to elude the patrol. Again and again, therefore, he returned to his hiding-place, and during his whole two months' liberty never went five miles from the Cross Keys. On the 25th of October, he was at last discovered by Mr. Francis, as he was emerging from a stack. A load of buckshot was instantly discharged at him, twelve of which passed through his hat as he fell to the ground. He escaped even then, but his pursuers were rapidly concentrating upon him, and it is perfectly astonishing that he could have eluded them for five days more.

On Sunday, October 30th, a man named Benjamin Phipps, going out for the first time on patrol duty, was passing at noon a clearing in the woods where a number of pine-trees had long since been felled. There was a motion among their boughs; he stopped to watch it; and through a gap in the branches he saw, emerging from a hole in the earth beneath, the face of Nat Turner. Aiming his gun instantly, Phipps called on him to surrender. The fugitive, exhausted with watching and privation, entangled in the branches, armed only with a sword, had nothing to do but to yield; sagaciously reflecting, also, as he afterwards explained, that the woods were full of armed men, and that he had better trust fortune for some later chance of escape, instead of desperately attempting it then. He was correct in the first impression, since there were fifty armed scouts within a circuit of two miles. His insurrection ended where it began; for this spot was only a mile and a half from the house of Joseph Travis. . . .

When Nat Turner was asked by Mr. T. R. Gray, the counsel assigned him, whether, although defeated, he still believed in his own Providential mission, he answered, as simply as one who came thirty years after him, "Was not Christ crucified?" In the same spirit, when arraigned before the court, "he answered, 'Not guilty,' saying to his counsel that he did not feel so." But apparently no argument was made in his favor by his counsel, nor were any witnesses called,—he being convicted on the testimony of Levi Waller, and upon his own confession, which was put in by Mr. Gray, and acknowledged by the prisoner before the six justices composing the court, as being "full, free, and voluntary." He was therefore placed in the paradoxical position of conviction by his own confession, under a plea of "Not guilty." The arrest took place on the thirtieth of October, 1831, the confession on the first of November, the trial and conviction on the fifth, and the execution on the following Friday, the eleventh of November, precisely at noon. He met his death with perfect composure, declined addressing the multitude assembled, and told the sheriff in a firm voice that he was ready. . . .

Petition for Equal Education, 1787*

To THE HONORABLE the Senate and House of Representatives of the Commonwealth of Massachusetts Bay, in General Court assembled.

The petition of a great number of blacks, freemen of this Commonwealth, humbly sheweth, that your petitioners are held in common with other freemen of this town and Commonwealth and have never been backward in paying our proportionate part of the burdens under which they have, or may labor under; and as we are willing to pay our equal part of these burdens, we are of the humble opinion that we have the right to enjoy the privileges of free men. But that we do not will appear in many instances, and we beg leave to men-

* Herbert Aptheker, ed., *A Documentary History of the Negro People in the United States* (New York: The Citadel Press, Inc., 1951), pp. 19-20. One of the organizers of this petition was the Negro leader, Prince Hall, who founded the Negro Masonic Order in 1787.

tion one out of many, and that is of the education of our children which now receive no benefit from the free schools in the town of Boston, which we think is a great grievance, as by woful experience we now feel the want of a common education. We, therefore, must fear for our rising offspring to see them in ignorance in a land of gospel light when there is provision made for them as well as others and yet can't enjoy them, and for no other reason can be given this they are black . . .

We therefore pray your Honors that you would in your wisdom make some provision . . . for the education of our dear children. And in duty bound shall ever pray.

Preamble of the Free African Society*

Philadelphia. [12th, 4th mo., 1778.]—WHEREAS, Absalom Jones and Richard Allen, two men of the African race, who, for their religious life and conversation have obtained a good report among men, these persons, from a love to the people of their complexion whom they beheld with sorrow, because of their irreligious and uncivilized state, often communed together upon this painful and important subject in order to form some kind of religious society, but there being too few to be found under the like concern, and those who were, differed in their religious sentiments; with these circumstances they labored for some time, till it was proposed, after a serious communication of sentiments, that a society should be formed, without regard to religious tenets, provided, the persons lived an orderly and sober life, in other to support one another in sickness, and for the benefit of their widows and fatherless children.

ARTICLES.

[17th, 5th mo., 1787.]—We, the free Africans and their descendants, of the City of Philadelphia, in the State of Pennsylvania, or elsewhere, do unanimously agree, for the benefit of each other, to advance one shilling in silver Pennsylvania currency a month; and after one year's subscription from the

---

* Rev. William Douglass, *Annals of the First African Church in the United States of America now styled the African Episcopal Church of St. Thomas, Philadelphia* (Philadelphia: King & Baird Printers, 1862), pp. 15-17.

date hereof, then to hand forth to the needy of this Society, if any should require, the sum of three shillings and nine pence per week of the said money: provided, this necessity is not brought on them by their own imprudence.

And it is further agreed, that no drunkard nor disorderly person be admitted as a member, and if any should prove disorderly after having been received, the said disorderly person shall be disjointed from us if there is not an amendment, by being informed by two of the members, without having any of his subscription money returned.

And if any should neglect paying his monthly subscription for three months, and after having been informed of the same by two of the members, and no sufficient reason appearing for such neglect, if he do not pay the whole the next ensuing meeting, he shall be disjointed from us, by being informed by two of the members as an offender, without having any of his subscription money returned.

Also, if any person neglect meeting every month, for every omission he shall pay three pence, except in case of sickness or any other complaint that should require the assistance of the Society, then, and in such a case, he shall be exempt from the fines and subscription during the said sickness.

Also, we apprehend it to be just and reasonable, that the surviving widow of a deceased member should enjoy the benefit of this Society as long as she remains his widow, complying with the rules thereof, excepting the subscriptions.

And we apprehend it to be necessary, that the children of our deceased members be under the care of the Society, so far as to pay for the education of their children, if they cannot attend the free school; also to put them out apprentices to suitable trades or places, if required.

Also, that no member shall convene the Society together; but, it shall be the sole business of the committee, and that only on special occasions, and to dispose of the money in hand to the best advantage for the use of the Society, after they are granted the liberty at a monthly meeting, and to transact all other business whatsoever, except that of Clerk and Treasurer.

And we unanimously agree to choose Joseph Clarke to be our Clerk and Treasurer; and whenever another should succeed him, it is always understood, that one of the people called Quakers, belonging to one of the three monthly meetings in Philadelphia, is to be chosen to act as Clerk and Treasurer of this useful Institution.

The following persons met, viz., Absalom Jones, Richard Allen, Samuel Baston, Joseph Johnson, Cato Freeman, Cæsar

Cranchell, and James Potter, also William White, whose early assistance and useful remarks we found truly profitable. This evening the articles were read, and after some beneficial remarks were made, they were agreed unto.

PART II

Antebellum Days

INTRODUCTION

BOTH PRO- AND anti-slavery forces were exceedingly active in
the period from the early nineteenth century through the ante-
bellum years. Slave-holders' fears of insurrection increased as
the slave population and anti-slavery agitation increased. The
slave population of the United States increased from under
700,000 in 1790 to over two million in 1830 and to 3,-
953,760 by 1860.

Anti-slavery forces were inspired to greater activity by the
ending of slavery by Great Britain in 1833, and the adoption
of the Fugitive Law of 1850, which provided for severe penalties for refusal to aid in the return of escaped slaves and for
hearings for accused fugitives. The hearings relied on the testimony of owners but the slaves themselves could not testify.
The trials of fugitives inflamed public sentiment against slavery, and in several instances abolitionists attempted to take
accused fugitives away from federal marshals by force.

Now the struggle against slavery became not the cause of
isolated individuals and of the slaves themselves, but of a
movement. Abolitionists dropped their earlier goal of gradual
abolition, and followed the revolutionary lead of William
Lloyd Garrison who demanded nothing less than immediate
emancipation. Garrison founded the *Liberator* in 1831 to es-
pouse the cause of immediate and total abolition in fiery
language.[1] In addition to holding advanced views on emanci-

[1] An interesting critique of the abolitionist movement is provided by
William Ellery Channing in *Slavery* (Boston: James Monroe & Co.,
1836). Channing argues for moderation by abolitionists and gives a
stirring defense of abolitionists' civil liberties, strongly condemning mob
action against them. Channing wrote: "The Abolitionsts have done
wrong, I believe; nor is their wrong to be winked at, because done
fanatically or with good intention; for how much mischief may be

pation Garrison was a vigorous defender of the rights of women, and was critical of churchmen on the grounds that they were not active enough in the anti-slavery cause.

Garrison was a guiding spirit of the American Anti-Slavery Society, a national organization founded in 1833, and active until slavery was abolished. By 1838 the Society had 1,350 affiliated state and local anti-slavery societies with a membership of a quarter of a million.

A large segment split from the society in 1840 to found the American and Foreign Anti-Slavery Society, but the earlier grouping continued to be the leading anti-slavery force until slavery was abolished during the Civil War. Abolitionist historian Louis Ruchames said of the split in the abolitionist movement: "It seems reasonable to conclude that it was not Garrison's language or his espousal of the rights of women or his attacks upon the churches for their indifference to slavery which brought down on the abolitionists the wrath of so many of America's political, economic and religious leaders, but the doctrine of immediate and unconditional emancipation, which was indeed a revolutionary doctrine for its time and represented a threat to what many believed to be the foundation of the existing social and economic order." [2]

The method of abolitionists up to 1840 had been public debate, but in that year the anti-Garrisonians turned to the Liberty Party for a political solution to the problem. The Garrisonians shunned politics and continued agitation through public speeches, newspapers, books and pamphlets. In this period Garrison took his most radical step in urging disunion, the secession of the North. He called the Constitution, "a convenant with death and an agreement with hell," and at a celebration on July 4, 1854, he burned a copy of it saying: "So perish all compromises with tyranny!"

The philosophy of the abolitionist movement was pacifism, though many of the abolitionist leaders including Garrison, Wendell Phillips, Ralph Waldo Emerson, Henry David Thoreau and Frederick Douglass supported the use of arms by John Brown. Phillips said at Brown's funeral:

Has the slave a right to resist his master? I will not argue that question to a people hoarse with shouting ever since July 4, 1776, that all men are created equal, that the right to liberty is inalienable, and that resistance to tyrants is obedience to God! . . . But

wrought with good design!" But, he wrote, "Abolition must not be put down by lawless design! The attempt so to destroy it ought to fail. Such attempts place Abolitionism on a new ground. They make it, not the cause of a few enthusiasts, but the cause of freedom."

[2] Louis Ruchames, *The Abolitionists* (New York: Capricorn Books, 1963), p. 23.

John Brown violated the law. Yes. On yonder desk lie the inspired words of men who died violent deaths for breaking the laws of Rome. Why do you listen to them so reverently? Huss and Wickliffe violated laws; why honor them? George Washington, had he been caught before 1783, would have died on the gibbet, for breaking the laws of his sovereign . . . Yes, you say, but these men broke *bad* laws. Just so. It is honorable, then, to break bad laws, and such lawbreaking history loves and God blesses! Who says then, that slave laws are not ten thousand times worse than any those men resisted? Whatever argument *excuses* them, makes John Brown a saint.[3]

Douglass, who knew about Brown's plans in advance and fled to Canada in advance of United States marshals who went to his Rochester home to question him, called Brown "the noble old hero whose one right hand has shaken the foundation of the American Union." He said of his position on the Harper's Ferry insurrection:

The tools to those that can use them. Let every man work for the abolition of Slavery in his own way. I would help all, and hinder none.[4]

The new militance was ushered in with the appearance of an eloquent and incendiary pamphlet, *An Appeal,* by a Boston free Negro, David Walker. Walker's pamphlet was strongly condemned by slave-holders, and several Southern states passed laws after the *Appeal's* appearance providing strong penalties for the circulation of abolitionist literature. Walker had written: "I speak Americans for your good. We must and shall be free I say, in spite of you. You may do your best to keep us in wretchedness and misery, to enrich you and your children; but God will deliver us from under you. And wo, wo, will be to you if we have to obtain our freedom by fighting. Throw away your fears and prejudices then, and enlighten us and treat us like men, and we will like you more than we do now hate you . . ."[5] The Mayor of Savannah, Georgia, demanded of Mayor Harrison Gray Otis of Boston that the pamphlet be suppressed there. Otis replied that he could not suppress it but that he held it in "deep disapprobation and abhorance [*sic*]."

There were others also who called for violent struggles

[3] Louis Filler, ed., *Wendell Phillips on Civil Rights and Freedom* (New York: Hill and Wang, American Century Series, 1956), pp. 107-08.

[4] *The Liberator,* November 11, 1859.

[5] David Walker, *An Appeal to the Coloured Citizens of the World* (Boston, 1829), p. 70. See below, pp. 84-89.

against slavery. Lysander Spooner, in an appeal to the non-slave-holders of the South, called for the overthrow of the Bourbons and an end to slavery. He advocated the formation of Leagues of Freedom to descend upon the South. Frederick Douglass called for resistance to the "kidnappers" who sought to reclaim fugitive slaves. "The only way to make the Fugitive Slave Law a dead letter, is to make half a dozen or more dead kidnappers," Douglass wrote.[6]

In May, 1854, Thomas W. Higginson led a group to the Boston courthouse to free the fugitive slave, Anthony Burns. They were repulsed, and in the course of the fighting a deputy was killed. Cavalry, marines and artillery units were called in by the United States Marshal, and Burns' hearing proceeded. The tremendous opposition to his return to his owner is described in the following:

It was a lovely, cloudless day in June when Burns was sent out of Boston. A large body of city police, twenty-two companies of Massachusetts soldiers, and a battery of artillery guarded the streets through which Burns and his guards must pass. The streets were cleared by a company of cavalry. . . .

No martial music here, only the dull tramp of feet and the clatter of horses' hoofs. The men gripped their muskets and stared stolidly down, closing their ears to the jeers and taunts of the crowd.

Windows along the line of march were draped in mourning and lines of crepe were stretched across the streets. From the window opposite Old State House was suspended a black coffin on which were the words, "The Funeral of Liberty." Farther on, the American flag, the Union down, was draped in mourning. The solemn procession was witnessed by fifty thousand people who hissed, groaned, and cried, "Kidnappers! Kidnappers! Shame! Shame! . . ."

Burns was the last fugitive ever seized on the soil of Massachusetts.[7]

While today one tends to think of the abolitionist movement as composed primarily of white people, Negroes played a major role. The best-known of Negro abolitionists was Douglass whose goals did not end with emancipation, but with nothing short of equality. Douglass was a prolific writer and published his paper, *North Star*, later *Frederick Douglass' Paper*, monthly from 1847 to 1863. He traveled widely in this country and abroad speaking against slavery, and made several tours in the company of Garrison during which

6 Frederick Douglass, *Frederick Douglass' Paper*, August 20, 1852.

7 Oscar Sherwin, "Sons of Otis and Hancock," *The New England Quarterly*, XIX (June 1946), pp. 221-23.

they met with hostility and sometimes violence from white persons opposed to such interracial socializing.[8]

But, national figures were not alone among Negro abolitionists; there was wide participation in the movement by ordinary folk. When it was founded, three-quarters of the subscribers to Garrison's *Liberator* were Negroes and in the end the paper was almost totally supported by Negroes.

There were many Negro and white abolitionists who, with Douglass, refused to limit their struggles to that for emancipation. Many participated in the fight for civil rights—equality before the law and political participation—and for education for the Negro and desegregation of public facilities. Some abolitionists felt bound even to struggle for social equality.

Regardless of public opposition and personal doubts, some abolitionists considered social intercourse with Negroes a demonstration of true devotion to the cause of their oppressed brethren. Although conceding that one could advocate "the civil emancipation of those whom he would still be unwilling to associate with," the American Anti-Slavery Society reprimanded its members for yielding too readily to prejudice. If color or public opinion alone explained an abolitionist's reluctance to associate with Negroes, then "he wrongs the cause in which he is engaged." When abolitionists did mix with Negroes, it became almost fashionable to tell others about this novel experience, treating it as a personal triumph over the amassed forces of prejudice and evil. Weld, for example, related at great length his daily intercourse with Negroes in Cincinnati. When Negro ministers and friends mixed with whites at the Weld-Angelina Grimke wedding, the new bride explained, "They were our invited guests and we thus had an opportunity to bear our testimony against the horrible prejudice which prevails against colored persons." [9]

Then as now the Negro-American, however, found foreigners to be more agreeable than Americans. On a ship bound for England Americans refused to eat with Frederick Douglass, so he dined with the ship's English captain. Douglass commented: "I declare it is enough to make a slave ashamed of the country which enslaved him."

Too, the "white backlash" was felt in this period of great Negro protest activity. The murder of abolitionist editor, Elijah Lovejoy, was the shocking climax of many a near-murder. Frederick Douglass was nearly killed by a mob in New-

[8] Douglass later split with Garrison and urged support of the Liberty Party as the best means of carrying on the abolition struggle.

[9] Leon F. Litwack, *North of Slavery* (Chicago: University of Chicago Press, 1961), p. 222-23.

castle, Indiana, while on an abolitionist tour. He was clubbed to the ground by the leader of a mob yelling, "Kill the nigger, kill the damn nigger." Garrison barely escaped lynching by a Boston mob when he sought to appear as a speaker at a meeting of the Boston Female Anti-Slavery Society. His clothes were torn off and he was beaten as he was dragged through the streets. The mayor and his posse managed to retrieve Garrison from the mob estimated at thousands and he was taken to jail for protection. He reported that the ladies were greeted with "taunts, hisses, and cheers of mobocratic triumph, from gentlemen of property and standing from all parts of the City." They yelled for him, he reported, "Garrison! We must have Garrison! Out with him! Lynch him." [10]

The abolitionist movement provided the dominant protest of the time, but the fight against segregation in the North was also carried on. The basis for over 50 years' sway of the separate but equal doctrine was laid during this period with the Supreme Court's decision in the Sarah Roberts Case. Charles Sumner and a Negro attorney, Robert Morris, Esq., argued that separate education was unequal in behalf of a five-year-old Negro girl, but the court ruled against her.[11] Protests against segregated transportation [12] continued also, the most famous of battlers in this arena being Sojourner Truth who also was an active fighter for women's rights.

One of the disagreements among Negro abolitionists in this period was the question of whether or not the Negro should seek entry into white American life. The American Moral Reform Society even urged the displacement of the terms "colored" and "African" by the term "oppressed American" in calling for the fullest integration possible. The Society opposed separate Negro organizations, such as the Negro Convention movement, vigorously supported by many Negro abolitionists. Completely opposed to the Moral Reform Society were the believers in colonization who achieved their greatest following in this period of 1835 to 1860. The colonizers stressed the African roots of American Negroes and their kinship with other colored peoples, and agitated for a complete break with white society and the building of black nations in non-white areas—Africa and the Caribbean.

[10] Account given in Harriet Beecher Stowe, *Men of Our Times* (Hartford, Conn.: Hartford Publishing Co., 1868), pp. 172-79.

[11] The Sumner argument is excerpted on pp. 96-102 below.

[12] One of the victories in this fight is recorded by William Still in "A Brief narrative of the Struggle for the rights of the colored people of Philadelphia in the City Railway cars and a Defense of William Still relating to his agency touching the passage of the late bill, et cetera" (Philadelphia: Merrihew & Son, Printers, 1867).

1. THE ABOLITIONISTS

Constitution of the American Anti-Slavery Society*

WHEREAS THE MOST High God "hath made of one blood all nations of men to dwell on the face of the earth," and hath commanded them to love their neighbors as themselves; and whereas, our National Existence is based upon this principle, as recognized in the Declaration of Independence, "that all mankind are created equal, and that they are endowed by their Creator with certain inalienable rights, among which are life, liberty, and the pursuit of happiness"; and whereas, after the lapse of nearly sixty years, since the faith and honor of the American people were pledged to this avowal, before Almighty God and the World, nearly one-sixth part of the nation are held in bondage by their fellow-citizens; and whereas, Slavery is contrary to the principles of natural justice, of our republican form of government, and of the Christian religion, and is destructive of the prosperity of the country, while it is endangering the peace, union, and liberties of the States; and whereas, we believe it the duty and interest of the masters immediately to emancipate their slaves, and that no scheme of expatriation, either voluntary or by compulsion, can remove this great and increasing evil; and whereas, we believe that it is practicable, by appeals to the consciences, hearts, and interests of the people, to awaken a public sentiment throughout the nation that will be opposed to the continuance of Slavery in any part of the Republic, and by effecting the speedy abolition of Slavery, prevent a general convulsion; and whereas, we believe we owe it to the oppressed, to our fellow-citizens who hold slaves, to our whole country, to posterity, and to God, to do all that is lawfully in our power to bring about the extinction of slavery, we do hereby agree, with a prayerful reliance on the Divine aid, to form ourselves into a society, to be governed by the following Constitution:—

ART. I.—This Society shall be called the AMERICAN ANTI-SLAVERY SOCIETY.

ART. II.—The object of this Society is the entire abolition

* Adopted at a convention in Philadelphia, December 4, 1833.

of Slavery in the United States. While it admits that each State, in which Slavery exists, has, by the Constitution of the United States, the exclusive right to *legislate* in regard to its abolition in said State, it shall aim to convince all our fellow-citizens, by arguments addressed to their understandings and consciences, that Slaveholding is a heinous crime in the sight of God, and that the duty, safety, and best interests of all concerned, require its *immediate abandonment*, without expatriation. The Society will also endeavor, in a constitutional way to influence Congress to put an end to the domestic Slave trade, and to abolish Slavery in all those portions of our common country which come under its control, especially in the District of Columbia,—and likewise to prevent the extension of it to any State that may be hereafter admitted to the Union.

Art. III.—This Society shall aim to elevate the character and condition of the people of color, by encouraging their intellectual, moral and religious improvement, and by removing public prejudice, that thus they may, according to their intellectual and moral worth, share an equality with the whites, of civil and religious privileges; but this Society will never, in any way, countenance the oppressed in vindicating their rights by resorting to physical force.

Art. IV.—Any person who consents to the principles of this Constitution, who contributes to the funds of this Society, and is not a Slaveholder, may be a member of this Society, and shall be entitled to vote at the meetings. . . .

The Liberator's *First Editorial**

WILLIAM LLOYD GARRISON

In the month of August, I issued proposals for publishing *"The Liberator"* in Washington City; but the enterprise, though hailed in different sections of the country, was palsied by public indifference. Since that time, the removal of the *Genius of Universal Emancipation* [1] to the Seat of Government has rendered less imperious the establishment of a similar periodical in that quarter.

During my recent tour for the purpose of exciting the minds of the people by a series of discourses on the subject

* *The Liberator*, Vol. I, January 1, 1831.

1 Abolitionist newspaper, published by Benjamin Lundy. Garrison was joint editor in 1829.

of slavery, every place that I visited gave fresh evidence of the fact, that a greater revolution in public sentiment was to be effected in the free states—*and particularly in New England*—than at the south. I found contempt more bitter, opposition more active, detraction more relentless, prejudice more stubborn, and apathy more frozen, than among slave owners themselves. Of course, there were individual exceptions to the contrary. This state of things afflicted, but did not dishearten me. I determined, at every hazard, to lift up the standard of emancipation in the eyes of the nation, *within sight of Bunker Hill and in the birth place of liberty*. That standard is now unfurled; and long may it float, unhurt by the spoliations of time or the missiles of a desperate foe—yea, till every chain be broken, and every bondman set free! Let Southern oppressors tremble—let their secret abettors tremble—let their Northern apologists tremble—let all the enemies of the persecuted blacks tremble.

I deem the publication of my original Prospectus unnecessary, as it has obtained a wide circulation. The principles therein inculcated will be steadily pursued in this paper, excepting that I shall not array myself as the political partisan of any man. In defending the great cause of human rights, I wish to derive the assistance of all religions and of all parties.

Assenting to the "self evident truth" maintained in the American Declaration of Independence, "that all men are created equal, and endowed by their Creator with certain inalienable rights—among which are life, liberty and the pursuit of happiness," I shall strenuously contend for the immediate enfranchisement of our slave population. In Park-Street Church, on the Fourth of July, 1829, in an address on slavery, I unreflectingly assented to the popular but pernicious doctrine of *gradual* abolition. I seize this opportunity to make a full and unequivocal recantation, and thus publicly to ask pardon of my God, of my country, and of my brethren the poor slaves, for having uttered a sentiment so full of timidity, injustice and absurdity. A similar recantation, from my pen, was published in the *Genius of Universal Emancipation* at Baltimore, in September, 1829. My conscience is now satisfied.

I am aware, that many object to the severity of my language; but is there not cause for severity? I *will be* as harsh as truth, and as uncompromising as justice. On this subject, I do not wish to think, or speak, or write, with moderation. No! No! Tell a man whose house is on fire, to give a moderate alarm; tell him to moderately rescue his wife from the hands of the ravisher; tell the mother to gradually extricate her babe from the fire into which it has fallen;—but urge me not to use moderation in a cause like the present. I am in earnest—I will not equivocate—I will not excuse—I will not retreat a single inch—*AND I WILL BE HEARD*. The apathy of the people is enough to make every statue leap from its pedestal, and to hasten the resurrection of the dead.

It is pretended, that I am retarding the cause of emancipation by the coarseness of my invective, and the precipitancy of my measures. *The charge is not true.* On this question my influence,—humble as it is,—is felt at this moment to a considerable extent, and shall be felt in coming years—not perniciously, but beneficially—not as a curse, but as a blessing; and posterity will bear testimony that I was right. I desire to thank God, that he enables me to disregard "the fear of man which bringeth a snare," and to speak his truth in its simplicity and power. . . .

American Slavery As It Is[*]

THEODORE WELD

As SLAVEHOLDERS AND their apologists are volunteer witnesses in their own cause, and are flooding the world with testimony that their slaves are kindly treated; that they are well fed, well clothed, well housed, well lodged, moderately worked, and bountifully provided with all things needful for their comfort, we propose—first, to disprove their assertions by the testimony of a multitude of impartial witnesses, and then to put slaveholders themselves through a course of cross-questioning which shall draw their condemnation out of their own mouths. We will prove that the slaves in the United States are treated with barbarous inhumanity; that they are overworked, underfed, wretchedly clad and lodged, and have insufficient sleep; that they are often made to wear round their necks iron collars armed with prongs, to drag heavy chains and weights at their feet while working in the field, and to wear yokes, and bells, and iron horns; that they

[*] Excerpts from Theodore Weld's introduction to American Anti-Slavery Society, *American Slavery As It Is,* compiled with introduction by Theodore Weld (New York, 1839), pp. 9-10. Weld was one of the founders of the American Anti-Slavery Society and as one of its agents traveled throughout the country speaking against slavery and gaining converts to abolitionism. The rest of this book was a compilation of the testimony of 1,000 witnesses culled from 20,000 newspapers.

are often kept confined in the stocks day and night for weeks together, made to wear gags in their mouths for hours or days, have some of their front teeth torn out or broken off, that they may be easily detected when they run away; that they are frequently flogged with terrible severity, have red pepper rubbed into their lacerated flesh, and hot brine, spirits of turpentine, &c., poured over the gashes to increase the torture; that they are often stripped naked, their backs and limbs cut with knives, bruised and mangled by scores and hundreds of blows with the paddle, and terribly torn by the claws of cats, drawn over them by their tormentors; that they are often hunted with blood hounds and shot down like beasts, or torn in pieces by dogs; that they are often suspended by the arms and whipped and beaten till they faint, and when revived by restoratives, beaten again till they faint, and sometimes till they die; that their ears are often cut off, their eyes knocked out, their bones broken, their flesh branded with red hot irons; that they are maimed, mutilated and burned to death over slow fires. All these things, and more, and worse, we shall *prove*. Reader, we know whereof we affirm, we have weighed it well; *more and worse* WE SHALL PROVE. Mark these words, and read on; we will establish all these facts by the testimony of scores and hundreds of eye witnesses, by the testimony of *slaveholders* in all parts of the slave states, by slaveholding members of Congress and of state legislatures, by ambassadors to foreign courts, by judges, by doctors of divinity, and clergymen of all denominations, by merchants, mechanics, lawyers and physicians, by presidents and professors in colleges and *professional* seminaries, by planters, overseers and drivers. We shall show, not merely that such deeds are committed, but that they are frequent; not done in corners, but before the sun; not in one of the slave states, but in all of them; not perpetrated by brutal overseers and drivers merely, but my magistrates, by legislators, by professors of religion, by preachers of the gospel, by governors of states, by "gentlemen of property and standing," and by delicate females moving in the "highest circles of society." We know, full well, the outcry that will be made by multitudes at these declarations; the multiform cavils, the flat denials, the charges of "exaggeration" and "falsehood" so often bandied, the sneers of affected contempt at the credulity that can believe such things, and the rage and imprecations against those who give them currency. We know, too, the threadbare sophistries by which slaveholders and their apologists seek to evade such testimony. If they admit that such deeds are committed, they tell us that they are exceedingly rare, and therefore furnish no grounds for judging of the general treatment of slaves; that occasionally a brutal wretch in the *free* states barbarously butchers his wife, but that no one thinks of inferring from that, the general treatment of wives at the North and West.

They tell us, also, that the slaveholders of the South are proverbially hospitable, kind, and generous, and it is incredible that they can perpetrate such enormities upon human beings; further, that it is absurd to suppose that they would thus injure their own property, that self-interest would prompt them to treat their slaves with kindness, as none but fools and madmen wantonly destroy their own property; further, that Northern visitors at the South come back testifying to the kind treatment of the slaves, and that the slaves themselves corroborate such representations. All these pleas, and scores of others, are bruited in every corner of the free States; and who that hath eyes to see, has not sickened at the blindness that saw not, at the palsy of heart that felt not, or at the cowardice and sycophancy that dared not expose such shallow fallacies? We are not to be turned from our purpose by such vapid babblings. In their appropriate places, we propose to consider these objections and various others, and to show their emptiness and folly.

The foregoing declarations touching the inflictions upon slaves, are not hap-hazard assertions, nor the exaggerations of fiction conjured up to carry a point; nor are they the rhapsodies of enthusiasm, nor crude conclusions, jumped at by hasty and imperfect investigation, nor the aimless outpourings either of sympathy or poverty; but they are proclamations of deliberate, well-weighed convictions, produced by accumulations of proof, by affirmations and affidavits, by written testimonies and statements of a cloud of witnesses who speak what they know and testify what they have seen, and all these impregnably fortified by proofs innumerable, in the relation of the slaveholder to his slave, the nature of arbitrary power, and the nature and history of man.

Of witnesses whose testimony is embodied in the following pages, a majority are slaveholders, many of the remainder have been slaveholders, but now reside in free States.

Another class whose testimony will be given, consists of those who have furnished the results of their own observation during periods of residence and travel in the slave States.

We will first present the reader with a few *Personal Narratives* furnished by individuals, natives of slave states and others, embodying, in the main, the results of their own observation in the midst of slavery—facts and scenes of which they were eye-witnesses.

In the next place, to give the reader as clear and definite a view of the actual condition of slaves as possible, we propose to make specific points; to pass in review the various particulars in the slave's condition, simply presenting sufficient testimony under each head to settle the question in every candid mind. The examination will be conducted by stating distinct propositions, and in the following order of topics.

1. *The Food of the Slaves, the Kinds, Quality and Quantity, also, the Number and Time of Meals Each Day, &c*
2. *Their hours of Labor and Rest*
3. *Their clothing*
4. *Their Dwellings*
5. *Their Privations and Inflictions*
6. *In conclusion,* a variety of *Objections and Arguments* will be considered which are used by the advocates of slavery to set aside the force of testimony, and to show that the slaves are kindly treated.

Between the larger divisions of the work, brief personal narratives will be inserted, containing a mass of facts and testimony, both general and specific. . . .

An Appeal to the Christian Women of the South

ANGELINA E. GRIMKÉ[*]

. . . WELL MAY THE poet exclaim in bitter sarcasm,

> "The fustian flag that proudly waves
> In solemn mockery *o'er a land of slaves.*"

Can you not, my friends, understand the signs of the times; do you not see the sword of retributive justice hanging over the South, or are you still slumbering at your posts?—Are

* Excerpts from Angelina E. Grimké, *An Appeal to the Christian Women of the South* (New York: American Anti-Slavery Society, 1836), pp. 23-35. The same year her sister, Sarah, published *An Epistle to the Clergy of the South.* The Grimké sisters were white Southerners active in the abolitionist movement. They were among the abolitionists who extended abolitionism to include social equality.

there no Shiphrahs, no Puahs among you, who will dare in Christian firmness and Christian meekness, to refuse to obey the *wicked laws* which require *woman to enslave, to degrade and to brutalize woman?* Are there no Miriams, who would rejoice to lead out the captive daughters of the Southern States to liberty and light? Are there no Huldahs there who will dare to *speak the truth* concerning the sins of the people and those judgments, which it requires no prophet's eye to see, must follow if repentance is not speedily sought? Is there no Esther among you who will plead for the poor devoted slave? Read the history of this Persian queen, it is full of instruction; she at first refused to plead for the Jews; but, hear the words of Mordecai, "Think not within thyself, that *thou* shalt escape in the king's house more than all the Jews, for *if thou altogether holdest thy peace at this time,* then shall there enlargement and deliverance arise to the Jews from another place: but *thou and thy father's house shall be destroyed.*" Listen, too, to her magnanimous reply to this powerful appeal; *"I will* go in unto the king, which is *not* according to the law, and if I perish, I perish." Yes! if there were but *one* Esther at the South, she *might* save her country from ruin; but let the Christian women there arise, as the Christian women of Great Britain did, in the majesty of moral power, and that salvation is certain. Let them embody themselves in societies and send petitions up to their different legislatures, entreating their husbands, fathers, brothers and sons, to abolish the institution of slavery; no longer to subject *woman* to the scourge and the chain, to mental darkness and moral degradation; no longer to tear husbands from their wives, and children from their parents; no longer to make men, women, and children, work *without wages;* no longer to make their lives bitter in hard bondage; no longer to reduce *American citizens* to the abject conditions of *slaves,* of "chattels personal;" no longer to barter the *image of God* in human shambles for corruptible things such as silver and gold.

The *women of the South can overthrow* this horrible system of oppression and cruelty, licentiousness and wrong. Such appeals to your legislatures would be irresistible, for there is something in the heart of man which *will bend under moral suasion.* There is a swift witness for truth in his bosom, which *will respond to truth* when it is uttered with calmness and dignity. If you could obtain but six signatures to such a petition in only one state, I would say, send up that petition, and be not in the least discouraged by the scoffs and jeers of the heartless, or the resolution of the house to lay it on the table. It will be a great thing if the subject can be introduced into your legislatures in any way, even by *women*, and *they* will be the most likely to introduce it there in the best possible manner, as a matter of *morals* and *religion*, not of expediency or politics. You may petition, too, the different ecclesiastical bodies of the slave states. Slavery must be attacked with the whole power of truth and the sword of the spirit. You must take it up on *Christian* ground, and fight against it with Christian weapons, whilst your feet are shod with the preparation of the gospel of. peace. And *you are now* loudly called upon by the cries of the widow and the orphan, to arise and gird yourselves for this great moral conflict, with the whole armour of righteousness upon the right hand and on the left.

There is every encouragement for you to labor and pray, my friends, because the abolition of slavery as well as its existence, has been the theme of prophecy. "Ethiopia (says the Psalmist) shall stretch forth her hands unto God." And is she not now doing so? Are not the Christian negroes of the south lifting their hands in prayer for deliverance, just as the Israelites did when their redemption was drawing nigh? Are they not sighing and crying by reason of the hard bondage? And think you, that He, of whom it was said, "and God heard their groaning, and their cry came up unto him by reason of the hard bondage," think you that his ear is heavy that he cannot *now* hear the cries of his suffering children? Or that He who raised up a Moses, an Aaron, and a Miriam, to bring them up out of the land of Egypt from the house of bondage, cannot now, with a high hand and a stretched out arm, rid the poor negroes out of the hands of their masters? Surely you believe that his arm is *not* shortened that he cannot save. And would not such a work of mercy redound to his glory? But another string of the harp of prophecy vibrates to the song of deliverance: "But they shall sit every man under his vine, and under his fig-tree, and *none shall make them afraid;* for the mouth of the Lord of Hosts hath spoken it." The *slave* never can do this as long as he is a *slave;* whilst he is a "chattel personal" he can own *no* property; but the time *is to come* when *every* man is to sit under *his own* vine and *his own* fig-tree, and no domineering driver, or irresponsible master, or irascible mistress, shall make him afraid of the chain or the whip. Hear, too, the sweet tones of another string: "Many shall run to and fro, and *knowledge* shall be increased." Slavery is an insurmountable barrier to the increase of knowledge in every community where it exists; *slavery, then, must be abolished before* this prediction can be fulfilled. The last chord I shall touch, will be this, "They shall *not* hurt nor destroy in all my holy mountain."

Slavery, then, must be overthrown before the prophecies can be accomplished, but how are they to be fulfilled? Will the wheels of the millennial car be rolled onward by miraculous power? No! God designs to confer this holy privilege upon *man;* it is through *his* instrumentality that the great and glorious work of reforming the world is to be done. And see you not how the mighty engine of *moral power* is dragging in its rear the Bible and peace societies, anti-slavery and temperance, sabbath schools, moral reform, and missions? or to adopt another figure, do not these seven philanthropic associations compose the beautiful tints in that bow of promise which spans the arch of our moral heaven? Who does not believe, that if these societies were broken up, their constitutions burnt, and the vast machinery with which they are laboring to regenerate mankind was stopped, that the black clouds of vengeance would soon burst over our world, and every city would witness the fate of the devoted cities of the plain? Each one of these societies is walking abroad through the earth scattering the seeds of truth over the wide field of our world, not with the hundred hands of a Briareus, but with a hundred thousand.

Another encouragement for you to labor, my friends, is, that you will have the prayers and co-operation of English and Northern philanthropists. You will never bend your knees in supplication at the throne of grace for the overthrow of slavery, without meeting there the spirits of other Christians, who will mingle their voices with yours, as the morning or evening sacrifice ascends to God. . . .

But I will now say a few words on the subject of Abolitionism. Doubtless you have all heard Anti-Slavery Societies denounced as insurrectionary and mischievous, fanatical and dangerous. It has been said they publish the most abominable untruths, and that they are endeavoring to excite rebellions at the South. Have you believed these reports, my friends? have *you* also been deceived by these false assertions? Listen to me, then, whilst I endeavor to wipe from the fair character of Abolitionism such unfounded accusations. You know that *I* am a Southerner; you know that my dearest relatives are now in a slave State. Can you for a moment believe I would prove so recreant to the feelings of a daughter and a sister, as to join a society which was seeking to overthrow slavery by falsehood, bloodshed, and murder? I appeal to you who have known and loved me in days that are passed, can *you* believe it? No! my friends. As a Carolinian, I was peculiarly jealous of any movements on this subject; and before I would join an Anti-Slavery Society, I took the precaution of becoming acquainted with some of the leading Abolitionists, of reading their publications and attending their meetings, at which I heard addresses from both colored and white men; and it was not until I was fully convinced that their principles were *entirely pacific,* and their efforts *only moral,* that I gave my name as a member to the Female Anti-Slavery Society of Philadelphia. Since that time, I have regularly taken the Liberator, and read many Anti-Slavery pamphlets and papers and books, and can assure you I *never* have seen a single insurrectionary paragraph, and never read any account of cruelty which I could not believe. Southerners may deny the truth of these accounts, but why do they not *prove* them to be false. Their violent expressions of horror at such accounts being believed, *may* deceive some, but they cannot deceive *me,* for I lived too long in the midst of slavery, not to know what slavery is. When *I* speak of this system, "I speak that I do know," and I am not at all afraid to assert, that Anti-Slavery publications have *not* overdrawn the monstrous features of slavery at all. And many a Southerner *knows* this as well as I do. A lady in North Carolina remarked to a friend of mine, about eighteen months since, "Northerners know nothing at all about slavery; they think it is perpetual bondage only; but of the *depth of degradation* that word involves, they have no conception; if they had, *they would never cease* their efforts until so *horrible* a system was overthrown." She did not know how faithfully some Northern men and Northern women had studied this subject; how diligently they had searched out the cause of "him who had none to help him," and how fearlessly they had told the story of the negro's wrongs. Yes, Northerners know *every* thing about slavery now. This monster of iniquity has been unveiled to the world, her frightful features unmasked, and soon, very soon will she be regarded with no more complacency by the American republic than is the idol of Juggernaut, rolling its bloody wheels over the crushed bodies of its prostrate victims. . . .

What can I say more, my friends, to induce *you* to set your hands, and heads, and hearts, to this great work of justice and mercy. Perhaps you have feared the consequences of immediate Emancipation, and been frightened by all those dreadful prophecies of rebellion, bloodshed and murder, which have been uttered. "Let no man deceive you;" they are the predictions of that same "lying spirit" which spoke through the four thousand prophets of old, to Ahab king of

Israel, urging him on to destruction. *Slavery* may produce these horrible scenes if it is continued five years longer, but Emancipation *never will*.

I can prove the *safety* of immediate Emancipation by history. In St. Domingo in 1793 six hundred thousand slaves were set free in a white population of forty-two thousand. That Island "marched as by enchantment towards its ancient splendor, cultivation prospered, every day produced perceptible proofs of its progress, and the negroes all continued quietly to work on the different plantations, until in 1802, France determined to reduce these liberated slaves again to bondage. It was at *this time* that all those dreadful scenes of cruelty occurred, which we so often *unjustly* hear spoken of, as the effects of Abolition. They were occasioned *not* by Emancipation, but by the base attempt to fasten the chains of slavery on the limbs of liberated slaves.

In Guadaloupe eighty-five thousand slaves were freed in a white population of thirteen thousand. The same prosperous effects followed manumission here, that had attended it in Hayti, every thing was quiet until Buonaparte sent out a fleet to reduce these negroes again to slavery, and in 1802 this institution was re-established in that Island. In 1834, when Great Britain determined to liberate the slaves in her West India colonies, and proposed the apprenticeship system; the planters of Bermuda and Antigua, after having joined the other planters in their representations of the bloody consequences of Emancipation, in order if possible to hold back the hand which was offering the boon of freedom to the poor negro; as soon as they found such falsehoods were utterly disregarded, and Abolition must take place, came forward voluntarily, and asked for the compensation which was due to them, saying, *they preferred immediate emancipation,* and were not afraid of any insurrection. And how is it with these islands now? They are decidedly more prosperous than any of those in which the apprenticeship system was adopted, and England is now trying to abolish that system, so fully convinced is she that immediate Emancipation is the *safest* and the best plan.

And why not try it in the Southern States, if it *never* has occasioned rebellion; if *not a drop of blood* has ever been shed in consequence of it, though it has been so often tried, why should we suppose it would produce such disastrous consequences now? "Be not deceived then, God is not mocked," by such false excuses for not doing justly and loving mercy. There is nothing to fear from immediate Emancipation, but *every thing* from the continuance of slavery.

Sisters in Christ, I have done. As a Southerner, I have felt it was my duty to address you. I have endeavoured to set before you the exceeding sinfulness of slavery, and to point you to the example of those noble women who have been raised up in the church to effect great revolutions, and to suffer for the truth's sake. I have appealed to your sympathies as women, to your sense of duty as *Christian women.* I have attempted to vindicate the Abolitionists, to prove the entire safety of immediate Emancipation, and to plead the cause of the poor and oppressed. I have done—I have sowed the seeds of truth, but I well know, that even if an Apollo were to follow in my steps to water them, *"God only* can give the increase." To Him then who is able to prosper the work of his servant's hand, I commend this Appeal in fervent prayer, that as he "hath *chosen the weak things of the world,* to confound the things which are mighty," so He may cause His blessing, to descend and carry conviction to the hearts of many Lydias through these speaking pages. Farewell—Count me not your "enemy because I have told you the truth," but believe me in unfeigned affection,

Your sympathizing Friend,

ANGELINA E. GRIMKÉ.

John Brown's Last Statement to Court, Nov. 2, 1859

I HAVE, MAY it please the Court, a few words to say.

In the first place, I deny everything but what I have all along admitted,—the design on my part to free the slaves. I intended certainly to have made a clean thing of that matter, as I did last winter, when I went into Missouri and there took slaves without the snapping of a gun on either side, moved them through the country, and finally left them in Canada. I designed to have done the same thing again, on a larger scale. That was all I intended. I never did intend murder, or treason, or the destruction of property, or to excite or incite slaves to rebellion, or to make insurrection.

I have another objection; and that is, it is unjust that I should suffer such a penalty. Had I interfered in the manner which I admit, and which I admit has been fairly proved (for I admire the truthfulness and candor of the greater portion of the witnesses who have testified in this case),—had I so interfered in behalf of the rich, the powerful, the intelligent, the so-called great, or in behalf of any of their friends,—either father, mother, brother, sister, wife, or children, or any of that class,—and suffered and sacrificed what I have in this interference, it would have been all right; and every man in this Court would have deemed it an act worthy of reward rather than punishment.

This Court acknowledges, as I suppose, the validity of the law of God. I see a book kissed here which I suppose to be the Bible, or at least the New Testament. That teaches me that all things whatsoever I would that man should do to me, I should do even so to them. It teaches me, further, to "remember them that are in bonds, as bound with them." I endeavored to act up to that instruction. I say, I am yet too young to understand that God is any respecter of persons. I believe that to have interfered as I have done—as I have always freely admitted I have done—in behalf of His despised poor, was not wrong, but right. Now, if it is deemed necessary that I should forfeit my life for the furtherance of the ends of justice, and mingle my blood further with the blood of my children and with the blood of millions in this slave country whose rights are disregarded by wicked, cruel, and unjust enactments,—I submit; so let it be done!

Let me say one word further.

I feel entirely satisfied with the treatment I have received on my trial. Considering all the circumstances, it has been more generous than I expected. But I feel no consciousness of guilt. I have stated from the first what was my intention, and what was not. I never had any design against the life of any person, nor any disposition to commit treason, or excite slaves to rebel, or make any general insurrection. I never encouraged any man to do so, but always discouraged any idea of that kind.

Let me say, also, a word in regard to the statements made by some of those connected with me. I hear it has been stated by some of them that I have induced them to join me. But the contrary is true. I do not say this to injure them, but as regretting their weakness. There is not one of them but joined me of his own accord, and the greater part of them at their own expense. A number of them I never saw, and never had a word of conversation with, till the day they came to me; and that was for the purpose I have stated.

Now I have done.

John Brown's Last Written Statement *

I, John Brown, am now quite *certain* that the crimes of this *guilty land* will never be purged away but with *blood*. I had, as I now think vainly, flattered myself that without very much bloodshed it might be done.

2. THE NEGRO VIEW

Editorial from North Star, *Vol. 1, No. 1*†

FREDERICK DOUGLASS

WE SOLEMNLY DEDICATE the "North Star" to the cause of our long oppressed and plundered fellow countrymen. May God bless the undertaking to your good! It shall fearlessly assert your rights, faithfully proclaim your wrongs, and earnestly demand for you instant and even-handed justice. Giving no quarter to slavery at the South, it will hold no truce with oppressors at the North. While it shall boldly advocate emancipation for our enslaved brethren, it will omit no opportunity to gain for the nominally free complete enfranchisement. Every effort to injure or degrade you or your cause—originating wheresoever, or with whomsoever—shall find in it a constant, unswerving and inflexible foe. . . .

Remember that we are one, that our cause is one, and that we must help each other, if we would succeed. We have drank to the dregs the bitter cup of slavery; we have worn the heavy yoke; we have sighed beneath our bonds, and writhed beneath the bloody lash;—cruel mementoes of our oneness are indelibly marked on our living flesh. We are one with you under the ban of prejudice and proscription—one with you under the slander of inferiority—one with you in social and political disfranchisement. What you suffer, we suffer; what you endure, we endure. We are indissolubly united, and must fall or flourish together. . . .

It is scarcely necessary for us to say that our desire to occu-

* The statement was handed to one of the guards on the morning of his execution, Dec. 2, 1859.

† Reprinted in Herbert Aptheker, *A Documentary History of the Negro People in the United States* (New York: Citadel Press, 1951) pp. 255-56.

py our present position at the head of an Anti-Slavery Journal, has resulted from no unworthy distrust or ungrateful want of appreciation of the zeal, integrity or ability of the noble band of white laborers in this department of our cause; but, from the sincere and settled conviction that such a Journal, if conducted with only moderate skill and ability, would do a most important and indispensable work, which it would be wholly impossible for our white friends to do for us.

It is neither a reflection on the fidelity, nor a disparagement of the ability of our friends and fellow-laborers, to assert what "common sense affirms and only folly denies," that the man who has *suffered the wrong* is the man to *demand redress*,—that the man STRUCK is the man to CRY OUT—and that he who has *endured the cruel pangs of Slavery* is the man to *advocate Liberty*. It is evident we must be our own representatives and advocates—not exclusively, but peculiarly—not distinct from, but in connection with our white friends. In the grand struggle for liberty and equality now waging it is meet, right and essential that there should arise in our ranks authors and editors, as well as orators, for it is in these capacities that the most permanent good can be rendered to our cause. . . .

David Walker's Appeal*

THE AMERICANS OF North and of South America, including the West India Islands—no trifling portion of whom were, for stealing, murdering, &c. compelled to flee from Europe, to save their necks or banishment, have effected their escape to this continent, where God blessed them with all the comforts of life—He gave them a plenty of every thing calculated to do them good—not satisfied with this, however, they wanted slaves, and wanted us for their slaves, who belong to the Holy Ghost, and no other, who we shall have to serve instead of tyrants.—I say, the Americans want us, the property of the Holy Ghost, to serve them. But there is a day fast approaching, when (unless there is a universal repentance on the part of the whites, which will scarcely take place, they

* Excerpts from David Walker, *An Appeal to the Coloured Citizens of the World* (Boston, 1829). Excerpts from Article IV, "Our Wretchedness in Consequence of the Colonizing Scheme." Walker was a free Negro born in North Carolina in 1785. He lived and died in Boston where he operated an old clothes shop. In the *Appeal* Walker noted that if anyone wished to enslave or murder him for the truth "know ye, that I am in the hand of God, and at your disposal." "I

have got to be so hardened in consequence of our blood, and so wise in their own conceit.) To be plain and candid with you, Americans! I say that the day is fast approaching, when there will be a greater time on the continent of America, than ever was witnessed upon this earth, since it came from the hand of its Creator. Some of you have done us so much injury, that you will never be able to repent.—Your cup must be filled.—You want us for your slaves, and shall have enough of us—God is just, *who will give you your fill of us*. . . .

If any of us see fit to go away, go to those who have been for many years, and are now our greatest earthly friends and benefactors—the English. If not so, go to our brethren, the Haytians, who, according to their word, are bound to protect and comfort us. The Americans say, that we are ungrateful —but I ask them for heaven's sake, what should we be grateful to them for—for murdering our fathers and mothers?—Or do they wish us to return thanks to them for chaining and handcuffing us, branding us, cramming fire down our throats, or for keeping us in slavery, and beating us nearly or quite to death to make us work in ignorance and miseries, to support them and their families. They certainly think that we are a gang of fools. Those among them, who have volunteered their services for our redemption, though we are unable to compensate them for their labours, we nevertheless thank them from the bottom of our hearts, and have our eyes steadfastly fixed upon them, and their labours of love for God and man.—But do slave-holders think that we thank them for keeping us in miseries, and taking our lives by the inches? . . . I have several times called the white Americans our *natural enemies*—I shall here define my meaning of the phrase. Shem, Ham and Japeth, together with their father Noah and wives, I believe were not natural enemies to each other. When the ark rested after the flood upon Mount Ararat, in Asia, they (eight) were all the people which could be found alive in all the earth—in fact if Scriptures be true, (which I believe are) there were no other living men in all the earth, notwithstanding some ignorant creatures hesitate not to tell us that we, (the blacks) are the seed of Cain the murderer of his brother Abel. But where or of whom those ignorant and avaricious wretches could have got their information, I am unable to declare. Did they receive it from the Bible? I have searched the Bible as well as they, if I am not as well learned as they are, and have never seen a verse which testifies wheth-

count my life not dear unto me," he wrote, "but I am ready to be offered at any moment." Walker was found dead in the doorway of his shop on June 28, 1830, shortly after the appearance of the third edition of the *Appeal*.

er we are the seed of Cain or of Abel. Yet those men tell us that we are the seed of Cain, and that God put a dark stain upon us, that we might be known as their slaves!!! Now, I ask those avaricious and ignorant wretches, who act more like the seed of Cain, by murdering the whites or the blacks? How many vessel loads of human beings have the blacks thrown into the seas? How many thousand souls have the blacks murdered in cold blood, to make them work in wretchedness and ignorance, to support them and their families? [1]—However, let us be the seed of *Cain, Harry, Dick,* or *Tom!!!* God will show the whites what we are, yet. I say, from the beginning, I do not think that we were natural enemies to each other. But the whites having made us so wretched, by subjecting us to slavery, and having murdered so many millions of us, in order to make us work for them, and out of devilishness—and they taking our wives, whom we love as we do ourselves—our mothers, who bore the pains of death to give us birth—our fathers and dear little children, and ourselves, and strip and beat us one before the other—chain, hand-cuff, and drag us about like rattlesnakes —shoot us down like wild bears, before each other's faces, to make us submissive to, and work to support them and their families. They (the whites) know well, if we are *men*—and there is a secret monitor in their hearts which tells them we are—they know, I say, if we *are* men, and see them treating us in the manner they do, that there can be nothing in our hearts but death alone, for them, notwithstanding we may appear cheerful, when we see them murdering our dear mothers and wives, because we cannot help ourselves. Man, in all ages and all nations of the earth, is the same. Man is a peculiar creature—he is the image of his God, though he may be subjected to the most wretched condition upon earth, yet the spirit and feeling which constitute the creature, man, can never be entirely erased from his breast, because the God who made him after his own image, planted it in his heart; he cannot get rid of it. The whites knowing this, they do not know what to do; they know that they have done us so much injury, they are afraid that we, being men, and not brutes, will retaliate, and woe will be to them; therefore, that dreadful fear, together with an avaricious spirit, and the natural love in them, to be called masters, (which term will yet honour them with to their sorrow) bring them to the resolve that

[1] How many millions souls of the human family have the blacks beat nearly to death, to keep them from learning to read the Word of God, and from writing. And telling lies about them, by holding them up to the world as a tribe of TALKING APES, void of INTELLECT!!!!! *incapable* of LEARNING, &c.

they will keep us in ignorance and wretchedness, as long as they possibly can,[2] and make the best of their time, while it lasts. Consequently they, themselves, (and not us) render themselves our natural enemies, by treating us so cruel. They keep us miserable now, and call us their property, but some of them will have enough of us by and by—their stomachs shall run over with us; they want us for their slaves, and shall have us to their fill. We are all in the world together!!—I said above, because we cannot help ourselves, (viz. we cannot help the whites murdering our mothers and our wives) but this statement is incorrect—for we can help ourselves; for, if we lay aside abject servility, and be determined to act like men, and not brutes—the murderers among the whites would be afraid to show their cruel heads. But O, my God! —in sorrow I must say it, that my colour, all over the world, have a mean, servile spirit. They yield in a moment to the whites, let them be right or wrong—the reason they are able to keep their feet on our throats. Oh! my coloured brethren, all over the world, when shall we arise from this death-like apathy?—And be men!! You will notice, if ever we become men, (I mean *respectable* men, such as other people are,) we must exert ourselves to the full. For remember, that it is the greatest desire and object of the greater part of the whites, to keep us ignorant, and make us work to support them and their families.—Here now, in the Southern and Western sections of this country, there are at least three coloured persons for one white, why is it, that those few weak, good-for-nothing whites, are able to keep so many able men, one of whom, can put to flight a dozen whites, in wretchedness and misery? It shows at once, what the blacks are, we are ignorant, abject, servile and mean—and the whites know it—they know that we are too servile to assert our rights as men—or they would not fool with us as they do. Would they fool with any other peoples as they do with us? No, they know too well, that they would get themselves ruined. Why do they not bring the inhabitants of Asia to be body servants to them? They know

---

[2] And still hold us up with indignity as being incapable of acquiring knowledge!!! See the inconsistency of the assertions of those wretches —they beat us inhumanely, sometimes almost to death, for attempting to inform ourselves by reading the *Word* of our Maker, and at the same time tell us, that we are beings *void of intellect!!!!* How admirably their practices agree with their professions in this case. Let me cry shame upon you Americans, for such outrages upon human nature!!! If it were possible for the whites always to keep us ignorant and miserable, and make us work to enrich them and their children, and insult our feelings by representing us as *talking Apes,* what would they do? But glory, honour and praise to Heaven's King, that the sons and daughters of Africa, will, in spite of all the opposition of their enemies, stand forth in all the dignity and glory that is granted by the Lord to his creature man.

that would get their bodies rent and torn from head to foot. Why do they not get the Aborigines of this country to be slaves to them and their children, to work their farms and dig their mines? They know well that the Aborigines of this country, (or Indians) would tear them from the earth. The Indians would not rest day or night, they would be up all times of night, cutting their cruel throats. But my colour, (some, not all,) are willing to stand still and be murdered by the cruel whites. In some of the West-Indies Islands, and over a large part of South America, there are six or eight coloured persons for one white.[3] Why do they not take possession of those places? Who hinders them? It is not the avaricious whites—for they are too busily engaged in laying up money —derived from the blood and tears of the blacks. The fact is, they are too servile, they love to have Masters too well!! Some of our brethren, too, who seeking more after self aggrandisement, than the glory of God, and the welfare of their brethren, join in with our oppressors, to ridicule and say all manner of evils falsely against our Bishop [Richard Allen]. They think, that they are doing great things, when they can get in company with the whites, to ridicule and make sport of

[3] For instance in the two States of Georgia, and South Carolina, there are, perhaps, not much short of six or seven hundred thousand persons of colour; and if I was a gambling character, I would not be afraid to stake down upon the board FIVE CENTS against TEN, that there are in the single State of Virginia, five or six hundred thousand Coloured persons. Four hundred and fifty thousand of whom (let them be well equipt for war) I would put against every white person on the whole continent of America. (Why? why because I know that the Blacks, once they get involved in a war, had rather die than to live, they either kill or be killed.) The whites know this too, which make them quake and tremble. To show the world further, how servile the coloured people are, I will only hold up to view, the one Island of Jamaica, as a specimen of our meanness.

In that Island, there are three hundred and fifty thousand souls—of whom fifteen thousand are whites, the remainder, three hundred and thirty-five thousand are coloured people! and this Island is ruled by the white people!!!!!!! (15,000) ruling and tyranizing over 335,000 persons!!!!!!!!—O! coloured men!! O! coloured men!!! O! coloured men!!! Look!! look!!! at this!!!! and, tell me if we are not abject and servile enough, how long, O! how long my colour shall we be dupes and dogs to the cruel whites?—I only passed Jamaica, and its inhabitants, in review as a specimen to show the world, the condition of the Blacks at this time, now coloured people of the whole world, I beg you to look at the (15000 white,) and (Three Hundred and Thirty-five Thousand coloured people) in that Island, and tell me how can the white tyrant of the world but say that we are not men, but were made to be slaves and Dogs to them and their children forever!!!!!!—why my friend only look at the thing!!!! (15000) whites keeping in wretchedness and degradation (335000) viz. 22 coloured persons for one white!!!!!!! when at the same time, an equal number (15000) Blacks, would almost take the whole of South America, because where they go as soldiers to fight death follows in their train.

those who are labouring for their good. Poor ignorant creatures, they do not know that the sole aim and object of the
whites, are only to make fools and slaves of them, and put
the whip to them, and make them work to support them and
their families. . . . Thus, we see, my brethren, the two very
opposite positions of those great men, who have written respecting this "Colonizing Plan." (Mr. Clay and his slave-holding party,) men who are resolved to keep us in eternal
wretchedness, are also bent upon sending us to Liberia. While
the Reverend Bishop Allen, and his party, men who have the
fear of God, and the wellfare of their brethren at heart. The
Bishop, in particular, whose labours for the salvation of his
brethren, are well known to a large part of those, who dwell
in the United States, are completely opposed to the plan—
and advise us to stay where we are. Now we have to determine whose advice we will take respecting this all important
matter, whether we will adhere to Mr. Clay and his slave-
holding party, who have always been our oppressors and
murderers, and who are for colonizing us, more through apprehension than humanity, or to this godly man who has
done so much for our benefit, together with the advice of all
the good and wise among us and the whites. Will any of us
leave our homes and go to Africa? I hope not.[4] Let them
commence their attack upon us as they did on our brethren
in Ohio.

Sojourner Truth[*]

WHILE SOJOURNER WAS engaged in the hospital, she often had
occasion to procure articles from various parts of the city for
the sick soldiers, and would sometimes be obliged to walk a
long distance, carrying her burdens upon her arm. She would
gladly have availed herself of the street cars; but, although
there was on each track one car called the Jim Crow car,
nominally for the accommodation of colored people, yet
should they succeed in getting on at all they would seldom

[4] Those who are ignorant enough to go to Africa, the coloured people ought to be glad to have them go, for if they are ignorant enough
to let the whites *fool* them off to Africa, they would be no small injury
to us if they reside in this country.

[*] Sojourner Truth, *Narrative of Sojourner Truth* (Boston, 1875), pp.
184-87. Sojourner Truth was born a slave in Ulster County, New
York, around 1800. She traveled in the North speaking against slavery
and for women's rights. She died in 1883 in Battle Creek, Mich.

have more than the privilege of standing, as the seats were usually filled with white folks. Unwilling to submit to this state of things, she complained to the president of the street railroad, who ordered the Jim Crow car to be taken off. A law was now passed giving the colored people equal car privileges with the white.

Not long after this, Sojourner, having occasion to ride, signaled the car, but neither conductor nor driver noticed her. Soon another followed, and she raised her hand again, but they also turned away. She then gave three tremendous yelps, "I want to ride! *I want to ride!!* I WANT TO RIDE!!!" Consternation seized the passing crowd—people, carriages, go-carts of every description stood still. The car was effectually blocked up, and before it could move on, Sojourner had jumped aboard. Then there arose a great shout from the crowd, "Ha! ha! ha!! She has beaten him," &c. The angry conductor told her to go forward where the horses were, or he would put her out. Quietly seating herself, she informed him that she was a passenger. "Go forward where the horses are, or I will throw you out," said he in a menacing voice. She told him that she was neither a Marylander nor a Virginian to fear his threats; but was from the Empire State of New York, and knew the laws as well as he did.

Several soldiers were in the car, and when other passengers came in, they related the circumstance and said, "You ought to have heard that old woman talk to the conductor." Sojourner rode farther than she needed to go; for a ride was so rare a privilege that she determined to make the most of it. She left the car feeling very happy, and said, "Bless God! I have had a ride."

Returning one day from the Orphan's Home at Georgetown, she hastened to reach a car; but they paid no attention to her signal, and kept ringing a bell that they might not hear her. She ran after it, and when it stopped to take other passengers, she succeeded in overtaking it and, getting in, said to the conductor, "It is a shame to make a lady run so." He told her if she said another word, he would put her off the car, and came forward as if to execute his threat. She replied, "If you attempt that, it will cost you more than your car and horses are worth." A gentleman of dignified and commanding manner, wearing a general's uniform, interfered in her behalf, and the conductor gave her no further trouble.

At another time, she was sent to Georgetown to obtain a nurse for the hospital, which being accomplished, they went to the station and took seats in an empty car, but had not proceeded far before two ladies came in, and seating themselves opposite the colored woman began a whispered conversation, frequently casting scornful glances at the latter. The nurse, for the first time in her life finding herself in one sense on a level with white folks and being much abashed, hung her poor old head nearly down to her lap; but Sojourner, nothing daunted, looked fearlessly about. At length one of the ladies called out, in a weak, faint voice, "Conductor, conductor, does niggers ride in these cars?" He hesitatingly answered, "Ye yea-yes," to which she responded, " 'Tis a shame and a disgrace. They ought to have a nigger car on the track." Sojourner remarked, "Of course colored people ride in the cars. Street cars are designed for poor white, and colored, folks, and will take them 2 or 3 miles for sixpence. Then ask for a nigger car!! Carriages are for ladies and gentlemen." Promptly acting upon this hint, they arose to leave. "Ah!" said Sojourner, "now they are going to take a carriage. Good by, ladies."

Mrs. Laura Haviland, a widely known philanthropist, spent several months in the same hospital and sometimes went about the city with Sojourner to procure necessaries for the invalids. Returning one day, being much fatigued, Mrs. Haviland proposed to take a car although she was well aware that a white person was seldom allowed to ride if accompanied by a black one. "As Mrs. Haviland signaled the car," says Sojourner, "I stepped one side as if to continue my walk and when it stopped I ran and jumped aboard. The conductor pushed me back, saying, 'Get out of the way and let this lady come in.' Whoop! said I, I am a lady too. We met with no further opposition till we were obliged to change cars. A man coming out as we were going into the next car, asked the conductor if 'niggers were allowed to ride.' The conductor grabbed me by the shoulder and jerking me around, ordered me to get out. I told him I would not. Mrs. Haviland took hold of my other arm and said, 'Don't put her out.' The conductor asked if I belonged to her. 'No,' replied Mrs. Haviland, 'She belongs to humanity.' 'Then take her and go,' said he, and giving me another push slammed me against the door. I told him I would let him know whether he could shove me about like a dog, and said to Mrs. Haviland, Take the number of this car.

"At this, the man looked alarmed, and gave us no more trouble. When we arrived at the hospital, the surgeons were called in to examine my shoulder and found that a bone was misplaced. I complained to the president of the road, who advised me to arrest the man for assault and battery. The Bureau furnished me a lawyer, and the fellow lost his situation.

It created a great sensation, and before the trial was ended, the inside of the cars looked like pepper and salt; and I felt, like Poll Parrot, 'Jack, I am riding.' A little circumstance will show how great a change a few weeks had produced: A lady saw some colored women looking wistfully toward a car, when the conductor, halting, said, 'Walk in, ladies.' Now they who had so lately cursed me for wanting to ride, could stop for black as well as white, and could even condescend to say, 'Walk in, ladies.' "

Speech Against Segregated Transportation*

CHARLES LENOX REMOND

MR. CHAIRMAN, AND Gentlemen of the Committee: In rising at this time, and on this occasion, being the first person of color who has ever addressed either of the bodies assembling in this building, I should, perhaps, in the first place, observe that, in consequence of the many misconstructions of the principles and measures of which I am the humble advocate, I may in like manner be subject to similar misconceptions from the moment I open my lips in behalf of the prayer of the petitioners for whom I appear, and therefore feel I have the right at least to ask, at the hands of this intelligent Committee, an impartial hearing; and that whatever prejudices they may have imbibed, be eradicated from their minds, if such exist. I have, however, too much confidence in their intelligence, and too much faith in their determination to do their duty as the representatives of this Commonwealth, to presume they can be actuated by partial motives. Trusting, as I do, that the day is not distant, when, on all questions touching the rights of the citizens of this State, men shall be considered great only as they are good, and not that it shall be told, and painfully experienced, that, in this country, this State, aye, this city, the Athens of America, the rights, privileges and immunities of its citizens are measured by complexion, or any other physical peculiarity or conformation, especially such as over which no man has any control. Complexion can in no sense be construed into crime, much less be

* Speech delivered before a committee of the Massachusetts House of Representatives, February, 1842. Reprinted in *The Liberator*, February 25, 1842. Remond was an active leader of the American Anti-Slavery Society.

rightfully made the criterion of rights. Should the people of color, through a revolution of Providence, become a majority, to the last I would oppose it upon the same principle; for, in either case, it would be equally reprehensible and unjustifiable—alike to be condemned and repudiated. It is JUSTICE I stand here to claim, and not FAVOR for either complexion.

And now, sir, I shall endeavor to confine my remarks to the same subject which has occupied the attention of the Committee thus far, and to stand upon the same principle which has been so ably and so eloquently maintained and established by my esteemed friend, Mr. [Wendell] Phillips.

Our right to citizenship in this State has been acknowledged and secured by the allowance of the elective franchise and consequent taxation; and I know of no good reason, if admitted in this instance, why it should be denied in any other.

With reference to the wrongs inflicted and injuries received on railroads by persons of color, I need not say they do not end with the termination of the route, but, in effect, tend to discourage, disparage and depress this class of citizens. All hope of reward for upright conduct is cut off. Vice in them becomes a virtue. No distinction is made by the community in which we live. The most vicious is treated as well as the most respectable, both in public and private.

But it is said we all look alike. If this is true, it is not true that we all behave alike. There is a marked difference; and we claim a recognition of this difference.

In the present state of things, they find God's provisions interfered with in such a way, by these and kindred regulations, that virtue may not claim her divinely appointed rewards. Color is made to obscure the brightest endowments, to degrade the fairest character, and to check the highest and most praiseworthy aspirations. If the colored man is vicious, it makes but little difference; if besotted, it matters not; if vulgar, it is quite as well; and he finds himself as well treated, and received as readily into society, as those of an opposite character. Nay, the higher our aspirations, the loftier our purposes and pursuits, does this iniquitous principle of prejudice fasten upon us, and especial pains are taken to irritate, obstruct and injure. No reward of merit, no remuneration for services, no equivalent is rendered the deserving. And I submit, whether this unkind and unchristian policy is not well calculated to make every man disregardful of his conduct, and every woman unmindful of her reputation.

The grievances of which we complain, be assured, sir, are not imaginary but real—not local, but universal—not occasional, but continual, every day matter of fact things—and have become, to the disgrace of our common country, matter of history. . . .

There is marked difference between social and civil rights. It has been well and justly remarked, by my friend Mr. Phillips, that we all claim the privilege of selecting our society and associations; but, in civil rights, one man has not the prerogative to define rights for another. For instance, sir, in public conveyances, for the rich man to usurp the privileges to himself to the injury of the poor man, would be submitted to in no well regulated society. And such is the position suffered by persons of color. On my arrival home from England, I went to the railway station, to go to Salem, being anxious to see my parents and sisters as soon as possible—asked for a ticket—paid 50 cents for it, and was pointed to the American designation car. Having previously received information of the regulations, I took my seat peaceably, believing it better to suffer wrong than do wrong. I felt then, as I felt on many occasions prior to leaving home, unwilling to descend so low as to bandy words with the superintendents, or contest my rights with conductors, or any others in the capacity of servants of any stage or steamboat company, or railroad corporation; although I never, by any means, gave evidence that, by my submission, I intended to sanction usages which would derogate from uncivilized, much less long and loud professing and high pretending America.

Bear with me while I relate an additional occurrence. On the morning after my return home, I was obliged to go to Boston again, and on going to the Salem station I met two friends, who enquired if I had any objection to their taking seats with me. I answered, I should be most happy. They took their seats accordingly, and soon afterwards one of them remarked to me—"Charles, I don't know if they will allow us to ride with you." It was some time before I could understand what they meant, and, on doing so, I laughed—feeling it to be a climax to every absurdity I had heard attributed to Americans. To say nothing of the wrong done those friends, and the insult and indignity offered me by the appearance of the conductor, who ordered the friends from the car in a somewhat harsh manner—they immediately left the carriage.

On returning to Salem some few evenings afterward, Mr. Chase, the superintendent on this road, made himself known to me by recalling bygone days and scenes, and then enquired if I was not glad to get home after so long an absence in Europe. I told him I was glad to see my parents and family again, and this was the only object I could have, unless he thought I should be glad to take a hermit's life in the great pasture; inasmuch as I never felt to loathe my American name so much as since my arrival. He wished to know my reasons for the remark. I immediately gave them, and wished to know of him, if, in the event of his having a brother with red hair, he should find himself separated while traveling because of this difference, he should deem it just. He could make no reply. I then wished to know if the principle was not the same; and if so, there was an insult implied by his question.

In conclusion, I challenged him as the instrument inflicting the manifold injuries upon all not colored like himself to the presentation of an instance in any other Christian or unchristian country, tolerating usages at once so disgraceful, unjust and inhuman. What if some few of the West or East India planters and merchants should visit our liberty-loving country, with their colored wives—how would he manage? Or, if R. M. Johnson, the gentleman who has been elevated to the second office in the gift of the people should be travelling from Boston to Salem, if he was prepared to separate him from his wife or daughters. [Involuntary burst of applause, instantly restrained.]

Sir, it happens to be my lot to have a sister a few shades lighter than myself; and who knows, if this state of things is encouraged, whether I may not on some future occasion be mobbed in Washington Street, on the supposition of walking with a white young lady! [Suppressed indications of sympathy and applause.]

Gentlemen of the Committee, these distinctions react in all their wickedness—to say nothing of their concocted and systematized odiousness and absurdity—upon those who instituted them; and particularly so upon those who are illiberal and mean enough to practise them.

Mr. Chairman, if colored people have abused any rights granted them or failed to exhibit due appreciation of favors bestowed, or shrunk from dangers or responsibility, let it be made to appear. Or if our country contains a population to compare with them in loyalty and patriotism, circumstances duly considered, I have it yet to learn. The history of our country must ever testify in their behalf. In view of these and many additional considerations, I unhesitatingly assert their claim, on the naked principle of merit, to every advantage set forth in the Constitution of this Commonwealth.

Finally, Mr. Chairman, there is in this and other States a large and growing colored population, whose residence in your midst has not been from choice (let this be understood and reflected upon), but by the force of circumstances over which they never had control. Upon the heads of their oppressors and calumniators be the censure and responsibility. If to ask at your hands redress for injuries, and protection in our rights and immunities as citizens, is reasonable, and dictated alike by justice, humanity and religion, you will not reject, I trust, the prayer of your petitioners.

Before sitting down, I owe it to myself to remark, that I was not apprised of the wish of my friends to appear here until passing through Boston a day or two since; and having been occupied with other matters, I have had no opportunity for preparation on this occasion. I feel much obliged to the Committee for their kind, patient, and attentive hearing. [Applause.]

The Sarah Roberts Case Against Segregated Education*

CHARLES SUMNER

MAY IT PLEASE YOUR HONORS:—

Can any discrimination on account of race or color be made among children entitled to the benefit of our Common Schools under the Constitution and Laws of Massachusetts? This is the question which the Court is now to hear, to consider, and to decide.

Or, stating the question with more detail, and with more particular application to the facts of the present case, are the Committee having superintendence of the Common Schools of Boston intrusted with *power* under the Constitution and Laws of Massachusetts, to exclude colored children from the schools, and compel them to find education at separate schools, set apart for colored children only, at distances

---

* Excerpts from "Equality before the Law: Unconstitutionality of Separate Colored Schools in Massachusetts. Argument before the Supreme Court of Massachusetts, in the Case of *Sarah C. Roberts v. the City of Boston,* December 4, 1849," in *The Works of Charles Sumner* (Vol. II; Boston: Lee and Shepard, 1870), pp. 327 ff. The decision against Miss Roberts, aged five, laid the basis for the separate but equal doctrine of *Plessy v. Ferguson* in 1896. Sumner's argument is reflected in the U.S. Supreme Court decision in *Brown v. Board of Education* in 1954.

from their homes less convenient than schools open to white children?

This important question arises in an action by a colored child only five years old, who, *by her next friend,* sues the city of Boston for damages on account of a refusal to receive her into one of the Common Schools.

It would be difficult to imagine any case appealing more strongly to your best judgment, whether you regard the parties or the subject. On the one side is the City of Boston, strong in wealth, influence, character; on the other side is a little child, of degraded color, of humble parents, and still within the period of natural infancy, but strong from her very weakness, and from the irrepressible sympathies of good men, which, by a divine compensation, come to succor the weak. This little child asks at your hands her *personal rights.* So doing, she calls upon you to decide a question which concerns the personal rights of other colored children,—which concerns the Constitution and Laws of the Commonwealth, —which concerns that *peculiar institution* of New England, the Common Schools,—which concerns the fundamental principles of human rights,—which concerns the Christian character of this community. Such parties and such interests justly challenge your earnest attention. . . .

Forgetting many of the topics and all of the heats heretofore mingling with the controversy, I shall strive to present the question in its juridical light, as becomes the habits of this tribunal. It is a question of jurisprudence on which you are to give judgment. But I cannot forget that the principles of morals and of natural justice lie at the foundation of all jurisprudence. Nor can any reference to these be inappropriate in a discussion before this Court.

Of Equality I shall speak, not only as a sentiment, but as a principle embodied in the Constitution of Massachusetts, and obligatory upon court and citizen. It will be my duty to show that this principle, after finding its way into our State Constitution, was recognized in legislation and judicial decisions. Considering next the circumstances of this case, it will be easy to show how completely they violate Constitution, legislation, and judicial proceedings,—*first,* by subjecting colored children to inconvenience inconsistent with the requirements of Equality, and, *secondly,* by establishing a system of Caste odious as that of the Hindoos,—leading to the conclusion that the School Committee have no such power as they have exercised, and that it is the duty of the Court to set aside their unjust by-law. In the course of this discussion I shall exhibit the true idea of our Common Schools, and the fallacy, of the pretension that any exclusion or discrimination founded on race or color can be consistent with Equal Rights.

In opening this argument, I begin naturally with the fundamental proposition which, when once established, renders the conclusion irresistible. According to the Constitution of Massachusetts, *all men, without distinction of race or color, are equal before the law*. In the statement of this proposition I use language which, though new in our country, has the advantage of precision . . .

But it is said that the School Committee, in thus classifying the children, have not violated any principle of Equality, inasmuch as they provide a school with competent instructors for colored children, where they have advantages equal to those provided for white children. It is argued, that, in excluding colored children from Common Schools open to white children, the Committee furnish an *equivalent*.

Here there are several answers. I shall touch them briefly, as they are included in what has been already said.

1. The separate school for colored children is not one of the schools established by the law relating to Public Schools. It is not a Common School. As such it has no legal existence, and therefore cannot be a *legal equivalent*. . . .

2. The second is that in point of fact the separate school is not an equivalent. We have already seen that it is the occasion of inconvenience to colored children, which would not arise, if they had access to the nearest Common School, besides compelling parents to pay an additional tax, and inflicting upon child and parent the stigma of Caste. Still further, —and this consideration cannot be neglected,—the matters taught in the two schools may be precisely the same, but a school exclusively devoted to one class must differ essentially in spirit and character from that Common School known to the law, where all classes meet together in Equality. It is a mockery to call it an equivalent.

3. But there is yet another answer. Admitting that it is an equivalent, still the colored children cannot be compelled to take it. Their rights are found in Equality before the Law; nor can they be called to renounce one jot of this. They have an equal right with white children to the Common Schools. A separate school, though well endowed, would not secure to them that precise Equality which they would enjoy in the Common Schools. The Jews in Rome are confined to a particular district called the Ghetto, and in Frankfort to a district known as the Jewish Quarter. It is possible that their accommodations are as good as they would be able to occupy, if left free to choose throughout Rome and Frankfort; but

this compulsory segregation from the mass of citizens is of itself an *inequality* which we condemn. It is a vestige of ancient intolerance directed against a despised people. It is of the same character with the separate schools in Boston.

Thus much for the doctrine of Equivalents as a substitute for Equality.

In determining that the School Committee have no *power* to make this discrimination we are strengthened by another consideration. If the power exists in the present case, it cannot be restricted to this. The Committee may distribute all the children into classes, according to mere discretion. They may establish a separate school for Irish or Germans, where each may nurse an exclusive nationality alien to our institutions. They may separate Catholics from Protestants, or, pursuing their discretion still further, may separate different sects of Protestants, and establish one school for Unitarians, another for Presbyterians, another for Baptists, and another for Methodists. They may establish a separate school for the rich, that the delicate taste of this favored class may not be offended by the humble garments of the poor. They may exclude the children of mechanics, and send them to separate schools. All this, and much more, can be done in the exercise of that high-handed power which makes a discrimination on account of race or color. The grand fabric of our Common Schools, the pride of Massachusetts,—where, at the feet of the teacher, innocent childhood should come, unconscious of all distinctions of birth,—where the equality of the Constitution and of Christianity should be inculcated by constant precept and example,—will be converted into a heathen system of proscription and Caste. We shall then have many different schools, representatives of as many different classes, opinions, and prejudices; but we shall look in vain for the true Common School of Massachusetts. Let it not be said that there is little danger that any Committee will exercise a discretion to this extent. They must not be intrusted with the power. Here is the only safety worthy of a free people.

The Court will declare the by-law of the School Committee unconstitutional and illegal, although there are no express words of prohibition in the Constitution and Laws.

It is hardly necessary to say anything in support of this proposition. Slavery was abolished in Massachusetts, under the Declaration of Rights in our Constitution, without any specific words of abolition in that instrument, or in any subsequent legislation. The same words which are potent to destroy Slavery must be equally potent against any institution founded on Inequality or Caste. . . . But authorities are not needed. The words of the Constitution are plain, and it will be the duty of the Court to see that they are applied to the discrimination now waiting for judgment. . . . According to familiar practice, judicial interpretation is made always in favor of life or liberty. So here the Court should incline in favor of Equality, that sacred right which is the companion of those other rights. In proportion to the importance of this right will the Court be solicitous to vindicate and uphold it. And in proportion to the opposition which it encounters from prejudices of society will the court brace themselves to this task. It has been pointedly remarked by Rousseau, that "it is precisely because the force of things tends always to destroy Equality that the force of legislation should always tend to maintain it." In similar spirit, and for the same reason, the Court should always tend to maintain Equality. . . .

But it is said that these separate schools are for the benefit of both colors, and of the Public Schools. In similar spirit Slavery is sometimes said to be for the benefit of master and slave, and of the country where it exists. There is a mistake in the one case as great as in the other. This is clear. Nothing unjust, nothing ungenerous, can be for the benefit of any person or any thing. From some seeming selfish superiority, or from the gratified vanity of class, short-sighted mortals may hope to draw permanent good; but even-handed justice rebukes these efforts and redresses the wrong. The whites themselves are injured by the separation. Who can doubt this? With the Law as their monitor, they are taught to regard a portion of the human family, children of God, created in his image, coequals in his love, as a separate and degraded class; they are taught practically to deny that grand revelation of Christianity, the Brotherhood of Man. Hearts, while yet tender with childhood, are hardened, and ever afterward testify to this legalized uncharitableness. Nursed in the sentiments of Caste, receiving it with the earliest food of knowledge, they are unable to eradicate it from their natures, and then weakly and impiously charge upon our Heavenly Father the prejudice derived from an unchristian school. Their characters are debased, and they become less fit for the duties of citizenship. . . .

Who can say that this does not injure the blacks? Theirs, in its best estate, is an unhappy lot. A despised class, blasted by prejudice and shut out from various opportunities, they feel this proscription from the Common Schools as a peculiar brand. Beyond this, it deprives them of those healthful, animating influences which would come from participation in the studies of their white brethren. It adds to their discouragements. It widens their separation from the community, and postpones that great day of reconciliation which is yet to come.

The whole system of Common Schools suffers also. It is a narrow perception of their high aim which teaches that they are merely to furnish an equal amount of knowledge to all, and therefore, provided all be taught, it is of little consequence where and in what company. The law contemplates not only that all shall be taught, but that *all* shall be taught *together*. They are not only to receive equal quantities of knowledge, but all are to receive it in the same way. All are to approach the same common fountain together; nor can there be any exclusive source for individual or class. The school is the little world where the child is trained for the larger world of life. It is the microcosm preparatory to the macrocosm, and therefore it must cherish and develop the virtues and the sympathies needed in the larger world. And since, according to our institutions, all classes, without distinction of color, meet in the performance of civil duties, so should they all, without distinction of color, meet in the school, beginning there those relations of Equality which the Constitution and Laws promise to all. . . .

Happily, our educational system, by the blending of all classes, draws upon the whole school that attention which is too generally accorded only to the favored few, and thus secures to the poor their portion of the fruitful sunshine. But the colored children, placed apart in separate schools, are deprived of this peculiar advantage. Nothing is more clear than that the welfare of classes, as well as of individuals, is promoted by mutual acquaintance. Prejudice is the child of ignorance. It is sure to prevail, where people do not know each other. Society and intercourse are means established by Providence for human improvement. They remove antipathies, promote mutual adaptation and conciliation, and establish relations of reciprocal regard. Whoso sets up barriers to these thwarts the ways of Providence, crosses the tendencies of human nature, and directly interferes with the laws of God.

May it please your Honors: Such are some of the things which I feel it my duty to say in this important cause. I have occupied much time, but the topics are not yet exhausted. Still, which way soever we turn, we are brought back to one single proposition,—*the Equality of men before the Law.* This stands as the mighty guardian of the colored children in this case. It is the constant, ever-present, tutelary genius of this Commonwealth, frowning upon every privilege of birth, every distinction of race, every institution of Caste. You cannot slight it or avoid it. You cannot restrain it. God grant that you may welcome it! Do this, and your words will be a "charter and freehold of rejoicing" to a race which by much suffering has earned a title to much regard. Your judgment will become a sacred landmark, not in jurisprudence only, but in the history of Freedom, giving precious encouragement to the weary and heavy-laden wayfarers in this great cause. Massachusetts, through you, will have fresh title to respect, and be once more, as in times past, an example to the whole land.

Already you have banished Slavery from this Commonwealth. I call upon you now to obliterate the last of its footprints, and to banish the last of the hateful spirits in its train. The law interfering to prohibit marriage between blacks and whites has been abolished by the Legislature. Railroads, which, imitating the Boston schools, placed colored people apart by themselves, are compelled, under the influence of an awakened public sentiment, to abandon this regulation, and to allow them the privileges of other travellers. Only recently I have read that his Excellency, our present Governor, took his seat in a train by the side of a negro. In the Caste Schools of Boston the prejudice of color seeks its final refuge. It is for you to drive it forth. You do well, when you rebuke and correct individual offences; but it is a higher office to rebuke and correct a vicious institution. Each individual is limited in influence; but an institution has the influence of numbers organized by law. The charity of one man may counteract or remedy the uncharitableness of another; but no individual can counteract or remedy the uncharitableness of an organized injury. Against it private benevolence is powerless. It is a monster to be hunted down by the public and the constituted authorities. And such is the institution of Caste in the Common Schools of Boston, which now awaits a just condemnation from a just Court. . . .

PART III

A Nation Divided

INTRODUCTION

EARLY IN THE Civil War, when the federal government still adhered to the notion that it was *not* a war over slavery, a debate was carried on among Negroes of the North over whether or not to offer their services. Many did attempt to enlist, but the sentiments of many others equalled that of one man who wrote:

I have observed with much indignation and shame, their willingness to take up arms in defence of this unholy, ill-begotten, would-be Republican government, that summons its skill, energy, and might, of money, men and false philosophy that a corrupt nation can bring to bear, to support, extend, and perpetuate that vilest of all vile systems, American slavery ...[1]

Yet many Negroes had sought to enlist, and attempts were continued until Congress authorized the use of Negro troops in 1862. Even after rejections Negroes had formed companies or military clubs and drilled, keeping themselves in readiness for the day when the government would decide they were fit, and needed and wanted in the fight. By the end of the war 186,017 Negroes had fought with the Union Army —over 100,000 of them recruited in the South.

Negroes of the South took a stand on the war in other ways also. Some refused to work altogether; others demanded wages for their labor. Many guided Union soldiers and gave information to federal troops. Probably the best-known Negro information-gatherer was Harriet Tubman [2] who was a

[1] Wesley W. Tate, letter to *Pine and Palm*, Nov. 23, 1861, in James M. McPherson, *The Negro's Civil War* (New York: Pantheon Books, 1965), p. 34.

[2] Harriet Tubman, a former slave, is best known for her work in the Underground Railway, for she made 19 trips into the South to aid hundreds of slaves to escape to Canada.

spy behind Confederate lines. In many cases slaves seized the property of their masters when Union troops arrived.

There are recorded cases of slave attacks on white civilians in the South, but despite the greatly increased fears of the Southern whites and widespread rumors of uprisings, there was no general insurrection. This is not surprising in view of the militarization of the South during the war which overlay the already established system of repression. In addition many observers agree that a general uprising was precluded by the accommodation of slaves to the slave system under the pressures of its elaborate techniques for preventing communication, and for breaking the will to resist by a combination of punishment and reward.[3] But while there was no general insurrection during the war slaves did reveal their sentiments, for thousands fled to the Union lines.

Once Negroes were accepted in the Union Army other struggles began. The War Department order providing for Negro enlistment also provided that black regiments were to have only white officers. Despite many appeals and petitions by soldiers, resolutions of Negro organizations, and representations by Negro leaders, not more than 100 Negroes received officers' commissions during the war.[4] A second struggle of black soldiers was the fight for equal pay. Two Massachusetts regiments, the Fifty-fourth and Fifty-fifth, refused to accept any pay at all until pay was equalized. When the Massachusetts legislature appropriated funds to make up the difference between their pay and that of white soldiers the Negro regiments still refused, holding out for a federal equal-pay order. As Congress debated the issue there were threats of strikes and mutinies. One sergeant, William Walker of the Third South Carolina Volunteers, led his company to the captain's tent and ordered them to stack their arms and resign from the army. He was court-martialed and shot for mutiny. The law providing for equal pay was passed six months after its introduction, but even then it had its faults. For those soldiers who had been free at the outbreak of the war, pay was made retroactive to the time of enlistment, for those who gained freedom through service in the war pay was retroactive only to January 1, 1864. Thus, the Congress made a distinction between those who were free before the

[3] Two recent studies of this aspect of the slave system are Stanley Elkins, *Slavery* (New York: Universal Library, Grosset & Dunlap, 1963) and Eugene Genovese, "The Legacy of Slavery," *Studies on the Left*, Vol. 6, 1966.

[4] Dudley Taylor Cornish, *The Sable Arm* (New York: W. W. Norton & Co., Inc., 1966), p. 214.

war and those who became free due to enlistment, providing full pay only for the former.[5]

The vacillation over equal pay was typical of the federal attitude toward the war and the Negro. In this issue as in others the government used the argument of popular tolerance—how much equality white people would accept—as the excuse for delay. Frederick Douglass, who went to President Lincoln to request equal pay and treatment for Negro soldiers, reported that Lincoln agreed with him "that Negroes should receive equal pay and should be promoted when they deserved it," but, he said, Lincoln told him that he "would have to wait until the nation became more accustomed to Negro soldiers." [6]

Indeed, there was evidence that the populace was not ready, for in an early form of the "white backlash" whites mobbed Negro soldiers in the streets of the nation's capital. In New York's draft riots of July, 1863, for four days whites burned Negro homes and lynched Negroes in the streets. Competition for jobs was among the reasons for riots in several Northern cities. Yet, temporizing over the role of the Negro may have been more the cause than the effect of the lack of popular support for a more forthright government policy. John Hope Franklin has noted rather wryly that "Perhaps it is not too much to suggest that there was discernible correlation between the uncertainty of federal policy and the hostile attitude of many white citizens in the North toward their darker fellows." [7]

From the beginning Lincoln had maintained that the aim of the war was to unite the country, and throughout he based his conservative approach on his desire to keep the border states loyal. He cited this when he revoked emancipation orders issued by two of his generals. Then, even when the time came for the admission that slavery was "at the root of the rebellion" the Emancipation Proclamation, so joyously hailed, was itself a reaffirmation of his caution, for it freed only the slaves in the rebel states. But even so the Proclamation was a

---

[5] James McPherson, *The Negro's Civil War* (New York: Pantheon Books, 1965), pp. 201-202. McPherson writes that the problem of unequal compensation that this distinction caused in the field was solved by one colonel's oath: "You do solemnly swear that you owed no man unrequited labor on or before the 19th day of April, 1861. So help you God." The oath became known as the "Quaker Oath" and former slaves took it in good conscience.

[6] John Hope Franklin, *The Emancipation Proclamation* (New York: Doubleday & Co., 1963), p. 150.

[7] John Hope Franklin, *From Slavery to Freedom* (New York: Alfred A. Knopf, 1967), p. 275.

decisive step for Lincoln who had heretofore put forward a plan of gradual emancipation to take place over thirty-seven years, with total emancipation to be effected by 1900. In addition, Lincoln's plan had called for administration of emancipation by the slave states themselves with compensation to slave-owners and for colonization of the freed slaves.

The government's vacillation extended also to treatment of Negroes freed by the war: some were treated as contraband of war, and were detained in Union-run camps, while others were returned to their masters. For those who were considered contraband there were contradictory policies. Much of the relief—clothing, food and medicine—which former slaves in contraband camps received came from private rather than government sources. Several private agencies joined together in 1865 to form the American Freedmen's Aid Commission which organized education for the freedmen and provided other relief. A government policy of aid initiated in 1862 by Rufus Saxton, commander of the Department of the South, was pretty much a failure. The plan was to provide ex-slaves with two acres of abandoned land per working hand, but the operation of the program depended upon the sense of fairness and interest of the administering superintendent whose performances varied greatly. By the last year of the war the private agencies had recruited at least 1,000 Northern men and women who established classes for Negroes in the South.[8]

Northern Negroes were active in the formation of these freedmen's aid societies to provide relief for the homeless ex-slaves, and they were active in setting up schools and teaching freedmen, both in the North and the South.

In addition Negroes continued the struggles begun in the North years before for equality of citizenship and against all forms of discrimination. Negroes of the District of Columbia, in a protest against taxation without representation, opened their petition this way: "The undersigned would press upon your attention a principle universally admitted by Americans; namely, that Governments derive their just power from the consent of the governed." [9]

The National Negro Convention held in Syracuse, New York, in 1864 had this to say on the franchise:

Whether the right to vote is a natural right or not, we are not here to determine. Natural or conventional, in either case we are

[8] *Ibid.,* pp. 270-72.

[9] Herbert Aptheker, *A Documentary History of the Negro in the United States* (New York: Citadel Press, 1951), p. 509.

amply supported in our appeal for its extension to us. If it is, as all the teachings of your Declaration of Independence imply, a natural right, to deny to us its exercise is a wrong done to our human nature. If, on the other hand, the right to vote is simply a conventional right, having no other foundation or significance than a mere conventional arrangement, which may be extended or contracted, given or taken away, upon reasonable grounds, we insist, that, even basing the right upon this uncertain foundation, we may reasonably claim a right to a voice in the election of the men who are to have at their command our time, our services, our property, our persons, and our lives. This command of our persons and lives is no longer theory, but now the positive practice of our Government.[10]

Not all of the protests were so strongly worded. In 1873 the National Civil Rights Convention met in Washington and presented a memorial to Congress urging equal education and representation on juries, and reminding the Congress that both national political conventions had platform planks for equal rights. But the Negro petition was respectfully presented as a "memorial of the National Convention of Colored Persons, praying to be protected in their civil rights." [11]

To most of those who had consistently seen the Civil War as a war to abolish slavery, the end of the war could not be the end of the struggle. Abolitionists in the Republican party which controlled Congress pushed for an extension of the Emancipation Proclamation to free slaves in the loyal states. On February 1, 1865, Congress sent the 13th Amendment abolishing slavery to the states for ratification. Nearly a year later, on December 18, 1865, it had been ratified by 27 of the 36 states. The following year the Congress, under the same abolitionist impetus, adopted the 14th Amendment to provide Constitutional guarantees of citizenship to all Americans, and ratification of the 14th Amendment was made a condition for readmission to the Union. The 15th Amendment, providing for male suffrage, was ratified in 1870. Between 1866 and 1875 Congress adopted seven Civil Rights Acts designed to implement the 13th, 14th, and 15th Amendments and specifically giving enforcement powers—with heavy penalties for violations—to the federal government.

The South was divided into five military districts, the Freedmen's Bureau was established to hear Negro complaints, suffrage was extended to all adult males loyal to the United States. In order to be a federal officeholder or regis-

10 *Ibid.*, p. 522. Note the reference to "your Declaration of Independence" as an example of this editor's comment on the feeling of separation prevalent among Negro Americans.

11 43rd Congress, 1st Session, *Mis. Doc. No. 21.* See pp. 158-59 below.

trar a Southerner had to take an "iron-clad" oath affirming that he had never voluntarily borne arms against the United States. Before the end of 1867 every rebel state except Texas had held elections for delegates to constitutional conventions. The number of Negro delegates to these conventions was proportionately much smaller than the Negro electorate; only one state, South Carolina, sent a majority of Negroes to the constitutional convention.

The picture of Reconstruction has been variously presented by historians of succeeding generations. In an article in which he was attempting to sort out the various views Bernard Weisberger has written: "Historians are not obliged, of course, to support the Negro's case unreservedly wherever it appears. They ought, nonetheless, to walk humbly when talking of the American Negro as slave, freedman, voter, or worker. He is known to us almost exclusively through the writings of white men, who, whether well-intentioned or not, were interested parties to a conflict." [12]

The constitutional conventions, made up mainly of Negroes and Radical Republicans, wrote constitutions which were better than any previous constitutions in the South. Negro officeholders[13] were not vindictive toward their former masters, and generally sought to remove disabilities from white participation in political and economic life. Reconstruction governments repaired or rebuilt public buildings, built roads and bridges and organized public school systems. In South Carolina, for example, in 1870 there were 30,448 children in 769 schools, and in 1876 there were 123,035 in 2,776 schools.[14] The white Southern charge has been that uncouth and uneducated Negroes, Northern carpetbaggers and Southern scalawags nearly wrecked the South through venality, corruption and graft. Professor Rembert Patrick points out that in the post-Civil War period graft was not a unique experience of the South, nor in the South of Southern Republicans. "Shortly after restoration of a 'white supremacy' government in Mississippi the Democratic state treasurer stole $315,612, a sum greater than the total taken by light-

[12] Bernard A. Weisberger, "The Dark and Bloody Ground of Reconstruction Historiography," *Journal of Southern History*, Vol. XXV, Nov., 1959, p. 438.

[13] There were no black governments of Southern states during Reconstruction. However, there were Negro members of several state legislatures, several lieutenant governors and two U.S. Senators and 16 members of the House of Representatives.

[14] John Hope Franklin, *Reconstruction: After the Civil War* (Chicago: University of Chicago Press, 1961), p. 141.

fingered Republicans during six years of their rule."
Moreover he points out:

During the Reconstruction era, legislators, governors, and other officeholders needed salaries sufficient to pay their living costs, approximately 4 million former slaves became citizens, public schools replaced private academies, and society assumed responsibility for more and more of its exceptional members . . . Rural, conservative whites never realized that the former philosophy of "what's good for the planter is good for the South" was being changed to a new concept of the most good for the most people, white and colored. Expenditures for public schools, courts, prisons, asylums, and hospitals increased state and local budgets.[15]

Radical Republicans who carried on the abolitionist tradition in the post-Civil War period and fought for full citizenship rights for the Negro were concerned that the South be reconstructed, but a political motivation of their behavior can also be discerned. They did not, for good reasons, want the control of the South to be returned to the hands of the former secessionist slave-holders and they did want to insure Republican victory nationally. Some critics even charged them with outright conspiracy to give Negroes the vote and deprive whites of the franchise for party power. The *Missouri Republican* said:

. . . they had the strongest interest to diminish the white vote. Before the final restriction was put on, the Radical managers at Washington had lists in their hands to guide them; and their only inquiry was: *How many whites must be struck off to insure a Radical majority*.[16]

But throughout this period the country continued in sullen resistance to the concept of equality for the Negro. In the South the resistance was violent. The Ku Klux Klan was founded in the winter of 1865-66, and the sporadic violence hitherto performed by roving bands of rebel soldiers became organized. A combination of violence by secret societies and vigilante groups, organized intimidation of Negroes at the polls and a withdrawal of federal pursuance of the goals of equality brought the downfall of Radical Reconstruction.

The completeness of the change in the federal attitude is exemplified by the Amnesty Act of 1872 which restored the

[15] Rembert W. Patrick, *The Reconstruction of the Nation* (New York: Oxford University Press, 1967), pp. 146-47.

[16] Quoted in William A. Russ, Jr., "The Negro and White Disfranchisement During Radical Reconstruction," *Journal of Negro History*, XIX (April, 1934), p. 179.

franchise to all but about 600 ex-Confederate officials. This provided the final blow to Radical Reconstruction. Then, the Supreme Court, in a series of opinions beginning in 1873, interpreted the Fourteenth and Fifteenth Amendments narrowly, and the "Compromise of 1877" which put Rutherford B. Hayes in the Presidency insured the white South that it might deal with its problems in its own way, for part of the compromise was a promise to withdraw federal troops from the South.

Among the foreign comments on the period was that of Czar Alexander II of Russia who said that he had done more for the emancipated Russian serf than Lincoln had for the Negro since he had not only freed the serf, but had given him land. In 1879 the Czar told an American, Wharton Barker, that he was at a loss to "understand how you Americans could have been so blind as to leave the Negro slave without tools to work out his salvation." [17]

The death of Radical Reconstruction and the return of the South to "home rule" put power back into the hands of landowners who had held it in 1861, but it also helped bring forth the strongest alliance of blacks and whites that the South has seen—the Populist Movement.

Commenting that it is altogether probable that Populism of the nineties brought "a greater comity of mind and harmony of political purpose" between Southern whites and Negroes than ever before or since, C. Vann Woodward explained the Populist tack:

The Populists steered clear of the patronizing approach that both the radical Republicans and the conservative Democrats took toward the freedmen. They neither pictured themselves as the keepers of the liberal conscience and the Negro as the ward of the nation, as did the Republican radicals, nor did they assume the pose of *noblesse oblige* and regard the Negro as an object of paternalistic protection as did the Southern conservatives. The Populists fancied themselves as exponents of a new realism on race, free from the delusions of doctrinaire and sentimental liberalism on the one hand, and the illusions of romantic paternalism on the other.[18]

The Populists and the Negro had "the kinship of a common grievance and a common oppressor."

The thrust of Populism put the Negro back into Southern

17 John Hope Franklin, *The Emancipation Proclamation* (New York: Doubleday & Co., 1963), p. 135.

18 C. Vann Woodward, *The Strange Career of Jim Crow* (New York: Oxford University Press, 1957), p. 42.

politics for a brief time: the North Carolina legislature in 1895, a fusion of Populists and Republicans, named 300 Negro magistrates. In answer, the white aristocracy began constitutional disfranchisement of the Negro.

In Louisiana in 1896 there were 164,088 whites registered, and 130,344 Negroes. In 1900, the first registration year after a new constitution had been adopted, there were 125,437 whites and 5,320 Negroes registered. By 1904 Negro registration had declined to 1,718, and white registration was 106,-360. This represented a 96 percent decrease in Negro registration, and a four percent decrease in white.[19]

In Alabama, Mississippi and South Carolina disfranchisement began earlier. In 1883 in Alabama there were only 3,-742 registered Negroes out of the 140,000 formerly registered.[20] In South Carolina Negro registration decreased from 92,081 in 1876 to 2,823 in 1898. In Mississippi the decrease was from 52,705 in 1876 to 3,573 in 1898.[21] Systematic exclusion continued up through the present time. Between 1920 and 1930 about 10,000 Negroes voted in Georgia out of a potential Negro electorate of 369,511, and in Virginia the Negro vote at any time in that decade was 12,000 to 18,000 out of a voting-age-or-over and literate Negro population of 248,347.[22]

The disfranchisement of Negroes was one step in the direction of separation of the races. The federal government lent a helping hand by establishing a legal justification of the separation in the Supreme Court's doctrine of "separate but equal" handed down in 1896 in *Plessy* v. *Ferguson.*

[19] Paul Lewinson, *Race, Class and Party* (New York: Oxford University Press, 1932), p. 81. A. B. W. Webb, *A History of Negro Voting in Louisiana, 1877-1906* (Baton Rouge, La.: Thesis, Louisiana State University, 1962), p. 68.

[20] Lewinson, *op. cit.,* p. 137.

[21] Rev. John Holmes, *The Disfranchisement of Negroes* (New York: National Association for the Advancement of Colored People, 191?), p. 8.

[22] C. A. Bacote, *The Negro in Georgia Politics, 1880-1908* (Chicago: Ph.D. Dissertation, University of Chicago, 1955), p. 347. Lewinson, *op. cit.,* appendices.

1. NEGROES AND THE WAR

Men of Color, to Arms!*

FREDERICK DOUGLASS

WHEN FIRST THE rebel cannon shattered the walls of Sumter and drove away its starving garrison, I predicted that the war then and there inaugurated would not be fought out entirely by white men. Every month's experience during these dreary years has confirmed that opinion. A war undertaken and brazenly carried on for the perpetual enslavement of colored men, calls logically and loudly for colored men to help suppress it. Only a moderate share of sagacity was needed to see that the arm of the slave was the best defense against the arm of the slaveholder. Hence, with every reverse to the national arms, with every exulting shout of victory raised by the slaveholding rebels, I have implored the imperiled nation to unchain against her foes her powerful black hand. Slowly and reluctantly that appeal is beginning to be heeded. Stop not now to complain that it was not heeded sooner. That it should not may or may not have been best. This is not the time to discuss that question. Leave it to the future. When the war is over, the country saved, peace established and the black man's rights are secured, as they will be, history with an impartial hand will dispose of that and sundry other questions. Action! action! not criticism, is the plain duty of this hour. Words are now useful only as they stimulate to blows. The office of speech now is only to point out when, where, and how to strike to the best advantage. There is no time to delay. The tide is at its flood that leads on to fortune. From East to West, from North to South, the sky is written all over, 'NOW OR NEVER.' Liberty won by white men would lose half its luster. 'Who would be free themselves must strike the blow.' 'Better even die free, than to live slaves.' This is the sentiment of every brave colored man amongst us. There are weak and cowardly men in all nations. We have them amongst us. They tell you this is the 'white man's war'; that you 'will be no better off after than before the war'; that the getting of you into the army is to 'sacrifice you on the first

* Frederick Douglass, *Life and Times of Frederick Douglass* (Boston: De Wolfe & Co., 1895), pp. 414-416.

opportunity.' Believe them not; cowards themselves, they do not wish to have their cowardice shamed by your brave example. Leave them to their timidity, or to whatever motive may hold them back. I have not thought lightly of the words I am now addressing you. The counsel I give comes of close observation of the great struggle now in progress, and of the deep conviction that this is your hour and mine. In good earnest, then, and after the best deliberation, I now, for the first time during this war, feel at liberty to call and counsel you to arms. By every consideration which binds you to your enslaved fellow-countrymen and to the peace and welfare of your country; by every aspiration which you cherish for the freedom and equality of yourselves and your children; by all the ties of blood and identity which make us one with the brave black men now fighting our battles in Louisiana and in South Carolina, I urge you to fly to arms, and smite with death the power that would bury the Government and your liberty in the same hopeless grave. I wish I could tell you that the State of New York calls you to this high honor. For the moment her constituted authorities are silent on the subject. They will speak by and by, and doubtless on the right side; but we are not compelled to wait for her. We can get at the throat of treason and slavery through the State of Massachusetts. She was first in the War of Independence; first to break the chains of her slaves; first to make the black man equal before the law; first to admit colored children to her common schools, and she was first to answer with her blood the alarm-cry of the nation, when its capital was menaced by rebels. You know her patriotic governor, and you know Charles Sumner. I need not add more.

Massachusetts now welcomes you to arms as soldiers. She has but a small colored population from which to recruit. She has full leave of the general government to send one regiment to the war, and she has undertaken to do it. Go quickly and help fill up the first colored regiment from the North. I am authorized to assure you that you will receive the same wages, the same rations, the same equipments, the same protection, the same treatment, and the same bounty, secured to white soldiers. You will be led by able and skillful officers, men who will take especial pride in your efficiency and success. They will be quick to accord to you all the honor you shall merit by your valor, and to see that your rights and feelings are respected by other soldiers. I have assured myself on these points, and can speak with authority. More than twenty years of unswerving devotion to our common cause may give me some humble claim to be trusted at this momentous crisis. I will not argue. To do so implies hesitation and doubt, and you do not hesitate. You do not doubt. The day dawns; the morning star is bright upon the horizon! The iron gate of our prison stands half open. One gallant rush from the North will fling it wide open, while four millions of our brothers and sisters shall march out into liberty. The chance is now given you to end in a day the bondage of centuries, and to rise in one bound from social degradation to the place of common equality with all other varieties of men. Remember Denmark Vessey [sic] of Charleston; remember Nathaniel Turner of South Hampton; remember Shields Green and Copeland, who followed noble John Brown, and fell as glorious martyrs for the cause of the slave. Remember that in a contest with oppression, the Almighty has no attribute which can take sides with oppressors. The case is before you. This is our golden opportunity. Let us accept it, and forever wipe out the dark reproaches unsparingly hurled against us by our enemies. Let us win for ourselves the gratitude of our country, and the best blessings of our posterity through all time. The nucleus of this first regiment is now in camp at Readville, a short distance from Boston. I will undertake to forward to Boston all persons adjudged fit to be mustered into the regiment, who shall apply to me at any time within the next two weeks.

ROCHESTER, March 2, 1863.

Army Life in a Black Regiment: The Struggle for Pay*

THOMAS WENTWORTH HIGGINSON

THE STORY OF the attempt to cut down the pay of the colored troops is too long, too complicated, and too humiliating, to be here narrated. In the case of my regiment there stood on record the direct pledge of the War Department to General Saxton that their pay should be the same as that of whites. So clear was this that our kind paymaster, Major W. J. Wood, of New Jersey, took upon himself the responsibility of paying the price agreed upon, for five months, till he was compelled by express orders to reduce it from thirteen dollars per month to ten dollars, and from that to seven dollars,—the pay of quartermaster's men and day-laborers. At the same time the "stoppages" from the payrolls for the loss of all

* From Thomas Wentworth Higginson, Army Life in a Black Regiment (Michigan State University Press, 1960), pp. 218-21, 227-28. First published in Boston in 1890. Higginson was a commander of a black regiment in the Civil War and an ardent abolitionist. By permission.

equipments and articles of clothing remained the same as for all other soldiers, so that it placed the men in the most painful and humiliating condition. Many of them had families to provide for, and between the actual distress, the sense of wrong, the taunts of those who had refused to enlist from the fear of being cheated, and the doubt how much farther the cheat might be carried, the poor fellows were goaded to the utmost. In the Third South Carolina Regiment, Sergeant William Walker was shot, by order of court-martial, for leading his company to stack arms before their captain's tent, on the avowed ground that they were released from duty by the refusal of the Government to fulfil its share of the contract. The fear of such tragedies spread a cloud of solicitude over every camp of colored soldiers for more than a year, and the following series of letters will show through what wearisome labors the final triumph of justice was secured. In these labors the chief credit must be given to my admirable Adjutant, Lieutenant G. W. Dewhurst. In the matter of bounty justice is not yet obtained; there is a discrimination against those colored soldiers who were slaves on April 19, 1861. Every officer, who through indolence or benevolent design claimed on his muster-rolls that all his men had been free on that day, secured for them the bounty; while every officer who, like myself, obeyed orders and told the truth in each case, saw his men and their families suffer for it, as I have done. A bill to abolish this distinction was introduced by Mr. Wilson at the last session, but failed to pass the House. It is hoped that next winter may remove this last vestige of the weary contest.

To show how persistently and for how long a period these claims had to be urged on Congress, I reprint such of my own printed letters on the subject as are now in my possession. There are one or two of which I have no copies. It was especially in the Senate that it was so difficult to get justice done; and our thanks will always be especially due to Hon. Charles Sumner and Hon. Henry Wilson for their advocacy of our simple rights. The records of those sessions will show who advocated the fraud.

To the Editor of the New York Tribune:

SIR,—No one can overstate the intense anxiety with which the officers of colored regiments in this Department are awaiting action from Congress in regard to arrears of pay of their men.

It is not a matter of dollars and cents only; it is a question of common honesty,—whether the United States Government has sufficient integrity for the fulfilment of an explicit business contract.

The public seems to suppose that all required justice will be done by the passage of a bill equalizing the pay of all soldiers for the future. But, so far as my own regiment is concerned, this is but half the question. My men have been nearly sixteen months in the service, and for them the immediate issue is the question of arrears.

They understand the matter thoroughly, if the public do not. Every one of them knows that he volunteered under an explicit *written assurance* from the War Department that he should have the pay of a white soldier. He knows that for five months the regiment received that pay, after which it was cut down from the promised thirteen dollars per month to ten dollars, for some reason to him inscrutable.

He does *not* know—for I have not yet dared to tell the men—that the Paymaster has been already reproved by the Pay Department for fulfilling even in part the pledges of the War Department; that at the next payment the ten dollars are to be further reduced to seven; and that, to crown the whole, all the previous overpay is to be again deducted or "stopped" from the future wages, thus leaving them a little more than a dollar a month for six months to come, unless Congress interfere!

Yet so clear were the terms of the contract that Mr. Solicitor Whiting, having examined the original instructions from the War Department issued to Brigadier-General Saxton, Military Governor, admits to me (under date of December 4, 1863,) that "the faith of the Government was thereby pledged to every officer and soldier enlisted under that call."

He goes on to express the generous confidence that "the pledge will be honorably fulfilled." I observe that every one at the North seems to feel the same confidence, but that, meanwhile, the pledge is unfulfilled. Nothing is said in Congress about fulfilling it. I have not seen even a proposition in Congress to pay the colored soldiers, *from date of enlistment,* the same pay with white soldiers; and yet anything short of that is an unequivocal breach of contract, so far as this regiment is concerned.

Meanwhile, the land sales are beginning, and there is danger of every foot of land being sold from beneath my soldiers' feet, because they have not the petty sum which Government first promised, and then refused to pay.

The officers' pay comes promptly and fully enough, and this makes the position more embarrassing. For how are we to explain to the men the mystery that Government can afford us a hundred or two dollars a month, and yet must keep back six of the poor thirteen which it promised them? Does it not naturally suggest the most cruel suspicions in regard to us? And yet nothing but their childlike faith in their officers, and in that incarnate soul of honor, General Saxton, has sustained their faith, or kept them patient, thus far.

There is nothing mean or mercenary about these men in general. Convince them that the Government actually needs their money, and they would serve it barefooted and on half-rations, and without a dollar—for a time. But, unfortunately, they see white soldiers beside them, whom they know to be in no way their superiors for any military service, receiving hundreds of dollars for re-enlisting from this impoverished Government which can only pay seven dollars out of thirteen to its black regiments. And they see, on the other hand, these colored men who refused to volunteer as soldiers, and who have found more honest paymasters than the United States Government, now exulting in well-filled pockets, and able to buy the little homesteads the soldiers need, and to turn the soldiers' families into the streets. Is this a school for self-sacrificing patriotism?

I should not speak thus urgently were it not becoming manifest that there is to be no promptness of action in Congress, even as regards the future pay of colored soldiers,— and that there is especial danger of the whole matter of *arrears* going by default. Should it be so, it will be a repudiation more ungenerous than any which Jefferson Davis advocated or Sydney Smith denounced. It will sully with dishonor all the nobleness of this opening page of history, and fix upon the North a brand of meanness worse than either Southerner or Englishman has yet dared to impute. The mere delay in the fulfilment of this contract has already inflicted untold suffering, has impaired discipline, has relaxed loyalty, and has begun to implant a feeling of sullen distrust in the very regiments whose early career solved the problem of the nation, created a new army, and made peaceful emancipation possible.

T. W. HIGGINSON,
Colonel commanding 1st S. C. Vols.
BEAUFORT, S. C., January 22, 1864.

* * * *

PETITION.

"To the Honorable Senate and House of Representatives of the United States in Congress assembled:—

"The undersigned respectfully petitions for the repeal of so much of Section IV. of the Act of Congress making appropriations for the army and approved July 4, 1864, as makes a distinction, in respect of pay due, between those colored soldiers who were free on or before April 19, 1861, and those who were not free until a later date;

"Or at least that there may be such legislation as to secure the fulfilment of pledges of full pay from date of enlistment, made by direct authority of the War Department to the colored soldiers of South Carolina, on the faith of which pledges they enlisted.

"THOMAS WENTWORTH HIGGINSON,
Late Colonel 1st S. C. Vols. (now 33d U. S. C. Vols.)
"NEWPORT, R.I., DECEMBER 9, 1864."

Negro Response to the Civil War*

JAMES M. McPHERSON

AT THE BEGINNING *of May 1861 the leaders of Philadelphia's sizable Negro population issued a public statement:*

Formidable difficulties prevent our service being made available to the country in this time of its extremity. First, the laws of the State debar 10,000 able-bodied colored citizens from bearing arms in defense of the State. . . .

The second, is, that the . . . colored citizens of this State are not invited, at this stage by the Government, to enroll themselves; still, in view of the present danger threatening the Commonwealth, we earnestly recommend that the colored citizens stand prepared, so that when officially solicited by the Government we may render such service as only men can render, who know how precious *Liberty* is.[1]

But another Philadelphia Negro, Henry Cropper, stated on May 4 that he would never fight for the Union unless the government accepted Negro volunteers on the same basis as whites:

We, the members of the first and only equipped military Company, have more knowledge of our duty, and also more dignity, than to offer our services to a Government, when knowing at the same time, that the laws call for none but white men to do military duty. . . . I, as the Captain, in behalf of the Company, am resolved never to offer or give service, except it be on equality with all other men.[2]

---

* From THE NEGRO'S CIVIL WAR, by James McPherson. ©
Copyright 1965 by James McPherson. Reprinted by permission of Pantheon Books, a Division of Random House, Inc.
  1 *Christian Recorder,* May 4, 1861.
  2 *Pine and Palm,* May 25, 1861.

A colored man in Chillicothe, Ohio, deplored the fact that Negroes were offering their services to the government even though they knew that such offers would be spurned.

Nevertheless, they say that when matters come to an adjustment, this offer of services can be used as a plea for our enfranchisement. But can it not be used as well against us? If the colored people, under all the social and legal disabilities by which they are environed, are ever ready to defend the government that despoils them of their rights, it may be concluded that it is quite safe to oppress them. . . . The truth is, if, in time of peace the fact of our having bled in defense of the country when it was struggling desperately for independence, avails nothing, it is absurd to suppose that the fact of tendering our services to settle a domestic war when we know that our services will be contemptuously rejected, will procure a practical acknowledgement of our rights.[3]

A group of Negroes in New York City held a meeting on May 1, at which the following resolution was discussed: "That several of the Southern States, being in open rebellion against the General Government, and the President, having called upon all loyal citizens to rally to the defence thereof, Therefore, that we tender our services to the Governor of this State, to serve during the war, either as firemen, during the absence of those firemen who may enlist for the war—to act as a Home Guard, or to go South, if the services should be required." *But several speakers at the meeting opposed the resolution on the ground that earlier offers by Negroes had been rejected, and they* "did not think that we should offer ourselves to be kicked and insulted, as others had been. . . . The whites knew that we were willing to fight, and therefore there was no need of laying ourselves liable to insult, simply for the privilege of saying so." *These speakers prevailed, and the resolution was defeated.*[4]

Nevertheless the Anglo-African, *a weekly Negro newspaper that circulated mainly among colored people in New York City and nearby areas, continued to urge black men to prepare themselves for any contingency:*

Colored men whose fingers tingle to pull the trigger, or clutch the knife aimed at the slave-holders in arms, will not have to wait much longer. Whether the foe attack Washington and succeed, or whether they attempt Maryland and fail, there is equal need for calling out the nation's "Reserve Guard"—the forlorn hope which will march to "Liberty or Death." . . .

3 *Ibid.*
4 *Ibid.*

There are men among our people who look upon this as the "white man's war," and such men openly say, let them fight it out among themselves. It is their flag, and their constitution which have been dishonored and set at naught. . . .

This is a huge fallacy. In proof of which let us ask ourselves some questions. . . . What rights have we in the free States? We have the "right to life, liberty and the pursuit of happiness." We have the right to labor, and are secure in the fruits of our labor; we have the right to our wives and our little ones; we have to a large extent the right to educate our children. . . .

Are these rights worth the having? If they are then they are worth defending with all our might, and at any cost. It is illogical, unpatriotic, nay mean and unmanly in us to shrink from the defence of these great rights and privileges. . . . But some will say that these rights of *ours* are not assailed by the South. Are they not? What in short is the programme or platform on which the South would have consented to remain in the Union? It was to spread slavery over all the States and territories. . . .

Hence, talk as we may, we *are* concerned in this fight and our fate hangs upon its issues. The South must be subjugated, or we shall be enslaved. In aiding the Federal government in whatever way we can, we are aiding to secure our own liberty; for this war can only end in the subjugation of the North or of the South. We do not affirm that the North is fighting in behalf of the black man's rights, as such—if this was the single issue, we even doubt whether they would fight at all. But circumstances have been so arranged by the decrees of Providence, that in struggling for their own nationality they are forced to defend our rights. . . . Let us be awake, therefore brethren; a generous emulation in a common patriotism, and a special call to defend our rights alike bid us to be on the alert to seize arms and drill as soon as the government shall be willing to accept our services.[5]. . .

A group of Northern Negroes sent a petition to President Lincoln:

We, the undersigned, respectfully represent to Your Excellency that we are native citizens of the United States, and that, notwithstanding much injustice and oppression which our race have suffered, we cherish a strong attachment for the land of our birth and for our Republican Government. We are filled with alarm at the formidable conspiracy for its overthrow, and lament the vast expense of blood and treasure which the present war involves. . . . We are anxious to use

[5] *Anglo-African*, August 24, September 14, 1861.

our power to give peace to our country and permanence to
our Government.

We are strong in numbers, in courage, and in patriotism,
and in behalf of our fellow countrymen of the colored race,
we offer to you and to the nation a power and a will sufficient to conquer rebellion, and establish peace on a permanent basis. We pledge ourselves, upon receiving the sanction
of Your Excellency, that we will immediately proceed to
raise an efficient number of regiments, and so fast as arms
and equipments shall be furnished, we will bring them into
the field in good discipline, and ready for action.[6]. . .

6 *Pine and Palm*, October 12, 1861.

Northerners Protest Discrimination*

THE CIVIL WAR *produced great changes in the status of
Northern Negroes. Some of the more important gains for
civil rights during the war were made on the national level.
The State Department ignored Chief Justice Roger Taney's
dictum in the Dred Scott case that a Negro could not be an
American citizen, and granted a passport in August 1861 to
Henry Highland Garnet. The passport explicitly stated that
Garnet was a "citizen of the United States."* [1] *In 1862 an
American revenue cutter detained a vessel in the coastwise
trade because the captain was a colored man. Under the
Dred Scott decision, Negroes were not citizens and hence
were not eligible to command ships flying the American flag.
Secretary of the Treasury Salmon P. Chase seized this opportunity to address a formal inquiry regarding the citizenship of
colored men to Attorney General Edward Bates. Bates replied with a lengthy statement which denied the principles of
the Dred Scott decision and affirmed that every free person
born in the United States was, "at the moment of birth,
prima facie a citizen."* [2]

*Under the leadership of Charles Sumner, Congress passed
several anti-discrimination measures during the war. In 1862
the Senate repealed an 1825 law barring colored persons
from carrying the mail. Democrats and conservative Republicans killed the bill in the House, but it finally passed both
Houses and became law on March 3, 1865. In 1862 Congress*

* McPherson, *op. cit.*, pp. 249-254.

1 *Douglass Monthly*, IV (November, 1861), p. 557.

2 Edward McPherson, *The Political History of the United States of
America, during the Great Rebellion* (Washington, 1865), pp. 378-84.

decreed that in all proceedings of District of Columbia courts there must be no exclusion of witnesses because of race, and in 1862 this legislation was broadened to cover every federal court in the nation.[3]

Negro leaders were active in several states in the movement to end discrimination and segregation at the state level. The following statement is from the salutatory editorial of the Pacific Appeal, *a Negro newspaper in San Francisco edited by Philip Bell from 1862 to 1864:*

We have nothing to disguise; we enter the field boldly, fearlessly, but with dignity and calmness to *Appeal* for the rights of the Colored Citizens of this State.

As we say in our Prospectus, our paper "is devoted to the interests of the Colored People of California and to their moral, intellectual and political advancement."

It will advocate their rights, their claims to humanity and justice; it will oppose the wrongs inflicted on them, and the disabilities under which they labor. It will urge the repeal of all oppressive laws, particularly that law which deprives them of the right to testify in courts, in cases in which a white person is a party.

Such laws are disgraceful to the statutes of our State, are relics of barbarism and slavery, retard the wheels of justice, degrade our manhood, and inflict irreparable injury on our rights and liberties.

We shall *Appeal* to the hearts and consciences of our rulers, not to their passions and prejudices; we shall *Appeal* to their sense of right and justice; not to their feelings of pity and commiseration.[4]

The California law barring Negroes from testifying against whites gave free license to whites to rob and beat colored persons without fear of arrest. As the Pacific Appeal *stated: "As long as those unjust laws which exclude our testimony in courts remain on the Statute books of California, so long will we be fitting subjects for assaults on our persons and property, by knavish and brutal white men, who, knowing we have no protection in law, think they can rob and murder us with impunity."*[5] *California Negroes worked hard to obtain repeal of the testimony law. They circulated petitions and gave speeches. In 1862 the legislature defeated a repeal motion by a narrow margin. The* Pacific Appeal *stated editorially:*

[3] Edward McPherson, *The Political History of the United States of America, during the Great Rebellion* (Washington, 1865), pp. 239-40, 242-43, 593; *U.S. Statutes at Large,* XII, 351, 407, XIII, 515.

[4] *Pacific Appeal,* April 5, 1862.

[5] *Ibid.*

Let our failure this year, be but the incentive to renewed exertion. Be active! Be vigilant! . . . Be not discouraged! Say not "it is useless, the whites will never grant us our legal rights." Be not governed by any such fallacy. Show the white man it is not only an act of justice and humanity, but it is one of deep interest to the community.

Another year, and the people of California will be convinced that it is no longer to their interest to yield obedience to the demands of the Slave Oligarchy. Chivalry will then be an extinct institution, and our State will be freed from the domineering influence of Secessionists.[6]

Buoyed up by such optimism, California Negroes stepped up their petition campaign. Their efforts were rewarded in 1863 when the California legislature repealed the testimony law. Colored men could henceforth testify in any court case.[7]

In Illinois, Negroes could not testify in any case to which a white person was a party. But the most severe feature of the Illinois "black laws," as they were called, was the law barring Negro immigration. Every colored person entering the state with intent to settle was subject to a heavy fine; in default of payment he could be sold at public auction to the person bidding the shortest period of service in return for payment of the fine. This law was seldom enforced, and Negroes continued to move into Illinois after the statute was enacted in 1853. But the influx of freed men during the war prompted the courts to begin enforcing the law: in 1863 eight Negroes were convicted of entering the state illegally, and seven of them were sold into temporary slavery to pay the fine.[8]

This was an intolerable situation, and Chicago Negroes, under the leadership of John Jones, a wealthy colored man, formed a "Repeal Association" in 1864. One of the wealthiest Negroes in America, Jones had been born free in North Carolina, where he taught himself to read and write and served as a tailor's apprentice. He came to Georgia in 1845 with $3.50 in his pocket. In the next fifteen years he made a small fortune out of his tailoring business, and became a militant race leader in Illinois. He was twice elected Cook County Commissioner after the war. In November 1864 Jones made the following appeal to Governor Richard Yates of Illinois:

Your petitioner, though humble in position, and having no political status in your State, notwithstanding I have resided in it for twenty-five years, and to-day am paying taxes on thir-

---

[6] *Ibid.*, May 3, 1862.

[7] *Ibid.*, July 5, August 2, September 6, 1862; Boston *Commonwealth*, April 17, 1863.

[8] Arthur Cole, *The Era of the Civil War, 1848-1870, Centennial History of Illinois*, Vol. II (Springfield, 1919), pp. 225-26, 333-35.

ty thousand dollars most humbly beseech you to recommend in your Message to the Legislature . . . the repeal of the Black Laws of this your State.

Jones also addressed an appeal to the legislature:

Gentlemen, we appeal directly to you. Our destiny is in your hands. Will you lift us out of our present degradation, and place us under the protection of wholesome laws, and make us responsible for the abuse of them as other citizens are? I beseech you, in behalf of seven thousand colored inhabitants of your State, try the experiment. In the States before mentioned, this experiment has been tried and there is no disposition in those States to return to their former unjust discrimination between their respective inhabitants. The petitions that will be presented to you this winter from all parts of your State will be signed by your most respected and influential citizens.

The Repeal Association circulated a petition in northern Illinois calling for repeal of the "black laws," and obtained eleven thousand signatures. Jones went to Springfield and made the following speech to a legislative committee:

We, the colored people of Illinois, charge upon that enactment, and lay at the doors of those who enacted it, our present degraded condition in this our great State. Every other nation, kindred and tongue have prospered and gained property, and are recognized as a part of the great Commonwealth, with the exception of our own: we have been treated as strangers in the land of our birth. . . . To-day a colored man cannot buy a *burying-lot* in the city of Chicago for his own use. All of this grows out of the proscriptive laws of this State, against our poor, unfortunate colored people. And, more than this, the cruel treatment that we receive daily at the hands of a portion of your foreign population, is all based upon these enactments. . . . They think we have no rights which white men are bound to respect, and according to your laws they think right. Then, fellow-citizens, in the name of the great Republic, and all that is dear to a man in this life, erase those nefarious and unnecessary laws, and give us your protection, and treat us as you treat other citizens of the State. We ask only even-handed justice, and all of our wrongs will be at an end by virtue of that act. May God in His goodness assist you to do the right. Will you do it? [9]

The contribution of colored soldiers to Union victory had produced a favorable climate for Jones's appeal, and the legislature in February repealed the "black laws" barring Negro immigration and testimony.[10] By the spring of 1865 Indiana

[9] *Anglo-African*, January 14, 1865.
[10] Cole, *Era of the Civil War*, pp. 336-37.

*was the only Northern state that retained such restrictions.
Indiana's Negroes had also worked for repeal of the black
laws during the Civil War. A short-lived monthly newspaper
published by Negroes in Spartanburg, Indiana, the* Students'
Repository, *urged the state legislature in 1863 to put an end
to racial discrimination:*

Look at the barbarous code of black laws with which the
Constitution and Statute books . . . are disgraced! By the
provisions of these barbarous laws, colored emigration [sic]
into the State is entirely prohibited, and twelve thousand of
the population of Indiana is wholly disfranchised. We are denied the right of suffrage, denied the right of holding office,
denied the right of testifying in courts of justice, denied the
benefit of the schools funds and at the same time compelled to
pay taxes for the support of the government. . . .

The worst and most deplorable feature of those proscriptive laws is, that they shut us out from the public schools,
and leave us (so far as the State is concerned) entirely without the means of education; and numbers of families that live
in white settlements, are growing up without education.

Republicans, how long! Oh! how long will this be the case?
When you support, by your votes and by your influence, the
other proscriptive laws of this State, you indeed commit a
crime against God and humanity of great magnitude; but
when you deprive us of the means of education, you commit
an outrage upon *the SOUL; a war upon THE IMMORTAL
PART!* . . .

The question of the colored man's rights in this country
has got to be met and settled before long. It may be delayed,
but it cannot be evaded.[11]

The Emancipation Proclamation*

JOHN HOPE FRANKLIN

THE CHARACTER OF the Civil War could not possibly have
been the same after the President issued the Emancipation
Proclamation as it had been before January 1, 1863. During
the first twenty months of the war, no one had been more

11 *Students' Repository*, I (July, 1863), 5.

* Excerpts pp. 136-45, 147-53 from THE EMANCIPATION PROCLAMATION,
by John Hope Franklin, Copyright © 1963 by John Hope Franklin. Reprinted by permission of Doubleday & Company, Inc.

careful than Lincoln himself to define the war merely as one to save the Union. He did this not only because such a definition greatly simplified the struggle and kept the border states fairly loyal, but also because he deeply felt that this was the only legitimate basis for prosecuting the war. When, therefore, he told Horace Greeley that if he could save the Union without freeing a single slave he made the clearest possible statement of his fundamental position. And he was holding to this position despite the fact that he had written the first draft of the Emancipation Proclamation at least six weeks before he wrote his reply to Greeley's famous "Prayer of Twenty Millions."

Lincoln saw no contradiction between the contents of his reply to Greeley and the contents of the Emancipation Proclamation. For he had come to the conclusion that in order to save the Union he must emancipate *some* of the slaves. His critics were correct in suggesting that the Proclamation was a rather frantic measure, an act of last resort. By Lincoln's own admission it was, indeed, a desperate act; for the prospects of Union success were not bright. He grabbed at the straw of a questionable victory at Antietam as the occasion for issuing the Preliminary Proclamation. If anything convinced him in late December that he should go through with issuing the final Proclamation, it was the ignominious defeat of the Union forces at Fredericksburg. *Something* needed to be done. Perhaps the Emancipation Proclamation would turn the trick!

The language of the Proclamation revealed no significant modification of the aims of the war. Nothing was clearer than the fact that Lincoln was taking the action under his authority "as Commander-in-Chief of the Army and Navy." The situation that caused him to take the action was that there was an "actual armed rebellion against the authority and government of the United States." He regarded the Emancipation Proclamation, therefore, as "a fit and necessary war measure for suppressing said rebellion." In another place in the Proclamation he called on the military and naval authorities to recognize and maintain the freedom of the slaves. Finally the President declared, in the final paragraph of the Proclamation, that the measure was "warranted by the Constitution upon military necessity." This was, indeed, a war measure, conceived and promulgated to put down the rebellion and save the Union.

Nevertheless, both by what it said and what it did not say, the Proclamation greatly contributed to the significant shift in 1863 in the way the war was regarded. It recognized the right of emancipated slaves to defend their freedom. The precise language was that they should "abstain from all violence, unless in necessary self-defence." It also provided that former slaves could now be received into the armed services. While it was clear that they were to fight to save the Union, the fact remained that since their own fate was tied to that of the Union, they would also be fighting for their own freedom. The Negro who, in December 1862, could salute his own colonel instead of blacking the boots of a Confederate colonel, as he had been doing a year earlier, had a stake in the war that was not difficult to define. However loyal to the Union the Negro troops were—and they numbered some 190,000 by April 1865—one is inclined to believe that they were fighting primarily for freedom for themselves and their brothers in the months that followed the issuance of the Emancipation Proclamation.

Despite the fact that the President laid great stress on the issuance of the Proclamation as a military necessity, he did not entirely overlook the moral and humanitarian significance of the measure. And even in the document itself he gave some indication of his appreciation of this particular dimension that was, in time, to eclipse many other considerations. He said that the emancipation of the slaves was "sincerely believed to be an act of justice. This conception of emancipation could hardly be confined to the slaves in states or parts of states that were in rebellion against the United States on January 1, 1863. It must be recalled, moreover, that in the same sentence that he referred to emancipation as an "act of justice" he invoked "the considerate judgment of mankind and the gracious favor of Almighty God." This raised the Proclamation above the level of just another measure for the effective prosecution of the war. And, in turn, the war became more than a war to save the integrity and independence of the Union. It became also a war to promote the freedom of mankind.

Throughout the previous year the President had held to the view that Negroes should be colonized in some other part of the world. And he advanced this view with great vigor wherever and whenever possible. He pressed the Cabinet and Congress to accept and implement his colonization views, and he urged Negroes to realize that it was best for all concerned that they should leave the United States. It is not without significance that Lincoln omitted from the Emancipation Proclamation any reference to colonization. It seems clear that the President had abandoned hope of gaining support for his scheme or of persuading Negroes to leave the only home they knew. Surely, moreover, it would have been a most incongruous policy as well as an ungracious act to have asked Negroes to perform one of the highest acts of citizenship—fighting for their country—and then invite them to leave. Thus, by inviting Negroes into the armed services and omitting all mention of colonization, the President indicated in the Proclamation that Negroes would enjoy a status that went beyond mere freedom. They were to be free persons, fighting for their *own* country, a country in which they were to be permitted to remain.

The impact of the Proclamation on slavery and Negroes was profound. Negroes looked upon it as a document of freedom, and they made no clear distinction between the areas affected by the Proclamation and those not affected by it. One has the feeling that the interest of the contrabands in Washington in seeing whether their home counties were excepted or included in the Proclamation was an academic interest so far as their own freedom was concerned. After all, they had proclaimed their own freedom and had put themselves beyond the force of the slave law or their masters. The celebration of the issuance of the Proclamation by thousands of Negroes in Norfolk illustrates the pervasive influence of the document. President Lincoln had said that Norfolk slaves were not emancipated by his Proclamation. Norfolk Negroes, however, ignored the exception and welcomed the Proclamation as the instrument of their own deliverance.

Slavery, in or out of the Confederacy, could not possibly have survived the Emancipation Proclamation. Slaves themselves, already restive under their yoke and walking off the plantation in many places, were greatly encouraged upon learning that Lincoln wanted them to be free. They proceeded to oblige him. There followed what one authority has called a general strike and another has described as widespread slave disloyalty throughout the Confederacy.[1] Lincoln understood the full implications of the Proclamation. That is one of the reasons why he delayed issuing it as long as he did. Once the power of the government was enlisted on the side of freedom in one place, it could not successfully be restrained from supporting freedom in some other place. It was too fine a distinction to make. Not even the slaveholders in the excepted areas could make it. They knew, therefore, that the Emancipation Proclamation was the beginning of the end

[1] W.E.B. DuBois, *Black Reconstruction* (New York, 1935), pp. 55-83; Wiley, *Southern Negroes*, pp. 63-84; and Harvey Wish, "Slave Disloyalty under the Confederacy," *Journal of Negro History*, XXIII (October, 1938), pp. 435-50.

of slavery for them. Many of them did not like it, but the realities of the situation clearly indicated what the future had in store for them. . . .

In the light of the demands they had been making, the language of the Emancipation Proclamation could hardly have been the source of unrestrained joy on the part of the abolitionists. The Proclamation did not represent the spirit of "no compromise" that had characterized their stand for a generation. There was no emancipation in the border states, with which the abolitionists had so little patience. Parts of states that were under Union control were excepted, much to the dismay of the abolitionists, whose view was ably set forth by Salmon Portland Chase. Obviously, the President was not completely under their sway, despite the claims of numerous critics of the Administration. For the most part, the Proclamation represented Lincoln's views. It was in no sense the result of abolitionist dictation.

And yet, when the Proclamation finally came, the abolitionists displayed a remarkable capacity for accommodating themselves to what was, from their point of view, an obvious compromise. Some of them took credit for the begrudging concessions that the compromise represented. . . .

The enthusiasm of the abolitionists was greater than that of a group that had reached the conclusion that half a loaf was better than none. Their initial reaction of dissatisfaction with the Preliminary Proclamation had been transformed into considerable pleasure over the edict of January 1. Most of them seemed to agree with [Frederick] Douglass that the Proclamation had, indeed, changed everything. Even if the Proclamation did not free a single slave, as Henry Ward Beecher admitted, it gave liberty a moral recognition. It was a good beginning, the most significant step that had been taken in a generation of crusading. It was only a beginning, however, as the delegation of antislavery leaders from Boston indicated to Lincoln when they visited him in late January. . . .

The broadening of the Union's war aims to include a crusade against slavery coincided with another important development. Serious grain shortages at home were forcing the British to look elsewhere for foodstuffs. The cotton supply was not yet acutely short, thanks to huge inventories at the beginning of the war, blockade-running during the war, and new sources of supply in India and Egypt. There were also new sources of grain supply, but the British had come to rely heavily on Northern wheat. Indeed, many thought it was indispensable. Perhaps, under the circumstances, the British government should not risk a rupture with the North, some leaders began to reason. As Her Majesty's Government began to look seriously at this problem, it also began to take cognizance of the pressures of the rank and file of the British people and the pressures of the Washington government. Hope for recognition of the Confederacy by Britain and the Continental powers faded away. The Emancipation Proclamation had played an important role in achieving this signal diplomatic victory.

In the months and years following January 1, 1863, Lincoln indicated in many ways that he fully appreciated the importance of the Emancipation Proclamation in the war effort. He knew that it could be an important factor in preventing European powers from moving closer to the Confederacy. He read with the greatest interest the reports from Charles Francis Adams about British reaction to the Proclamation. He even sought to influence British response to the Proclamation by suggesting the form that resolutions adopted in British meetings might take. . . .

Despite the fact that the immediate results of the Emancipation Proclamation were not always measurable, Lincoln was pleased with what he had done. Over and over again he expressed the view that he had done the right thing. It had not had an adverse effect on the course of the war. The war, he told a correspondent in the summer of 1863, had "certainly progressed as favorably for us, since the issue of the proclamation as before." The Proclamation was valid, and he would never retract it. Moreover, it reflected his own repugnance to slavery. As an antislavery man, he wrote Major General Nathaniel P. Banks, he had a motive for issuing the Proclamation that went beyond military considerations. At last he had been able to strike the blow for freedom that he had long wanted to do.

Finally, Lincoln hoped that the Proclamation would provide the basis for a new attitude and policy for Negroes. That all slaves would soon be free was a reality that all white men should face. "Those who shall have tasted actual freedom I believe can never be slaves, or quasi slaves again." He hoped, therefore, that the several states would adopt some practical system "by which the two races could gradually live themselves out of their old relation to each other, and both come out better prepared for the new." He hoped that states would provide for the education of Negroes, and he went so far as to suggest to Governor Michael Hahn of Louisiana that his state might consider extending the franchise to free Negroes of education and property. [2]

Thus, in many ways the Proclamation affected the course of the war as well as Lincoln's way of thinking about the problem of Negroes in the United States. Abroad, it rallied large numbers of people to the North's side and became a valuable instrument of American foreign policy. At home it sharpened the issues of the war and provided a moral and humanitarian ingredient that had been lacking. It fired the leaders with a new purpose and gave to the President a new weapon. Small wonder that he no longer promoted the idea of colonization. Small wonder that he began to advocate education and the franchise for Negroes. They were a new source of strength that deserved to be treated as the loyal citizens that they were. . . .

2. RECONSTRUCTION

New Orleans Tribune *on Reconstruction**

AFTER THREE YEARS' hesitation and delay the National Government concluded at last to take the right step for reconstruction. Every way was first tried except the sound and logical one. The first attempt at reconstruction was through military power. Provisional officers, taken from the army, were appointed as governors and mayors; provost marshals and freedmen's bureau agents were intrusted with the supervision of affairs in the country parishes. They understood very little of the political situation. Governor Shepley discarded the propositions of the Free State Committee. Provost marshals showed the rebels more courtesy and granted them more favors than they did to poor but devoted Union men. Agents of the Freedmen's Bureau might have been designated better as planters' agents. They took more trouble to procure hands for the owners of large plantations than to protect the freed people and defend their rights. We still recollect Gen. Banks' order on "small-pox passes," by which, under the absurd plea of preventing the spreading of small-pox, the colored people were placed under a law of exception as far as

---

[2] Lincoln, *Collected Works,* vol. VI, pp. 358, 408; vol. VII, p. 243.

* This editorial was published in the *Tribune,* the first Negro daily, on Nov. 22, Nov. 24, 1867.

their movements were concerned. They were not allowed to change plantations, they could not leave a place and hunt for work—which is the natural right of all free laborers—unless they first obtained a pass from their former employer, who, of course, refused to give them any. The hypocritical "small-pox passes" remain on Gen. Banks' record, as one of the most flagrant failures to understand and to establish freedom.

The pro-slavery spirit inspired the act of the military administration. The military was not the power to understand civil liberty; generals used to arbitrary command, felt better disposed in favor of the chiefs of the plantations than in favor of the common laborers. They were, moreover, unwilling to take the responsibility of any important change. And after Butler—who was an exception to the rule—had left us, they did, perhaps unconsciously, as much as they could for the slave power, and as little as they could for the cause of liberty and the rights of men.

At last, however, the military government relinquished its hold. The Convention of 1864 assembled, and under the Constitution they framed, a civil government having its legislative, its executive, and judicial officers, was inaugurated. The attempt was made under the inspiration of the military, and could be, of course, but a continuance of the same errors already made. A very small number of the people of a small number of parishes was called upon to vote. The representatives of the old Union minority of white men met at the City Hall, and ignoring the change of the times, believing themselves the legitimate successors of King Cotton, they made an oligarchical Constitution, nearly as bad, for it was as partial as that of 1852. They forgot through pride and presumption, that they had no power by themselves to uphold the white Union oligarchy thus created. The fact is that the very day when military rule came to an end, and the qualified voters —the white voters—under the Constitution of 1864 went to the polls, the Union oligarchs were put aside and rebel oligarchs reinstated in their stead. It did not take great power of intellect to foresee that result. The UNION and subsequently the *Tribune* warned our white friends, at the time, of the evident fate in store for them. Still they kept up their illusions; for could they listen to a black organ? The dullest among them believed himself smarter than any colored man in the land; and down they went, having consummated their own ruin. Gov. Wells vindicated our forebodings. He promptly turned them out of office; and then they could see whether the black organ had seen things correctly or not. From that day they began to call again at our office; they said they were ready to retrieve their faults, and to proclaim universal suf-

frage. But the golden opportunity had passed away, they had
been blind at the opportune time; they had played in their
enemies hands. And rebels showed at the Mechanics' Institute how they intended to treat them.

This was the end of the Union white man's government.
Since the eventful day of the 30th of July, 1866, we have
lived under the grasp of the rebel oligarchy, restored to
power. But Congress has finally given us the means of relief.
After governments of minorities, we are at last enabled to
organize a government of the people. Let us hope that the
Convention of 1867 will have more foresight, a sounder judgment and more liberalism than had the Convention of 1864.
They have to work in the interest of the whole people and
secure the rights of all classes of citizens, of whatever race
or color, unless they want to see the fabric they will attempt
to build up crumble to pieces, and partake of the fate of the
government erected in 1864.

Reconstruction*

FREDERICK DOUGLASS

. . . WHETHER THE TREMENDOUS war so heroically fought
and so victoriously ended shall pass into history, a miserable
failure, barren of permanent results,—a scandalous and
shocking waste of blood and treasure,—a strife for empire, as
Earl Russell characterized it, of no value to liberty or civilization,—an attempt to re-establish a Union by force, which
must be the merest mockery of a Union,—an effort to bring
under Federal authority States into which no loyal man from
the North may safely enter, and to bring men into the national councils who deliberate with daggers and vote with revolvers, and who do not even conceal their deadly hate of the
country that conquered them; or whether, on the other hand,
we shall, as the rightful reward of victory over treason, have a
solid nation, entirely delivered from all contradictions and social antagonisms, based upon loyalty, liberty, and equality,
must be determined one way or the other by the present session of Congress. The last session really did nothing which
can be considered final as to these questions. The Civil Rights

* Frederick Douglass, "Reconstruction," *Atlantic Monthly,* XVIII
(December, 1866), pp. 761-65.

Bill and the Freedmen's Bureau Bill and the proposed constitutional amendments, with the amendment already adopted
and recognized as the law of the land, do not reach the difficulty, and cannot, unless the whole structure of the government is changed from a government by States to something
like a despotic central government, with power to control
even the municipal regulations of States, and to make them
conform to its own despotic will. While there remains such
an idea as the right of each State to control its own local
affairs,—an idea, by the way, more deeply rooted in the
minds of men of all sections of the country than perhaps any
one other political idea,—no general assertion of human
rights can be of any practical value. To change the character
of the government at this point is neither possible nor desirable. All that is necessary to be done is to make the government consistent with itself and render the rights of the States
compatible with the sacred rights of human nature.

The arm of the Federal government is long, but it is far
too short to protect the rights of individuals in the interior of
distant States. They must have the power to protect themselves, or they will go unprotected, in spite of all the laws
the Federal government can put upon the national statute-
book.

Slavery, like all other great systems of wrong, founded in
the depths of human selfishness, and existing for ages, has not
neglected its own conservation. It has steadily exerted an influence upon all around it favorable to its own continuance.
And to-day it is so strong that it could exist, not only without
law, but even against law. Custom, manners, morals, religion,
are all on its side everywhere in the South; and when you add
the ignorance and servility of the ex-slave to the intelligence
and accustomed authority of the master, you have the conditions, not out of which slavery will again grow, but under
which it is impossible for the Federal government to wholly
destroy it, unless the Federal government be armed with despotic power, to blot out State authority, and to station a Federal officer at every cross-road. This, of course, cannot be
done, and ought not even if it could. The true way and the
easiest way is to make our government entirely consistent
with itself, and give to every loyal citizen the elective franchise,—a right and power which will be ever present, and
will form a wall of fire for his protection.

One of the invaluable compensations of the late Rebellion is
the highly instructive disclosure it made of the true source of
danger to republican government. Whatever may be tolerated
in monarchical and despotic governments, no republic is safe

that tolerates a privileged class, or denies to any of its citizens equal rights and equal means to maintain them. What was theory before the war has been made fact by the war. . .

It is asked, said Henry Clay, on a memorable occasion, Will slavery never come to an end? That question, said he, was asked fifty years ago, and it has been answered by fifty years of unprecedented prosperity. In spite of the eloquence of the earnest abolitionists,—poured out against slavery during thirty years,—even they must confess, that, in all the probabilities of the case, that system of barbarism would have continued its horrors far beyond the limits of the nineteenth century but for the Rebellion, and perhaps only have disappeared at last in a fiery conflict, even more fierce and bloody than that which has now been suppressed.

It is no disparagement to truth, that it can only prevail where reason prevails. War begins where reason ends. The thing worse than rebellion is the thing that causes rebellion. What that thing is, we have been taught to our cost. It remains now to be seen whether we have the needed courage to have that cause entirely removed from the Republic. At any rate, to this grand work of national regeneration and entire purification Congress must now address itself, with full purpose that the work shall this time be thoroughly done. The deadly upas, root and branch, leaf and fibre, body and sap, must be utterly destroyed. The country is evidently not in a condition to listen patiently to pleas for postponement, however plausible, nor will it permit the responsibility to be shifted to other shoulders. Authority and power are here commensurate with the duty imposed. There are no cloud-flung shadows to obscure the way. Truth shines with brighter light and intenser heat at every moment, and a country torn and rent and bleeding implores relief from its distress and agony.

If time was at first needed, Congress has now had time. All the requisite materials from which to form an intelligent judgment are now before it. Whether its members look at the origin, the progress, the termination of the war, or at the mockery of a peace now existing, they will find only one unbroken chain of argument in favor of a radical policy of reconstruction. . . . Radicalism, so far from being odious, is now the popular passport to power. The men most bitterly charged with it go to Congress with the largest majorities, while the timid and doubtful are sent by lean majorities, or else left at home. The strange controversy between the President and Congress, at one time so threatening, is disposed of by the people. The high reconstructive powers which he so confidently, ostentatiously, and haughtily claimed, have been disallowed, denounced, and utterly repudiated; while those claimed by Congress have been confirmed.

Without attempting to settle here the metaphysical and somewhat theological question (about which so much has already been said and written), whether once in the Union means always in the Union,—agreeably to the formula, Once in grace always in grace,—it is obvious to common sense that the rebellious States stand to-day, in point of law, precisely where they stood when, exhausted, beaten, conquered, they fell powerless at the feet of Federal authority. Their State governments were overthrown, and the lives and property of the leaders of the Rebellion were forfeited. In reconstructing the institutions of these shattered and overthrown States, Congress should begin with a clean slate, and make clean work of it. Let there be no hesitation. It would be a cowardly deference to a defeated and treacherous President, if any account were made of the illegitimate, one-sided, sham governments hurried into existence for a malign purpose in the absence of Congress. These pretended governments, which were never submitted to the people, and from participation in which four millions of the loyal people were excluded by Presidential order, should now be treated according to their true character, as shams and impositions, and supplanted by true and legitimate governments, in the formation of which loyal men, black and white, shall participate.

It is not, however, within the scope of this paper to point out the precise steps to be taken, and the means to be employed. The people are less concerned about these than the grand end to be attained. They demand such a reconstruction as shall put an end to the present anarchical state of things in the late rebellious States,—where frightful murders and wholesale massacres are perpetrated in the very presence of Federal soldiers. This horrible business they require shall cease. They want a reconstruction such as will protect loyal men, black and white, in their persons and property; such a one as will cause Northern industry, Northern capital, and Northern civilization to flow into the South, and make a man from New England as much at home in Carolina as elsewhere in the Republic. No Chinese wall can now be tolerated. The South must be opened to the light of law and liberty, and this session of Congress is relied upon to accomplish this important work.

The plain, common-sense way of doing this work, as intimated at the beginning, is simply to establish in the South one law, one government, one administration of justice, one condition to exercise of the elective franchise, for men of all races and colors alike. This great measure is sought as earnestly by loyal white men as by loyal blacks, and is needed alike by both. Let sound political prescience but take the place of an unreasoning prejudice, and this will be done.

Men denounce the negro for his prominence in this discussion; but it is no fault of his that in peace as in war, that in conquering Rebel armies as in reconstructing the rebellious States, the right of the negro is the true solution of our national troubles. The stern logic of events which goes directly to the point, disdaining all concern for the color or features of men, has determined the interests of the country as identical with and inseparable from those of the negro.

The policy that emancipated and armed the negro—now seen to have been wise and proper by the dullest—was not certainly more sternly demanded than is now the policy of enfranchisement. If with the negro was success in war, and without him failure, so in peace it will be found that the nation must fall or flourish with the negro.

Fortunately, the Constitution of the United States knows no distinction between citizens on account of color. Neither does it know any difference between a citizen of a State and a citizen of the United States. Citizenship evidently includes all the rights of citizens, whether State or national. If the Constitution knows none, it is clearly no part of the duty of a Republican Congress now to institute one. The mistake of the last session was the attempt to do this very thing by a renunciation of its power to secure political rights to any class of citizens, with the obvious purpose to allow the rebellious States to disfranchise, if they should see fit, their colored citizens. This unfortunate blunder must now be retrieved, and the emasculated citizenship given to the negro supplanted by that contemplated in the Constitution of the United States, which declares that the citizens of each State shall enjoy all the rights and immunities of citizens of the several States, —so that a legal voter in any State shall be a legal voter in all the States.

Of the Dawn of Freedom*

W. E. B. Du BOIS

THE PROBLEM OF the twentieth century is the problem of the color-line,—the relation of the darker to the lighter races of men in Asia and Africa, in America and the islands of the sea. It was a phase of this problem that caused the Civil War; and however much they who marched South and North in 1861 may have fixed on the technical points of union and local autonomy as a shibboleth, all nevertheless knew, as we know, that the question of Negro slavery was the real cause of the conflict. Curious it was, too, how this deeper question ever forced itself to the surface despite effort and disclaimer. No sooner had Northern armies touched Southern soil than this old question, newly guised, sprang from the earth,— What shall be done with Negroes? Peremptory military commands, this way and that, could not answer the query; the Emancipation Proclamation seemed but to broaden and intensify the difficulties; and the War Amendments made the Negro problems of to-day.

It is the aim of this essay to study the period of history from 1861 to 1872 so far as it relates to the American Negro. In effect, this tale of the dawn of Freedom is an account of that government of men called the Freedman's Bureau,—one of the most singular and interesting of the attempts made by a great nation to grapple with the vast problems of race and social condition. . . .

It was a Pierce of Boston who pointed out the way, and thus became in a sense the founder of the Freedmen's Bureau. He was a firm friend of Secretary Chase; and when, in 1861, the care of slaves and abandoned lands developed upon the Treasury officials, Pierce was specially detailed from the ranks to study the conditions. . . . Before his experiment was barely started, however, the problem of the fugitives had assumed such proportions that it was taken from the hands of the over-burdened Treasury Department and given to the army officials. . . .

Then came the Freedmen's Aid societies, born of the

* Excerpts from W.E.B. Du Bois, *The Souls of Black Folk* (New York: Fawcett Publications), pp. 23-41. First published by A. C. McClurg & Co., 1903.

touching appeals from Pierce and from these other centers of
distress. There was the American Missionary Association,
sprung from the *Amistad*, and now full-grown for work; the
various church organizations, the National Freedmen's Relief
Association, the American Freedmen's Union, the Western
Freedmen's Aid Commission,—in all fifty or more active organizations, which sent clothes, money, school-books, and
teachers southward. All they did was needed, for the destitution of the freedmen was often reported as "too appalling for
belief," and the situation was daily growing worse rather than
better.

And daily, too, it seemed more plain that this was no ordinary matter of temporary relief, but a national crisis; for here
loomed a labor problem of vast dimensions. Masses of
Negroes stood idle, or, if they worked spasmodically, were
never sure of pay; and if perchance they received pay, squan-
dered the new thing thoughtlessly. In these and other ways
were camp-life and the new liberty demoralizing the freedmen. The broader economic organization thus clearly
demanded sprang up here and there as accident and local
conditions determined. . . .

Petitions came in to President Lincoln from distinguished
citizens and organizations, strongly urging a comprehensive
and unified plan of dealing with the freedmen, under a bureau
which should be "charged with the study of plans and execution of measures for easily guiding, and in every way judicious-
ly and humanely aiding, the passage of our emancipated and
yet to be emancipated blacks from the old condition of forced
labor to their new state of voluntary industry."

Some half-hearted steps were taken to accomplish this, in
part, by putting the whole matter again in charge of the special Treasury agents. Laws of 1863 and 1864 directed them
to take charge of and lease abandoned lands for periods not
exceeding twelve months, and to "provide in such leases, or
otherwise, for the employment and general welfare" of the
freedmen. Most of the army officers greeted this as a welcome relief from perplexing "Negro affairs," and Secretary
Fessenden, July 29, 1864, issued an excellent system of regulations, which were afterward closely followed by General
al Howard. Under Treasury agents, large quantities of land
were leased in the Mississippi Valley, and many Negroes were
employed; but in August, 1864, the new regulations were suspended for reasons of "public policy," and the army was
again in control. . . .

A Bureau [of Freedmen] was created, [by Congress]
"to continue during the present War of Rebellion, and for

one year thereafter," to which was given "the supervision and management of all abandoned lands and the control of all subjects relating to refugees and freedmen," under "such rules and regulations as may be presented by the head of the Bureau and approved by the President." A Commissioner, appointed by the President and Senate, was to control the Bureau, with an office force not exceeding ten clerks. The President might also appoint assistant commissioners in the seceded States, and to all these offices military officials might be detailed at regular pay. The Secretary of War could issue rations, clothing, and fuel to the destitute, and all abandoned property was placed in the hands of the Bureau for eventual lease and sale to ex-slaves in forty-acre parcels.

Thus did the United States government definitely assume charge of the emancipated Negro as the ward of the nation. It was a tremendous undertaking. Here at the stroke of the pen was erected a government of millions of men,—and not ordinary men either, but black men emasculated by a peculiarly complete system of slavery, centuries old; and now, suddenly, violently, they come into a new birthright, at a time of war and passion, in the midst of the stricken and embittered population of their former masters.

Less than a month after the weary Emancipator passed to his rest, his successor assigned Major-Gen. Oliver O. Howard to duty as Commissioner of the new Bureau. . . .

On May 12, 1865, Howard was appointed; and he assumed the duties of his office promptly on the 15th, and began examining the field of work. A curious mess he looked upon: little despotisms, communistic experiments, slavery, peonage, business speculations, organized charity, unorganized almsgiving,—all reeling on under the guise of helping the freedmen, and all enshrined in the smoke and blood of war and the cursing and silence of angry men. On May 19 the new government—for a government it really was—issued its constitution; commissioners were to be appointed in each of the seceded states, who were to take charge of "all subjects relating to refugees and freedmen," and all relief and rations were to be given by their consent alone. The Bureau invited continued coöperation with benevolent societies, and declared: "It will be the object of all commissioners to introduce practicable systems of compensated labor," and to establish schools. . . . Forthwith nine assistant commissioners were appointed. They were to hasten to their fields of work; seek gradually to close relief establishments, and make the destitute self-supporting; act as courts of law where there were no courts, or where Negroes were not recognized in them as free; establish the institution of marriage among ex-slaves, and keep records; see that freedmen were free to choose their employers, and help in making fair contracts for them; and finally, the circular said: "Simple good faith, for which we hope on all hands for those concerned in the passing away of slavery, will especially relieve the assistant commissioners in the discharge of their duties toward the freedmen, as well as promote the general welfare."

After a year's work, vigorously as it was pushed, the problem looked even more difficult to grasp and solve than at the beginning. Nevertheless, three things that year's work did, well worth the doing: it relieved a vast amount of physical suffering; it transported seven thousand fugitives from congested centers back to the farm; and, best of all, it inaugurated the crusade of the New England schoolma'am. . . . In that first year they taught one hundred thousand souls, and more.

Evidently, Congress must soon legislate again on the hastily organized Bureau, which had so quickly grown into wide significance and vast possibilities. An institution such as that was well-nigh as difficult to end as to begin. Early in 1866 Congress took up the matter, when Senator Trumbull, of Illinois, introduced a bill to extend the Bureau and enlarge its powers. This measure received, at the hands of Congress, far more thorough discussion and attention than its predecessor. . . . The bill which finally passed enlarged and made permanent the Freedmen's Bureau. It was promptly vetoed by President Johnson as "unconstitutional," "unnecessary," and "extrajudicial," and failed of passage over the veto. Meantime, however, the breach between Congress and President began to broaden, and a modified form of the lost bill was finally passed over the President's second veto, July 16.

The act of 1866 gave the Freedmen's Bureau its final form, —the form by which it will be known to posterity and judged of men. It extended the existence of the Bureau to July, 1868; it authorized additional assistant commissioners, the retention of army officers mustered out of regular service, the sale of certain forfeited lands to freedmen on nominal terms, the sale of Confederate public property for Negro schools, and a wider field of judicial interpretation and cognizance. The government of the unreconstructed South was thus put very largely in the hands of the Freedmen's Bureau, especially as in many cases the departmental military commander was now made also assistant commissioner. It was thus that the Freedmen's Bureau became a full-fledged government of men. It made laws, executed them and interpreted them; it laid and collected taxes, defined and punished crime, maintained and used military force, and dictated such measures as it thought necessary and proper for the accomplishment of its varied ends. . . .

To understand and criticise intelligently so vast a work, one must not forget an instant the drift of things in the later sixties. Lee had surrendered, Lincoln was dead, and Johnson and Congress were at loggerheads; the Thirteenth Amendment was adopted, the Fourteenth pending, and the Fifteenth declared in force in 1870. Guerrilla raiding, the ever-present flickering after-flame of war, was spending its forces against the Negroes, and all the Southern land was awakening as from some wild dream to poverty and social revolution. In a time of perfect calm, amid willing neighbors and streaming wealth, the social uplifting of four million slaves to an assured and self-sustaining place in the body politic and economic would have been a herculean task; but when to the inherent difficulties of so delicate and nice a social operation were added the spite and hate of conflict, the hell of war; when suspicion and cruelty were rife, and gaunt Hunger wept beside Bereavement,—in such a case, the work of any instrument of social regeneration was in large part foredoomed to failure. The very name of the Bureau stood for a thing in the South which for two centuries and better men had refused even to argue,—that life amid free Negroes was simply unthinkable, the maddest of experiments.

. . . Curiously incongruous elements were left arrayed against each other,—the North, the government, the carpetbagger, and the slave, here; and there, all the South that was white, whether gentleman or vagabond, honest man or rascal, lawless murderer or martyr to duty.

Thus it is doubly difficult to write of this period calmly, so intense was the feeling, so mighty the human passions that swayed and blinded men.

Here, then, was the field of work for the Freedmen's Bureau; and since, with some hesitation, it was continued by the act of 1868 until 1869, let us look upon four years of its work as a whole. There were, in 1868, nine hundred Bureau officials scattered from Washington to Texas, ruling, directly and indirectly, many millions of men. The deeds of these rulers fall mainly under seven heads: the relief of physical suffering, the overseeing of the beginnings of free labor, the buying and selling of land, the establishment of schools, the paying of bounties, the administration of justice, and the financiering of all these activities. . . .

In the work of establishing the Negroes as peasant proprietors, the Bureau was from the first handicapped and at last absolutely checked. Something was done, and larger things were planned; abandoned lands were leased so long as they remained in the hands of the Bureau, and a total revenue of nearly half a million dollars derived from black tenants. Some other lands to which the nation had gained title were sold on easy terms, and public lands were opened for settlement to the very few freedmen who had tools and capital. But the vision of "forty acres and a mule"—the righteous and reasonable ambition to become a landholder, which the nation had all but categorically promised the freedmen—was destined in most cases to bitter disappointment. And those men of marvellous hindsight who are today seeking to preach the Negro back to the present peonage of the soil know well, or ought to know, that the opportunity of binding the Negro peasant willingly to the soil was lost on that day when the Commissioner of the Freedmen's Bureau had to go to South Carolina and tell the weeping freedmen, after their years of toil, that their land was not theirs, that there was a mistake —somewhere. If by 1874 the Georgia Negro alone owned three hundred and fifty thousand acres of land, it was by the grace of his thrift rather than by bounty of the government.

The greatest success of the Freedmen's Bureau lay in the planting of the free school among Negroes, and the idea of free elementary education among all classes in the South. . . .

The most perplexing and least successful part of the Bureau's work lay in the exercise of its judicial functions. The regular Bureau court consisted of one representative of the employer, one of the Negro, and one of the Bureau. If the Bureau could have maintained a perfectly judicial attitude, this arrangement would have been ideal, and must in time have gained confidence; but the nature of its other activities and the character of its *personnel* prejudiced the Bureau in favor of the black litigants, and led without doubt to much injustice and annoyance. On the other hand, to leave the Negro in the hands of the Southern courts was impossible. In a distracted land where slavery had hardly fallen, to keep the strong from wanton abuse of the weak, and the weak from bloating insolently over the half-shorn strength of the strong, was a thankless, hopeless task. The former masters of the land were peremptorily ordered about, seized, and imprisoned, and punished over and again, with scant courtesy from army officers. The former slaves were intimidated, beaten, raped, and butchered by angry and revengeful men. Bureau courts tended to become centers simply for punishing whites, while the regular civil courts tended to become solely institutions for perpetuating the slavery of blacks. Almost every law and method ingenuity could devise was employed by the legislatures to reduce the Negroes to serfdom,—to make them the slaves of the State, if not of individual owners; while the Bureau officials too often were found striving to put the "bottom rail on top," and gave the freedmen a power and independence which they could not yet use. It is all well enough for us of another generation to wax wise with advice to those who bore the burden in the heat of the day. It is full easy now to see that the man who lost home, fortune, and family at a stroke, and saw his land ruled by "mules and niggers," was really benefited by the passing of slavery. It is not difficult now to say to the young freedman, cheated and cuffed about who has seen his father's head beaten to a jelly and his own mother namelessly assaulted, that the meek shall inherit the earth. Above all, nothing is more convenient than to heap on the Freedmen's Bureau all the evils of that evil day, and damn it utterly for every mistake and blunder that was made.

All this is easy, but it is neither sensible nor just. Someone had blundered, but that was long before Oliver Howard was born; there was criminal aggression and heedless neglect, but without some system of control there would have been far more than there was. Had the control been from within, the Negro would have been reenslaved, to all intents and purposes. Coming as the control did from without, perfect men and methods would have bettered all things; and even with imperfect agents and questionable methods, the work accomplished was not undeserving of commendation.

Such was the dawn of Freedom; such was the work of the Freedmen's Bureau, which, summed up in brief, may be epitomized thus: for some fifteen million dollars, beside the sums spent before 1865, and the dole of benevolent societies, this Bureau set going a system of free labor, established a beginning of peasant proprietorship, secured the recognition of black freedmen before courts of law, and founded the free common school in the South. On the other hand, it failed to begin the establishment of good-will between ex-masters and freedmen, to guard its work wholly from paternalistic methods which discouraged self-reliance, and to carry out to any considerable extent its implied promises to furnish the freedmen with land. Its successes were the result of hard work, supplemented by the aid of philanthropists and the eager striving of black men. Its failures were the result of bad local agents, the inherent difficulties of the work, and national neglect.

Such an institution, from its wide powers, great responsibilities, large control of moneys, and generally conspicuous position, was naturally open to repeated and bitter attack. It sustained a searching Congressional investigation at the instance of Fernando Wood in 1870. Its archives and few remaining functions were with blunt discourtesy transferred from Howard's control, in his absence, to the supervision of Secretary of War Belknap in 1872, on the Secretary's recommendation. Finally, in consequence of grave intimations of wrong-doing made by the Secretary and his subordinates, General Howard was court-martialed in 1874. In both of these trials the Commissioner of the Freedmen's Bureau was officially exonerated from any wilful misdoing, and his work commended. Nevertheless, many unpleasant things were brought to light,—the methods of transacting the business of the Bureau were faulty; several cases of defalcation were proved, and other frauds strongly suspected; there were some business transactions which savored of dangerous speculation, if not dishonesty; and around it all lay the smirch of the Freedmen's Bank.

Morally and practically, the Freedmen's Bank was part of the Freedmen's Bureau, although it had no legal connection with it. With the prestige of the government back of it, and a directing board of unusual respectability and national reputation, this banking institution had made a remarkable start in the development of that thrift among black folk which slavery had kept them from knowing. Then in one sad day came the crash,—all the hard-earned dollars of the freedmen disappeared; but that was the least of the loss,—all the faith in saving went too, and much of the faith in men; and that was a loss that a Nation which to-day sneers at Negro shiftlessness has never yet made good. Not even ten additional years of slavery could have done so much to throttle the thrift of the freedmen as the mismanagement and bankruptcy of the series of savings banks chartered by the Nation for their especial aid. Where all the blame should rest, it is hard to say; whether the Bureau and the Bank died chiefly by reason of the blows of its selfish friends or the dark machinations of its foes, perhaps even time will never reveal, for here lies unwritten history.

Of the foes without the Bureau, the bitterest were those who attacked not so much its conduct or policy under the law as the necessity for any such institution at all. Such attacks came primarily from the border States and the South; and they were summed up by Senator Davis, of Kentucky, when he moved to entitle the act of 1866 a bill "to promote strife and conflict between the white and black races . . . by a grant of unconstitutional power." The argument gathered tremendous strength South and North; but its very strength was its weakness. For, argued the plain common-sense of the nation, if it is unconstitutional, unpractical, and futile for the nation to stand guardian over its helpless wards, then there is left but one alternative,—to make those wards their own guardians by arming them with the ballot. Moreover, the path of the practical politician pointed the same way; for, argued this opportunist, if we cannot peacefully reconstruct the South with white votes, we certainly can with black votes. So justice and force joined hands.

The alternative thus offered the nation was not between full and restricted Negro suffrage; else every sensible man, black and white, would easily have chosen the latter. It was rather a choice between suffrage and slavery, after endless blood and gold had flowed to sweep human bondage away. Not a single Southern legislature stood ready to admit a Negro, under any conditions, to the polls; not a single Southern legislature believed free Negro labor was possible without a system of restrictions that took all its freedom away; there was scarcely a white man in the South who did not honestly regard Emancipation as a crime, and its practical nullification as a duty. In such a situation, the granting of the ballot to the black man was a necessity, the very least a guilty nation could grant a wronged race, and the only method of compelling the South to accept the results of the war. Thus Negro suffrage ended a civil war by beginning a race feud. And some felt gratitude toward the race thus sacrificed in its swaddling clothes on the altar of national integrity; and some felt and feel only indifference and contempt.

Had political exigencies been less pressing, the opposition to government guardianship of Negroes less bitter, and the attachment to the slave system less strong, the social seer can well imagine a far better policy,—a permanent Freedmen's Bureau, with a national system of Negro schools; a carefully supervised employment and labor office; a system of impartial protection before the regular courts; and such institutions for social betterment as savings-banks, land and building associations, and social settlements. All this vast expenditure of money and brains might have formed a great school of prospective citizenship, and solved in a way we have not yet solved the most perplexing and persistent of the Negro problems.

That such an institution was unthinkable in 1870 was due in part to certain acts of the Freedmen's Bureau itself. It came to regard its work as merely temporary, and Negro suffrage as a final answer to all present perplexities. The political ambition of many of its agents and *protégés* led it far afield into questionable activities, until the South, nursing its own deep prejudices, came easily to ignore all the good deeds of the Bureau and hate its very name with perfect hatred. So the Freedmen's Bureau died, and its child was the Fifteenth Amendment.

The passing of a great human institution before its work is done, like the untimely passing of a single soul, but leaves a legacy of striving for other men. The legacy of the Freedmen's Bureau is the heavy heritage of this generation. To-day, when new and vaster problems are destined to strain every fibre of the national mind and soul, would it not be well to count this legacy honestly and carefully? For this much all men know: despite compromise, war, and struggle, the Negro is not free. In the backwoods of the Gulf States, for miles and miles, he may not leave the plantation of his birth; in well-nigh the whole rural South the black farmers are peons, bound by law and custom to an economic slavery, from which the only escape is death or the penitentiary. In the most cultured sections and cities of the South the Negroes are a segregated servile caste, with restricted rights and privileges. Before the courts, both in law and custom, they stand on a different and peculiar basis. Taxation without representation is the rule of their political life. And the result of all this is, and in nature must have been, lawlessness and crime. That is the large legacy of the Freedmen's Bureau, the work it did not do because it could not.

I have seen a land right merry with the sun, where children sing, and rolling hills lie like passioned women wanton with harvest. And there in the King's Highway sat and sits a figure veiled and bowed, by which the traveller's footsteps hasten as they go. On the tainted air broods fear. Three centuries' thought has been the raising and unveiling of that bowed human heart, and now behold a century new for the duty and the deed. The problem of the twentieth century is the problem of the color-line.

THE BLACK CODES

(a) Louisiana, 1865*

1. AN ACT TO PROVIDE FOR AND REGULATE LABOR CONTRACTS FOR AGRICULTURAL PURSUITS.

Sec. 1. Be it enacted by the Senate and House of Representatives of the State of Louisiana in general assembly convened, That all persons employed as laborers in agricultural pursuits shall be required, during the first ten days of the month of January of each year, to make contracts for labor for the then ensuing year, or for the year next ensuing the termination of their present contracts. All contracts for labor for agricultural purposes shall be made in writing, signed by the employer, and shall be made in the presence of a Justice of the Peace and two disinterested witnesses, in whose presence the contract shall be read to the laborer, and when assented to and signed by the latter, shall be considered as binding for the time prescribed. . . .

Sec. 2. Every laborer shall have full and perfect liberty to choose his employer, but, when once chosen, he shall not be allowed to leave his place of employment until the fulfillment of his contract . . . and if they do so leave, without cause or permission, they shall forfeit all wages earned to the time of abandonment. . . .

Sec. 7. All employers failing to comply with their contracts, shall, upon conviction, be fined an amount double that due the laborer . . . to be paid to the laborer; and any inhumanity, cruelty, or neglect of duty on the part of the employer shall be summarily punished by fines . . . to be paid to the injured party. . . .

Sec. 8. Be it further enacted, &c., That in case of sickness of the laborer, wages for the time lost shall be deducted, and where the sickness is feigned for purposes of idleness, and also on refusal to work according to contract, double the amount of wages shall be deducted for the time lost; and also

* Acts of the General Assembly of Louisiana Regulating Labor. Extra Session, 1865, p. 3ff. Reprinted in Henry Steele Commager, *Documents of American History* (New York: Appleton-Century-Crofts, Inc., 1958), p. 455.

where rations have been furnished; and should the refusal to work continue beyond three days, the offender shall be reported to a Justice of the Peace, and shall be forced to labor on roads, levees, and other public works, without pay, until the offender consents to return to his labor.

Sec. 9. Be it further enacted, &c., That, when in health, the laborer shall work ten hours during the day in summer, and nine hours during the day in winter, unless otherwise stipulated in the labor contract; he shall obey all proper orders of his employer or his agent; take proper care of his work-mules, horses, oxen, stock; also of all agricultural implements; and employers shall have the right to make a reasonable deduction from the laborer's wages for injuries done to animals or agricultural implements committed to his care, or for bad or negligent work. Bad work shall not be allowed. Failing to obey reasonable orders, neglect of duty, and leaving home without permission will be deemed disobedience; impudence, swearing, or indecent language to or in the presence of the employer, his family, or agent, or quarreling and fighting with one another, shall be deemed disobedience. For any disobedience a fine of one dollar shall be imposed on and paid by the offender. For all lost time from work-hours, unless in case of sickness, the laborer shall be fined twenty-five cents per hour. For all absence from home without leave he will be fined at the rate of two dollars per day. Laborers will not be required to labor on the Sabbath unless by special contract. For all thefts of the laborer from the employer of agricultural products, hogs, sheep, poultry, or any other property of the employer, or willful destruction of property or injury, the laborer shall pay the employer double the amount of the value of the property stolen, destroyed, or injured, one-half to be paid to the employer and the other half to be placed in the general fund provided for in this section. No live stock shall be allowed to laborers without the permission of the employer. Laborers shall not receive visitors during work-hours. All difficulties arising between the employers and laborers, under this section, shall be settled by the former; if not satisfactory to the laborers, an appeal may be had to the nearest Justice of the Peace and two freeholders, citizens, one of said citizens to be selected by the employer and the other by the laborer; and all fines imposed and collected under this section shall be deducted from wages due, and shall be placed in a common fund, to be divided among the other laborers on the plantation, except as provided for above. . . .

Sec. 10. Be it further enacted, &c., That for gross misconduct on the part of the laborer, such as insubordination, habitual laziness, frequent acts of violation of his contract or the laws of the State, he may be dismissed by his employer; nevertheless, the laborer shall have the right to resist his dismissal and to a redress of his wrongs by an appeal to a Justice of the Peace and two freeholders, citizens of the parish, one of the freeholders to be selected by himself and the other by his employer.

2. An Act Relative to Apprentices and Indentured Servants

Sec. 1. Be it enacted . . . That it shall be the duty of Sheriffs, Justices of the Peace, and other Civil officers of this State, to report . . . for each and every year, all persons under the age of eighteen years, if females, and twenty-one, if males, who are orphans, or whose parents, . . . have not the means, or who refuse to provide for and maintain said minors; and thereupon it shall be the duty of the Clerk of the District Courts . . . to examine whether the party or parties so reported from time to time, come within the purview and meaning of this Act, and, if so, to apprentice said minor or minors, in manner and form as prescribed by the Civil Code. . . .

Sec. 2. That persons, who have attained the age of majority, . . . may bind themselves to services to be performed in this State, for the term of five years, on such terms as they may stipulate, as domestic servants, and to work on farms, plantations, or in manufacturing establishments, which contracts shall be valid and binding on the parties to the same.

Sec. 3. That in all cases where the age of the minor can not be ascertained by record testimony, the Clerk of the District Courts, Mayor and President of the Police Jury, or Justices of the Peace aforesaid, shall fix the age, according to the best evidence before them. . . .

(b) Mississippi, 1865*

1. Civil Rights of Freedmen in Mississippi

Sec. 1. *Be it enacted,* . . . That all freedmen, free negroes, and mulattoes may sue and be sued, implead and be implead-

* Laws of Mississippi, 1865, p. 82ff, reprinted in *ibid.,* p. 452.

ed, in all the courts of law and equity of this State, and may acquire personal property, and choses in action, by descent or purchase, and may dispose of the same in the same manner and to the same extent that white persons may: *Provided,* That the provisions of this section shall not be so construed as to allow any freedman, free negro, or mulatto to rent or lease any lands or tenements except in incorporated cities or towns, in which places the corporate authorities shall control the same. . . .

Sec. 3. . . . All freedmen, free negroes, or mulattoes who do now and have herebefore lived and cohabited together as husband and wife shall be taken and held in law as legally married, and the issue shall be taken and held as legitimate for all purposes; that it shall not be lawful for any freedman, free negro, or mulatto to intermarry with any white person; nor for any white person to intermarry with any freedman, free negro, or mulatto; and any person who shall so intermarry, shall be deemed guilty of felony, and on conviction thereof shall be confined in the State penitentiary for life; and those shall be deemed freedmen, free negroes, and mulattos who are of pure negro blood, and those descended from a negro to the third generation, inclusive, though one ancestor in each generation may have been a white person. . . .

Sec. 6. . . . All contracts for labor made with freedmen, free negroes, and mulattoes for a longer period than one month shall be in writing, and in duplicate, attested and read to said freedman, free negro, or mulatto by a beat, city or county officer, or two disinterested white persons of the county in which the labor is to be performed, of which each party shall have one; and said contracts shall be taken and held as entire contracts, and if the laborer shall quit the service of the employer before the expiration of his term of service, without good cause, he shall forfeit his wages for that year up to the time of quitting.

Sec. 7. . . . Every civil officer shall, and every person may, arrest and carry back to his or her legal employer any freedman, free negro, or mulatto who shall have quit the service of his or her employer before the expiration of his or her term of service without good cause; and said officer and person shall be entitled to receive for arresting and carrying back every deserting employe aforesaid the sum of five dollars, and ten cents per mile from the place of arrest to the place of delivery; and the same shall be paid by the employer, and held as a set-off for so much against the wages of said deserting employe: *Provided,* that said arrested party, after being so returned, may appeal to the justice of the peace or member of the board of police of the county, who, on notice to the alleged employer, shall try summarily whether said appellant is legally employed by the alleged employer, and has good cause to quit said employer . . .

2. MISSISSIPPI APPRENTICE LAW

Sec. 1. . . . It shall be the duty of all sheriffs, justices of the peace, and other civil officers of the several counties in this State, to report to the probate courts of their respective counties semi-annually, at the January and July terms of said courts, all freedmen, free negroes, and mulattoes, under the age of eighteen, in their respective counties, beats or districts, who are orphans, or whose parent or parents have not the means or who refuse to provide for and support said minors; and thereupon it shall be the duty of said probate court to order the clerk of said court to apprentice said minors to some competent and suitable person, on such terms as the court may direct, having a particular care to the interest of said minor: *Provided*, that the former owner of said minors shall have the preference when, in the opinion of the court, he or she shall be a suitable person for that purpose.

Sec. 2. . . . The said court shall be fully satisfied that the person or persons to whom said minor shall be apprenticed shall be a suitable person to have the charge and care of said minor, and fully to protect the interest of said minor. The said court shall require the said master or mistress to execute bond and security, payable to the State of Mississippi, conditioned that he or she shall furnish said minor with sufficient food and clothing; to treat said minor humanely; furnish medical attention in case of sickness; teach, or cause to be taught, him or her to read and write, if under fifteen years old, and will conform to any law that may be hereafter passed for the regulation of the duties and relation of master and apprentice. . . .

Sec. 3. . . . In the management and control of said apprentice, said master or mistress shall have the power to inflict such moderate corporal chastisement as a father or guardian is allowed to inflict on his or her child or ward at common law: *Provided*, that in no case shall cruel or inhuman punishment be inflicted.

Sec. 4. . . . If any apprentice shall leave the employment of his or her master or mistress, without his or her consent, said master or mistress may pursue and recapture said apprentice, and bring him or her before any justice of the peace of the county, whose duty it shall be to remand said apprentice to the service of his or her master or mistress; and in the event of a refusal on the part of said apprentice so to return, then said justice shall commit said apprentice to the jail of said county, on failure to give bond, to the next term of the county court; and it shall be the duty of said court at the first term thereafter to investigate said case, and if the court shall be of opinion that said apprentice left the employment of his or her master or mistress without good cause, to order him or her to be punished, as provided for the punishment of hired freedmen, as may be from time to time provided for by law for desertion, until he or she shall agree to return to the service of his or her master or mistress: . . . if the court shall believe that said apprentice had good cause to quit his said master or mistress, the court shall discharge said apprentice from said indenture, and also enter a judgment against the master or mistress for not more than one hundred dollars, for the use and benefit of said apprentice. . . .

3. MISSISSIPPI VAGRANT LAW

Sec. 1. *Be it enacted,* etc., . . . That all rogues and vagabonds, idle and dissipated persons, beggars, jugglers, or persons practicing unlawful games or plays, runaways, common drunkards, common night-walkers, pilferers, lewd, wanton, or lascivious persons, in speech or behavior, common railers and brawlers, persons who neglect their calling or employment, misspend what they earn, or do not provide for the support of themselves or their families, or dependents, and all other idle and disorderly persons, including all who neglect all lawful business, habitually misspend their time by frequenting houses of ill-fame, gaming-houses, or tippling shops, shall be deemed and considered vagrants, under the provisions of this act, and upon conviction thereof shall be fined not exceeding one hundred dollars, with all accruing costs, and be imprisoned at the discretion of the court, not exceeding ten days.

Sec. 2. . . . All freedmen, free negroes and mulattoes in this State, over the age of eighteen years, found on the second Monday in January, 1866, or thereafter, with no lawful employment or business, or found unlawfully assembling themselves together, either in the day or night time, and all white persons so assembling themselves with freedmen, free negroes or mulattoes, or usually associating with freedmen, free negroes or mulattoes, on terms of equality, or living in adultery or fornication with a freed woman, free negro or mulatto, shall be deemed vagrants, and on conviction thereof shall be fined in a sum not exceeding, in the case of a freedman, free negro or mulatto, fifty dollars, and a white man two hundred dollars, and imprisoned at the discretion of the court, the free negro not exceeding ten days, and the white man not exceeding six months. . . .

4. Penal Laws of Mississippi

Sec. 1. *Be it enacted.* . . . That no freedman, free negro or mulatto, not in the military service of the United States government, and not licensed so to do by the board of police of his or her county, shall keep or carry fire-arms of any kind, or any ammunition, dirk or bowie knife, and on conviction thereof in the county court shall be punished by fine, not exceeding ten dollars, and pay the costs of such proceedings, and all such arms or ammunition shall be forfeited to the informer; and it shall be the duty of every civil and military officer to arrest any freedman, free negro, or mulatto found with any such arms or ammunition, and cause him or her to be committed to trial in default of bail.

2. . . . Any freedman, free negro, or mulatto committing riots, routs, affrays, trespasses, malicious mischief, cruel treatment to animals, seditious speeches, insulting gestures, language, or acts, or assaults on any person, disturbance of the peace, exercising the function of a minister of the Gospel without a license from some regularly organized church, vending spirituous or intoxicating liquors, or committing any other misdemeanor, the punishment of which is not specifically provided for by law, shall, upon conviction thereof in the county court, be fined not less than ten dollars, and not more than one hundred dollars, and may be imprisoned at the discretion of the court, not exceeding thirty days. . . .

Sec. 5. . . . If any freedman, free negro, or mulatto, convicted of any of the misdemeanors provided against in this act, shall fail or refuse for the space of five days, after conviction, to pay the fine and costs imposed, such person shall be hired out by the sheriff or other officer, at public outcry, to any white person who will pay said fine and all costs, and take said convict for the shortest time.

Petition to Congress Against Violence*

To the Senate and house of Representatives in Congress assembled: We the Colored Citizens of Frankfort and vicinity do this day memorialize your honorable bodies upon the condition of affairs now existing in this the state of Kentucky.

* U.S. Senate, 42d Congress, 1st Session.

We would respectfully state that life, liberty and property are unprotected among the colored race of this state. Organized Bands of desperate and lawless men mainly composed of soldiers of the late Rebel Armies, Armed disciplined and disguised and bound by Oath and secret obligations, have by force terror and violence subverted all civil society among Colored people, thus utterly rendering insecure the safety of persons and property overthrowing all those rights which are the primary basis and objects of the Government which are expressly guaranteed to us by the Constitution of the United States as amended; We believe you are not familiar with the description of the Ku Klux Klans riding nightly over the country going from County to County and in the County towns spreading terror wherever they go, by robbing whipping ravishing and killing our people without provocation, compelling Colored people to brake the ice and bathe in the Chilly waters of the Kentucky River.

The Legislature has adjourned they refused to enact any laws to suppress Ku Klux disorder. We regard them as now being licensed to continue their dark and bloody deeds under cover of the dark night. They refuse to allow us to testify in the state Courts where a white man is concerned. We find their deeds are perpetrated only upon Colored men and white Republicans. We also find that for our services to the Government and our race we have become the special object of hatred and persecution at the hands of the Democratic party. Our people are driven from their homes in great numbers having no redress only the U.S. Courts which is in many cases unable to reach them. We would state that we have been law abiding citizens, pay our tax and in many parts of the state our people have been driven from the poles [sic], refused the right to vote. Many have been slaughtered while attempting to vote, we ask how long is this state of things to last.

We appeal to you as law abiding citizens to enact some laws that will protect us. And that will enable us to exercise the rights of citizens. We see that the senator from this state denies there being organized Bands of desperaders in the state, for information we lay before you an number of violent acts occurred during his Administration. Although he Stevenson * says half Dozen instances of violence did occur these are not more than one half the acts that have occured. The Democratic party has here a political organization composed only of Democrats not a single Republican can join them where many of these acts have been committed it has been proven that

* Governor–later, Senator–John W. Stevenson.

they were the men, don with Armies from the State Arsenal. We pray you will take steps to remedy these evils.

Don by a Committee of Grievances appointed at a meeting of all the Colored Citizens of Frankfort & vicinity.

Mar. 25th, 1871

Henry Marrs, Teacher colored school   Samuel Damsey,
Henry Lynn, Livery stable keeper   B. Smith [Blacksmith]
N. N. Trumbo, Grocer   B. T. Crampton, Barber

COMMITTEE

1. A mob visited Harrodsburg in Mercer County to take from jail a man name Robertson, Nov. 14, 1867.

2. Smith attacked and whipped by regulation in Zelun County Nov. 1867.

3. Colored school house burned by incendiaries in Breckinridge Dec. 24, 1867.

4. A Negro Jim Macklin taken from jail in Frankfort and hung by mob January 28, 1868.

5. Sam Davis hung by mob in Harrodsburg May 28, 1868.

6. Wm. Pierce hung by a mob in Christian July 12, 1868.

7. Geo. Roger hung by a mob in Bradsfordsville Martin County July 11, 1868.

8. Colored school Exhibition at Midway attacked by a mob July 31, 1868.

9. Seven person ordered to leave their homes at Standford, Ky. Aug. 7, 1868.

10. Silas Woodford age sixty badly beaten by disguised mob. Mary Smith Curtis and Margaret Mosby also badly beaten, near Keene Jessemine County Aug. 1868.

11. Cabe Fields shot—and killed by disguise men near Keene Jessamine County Aug. 3, 1868.

12. James Gaines expelled from Anderson by Ku Klux Aug. 1868.

13. James Parker killed by Ku Klux Pulaski, Aug. 1868.

14. Noah Blankenship whipped by a mob in Pulaski County Aug. 1868.

15. Negroes attacked robbed and driven from Summerville in Green County Aug. 21, 1868.

16. William Gibson and John Gibson hung by a mob in Washington County Aug. 1868.

17. F. H. Montford hung by an mob near Cogers landing in Jessamine County Aug. 28, 1868.

18. Wm. Glassgow killed by a mob in Warren County Sep. 5, 1868.

19. Negro hung by a mob Sep. 1868.

20. Two Negros beaten by Ku Klux in Anderson County Sept. 11, 1868.

21. Mob attacked house of Oliver Stone in Fayette County Sept. 11, 1868.

22. Mob attacked Cumins house in Pulaski County. Cumins his daughter and a man name Adams killed in the attack Sept. 18, 1868.

23. U.S. Marshall Meriwether attacked captured and beatened with death in Larue County by mob Sept. 1868.

24. Richardson house attacked in Conishville by mob and Crasban killed Sept. 28, 1868.

25. Mob attacks Negro cabin at hanging forks in Lincoln County. John Mosteran killed & Cash & Coffey killed Sept. 1869.

26. Terry Laws & James Ryan hung by mob at Nicholasville Oct. 26, 1868.

27. Attack on Negro cabin in Spencer County—a woman outraged Dec. 1868.

28. Two Negroes shot by Ku Klux at Sulphur Springs in Union County Dec. 1868.

29. Negro shot at Morganfield Union County, Dec. 1868.

30. Mob visited Edwin Burris house in Mercer County, January, 1869.

31. William Parker whipped by Ku Klux in Lincoln County Jan. 20/69.

32. Mob attacked and fired into house of Jesse Davises in Lincoln County Jan. 20, 1868.

33. Spears taken from his room at Harrodsburg by disguise men Jan. 19, 1869.

34. Albert Bradford killed by disguise men in Scott County, Jan. 20, 1869.

35. Ku Klux whipped boy at Standford March 12, 1869.

36. Mob attacked Frank Bournes house in Jessamine County. Roberts killed March 1869.

37. Geo Bratcher hung by mob on sugar creek in Garrard County March 30, 1869.

38. John Penny hung by a mob at Nevada Mercer county May 29, 1869.

39. Ku Klux whipped Lucien Green in Lincoln county June 1869.

40. Miller whipped by Ku Klux in madison county July 2d, 1869.

41. Chas Henderson shot & his wife killed by mob on silver creek Madison county July 1869.

42. Mob decoy from Harrodsburg and hangs Geo Bolling July 17, 1869.

43. Disguise band visited home of I. C. Vanarsdall and T. J. Vanarsdall in Mercer county July 18/69.

44. Mob attack Ronsey's house in Casey county three men and one woman Killed July 1869.

45. James Crowders hung by mob near Lebanon Merion county Augt 9, 1869.

46. Mob tar and feather a citizen of Cynthiana in Harrison county Aug. 1869.

47. Mob whipped and bruised a Negro in Davis county Sept. 1869.

48. Ku Klux burn colored meeting-house in Carrol county Sept. 1869.

49. Ku Klux whipped a Negro at John Carmins's farm in Fayette county Sept. 1869.

50. Wiley Gevens killed by Ku Klux at Dixon Webster county Oct. 1869.

51. Geo Rose killed by Klu Klux near Kirkville in Madison county Oct. 18, 1869.

52. Ku Klux ordered Wallace Sinkhorn to leave his home near Parkville Boyle county Oct. 1869.

53. Man named Shepherd shot by mob near Parksville Oct. 1869.

54. Regulator killed Geo Tanhely in Lincoln county Nov. 2d. 1869.

55. Ku Klux attacked Frank Searcy house in madison county one man shot Nov. 1869.

56. Searcy hung by mob madison county at Richmond Nov. 4th, 1869.

57. Ku Klux killed Robt Mershon daughter shot Nov. 1869.

58. Mob whipped Pope Hall and Willett in Washington county Nov. 1869.

59. Regulators whipped Cooper in Pulaski County Nov. 1869.

60. Ku Klux ruffians outraged Negroes in Hickman county Nov. 20, 1869.

61. Mob take two Negroes from jail Richmond Madison county one hung one whipped Dec. 12, 1869.

62. Two Negroes killed by mob while in civil custody near mayfield Graves county Dec. 1869.

63. Allen Cooper killed by Ku Klux in Adair county Dec. 24th, 1869.

64. Negroes whipped while on Scott's farm in Franklin county Dec. 1869.

Petition to Congress for Civil Rights*

MEMORIAL

OF THE

NATIONAL CONVENTION OF COLORED PERSONS,

PRAYING

To be protected in their civil rights.

DECEMBER 19, 1873.—Ordered to lie on the table and be printed.

NATIONAL CIVIL-RIGHTS CONVENTION,
Washington, D. C., December, 1873.

Honorable Senate and House of Representatives in Congress assembled:

* U.S. Senate, 43d Congress, 1st Session, *Mis. Doc. No. 21.*

We regret the necessity which compels us to again come before you and say "we are aggrieved." We are authorized to say to those in authority, to Congress, to the people whom it represents, that there are nearly five millions of American citizens who are shamefully outraged; who are thus treated without cause. The recognitions made within a few years respecting in part our rights, make us more sensitive as to the denial of the rest.

Late declarations recognizing our entitlement to all of our rights, with essential ones withheld, render the grievances even more intolerable. Our grievances are many; our inconveniences through the denial of rights are great; but we shall refer only to those that may be affected through the action of Congress, by statutes forbidding them under penalties. We shall take it for granted that action will be had by Congress, protecting us from invidious distinctions in the enjoyment of common carriers, hotels and other public places of convenience and refreshment, in public places of amusement, and in enjoying other civil rights; but there are indications that there may be some objection made to Federal action against discrimination as to race and color in the management of public instruction, and in impaneling juries, the objectors alleging that it is unconstitutional for Congress to legislate to affect these cases. We propose to notice these objections briefly. They come from lawyers, who, like men in other callings, have their thoughts circumscribed by their training and habits of reflection. We do not feel bound, in a matter involving rights, to be circumscribed thereby. Language should be used, whenever it may without outraging it, to best subserve equity and justice. A decision of the supreme judiciary is binding and irrevocable, as affecting the particular case adjudicated, but is to be regarded only as a light which may be used, nay, should be, in any other case before that judiciary, to assist in finding a proper solution of the case. It has no imperative binding force upon any subsequent case.

The force of recorded decisions as to the powers of Congress is somewhat impaired, because they were rendered under a bias or influence differing from the present.

The interest of slavery, a state institution, was so great and overshadowing as to subjugate church as well as state, morality as well as the laws of the land; decisions were rendered in its interests; it was ever keen, active, resolute, extremely suspicious. The State-rights theory, one essential to slavery, was persistently urged. How it was adhered to may be seen in its producing the late rebellion, its grave-yard. Therefore the leanings of legal minds, through decisions and opinions made popular by this State-rights theory, must not be permitted to have the controlling sway some lawyers are disposed to give them; hence we are emboldened to take exceptions to the theory that Congress may not interpose except in the United States courts to secure unto a citizen an impartial jury. We affirm there is no prohibitory clause of the Constitution denying this right. On the other hand, we affirm that it ranges itself among the powers delegated to Congress, at least by implication; that it is a power inherent in the Government from its character, one supported by the principles of common law. It is in maintenance of a national right. We are at a loss to find the part of the Constitution which admits Congress to go as far as it has gone in protecting the civil rights of citizens in the several States, assented to by objecting Senators, but which forbids its going far enough to effectually protect the civil rights of a citizen wherever the stars and stripes have sway.

If Congress may throw the protecting arm of the law around any citizen of the United States, in every State, so as to forbid any denial or discrimination in hotels and in public conveyances on account of race and color, it certainly may do so in protecting him from invidious rules impairing the right of property; it may say the common school, paid for and owned by all citizens in common, shall not be made to serve to the degradation and humiliation of any class thereof; that a branch of the Government, maintained to train the child as to his proper relation to his Government and his fellow-citizens, must not therein be trained in opposition to the Government's fundamental principles. . . .

This same argument applies to the constituting of juries, and we shall apply it in considering whether Congress has the right to secure to any citizen the benefit of an impartial jury of his peers.

Article 1st, section 8th, of the Constitution, says: "Congress shall have power to make all laws which shall be necessary and proper for carrying into execution the powers vested by the Constitution in the Government of the United States." The Constitution further says: "The Constitution, and the laws of the United States which shall be made in pursuance thereof, are the supreme law of the land, and the judges in every State shall be bound thereby." The Constitution, by implication as well as by direct words, affirms an impartial jury to be a constitutional right, of course to be maintained as such, to be a supreme law of the land, anything in the constitution and laws of any State to the contrary notwithstanding; which amounts to a prohibition on a State from refusing an impartial jury. From all of which it is evident, as well as from the binding force of the common law in securing an impartial jury, that Congress has power to protect, by law, the citizen in this great national and common right under civilized government.

The fact that Federal legislation has been had and acquiesced in, and judicial decisions have enforced the same, establishing the theory that the National Government may interpose and regulate the judiciary of the States, restraining them from proscribing citizens because of their race or color, as, for instance, actions had under the present existing civil-rights laws, which regulate the receiving of testimony in the several States, shows that the power exists to protect us from the injustice of which we complain. . . .

It is not complete liberty and exact equality to be compelled to go to a proscribed school; to be tried by a jury from which every individual of the class to which the party tried belongs is excluded because he is of that class. The republican party, now in power, said there should be efficient and appropriate State and Federal legislation against the same. It is quite significant that the opponents of the republicans in the presidential canvass went into it with a platform which, as to civil rights, was not opposed to this position of the republicans; and in all subsequent elections, in which the democrats have alluded to everything they could think of to represent the republican party in the most odious light, referring to Credit Mobilier, back pay, and other things, they did not think it would be politic and effectual in arousing indignation against the party to make the platform of the party as to civil rights, committing it to Federal action, a subject of condemnation.

In making this appeal, we confidently expect at the hands of our own party a favorable response, which expectation is increased by manifestations exhibited by parties who have hitherto bitterly opposed us. May we not beseech such to fully fraternize with our friends?

Very respectfully, your memorialists, &c.,

GEO. T. DOWNING,
Acting President.

Copy of resolutions unanimously adopted by the convention.

Whereas a large class of citizens of the United States of America, numbering nearly five million of souls, are still laboring under certain disabilities on account of color, as is generally admitted throughout the country, namely, a non-recognition of their equal rights to all the public privileges properly attaching to American citizenship, among which we number the right to enjoy upon equal terms with other citizens the benefits of the public schools, common carriers, public places of amusement or resort; and

Whereas these disabilities under which we labor can only be removed effectually by national law, to be made as far-reaching as the jurisdiction of the National Government itself; and

Whereas the whole people of the country, more than a year since, speaking through the conventions of both great political parties, made solemn declaration, at Philadelphia, that "complete liberty and exact equality in the enjoyment of all civil, political, and public rights should be established and effectually maintained throughout the Union by efficient and appropriate State and Federal legislation;" and that "neither law nor its administration should admit of any discrimination in respect to the citizen by reason of race, creed, color, or previous condition of servitude;" and, at Cincinnati and Baltimore, "that we recognize the equality of all men before the law, and hold that the Government in its dealings with the people should mete out equal and exact justice to all, of whatever nativity, race, color or persuasion, religious or political:" Therefore,

Resolved, That the protection of civil rights in the persons of every inhabitant of the country is the first and most imperative duty of the Government, in order that freedom in this country and American citizenship may be made valuable to us.

Resolved, That no people can aid in sustaining and upholding either themselves or the nation unless they are fully protected in their pursuit of happiness.

Resolved, That we earnestly petition the Congress of the United States, representing, as it does, the two great political parties above referred to, being committed, as they are, to the doctrine of civil rights, to pass at the earliest practical moment, in the interest of justice and humanity, the civil-rights bill now pending in the United States Senate, and known as Senate bill No. 1, or some equally comprehensive and just measure.

GEORGE T. DOWNING,
Chairman.

Attest:
A. M. GREEN,
Secretary of the Convention.

S. Mis. 21——2

A Negro Attorney Testifies Against Segregated Travel, 1883*

THERE HAS BEEN a universal discrimination here in Alabama, and, indeed, all over the South, in the treatment of the colored people as to cars they are permitted to ride in. The white people have always labored under the impression that whenever a colored man attempted to go into a ladies' car, he did it simply because it was a car for white people. Now if the white people looked at it as we look at it, taking a common-sense view of it, they would see that that idea is erroneous and false. We go into those cars simply because there are better accommodations there, and because we secure better protection in the ladies' car, for the general sentiment of the white men certainly protects their ladies. But in the cars allotted to the colored people a white man comes in and smokes cigars, and chews tobacco, and curses and swears, and all that kind of thing, and the conductors on the various roads don't exercise their powers for the protection of the colored passengers. We made these complaints to the railroad commission, and the president of the commission told us that it was a matter within their jurisdiction, and that they would take cognizance of it, and would see that those complaints were looked into, and those evils remedied. We asked simply for equal accommodation and protection with the white people in riding on the railroads, and the 22d day of this month was set for a final hearing, and the superintendent of railroads was summoned to be there at the final hearing of the matter, and we have the assurance of the gentlemen of the commission that the subject will be acted upon promptly, and that the vexed question—for this is one of the most vexed questions that we have to deal with in the South—will be settled. We expect, therefore, that so far as Alabama is concerned, the people of both races will have equal accommoda-

* *Senate Report on Labor and Capital*, testimony, vol. iv, p. 382 [1883]. Statement of J. A. Scott of Birmingham, Ala. In Walter L. Fleming, *Documentary History of Reconstruction* (New York: McGraw Hill Book Co., 1966), II, pp. 446-47. First published by Arthur H. Clark Co., Cleveland, 1906-07.

tion. Our people do not care whether they are put in the front of the train or in the middle or at the tail end, so long as they have proper accommodation and proper protection.

Justice for the Outcast: The Negro*

THOMAS E. WATSON

. . . NEVER BEFORE DID two distinct races dwell together under such conditions.

And the problem is, can these two races, distinct in color, distinct in social life, and distinct as political powers, dwell together in peace and prosperity?

Upon a question so difficult and delicate no man should dogmatize—nor dodge. The issue is here; grows more urgent every day, and must be met.

It is safe to say that the present status of hostility between the races can only be sustained at the most imminent risk to both. It is leading by logical necessity to results which the imagination shrinks from contemplating. And the horrors of such a future can only be averted by honest attempts at a solution of the question which will be just to both races and beneficial to both.

Having given this subject much anxious thought, my opinion is that the future happiness of the two races will never be assured until the political motives which drive them asunder, into two distinct and hostile factions, can be removed. There must be a new policy inaugurated, whose purpose is to allay the passions and prejudices of race conflict, and which makes its appeal to the sober sense and honest judgment of the citizen regardless of his color.

To the success of this policy two things are indispensable —a common necessity acting upon both races, and a common benefit assured to both—without injury or humiliation to either.

Then, again, outsiders must let us alone. We must work out our own salvation. In no other way can it be done. Suggestions of Federal interference with our elections post-

---

* Excerpts from Thomas E. Watson, "The Negro Question in the South," *Arena*, VI (October, 1892), pp. 540-50. Watson, leader of the Populist movement, in later years turned against Negroes, and the Populist black-white alliance ended.

pone the settlement and render our task the more difficult. Like all free people, we love home rule, and resent foreign compulsion of any sort. . . . .

As long as there was no choice, except as between the Democrats and the Republicans, the situation of the two races was bound to be one of antagonism. The Republican Party represented everything which was hateful to the whites; the Democratic Party, everything which was hateful to the blacks.

Therefore a new party was absolutely necessary. It has come, and it is doing its work with marvellous rapidity.

Why does a Southern Democrat leave his party and come to ours?

Because his industrial condition is pitiably bad; because he struggles against a system of laws which have almost filled him with despair; because he is told that he is without clothing because he produces too much cotton, and without food because corn is too plentiful; because he sees everybody growing rich off the products of labor except the laborer; because the millionaires who manage the Democratic Party have contemptuously ignored his plea for a redress of grievances and have nothing to say to him beyond the cheerful advice to "work harder and live closer."

Why has this man joined the PEOPLE'S PARTY? Because the same grievances have been presented to the Republicans by the farmer of the West, and the millionaires who control that party have replied to the petition with the soothing counsel that the Republican farmer of the West should "work more and talk less."

Therefore, if he were confined to a choice between the two old parties, the question would merely be (on these issues) whether the pot were larger than the kettle—the color of both being precisely the same.

The key to the new political movement called the People's Party has been that the Democratic farmer was as ready to leave the Democratic ranks as the Republican farmer was to leave the Republican ranks. In exact proportion as the West received the assurance that the South was ready for a new party, it has moved. In exact proportion to the proof we could bring that the West had broken Republican ties, the South has moved. *Without* a decided break in both sections, neither would move. *With* that decided break, both moved.

The very same principle governs the race question in the

South. The two races can never act together permanently, harmoniously, beneficially, till each race demonstrates to the other a readiness to leave old party affiliations and to form new ones, based upon the profound conviction that, in acting together, both races are seeking new laws which will benefit both. On no other basis under heaven can the "Negro Question" be solved.

Now, suppose that the colored man were educated upon these questions just as the whites have been; suppose he were shown that his poverty and distress came from the same sources as ours; suppose we should convince him that our platform principles assure him an escape from the ills he now suffers, and guarantee him the fair measure of prosperity his labor entitles him to receive,—would he not act just as the white Democrat who joined us did? Would he not abandon a party which ignores him as a farmer and laborer; which offers him no benefits of an equal and just financial system; which promises him no relief from oppressive taxation; which assures him of no legislation which will enable him to obtain a fair price for his produce?

Granting to him the same selfishness common to us all: granting him the intelligence to know what is best for him and the desire to attain it, why would he not act from that motive just as the white farmer has done?

That he would do so, is as certain as any future event can be made. Gratitude may fail; so may sympathy and friendship and generosity and patriotism; but in the long run, self-interest *always* controls. Let it once appear plainly that it is to the interest of a colored man to vote with the white man, and he will do it. Let it plainly appear that it is to the interest of the white man that the vote of the Negro should supplement his own, and the question of having that ballot freely cast and fairly counted, becomes vital to the *white man*. He will see that it is done. . . .

The People's Party will settle the race question. First, by enacting the Australian ballot system. Second, by offering to white and black a rallying point which is free from the odium of former discords and strifes. Third, by presenting a platform immensely beneficial to both races and injurious to neither. Fourth, by making it to the *interest* of both races to act together for the success of the platform. Fifth, by making it to the *interest* of the colored man to have the same patriotic zeal for the welfare of the South that the whites possess.

Now to illustrate. Take two planks of the People's Party platform: that pledging a free ballot under the Australian system and that which demands a distribution of currency to the people upon pledges of land, cotton, etc.

The guaranty as to the vote will suit the black man better than the Republican platform, because the latter contemplates Federal interference, which will lead to collisions and bloodshed. The Democratic platform contains no comfort to the Negro, because, while it denounces the Republican programme, as usual, it promises nothing which can be specified. It is a generality which does not even possess the virtue of being "glittering."

The People's Party, however, not only condemns Federal interference with elections, but also distinctly commits itself to the method by which every citizen shall have his constitutional right to the free exercise of his electoral choice. We pledge ourselves to isolate the voter from all coercive influences and give him the free and fair exercise of his franchise under state laws.

Now couple this with the financial plank which promises equality in the distribution of the national currency, at low rates of interest.

The white tenant lives adjoining the colored tenant. Their houses are almost equally destitute of comforts. Their living is confined to bare necessities. They are equally burdened with heavy taxes. They pay the same high rent for gullied and impoverished land.

They pay the same enormous prices for farm supplies. Christmas finds them both without any satisfactory return for a year's toil. Dull and heavy and unhappy, they both start the plows again when "New Year's" passes.

Now the People's Party says to these two men, "You are kept apart that you may be separately fleeced of your earnings. You are made to hate each other because upon that hatred is rested the keystone of the arch of financial despotism which enslaves you both. You are deceived and blinded that you may not see how this race antagonism perpetuates a monetary system which beggars both."

This is obviously true it is no wonder both these unhappy laborers stop to listen. No wonder they begin to realize that no change of law can benefit the white tenant which does not benefit the black one likewise; that no system which now does injustice to one of them can fail to injure both. Their every material interest is identical. The moment this becomes a conviction, mere selfishness, the mere desire to better their conditions, escape onerous taxes, avoid usurious charges, lighten their rents, or change their precarious tenements into smiling, happy homes, will drive these two men together, just as their mutually inflamed prejudices now drive them apart.

Suppose these two men now to have become fully imbued with the idea that their material welfare depends upon the reforms we demand. Then they act together to secure them. Every white reformer finds it to the vital interest of his home, his family, his fortune, to see to it that the vote of the colored reformer is freely cast and fairly counted.

Then what? Every colored voter will be thereafter a subject of industrial education and political teaching.

Concede that in the final event, a colored man will vote where his material interests dictate that he should vote; concede that in the South the accident of color can make no possible difference in the interests of farmers, croppers, and laborers; concede that under full and fair discussion the people can be depended upon to ascertain where their interests lie—and we reach the conclusion that the Southern race question can be solved by the People's Party on the simple proposition that each race will be led by self-interest to support that which benefits it, when so presented that neither is hindered by the bitter party antagonisms of the past.

Let the colored laborer realize that our platform gives him a better guaranty for political independence; for a fair return for his work; a better chance to buy a home and keep it; a better chance to educate his children and see them profitably employed; a better chance to have public life freed from race collisions; a better chance for every citizen to be considered as a *citizen* regardless of color in the making and enforcing of laws,—let all this be fully realized, and the race question [in] the South will have settled itself through the evolution of a political movement in which both whites and blacks recognize their surest way out of wretchedness into comfort and independence.

The illustration could be made quite as clearly from other planks in the People's Party platform. On questions of land, transportation and finance, especially, the welfare of the two races so clearly depends upon that which benefits either, that intelligent discussion would necessarily lead to just conclusions. Why should the colored man always be taught that the white man of his neighborhood hates him, while a Northern man, who taxes every rag on his back, loves him? Why should not my tenant come to regard me as his friend rather than the manufacturer who plunders us both? Why should we perpetuate a policy which drives the black man into the arms of the Northern politician?

Why should we always allow Northern and Eastern Democrats to enslave us forever by threats of the Force Bill?

Let us draw the supposed teeth of this fabled dragon by founding our new policy upon justice—upon the simple but profound truth that, if the voice of passion can be hushed, the self-interest of both races will drive them to act in concert. There never was a day during the last twenty years when the South could not have flung the money power into the dust by patiently teaching the Negro that we could not be wretched under any system which would not afflict him likewise; that we could not prosper under any law which would not also bring its blessings to him.

To the emasculated individual who cries "Negro supremacy!" there is little to be said. His cowardice shows him to be a degeneration from the race which has never yet feared any other race. Existing under such conditions as they now do in this country, there is no earthly chance for Negro domination, unless we are ready to admit that the colored man is our superior in will power, courage, and intellect.

Not being prepared to make any such admission in favor of any race the sun ever shone on, I have no words which can portray my contempt for the white men, Anglo-Saxons, who can knock their knees together, and through their chattering teeth and pale lips admit that they are afraid the Negroes will "dominate us."

The question of social equality does not enter into the calculation at all. That is a thing each citizen decides for himself. No statute ever yet drew the latch of the humblest home —or ever will. Each citizen regulates his own visiting list— and always will.

The conclusion, then, seems to me to be this: the crushing burdens which now oppress both races in the South will cause each to make an effort to cast them off. They will see a similarity of cause and a similarity of remedy. They will recognize that each should help the other in the work of repealing bad laws and enacting good ones. They will become political allies, and neither can injure the other without weakening both. It will be to the interest of both that each should have justice. And on these broad lines of mutual interest, mutual forbearance, and mutual support the present will be made the stepping-stone to future peace and prosperity.

Separate but Equal—
the Plessy v. Ferguson Decision*

. . . MR. JUSTICE BROWN, after stating the facts in the fore-going language, delivered the opinion of the court.

This case turns upon the constitutionality of an act of the general assembly of the state of Louisiana, passed in 1890, providing for separate railway carriages for the white and colored races. Acts 1890, No. 111, p. 152.

The first section of the statute enacts "that all railway companies carrying passengers in their coaches in this state, shall provide equal but separate accommodations for the white, and colored races, by providing two or more passenger coaches for each passenger train, or by dividing the passenger coaches by a partition so as to secure separate accommodations: provided, that this section shall not be construed to apply to street railroads. No person or persons shall be permitted to occupy seats in coaches, other than the ones assigned to them, on account of the race they belong to." . . .

The constitutionality of this act is attacked upon the ground that it conflicts both with the thirteenth amendment of the constitution, abolishing slavery, and the fourteenth amendment, which prohibits certain restrictive legislation on the part of the states.

1. That it does not conflict with the thirteenth amendment, which abolished slavery and involuntary servitude, except as a punishment for crime, is too clear for argument. Slavery implies involuntary servitude,—a state of bondage; the ownership of mankind as a chattel, or, at least, the control of the labor and services of one man for the benefit of another, and the absence of a legal right to the disposal of his own person, property, and services. This amendment was said in the Slaughter-House Cases, 16 Wall. 36, to have been intended primarily to abolish slavery, as it had been previously known in this country, and that it equally forbade Mexican peonage or the Chinese coolie trade, when they amounted to slavery

---

* 163 U.S. 537 [1896]. Excerpts. Mr. Justice Harlan's dissent, omitted here for space reasons, termed the arbitrary separation of citizens on the basis of race a badge of servitude, inconsistent with the equality before the law established by the 13th, 14th, and 15th Amendments to the Constitution.

or involuntary servitude, and that the use of the word "servitude" was intended to prohibit the use of all forms of involuntary slavery, of whatever class or name. It was intimated, however, in that case, that this amendment was regarded by the statesmen of that day as insufficient to protect the colored race from certain laws which had been enacted in the Southern states, imposing upon the colored race onerous disabilities and burdens, and curtailing their rights in the pursuit of life, liberty, and property to such an extent that their freedom was of little value; and that the fourteenth amendment was devised to meet this exigency.

So, too, in the Civil Rights Cases, 109 U.S. 3, 3 Sup. Ct. 18, it was said that the act of a mere individual, the owner of an inn, a public conveyance or place of amusement, refusing accommodations to colored people, cannot be justly regarded as imposing any badge of slavery or servitude upon the applicant, but only as involving an ordinary civil injury, properly cognizable by the laws of the state, and presumably subject to redress by those laws until the contrary appears. "It would be running the slavery question into the ground," said Mr. Justice Bradley, "to make it apply to every act of discrimination which a person may see fit to make as to the guests he will entertain, or as to the people he will take into his coach or cab or car, or admit to his concert or theater, or deal with in other matters of intercourse or business."

A statute which implies merely a legal distinction between the white and colored races—a distinction which is founded in the color of the two races, and which must always exist so long as white men are distinguished from the other race by color—has no tendency to destroy the legal equality of the two races, or re-establish a state of involuntary servitude. Indeed, we do not understand that the thirteenth amendment is strenuously relied upon by the plaintiff in error in this connection.

2. By the fourteenth amendment, all persons born or naturalized in the United States, and subject to the jurisdiction thereof, are made citizens of the United States and of the state wherein they reside; and the states are forbidden from making or enforcing any law which shall abridge the privileges or immunities of citizens of the United States, or shall deprive any person of life, liberty, or property without due process of law, or deny to any person within their jurisdiction the equal protection of the laws. . . .

The object of the amendment was undoubtedly to enforce the absolute equality of the two races before the law, but, in the nature of things, it could not have been intended to abolish distinctions based upon color, or to enforce social, as distinguished from political, equality, or a commingling of the two races upon terms unsatisfactory to either. Laws permitting, and even requiring, their separation, in places where they are liable to be brought into contact, do not necessarily imply the inferiority of either race to the other, and have been generally, if not universally, recognized as within the competency of the state legislatures in the exercise of their police power. The most common instance of this is connected with the establishment of separate schools for white and colored children, which have been held to be a valid exercise of the legislative power even by courts of states where the political rights of the colored race have been longest and most earnestly enforced.

One of the earliest of these cases is that of Roberts v. City of Boston, 5 Cush. 198, in which the supreme judicial court of Massachusetts held that the general school committee of Boston had power to make provision for the instruction of colored children in separate schools established exclusively for them, and to prohibit their attendance upon the other schools. "The great principle," said Chief Justice Shaw, "advanced by the learned and eloquent advocate for the plaintiff [Mr. Charles Sumner], is that, by the constitution and laws of Massachusetts, all persons, without distinction of age or sex, birth or color, origin or condition, are equal before the law. * * * But, when this great principle comes to be applied to the actual and various conditions of persons in society, it will not warrant the assertion that men and women are legally clothed with the same civil and political powers, and that children and adults are legally to have the same functions and be subject to the same treatment; but only that the rights of all, as they are settled and regulated by law, are equally entitled to the paternal consideration and protection of the law for their maintenance and security." It was held that the powers of the committee extended to the establishment of separate schools for children of different ages, sexes and colors, and that they might also establish special schools for poor and neglected children, who have become too old to attend the primary school, and yet have not acquired the rudiments of learning, to enable them to enter the ordinary schools. . . . It is also suggested by the learned counsel for the plaintiff in error that the same argument that will justify the state legislature in requiring railways to provide separate accommodations for the two races will also authorize them to require separate cars to be provided for people whose hair is of a certain color, or who are aliens, or who belong to certain nationalities, or to enact laws requiring colored people to walk upon one side of the street, and white people upon the other, or requiring white men's houses to be painted white, and colored men's black, or their vehicles or business signs to be of different colors, upon the theory that one side of the street is as good as the other, or that a house or vehicle of one color is as good as one of another color. The reply to all this is that every exercise of the police power must be reasonable, and extend only to such laws as are enacted in good faith for the promotion of the public good, and not for the annoyance or oppression of a particular class. . . .

So far, then, as a conflict with the fourteenth amendment is concerned, the case reduces itself to the question whether the statute of Louisiana is a reasonable regulation, and with respect to this there must necessarily be a large discretion on the part of the legislature. In determining the question of reasonableness, it is at liberty to act with reference to the established usages, customs, and traditions of the people, and with a view to the promotion of their comfort, and the preservation of the public peace and good order. Gauged by this standard, we cannot say that a law which authorizes or even requires the separation of the two races in public conveyances is unreasonable, or more obnoxious to the fourteenth amendment than the acts of congress requiring separate schools for colored children in the District of Columbia, the constitutionality of which does not seem to have been questioned, or the corresponding acts of state legislatures.

We consider the underlying fallacy of the plaintiff's argument to consist in the assumption that the enforced separation of the two races stamps the colored race with a badge of inferiority. If this be so, it is not by reason of anything found in the act, but solely because the colored race chooses to put that construction upon it. The argument necessarily assumes that if, as has been more than once the case, and is not unlikely to be so again, the colored race should become the dominant power in the state legislature, and should enact a law in precisely similar terms, it would thereby relegate the white race to an inferior position. We imagine that the white race, at least, would not acquiesce in this assumption. The argument also assumes that social prejudices may be overcome by legislation, and that equal rights cannot be secured to the negro except by an enforced commingling of the two races.

We cannot accept this proposition. If the two races are to meet upon terms of social equality, it must be the result of natural affinities, a mutual appreciation of each other's merits, and a voluntary consent of individuals. . . .

PART IV

The Early Twentieth Century

INTRODUCTION

THE FIRST TWO decades of the twentieth century were violent years in both North and South. The white Southern "Redeemers" sought total subjection of the Negro, and all the methods which are now familiar were brought to bear. In addition to murder and physical torture economic pressures were employed. Negro landowners lost their land through chicanery; tenant farmers and share-croppers were trapped in an endless debt to a white landlord; a system of peonage was introduced whereby Negro prisoners were rented out by the county to work off sentences and fines.

In the years 1882 to 1927, 3,513 Negroes were known to have been lynched. Economic conditions, disfranchisement and murder drove thousands of Negroes to the North.

In the North Negroes met nearly as much hostility. Some Northern cities did not even permit Negroes in the city limits. In others there were lynchings and riots. One of the most shocking of the Northern riots was that in Springfield, Illinois, in 1908, during which two Negroes were lynched, four white men killed, and 70 persons injured. Fifty indictments were returned against leaders of the lynch-mob, but no one was punished.

The Negro protest moved in two directions: toward separation and toward integration. The two foremost Negro leaders were Booker T. Washington, who advocated self-help and training for jobs and business through which the Negro could become independent, though socially useful; and W.E.B. Du Bois, who also stressed education, but whose ultimate goal was integration of the Negro into American society with full equality. Du Bois put forth the idea of the "Talented Tenth"

175

—an educated elite as the key to uplifting the race, rather than the manual training of Washington.

Du Bois reflected later on his differences with Washington:

> There was first of all the ideological controversy. I believed in the higher education of a Talented Tenth who through their knowledge of modern culture could guide the American Negro into a higher civilization. I knew that without this the Negro would have to accept white leadership, and that such leadership could not always be trusted to guide this group into self-realization and to its highest cultural possibilities. . . .
> But beyond this difference of ideal lay another and more bitter and insistent controversy. This started with the rise at Tuskegee Institute, and centering around Booker T. Washington, of what I may call the Tuskegee Machine. . . ."[1]

Du Bois criticized Washington for decrying political activities among Negroes while dictating political objectives from Tuskegee, a course which provoked the label, "Tuskegee Machine." Washington told Negroes that they should not be too aggressive in demands for political rights, that they should depend upon "the slow but sure influences that proceed from the possession of property, intelligence, and high character."[2]

Washington became the government's chief advisor on Negro affairs both domestically and internationally, and he was frequently consulted by Presidents Theodore Roosevelt and William Howard Taft. Tuskegee Institute was an educational center not only for American Negroes, but for Africans as well. Washington's approach to black Africa was the same as toward black America. He urged the same policy of self-help within the existing political and racial order. To colonial officials in South Africa who sought his advice Washington wrote: "Since blacks are to live under the English Government, they should be taught to love and revere that government better than any other institution. To teach them this, they should receive their education and training for citizenship from or through the government. It is not always true that the missions teach respect for the rulers in power."[3]

The essence of Washington's philosophy is set forth in his Atlanta Exposition Address (which Du Bois refers to as the "Atlanta Compromise") in which he said that the relationship of Negro and white should be like "the five fingers on

---

[1] W. E. Burghardt Du Bois, *Dusk of Dawn: An Essay Toward an Autobiography of a Race Concept* (New York: Harcourt, Brace and Co. Inc., 1940), pp. 70-71.

[2] Booker T. Washington, *Up from Slavery: An Autobiography* (New York: Doubleday, Page & Co., 1901), p. 236.

[3] Louis R. Harlan, "Booker T. Washington and the White Man's Burden," *American Historical Review*, 71 (January, 1966), p. 449. Letter to Mrs. Grace Lathrop Luling, Jan. 23, 1905 in Washington Papers. Library of Congress.

one hand." [4] Washington acknowledged mutual need and advocated white support of separate educational institutions for Negroes.

As Washington preached the doctrine of separation of the races, and both the North and South adopted segregation laws, Du Bois pursued equality through agitation. He was instrumental in setting up the Niagara Movement, and later was a founder of the interracial National Association for the Advancement of Colored People.[5] The immediate stimulus for the founding of the new organization was a rising tide of racism in the country exemplified by the Springfield, Illinois race riot. One of the first crusades the NAACP launched was a campaign for anti-lynch legislation which lasted through the 1940's.

With America's entry into World War I, the war to make the world safe for democracy, Negroes flocked to the armed forces once more to fight for the cause of freedom. There were 360,000 Negroes in the armed services. Once again the Negro, hearing the nation shouting its commitment to democracy, found new hope that it would be extended to him. Southern Negroes went North in large numbers to seek jobs in the booming war industries to be met by ever-increasing race hate. They were rebuffed by the trade unions, banned from white neighborhoods and attacked on the streets; still they fared better there than in the poorer South.

Negro hopes were shortlived. The Ku Klux Klan had been revived in the Southern states in 1915, and it spread rapidly in the West and North as well. In East St. Louis in July, 1917, a bloody race riot grew out of employment of Negroes in a factory on strike. Many blamed local union leaders who provoked anti-Negro hysteria. Estimates of the number killed vary considerably. A Congressional investigating committee reported at least 39 Negroes and eight whites killed and hundreds of Negroes wounded and maimed; one NAACP investigation put the number of deaths at 175 and the NAACP magazine, *Crisis,* reported 125. Approximately 6,000 Negroes were left homeless. There was widespread protest including a Silent Protest Parade in New York in which eight to ten thousand marched down Fifth Avenue to muffled drums with banners reading, "Mr. President, why not make America safe for Democracy?" In the end ten Negroes and four whites were convicted of murder while most of the white persons arrested were acquitted or given short sentences. In the first six months of 1919 there were 25 race riots, and in the first year after the

---

[4] See pp. 195-99 below for text for the address.

[5] See Langston Hughes, *Fight for Freedom, the Story of the NAACP* excerpt on pp. 210-14 below.

war more than 70 Negroes were lynched, several of them
veterans in uniform.

Another serious race riot took place in Chicago in July,
1919. The growth of the city's Negro population pushed the
walls of the ghetto outward into surrounding white areas, and
tension was high. The riot which started with the drowning of
a Negro youngster in the customarily white section of Lake
Michigan ended 13 days later after 38 persons had been
killed and over 500 injured.

The NAACP published a study, *Thirty Years of Lynching
in the United States, 1889-1918,* and was the spearhead of an
intensive campaign which included full-page advertisements
in leading daily newspapers and over 200 protest meetings. A
federal anti-lynch bill passed in the House by a vote of 230
to 119 in 1922, but a Southern filibuster killed it in the Senate.

Other struggles in the war years were against segregation
of federal employes, discriminatory dismissals of Negroes in
federal employment and protests of the treatment of Negro
soldiers, particularly in France where U.S. authorities asked
the French not to permit fraternization with Negroes.

After the war Negroes showing concern for international
affairs sent delegations to the Peace Conference to fight for
the independence of former African colonies, and against the
spread of imperialism. One of the active participants in these
struggles was the militant James Monroe Trotter, editor of
the Boston *Guardian.* Trotter had visited President Woodrow
Wilson in 1914 to appeal for an end to the segregation in
federal agencies instituted during Wilson's administration. Wilson angrily ended the interview after Trotter said Negro leaders were being called traitors by their people for having supported the Democratic ticket headed by Wilson. At the Peace
Conference Trotter called for international guarantees of the
rights of American Negroes. Du Bois also attended the Peace
Conference and the Pan-African Congress of which he was
the prime organizer. Another manifestation of this new international interest was the NAACP's campaign for Haitian independence, then under U.S. occupation.

The strong language in which all of these protests were
voiced led to the inclusion of the NAACP along with more
radical organizations in the attacks of Attorney General A.
Mitchell Palmer on "Bolshevism."

The main focus of this interest in the international scene
had been Africa and Haiti—black nations—and this interest
found a comparable expression domestically in the cultural
boom known as the Harlem Renaissance, and in the black

nationalist movement of Marcus Garvey. There was a great resurgence of interest in the Negro. But despite the wide popularity of such writers as Alain Locke, Zora Neale Thurston, Langston Hughes, Claude McKay, Countee Cullen, James Weldon Johnson, George Schuyler and Jean Toomer, the image of the Negro was grossly distorted. In the "new Negro" the roaring twenties saw a "gay," "happy," "laughing," "primitive" being. Questioning the extent of interracial understanding of the whites who indulged in a Negro cult Gilbert Osofsky said, "They saw Negroes not as people but as symbols of everything America was not." [6]

The Harlem Renaissance was not what the whites downtown saw and reveled in; it was part of the general Negro interest in himself, his people, his culture, and his roots. Both the literature and the largest Negro mass movement of the 20's, Garvey's Universal Negro Improvement Association, were rooted in race pride, the dignity and beauty of blackness. The Garvey movement attracted millions of members and sympathizers from among the Negro masses. The goals of the UNIA were to instill race pride, develop an independent black colony in Africa, and gain economic and political control of black communities in the United States; in short, economic cooperation among black Americans and with black people all over the world. The movement disintegrated after Garvey was jailed in 1925 after a conviction for using the mails to defraud. President Coolidge commuted his sentence in 1927, and Garvey was deported.[7]

The middle-class intellectual leaders of the Negro movement, who had been extremely critical of Garvey and whose following was mainly drawn from the middle-class, continued their agitation for legal reforms until the Great Depression brought the plight of the laboring masses of people to the center of the stage.

[6] Gilbert Osofsky, *Harlem: The Making of a Ghetto* (New York: Harper & Row, Publishers, 1965), p. 183.

[7] Excerpts from *The Philosophy and Opinions of Marcus Garvey* are on pp. 199-203.

1. NORTHERN MIGRATION

Letters of Negro Migrants[*]

EMMETT J. SCOTT

LETTERS ABOUT LABOR AGENTS

MOBILE, ALA., 4-26-17.

Dear Sir Bro.: I take great pane in droping you a few lines hopeing that this will find you enjoying the best of health as it leave me at this time present. Dear sir I seen in the Defender where you was helping us a long in securing a poission an I can do cement work an stone work. I written to a firm in Birmingham an they sent me a blank stateing $2.00 would get me a ticket an pay 10 per ct of my salary for the 1st month and $24.92c would be paid after I reach Detroit and went to work where they sent me to work. I had to stay there until I pay them the sum of $24.92c so I want to leave Mobile for there. If there nothing there for me to make a support for my self and family. My wife is seamstress. We want to get away the 15 or 20 of May so please give this matter your earnest consideration an let me hear from you by return mail as my bro. in law want to get away to. He is a carpenter by trade. So please help us as we are in need of your help as we wanted to go to Detroit but if you says no we go where ever you sends us until we can get to Detroit. We expect to do whatever you says. There is nothing here for the colored man but a hard time wich these southern crackers gives us. We has not had any work to do in 4 wks. and every thing is high to the colored man so please let me hear from you by return mail. Please do this for your brother.

ALGIERS, LA., May 16-17.

Sir: I saw sometime ago in the Chicago Defender, that you needed me for different work, would like to state that I can bring you all the men that you need, to do anything of work.

* Emmett J. Scott, ed., "Letters of Negro Migrants, 1917-18," *Journal of Negro History*, II (July, 1919), pp. 305-6, 308, 329, 331-336. Reprinted by permission.

or send them, would like to Come my self Con recommend all the men I bring to do any kind of work, and will give satisfaction; I have bin foreman for 20 yrs over some of these men in different work from R. R. work to Boiler Shop machine shop Blacksmith shop Concreet finishing or puting down pipe or any work to be did. they are all hard working men and will work at any kind of work also plastering anything in the labor line, from Clerical work down, I will not bring a man that is looking for a easy time only hard working men, that want good wages for there work, let me here from you at once.

MEMPHIS, TENN., May 12.

Dear Sir: I am a constant reader of your paper which can be purchased here at the Panama Cafe news stand. Mr. ———— at present I am employed as agent for the Interstate Life and acc'd ins. Co. but on account of the race people leaving here so very fast my present job is no longer a profitable one. I have a number of young friends in your city who are advising me to come to Chicago and I have just about made up my mind to come. but before leaving here I wanted to ask Some advice from you along certain lines. I am buying property here and taking up notes each month on Same these notes now are aroun $14 per month. and with my present Salary and the unusual high price on everything I can't possibly protect myself very long against a foreclosure on above mentioned property on account of my Salary being less than $50.00 per month. Mr. ———— do you think I could come to your city with myself and wife rent this place out here and better my condition financially? I am strong and able to do anything kind of work so long as the Salary is O. K. I have a fair experience as a meat cutter and can furnish the best of reference from business houses one of them is Swift & Co of this city. I hope you can understand me clearly, it is my aim to make an honest living and would not dream of any other method. I am prepared to leave here at any time and must go Some place but Chicago is the place that impress me most. and having the confidence in you as a great race man I am writing you for your honest opinion concerning the facts in the matter. Many thanks for the information in today's paper under the Caption ("Know thyself") hoping this will meet with your hearty Cooperation.

P. S. What is about the average salaries paid there for unskilled laborers and what is board and room rent? if I come would it be advisable to come alone and Secure location and everything and then have my wife come later?

LETTERS ABOUT THE GREAT NORTHERN DRIVE OF 1917

PENSACOLA, FLA., 4-21-17.

Sir: You will please give us the names of firms where we can secure employment. Also please explain the Great Northern Drive for May 15th. We will come by the thousands. Some of us like farm work. The colored people will leave if you will assist them.

MOBILE, ALA., April 25, 1917.

Sir: I was reading in theat paper about the Colored race and while reading it I seen in it where cars would be here for the 15 of May which is one month from to day. Will you be so kind as to let me know where they are coming to and I will be glad to know because I am a poor woman and have a husband and five children living and three dead one single and two twin girls six months old today and my husband can hardly make bread for them in Mobile. This is my native home but it is not fit to live in just as the Chicago Defender say it says the truth and my husband only get $1.50 a day and pays $7.50 a month for house rent and can hardly feed me and his self and children. I am the mother of 8 children 25 years old and I want to get out of this dog hold because I dont know what I am raising them up for in this place and I want to get to Chicago where I know they will be raised and my husband crazy to get there because he know he can get more to raise his children and will you please let me know where the cars is going to stop to so that he can come where he can take care of me and my children. He get there a while and then he can send for me. I heard they wasnt coming here so I sent to find out and he can go and meet them at the place they are going and go from there to Chicago. No more at present. hoping to hear from you soon from your needed and worried friend.

MONTGOMERY, ALA., May 7, 1917.

My dear Sir: I am writing to solicit your aid and advice as to how I may best obtain employment at my trade in your city. I shall be coming that way on the 15th of May and I wish to find immediate employment if possible.

I have varied experience as a compositor and printer. Job composition is my hobby. I have not experience as linotype operator, but can fill any other place in a printing office. Please communicate with me at the above address at once. Thanking you in advance for any assistance and information in the matter.

ROME, GA., May 13, 1917.

Dear Sir: I am writing you in regards to present conditions in Chicago in getting employment. I am an experienced hotel man—in all departments, such as bellman, waiter, buss boy, or any other work pertaining to hotel and would like to know in return could you furnish me transportation to Chicago as you advertise in the Chicago Defender. Am good honest and sober worker, can furnish recermendations if necessary. Have worked at the Palmer House during year 1911 as bus boy in Cafe. But returned South for awhile and since the Northern Drive has begun I have decided to return to Chicago as I am well acquainted with the city. Hope to hear from you soon on this matter as it is of great importance to me.

NEW ORLEANS, LA., 4-23-17.

Dear Editor: I am a reader of the Defender and I am askeso much about the great Northern drive on the 15th of May. We want more understanding about it for there is a great many wants to get ready for that day & the depot agents never gives us any satisfaction when we ask for they dont want us to leave here, I want to ask you to please publish in your next Saturdays paper just what the fair will be on that day so we all will know & can be ready. So many women here are wanting to go that day. They are all working women and we cant get work here so much now, the white women tell us we just want to make money to go North and we do so please kindly ans. this in your next paper if you do I will read it every word in the Defender, had rather read it then to eat when Saturday comes, it is my hearts delight & hope your paper will continue on in the south until every one reads it for it is a God sent blessing to the Race.

Will close with best wishes.

NEW ORLEANS, LA., May 2, 1917.

Dear Sir: Please Sir will you kindly tell me what is meant by the Great Northern Drive to take place May the 15th on tuesday. It is a rumor all over town to be ready for the 15th of May to go in the drive. the Defender first spoke of the drive the 10th of February. My husband is in the north already preparing for our family but hearing that the excursion will be $6.00 from here north on the 15 and having a large family, I could profit by it if it is really true. Do please write me at once and say is there an excursion to leave the south.

Nearly the whole of the south is getting ready for the drive or excursion as it is termed. Please write at once. We are sick to get out of the solid south.

AUGUSTA, GA., May 12, 1917.

Dear Sir: Just for a little infermation from you i would like to know wheather or not i could get in tuch with some good people to work for with a firm because things is afful hear in the south let me here from you soon as poseble what ever you do dont publish my name in your paper but i think peple as a race ought to look out for one another as Christians friends i am a schuffur and i cant make a living for my family with small pay and the people is getting so bad with us black peple down south hear. now if you ever help your race now is the time to help me to get my family away. food stuf is so high. i will look for answer by return mail. dont publish my name in your paper but let me hear from you at once.

Close Ranks*

W.E.B. DU BOIS

THIS IS THE crisis of the world. For all the long years to come men will point to the year 1918 as the great Day of Decision, the day when the world decided whether it would submit to military despotism and an endless armed peace—if peace it could be called—or whether they would put down the menace of German militarism and inaugurate the United States of the World.

We of the colored race have no ordinary interest in the outcome. That which the German power represents today spells death to the aspirations of Negroes and all darker races for equality, freedom and democracy. Let us not hesitate. Let us, while this war lasts, forget our special grievances and close our ranks shoulder to shoulder with our own white fellow citizens and the allied nations that are fighting for democracy. We make no ordinary sacrifice, but we make it gladly and willingly with our eyes lifted to the hills.

* Editorial, *The Crisis*, Vol. XVI (July, 1918). Reprinted by permission of The Crisis Publishing Co.

The Descent of Du Bois*

HUBERT H. HARRISON

IN A RECENT bulletin of the War Department it was declared that "justifiable grievances" were producing and had produced "not disloyalty, but an amount of unrest and bitterness which even the best efforts of their leaders may not be able always to guide." This is the simple truth. The essence of the present situation lies in the fact that the people whom our white masters have "recognized" as our leaders (without taking the trouble to consult us) and those who, by our own selection, had actually attained to leadership among us are being revaluated and, in most cases, rejected.

The most striking instance from the latter class is Dr. W. E. Du Bois, the editor of the *Crisis*. Du Bois's case is the more significant because his former services to his race have been undoubtedly of a high and courageous sort. Moreover, the act by which he has brought upon himself the stormy outburst of disapproval from his race is one which of itself, would seem to merit no such stern condemnation. To properly gauge the value and merit of this disapproval one must view it in the light of its attendant circumstances and of the situation in which it arose.

Dr. Du Bois first palpably sinned in his editorial "Close Ranks" in the July number of the *Crisis*. But this offense (apart from the trend and general tenor of the brief editorial) lies in a single sentence: "Let us, while this war lasts, *forget our special grievances* and close our ranks, shoulder to shoulder with our white fellow-citizens and the allied nations that are fighting for democracy." From the latter part of the sentence there is no dissent, so far as we know. The offense lies in that part of the sentence which ends with the italicized words. It is felt by all his critics, that Du Bois, of all Negroes, knows best that our "special grievances" which the War Department Bulletin describes as "justifiable" consist of lynching, segregation and disfranchisement, and that the Negroes of America can not preserve either their lives, their

* Hubert H. Harrison, *When Africa Awakes* (New York: Porro Press, 1920). Harrison, once a Socialist Party adherent, later founded the Liberty League of Negro-Americans, out of which, he claimed, Garveyism grew. He was criticized by other Negro leaders including A. Philip Randolph, Chandler Owen and Du Bois for his "race first" approach.

manhood or their vote (which is their political life and liberties) with these things in existence. The doctor's critics feel that America can not use the Negro people to any good effect unless they have life, liberty and manhood assured and guaranteed to them. Therefore, instead of the war for democracy making these things less necessary, it makes them more so.

"But," it may be asked, "why should not these few words be taken merely as a slip of the pen or a venal error in logic? Why all this hubbub?" It is because the so-called leaders of the first-mentioned class have already established an unsavory reputation by advocating this same surrender of life, liberty and manhood, masking their cowardice behind the pillars of war-time sacrifice? Du Bois's statement, then, is believed to mark his entrance into that class, and is accepted as a "surrender" of the principles which brought him into prominence—and which alone kept him there.

Later, when it was learned that Du Bois was being preened for a berth in the War Department as a captain-assistant (adjutant) to Major Spingarn, the words used by him in the editorial acquired a darker and more sinister significance. The two things fitted too well together as motive and self-interest.

For these reasons Du Bois is regarded much in the same way as a knight in the middle ages who had had his armor stripped from him, his arms reversed and his spurs hacked off. This ruins him as an influential person among Negroes at this time, alike whether he becomes a captain or remains an editor.

But the case has its roots much farther back than the editorial in July's *Crisis*. Some time ago when it was learned that the *Crisis* was being investigated by the government for an alleged seditious utterance a great clamor went up, although the expression of it was not open. Negroes who dared to express their thoughts seemed to think the action tantamount to a declaration that protests against lynching, segregation and disfranchisement were outlawed by the government. But nothing was clearly understood until the conference of editors was called under the assumed auspices of Emmet Scott and Major Spingarn. Then it began to appear that these editors had not been called without a purpose. The desperate ambiguity of the language which they used in their report (in the War Department Bulletin), coupled with the fact that not one of them, upon his return would tell the people anything of the proceedings of the conference—all this made the Negroes feel less and less confidence in them and their leadership; made them (as leaders) less effective instruments for the influential control of the race's state of mind.

Now Du Bois was one of the most prominent of those editors "who were called." The responsibility, therefore, for a course of counsel which stresses the servile virtues of acquiescence and subservience falls squarely on his shoulders. The offer of a captaincy and Du Bois's flirtation, with that offer following on the heels of these things seemed, even in the eyes of his associate members of the N. A. A. C. P. to afford clear proof of that which was only a suspicion before, viz: that the racial resolution of the leaders had been tampered with, and that Du Bois had been privy to something of the sort. The connection between the successive acts of the drama (May, June, July) was too clear to admit of any interpretation other than that of deliberate, cold-blooded, purposive planning. And the connection with Spingarn seemed to suggest that personal friendships and public faith were not good working teammates.

For the sake of the larger usefulness of Dr. Du Bois we hope he will be able to show that he can remain as editor of the *Crisis;* but we fear that it will require a good deal of explaining. For, our leaders, like Caesar's wife, must be above suspicion.

—July, 1918

Race Riot, Chicago, 1919*

ST. CLAIR DRAKE AND HORACE R. CAYTON

HERE AND THERE throughout America, the tensions of postwar readjustment flared into open violence. On the labor front and along the color-line, deep-laid frustrations, uneasy fears, and latent suspicions bobbed to the surface. Group antagonisms suppressed and sublimated by the war effort now returned with doubled fury. For labor, there were the "Palmer raids"; for the Negro, lynchings and riots. The South, particularly, was nervous. Returning Negro soldiers, their horizons widened through travel, constituted a threat to the caste system. They must be kept in their place. A wave of interracial conflicts swept the country involving communities in the North as well as in the South.

* St. Clair Drake and Horace R. Cayton. *Black Metropolis: A Study of Negro Life in a Northern City,* pp. 65-73. Copyright 1945 by St. Clair Drake and Horace R. Cayton. Reprinted by permission of Harcourt, Brace & World, Inc.

Chicago was not spared its measure of violence. The sporadic bombing of Negro homes in 1918 was but the prelude to a five-day riot in 1919 which took at least thirty-eight lives, resulted in over five hundred injuries, destroyed $250,-000 worth of property, and left over a thousand persons homeless. For the first time since 1861 the Negro was the center of a bloody drama. Then he was the hero; now he was the villain.[1]

The generally disturbed background out of which the Chicago riot exploded is revealed by a news item in the Chicago *Tribune* for July 4, 1917, reporting a protest meeting against a bloody riot which had occurred in East St. Louis, Illinois. The article, headlined, "LAWYER WARNS NEGROES HERE TO ARM SELVES," quoted one of Chicago's most respected and conservative Negro leaders as saying, "Arm yourselves now with guns and pistols." Another equally prominent leader was quoted as declaring that he "hoped God would demand 100,000 white lives in the War for each Negro slaughtered in East St. Louis." [2]

The Chicago riot began on a hot July day in 1919 as the result of an altercation at a bathing beach. A colored boy swam across the imaginary line which was supposed to separate Negroes from whites at the Twenty-ninth Street beach. He was stoned by a group of white boys. During the ensuing argument between groups of Negro and white bathers, the boy was drowned. Colored bathers were enraged. Rumor swept the beach, "White people have killed a Negro." The resulting fight, which involved the beach police and the white and colored crowd, set off six days of rioting.

Pitched battles were fought in the Black Belt streets. Negroes were snatched from streetcars and beaten; gangs of hoodlums roamed the Negro neighborhood, shooting at random. Instead of the occasional bombings of two years before, this was a pogrom. But the Negroes fought back.

Attacks and reprisals were particularly bitter up and down the western and southern boundary between the Irish neighborhoods and the Black Belt. Here youthful white gangs—the so-called athletic clubs—functioning with the tacit approval of the ward politicians who sponsored them, raided the Negro community, attacking the people whom for years they had derided as "jigs," "shines," "dinges," "smokes," and "niggers," and who were now fair game. The rising smoke from burning homes in the white neighborhoods around the stock-

[1] Chicago Commission on Race Relations, *The Negro in Chicago* (University of Chicago, 1922), pp. 12-20.

[2] Chicago *Tribune*, July 4, 1917.

yards and the railroad tracks, during the next two days, was silent evidence of the embittered Negroes' reprisals.

The reaction of most colored civic leaders was ambivalent. Publicly they were constrained to be conciliatory and to curb the masses who did the actual fighting. Privately, despite a recognition of the horrors of the riot, like Negroes of all classes they justified the fighting as self-defense and as proof that Negroes would not supinely suffer mistreatment. They did not view a riot as unmitigated evil if it focused attention upon injustices. To them it held the same paradoxical elements of good emerging from evil that Wilson saw in the First World War or Lenin in the Russian Revolution.

There were some, however, particularly among Old Settlers,* who viewed the riot as the tragic end of a golden age of race relations. They were very bitter against the southern Negroes, who, they felt, had brought this catastrophe upon them. A group of representative business and professional men met to devise means for ending the disorder. Among the speakers was a lawyer who had come to Chicago from Georgia by way of Canada in 1893, studied law, and amassed some wealth. He insisted that "a lot of the trouble is due to Negroes from the South" and called upon "some representative Negroes from the same part of the country [to] do what they can to help quiet things down."

Many Negroes expressed their resentment against one Old Settler who began his address by placing the blame for the riot on the colored population, stating that "One of the chief causes of the trouble is that the colored men have been taught they must act on the policy of an eye for an eye and a tooth for a tooth."

They condemned him as an "Uncle Tom" † when he continued:

This starts a series of reprisals that is likely to go on until the white man will get mad, and if he does we know what will happen to the man of color. Some of us forget that the white man has given us freedom, the right to vote, to live on terms of equality with him, to be paid well for our work, and to receive many other benefits.

They ridiculed him as a "white man's nigger" for his warning:

* A term used by both Negroes and whites in Chicago to designate persons who lived in Chicago prior to the First World War.

† "Uncle Tom," the hero of Harriet Beecher Stowe's famous novel of the abolitionist era, has become for colored people a symbol of the subservient Negro. The term thus serves as a satirical condemnation of any Negro who is thought to be currying favor with white people.

If the white man should decide that the black man has proved he is not fit to have the right to vote, that right may be taken away. We might also find it difficult to receive other favors to which we have been accustomed, and then what would happen to us? We must remember that this is a white man's country. Without his help we can do nothing. When we fight the white man we fight ourselves. We can start a riot but it takes the white man to stop it. We are not interested now in what started the riot, but how to stop it. The Germans thought these same people were so easy-going that they wouldn't fight, and they kept stirring things up until the Americans got mad. That ought to be warning enough! If this thing goes on for three days more there will be no jobs for our men to go back to.

They agreed, however, with his solution, provided it were impartially applied: "If the city cannot restore order then let us with the aid of the militia, have martial law, and take the arms away from the hoodlums." [3]

The bitterness felt by even the more conservative Negro leaders is plainly revealed in the tone of the annual report of Provident Hospital for 1919. Proud of the efficiency with which it handled riot casualties, the hospital board detailed its activities as follows: [4]

. . . A crowd of young white toughs from in and near Wentworth Avenue, mainly mere boys, began raids into the colored district, destroying, wounding and killing as they went. On one of these trips the raiders shot into the hospital. That evening fifteen victims were treated at the hospital, one white, the rest colored . . . the majority stabbed or clubbed, and a few shot.

As early as three o'clock in the afternoon on Monday, a mob gathered about the hospital. Feeling was running high. Many of the nurses, worn and tired by long hours of excitement and hard work, found human nature too weak to stand the hideous sights and bloodshed and begged to be taken away . . . but except for short spells of hysteria they were at their posts every minute of the time without sleep and without proper nourishment, for it was difficult from the start to get food into the hospital.

During the twenty-four hours from midnight Sunday to midnight Monday, seventy-five victims were taken care of. A number were taken by friends after having received treatment and a number died. Of these patients nine were white. Cots were placed in the wards and in the emergency room until every available space was occupied; then the victims had to lie upon the floor.

The demand on the hospital surgical supplies and food supplies was heavy; furnishings and equipment suffered; surgical instru-

[3] Quoted from a manuscript document, Cayton-Warner Research.

[4] Annual Report of Provident Hospital and Training School, 1919, *Provident Hospital in the Race Riot of July, 1919,* issued by Authority of the Board of Trustees.

ments were lost and broken; mattresses were ruined, and furniture was wrecked.

The references to the treatment of white patients were a deliberate build-up for two devastating paragraphs:

It should be borne in mind that the conditions in the colored district were exactly reversed in certain white localities where any offending colored person who appeared was ruthlessly slaughtered, whether man, woman, or baby. From these localities came the raiding parties that caused substantially all the trouble.

The white doctors, of course, were not in attendance during this time and many of the colored staff doctors and the three colored house internes worked day and night; sometimes six operations were in progress at one time.

The daily newspapers headlined the Riot as big news, at the same time editorializing against it. The *New Majority*, organ of the Chicago Federation of Labor, prominently displayed an article, "FOR WHITE UNION MEN TO READ," reminding the workers of their "hatred of violence on the picket line" and insisting that a heavy responsibility rested on them "not because they had anything to do with starting the present trouble, but because of their advantageous position to help end it." [5] The general public watched and read, but did not participate. Probably its sympathies were divided and its loyalties confused.

The Riot was ended on its sixth day by the state militia, belatedly called after the police had shown their inability, and in some instances their unwillingness, to curb attacks on Negroes.

RECONCILIATION (1920-1922)

One result of the Riot was an increased tendency on the part of white Chicagoans to view Negroes as a "problem." The rapid influx from the South had stimulated awareness of their presence. The elections of 1915 and 1917 had indicated their growing political power in the Republican machine—a circumstance viewed with apprehension by both the Democratic politicians and the "good government" forces. Now the Riot, the screaming headlines in the papers, the militia patrolling the streets with fixed bayonets, and the accompanying hysteria imbedded the "Negro problem" deeply in the city's consciousness.

Civic leaders, particularly, were concerned. They decided

5 Quoted in *The Negro in Chicago*, p. 45.

that the disaster demanded study, so Governor Lowden appointed the non-partisan, interracial Chicago Commission on Race Relations to investigate the causes of the Riot and to make recommendations. For the next twenty years its suggestions set the pattern of activity for such civic groups as the Urban League, the YMCA, and various public agencies. The Commission's report was the first formal codification of the Negro-white relations in Chicago since the days of the Black Code.

After a year of study the Commission reported that it could suggest no "ready remedy," no "quick means of assuring harmony between the races," but it did offer certain suggestions in the hope that "mutual understanding and sympathy between the races will be followed by harmony and co-operation." It based its faith on "the civic conscience of the community" and opined that "progress should begin in a direction steadily away from the disgrace of 1919."

Immediately after the Riot there had been some sentiment favoring a segregation ordinance. The alderman of one white ward introduced a resolution in the City Council asking for an interracial commission to investigate the causes of the Riot and "to equitably fix a zone or zones . . . for the purpose of limiting within its borders the residence of only colored or white persons." Alderman Louis B. Anderson, Mayor Thompson's colored floor leader, "spoke with acerbity and resentment" [6] against the resolution, and it was referred to the judiciary committee and subsequently dropped. The Governor's Commission, too, was emphatic in its repudiation of such a solution, declaring that:

"We are convinced by our inquiry . . . that measures involving or approaching deportation or segregation are illegal, impracticable and would not solve, but would accentuate, the race problem and postpone its just and orderly solution by the process of adjustment."

The Negro had come to Chicago to stay!

The Commission was very specific in its charges and did not hesitate to allocate responsibility for the conditions which produced the Riot. Even governmental agencies were asked to assume their share of the blame. To the police, militia, state's attorney, and courts, the Commission recommended the correction of "gross inequalities of protection" at beaches and playgrounds and during riots; rebuked the courts for facetiousness in dealing with Negro cases, and the police for

6 Chicago *Daily News,* Aug. 5, 1919.

unfair discrimination in arrests. It suggested the closing of the white adolescent "athletic clubs." It asked the authorities to "promptly rid the Negro residence areas of vice resorts, whose present exceptional prevalence in such areas is due to official laxity." The City Council and administrative boards were asked to be more vigilant in the condemnation and razing of "all houses unfit for human habitation, many of which the Commission has found to exist in the Negro residence areas." In such matters as rubbish and garbage disposal, as well as street repair, Negro communities were said to be shamefully neglected. Suggestions were made that more adequate recreational facilities be extended to Negro neighborhoods, but also that Negroes should be protected in their right to use public facilities anywhere in the city.

The Board of Education was asked to exercise special care in selecting principals and teachers in Negro communities; to alleviate overcrowding and double-shift schools; to enforce more carefully the regulations regarding truancy and work-permits for minors, and to establish adequate night schools. Restaurants, theaters, stores, and other places of public accommodation were informed that "Negroes are entitled by law to the same treatment as other persons" and were urged to govern their policies and actions accordingly.

Employers and labor organizations were admonished in some detail against the use of Negroes as strike-breakers and against excluding them from unions and industries. "Deal with Negroes as workmen on the same plane as white workers," was the suggestion. Negroes were urged to join labor unions. "Self-seeking agitators, Negro or white, who use race sentiment to establish separate unions in trades where existing unions admit Negroes to equal membership" were roundly condemned.

As to the struggle for living space, a section of the report directed toward the white members of the public reiterated the statement that Negroes were entitled to live anywhere in the city. It pointed out several neighborhoods where they had lived harmoniously with white neighbors for years, insisted that property depreciation in Negro areas was often due to factors other than Negro occupancy, condemned arbitrary advance of rents, and designated the amount and quality of housing as "an all-important factor in Chicago's race problem." The final verdict was that "this situation will be made worse by methods tending toward forcible segregation or exclusion of Negroes."

Not all of the Commission's advice and criticism was directed at public agencies and white persons, however. The

Negro workers who had so recently become industrialized were admonished to "abandon the practice of seeking petty advance payments on wages and the practice of laying off work without good cause." There was an implied criticism of the colored community, too, in a statement urging Negroes "to contribute more freely of their money and personal effort to the social agencies developed by public-spirited members of their group; also to contribute to the general social agencies of the community." Negroes were asked to protest "vigorously and continuously . . . against the presence in their residence areas of any vicious resort" and to assist in the prevention of vice and crime.

The Commission expressed particular concern over growing race consciousness, a phenomenon of which the riot itself was evidence. The Negro community was warned that "while we recognize the propriety and social values of race pride among Negroes . . . thinking and talking too much in terms of race alone are calculated to promote separation of race interests and thereby to interfere with racial adjustment." Negro newspapers were advised to exercise greater care and accuracy in reporting incidents involving whites and Negroes and to abandon sensational headlines and articles on racial questions. The investigation had revealed the existence of several small Negro groups, such as the Garveyites and Abyssinians, who were bitterly opposed to any interracial collaboration. The Commission rebuked them indirectly: "We recommend to Negroes the promulgation of sound racial doctrines among the uneducated members of their group, and the discouragement of propaganda and agitators seeking to inflame racial animosity and to incite Negroes to violence." There was, finally, a word of commendation for the work of "the Chicago Urban League, the Negro churches, and other organizations in facilitating the adjustment of migrant Negroes from the South to the conditions of living in Chicago."

In addition to specific recommendations of the type referred to above, the report proposed a long-range educational program grounded in the belief that "no one, white or Negro, is wholly free from an inheritance of prejudice in feeling and in thinking. . . . Mutual understanding and sympathy . . . can come completely only after the disappearance of prejudice. Thus the remedy is necessarily slow."

Social and civic organizations, labor unions and churches, were asked "to dispel false notions of each race about the other," such as "the common disposition, arising from erroneous tradition and literature, to regard all Negroes as belonging to one homogeneous group and as being inferior in mentality and morality, given to emotionalism, and having an innate tendency toward crime, especially sex crime." Prominent among the myths which the Commission sought to explode was one which drew the following comment: "We commend to the attention of employers who fear clashes or loss of white workers by taking on Negro workers the fact that in 89 percent of the industries investigated by this Commission, Negroes were found working in close association with white employees, and that friction between these elements had rarely been manifested."

In implementing such a program, a frequent interchange of speakers between Negro and white groups was urged. Public-school principals and teachers were asked to "encourage participation by children of both races in student activities as a means of promoting mutual understanding and good race relations in such schools and in the community." The daily press, which had been excoriated by the report, was asked to tone down its sensational treatment of Negro crime and to print more news about Negro achievement. And as a concession to that touchy aspect of Negro-white relations referred to in the Eighties by the *Conservator,* the Commission recommended the capitalization of the word "Negro" in racial designations, and avoidance of the word *nigger* "as contemptuous and needlessly provocative." [7]

2. SEPARATISM VS. ALLIANCE

*Atlanta Exposition Address**

BOOKER T. WASHINGTON

MR. PRESIDENT AND GENTLEMEN OF THE BOARD OF DIRECTORS AND CITIZENS.

One-third of the population of the South is of the Negro race. No enterprise seeking the material, civil, or moral welfare of this section can disregard this element of our population and reach the highest success. I but convey to you, Mr. President and Directors, the sentiment of the masses of my

[7] *The Negro in Chicago,* pp. 595-651.

* Booker T. Washington, *Up From Slavery: An Autobiography* (New York: Doubleday, Page & Co., 1901), pp. 218-225.

race when I say that in no way have the value and manhood of the American Negro been more fittingly and generously recognized than by the managers of this magnificent Exposition at every stage of its progress. It is a recognition that will do more to cement the friendship of the two races than any occurrence since the dawn of our freedom.

Not only this, but the opportunity here afforded will awaken among us a new era of industrial progress. Ignorant and inexperienced, it is not strange that in the first years of our new life we began at the top instead of at the bottom; that a seat in Congress or the state legislature was more sought than real estate or industrial skill; that the political convention or stump speaking had more attractions than starting a dairy farm or truck garden.

A ship lost at sea for many days suddenly sighted a friendly vessel. From the mast of the unfortunate vessel was seen a signal, "Water, water; we die of thirst!" The answer from the friendly vessel at once came back, "Cast down your bucket where you are." A second time the signal, "Water, water; send us water!" ran up from the distressed vessel, and was answered, "Cast down your bucket where you are." And a third and fourth signal for water was answered, "Cast down your bucket where you are." The captain of the distressed vessel, at last heeding the injunction, cast down his bucket, and it came up full of fresh, sparkling water from the mouth of the Amazon River. To those of my race who depend on bettering their condition in a foreign land or who underestimate the importance of cultivating friendly relations with the Southern white man, who is their next-door neighbour, I would say: "Cast down your bucket where you are"—cast it down in making friends in every manly way of the people of all races by whom we are surrounded.

Cast it down in agriculture, mechanics, in commerce, in domestic service, and in the professions. And in this connection it is well to bear in mind that whatever other sins the South may be called to bear, when it comes to business, pure and simple, it is in the South that the Negro is given a man's chance in the commercial world, and in nothing is this Exposition more eloquent than in emphasizing this chance. Our greatest danger is that in the great leap from slavery to freedom we may overlook the fact that the masses of us are to live by the productions of our hands, and fail to keep in mind that we shall prosper in proportion as we learn to dignify and glorify common labour and put brains and skill into the common occupations of life; shall prosper in proportion as we learn to draw the line between the superficial and the substantial, the ornamental gewgaws of life and the useful.

No race can prosper till it learns that there is as much dignity in tilling a field as in writing a poem. It is at the bottom of life we must begin, and not at the top. Nor should we permit our grievances to overshadow our opportunities.

To those of the white race who look to the incoming of those of foreign birth and strange tongue and habits for the prosperity of the South, were I permitted I would repeat what I say to my own race, "Cast down your bucket where you are." Cast it down among the eight millions of Negroes whose habits you know, whose fidelity and love you have tested in days when to have proved treacherous meant the ruin of your firesides. Cast down your bucket among these people who have, without strikes and labour wars, tilled your fields, cleared your forests, builded your railroads and cities, and brought forth treasures from the bowels of the earth, and helped make possible this magnificent representation of the progress of the South. Casting down your bucket among my people, helping and encouraging them as you are doing on these grounds, and to education of head, hand, and heart, you will find that they will buy your surplus land, make blossom the waste places in your fields, and run your factories. While doing this, you can be sure in the future, as in the past, that you and your families will be surrounded by the most patient, faithful, law-abiding, and unresentful people that the world has seen. As we have proved our loyalty to you in the past, in nursing your children, watching by the sick-bed of your mothers and fathers, and often following them with tear-dimmed eyes to their graves, so in the future, in our humble way, we shall stand by you with a devotion that no foreigner can approach, ready to lay down our lives, if need be, in defence of yours, interlacing our industrial, commercial, civil, and religious life with yours in a way that shall make the interests of both races one. In all things that are purely social we can be as separate as the fingers, yet one as the hand in all things essential to mutual progress.

There is no defence or security for any of us except in the highest intelligence and development of all. If anywhere there are efforts tending to curtail the fullest growth of the Negro, let these efforts be turned into stimulating, encouraging, and making him the most useful and intelligent citizen. Effort or means so invested will pay a thousand per cent interest. These efforts will be twice blessed—"blessing him that gives and him that takes."

There is no escape through law of man or God from the inevitable:—

The laws of changeless justice bind

Oppressor with oppressed;
And close as sin and suffering joined
We march to fate abreast.

Nearly sixteen millions of hands will aid you in pulling the load upward, or they will pull against you the load downward. We shall constitute one-third and more of the ignorance and crime of the South, or one-third its intelligence and progress; we shall contribute one-third to the business and industrial prosperity of the South, or we shall prove a veritable body of death, stagnating, depressing, retarding every effort to advance the body politic.

Gentlemen of the Exposition, as we present to you our humble effort at an exhibition of our progress, you must not expect overmuch. Starting thirty years ago with ownership here and there in a few quilts and pumpkins and chickens (gathered from miscellaneous sources), remember the path that has led from these to the inventions and production of agricultural implements, buggies, steam-engines, newspapers, books, statuary, carving, paintings, the management of drug-stores and banks, has not been trodden without contact with thorns and thistles. While we take pride in what we exhibit as a result of our independent efforts, we do not for a moment forget that our part in this exhibition would fall far short of your expectations but for the constant help that has come to our educational life, not only from the Southern states, but especially from Northern philanthropists, who have made their gifts a constant stream of blessing and encouragement.

The wisest among my race understand that the agitation of questions of social equality is the extremest folly, and that progress in the enjoyment of all the privileges that will come to us must be the result of severe and constant struggle rather than of artificial forcing. No race that has anything to contribute to the markets of the world is long in any degree ostracized. It is important and right that all privileges of the law be ours, but it is vastly more important that we be prepared for the exercises of these privileges. The opportunity to earn a dollar in a factory just now is worth infinitely more than the opportunity to spend a dollar in an opera-house.

In conclusion, may I repeat that nothing in thirty years has given us more hope and encouragement, and drawn us so near to you of the white race, as this opportunity offered by the Exposition; and here bending, as it were, over the altar that represents the results of the struggles of your race and mine, both starting practically empty-handed three decades ago, I pledge that in your effort to work out the great and intricate problem which God has laid at the doors of the

South, you shall have at all times the patient, sympathetic help of my race; only let this be constantly in mind, that, while from representations in these buildings of the product of field, of forest, of mine, of factory, letters, and art, much good will come, yet far above and beyond material benefits will be that higher good, that, let us pray God, will come, in a blotting out of sectional differences and racial animosities and suspicions, in a determination to administer absolute justice, in a willing obedience among all classes to the mandates of law. This, coupled with material prosperity, will bring into our beloved South a new heaven and a new earth.

The Philosophy of Marcus Garvey*

MARCUS GARVEY

The Future As I See It

IT COMES TO the individual, the race, the nation, once in a life time to decide upon the course to be pursued as a career. The hour has now struck for the individual Negro as well as the entire race to decide the course that will be pursued in the interest of our own liberty.

We who make up the Universal Negro Improvement Association have decided that we shall go forward, upward and onward toward the great goal of human liberty. We have determined among ourselves that all barriers placed in the way of our progress must be removed, must be cleared away for we desire to see the light of a brighter day.

The Negro Is Ready

The Universal Negro Improvement Association for five years has been proclaiming to the world the readiness of the Negro to carve out a pathway for himself in the course of life. Men of other races and nations have become alarmed at this attitude of the Negro in his desire to do things for himself and by himself. This alarm has become so universal that organizations have been brought into being here, there and everywhere for the purpose of deterring and obstructing this

* A. J. Garvey, ed., *The Philosophy and Opinions of Marcus Garvey* (New York: Universal Publishing House, 1923), I, pp. 73-78.

forward move of our race. Propaganda has been waged here, there and everywhere for the purpose of misinterpreting the intention of this organization; some have said that this organization seeks to create discord and discontent among the races; some say we are organized for the purpose of hating other people. Every sensible, sane and honest-minded person knows that the Universal Negro Improvement Association has no such intention. We are organized for the absolute purpose of bettering our condition, industrially, commercially, socially, religiously and politically. We are organized not to hate other men, but to lift ourselves, and to demand respect of all humanity. We have a program that we believe to be righteous; we believe it to be just, and we have made up our minds to lay down ourselves on the altar of sacrifice for the realization of this great hope of ours, based upon the foundation of righteousness. We declare to the world that Africa must be free, that the entire Negro race must be emancipated from industrial bondage, peonage and serfdom; we make no compromise, we make no apology in this our declaration. We do not desire to create offense on the part of other races, but we are determined that we shall be heard, that we shall be given the rights to which we are entitled. . . .

"Crocodiles" As Friends

Men of the Negro race, let me say to you that a greater future is in store for us; we have no cause to lose hope, to become faint-hearted. We must realize that upon ourselves depend our destiny, our future; we must carve out that future, that destiny, and we who make up the Universal Negro Improvement Association have pledged ourselves that nothing in the world shall stand in our way, nothing in the world shall discourage us, but opposition shall make us work harder, shall bring us closer together so that as one man the millions of us will march on toward that goal that we have set for ourselves. The new Negro shall not be deceived. The new Negro refuses to take advice from anyone who has not felt with him, and suffered with him. We have suffered for three hundred years, therefore we feel that the time has come when only those who have suffered with us can interpret our feelings and our spirit. It takes the slave to interpret the feelings of the slave; it takes the unfortunate man to interpret the spirit of his unfortunate brother; and so it takes the suffering Negro to interpret the spirit of his comrade. It is strange that so many people are interested in the Negro now, willing to advise him how to act, and what organizations he should join, yet nobody was interested in the Negro to the extent of not making him a slave for two hundred and fifty years, reducing him to industrial peonage and serfdom after he was freed; it is strange that the same people can be so interested in the Negro now, as to tell him what organization he should follow and what leader he should support.

Whilst we are bordering on a future of brighter things, we are also at our danger period, when we must either accept the right philosophy, or go down by following deceptive propaganda which has hemmed us in for many centuries.

Deceiving The People

There is many a leader of our race who tells us that everything is well, and that all things will work out themselves and that a better day is coming. Yes, all of us know that a better day is coming; we all know that one day we will go home to Paradise; but whilst we are hoping by our Christian virtues to have an entry into Paradise we also realize that we are living on earth, and that the things that are practised in Paradise are not practiced here. You have to treat this world as the world treats you; we are living in a temporal, material age, an age of activity, an age of racial, national selfishness. What else can you expect but to give back to the world what the world gives you, and we are calling upon the four hundred million Negroes of the world to take a decided stand, a determined stand, that we shall occupy a firm position; that position shall be an emancipated race and a free nation of our own. We are determined that we shall have a free country; we are determined that we shall have a flag; we are determined that we shall have a government, second to none in the world.

An Eye For An Eye

Men may spurn the idea, they may scoff at it; the metropolitan press of this country may deride us; yes, white men may laugh at the idea of Negroes talking about government; but let me tell you there is going to be a government, and let me say to you also that whatsoever you give, in like measure it shall be returned to you. The world is sinful, and therefore man believes in the doctrine of an eye for an eye, a tooth for a tooth. Everybody believes that revenge is God's, but at the same time we are men, and revenge sometimes springs up, even in the most Christian heart.

Why should man write down a history that will react

against him? Why should man perpetrate deeds of wickedness upon his brother which will return to him in like measure? Yes, the Germans maltreated the French in the Franco-Prussian war of 1870, but the French got even with the Germans in 1918. It is history, and history will repeat itself. Beat the Negro, brutalize the Negro, kill the Negro, burn the Negro, imprison the Negro, scoff at the Negro, deride the Negro, it may come back to you one of these fine days, because the supreme destiny of man is in the hands of God. God is no respecter of persons, whether that person be white, yellow or black. Today the one race is up, tomorrow it has fallen; today the Negro seems to be the footstool of the other races and nations of the world; tomorrow the Negro may occupy the highest rung of the great human ladder.

But, when we come to consider the history of man, was not the Negro a power, was he not great once? Yes, honest students of history can recall the day when Egypt, Ethiopia and Timbuctoo towered in their civilizations, towered above Europe, towered above Asia. When Europe was inhabited by a race of cannibals, a race of savages, naked men, heathens and pagans, Africa was peopled with a race of cultured black men, who were masters in art, science and literature; men who were cultured and refined; men who, it was said, were like the gods. Even the great poets of old sang in beautiful sonnets of the delight it afforded the gods to be in companionship with the Ethiopians. Why, then, should we lose hope? Black men, you were once great; you shall be great again. Lose not courage, lose not faith, go forward. The thing to do is to get organized; keep separated and you will be exploited, you will be robbed, you will be killed. Get organized, and you will compel the world to respect you. If the world fails to give you consideration because you are black men, because you are Negroes, four hundred millions of you shall, through organization, shake the pillars of the universe and bring down creation, even as Samson brought down the temple upon his head and upon the heads of the Philistines.

An Inspiring Vision

So Negroes, I say, through the Universal Negro Improvement Association, that there is much to live for. I have a vision of the future, and I see before me a picture of a redeemed Africa, with her dotted cities, with her beautiful civilization, with her millions of happy children, going to and fro. Why should I lose hope, why should I give up and take a back place in this age of progress? Remember that you are

men, that God created you Lords of this creation. Lift up
yourselves, men, take yourselves out of the mire and hitch
your hopes to the stars; yes, rise as high as the very stars
themselves. Let no man pull you down, let no man destroy
your ambition, because man is but your companion, your
equal; man is your brother; he is not your lord; he is not
your sovereign master.

We of the Universal Negro Improvement Association feel
happy; we are cheerful. Let them connive to destroy us; let
them organize to destroy us; we shall fight the more. Ask me
personally the cause of my success, and I say opposition; oppose me, and I fight the more, and if you want to find out the
sterling worth of the Negro, oppose him, and under the leadership of the Universal Negro Improvement Association he
shall fight his way to victory, and in the days to come, and I
believe not far distant, Africa shall reflect a splendid demonstration of the worth of the Negro, of the determination of
the Negro, to set himself free and to establish a government
of his own.

National Negro Committee Criticizes
Booker T. Washington*

The National Negro Committee on Mr. Washington, 1910

To The People of Great Britain and Europe—

The undersigned Negro-Americans have heard, with great
regret, the recent attempt to assure England and Europe that
their condition in America is satisfactory. They sincerely wish
that such were the case, but it becomes their plain duty to say
that if Mr. Booker T. Washington, or any other person, is
giving the impression abroad that the Negro problem in
America is in process of satisfactory solution, he is giving an
impression which is not true.

We say this without personal bitterness toward Mr. Washington. He is a distinguished American and has a perfect
right to his opinions. But we are compelled to point out that
Mr. Washington's large financial responsibilities have made

* In *A Documentary History of the Negro People in the United
States,* Herbert Aptheker, ed. (New York: The Citadel Press, 1951),
pp. 884-886. A printed brochure, "Race Relations in the United States"
[1910] in Du Bois MSS. By permission.

him dependent on the rich charitable public and that, for this reason, he has for years been compelled to tell, not the whole truth, but that part of it which certain powerful interests in America wish to appear as the whole truth. . . .

Our people were emancipated in a whirl of passion, and then left naked to the mercies of their enraged and impoverished ex-masters. As our sole means of defence we were given the ballot, and we used it so as to secure the real fruits of the War. Without it we would have returned to slavery; with it we struggled toward freedom. No sooner, however, had we rid ourselves of nearly two-thirds of our illiteracy, and accumulated $600,000,000 worth of property in a generation, than this ballot, which had become increasingly necessary to the defence of our civil and property rights, was taken from us by force and fraud.

Today in eight States where the bulk of the Negroes live, Black men of property and university training can be, and usually are, by law denied the ballot, while the most ignorant White man votes. This attempt to put the personal and property rights of the Blacks at the absolute political mercy of the worst of the Whites is spreading each day.

Along with this has gone a systematic attempt to curtail the education of the Black race. Under a widely advertised system of "universal" education, not one Black boy in three today has in the United States a chance to learn to read and write. The proportion of school funds due to Black children are often spent on Whites, and the burden on private charity to support education, which is a public duty, has become almost intolerable.

In every walk of life we meet discrimination based solely on race and color, but continually and persistently misrepresented to the world as the natural difference due to condition.

We are, for instance, usually forced to live in the worst quarters, and our consequent death rate is noted as a race trait, and reason for further discrimination. When we seek to buy property in better quarters we are sometimes in danger of mob violence, or, as now in Baltimore, of actual legislation to prevent.

We are forced to take lower wages for equal work, and our standard of living is then criticised. Fully half the labor unions refuse us admittance, and then claim that as "scabs" we lower the price of labor.

A persistent caste proscription seeks to force us and confine us to menial occupations where the conditions of work are worst.

Our women in the South are without protection in law and

custom, and are then derided as lewd. A widespread system of deliberate public insult is customary, which makes it difficult, if not impossible, to secure decent accommodation in hotels, railway trains, restaurants and theatres, and even in the Christian Church we are in most cases given to understand that we are unwelcome unless segregated.

Worse than all this is the wilful miscarriage of justice in the courts. Not only have 3,500 Black men been lynched publicly by mobs in the last twenty-five years without semblance or pretence of trial, but regularly every day throughout the South the machinery of the courts is used, not to prevent crime and correct the wayward among Negroes, but to wreak public dislike and vengeance, and to raise public funds. This dealing in crime as a means of public revenue is a system well-nigh universal in the South, and while its glaring brutality through private lease has been checked, the underlying principle is still unchanged.

Everywhere in the United States the old democratic doctrine of recognising fitness wherever it occurs is losing ground before a reactionary policy of denying preferment in political or industrial life to competent men if they have a trace of Negro blood, and of using the weapons of public insult and humiliation to keep such men down. It is today a universal demand in the South that on all occasions social courtesies shall be denied any person of known Negro descent, even to the extent of refusing to apply the titles of "Mr.," "Mrs.," and "Miss."

Against this dominant tendency strong and brave Americans, White and Black, are fighting, but they need, and need sadly, the moral support of England and of Europe in this crusade for the recognition of manhood, despite adventitious differences of race, and it is like a blow in the face to have one, who himself suffers daily insult and humiliation in America, give the impression that all is well. It is one thing to be optimistic, self-forgetful and forgiving, but it is quite a different thing, consciously or unconsciously, to misrepresent the truth.

(Signed)
J. Max Barber, B.A., Editor of *The Voice of the Negro*.
C. E. Bentley, formerly Chairman of Dental Clinics, St. Louis Exposition.
W. Justin Carter, Barrister, Harrisburg, Pa.
S. L. Corrothers, D.D., Pastor African M.E. Zion Church, Washington, D.C.
George W. Crawford, B.A., LL.B., Barrister, formerly Clerk of Court, New Haven, Ct.

James R. L. Diggs, M.A., President of Virginia Seminary and College, Va.

W. E. Burghardt Du Bois, Ph.D., Author of *Souls of Black Folk*, &c., Fellow of the American Association for the Advancement of Science, Member of International Law Society and Secretary of the National Afro-American Committee.

Archibald H. Grimké, late U.S. Consul to San Domingo.

N. B. Marshall, B.A., LL.B., Barrister, Counsel in the Brownsville Soldiers Court Martial.

Frederick L. McGhee, Barrister, St. Paul, Minn.

G. W. Mitchell, B.A., LL.B., Barrister, Philadelphia.

Clement G. Morgan, B.A., LL.B., Barrister, formerly Alderman of Cambridge, Mass.

Edward H. Morris, Grand Master of the Grand United Order of Odd Fellows in America.

N. F. Mossell, M.D., Medical Director of Douglass Hospital, Philadelphia, Pa.

James L. Neill, Recording Secretary of the National Independent League.

William Pickens, B.A., Professor of Latin, Talladega College, Ala.

William A. Sinclair, Author of *The Aftermath of Slavery*, and Field Secretary of the Constitution League, which represents nine-tenths of the American Negroes, and has 15,000 coloured Ministers in affiliated relations with it.

Harry C. Smith, Editor of *The Cleveland Gazette*, for six years Member of the Legislature of Ohio.

B. S. Smith, Barrister, formerly Assistant States Attorney, State of Kansas.

William Monroe Trotter, B.A., Editor of *The Boston Guardian*.

J. Milton Waldron, D.D., Pastor of Shiloh Baptist Church, Washington, D.C.

Owen M. Waller, M.D., Physician, Brooklyn, New York.

Alexander Walters, D.D., Bishop of the African M.E. Zion Church.

*The Niagara Movement** *Declaration of Principles*

PROGRESS: THE MEMBERS of the conference, known as the Niagara Movement, assembled in annual meeting at Buffalo, July 11th, 12th and 13th, 1905, congratulate the Negro-Americans on certain undoubted evidences of progress in the last decade, particularly the increase of intelligence, the buying of property, the checking of crime, the uplift in home life, the advance in literature and art, and the demonstration of con-

* 1905. Statement probably drafted by Dr. W.E.B. Du Bois, the founder of the Niagara Movement.

structive and executive ability in the conduct of great religious,
economic and educational institutions.

Suffrage: At the same time, we believe that this class of
American citizens should protest emphatically and continually against the curtailment of their political rights. We believe in manhood suffrage; we believe that no man is so good,
intelligent or wealthy as to be entrusted wholly with the welfare of his neighbor.

Civil Liberty: We believe also in protest against the curtailment of our civil rights. All American citizens have the right
to equal treatment in places of public entertainment according to their behavior and deserts.

Economic Opportunity: We especially complain against the
denial of equal opportunities to us in economic life; in the
rural districts of the South this amounts to peonage and vir-
tual slavery; all over the South it tends to crush labor and
small business enterprises; and everywhere American prejudice, helped often by iniquitous laws, is making it more difficult for Negro-Americans to earn a decent living.

Education: Common school education should be free to all
American children and compulsory. High school training
should be adequately provided for all, and college training
should be the monopoly of no class or race in any section of
our common country. We believe that, in defense of our own
institutions, the United States should aid common school education, particularly in the South, and we especially recommend concerted agitation to this end. We urge an increase in
public high school facilities in the South, where the Negro-
Americans are almost wholly without such provisions. We
favor well-equipped trade and technical schools for the training of artisans, and the need of adequate and liberal endow-
ment for a few institutions of higher education must be patent
to sincere well-wishers of the race.

Courts: We demand upright judges in courts, juries selected without discrimination on account of color and the
same measure of punishment and the same efforts at reforma-
tion for blacks as for white offenders. We need orphanages
and farm schools for dependent children, juvenile reformato-
ries for delinquents, and the abolition of the dehumanizing
convict-lease system.

Public Opinion: We note with alarm the evident retrogres-
sion in this land of sound public opinion on the subject of
manhood rights, republican government and human brotherhood, and we pray God that this nation will not degenerate
into a mob of boasters and oppressors, but rather will return

to the faith of the fathers, that all men were created free and equal, with certain unalienable rights.

Health: We plead for health—for an opportunity to live in decent houses and localities, for a chance to rear our children in physical and moral cleanliness.

Employers and Labor Unions: We hold up for public execration the conduct of two opposite classes of men: The practice among employers of importing ignorant Negro-American laborers in emergencies, and then affording them neither protection nor permanent employment; and the practice of labor unions in proscribing and boycotting and oppressing thousands of their fellow-toilers, simply because they are black. These methods have accentuated and will accentuate the war of labor and capital, and they are disgraceful to both sides.

Protest: We refuse to allow the impression to remain that the Negro-American assents to inferiority, is submissive under oppression and apologetic before insults. Through helplessness we may submit, but the voice of protest of ten million Americans must never cease to assail the ears of their fellows, so long as America is unjust.

Color-Line: Any discrimination based simply on race or color is barbarous, we care not how hallowed it be by custom, expediency or prejudice. Differences made on account of ignorance, immorality, or disease are legitimate methods of fighting evil, and against them we have no word of protest; but discriminations based simply and solely on physical peculiarities, place of birth, color of skin, are relics of that unreasoning human savagery of which the world is and ought to be thoroughly ashamed.

"Jim Crow" Cars: We protest against the "Jim Crow" car, since its effect is and must be to make us pay first-class fare for third-class accommodations, render us open to insults and discomfort and to crucify wantonly our manhood, womanhood and self-respect.

Soldiers: We regret that this nation has never seen fit adequately to reward the black soldiers who, in its five wars, have defended their country with their blood, and yet have been systematically denied the promotions which their abilities deserve. And we regard as unjust, the exclusion of black boys from the military and naval training schools.

War Amendments: We urge upon Congress the enactment of appropriate legislation for securing the proper enforcement of those articles of freedom, the thirteenth, fourteenth and fifteenth amendments of the Constitution of the United States.

Oppression: We repudiate the monstrous doctrine that the oppressor should be the sole authority as to the rights of the oppressed. The Negro race in America stolen, ravished and degraded, struggling up through difficulties and oppression, needs sympathy and receives criticism; needs help and is given hindrance, needs protection and is given mob-violence, needs justice and is given charity, needs leadership and is given cowardice and apology, needs bread and is given a stone. This nation will never stand justified before God until these things are changed.

The Church: Especially are we surprised and astonished at the recent attitude of the church of Christ—of an increase of a desire to bow to racial prejudice, to narrow the bounds of human brotherhood, and to segregate black men to some outer sanctuary. This is wrong, unchristian and disgraceful to the twentieth century civilization.

Agitation: Of the above grievances we do not hesitate to complain, and to complain loudly and insistently. To ignore, overlook, or apologize for these wrongs is to prove ourselves unworthy of freedom. Persistent manly agitation is the way to liberty, and toward this goal the Niagara Movement has started and asks the cooperation of all men of all races.

Help: At the same time we want to acknowledge with deep thankfulness the help of our fellowmen from the abolitionist down to those who today still stand for equal opportunity and who have given and still give of their wealth and of their poverty for our advancement.

Duties: And while we are demanding, and ought to demand, and will continue to demand the rights enumerated above, God forbid that we should ever forget to urge corresponding duties upon our people:

The duty to vote.

The duty to respect the rights of others.

The duty to work.

The duty to obey the laws.

The duty to be clean and orderly.

The duty to send our children to school.

The duty to respect ourselves, even as we respect others.

This statement, complaint and prayer we submit to the American people, and Almighty God.

The Formation of the NAACP*

LANGSTON HUGHES

THE LETTER WHICH eventually led to the founding of the
NAACP was written to William English Walling by Mary
White Ovington immediately after she read his moving account of the Springfield, Illinois, race riots in the *Independent*. Walling's story vividly described how for two days a mob
surged through the streets of that city in the summer of 1908
looting and burning Negro homes; they lynched a Negro barber and an 84-year-old man for no reason at all except that
the prisoners the whites were looking for were not in the jail.
The mob seriously injured some 70 persons, and drove hundreds of Negroes from the city. All this violence occurred
near the Lincoln mansion and less than two miles from the
Great Emancipator's grave. Walling concluded his article,
which he called "Race War in the North," by invoking "the
spirit of the abolitionists, of Lincoln and of Lovejoy" to help
alleviate the repressive condition of the Negro. "Who realizes," he asked, "the seriousness of the situation, and what
large and powerful body of citizens is ready to come to their
aid?"

In her letter to Walling, Miss Ovington suggested that they
explore what could be done to remedy the deplorable state of
race relations in the North and South. In the decade preceding the Springfield riots there were over 1000 lynchings in the
United States. In 1901 alone, 105 Negroes were publicly
done to death by mobs in mass orgies of violence; they had
no protection from the police and their lynchers were not
brought to trial. Since 1900 an epidemic of race riots had
swept the country from Texas and Georgia as far north as
Pennsylvania, Ohio, and Illinois, causing millions of dollars'
worth of property damage and killing or wounding hundreds
of people. All this violence, added to the everyday handicaps
which Negroes already suffered, presented a dire picture indeed.

* From Langston Hughes, *Fight for Freedom, the Story of the
NAACP* (New York: W. W. Norton & Co., Inc., 1962), pp. 20-24, p.
25, pp. 27-28. Reprinted by permission of Berkley Publishing Corp.

To discuss this sorry situation, three people met in Walling's apartment in Manhattan in the first week of the new year 1909. These three—Miss Ovington, a wealthy Northerner who had made a thorough study of racial problems; William English Walling, a Southern journalist with liberal racial views; and Henry Moskovitz, a Jewish social worker—all were concerned with democracy and the Negro. They decided to issue a call for a conference to be signed by a number of prominent Americans. It would be released on February 12, 1909, the 100th anniversay of Abraham Lincoln's birth. Written by Oswald Garrison Villard of the *New York Post,* the call read in part:

The Celebration of the Centennial of the birth of Abraham Lincoln, widespread and grateful as it may be, will fail to justify itself if it takes no note of and makes no recognition of the colored men and women for whom the Great Emancipator labored to assure freedom. . . . If Mr. Lincoln could revisit this country in the flesh, he would be disheartened and discouraged. He would learn that on January 1, 1909, Georgia had rounded out a new confederacy by disfranchising the Negro, after the manner of all the other Southern States. He would learn that the Supreme Court of the United States, supposedly a bulwark of American liberties, had refused every opportunity to pass squarely upon the disfranchisement of millions. . . . He would learn that the Supreme Court . . . had laid down the principle that if an individual State chooses, it may "make it a crime for white and colored persons to frequent the same market place at the same time, or appear in an assemblage of citizens convened to consider questions of a public or political nature in which all citizens, without regard to race, are equally interested."

In many States Lincoln would see the black men and women, for whose freedom a hundred thousand soldiers gave their lives, set apart in trains, in which they pay first-class fares for third-class service, and segregated in railway stations and in places of entertainment; he would observe that State after State declines to do its elementary duty in preparing the Negro through education for the best exercise of citizenship. Added to this, the spread of lawless attacks upon the Negro, North, South, and West—even in the Springfield made famous by Lincoln . . . could but shock the author of the sentiment that "government of the people, by the people, for the people, should not perish from the earth."

Silence under these conditions means tacit approval. . . . Hence we call upon all the believers in democracy to join in a National Conference for the discussion of present evils, the voicing of protests, and the renewal of the struggle for civil and political liberty.

This document was signed by sixty persons of distinction —among them, Jane Addams, the famous founder of Hull House; Francis J. Grimké, Washington's militant Negro minister; John Dewey of Columbia University; William Lloyd

Garrison of Boston; the Reverend John Haynes Holmes; Alexander Walters, bishop of the African Methodist Episcopal Zion Church; Rabbi Stephen S. Wise; Ida B. Wells Barnett; J. G. Phelps Stokes, the philanthropist; Lincoln Steffens, the famous journalist; Mary E. Woolley, president of Mount Holyoke College; Ray Stannard Baker; Mary Church Terrell; Lillian D. Wald; Brand Whitlock, mayor of Toledo; and Dr. W. E. B. Du Bois.

The conference that resulted from this call began on May 30, 1909, with an interracial reception at the Henry Street Settlement in New York, and ended on June 1 with a mass meeting at Cooper Union. From these sessions there emerged an organization called the National Negro Committee, consisting of 40 persons. It held four well-attended public meetings during the year and enrolled many additional members.

At the second annual meeting of the National Negro Committee in May, 1910, a new name was chosen, the National Association for the Advancement of Colored People. As such, the organization was incorporated under the laws of the State of New York, and its purposes officially recorded: "To promote equality of rights and eradicate caste or race prejudice among the citizens of the United States; to advance the interest of colored citizens; to secure for them impartial suffrage; and to increase their opportunities for securing justice in the courts, education for their children, employment according to their ability, and complete equality before the law." Among those signing the papers of incorporation were Mary White Ovington, W. E. B. Du Bois, Oswald Garrison Villard (a grandson of William Lloyd Garrison), John Haynes Holmes, and Walter E. Sachs. Although the NAACP did not receive its name until May, 1910, and was not incorporated until the following year, the date of its founding has always been considered to be the date of the call written by Villard—February 12, 1909, the centennial of Lincoln's birth.

The first president of the NAACP was Moorfield Storey, the distinguished Boston lawyer; William English Walling became chairman of the Executive Committee; John E. Milholland, treasurer; Oswald Garrison Villard, disbursing treasurer; Frances Blascoer, executive secretary; and W. E. B. Du Bois, director of publicity and research. Thanks to Oswald Garrison Villard, the NAACP obtained a rent-free office in the *Evening Post* building on Vesey Strreet. From the beginning the organization and its workers were interracial. Its Board of Directors included eight former members of the Niagara Movement.

Within three months after its organization the NAACP opened its first local office in Chicago. That summer also its legal work, which was eventually to have so great an effect upon American racial patterns, began, when NAACP lawyers filed a petition of pardon for a Negro sharecropper in South Carolina. This man had been given the death penalty for slaying a constable who burst into his cabin after midnight to charge him with breach of contract. The young NAACP initiated an intensive publicity campaign by means of press releases and pamphlets exposing acts of racial injustice and setting forth the Association's objectives. The first issue of its official organ, *The Crisis*, appeared in November under the editorship of Dr. Du Bois. . . .

As a result of his brilliant editorials in *The Crisis*, that periodical achieved unprecedented circulation among Negro readers and attracted the attention of many whites as well. The initial issue of 1000 copies was soon exhausted. By the end of its first year it had 12,000 readers. Eventually its circulation rose to more than 100,000. It spotlighted distinguished Negro "Men of the Month" and in "Following the Color Line" featured news of race problems and progress around the world. There was a month-to-month résumé of NAACP activities, and each year a roundup with photographs of Negro college graduates, records of advanced degrees, Phi Beta Kappa selections, and other academic achievements. Reviews of books and plays relating to Negro life were an important part of the contents. Young writers published their poems and stories in *The Crisis*. The poetnovelist, Jessie Redmon Fauset, was appointed to the staff as managing editor. Harvard-trained Augustus Granville Dill was business manager.

In the first issue Du Bois stated that *The Crisis* would stand for "the highest ideals of American democracy, and for reasonable but earnest and persistent attempts to gain these rights and realize these ideals." The *Crisis* became America's leading publication devoted to the Negro, a position it held for well over a quarter of a century. When it became self-supporting, with its staff paid from its own income rather than with Association funds, *The Crisis* became the only magazine in the country devoted to social service that was not dependent upon subsidy. Its founding was one of the great contributions of the NAACP to national cultural life. . . .

By the end of 1913 the National Association for the Advancement of Colored People had 24 branches in the United

States, and its budget had increased to $16,000. But violence and racial discrimination were increasing, not diminishing. That year 79 persons were lynched. In 1912 the count was 63 —an average of more than one mass murder a week. An expanded NAACP was a national necessity. . . . By the end of 1914 there were 50 branches of the NAACP in the United States. . . .

Off to a good start, the young Association still had a long haul. The going was far from easy. Powerful philanthropists, mostly of the Booker T. Washington school of thought, gave the NAACP no aid. Conservative whites and even some prominent Negroes attacked it as "radical." They charged that its program of complete equality was impractical, if not utopian. Some even said that the NAACP platform did race relations in America more harm than good. Few newspapers anywhere gave its activities sympathetic coverage. It was denounced violently in the South. In some cities *The Crisis* could not be sold openly. And there were places in the South where it was impossible to organize branches for fear of mob reprisals.

PART V

Depression and War

INTRODUCTION

MARCUS GARVEY had attracted the allegiance of the masses
of Negro people more than any other leader, yet his program
lacked action in which to involve them. They could join the
UNIA and send in their dues and expressions of support, but
otherwise there was little for them beyond the satisfaction
people could derive from his publicly extolling the virtues of
blackness. With the Great Depression other organizations
arose which involved the common man in action. The depression hit the Negro hardest of all Americans since he had always been on the lowest level of the economy. It was estimated in 1933 that 66% of the potential labor force of Harlem
was unemployed.

Charles Johnson in *The Economic Status of Negroes* said
that in Philadelphia the unemployment rate of whites in 1929
was 9.0 and of Negroes 15.7, and in 1932 the rate was 39.7
for whites and 56.0 for Negroes.[1] Tom Kahn, in a study for
the League for Industrial Democracy, said that after eight
years of the New Deal "25% of the Negro work force was
still unemployed as against 13% of the white." [2]

In 1935 there were over two million Negroes on relief.
Everywhere the proportion of Negroes on relief was much
higher than whites: in Detroit four times as many, and in St.
Louis, New York and Birmingham three times as many.[3]

[1] Charles Johnson, *The Economic Status of Negroes* (Nashville: Fisk
University Press, 1933), p. 19.

[2] Tom Kahn, *The Economics of Equality* (New York: League for
Industrial Democracy, 1964), p. 17. Kahn said that World War II, not
the New Deal was responsible for a gain in Negro income between
1940 and 1954. Negro median family income went from 37% of white
income to 56%.

[3] C. S. Johnson, "The Negro and the Present Crisis," *Journal of
Negro Education,* 10 (July, 1941), p. 588.

Negroes joined the Unemployed Councils, and participated in "hunger marches" in many parts of the country. The aims of the councils were immediate relief first, and second, unemployment compensation legislation; in addition the councils preached racial solidarity.

During this period of radicalization the Communist Party became one of the foremost champions of Negro rights and achieved a steady growth in Negro membership. In addition to its activities in the economic sphere the Communist Party carried on active campaigns in defense of such victims of Southern justice as the Scottsboro boys, accused of rape in the lynch atmosphere of Alabama. Such campaigns, substantial contributions to the fight for civil liberties and for equal justice, also attracted Negroes to the Party.

The New York *Herald Tribune* said on October 8, 1933, that the increased number of Negro Communists indicated "a militant and aggressive ambition for betterment." The paper concluded: "This is what the depression has wrought—resentment directed mainly against the white man; restlessness, and a flaming desire for advancement. And this is all strange and new—opposed to all the traditions that have been built up by the Negro people. Ambition has supplanted fatalism; longing has replaced resignation—yet those first traditions have not been entirely swept away. And even in a hungry and rebellious Harlem some of the old chords still are stirred."

The thirties saw the rise of the Congress of Industrial Organizations and its challenge to the old craft union set-up of the American Federation of Labor. Industrial unionism opened the door to organizing Negro workers. Herbert Hill, labor secretary of the NAACP, said that the Negro "had established his first beachheads in industry during World War I, but most AFL unions still practiced a rigorous exclusionist policy throughout the 1930's." Hill points out that in the early years of the CIO "for the first time in American labor history, tens of thousands of American Negroes became union members." [4]

Negroes formed new organizations of their own. In Harlem the Harlem Labor Union fought for jobs on 125th Street where "don't buy where you can't work"-pickets marched.

As had happened in the past, the war created jobs for both whites and Negroes. Negroes applied to defense industries in large numbers and volunteered for the armed forces. Also, as in earlier days, Negroes were rebuffed at first until the need for manpower became so great that the armed services and

4 Herbert Hill, "Labor Unions and the Negro, The Record of Discrimination," *Commentary,* 28 (December, 1959), p. 482. Excerpted on pp. 480-88 below.

industries which had up to now been closed to them began to accept Negroes. In the winter of 1940, 75 percent of the defense industry was barred to Negroes. By 1944 a million more Negroes were employed in civilian jobs than in 1940. "Despite continuing resistance to the upgrading of Negroes, the number employed as skilled craftsmen and foremen doubled from 1940 to 1944; the number of those in semi-skilled jobs also doubled. The number of Negro women in industry has quadrupled since the war," Carey McWilliams wrote in 1946.[5]

In the Army over 70 percent of all Negro overseas troops were assigned to unskilled non-combat duties, and in the Navy 80 percent were cooks, stewards and steward's mates; only two percent of white sailors were so assigned. *The Negro Handbook, 1944,* estimated that "approximately two-thirds of the Negro troops appeared to be in service units of various types."

With the desperate need of troops created by the "Battle of the Bulge" (when German troops broke through Allied lines in Normandy) in the winter and spring of 1944 and 1945, Negro volunteers from communications zone units were accepted as infantry replacements. Negro volunteers were organized into platoons and assigned one platoon to a white company.[6]

Once more the Negro found himself fighting for the opportunity to be allowed to fight for his country, and many struggles were waged over segregation in the armed forces and discrimination on and off military bases. Agitation finally resulted in 1948 in President Truman's executive order desegregating the armed forces. On the home front the threat of a massive march on Washington had persuaded President Roosevelt to issue a Fair Employment Practices order. The order was hailed by many Negro leaders, but some took a wait-and-see attitude. Roy Wilkins wrote in the *Amsterdam News:* "Well, the President has spoken out on Negroes in defense and in the most effective way he could have spoken—through an executive order. It remains now to be seen how much compliance will be secured."

To get a government order for non-discrimination in employment Negroes had refused to heed two arguments presented before and since by government leaders faced with the prospect of a massive Negro protest. One argument, in the

[5] Carey McWilliams, "How the Negro Fared in the War," *Negro Digest,* IV (May, 1946), p. 72-73.
[6] Paul C. Davis, "The Negro in the Armed Services," *Virginia Quarterly Review,* 24, 1948, pp. 508-09.

words of Lester Granger, was that it "would have been notice to foreign critics of our domestic disunity at a time when a semblance of unity was most essential to national prestige." [7] The other argument was that of Mrs. Eleanor Roosevelt who wrote to Randolph, "I am afraid it will set back the progress which is being made, in the Army at least, towards better opportunities and less segregation." She added that "one must face situations as they are and not as one wishes them to be." [8] Mrs. Roosevelt's reaction, though she had demonstrated her concern for Negro rights, was similar to that of President Lincoln who had told a group of Negro leaders petitioning for equal pay for Negro soldiers in the Civil War that the country was not ready.

At the end of the war, Negroes returning home were even more disillusioned by their treatment as civilians. Veterans, who had lived another kind of life overseas and who, after all, had served in the cause of freedom, found that they were expected to fall back into place at home. In the South again there was a wave of violence. Six veterans were lynched between July 20 and August 8, 1946, and additional bodies were found floating in the Mississippi River. Many Negroes migrated North and many veterans re-enlisted. "Although Negroes made up only one-thirteenth of the total number who served during the war, 25 percent of all volunteers from September, 1945, to September, 1946, were Negro veterans. Finally, in early September, 1946, the War Department set a quota on Negro enlistments. This quota, supposedly based on the over-all percentage of Negroes in the population, has remained intact despite vigorous protests from enlightened groups who saw in the order the curtailing of still another opportunity for full participation by Negro veterans. The large percentage of Negroes who want to re-enlist is not so much a commentary upon the advantages in the armed forces as an indication that life back home is still insecure and lacking in the promise of fruitful living." [9]

During the war, and in the postwar period, the civil rights movement developed a nationwide struggle to increase Negro voter registration. The NAACP had fought and won several court cases concerned with Negro voting paving the way for a massive voter registration drive. Between 1915 and 1948

[7] Lester B. Granger, "Barriers to Negro War Employment," *The Annals of the American Academy of Political and Social Science*, 223 (September, 1942), p. 78.

[8] Quoted in Louis Ruchames' excellent study of the FEPC, *Race, Jobs and Politics* (New York: Columbia University Press, 1953), p. 17.

[9] Charles G. Volte and Louis Harris, *Our Negro Veterans*, Public Affairs Pamphlet No. 128, 1947, p. 26.

the NAACP won 24 of 26 cases it argued before the U. S. Supreme Court. Among the voting cases were *Guinn v. United States* (1915) in which the "grandfather clause" [10] was declared unconstitutional, and *Nixon v. Herndon* (1927), *Nixon v. Condon* (1932) and *Smith v. Allwright* (1944) which outlawed "white primaries." In 12 Southern states between 1940 and 1947 Negro voter registration increased by about 26 percent. Increased registration was greatest in urban areas and Negroes by 1946 held the balance of power in a few Southern cities. Still the increase in registration represented only a small fraction of the potential voting power. In only two [11] of the states were 25 percent of Negroes of voting age registered—Oklahoma with 29.6 and Tennessee with 25.8. In three Deep South states the percentages were: Louisiana, 2.6; Alabama, 1.2, and Mississippi, 0.9.[12]

Despite these low percentages in the South by 1944, the Negro held the balance of power nationally. After the election of Roosevelt in 1944, Republican National Committee Chairman Herbert Brownell, Jr. said that "a shift of 303,414 votes in fifteen states outside of the South would have enabled Governor Thomas E. Dewey to capture 175 additional electoral votes and to win the presidency with an eight electoral-vote margin." Henry Lee Moon commented: "In at least eight of the fifteen states listed by Brownell, the Negro vote exceeded the number needed to shift in order to place them in the Republican column." [13]

Moon described this balance of power:

The Negro's political influence in national elections derives not so much from its numerical strength as from its strategic diffusion in the balance-of-power and marginal states in which a shift of 5 percent or less of the popular vote would have reversed the electoral votes cast by these states. In twelve of these, with a total of 228 electoral college votes, the potential Negro vote exceeds the number required to shift the states from one column to the other. Two of these marginal states—Ohio with 25 votes and Indiana with 13—went Republican. The ten remaining states—New York, New Jersey, Pennsylvania, Illinois, Michigan, Missouri, Delaware,

[10] The grandfather clause excused persons from literacy tests required for voter registration who had been entitled to vote on January 1, 1866 or before, or who lived in a foreign nation at that time, and any lineal descendant of such a person.

[11] Current voting studies of the South usually cover 11 states, excluding Oklahoma.

[12] Luther P. Jackson, "Race and Suffrage in the South Since 1940," *New South* (Atlanta, Ga.: Southern Regional Council), 3, Nos. 5 & 6, (June-July, 1948), p. 3.

[13] Henry Lee Moon, *Balance of Power: The Negro Vote* (Garden City, N.Y.: Doubleday & Co., 1948), p. 35.

Maryland, West Virginia and Kentucky—gave to Mr. Roosevelt 190 electoral college votes essential to his victory. The closeness of the popular vote in the marginal states accented the decisive potential of the Negro's ballot.[14]

During the 1940's Negroes conducted intensive voter registration drives. In the South the NAACP spurred the establishment of dozens of local "voters' leagues" which conducted voter education classes and took people to the courthouse to register.

With the end of the war, the United States had secured its place as the world's leading power and the nation had not retreated into isolationism, but continued its involvement in international affairs. The Negro movement took advantage of this international focus, and appealed to the United Nations for aid in obtaining full citizenship. The NAACP presented the document "An Appeal to the World!" to the UN in 1947. Written under the editorial supervision of W. E. B. Du Bois, the document was subtitled "A Statement on the Denial of Human Rights to Minorities in the Case of Citizens of Negro Descent in the United States of America and an Appeal to the United Nations for Redress." It was a factual study of the denial of the right to vote and denial of legal, educational and social rights.

Again in 1951 Negroes turned to the UN with another petition. This one, "We Charge Genocide," was a catalog of lynchings and other acts of violence against Negroes which asked for UN action under Article II, the Genocide Convention. The petition was edited, prepared and presented to the UN by William L. Patterson, national executive secretary of the Civil Rights Congress.

An extensive campaign was conducted during this period by many professional and other private groups to remedy one of the most stinging insults faced by Negroes—segregation in the nation's capital. Until the spring of 1951 Negroes were barred from theaters, movie houses, hotels and "white" restaurants in Washington. In 1952 the last segregated dimestore chain opened its lunch counters to Negroes; in 1953 the first desegregated swimming pool was opened by the District of Columbia and that year the District announced a policy of non-discrimination in employment and in facilities and services. Not until 1954 were downtown motion picture theaters opened to Negroes. That same year, immediately after the decision in Brown v. Board of Education, the District Board of Education ordered schools desegregated. However, as in

14 Ibid., p. 198.

Northern cities, school segregation increased in the following years as white residents fled to the suburbs and white suburban schools. But in terms of public accommodations the battle for equal treatment in the Capital was won by the mid-fifties.

1. NEGRO AND LABOR

The A. F. of L. and the Negro*

IT IS OFTEN asserted that black workers have been slow in accepting the doctrines and methods of organized labor. The most exploited workers in the United States, they have remained the least organized and therefore the most feeble in achieving either security in their employment or living wages and decent working conditions. This apparent indifference of the black worker to the benefits of trade unionism has served to draw the fire of various officials of the American Federation of Labor who, when accused of apathy to the fate of Negro labor, have replied from time to time that the Negro worker was unorganizable, and was as yet incapable of appreciating the necessity of identifying himself with the American Labor Movement.

The recent convention of the American Federation of Labor in Toronto lacked much of being able to convince observers that it is the pillar of flame by night and a cloud by day to lead the black worker, or for that matter the white worker, out of the wilderness. Out of the thirty million workers in America less than three million are enrolled in the American Federation. And the number of accessions this year of our Lord, which was to see a great drive in the South, even as reported, was a scanty 35,000.

The American Federation of Labor then not only has failed to unionize the black worker; it has failed to unionize the white worker. It is the citadel not of labor in the large sense but of crafts, and as a craft organization it necessarily has failed to embrace that great mass of unskilled labor with which the bulk of the black workers is identified.

Only in those occupations, generally semi-skilled or un-

* Editorial, *Opportunity*, VII (November, 1929), pp. 335-36. Reprinted with permission from *Opportunity: Journal of Negro Life*, a publication of the National Urban League, Inc.

skilled, which attract large numbers of Negroes, such as long-shoremen, hod-carriers, common building laborers, or those in which Negroes enjoy a comparative monopoly, such as dining-car waiters and Pullman porters; or those in which Negro competition is able to cope successfully with the competition of white workers, as in the coal mining industry, only in these has American organized labor made any real effort to enlist the black worker in its ranks. The Negro, contrary to general opinion, is not slow to organize. There are approximately 100,000 Negro workers who are affiliated with some form of labor organization, a remarkable number when one considers that the Negro not only is outside of the pale of the skilled craft organizations, but also is compelled oft times to face the opposition of white labor, organized and unorganized, in order to gain a foothold in industry.

It is true that the American Federation of Labor has issued several lofty pronouncements to the effect that no discrimination because of race or color should govern admission to unions. It is also true that only eleven unions affiliated with the Federation specifically deny Negroes membership. But, so far, even when racial prejudice does not operate effectively to keep Negroes out, craft limitations and restrictions achieve the same result.

The statesmanship of the American Federation of Labor has failed to meet the problem of the unskilled worker, therefore it has been inadequate in so far as black workers are concerned. And there will be but little hope for the black worker in the American Federation as long as it is the so-called "aristocracy of labor," as long as it remains structurally a craft organization. And there will not be much hope for the unskilled white worker either in those great industries where crafts give way before the introduction of machinery and the increasing specialization of tasks. Where this has occurred to a considerable degree, the American Federation of Labor has made but little progress; the automobile industry; the packing industry; the rising rayon industries, these three are significant and striking examples of the failure of the Federation to keep pace with modern industrial trends.

In the South, where the Federation contemplates a mighty effort to organize the worker, a higher type of statesmanship will have to be evolved than has hitherto been revealed by the guiding geniuses of the Federation. Any attempt to organize the workers which ignores the presence of the two million black workers will be fraught with disaster. It will take more

than official pronouncements of policy. It will demand the resolute facing of the fact that the problems of white labor and
the problems of black labor are identical.

*Why We March**

OUR MOST IMMEDIATE problem and task is to make sure
that:
*Not one unemployed worker or his family shall be without
decent housing, food and clothing during the coming winter.*

Our every action must have as its first purpose to assure
that this immediate aim shall be realized.

To this end, we are bending all our efforts to develop a
mighty united movement of all victims of the crisis and the
bosses' hunger war. This essential unity must be developed in
every neighborhood, in every place of assembly, at every
point where workers are confronted with the problems of
housing, food and clothing. At all such points we urge the
workers to come together, discuss their problems, elect a
Committee of Action out of their own ranks and unitedly
conduct struggle around every case where any worker is deprived of these essentials.

The National Hunger March is first of all intended to give
impetus to the development of this unity and of countless
daily struggles for the most immediate needs of the workers.

We march in order to carry the message of unity and organization to millions of workers in thousands of cities and
towns.

We march in order to provide a living demonstration and
example of the growing unity of Negro and white, native and
foreign born, men and women, young and old in the common
struggle against poverty and mass starvation.

We march in order to lend additional encouragement, inspiration and leadership to these necessary struggles.

We march in order that the forces of the entire country
may be consolidated into a mighty counter-offensive against
the attacks of the bosses and their government.

*We march to force the federal government to supplement
local relief, by giving every unemployed worker $50.00 cash
winter relief, plus $10.00 for each such worker's dependent.*

* Excerpts from a pamphlet issued by National Committee of Unemployed Councils (New York: Workers Library Publishers, November,
1932).

Unemployment is no longer a temporary problem. Millions of workers have been permanently expelled from industry. These millions of dis-employed have been replaced by "labor-saving" machinery. Their jobs have been lost in consequence of the terrific speed-up methods that have been introduced in all industries.

We march in order to rouse greater masses to a realization of the need for measures that will provide permanent security of the masses who are suffering from and threatened by permanent unemployment.

We march in order to expose the fraudulent schemes that are being constantly brought forward by the various agents of the bosses in the effort to confuse and deceive us.

We march in order to demonstrate that ever greater masses are becoming aware of the need for a system of unemployment insurance, that can assure an income to workers who are deprived of the opportunity to earn a livelihood for themselves and their families.

We march in order to present to Congress and to the President our demand for—

Immediate unemployment insurance at the expense of the government and the employers.

WE CAN WIN THROUGH UNITED MASS STRUGGLE

Every effort will be made by all the enemies of the masses to defeat these demands.

Their propagandists will tell us that our demands are "unreasonable." The same Congress that appropriated four billion dollars for the bankers, insurance and railroad companies will tell us that they can't afford to provide relief and insurance for the starving masses.

They will try to mobilize "public opinion" by raising the cry that federal relief and unemployment insurance will increase the tax burden.

We march to give our answer, the answer of the toiling masses, to these alibis and to this propaganda.

We march to expose and blast these baseless claims.

We march to demand that the government shall stop the billion dollar subsidies for the bankers and trusts.

We march to demand that the government shall stop the billion dollar expenditures for war preparations.

We march to demand that the government shall stop the rebates of hundreds of millions in taxes to the multi-millionaires and their corporations.

We march to demand that the government shall levy upon the capital of these multi-billionaires some of whom, such as

Andy Mellon, control fortunes equal to twice the wealth in the United States treasury.

We march to demand:

Not a penny off the wages; not a penny of taxation on articles of mass consumption; not a cent for war!

WE DEMAND UNEMPLOYMENT INSURANCE AT THE EXPENSE OF THE GOVERNMENT AND EMPLOYERS!

We march to declare our determination to fight for these demands; to demonstrate our confidence in the possibility of winning them and to mobilize the mass power which alone can make the ruling class and its government concede these demands.

We march as workers who have participated in the many struggles of the past three years and more, and who know from our experience in these struggles that it is possible to win concessions through militant mass struggles.

We march as delegates of great masses of workers who have elected us and who are pledged to carry forward the struggle.

We march as the representatives of the needs and interests of millions of Negro and white toilers and of their children.

We march in the face of the bitter hostility of all forces of the ruling class; under conditions of great hardship; through lines of professional sluggers and gunmen clothed with the authority of the state, supplemented by the extra legal forces of violence.

These are also the conditions under which our every struggle is conducted. We will not be terrified. We are fortified by the support of the masses of workers and poor farmers in every city and town. This support is the effective defense as well as the means for achieving our aims.

The toiling masses of this country, the employed and unemployed, the workers on land and in industry, face the alternative of death by slow starvation or united struggle to defeat the capitalist hunger program.

On the side of our enemy, of those responsible for mass unemployment and of those co-operating in the effort to solve the deepening crisis at the expense of the toiling population, are the forces of the government, the combined press, the owners of all other agencies of publicity as the radio and movies, the spokesmen of the subsidized churches, the corrupt leaders of the A. F. of L. unions, the numerous ambitious politicians of the Republican, Democratic and Socialist Parties.

On the side of those who suffer from the crisis are the great mass of producers, the workers of hand and brain who constitute 90% of the population of this country, who have already been made destitute or face the prospect of unrelieved destitution.

Theirs is the control of the institutions. We are the mass whose power is in our organized numbers.

We march, in order to develop organization, unity and struggle that will involve the millions and defeat the small clique of multi-billionaires. We are confident of ultimate success, because we know that the workers and impoverished farmers of the United States will not consent to starve. We know that every self-respecting worker would rather die fighting than die of slow starvation like a trapped rat in a hole.

We march, several thousand strong, backed by hundreds of thousands, who have already demonstrated in countless struggles that the workers of this country have the courage, the will, the capacity to organize and fight for the right to live.

Workers! Employed and unemployed! Negro and white! Rally in the common struggle! Build Committees of Action in your community and organization! Force your local authorities to provide adequate housing, food and clothing for every unemployed worker and his family!

Rally in support of the demands of the starving masses as presented by the National Hunger March!

Force the federal government and the bosses to provide:

Winter relief of $50 for every unemployed worker, plus $10 for each such worker's dependent as a supplement to local relief.

Immediate unemployment insurance for every worker who is unemployed through no fault of his own.

Immediate payment of the so-called bonus to all veterans.

FORWARD IN THE UNITED STRUGGLE AGAINST HUNGER!

You Cannot Kill the Working Class*

ANGELO HERNDON

THEY SAY THAT once a miner, always a miner. I don't know if that's so, but I do know that my father never followed any

---

* Angelo Herndon, *You Cannot Kill the Working Class* (New York: The International Labor Defense and the League of Struggle for Negro Rights, n.d. [circa, 1934]). Herndon was the plaintiff in *Herndon v. Lowry*, 301 U.S. 242 (1937), which overturned Georgia's insurrection statute.

other trade. His sons never doubted that they would go down into the mines as soon as they got old enough. The wail of the mine whistle morning and night, and the sight of my father coming home with his lunch-pail, grimy from the day's coating of coal-dust, seemed a natural and eternal part of our lives.

Almost every working-class family, especially in those days, nursed the idea that one of its members, anyway, would get out of the factory, and wear clean clothes all the time and sit at a desk. My family was no exception. They hoped that I would be the one to leave the working-class. They were ready to make almost any sacrifices to send me through high-school and college. They were sure that if a fellow worked hard and had intelligence and grit, he wouldn't have to be a worker all his life.

I haven't seen my mother or most of my family for a long time—but I wonder what they think of that idea now!

My father died of miner's pneumonia when I was very small, and left my mother with a big family to care for. Besides myself, there were six other boys and two girls. We all did what we could. Mother went out to do housework for rich white folks. An older brother got a job in the steel mills. I did odd jobs, working in stores, running errands, for $2 and $3 a week. They still had the idea they could scrimp and save and send me through college. But when I was 13, we saw it wouldn't work.

So one fine morning in 1926, my brother Leo and I started off for Lexington, Ky. It was just across the border, and it had mines, and we were miner's kids.

A few miles outside of Lexington, we were taken on at a small mine owned by the powerful DeBardeleben Coal Corporation. . . .

We lived in the company town. It was pretty bad. The houses were just shacks on unpaved streets. We seldom had anything to eat that was right. We had to buy everything from the company store, or we'd have lost our jobs. They kept our pay low and paid only every two weeks, so we had to have credit between times. We got advances in the form of clackers, which could be used only in the company store. Their prices were very high. I remember paying 30 cents a pound for pork-chops in the company store and then noticing that the butcher in town was selling them for 20 cents. The company store prices were just robbery without a pistol.

The safety conditions in the mine were rotten. The escape-ways were far from where we worked, and there was never enough timbering to keep the rocks from falling. There were some bad accidents while I was there. I took all the skin off my right hand pushing a car up into the facing. The cars didn't have enough grease and there were no cross-ties just behind me to brace my feet against. That was a bit of the company's economy. The car slipped, the track turned over, and the next thing I knew I had lost all the skin and a lot of the flesh off my right hand. The scars are there to this day.

This DeBardeleben mine in Lexington was where the Jim-Crow system first hit me. The Negroes and whites very seldom came in contact with each other. Of course there were separate company patches for living quarters. But even in the mine the Negroes and the whites worked in different places. The Negroes worked on the North side of the mine and the whites on the South.

The Negroes never got a look-in on most of the better-paying jobs. They couldn't be section foremen, or electricians, or surveyors, or head bank boss, or checkweighman, or steel sharpeners, or engineers. They could only load the coal, run the motors, be mule-boys, pick the coal, muck the rock. In other words, they were only allowed to do the muscle work.

Besides that, the Negro miners got the worst places to work. We worked in the low coal, only 3 or 4 feet high. We had to wear knee pads, and work stretched flat on our bellies most of the time.

One day the company put up a notice that due to large overhead expenses, they would have to cut our pay from 42 to 31 cents a ton. We were sore as hell. But there wasn't any union in the mine, and practically none of us had any experience at organization, and though we grumbled plenty we didn't take any action. We were disgusted, and some of us quit. Whites and Negroes both.

I was one of those who quit. My contact with unions, and with organization, and the Communist Party, and unity between black and white miners—all that was still in the future. The pay-cut and the rotten conditions got my goat, and I walked off, because as yet I didn't know of anything else to do. . . .

The Jim-Crow system was in full force in the mines of the Tennessee Coal and Iron Company, and all over Birmingham. It had always burnt me up, but I didn't know how to set about fighting it. My parents and grandparents were hard-boiled Republicans, and told me very often that Lincoln had freed the slaves, and that we'd have to look to the Republican Party for everything good. I began to wonder about that. Here I was, being Jim-Crowed and cheated. Every couple of weeks I read about a lynching somewhere in the South.

Yet there sat a Republican government up in Washington, and they weren't doing a thing about it.

My people told me to have faith in God, and he would make everything come right. I read a lot of religious tracts, but I got so I didn't believe them. I figured that there was no use for a Negro to go to heaven, because if he went there it would only be to shine some white man's shoes.

I wish I could remember the exact date when I first attended a meeting of the Unemployment Council, and met up with a couple of members of the Communist Party. That date means a lot more to me than my birthday, or any other day in my life.

The workers in the South, mostly deprived of reading-matter, have developed a wonderful grapevine system for transmitting news. It was over this grapevine that we first heard that there were "reds" in town.

The foremen—when they talked about it—and the newspapers, and the big-shot Negroes in Birmingham, said that the "reds" were foreigners, and Yankees, and believed in killing people, and would get us in a lot of trouble. But out of all the talk I got a few ideas clear about the Reds. They believed in organizing and sticking together. They believed that we didn't have to have bosses on our backs. They believed that Negroes ought to have equal rights with whites. It all sounded O.K. to me. But I didn't meet any of the Reds for a long time.

One day in June, 1930, walking home from work, I came across some handbills put out by the Unemployment Council in Birmingham. They said: "Would you rather fight—or starve?" They called on the workers to come to a mass meeting at 3 o'clock.

Somehow I never thought of missing that meeting. I said to myself over and over: "It's war! It's war! And I might as well get into it right now!" I got to the meeting while a white fellow was speaking. I didn't get everything he said, but this much hit me and stuck with me: that the workers could only get things by fighting for them, and that the Negro and white workers had to stick together to get results. The speaker described the conditions of the Negroes in Birmingham, and I kept saying to myself: "That's it." Then a Negro spoke from the same platform, and somehow I knew that this was what I'd been looking for all my life.

At the end of the meeting I went up and gave my name. From that day to this, every minute of my life has been tied up with the workers' movement.

I joined the Unemployment Council, and some weeks later

the Communist Party. I read all the literature of the movement that I could get my hands on, and began to see my way more clearly.

I had some mighty funny ideas at first, but I guess that was only natural. For instance, I thought that we ought to start by getting all the big Negro leaders like DePriest and DuBois and Walter White into the Communist Party, and then we would have all the support we needed. I didn't know then that DePriest and the rest of the leaders of that type are on the side of the bosses, and fight as hard as they can against the workers. They don't believe in fighting against the system that produces Jim-Crowism. They stand up for that system, and try to preserve it, and so they are really on the side of Jim-Crowism and inequality. I got rid of all these ideas after I heard Oscar Adams and others like him speak in Birmingham.

That happened this way:

Birmingham had just put on a Community Chest drive. The whites gave and the Negroes gave. Some gave willingly, thinking it was really going to help feed the unemployed, and the rest had it taken out of their wages. There was mighty little relief handed out to the workers, even when they did get on the rolls. The Negroes only got about half what the whites got. Some of the workers waiting at the relief station made up a take-off on an old prison song. I remember that the first two lines of it went:

> I've counted the beans, babe,
> I've counted the greens. . . .

The Unemployment Council opened a fight for cash relief, and aid for single men, and equal relief for Negro and white. They called for a meeting in Capitol Park, and we gathered about the Confederate Monument, about 500 of us, white and Negro, and then we marched on the Community Chest headquarters. There were about 100 cops there. The officials of the Community Chest spoke, and said that the best thing for the Negroes to do was to go back to the farms. They tried very hard to give the white workers there the idea that if the Negroes went back to the farms, the whites would get a lot more relief.

Of course our leaders pointed out that the small farmers and share-croppers and tenants on the cotton-lands around Birmingham were starving, and losing their land and stock, and hundreds were drifting into the city in the hope of getting work.

Then Oscar Adams spoke up. He was the editor of the *Birmingham Reporter,* a Negro paper. What he said opened my eyes—but not in the way he expected. He said we shouldn't be misled by the leaders of the Unemployment Council, that we should go politely to the white bosses and officials and ask them for what they wanted, and do as they said.

Adams said: "We Negroes don't want social equality." I was furious. I said inside of myself: "Oscar Adams, we Negroes want social and every other kind of equality. There's no reason on God's green earth why we should be satisfied with anything less."

That was the end of any ideas I had that the big-shots among the recognized Negro leaders would fight for us, or really put up any struggle for equal rights. I knew that Oscar Adams and the people like him were among our worst enemies, especially dangerous because they work from inside our ranks and a lot of us get the idea that they are with us and of us.

I look back over what I've written about those days since I picked up the leaflet of the Unemployment Council, and wonder if I've really said what I mean. I don't know if I can get across to you the feeling that came over me whenever I went to a meeting of the Council, or of the Communist Party, and heard their speakers and read their leaflets. All my life I'd been sweated and stepped on and Jim-Crowed. I lay on my belly in the mines for a few dollars a week, and saw my pay stolen and slashed, and my buddies killed. I lived in the worst section of town, and rode behind the "Colored" signs on streetcars, as though there was something disgusting about me. I heard myself called "nigger" and "darky," and I had to say "Yes, sir" to every white man, whether he had my respect or not.

I had always detested it, but I had never known that anything could be done about it. And here, all of a sudden, I had found organizations in which Negroes and whites sat together, and worked together, and knew no difference of race or color. Here were organizations that weren't scared to come out for equality for the Negro people, and for the rights of the workers. The Jim-Crow system, the wage-slave system, weren't everlasting after all! It was like all of a sudden turning a corner on a dirty, old street and finding yourself facing a broad, shining highway.

The bosses, and the Negro misleaders like Oscar Adams, told us that these Reds were "foreigners" and "strangers" and that the Communist program wasn't acceptable to the workers in the South. I couldn't see that at all. The leaders of the Communist Party and the Unemployment Council seemed people very much like the ones I'd always been used to. They were workers, and they talked our language. Their talk sure sounded better to me than the talk of Oscar Adams, or the President of the Tennessee Coal, Iron and Railroad Co. who addressed us every once in a while. As for the program not being acceptable to us, I felt, and I know now, that the Communist program is the only program that the Southern workers—whites and Negroes both—can possibly accept in the long run. It's the only program that does justice to the Southern worker's ideas that everybody ought to have an equal chance, and that every man has rights that must be respected. . . .

We organized a number of block committees of the Unemployment Councils, and got rent and relief for a large number of families. We agitated endlessly for unemployment insurance.

In the middle of June, 1932, the state closed down all the relief stations. A drive was organized to send all the jobless to the farms.

We gave out leaflets calling for a mass demonstration at the courthouse to demand that the relief be continued. About 1000 workers came, 600 of them white. We told the commissioners we didn't intend to starve. We reminded them that $800,000 had been collected in the Community Chest drive. The commissioners said there wasn't a cent to be had.

But the very next day the commission voted $6,000 for relief to the jobless!

On the night of July 11, I went to the Post Office to get my mail. I felt myself grabbed from behind and turned to see a police officer.

I was placed in a cell, and was shown a large electric chair, and told to spill everything I knew about the movement. I refused to talk, and was held incommunicado for eleven days. Finally I smuggled out a letter through another prisoner, and the International Labor Defense got on the job.

Assistant Solicitor John Hudson rigged up the charge against me. . . .

The trial was set for January 16, 1933. The state of Georgia displayed the literature that had been taken from my room, and read passages of it to the jury. They questioned me in great detail. Did I believe that the bosses and government ought to pay insurance to unemployed workers? That Negroes should have complete equality with white people? Did I believe in the demand for the self-determination of the Black Belt—that the Negro people should be allowed to rule the Black Belt territory, kicking out the white landlords and government officials? Did I feel that the working-class could run the mills and mines and government? That it wasn't necessary to have bosses at all?

I told them I believed all of that—and more.

The courtroom was packed to suffocation. The I.L.D. attorneys, Benjamin J. Davis, Jr., and John H. Geer, two young Negroes—and I myself—fought every step of the way. We were not really talking to that judge, nor to those prosecutors, whose questions we were answering. Over their heads we talked to the white and Negro workers who sat on the benches, watching, listening, learning. And beyond them we talked to the thousands and millions of workers all over the world to whom this case was a challenge.

We demanded that Negroes be placed on jury rolls. We demanded that the insulting terms, "nigger" and "darky," be dropped in that court. We asserted the right of the workers to organize, to strike, to make their demands, to nominate candidates of their choice. We asserted the right of the Negro people to have complete equality in every field.

The state held that my membership in the Communist Party, my possession of Communist literature, was enough to send me to the electric chair. They said to the jury: "Stamp this damnable thing out now with a conviction that will automatically carry with it a penalty of electrocution."

And the hand-picked lily-white jury responded:

"We, the jury, find the defendant guilty as charged, but recommend that mercy be shown and fix his sentence at from 18 to 20 years."

I had organized starving workers to demand bread, and I was sentenced to live out my years on the chain-gang for it. But I knew that the movement itself would not stop. I spoke to the court and said:

"They can hold this Angelo Herndon and hundreds of others, but it will never stop these demonstrations on the part of Negro and white workers who demand a decent place to live in and proper food for their kids to eat."

I said: "You may do what you will with Angelo Herndon. You may indict him. You may put him in jail. But there will come thousands of Angelo Herndons. If you really want to do anything about the case, you must go out and indict the social system. But this you will not do, for your role is to defend the system under which the toiling masses are robbed and oppressed.

"You may succeed in killing one, two, even a score of working-class organizers. But you cannot kill the working class." . . .

The Negro—Friend or Foe
of Organized Labor?*

LESTER B. GRANGER

WHO HOLDS FIRST claim on the loyalty of the Negro worker—
his fellow workers who toil side by side with him, or his employer who hires and pays him, sometimes against the wishes
of white labor? Is it wisdom for Negro workers to protect the
interest of white labor, which has so often kicked them in the
face, or should they line up with employers against labor
unions, even to the point of scabbing and strike-breaking?

This is no longer an academic question to be disputed to
hairline extremities by soft-handed theoreticians. It is an urgent problem facing the black man in the street every day,
the answer to which will have tremendous effect upon the
fortunes of Negro populations in every large city of America
within the next ten years. Visible results may come even sooner, so amazing is the speed with which our national industrial
picture is being transformed under the pressure of economic
upheaval. Every day comes account of some new development in Negro-white labor relations—some new problem to
be solved presently by black workers for their permanent
profit or loss.

A few months ago the staff of a New Jersey white daily
newspaper protested to the publisher against unfair working
conditions. They were members of the Newspaper Guild, and
when their demands were not met they went out on strike.
On the staff, and a member of the Guild, was a Negro editorial writer who had been given his chance and promoted
from the ranks by the publisher personally. He refused to
strike with his fellow union members, stating that the publisher needed him and he could not desert his employer-friend in
this hour of need.

* Lester B. Granger, "The Negro—Friend or Foe of Organized
Labor?," *Opportunity*, XII (May, 1935), pp. 142-44. Reprinted with
permission from *Opportunity: Journal of Negro Life*, a publication of
the National Urban League, Inc.

In New York, on the other hand, sixty employees of a wholesale drug company went out on strike to protest the dismissal of three workers because of union activities. Among the strikers was a Negro who held an excellent job and stood high in the employer's favor. He walked out on strike, not because of any personal dissatisfaction, but because he resented the boss's attempt to break up the union—because he felt that his own job could not be safe unless his fellow workers were also secure.

Which Negro acted wisely? Was the drug clerk a scatterbrained young fool, as his friends advised, to risk his own prospects in joining with his white fellow workers? Was the newspaper man a treacherous scab, to violate his union pledge and betray the strike for better working conditions? It is a question which comes up with increasing frequency to plague the Negro worker employed with a small concern where close personal relationships are established between worker and boss.

Such individual problems, however, fade into relative insignificance beside the huge problem posed before Negro labor in the mass. For generations organized labor for the most part has been indifferent, if not actively hostile, to participation by black workers. This has been partly due to race prejudice, and partly due to that group selfishness typical of craft unionism. Recently there has been a change of attitude. As the great mass of America's workers have gradually become more intelligent regarding the nature of the struggle between Labor and Capital, they have begun to realize the essential solidarity of interests of all labor. There has been a decided movement away from craft toward industrial unionism; there are signs that race prejudice is weakening.

The partial success of the Randolph resolution at the 1934 A.F. of L. convention was one indication. A western local of the Railway Clerks Union recently defied the color bar of the International's constitution and admitted a Negro member. These and other events are faint cracks appearing in the solid wall of race prejudice which has heretofore baffled the attempts of Negroes to cooperate closely with white workers. Black labor's reaction to this new situation will largely determine the future of Negroes in the organized labor movement, and also influence the ultimate success of Labor's struggle against Capital.

The individual cases of the Negro newspaperman and the drug clerk are comparatively easy to judge. The former joined a union of fellow employees without color bar and pledged himself to support union action. He simply weighed the union's chances of winning and his own chances of finding another job against the ethics of the situation—and tossed ethics into the ashcan. The drug clerk, being younger and braver, kept faith with his fellow workers and his manhood.

A different situation faces Negro workers in industries where they have become established without the support of organized labor, and where organized labor is now beginning to woo their membership, more from reasons of self-defense than brotherly love. For instance, in the city of Dayton, Ohio, locals of the International Moulders Union during prosperous years discouraged the applications for membership of Negro foundry moulders, using the obvious expedient of boosting initiation fees to a prohibitive figure. Negroes found jobs at lower wages in open-shop foundries where the company union plan of employee organization was effective in keeping out the A.F. of L. union. Lean depression years have starved the International's treasuries, and now the Dayton locals are soliciting as members the Negroes whom they once rebuffed. Black workers refuse to join and stand by the company union.

There are a thousand colored foundrymen in that city, and upon their prosperity depends the economic security of black Dayton. What does that security demand—that Negroes repay the stupid prejudice of white moulders with an unrelenting opposition to organized action, or that they drop their justified grudge and seize this chance to establish better relations with white workers? Can Negroes trust this gesture of friendship by the International, or do they seriously imperil their present jobs when they desert the company union?

Traditional college-bred, white-collar leadership among Negroes has usually insisted the latter probability. A Chicago garment factory employs hundreds of Negroes, working and paying them by sub-union standards and offering them certain recreational and "welfare" services. The International Ladies' Garment Workers' Union tries vainly to organize the Sopkin employees and meets the opposition of numerous influential Negro citizens. Critics of the International say that its past policy in Chicago toward Negro workers has been unsatisfactory, and that undercover discrimination exists in locals even today. They urge Sopkin employees to stick to the company union until the International gives more complete proof of what protection it can and will offer. "Any job," they say, "is better than no job at all—even a sweatshop job. Our lower wage is the employer's profit, and that profit insures our job security." One inspired Sopkin employee even rushes into print with an article entitled, "Thumbs Down on Unions!"

The International's supporters and organizers denounce these "leaders" as paid mouthpieces of Big Money, or as short-sighted opportunists who betray the very cause they seek to protect. The International points to its record as one of the most liberal of all A. F. of L. organizations, to its membership of 6,000 Negroes in New York, to its rapid gains among the Negro workers of Cleveland and Philadelphia, as proof of the fact that the rights of colored union members would be fully protected. They warn that refusal of Negroes to join the organized movement now only widens the breach that may have existed formerly, and increases the danger that colored workers may be shut out of the industry almost entirely if and when Chicago is as successfully unionized as New York City. The air is black with charges and counter-charges, while, true to precedent, the Negro workers themselves give little or no serious thought to the problem which is ready to smack them in the face.

So with the rubber workers of Ohio, the tobacco workers of North Carolina, the steel workers of Pennsylvania, the longshoremen of California—the list can be multiplied indefinitely of instances where Negro workers have problems similar to these thrust upon them for immediate decision. Their decision is not made more easy by the conflicting advice coming from disputant groups of "leaders." The defeatists lament that industry holds no future for Negro workers and urge a hasty retreat back to the farm. The middle-of-the-roaders advise Negroes to stick with the employers and the company union until Labor's fight has been won or lost, when they can choose their new allegiance. Professional labor organizers insist that Negro workers should rush pell mell into the A. F. of L. ranks at first opportunity.

The truth is that none of this advice reaches the Negro's needs. It is perfectly true that there are industries where white workers, already organized, have fought bitterly the employment of Negroes and have barred them from unions. In such cases Negro labor has no alternative other than to stick with the employer and accept whatever protection is afforded by company unions. While accepting the company union, however, as a shelter in the time of storm, black workers must realize that the shelter won't last long—while the storm will. The company union does not, and cannot adequately protect the interests of workers, for it opposes the very things which true unionism seeks to produce—unity of all workers, freedom from employer interference, independence of leadership, and bargaining strength through numbers.

Therefore, even when forced to accept temporarily the dubious benefits of the company union, Negro workers must still seek a favorable opportunity to force terms on organized labor and enter its ranks. Sometimes no pressure is needed, as in the case of the I.L.G.W.U., which realized some time ago the necessity of organizing the thousands of Negro garment workers in the East. Sometimes a bitter lesson must be learned by white workers, as with the San Francisco dock workers, who barred Negroes from union membership until colored longshoremen helped to break the docks strike of 1934—after which they were admitted to unions to prevent future strike-breaking. Again, in times of crisis, Negro labor often has a chance to drive a bargain with organized labor and force concessions previously withheld. For instance, Negro longshoremen of Los Angeles refrained from strike-breaking on condition that they would be admitted freely to the union and receive their share of work—a bargain made and kept by the union.

Sometimes, for one reason or another, Negroes are unable or unwilling to join a union, but form separate organizations having an understanding with white workers regarding mutual protection of wages and hours. This is an arrangement adopted by motion picture projectionists in several large cities, but it is plainly a less satisfactory arrangement than full union membership.

He is a light-hearted optimist indeed who believes that all of the problems of Negro labor can be solved thus directly. Neither diplomacy, strategem nor threat is likely to have any effect, for instance, on the anti-Negro policy of the four railroad brotherhoods, aristocrats of American labor, which for fifty years have maintained an arrogant disdain for other groups of workers. There can be no parleying with the railway unions of the South which have bargained with railroad heads to put Negroes out of jobs—whose members have lain in ambush and murdered Negro trainmen in a terrorist campaign. Such unions as these—internationals and locals— Negroes must fight openly as enemies not only of black labor but of organized labor as a whole.

Against them there is a weapon of defense which Negro labor has not used enough in the past—legal action. With millions of taxpayers' dollars going into railway construction and public works projects, it is possible as never before for skilled legal talent to find ways of bringing suits on behalf of black workers which might hold up appropriations until justice is given them.

All of the above indicates the utter hopelessness of expecting the intellectuals and professionals of the race to plan the way for Negro labor. Their leadership is bound inevitably to end up in a blind alley of futile compromise. The Negro Workers' Councils created by the National Urban League are a frank recognition of this fact, and an attempt to set up a form of organization in which workers, without the interference of outsiders, may meet to discuss their mutual problems and learn ways of facing them. They are a vehicle for wider spread of workers' education among Negroes, which is the first step toward workers' action. In Pittsburgh and Columbus, in New York and Newark, in Raleigh and Greensboro, in St. Louis and Kansas City, in Atlanta and New Orleans—all over the country these Councils are forming groups of black workers who are facing soberly a future of bitter struggle in the American industrial scene.

They realize that there can be no neutrality for Negroes in this struggle. In any bitter conflict the neutral becomes the buffer, and Belgium discovered in 1914 how hapless is the buffer's fate. If Negro workers would avoid a similar fate they must choose shortly whether they will be friend or foe of organized labor.

Essential to a proper decision is their understanding of the aims and methods of unions—their realization that Negroes are not the only group unfairly treated by unions, nor the only workers dissatisfied with labor leadership. They must learn that organized labor and A. F. of L. are not necessarily synonymous, but sometimes antithetical—that to uphold the interest of the one may be to attack the plan of the other.

In short, when Negro workers assume their own leadership and attack their own problems they will recognize that a blow at organized labor is a blow at their own safety. Only continued stupidity on the part of white labor leadership can prevent black workers from lining up with the cause of organized labor.

2. MASS MARCHES BEGIN

National Negro Congress*
The Call

A New Crisis Confronts the Negro People

TODAY THE WHOLE of the United States faces the crisis of mass unemployment, lower standards of living, hunger and misery. For Negroes this crisis shakes the foundation of their social and economic existence in the nation. For them six terrible years of depression have meant an intolerable double exploitation both as Negroes and as workers.

Negro workers on farms, in factories and in households as servants see their wages fall while prices increase. Discrimination against them has increased on the job. They can no longer be certain that tomorrow will find them employed. Negro miners are attacked and railroad workers are intimidated by white gangs inspired by bosses into quitting work; and an increasing number of barriers are erected against Negroes getting jobs by unions, which, following anti-working class policies, deny Negroes union privileges and union membership. Negro women are being literally driven out of industrial employment. Negro youth find less and less opportunity to earn a living. This growing futility stunts the growth of a whole generation of Negro people. On government building projects discrimination against employment of Negro artisans continues. Even so-called "Negro" jobs are no longer available. Unemployment spreads, and in every section of the nation the Negro is fast becoming a jobless race.

The Negro farm population in the South is fast becoming landless. We face the fact that within the past fifteen years not only have Negroes not gained in land ownership but they have lost possession of more than four million acres of farm land; and, furthermore, there is a steady decline in the already pitiable farm wage.

* From the original call to the Congress held in 1935. The Congress adopted resolutions urging unionization of Negro women workers, desegregation of public accommodations and schools, protection of migrant workers, and anti-lynch legislation. They also approved resolutions against war and fascism.

Negro youth is deprived of adequate educational opportunities. A striking manifestation of this appears in the professional and technical fields. Moreover, the present marked retrenchment in education affects Negro students in the South especially, since their separate schools, inadequate at best, are always curtailed first and disproportionately.

A SOCIAL AND POLITICAL CONTRAST

Not hunger and poverty alone plague the existence of Black America. The denial of citizenship rights creates a double burden. The ballot, the most elemental right of a citizen, is effectively denied two-thirds of the entire Negro population. In the courts of the land, the Negro is denied justice. He is illegally kept from jury service, and made to face daily unfair trials and inhuman sentences. Negroes are mobbed and lynched while Congress cynically refuses to enact a federal anti-lynching law. They are excluded from public places, even from restaurants in the nation's Capitol. All of these manifestations of injustice have become more severe.

Negroes in America observe with deep indignation the war on Ethiopia by fascist Italy, threatening, as it does, to throw the entire world into a terrible war. The memory of the human slaughter of the last war, of Jim-Crow stevedore battalions for Negroes, of Negro Gold Star Mothers forced into Jim-Crow ships to visit the graves of their dead sons overseas, makes Negroes oppose war. The full knowledge of the impoverishment which war and fascism bring to the entire nation make them strong in their desire for peace, resolute in their fight against war and fascism.

TRADITIONS OF NEGROES REFUTE MEEK ACCEPTANCE

The problems facing the Negro make him more determined to struggle against injustice. The unconquerable spirits of Nat Turner and Denmark Vesey, of Frederick Douglass, Harriet Tubman and Sojourner Truth symbolize a spirit no less alive today. We see semblances of these traditions today in the struggles of the National Association for the Advancement of Colored People to win for the Negro equal school facilities, to win for the Negro in the South freedom from mob-violence and lynching; in the fight of the National Urban Leagues and the International Brotherhood of Sleeping Car Porters to organize Negro workers into militant unions. That spirit is alive today in thousands of Negro churches where voices are lifted up in defense of Ethiopia. It lives in the efforts of hundreds of thousands of Negro citizens to win complete freedom for Angelo Herndon and the Scottsboro Boys. In hundreds of communities Negro citizens have organized in many varied ways, fighting against social and economic oppression. And today larger and larger numbers of men and women of other races are beginning to feel the common interest of the oppressed. White sharecroppers of Arkansas and Alabama no less than white intellectuals and workers of the North, are joining in the fight for Negro rights.

PRESENT CRISIS CALLS FOR UNITED ACTION

Every problem presented here calls for greater united action. For this reason we who sign this declaration call for the united action of all organizations and individuals to whom it is addressed, to work for a National Negro Congress to be composed of delegates representing all Negro organizations, and such other organizations—mixed or white—as will take a stand for equal rights for the Negro. This Congress is called to meet in Chicago, Illinois on February 14, 1936, on the historic occasion of the anniversary of the birth of Frederick Douglass.

We believe that this Congress will furnish the opportunity for considering the problems that face the Negro people and that a plan of action—the collective wisdom of all freedom-loving sections of our population—can be intelligently worked out for the solution of these problems. By unity of action we can create a nation-wide public opinion which will force real consideration from public officials, such as no single organization can hope to muster. The sincerity of purpose of all organizations to whom this call is addressed assures harmonious cooperation in the common cause for justice.

WHAT WILL A NEGRO CONGRESS DO?

The NATIONAL NEGRO CONGRESS will be no new organization, nor does it seek to usurp the work of existing organizations. It will seek rather to accomplish unity of action of existing organizations.

It is with these objectives clearly in mind that we propose for discussion and action by the Congress the issues outlined below:

1. The right of Negroes to jobs at decent living wages and for the right to join all trade unions. For the right to equal wages and equal labor conditions with other workers. For the or-

ganization of Negro workers with their fellow white workers into democratically controlled trade unions.

2. Relief and security for every needy Negro family; and, for genuine social and unemployment insurance without discrimination.

3. Aid to the Negro farm population, to ease the burden of debts and taxation; for the right of farmers, tenants and sharecroppers to organize and bargain collectively.

4. A fight against lynching, mob violence and police brutality; for enactment of a federal anti-lynching law; for the right to vote, serve on juries and enjoy complete civil liberty.

5. The right of Negro youth to equal opportunity in education and in the economic life of the community.

6. For complete equality for Negro women; for their right, along with all women, to equal pay for equal work; for their right to a suitable environment for themselves and their children—an environment which demands adequate housing, good schools, and recreational facilities; for their right to organize as consumers.

7. To oppose war and fascism, the attempted subjugation of Negro people in Ethiopia, the oppression of colonial nations throughout the world; for the independence of Ethiopia.

*The March on Washington Movement**

A. PHILIP RANDOLPH

FELLOW MARCHERS AND delegates to the Policy Conference of the March on Washington Movement and Friends:

We have met at an hour when the sinister shadows of war are lengthening and becoming more threatening. As one of the sections of the oppressed darker races, and representing a part of the exploited millions of the workers of the world, we are deeply concerned that the totalitarian legions of Hitler, Hirohito, and Mussolini do not batter the last bastions of democracy. We know that our fate is tied up with the fate of the democratic way of life. And so, out of the depth of our

* Excerpts from Keynote Address to the Policy Conference of the March on Washington Movement (Detroit, Michigan, September 26, 1942). Reprinted by permission of A. Philip Randolph.

hearts, a cry goes up for the triumph of the United Nations. But we would not be honest with ourselves were we to stop with a call for a victory of arms alone. We know this is not enough. We fight that the democratic faiths, values, heritages and ideals may prevail.

Unless this war sounds the death knell to the old Anglo-American empire systems, the hapless story of which is one of exploitation for the profit and power of a monopoly-capitalist economy, it will have been fought in vain. Our aim then must not only be to defeat nazism, fascism, and militarism on the battlefield but to win the peace, for democracy, for freedom and the Brotherhood of Man without regard to his pigmentation, land of his birth or the God of his fathers.

We therefore sharply score the Atlantic Charter as expressing a vile and hateful racism and a manifestation of the tragic and utter collapse of an old, decadent democratic political liberalism which worshipped at the shrine of a world-conquering monopoly-capitalism. This system grew fat and waxed powerful off the flesh, blood, sweat and tears of the tireless toilers of the human race and the sons and daughters of color in the underdeveloped lands of the world.

When this war ends, the people want something more than the dispersal of equality and power among individual citizens in a liberal, political democratic system. They demand with striking comparability the dispersal of equality and power among the citizen-workers in an economic democracy that will make certain the assurance of the good life—the more abundant life—in a warless world.

But, withal this condition of freedom, equality and democracy is not the gift of the gods. It is the task of men, yes, men, brave men, honest men, determined men.

This is why we have met in Detroit in this Policy Conference of the March on Washington Movement. We have come to set forth our goals, declare our principles, formulate our policies, plan our program and discuss our methods, strategy, and tactics. This is the job of every movement which seeks to map out clearly the direction in which it is going as well as build up and strengthen the motivations.

Now our goals are what we hope to attain. They are near and remote, immediate and ultimate. This requires the long and short range program.

Thus our feet are set in the path toward equality—economic, political and social and racial. Equality is the heart and essence of democracy, freedom and justice. Without equality of opportunity in industry, in labor unions, schools and colleges, government, politics and before the law, without equality in social relations and in all phases of human endeavor, the Negro is certain to be consigned to an inferior status. There must be no dual standards of justice, no dual rights, privileges, duties or responsibilities of citizenship. No dual forms of freedom.

If Negroes are not the equal of white citizens, then they are unequal, either above or below them. But if they are to set the standards, Negroes will be below them. And if Negroes are considered unequal on a sub-standard basis, then they will receive unequal or inferior treatment.

Justice for the slave is not the same justice for the freeman. Treatment of a thoroughbred is not the same as the treatment of a workhorse.

But our nearer goals include the abolition of discrimination, segregation, and jim-crow in the Government, the Army, Navy, Air Corps, U. S. Marine, Coast Guard, Women's Auxiliary Army Corps and the Waves, and defense industries; the elimination of discriminations in hotels, restaurants, on public transportation conveyances, in educational, recreational, cultural, and amusement and entertainment places such as theatres, beaches and so forth.

We want the full works of citizenship with no reservations. We will accept nothing less.

But goals must be achieved. They are not secured because it is just and right that they be possessed by Negro or white people. Slavery was not abolished because it was bad and unjust. It was abolished because men fought, bled and died on the battlefield in the Union Army and conquered the Confederate forces in the Civil War. Of course slavery was uneconomic and would have disappeared in time but this economic axiom involves no moral judgment.

Therefore, if Negroes secure their goals, immediate and remote, they must win them and to win them they must fight, sacrifice, suffer, go to jail and, if need be, die for them. These rights will not be given. They must be taken.

Democracy was fought for and taken from political royalists—the kings. Industrial democracy, the rights of the workers to organize and designate the representatives of their own choosing to bargain collectively is being won and taken from the economic royalists—big business.

Now the realization of goals and rights by a nation, race or class requires belief in and loyalty to principles and policies. Principles represent the basic and deep human and social convictions of a man or a people such as democracy, equality, freedom of conscience, the deification of the state, protestantism. Policies rest upon principles. Concretely a policy sets forth one's position on vital public questions such as political affiliations, religious alliances. The March on Washington Movement must be opposed to partisan political commitments, religious or denominational alliances. We cannot sup with the Communists, for they rule or ruin any movement. This is their policy. Our policy must be to shun them. This does not mean that Negro Communists may not join the March on Washington Movement.

As to the composition of our movement. Our policy is that it be all-Negro, and pro-Negro but not anti-white, or anti-Semitic or anti-labor, or anti-Catholic. The reason for this policy is that all oppressed people must assume the responsibility and take the initiative to free themselves. Jews must wage their battle to abolish anti-semitism. Catholics must wage their battle to abolish anti-catholicism. The workers must wage their battle to advance and protect their interests and rights.

But this does not mean that because Jews must take the responsibility and initiative to solve their own problems that they should not seek the cooperation and support of Gentiles, or that Catholics should not seek the support of Negroes, or that the workers should not attempt to enlist the backing of Jews, Catholics, and Negroes in their fight to win a strike; but the main reliance must be upon the workers themselves. By the same token because Negroes build an all-Negro movement such as the March, it does not follow that our movement should not call for the collaboration of Jews, Catholics, trade unions and white liberals to help restore the President's Fair Employment Practice Committee to its original status of independence, with responsibility to the President. That was done. William Green, President of the A. F. of L. and Philip Murray, President of C. I. O. were called upon to send telegrams to the President to restore the Committee to its independence. Both responded. Their cooperation had its effects. Workers have formed citizens committees to back them while on strike, but this does not mean that they take those citizens into their unions as members. No, not at all.

And while the March on Washington Movement may find it advisable to form a citizens committee of friendly white citizens to give moral support to a fight against the poll tax or white primaries, it does not imply that these white citizens or citizens of any racial group should be taken into the March on Washington Movement as members. The essential value of an all-Negro movement such as the March on Washington is that it helps to create faith by Negroes in Negroes. It develops a sense of self-reliance with Negroes depending on Negroes in vital matters. It helps to break down the slave psychology and inferiority-complex in Negroes which comes and is nourished with Negroes relying on white people for direction and support. This inevitably happens in mixed organizations that are supposed to be in the interest of the Negro.

Now, in every community there are many and varied problems. Some are specialized and others are generalized. For instance the problem of anti-semitism is a specialized one and must be attacked by the Jews through a Jewish organization which considers this question its major interest. The organization of the unorganized workers and the winning of wage increases, shorter hours, and better working conditions, is a specialized problem of workers which must be handled through a trade union composed of workers, not lawyers, doctors, preachers, or business men or by an organization of Catholics or Negroes.

The problem of lynching is a specialized one and Negroes must take the responsibility and initiative to solve it, because Negroes are the chief victims of it just as the workers are the victims of low wages and must act to change and raise them.

But the problems of taxation, sanitation, health, a proper school system, an efficient fire department, and crime are generalized problems. They don't only concern the workers or Jews or Negroes or Catholics, but everybody and hence it is sound and proper social strategy and policy for all of these groups in the community to form a generalized or composite movement, financed by all, to handle these problems that are definitely general in nature. Neither group can depend upon the other in dealing with a general social problem. No one group can handle it properly. But this same general organization could not be depended upon to fight for the abolition of segregation of Negroes in the government, or to abolish company unionism in the interest of the workers, or to fight anti-semitism. Its structure is too general to qualify it to attempt to solve a special problem. And, by the same logic, the Zionist Movement, or the Knights of Columbus, or the Longshoremen's Union is too special in structure and purpose to be qualified to deal with such a general problem as crime, or health, or education in a community.

Therefore, while the March on Washington Movement is interested in the general problems of every community and will lend its aid to help solve them, it has as its major interest and task the liberation of the Negro people, and this is sound social economy. It is in conformity with the principle of the division of labor. No organization can do everything. Every organization can do something, and each organization is charged with the social responsibility to do that which it can do, it is built to do.

I have given quite some time to the discussion of this question of organizational structure and function and composition, because the March on Washington Movement is a mass movement of Negroes which is being built to achieve a definite objective, and is a departure from the usual pattern of Negro efforts and thinking. As a rule, Negroes do not choose to be to themselves in anything, they are only to themselves as a result of compulsive segregation. Negroes are together voluntarily for the same reason workers join voluntarily into a trade union. But because workers only join trade unions, does not mean that the very same workers may not join organizations composed of some non-workers, such as art museums or churches or fraternal lodges that have varying purposes. This same thing is true of Negroes. Because Negroes only can join the March on Washington Movement, does not indicate that Negroes in the M.O.W.M. may not join an inter-racial golf club or church or Elks Lodge or debating society or trade union.

No one would claim that a society of Filipinos is undemocratic because it does not take in Japanese members, or that Catholics are anti-Jewish because the Jesuits won't accept Jews as members or that trade unions are not liberal because they deny membership to employers. Neither is the March on Washington Movement undemocratic because it confines its members to Negroes. Now this reasoning would not apply to a public school or a Pullman Car because these agencies are public in nature and provide a service which is necessary to all of the people of a community.

Now, the question of policy which I have been discussing involves, for example, the March on Washington Movement's position on the war. We say that the Negro must fight for his democratic rights now for after the war it may be too late. This is our policy on the Negro and the war. But this policy raises the question of method, programs, strategy, and tactics; namely, how is this to be done. It is not sufficient to say that Negroes must fight for their rights now, during the war. Some methods must be devised, program set up, and strategy outlined.

This Policy Conference is designed to do this very thing. The first requirement to executing the policies of the March on Washington Movement is to have something to execute them with. This brings me to the consideration of organization. Organization supplies the power. The formulation of policies and the planning process furnish direction. Now there is organization and organization. Some people say, for instance, Negroes are already organized and they cite, The Sisters of the Mysterious Ten, The Sons and Daughters of I Will Arise, the Holy Rollers, the social clubs, and so forth. But these organizations are concerned about the individual interest of helping the sick and funeralizing the dead or providing amusement and recreation.

They deal with no social or racial problem which concerns the entire people. The Negro people as a whole is not interested in whether Miss A. plays Contract Bridge on Friday or not, or whether the deacon of the Methodist Church has a 200 or 500 dollar casket when he dies. These are personal questions. But the Negro race is concerned about Negroes being refused jobs in defense plants, or whether a Negro can purchase a lower in a Pullman Car, or whether the U. S. Treasury segregates Negro girls. Thus, while it is true Negroes are highly organized, the organizations are not built to deal with and manipulate the mechanics of power. Nobody cares how many Whist Clubs or churches or secret lodges Negroes establish because they are not compulsive or coercive. They don't seek to transform the socio-economic racial milieu. They accept and do not challenge conditions with an action program.

Hence, it is apparent that the Negro needs more than organization. He needs mass organization with an action program, aggressive, bold and challenging in spirit. Such a movement is our March on Washington.

Our first job then is actually to organize millions of Negroes, and build them into block systems with captains so that they may be summoned to action over night and thrown into physical motion. Without this type of organization, Negroes will never develop mass power which is the most effective weapon a minority people can wield. Witness the strategy and maneuver of the people of India with mass civil disobedience and non-cooperation and the marches to the sea to make salt. It may be said that the Indian people have not won their freedom. This is so, but they will win it. . . .

We must develop huge demonstrations because the world is used to big dramatic affairs. They think in terms of hundreds of thousands and millions and billions. Millions of Germans and Russians clash on the Eastern front. Billions of dollars are appropriated at the twinkling of an eye. Nothing little counts.

Besides, the unusual attracts. We must develop a series of marches of Negroes at a given time in a hundred or more cities throughout the country, or stage a big march of a hundred thousand Negroes on Washington to put our cause into the main stream of public opinion and focus the attention of world interests. This is why India is in the news.

Therefore, our program is in part as follows:

1. A national conference for the integration and expression of the collective mind and will of the Negro masses.

2. The mobilization and proclamation of a nation-wide series of mass marches on the City Halls and City Councils to awaken the Negro masses and center public attention upon the grievances and goals of the Negro people and serve as training and discipline of the Negro masses for the more strenuous struggle of a March on Washington, if, as, and when an affirmative decision is made thereon by the Negro masses of the country through our national conference.

3. A march on Washington as an evidence to white America that black America is on the march for its rights and means business.

4. The picketing of the White House following the March on Washington and maintain the said picket line until the country and the world recognize the Negro has become of age and will sacrifice his all to be counted as men, free men.

This program is drastic and exacting. It will test our best mettle and stamina and courage. Let me warn you that in these times of storm and stress, this program will be opposed. Our Movement therefore must be well-knit together. It must have moral and spiritual vision, understanding, and wisdom . . .

PART VI

The Birth of a Movement

INTRODUCTION

THE STYLE OF the Negro protest movement changed drastically in the 1960's with the large-scale use of the technique of non-violent resistance. Other methods of protest were by no means abandoned, but a qualitative change took place when the youth shifted the emphasis from the slow process of court suits to direct confrontations.

The first decisive step toward nonviolent mass action, however, was taken by an adult—a quiet, reserved woman named Mrs. Rosa Parks who on December 4, 1955 refused to give up her seat on a Montgomery, Alabama, city bus and move to the "colored section." This action signaled the beginning of a new surge of activity in the Negro movement. Before the city officials and white civic leaders of Montgomery knew what had happened to them 42,000 Negro men and women were walking to work each morning and home each evening. A black boycott of the city transportation system was in full swing. The city buses were empty for 381 days. Boycott demands were a guarantee of courteous treatment by bus operators, seating on a first come first served basis with Negroes sitting from the back toward the front and whites from the front toward the back and employment of Negro drivers on predominantly Negro routes. The Montgomery Improvement Association (MIA) was formed to coordinate boycott activities and its twice-weekly mass meetings were overflowing.

When the city proposed a compromise solution which did not include Negro employment, it was rejected. In one church the pastor and assistant pastor voted to accept the compromise, but the mass meeting voted 3,998 to two to reject it. Indignation and demands for action swept everyone

251

along, and that pastor joined 90 others in jail for violation of Alabama's anti-boycott law. Also jailed were Mrs. Parks, Rev. Martin Luther King Jr., the president of MIA, and E. D. Nixon, the initiator of the boycott. Just over a year after it had begun the boycott ended with the desegregation of the city buses on December 21, 1956, after the Supreme Court had ruled bus segregation illegal.

The kind of movement which has developed in the past few years was sparked by this mass action, by the fact that the total Negro population of a Southern city moved together for a common goal, by the fact that the motivation of the Negroes of Montgomery struck a chord for Negroes throughout the country. Mrs. Parks was tired of moving to the back of the bus, just fed up. Other black people in Montgomery and elsewhere were fed up too.

Usually the Supreme Court decision in *Brown v. Board of Education* is thought of in connection with the beginning of the current civil rights movement. But the decision itself did not hurtle Negroes into the dramatic action to secure equal education, nor was it a command to Southern school officials to end segregation immediately. As a matter of fact in a footnote to the decision the court raised questions as to how much authority it had and how to proceed toward getting compliance.[1] These questions cast some doubt on how meaningful the decision would be. It was, however, a landmark decision in that it overturned a legal policy established in 1896 in *Plessy v. Ferguson* that requirements of the 14th Amendment were satisfied by providing "separate but equal" facilities for Negroes. For many years the civil rights movement had accepted the policy of separate but equal in its own drive. It had waged a fight, which it never won, for equal pay for teachers and for equal school facilities, and it had fought for equal library, recreational facilities and health services. Just as the *Plessy v. Ferguson* decision had affected the tenor of the Negro struggle so did the decision which struck it down.

In a series of decisions the Supreme Court had led up to *Brown* by ruling first that white universities must admit Negroes to graduate facilities, if a desired course of study was not available in a Negro institution. Then, in 1948, in *Sipuel v. Board of Regents of the University of Oklahoma,* the Court ruled on the same basis that Negroes must be admitted to state universities. In 1950 the Court ruled in *Sweatt v. Painter* that a separate Negro law school, established for Sweatt after he sued for admission to the University of Texas

---

[1] See pp. 261-68 for text of decision.

Law School, was unequal not only in physical facilities and curriculum, but in reputation and opportunity for stimulating professional contact. Also, in 1950, the Court ruled in *Mc- Laurin v. Oklahoma State Regents* that the state violated the separate but equal doctrine in requiring isolated cafeteria and classroom seats of Negro students which produced an inequality in educational opportunity.

The Brown decision, which in effect said that separate schools were *ipso facto un*equal, gave a positive thrust to the movement which took up this legal challenge to segregation, and began to struggle for full equality once again.[2] *Brown* also influenced the movement in a negative way, for the very fact that little progress toward school desegregation had been made by 1960, six years after the decision, was a motivating factor in the student protest.

There had been in the intervening years attempts by NAACP chapters to encourage Negro parents to send their children to "white" schools, and there had been retaliation against those who did. There had also been three mass marches to Washington on the school issue. On May 18, 1957, the anniversary of the *Brown* decision, about 35,000 people attended a Prayer Pilgrimage for integrated schools sponsored by both Northern and Southern civil rights leaders, the first such joint effort for a mass demonstration. In the next two years youth marches for integrated schools were held. In 1959, 400,000 signatures were presented to Congressman Charles Diggs petitioning the President and Congress for a program to insure the orderly and speedy integration of schools. But the time for marches for integrated schools was over.

The legal struggle itself dragged on in the years immediately following the *Brown* decision. Southern school boards and state governments brought suit after suit to emasculate *Brown*. Under the theory of "interposition" they devised a wide variety of schemes to get around the intent of the decision. And in those few localities, where at least minimum compliance was attempted, the South resorted to intimidation and violence to keep white schools white.

But the *Brown* decision provided the setting for major confrontations between the federal government and the states,

[2] While the concept of separate but equal did provide a framework for much civil rights activity, I do not mean to imply that the movement relied on this theory exclusively. There were struggles for the desegregation of transportation, particularly after the decision in *Morgan v. Virginia* and a campaign was conducted for nondiscriminatory hiring and for integration of the armed forces. However, there was a marked shift in attitude when the concept of separate but equal was abandoned by the Court.

and the Negro and white population of several Southern cities. *New York Times* reporter Anthony Lewis, in a study of school desegregation, points out that there were rapid steps taken toward desegregation in Kansas, Arizona, Washington, D.C. and Baltimore. "Altogether, in the years 1954, 1955, 1956 several hundred school districts throughout the country abandoned racially segregated classes." However, Lewis says that by 1956 "after a first calm and responsible reaction to the Supreme Court decision, most of the political leaders of the South had come around to a position of defiance." [3]

An example is Clinton, Tennessee, where the school board members and other white citizens faced down a mob led by John Kasper in September of 1956, but where the high school was bombed in 1958. It was in 1956, however, that Autherine Lucy's presence set off rioting at the University of Alabama and University authorities forced her withdrawal. The federal government did not respond to the University's request to Attorney General Herbert Brownell for aid. In 1962 James Meredith entered the University of Mississippi despite serious rioting, but federal troops had been called out by President Kennedy. Perhaps as shocking as the inability of the federal government to prevent riots especially such as that at the University of Mississippi [4] is the fact that one county in the United States had no public schools at all from 1959 to 1964. Prince Edward County in Virginia closed its schools in 1959 rather than desegregate them, and did not reopen them until the Supreme Court ruled that they must. Seventeen hundred Negro children had no schooling from 1959 until 1963 when Negroes formed The Prince Edward County Free School which operated from Fall, 1963 to June, 1964.

Little Rock, Arkansas, was the site of a confrontation of major significance to the future movement, for the whole world read about the 15-year-old Negro girl who in 1957 was turned away from Little Rock Central High School by a National Guardsman into a white mob screaming, "Lynch her! Lynch her!" "Drag her over to this tree! Let's take care of the nigger." People the world over read it and Negroes

[3] Anthony Lewis and The New York Times, *Portrait of a Decade: The Second American Revolution* (New York: Random House, 1964), p. 33, 43.

[4] There was an understanding between Attorney General Robert Kennedy and Mississippi Governor Ross Barnett that Mississippi law enforcement officers would maintain calm. I will never forget the horror of watching President Kennedy on television appeal to white Mississippians' sense of honor at the very moment that the federalized National Guard was near to being overwhelmed by an on-rushing mob and shots were ringing out on the campus. Two journalists were killed on the campus that night.

read it, and Negroes, particularly those who were in high school themselves, did not forget.

Then on February 1, 1960, it started. Four young students at A and T College in Greensboro, North Carolina, decided that they, too, had had enough. They went to the local Woolworth store where they could buy pencils, but could not eat and sat down at the white-only lunch counter until they were arrested.

The "sit-in" technique had been developed many years earlier primarily by members of the Congress of Racial Equality who conducted successful campaigns against discriminatory lunch counters and restaurants as early as 1943 in Chicago, and then in 1949 and 1953 in St. Louis and Baltimore. The NAACP Youth Council in Oklahoma City conducted sit-ins in 1958.

But it was in 1960 that sit-ins caught on. In the next few weeks after February 1, the sit-ins spread to a dozen or more Southern cities with nearby Negro colleges. The students had begun to move. In the next two years the technique was refined and developed almost to guerilla war proportions. In February of 1960, in Orangeburg, South Carolina 1,000 students marched through downtown and over 350 were arrested and placed in an open-air stockade. In the rain they sang the "Star-Spangled Banner" and held a prayer meeting. Two years later in Atlanta, Georgia, students from the Atlanta University complex staged a succession of sit-ins at all of the downtown chain and drug stores timed to the split second, with a chain of command running from lieutenant on down, and utilizing walkie-talkies to communicate between sit-in groups downtown and the command post in the Negro community.

Estimates are that nearly 20,000 persons were arrested in direct action demonstrations across the South between 1960 and 1963. The situation roused Northerners to support action —pickets at Northern branches and headquarters of chains with segregated Southern outlets and fund-raising for bail— and, more significantly, it stirred Northern campuses into a vigorous pursuit of social change. The Student Nonviolent Coordinating Committee, which started in April, 1960 as a coordinating body made up of representatives of the dozens of "protest areas" of the South, was the precursor of many Northern student groups and protests. Bayard Rustin, civil rights activist, credited the Southern sit-in movement with having "banished the ugliest features of McCarthyism from the American campus and resurrected political debate," [5] as it galvanized white students into action.

The aims of the Southern protest were quickly broadened

[5] Bayard Rustin, "From Protest to Politics: The Future of the Civil Rights Movement," *Commentary*, 40 (February, 1964), p. 28.

to include areas other than the lunch counters. There were wade-ins at beaches, kneel-ins at churches, stand-ins at theaters. In many places city-wide committees were formed, as in Nashville where the Nashville movement conducted massive demonstrations throughout the Spring of 1963 for an "open city," that is, desegregation of all public facilities.

The courage of the students who were taunted, clubbed, tear-gassed and jailed in the course of their sit-ins, marches and picket lines engendered adult participation in many cities. In the Atlanta campaign, for example, Negro businesses supplied hot coffee and lunches to the picket lines and Negro taxis ran free ferry services from campus to lunch counter. In every city, churches were the meeting centers and the ministers, reluctant at first, were swept along.

Encouragement of adult participation had also come from the Southern Christian Leadership Conference (SCLC) founded in 1957 as the Southern Leadership Conference on Transportation and Non-violent Integration. The Rev. Martin Luther King Jr., its president and leading exponent of the philosophy of nonviolence, had been catapulted to national fame as head of the Montgomery Improvement Association which conducted the Montgomery bus boycott. In a history of the SCLC, L.D. Reddick wrote that "in a sense SCLC was a child of the MIA." "In another sense," he said, "SCLC was the organizational vehicle that was required for Martin Luther King after he had achieved national prominence during the Montgomery protest. In order not to waste the public build-up or to limit the voice of this new spokesman to one locality, some Southwide body was a logical consequence." SCLC's strongest base was in Birmingham, where immediately after the Supreme Court decision declaring bus segregation illegal in the Montgomery case the city's Negroes under the leadership of Rev. Fred L. Shuttlesworth began testing Birmingham bus segregation. In May, 1956, the NAACP was outlawed in Alabama, and in answer the Alabama Christian Movement for Human Rights was formed with Shuttlesworth as president. The ACMHR and groups which had conducted bus boycotts in cities like Baton Rouge, Louisiana and Tallahassee, Florida, formed the bases of SCLC.

After the 1960 sit-ins began Dr. King counseled the students and addressed the student protest leaders at the conference of the Temporary Student Nonviolent Coordinating Committee organized by SCLC's executive secretary Ella J. Baker at Raleigh, North Carolina, in April, 1960.

The nonviolent technique (and ethic for many) which propelled the direct action demonstrations of the early sixties was never played out without the counterpoint of violence. What thrilled and astounded Northern sympathizers about the nonviolent movement—that Negroes stood tall and walked through screaming armed mobs to the courthouse or school in quiet, dignified demonstrations of determination, courage and *will*—infuriated their enemies, i.e., much of the white South. Thus, while there had already been an adult movement on the rise, the student movement of 1960, generated even more activity as a result of its direct action protests.

In all of the mass demonstrations of 1960 through 1963, a high point for mass marches and mass arrests, the demonstrators were nonviolent, but the police were not. In Danville one bloody night 47 out of 65 demonstrators received emergency medical treatment. In Birmingham police washed demonstrators head over heels down the streets with high-powered fire hoses, and state troopers beat Negroes sitting on their porches back into their houses with swinging billy clubs. That was in the summer of 1963, when movement demands were employment, and in Birmingham, desegregation of department store fitting rooms and restaurants. Law enforcement officials by no means had a monopoly on violence against demonstrators. Throughout the rural South Negro churches, where movement mass meetings were held, were burned to the ground: homes were fire-bombed and shot into. On May 10 in Birmingham the demonstration headquarters, the A.D. Gaston motel, and the home of Rev. A.D. King, one of the demonstration leaders, were bombed. The next night, in response, more than 2,500 Negroes threw bricks at firemen and policemen, and overturned taxis and police cars, and set them afire.

On June 12, 1963, Mississippi State NAACP field secretary Medgar Evers was ambushed outside his home in Jackson and killed. Gov. Ross Barnett visited Evers' accused killer, Byron de la Beckwith, in jail, and Beckwith, acquitted, still mutters threats to civil rights workers in and around his home town of Greenwood, Mississippi. Four little Negro girls were killed in Sunday School at the 16th Street Baptist Church of Birmingham when bombs were thrown through its windows. The scenes of these events, shown on nationwide television and publicized around the world, disturbed the national conscience at home, and damaged the United States' reputation abroad.

Sometimes the violence the Negroes faced was direct action by the law enforcement officers, sometimes it came because of official inaction. The police, though alerted to the arrival of a desegregated bus at the Birmingham bus terminal in 1961, stayed out of sight until a white mob had had time to vent its fury on the Freedom Riders.

In many situations, particularly in the rural South, there is collusion between officials and white citizenry in carrying out acts of violence, in encouragement of acts of violence, and in the creation of a general atmosphere in which violence is condoned. Sheriff Z.T. Matthews of Baker County in rural Southwest, Georgia, told the U.S. Commission on Civil Rights that "it's fear that keeps the niggers down." Once the Negroes had begun to brave the mobs and the police dogs in nonviolent demonstrations they lost that fear and would not stay down.

As mass demonstrations for public accommodations and jobs went on a political drive was also under way. Young workers of SNCC and CORE, who had left college for a year or more of work in the Black Belt South, were attempting to convince fear-ridden rural Negroes to go to the white courthouse and register to vote. The SCLC was operating a citizenship school for voter registration. Northern foundations funded a Voter Education Project which provided funds to these two organizations, and to the NAACP and several local voters' leagues for voter registration work.

Voter registration drives in the cities were highly successful, but in the rural areas Negroes who attempted to register were subjected to harassment, intimidation, economic reprisals and physical assault. While demonstrations at the courthouse were nonviolent, most people practiced armed defense. One of the heroes of the Southern movement is a small, wiry elderly man, E.W. Steptoe of Amite County, Mississippi. When Steptoe's house was bombed after he attempted to register to vote, he fired at the fleeing bombers. But Steptoe's action is not an isolated incident. It became common throughout the Deep South for guards to be posted at homes where civil rights workers lived, and around halls or Freedom Houses when meetings were in progress. Many shot back when their homes were fired upon. Curtis C. Bryant, President of the Pike County, Mississippi branch of the NAACP told the U.S. Commission on Civil Rights:

On the night of April 28 there was a bomb thrown in my barbershop. . . .

On June 22, I think it was, 1964—I don't recall exactly when. On the night of that, my son and another boy, a young man, were guarding my home. I had reached the point where we felt that it was very hazardous. We had received numerous phone calls threatening our lives, not only my life, but that of my entire family. And the Pike County branch of the NAACP had employed this young man to guard my home. . . .

. . . on the night of June 22, the bomb was thrown—I mean the dynamite was thrown about 19 feet from the car in which my son and the other young man were sitting. It really had an impact. The first thing I thought of, that they had been killed. I immediately ran out. I had acquired a high-powered rifle in order to try and protect my home and my family. I discharged, I think, one or two shots with the rifle, and when we finally found out that my son and the other young man were safe, we felt somewhat more secure.[6]

For a period during the summer of 1964 Burgland, the Negro section of McComb, the first Mississippi town to begin voter registration activity in the current period, was an off-limits area to all but persons known to the community guards at the outskirts of Burgland. All cars seeking to enter Burgland were stopped at a roadblock and asked for identification.

For the most part civil rights workers relied on nonviolent techniques for protection. Skilled driving in fast cars to speed away from local white citizens harassing them on the roads; two-way radio equipment so that workers traveling from place to place on the road could keep headquarters advised of their whereabouts and get help to those in danger quickly.

The new movement up through the end of the summer of 1964 had a dual thrust. The older and more conservative NAACP participated with the youngsters of SNCC and CORE in an over-all organization, the Council of Federated Organizations, set up to channel all efforts in Mississsippi; and nationally the major civil rights groups met as the United Council of Civil Rights Leadership [7] to hold periodic consultations at the top leadership level on strategy. While the thrust of this grouping was toward "coalition politics"—essentially a drive to invigorate the liberal-labor elements around the Democratic Party as a pressure group to push for civil rights —a simultaneous thrust was beginning within the younger and more militant civil rights organizations toward independent political action.

The mass actions of 1963 were so large and so frequent, often lasting weeks or months, that the term "revolution" was

[6] *Hearings before the United States Commission on Civil Rights*, II, Administration of Justice, Hearings held in Jackson, Miss., February 16-20, 1965, pp. 65-66.

[7] The council was made up of representatives of the National Urban League, Congress of Racial Equality, the National Council of Negro Women, the NAACP, the NAACP Legal Defense Fund, Inc., the Southern Christian Leadership Conference and the Student Nonviolent Coordinating Committee.

often applied to the Negro protest. These included Birmingham demonstrations in the Spring which were climaxed by serious riots, and Jackson, Mississippi demonstrations which barely avoided a bloody confrontation of angry students and police at the funeral of slain civil rights leader Medgar Evers. The National Guard governed Cambridge, Maryland, which was under martial law for a year after long and large demonstrations there in which hundreds were arrested. In May 1,000 were arrested in Greensboro, North Carolina, and 1,400 in Durham, North Carolina and in September, 1,400 in Orangeburg, South Carolina.

But the marches and protests, even the march of 200,000 to Washington, D.C. in August, 1963,[8] and the Mississippi drive of the summer of 1964 came to be seen by militants and by the masses of Negroes as a series of rebuffs, disappointments, even failures. Many of the mass actions had ended after weeks of marches and beatings and jailings in compromises which halted demonstrations, but failed to fulfill Negro demands. The nation's attention was transferred to another city. The situation for Negroes in Albany or Cambridge, in Danville or in Selma, in Jackson or in Birmingham remained pretty much the same after the upheaval as it had been before. This was true also for the Negroes in Northern ghettos. *De facto* segregation was increasing in Northern schools, unemployment was rising, the gap between Negro and white income increased. The picket lines in Northern cities against discrimination in employment did not create enough Negro jobs. The other mode of protest in Northern ghettos—riots—provided a fleeting emotional outlet but little else.

More and more Negro intellectuals were publicly saying "farewell to the liberals" as early as 1962. By 1964 they had been joined by the ordinary Negro man in the street who began to try to change his own condition, in effect saying farewell to the white folks.

---

[8] The march was organized by the major national civil rights organizations plus representatives of church, labor and civic groups and was coordinated by civil rights activist Bayard Rustin.

1. THE EARLY CHALLENGES

Separate Education is Unequal
The Supreme Court Opinion in Brown *v.*
Board of Education*

MR. CHIEF JUSTICE Warren delivered the opinion of the Court.

These cases come to us from the States of Kansas, South Carolina, Virginia, and Delaware. They are premised on different facts and different local conditions, but a common legal question justifies their consideration together in this consolidated opinion.[1]

* Brown v. Board of Education, 347 U. S. 483 (1954).

[1] In the Kansas case, *Brown* v. *Board of Education,* the plaintiffs are Negro children of elementary school age residing in Topeka. They brought this action in the United States District Court for the District of Kansas to enjoin enforcement of a Kansas statute which permits, but does not require, cities of more than 15,000 population to maintain separate school facilities for Negro and white students. Kan. Gen. Stat. § 72-1724 (1949). Pursuant to that authority, the Topeka Board of Education elected to establish segregated elementary schools. Other public schools in the community, however, are operated on a nonsegregated basis. The three-judge District Court, convened under 28 U. S. C. §§ 2281 and 2284, found that segregation in public education has a detrimental effect upon Negro children, but denied relief on the ground that the Negro and white schools were substantially equal with respect to buildings, transportation, curricula, and educational qualifications of teachers. 98 F. Supp. 797. The case is here on direct appeal under 28 U. S. C. § 1253.

In the South Carolina case, *Briggs* v. *Elliott,* the plaintiffs are Negro children of both elementary and high school age residing in Clarendon County. They brought this action in the United States District Court for the Eastern District of South Carolina to enjoin enforcement of provisions in the state constitution and statutory code which require the segregation of Negroes and whites in public schools. S. C. Const., Art. XI, § 7; S. C. Code § 5377 (1942). The three-judge District Court, convened under 28 U. S. C. §§ 2281 and 2284, denied the requested relief. The court found that the Negro schools were inferior to the white schools and ordered the defendants to begin immediately to equalize the facilities. But the court sustained the validity of the contested provisions and denied the plaintiffs admission to the white schools during the equalization program. 98 F. Supp. 529. This Court vacated the District Court's judgment and remanded the case for the purpose of obtaining the court's views on a report filed by the defendants concerning the progress made in the equalization program. 342 U. S. 350. On remand, the District Court found that substantial equality had been achieved except for buildings and that the defendants were proceeding to rectify this inequality as well. 103 F. Supp. 920. The case is again

In each of the cases, minors of the Negro race, through their legal representatives, seek the aid of the courts in obtaining admission to the public schools of their community on a nonsegregated basis. In each instance, they had been denied admission to schools attended by white children under laws requiring or permitting segregation according to race. This segregation was alleged to deprive the plaintiffs of the equal protection of the laws under the Fourteenth Amendment. In each of the cases other than the Delaware case, a three-judge federal district court denied relief to the plaintiffs on the so-called "separate but equal" doctrine announced by this Court in *Plessy* v. *Ferguson*, 163 U. S. 537. Under that doctrine, equality of treatment is accorded when the races are provided substantially equal facilities, even though these facilities be separate. In the Delaware case, the Supreme Court of Delaware adhered to that doctrine, but ordered that the

here on direct appeal under 28 U. S. C. § 1253.

In the Virginia case, *Davis* v. *County School Board*, the plaintiffs are Negro children of high school age residing in Prince Edward County. They brought this action in the United States District Court for the Eastern District of Virginia to enjoin enforcement of provisions in the state constitution and statutory code which require the segregation of Negroes and whites in public schools. Va. Const., § 140; Va. Code § 22–221 (1950). The three-judge District Court, convened under 28 U. S. C. §§ 2281 and 2284, denied the requested relief. The court found the Negro school inferior in physical plant, curricula, and transportation, and ordered the defendants forthwith to provide substantially equal curricula and transportation and to "proceed with all reasonable diligence and dispatch to remove" the inequality in physical plant. But, as in the South Carolina case, the court sustained the validity of the contested provisions and denied the plaintiffs admission to the white schools during the equalization program. 103 F. Supp. 337. The case is here on direct appeal under 28 U. S. C. § 1253.

In the Delaware case, *Gebhart* v. *Belton*, the plaintiffs are Negro children of both elementary and high school age residing in New Castle County. They brought this action in the Delaware Court of Chancery to enjoin enforcement of provisions in the state constitution and statutory code which require the segregation of Negroes and whites in public schools. Del. Const., Art. X, § 2; Del. Rev. Code § 2631 (1935). The Chancellor gave judgment for the plaintiffs and ordered their immediate admission to schools previously attended only by white children, on the ground that the Negro schools were inferior with respect to teacher training, pupil-teacher ratio, extracurricular activities, physical plant, and time and distance involved in travel. 87 A. 2d 862. The Chancellor also found that segregation itself results in an inferior education for Negro children (see note 10, *infra*), but did not rest his decision on that ground. *Id.*, at 865. The Chancellor's decree was affirmed by the Supreme Court of Delaware, which intimated, however, that the defendants might be able to obtain a modification of the decree after equilization of the Negro and white schools had been accomplished. 91 A. 2d 137, 152. The defendants, contending only that the Delaware courts had erred in ordering the immediate admission of the Negro plaintiffs to the white schools, applied to this Court for certiorari. The writ was granted, 344 U. S. 891. The plaintiffs, who were successful below, did not submit a cross-petition.

plaintiffs be admitted to the white schools because of their superiority to the Negro schools.

The plaintiffs contend that segregated public shools are not "equal" and cannot be made "equal," and that hence they are deprived of the equal protection of the laws. Because of the obvious importance of the question presented, the Court took jurisdiction.[2] Argument was heard in the 1952 Term, and reargument was heard this Term on certain questions propounded by the Court.[3]

Reargument was largely devoted to the circumstances surrounding the adoption of the Fourteenth Amendment in 1868. It covered exhaustively consideration of the Amendment in Congress, ratification by the states, then existing practices in racial segregation, and the views of proponents and opponents of the Amendment. This discussion and our own investigation convince us that, although these sources cast some light, it is not enough to resolve the problem with which we are faced. At best, they are inconclusive. The most avid proponents of the post-War Amendments undoubtedly intended them to remove all legal distinctions among "all persons born or naturalized in the United States." Their opponents, just as certainly, were antagonistic to both the letter and the spirit of the Amendments and wished them to have the most limited effect. What others in Congress and the state legislatures had in mind cannot be determined with any degree of certainty.

An additional reason for the inconclusive nature of the Amendment's history, with respect to segregated schools, is the status of public education at that time.[4] In the South, the

2 344 U. S. 1, 141, 891.

3 345 U. S. 972. The Attorney General of the United States participated both Terms as *amicus curiae.*

4 For a general study of the development of public education prior to the Amendment, see Butts and Cremin, *A History of Education in American Culture* (1953), Pts. I, II; Cubberley, *Public Education in the United States* (1934 ed.), cc. II–XII. School practices current at the time of the adoption of the Fourteenth Amendment are described in Butts and Cremin, *supra,* at 269–275; Cubberley, *supra,* at 288–339, 408–431; Knight, *Public Education in the South* (1922), cc. VIII, IX. See also H. Ex. Doc. No. 315, 41st Cong., 2d Sess. (1871). Although the demand for free public schools followed substantially the same pattern in both the North and the South, the development in the South did not begin to gain momentum until about 1850, some twenty years after that in the North. The reasons for the somewhat slower development in the South (*e.g.,* the rural character of the South and the different regional attitudes toward state assistance) are well explained in Cubberley, *supra,* at 408–423. In the country as a whole, but particularly in the South, the War virtually stopped all progress in public education. *Id.,* at 427–428. The low status of Negro education in all sections of the country, both before and immediately after the War,

movement toward free common schools, supported by general taxation, had not yet taken hold. Education of white children was largely in the hands of private groups. Education of Negroes was almost nonexistent, and practically all of the race were illiterate. In fact, any education of Negroes was forbidden by law in some states. Today, in contrast, many Negroes have achieved outstanding success in the arts and sciences as well as in the business and professional world. It is true that public school education at the time of the Amendment had advanced further in the North, but the effect of the Amendment on Northern States was generally ignored in the congressional debates. Even in the North, the conditions of public education did not approximate those existing today. The curriculum was usually rudimentary; ungraded schools were common in rural areas; the school term was but three months a year in many states; and compulsory school attendance was virtually unknown. As a consequence, it is not surprising that there should be so little in the history of the Fourteenth Amendment relating to its intended effect on public education.

In the first cases in this Court construing the Fourteenth Amendment, decided shortly after its adoption, the Court interpreted it as proscribing all state-imposed discriminations against the Negro race.[5] The doctrine of "separate but equal" did not make its appearance in this Court until 1896 in the case of *Plessy* v. *Ferguson, supra,* involving not education

---

is described in Beale, *A History of Freedom of Teaching in American Schools* (1941), 112–132, 175–195. Compulsory school attendance laws were not generally adopted until after the ratification of the Fourteenth Amendment, and it was not until 1918 that such laws were in force in all the states. Cubberley, *supra,* at 563–565.

[5] *Slaughter-House Cases,* 16 Wall. 36, 67–72 (1873); *Strauder* v. *West Virginia,* 100 U. S. 303, 307–308 (1880):
"It ordains that no State deprive any person of life, liberty, or property, without due process of law, or deny to any person within its jurisdiction the equal protection of the laws. What is this but declaring that the law in the States shall be the same for the black as for the white; that all persons, whether colored or white, shall stand equal before the laws of the States, and, in regard to the colored race, for whose protection the amendment was primarily designed, that no discrimination shall be made against them by law because of their color? The words of the amendment, it is true, are prohibitory, but they contain a necessary implication of a positive immunity, or right, most valuable to the colored race,—the right to exemption from unfriendly legislation against them distinctively as colored,—exemption from legal discriminations, implying inferiority in civil society, lessening the security of their enjoyment of the rights which others enjoy, and discriminations which are steps towards reducing them to the condition of a subject race."
See also *Virginia* v. *Rives,* 100 U. S. 313, 318 (1880); *Ex parte Virginia,* 100 U. S. 339, 344–345 (1880).

but transportation.[6] American courts have since labored with the doctrine for over half a century. In this Court, there have been six cases involving the "separate but equal" doctrine in the field of public education.[7] In *Cumming* v. *County Board of Education,* 175 U. S. 528, and *Gong Lum* v. *Rice,* 275 U. S. 78, the validity of the doctrine itself was not challenged.[8] In more recent cases, all on the graduate school level, inequality was found in that specific benefits enjoyed by white students were denied to Negro students of the same educational qualifications. *Missouri ex rel. Gaines* v. *Canada,* 305 U. S. 337; *Sipuel* v. *Oklahoma,* 332 U. S. 631; *Sweatt* v. *Painter,* 339 U. S. 629; *McLaurin* v. *Oklahoma State Regents,* 339 U. S. 637. In none of these cases was it necessary to re-examine the doctrine to grant relief to the Negro plaintiff. And in *Sweatt* v. *Painter, supra,* the Court expressly reserved decision on the question whether *Plessy* v. *Ferguson* should be held inapplicable to public education.

In the instant cases, that question is directly presented. Here, unlike *Sweatt* v. *Painter,* there are findings below that the Negro and white schools involved have been equalized, or are being equalized, with respect to buildings, curricula, qualifications and salaries of teachers, and other "tangible" factors.[9] Our decision, therefore, cannot turn on merely a comparison of these tangible factors in the Negro and white

[6] The doctrine apparently originated in *Roberts* v. *City of Boston,* 59 Mass. 198, 206 (1850), upholding school segregation against attack as being violative of a state constitutional guarantee of equality. Segregation in Boston public schools was eliminated in 1855. Mass. Acts 1855, c. 256. But elsewhere in the North segregation in public education has persisted in some communities until recent years. It is apparent that such segregation has long been a nationwide problem, not merely one of sectional concern.

[7] See also *Berea College* v. *Kentucky,* 211 U. S. 45 (1908).

[8] In the *Cumming* case, Negro taxpayers sought an injunction requiring the defendant school board to discontinue the operation of a high school for white children until the board resumed operation of a high school for Negro children. Similarly, in the *Gong Lum* case, the plaintiff, a child of Chinese descent, contended only that state authorities had misapplied the doctrine by classifying him with Negro children and requiring him to attend a Negro school.

[9] In the Kansas case, the court below found substantial equality as to all such factors. 98 F. Supp. 797, 798. In the South Carolina case, the court below found that the defendants were proceeding "promptly and in good faith to comply with the court's decree." 103 F. Supp. 920, 921. In the Virginia case, the court below noted that the equalization program was already "afoot and progressing" (103 F. Supp. 337, 341); since then, we have been advised, in the Virginia Attorney General's brief on reargument, that the program has now been completed. In the Delaware case, the court below similarly noted that the state's equalization program was well under way. 91 A. 2d 137, 149.

schools involved in each of the cases. We must look instead to the effect of segregation itself on public education.

In approaching this problem, we cannot turn the clock back to 1868 when the Amendment was adopted, or even to 1896 when *Plessy* v. *Ferguson* was written. We must consider public education in the light of its full development and its present place in American life throughout the Nation. Only in this way can it be determined if segregation in public schools deprives these plaintiffs of the equal protection of the laws.

Today, education is perhaps the most important function of state and local governments. Compulsory school attendance laws and the great expenditures for education both demonstrate our recognition of the importance of education to our democratic society. It is required in the performance of our most basic public responsibilities, even service in the armed forces. It is the very foundation of good citizenship. Today it is a principal instrument in awakening the child to cultural values, in preparing him for later professional training, and in helping him to adjust normally to his environment. In these days, it is doubtful that any child may reasonably be expected to succeed in life if he is denied the opportunity of an education. Such an opportunity, where the state has undertaken to provide it, is a right which must be made available to all on equal terms.

We come then to the question presented: Does segregation of children in public schools solely on the basis of race, even though the physical facilities and other "tangible" factors may be equal, deprive the children of the minority group of equal educational opportunities? We believe that it does.

In *Sweatt* v. *Painter, supra,* in finding that a segregated law school for Negroes could not provide them equal educational opportunities, this Court relied in large part on "those qualities which are incapable of objective measurement but which make for greatness in a law school." In *McLaurin* v. *Oklahoma State Regents, supra,* the Court, in requiring that a Negro admitted to a white graduate school be treated like all other students, again resorted to intangible considerations: ". . . his ability to study, to engage in discussions and exchange views with other students, and, in general, to learn his profession." Such considerations apply with added force to children in grade and high schools. To separate them from others of similar age and qualifications solely because of their race generates a feeling of inferiority as to their status in the community that may affect their hearts and minds in a way unlikely ever to be undone. The effect of this separation on their educational opportunities was well stated by a finding in the Kansas case by a court which nevertheless felt compelled to rule against the Negro plaintiffs:

Segregation of white and colored children in public schools has a detrimental effect upon the colored children. The impact is greater when it has the sanction of the law; for the policy of separating the races is usually interpreted as denoting the inferiority of the negro group. A sense of inferiority affects the motivation of a child to learn. Segregation with the sanction of law, therefore, has a tendency to [retard] the educational and mental development of negro children and to deprive them of some of the benefits they would receive in a racial[ly] integrated school system.[10]

Whatever may have been the extent of psychological knowledge at the time of *Plessy* v. *Ferguson,* this finding is amply supported by modern authority.[11] Any language in *Plessy* v. *Ferguson* contrary to this finding is rejected.

We conclude that in the field of public education the doctrine of "separate but equal" has no place. Separate educational facilities are inherently unequal. Therefore, we hold that the plaintiffs and others similarly situated for whom the actions have been brought are, by reason of the segregation complained of, deprived of the equal protection of the laws guaranteed by the Fourteenth Amendment. This disposition makes unnecessary any discussion whether such segregation also violates the Due Process Clause of the Fourteenth Amendment.[12]

Because these are class actions, because of the wide applicability of this decision, and because of the great variety of local conditions, the formulation of decrees in these cases presents problems of considerable complexity. On reargument, the consideration of appropriate relief was necessarily subordinated to the primary question—the constitutionality

[10] A similar finding was made in the Delaware case: "I conclude from the testimony that in our Delaware society, State-imposed segregation in education itself results in the Negro children, as a class, receiving educational opportunities which are substantially inferior to those available to white children otherwise similarly situated." 87 A. 2d 862, 865.

[11] K. B. Clark, *Effect of Prejudice and Discrimination on Personality Development* (Midcentury White House Conference on Children and Youth, 1950); Witmer and Kotinsky, *Personality in the Making* (1952), c. VI; Deutscher and Chein, *The Psychological Effects of Enforced Segregation: A Survey of Social Science Opinion,* 26 J. Psychol. 259 (1948); Chein, *What are the Psychological Effects of Segregation Under Conditions of Equal Facilities?,* 3 Int. J. Opinion and Attitude Res. 229 (1949); Brameld, *Educational Costs, in Discrimination and National Welfare* (MacIver, ed., 1949), 44–48; Frazier, *The Negro in the United States* (1949), 674–681. And see generally Myrdal, *An American Dilemma* (1944).

[12] See *Bolling* v. *Sharpe,* 347 U. S. 497, concerning the Due Process Clause of the Fifth Amendment.

of segregation in public education. We have now announced
that such segregation is a denial of the equal protection of the
laws. In order that we may have the full assistance of the parties in formulating decrees, the cases will be restored to the
docket, and the parties are requested to present further argument on Questions 4 and 5 previously propounded by the
Court for the reargument this Term. [13] The Attorney General
of the United States is again invited to participate. The Attorneys General of the states requiring or permitting segregation
in public education will also be permitted to appear as *amici
curiae* upon request to do so by September 15, 1954, and
submission of briefs by October 1, 1954.[14]

It is so ordered.

[13] "4. Assuming it is decided that segregation in public schools violates the Fourteenth Amendment

"(*a*) would a decree necessarily follow providing that, within the
limits set by normal geographic school districting, Negro children
should forthwith be admitted to schools of their choice, or

"(*b*) may this Court, in the exercise of its equity powers, permit an
effective gradual adjustment to be brought about from existing segregated systems to a system not based on color distinctions?

"5. On the assumption on which questions 4 (*a*) and (*b*) are based,
and assuming further that this Court will exercise its equity powers to
the end described in question 4 (*b*),

"(*a*) should this Court formulate detailed decrees in these cases;

"(*b*) if so, what specific issues should the decrees reach;

"(*c*) should this Court appoint a special master to hear evidence
with a view to recommending specific terms for such decrees;

"(*d*) should this Court remand to the courts of first instance with
directions to frame decrees in these cases, and if so what general directions should the decrees of this Court include and what procedures
should the courts of first instance follow in arriving at the specific
terms of more detailed decrees?"

[14] See Rule 42, Revised Rules of this Court (effective July 1, 1954).

Defiance
The Southern Manifesto[*]

DECLARATION OF CONSTITUTIONAL PRINCIPLES

THE UNWARRANTED DECISION of the Supreme Court in the
public school cases is now bearing the fruit always produced
when men substitute naked power for established law.

* U.S., *Congressional Record*, 84th Cong., 2nd Sess., 1956, 4515–16.

The Founding Fathers gave us a Constitution of checks and balances because they realized the inescapable lesson of history that no man or group of men can be safely entrusted with unlimited power. They framed this Constitution with its provisions for change by amendment in order to secure the fundamentals of government against the dangers of temporary popular passion or the personal predilections of public officeholders.

We regard the decision of the Supreme Court in the school cases as a clear abuse of judicial power. It climaxes a trend in the Federal judiciary undertaking to legislate, in derogation of the authority of Congress, and to encroach upon the reserved rights of the States and the people.

The original Constitution does not mention education. Neither does the 14th amendment nor any other amendment. The debates preceding the submission of the 14th amendment clearly show that there was no intent that it should affect the systems of education maintained by the States.

The very Congress which proposed the amendment subsequently provided for segregated schools in the District of Columbia.

When the amendment was adopted, in 1868, there were 37 States of the Union. Every one of the 26 States that had any substantial racial differences among its people either approved the operation of segregated schools already in existence or subsequently established such schools by action of the same lawmaking body which considered the 14th amendment.

As admitted by the Supreme Court in the public school case (*Brown* v. *Board of Education*), the doctrine of separate but equal schools "apparently originated in *Roberts* v. *City of Boston* * * * (1849), upholding school segregation against attack as being violative of a State constitutional guarantee of equality." This constitutional doctrine began in the North—not in the South, and it was followed not only in Massachusetts, but in Connecticut, New York, Illinois, Indiana, Michigan, Minnesota, New Jersey, Ohio, Pennsylvania, and other northern States until they, exercising their rights as States through the constitutional processes of local self-government, changed their school systems.

In the case of *Plessy* v. *Ferguson,* in 1896, the Supreme Court expressly declared that under the 14th amendment no person was denied any of his rights if the States provided separate but equal public facilities. This decision has been followed in many other cases. It is notable that the Supreme Court, speaking through Chief Justice Taft, a former President of the United States, unanimously declared, in 1927, in *Lum* v. *Rice,* that the "separate but equal" principle is "within the discretion of the State in regulating its public schools and does not conflict with the 14th amendment."

This interpretation, restated time and again, became a part of the life of the people of many of the States and confirmed their habits, customs, traditions, and way of life. It is founded on elemental humanity and commonsense, for parents should not be deprived by Government of the right to direct the lives of and education of their own children.

Though there has been no constitutional amendment or act of Congress changing this established legal principle almost a century old, the Supreme Court of the United States, with no legal basis for such action, undertook to exercise their naked judicial power and substituted their personal political and social ideas for the established law of the land.

This unwarranted exercise of power by the Court, contrary to the Constitution, is creating chaos and confusion in the States principally affected. It is destroying the amicable relations between the white and Negro races that have been created through 90 years of patient effort by the good people of both races. It has planted hatred and suspicion where there has been heretofore friendship and understanding.

Without regard to the consent of the governed, outside agitators are threatening immediate and revolutionary changes in our public-school systems. If done, this is certain to destroy the system of public education in some of the States.

With the gravest concern for the explosive and dangerous condition created by this decision and inflamed by outside meddlers:

We reaffirm our reliance on the Constitution as the fundamental law of the land.

We decry the Supreme Court's encroachments on rights reserved to the States and to the people, contrary to established law and to the Constitution.

We commend the motives of those States which have declared the intention to resist forced integration by any lawful means.

We appeal to the States and people who are not directly affected by these decisions to consider the constitutional principles involved against the time when they, too, on issues vital to them, may be the victims of judicial encroachment.

Even though we constitute a minority in the present Congress, we have full faith that a majority of the American people believe in the dual system of Government which has enabled us to achieve our greatness and will in time demand that the reserved rights of the State and of the people be made secure against judicial usurpation.

We pledge ourselves to use all lawful means to bring about a reversal of this decision which is contrary to the Constitution and to prevent the use of force in its implementation.

In this trying period, as we all seek to right this wrong, we appeal to our people not to be provoked by the agitators and troublemakers invading our States and to scrupulously refrain from disorders and lawless acts.

Signed by:

Members of the United States Senate: WALTER F. GEORGE; RICHARD B. RUSSELL; JOHN STENNIS; SAM J. ERVIN, JR.; STROM THURMOND; HARRY F. BYRD; A. WILLIS ROBERTSON; JOHN L. MC-CLELLAN; ALLEN J. ELLENDER; RUSSELL B. LONG; LISTER HILL; JAMES O. EASTLAND; W. KERR SCOTT; JOHN SPARKMAN; OLIN D. JOHNSTON; PRICE DANIEL; J. W. FULBRIGHT; GEORGE A. SMATHERS; SPESSARD L. HOLLAND.

Members of the United States House of Representatives:

Alabama: FRANK W. BOYKIN; GEORGE M. GRANT; GEORGE W. ANDREWS; KENNETH A. ROBERTS; ALBERT RAINS; ARMISTEAD I. SELDEN, JR.; CARL ELLIOTT; ROBERT E. JONES; GEORGE HUDDLESTON, JR.

Arkansas: E. C. GATHINGS; WILBUR D. MILLS; JAMES W. TRIMBLE; OREN HARRIS; BROOKS HAYS; W. F. NORRELL.

Florida: CHARLES E. BENNETT; ROBERT L. F. SIKES; A. S. HERLONG, JR.; PAUL G. ROGERS; JAMES A. HALEY; D. R. MATTHEWS; WILLIAM C. CRAMER.

Georgia: PRINCE H. PRESTON; JOHN L. PILCHER; E. L. FORRESTER; JOHN JAMES FLYNT, JR.; JAMES C. DAVIS; CARL VINSON; HENDERSON LANHAM; IRIS F. BLITCH; PHIL M. LANDRUM; PAUL BROWN.

Louisiana: F. EDWARD HÉBERT; HALE BOGGS; EDWIN E. WILLIS; OVERTON BROOKS; OTTO E. PASSMAN; JAMES H. MORRISON; T. ASHTON THOMPSON; GEORGE S. LONG.

Mississippi: THOMAS G. ABERNETHY; JAMIE L. WHITTEN; FRANK E. SMITH; JOHN BELL WILLIAMS; ARTHUR WINSTEAD; WILLIAM M. COLMER.

North Carolina: HERBERT C. BONNER; L. H. FOUNTAIN; GRAHAM A. BARDEN; CARL T. DURHAM; F. ERTEL CARLYLE; HUGH Q. ALEXANDER; WOODROW W. JONES; GEORGE A. SHUFORD; CHARLES R. JONAS.

South Carolina: L. MENDEL RIVERS; JOHN J. RILEY; W. J. BRYAN DORN; ROBERT T. ASHMORE; JAMES P. RICHARDS; JOHN L. MC-MILLAN.

Tennessee: JAMES B. FRAZIER, JR.; TOM MURRAY; JERE COOPER; CLIFFORD DAVIS; ROSS BASS; JOE L. EVINS.

Texas: WRIGHT PATMAN; JOHN DOWDY; WALTER ROGERS; O. C. FISHER; MARTIN DIES.

Virginia: EDWARD J. ROBESON, JR.; PORTER HARDY, JR.; J. VAUGHAN GARY; WATKINS M. ABBITT; WILLIAM M. TUCK; RICHARD

H. Poff; Burr P. Harrison; Howard W. Smith; W. Pat Jennings; Joel T. Broyhill.

She Walked Alone*

DAISY BATES

Dr. Benjamin Fine was then education editor of *The New York Times*. He had years before won for his newspaper a Pulitzer prize. He was among the first reporters on the scene to cover the Little Rock story.

A few days after the National Guard blocked the Negro children's entrance to the school, Ben showed up at my house. He paced the floor nervously, rubbing his hands together as he talked.

"Daisy, they spat in my face. They called me a 'dirty Jew.' I've been a marked man ever since the day Elizabeth tried to enter Central. I never told you what happened that day. I tried not to think about it. Maybe I was ashamed to admit to you or to myself that white men and women could be so beastly cruel.

"I was standing in front of the school that day. Suddenly there was a shout—'They're here! The niggers are coming!' I saw a sweet little girl who looked about fifteen, walking alone. She tried several times to pass through the guards. The last time she tried, they put their bayonets in front of her. When they did this, she became panicky. For a moment she just stood there trembling. Then she seemed to calm down and started walking toward the bus stop with the mob baying at her heels like a pack of hounds. The women were shouting, 'Get her! Lynch her!' The men were yelling, 'Go home, you bastard of a black bitch!' She finally made it to the bus stop and sat down on the bench. I sat down beside her and said, 'I'm a reporter from *The New York Times*, may I have your name?' She just sat there, her head down. Tears were streaming down her cheeks from under her sun glasses. Daisy, I don't know what made me put my arm around her, lifting her chin, saying, 'Don't let them see you cry.' Maybe she reminded me of my fifteen-year-old daughter, Jill.

* Daisy Bates, *The Long Shadow of Little Rock* (New York: David McKay, 1962), pp. 69-76. Reprinted by permission of David McKay Company, Inc. This chapter is the story of Elizabeth Eckford, one of the "Little Rock Nine" who sought to enter the city's all-white Central High School in 1957.

"There must have been five hundred around us by this time. I vaguely remember someone hollering, 'Get a rope and drag her over to this tree.' Suddenly I saw a white-haired, kind-faced woman fighting her way through the mob. She looked at Elizabeth, and then screamed at the mob, 'Leave this child alone! Why are you tormenting her? Six months from now, you will hang your heads in shame.' The mob shouted, 'Another nigger-lover. Get out of here!' The woman, who I found out later was Mrs. Grace Lorch, the wife of Dr. Lee Lorch, professor at Philander Smith College, turned to me and said, 'We have to do something. Let's try to get a cab.'

"We took Elizabeth across the street to the drugstore. I remained on the sidewalk with Elizabeth while Mrs. Lorch tried to enter the drugstore to call a cab. But the hoodlums slammed the door in her face and wouldn't let her in. She pleaded with them to call a cab for the child. They closed in on her saying, 'Get out of here, you bitch!' Just then the city bus came. Mrs. Lorch and Elizabeth got on. Elizabeth must have been in a state of shock. She never uttered a word. When the bus pulled away, the mob closed in around me. 'We saw you put your arm around that little bitch. Now it's your turn.' A drab, middle-aged woman said viciously, 'Grab him and kick him in the balls!' A girl I had seen hustling in one of the local bars screamed, 'A dirty New York Jew! Get him!' A man asked me, 'Are you a Jew?' I said, 'Yes.' He then said to the mob, 'Let him be! We'll take care of him later.'

"The irony of it all, Daisy, is that during all this time the national guardsmen made no effort to protect Elizabeth or to help me. Instead, they threatened to have me arrested—for inciting to riot."

Elizabeth, whose dignity and control in the face of jeering mobsters had been filmed by television cameras and recorded in pictures flashed to newspapers over the world, had overnight become a national heroine. During the next few days newspaper reporters besieged her home, wanting to talk to her. The first day that her parents agreed she might come out of seclusion, she came to my house where the reporters awaited her. Elizabeth was very quiet, speaking only when spoken to. I took her to my bedroom to talk before I let the reporters see her. I asked how she felt now. Suddenly all her pent-up emotion flared.

"Why am I here?" she said, turning blazing eyes on me. "Why are you so interested in my welfare now? You didn't care enough to notify me of the change of plans—"

I walked over and reached out to her. Before she turned her

back on me, I saw tears gathering in her eyes. My heart was breaking for this young girl who stood there trying to stifle her sobs. How could I explain that frantic early morning when at three o'clock my mind had gone on strike?

In the ensuing weeks Elizabeth took part in all the activities of the nine—press conferences, attendance at court, studying with professors at nearby Philander Smith College. She was present, that is, but never really a part of things. The hurt had been too deep.

On the two nights she stayed at my home I was awakened by the screams in her sleep, as she relived in her dreams the terrifying mob scenes at Central. The only times Elizabeth showed real excitement were when Thurgood Marshall met the children and explained the meaning of what had happened in court. As he talked, she would listen raptly, a faint smile on her face. It was obvious he was her hero.

Little by little Elizabeth came out of her shell. Up to now she had never talked about what happened to her at Central. Once when we were alone in the downstairs recreation room of my house, I asked her simply, "Elizabeth, do you think you can talk about it now?"

She remained quiet for a long time. Then she began to speak.

"You remember the day before we were to go in, we met Superintendent Blossom at the school board office. He told us what the mob might say and do but he never told us we wouldn't have any protection. He told our parents not to come because he wouldn't be able to protect the children if they did.

"That night I was so excited I couldn't sleep. The next morning I was about the first one up. While I was pressing my black and white dress—I had made it to wear on the first day of school—my little brother turned on the TV set. They started telling about a large crowd gathered at the school. The man on TV said he wondered if we were going to show up that morning. Mother called from the kitchen, where she was fixing breakfast, 'Turn that TV off!' She was so upset and worried. I wanted to comfort her, so I said, 'Mother, don't worry.'

"Dad was walking back and forth, from room to room, with a sad expression. He was chewing on his pipe and he had a cigar in his hand, but he didn't light either one. It would have been funny, only he was so nervous.

"Before I left home Mother called us into the living-room. She said we should have a word of prayer. Then I caught the bus and got off a block from the school. I saw a large crowd of people standing across the street from the soldiers guarding Central. As I walked on, the crowd suddenly got very quiet.

Superintendent Blossom had told us to enter by the front door. I looked at all the people and thought, 'Maybe I will be safer if I walk down the block to the front entrance behind the guards.'

"At the corner I tried to pass through the long line of guards around the school so as to enter the grounds behind them. One of the guards pointed across the street. So I pointed in the same direction and asked whether he meant for me to cross the street and walk down. He nodded 'yes.' So, I walked across the street conscious of the crowd that stood there, but they moved away from me.

"For a moment all I could hear was the shuffling of their feet. Then someone shouted, 'Here she comes, get ready!' I moved away from the crowd on the sidewalk and into the street. If the mob came at me I could then cross back over so the guards could protect me.

"The crowd moved in closer and then began to follow me, calling me names. I still wasn't afraid. Just a little bit nervous. Then my knees started to shake all of a sudden and I wondered whether I could make it to the center entrance a block away. It was the longest block I ever walked in my whole life.

"Even so, I still wasn't too scared because all the time I kept thinking that the guards would protect me.

"When I got right in front of the school, I went up to a guard again. But this time he just looked straight ahead and didn't move to let me pass him. I didn't know what to do. Then I looked and saw that the path leading to the front entrance was a little further ahead. So I walked until I was right in front of the path to the front door.

"I stood looking at the school—it looked so big! Just then the guards let some white students go through.

"The crowd was quiet. I guess they were waiting to see what was going to happen. When I was able to steady my knees, I walked up to the guard who had let the white students in. He too didn't move. When I tried to squeeze past him, he raised his bayonet and then the other guards closed in and they raised their bayonets.

"They glared at me with a mean look and I was very frightened and didn't know what to do. I turned around and the crowd came toward me.

"They moved closer and closer. Somebody started yelling, 'Lynch her! Lynch her!'

"I tried to see a friendly face somewhere in the mob—someone who maybe would help. I looked into the face of an old woman and it seemed a kind face, but when I looked at her again, she spat on me.

"They came closer, shouting, 'No nigger bitch is going to get in our school. Get out of here!'

"I turned back to the guards but their faces told me I wouldn't get help from them. Then I looked down the block and saw a bench at the bus stop. I thought, 'If I can only get there I will be safe.' I don't know why the bench seemed a safe place to me, but I started walking toward it. I tried to close my mind to what they were shouting, and kept saying to myself, 'If I can only make it to the bench I will be safe.'

"When I finally got there, I don't think I could have gone another step. I sat down and the mob crowded up and began shouting all over again. Someone hollered, 'Drag her over to this tree! Let's take care of the nigger.' Just then a white man sat down beside me, put his arm around me and patted my shoulder. He raised my chin and said, 'Don't let them see you cry.'

"Then, a white lady—she was very nice—she came over to me on the bench. She spoke to me but I don't remember now what she said. She put me on the bus and sat next to me. She asked me my name and tried to talk to me but I don't think I answered. I can't remember much about the bus ride, but the next thing I remember I was standing in front of the School for the Blind, where Mother works.

"I thought, 'Maybe she isn't here. But she has to be here!' So I ran upstairs, and I think some teachers tried to talk to me, but I kept running until I reached Mother's classroom.

"Mother was standing at the window with her head bowed, but she must have sensed I was there because she turned around. She looked as if she had been crying, and I wanted to tell her I was all right. But I couldn't speak. She put her arms around me and I cried."

Montgomery Bus Boycott*

MRS. ROSA PARKS

WE THINK YOU would like to share with us Mrs. Rosa Parks' story of her role in the Montgomery Bus Protest. This is the

* Mrs. Parks reports on the Montgomery, Alabama bus boycott at a workshop at the Highlander Folk School, Monteagle, Tennessee, March, 1956. Included are comments by Myles Horton, director of the school and Beulah Johnson, a public school teacher in Tuskegee, Alabama. Reprinted from a mimeographed report, by permission of Myles Horton.

story of how her quiet refusal to move to the back of a bus touched off what is being called the first Passive Resistance Movement in the South. Rosa was a student at Highlander last summer. The following was recorded here during the March 3-4, 1956 Planning Conference on a series of Public School Integration Workshops.

ROSA PARKS: Montgomery today is nothing at all like it was as you knew it last year. It's just a different place altogether since we demonstrated, which marked the time of my arrest on the city line bus for not moving out of the seat I had already occupied. For a white person to take the seat I would have had to stand. It was not at all pre-arranged. It just happened that the driver made a demand and I just didn't feel like obeying his demand. He called a policeman and I was arrested and placed in jail, later released on a $100 bond and brought to trial on December 5th. This was the first date that the Negroes of Montgomery set to not ride the bus and from December to this date they are still staying off the bus in large numbers, almost 100%. Once in a while you may see one or two but very seldom do you see any riding the city line buses. It attracted much attention all over the nation and world wide, you may say. There was attention even as far away as London. We had a correspondent at one of our meetings. There was a correspondent from even as far away as Tokyo, Japan. People all over the country have called in to see what's going on, what's being done and what is the reaction to it.

MYLES HORTON: What you did was a very little thing just to sit there, you know, to touch off such a fire. Why did you do it; what moved you not to move? I'm interested in motivations —what makes people do things. What went on in your mind, Rosa?

ROSA PARKS: Well, in the first place, I had been working all day on the job. I was quite tired after spending a full day working. I handle and work on clothing that white people wear. That didn't come in my mind but this is what I wanted to know; when and how would we ever determine our rights as human beings? The section of the bus where I was sitting was what we called the colored section, especially in this neighborhood because the bus was filled more than two-thirds with Negro passengers and a number of them were standing. And just as soon as enough white passengers got on the bus to take what we consider their seats and then a few over, that meant that we would have to move back for them even though there was no room to move back. It was an imposition as far as I was concerned.

MYLES HORTON: Well, had you ever moved before?

ROSA PARKS: I hadn't for quite a long while. It has happened in the past and I did obey somewhat reluctantly. The times that I had to move back I think a colored man gave me his seat. Just having paid for a seat and riding for only a couple of blocks and then having to stand, was too much. These other persons had got on the bus after I did—it meant that I didn't have a right to do anything but get on the bus, give them my fare and then be pushed wherever they wanted me.

MYLES HORTON: You just decided that you wouldn't be moved again, is that it?

ROSA PARKS: That is what I felt like. . . .

MYLES HORTON: They have tried their patience for a long time. Why, suddenly, does somebody—who happens to be somebody we know and admire and are proud of—say, "Now —this is it." It seems to me what has happened in Montgomery is a new high in American protest, in the sense of people using passive resistance instead of the more conventional methods. Now why, in the first place, did Rosa do this instead of its just being another time when she'd move—and then, equally important, why did the fact touch off the tremendous response that it did in Montgomery? These are significant questions. I don't know whether we can get the answers to them. You couldn't have the highest paid public relations people or the highest paid organizers in the country do this, you know, George. It's just the kind of job that you couldn't set up, plan and carry out. We had heard last summer when Rosa was here that the Negroes in Montgomery were timid and would not act. In fact some of the leaders in Montgomery wrote us to that effect. They said they couldn't get any interest stirred up there, that the Negroes wouldn't stand together. Then Rosa refused to move and as a result of her arrest something big happened. Was it an accident—how do you feel about it, Rosa?

ROSA PARKS: None of us seem to know exactly ourselves unless it was because this incident had been experienced by so many others—many Negroes had been subjected to this type of humiliation. I think they responded because each person had experienced something of the same thing.

MYLES HORTON: And your protest made the rest of them realize that the time had come.

ROSA PARKS: We at least could give it a try! . . .

MYLES HORTON: I am sure that Rosa heard all the discussions up here last summer and other people from Montgomery who weren't here heard the radio and read the papers. This certainly was background preparation but there was the same background preparation for a lot of other places where this didn't happen.

BEULAH JOHNSON: You ask what has happened to Rosa. I think I can tell you what happened to her. It is the same thing that happened to me and that man on the L&N railroad. I was tired of insults. You know that the law is on your side and you get tired of being run over. You say, "Well, let's fight it out—if it means going to jail then go to jail." That's just the whole attitude—when you get tired then you get tired of people asking you to get up and move. I'm just pretty certain that that's just one of those days that happened to Rosa. There comes a time in your life when you just decide that you don't give a rap. Many of us have reached that point. I don't live in Montgomery but I'm in Montgomery every week and I know the situation. Now that's what happened to Rosa here. You ask the question why people fell in line.

We have had NAACP meetings and we've had the things we discussed when we were here last summer. We have been very much concerned with getting people registered in the state of Alabama. We've been talking about those things and we've been reviewing what has happened all around as far as the court decisions go.

MYLES HORTON: Well, that answers a lot of questions in my mind—but it still doesn't explain why it took the passive resistance form that it did.

ROSA PARKS: I think I can account for that because in the organization the ministers came together and took the lead and made the announcements from their pulpits and we also had these spiritual mass meetings twice weekly.

BEULAH JOHNSON: Well, I tell you I think you are going to have to keep in mind that for the last five years we have been calling on ministers throughout the United States and we have been letting them know that it is strictly a job that ministers should undertake. There has been beautiful support from the ministers—they are really coming out and working. I think they are simply doing what should have been done a long time ago.

MYLES HORTON: You agree with Rosa then that the ministers probably gave the situation a little different flavor from what it would have been if there hadn't been that kind of church leadership.

BEULAH JOHNSON: Yes.

MYLES HORTON: I don't know of any other case where ministers have taken the lead and become spokesmen so spontaneously. Some of us talked about passive resistance—we talked about it in labor unions, we talked about it in India and

Africa. But somehow the Montgomery movement seems to be unplanned, unpremeditated, a sort of natural movement with religious motivation—a protest movement. As far as I know nobody called it a passive resistance movement down there; they just said let's protest and as religious leaders the only way to protest is non-violently. Would that be a correct way to evaluate the situation?

ROSA PARKS: Yes, I think so. . . .

BEULAH JOHNSON: It is not only the Negroes in Montgomery—but Negroes all over the country are sticking together. This is a new day. I think Langston Hughes wrote a poem— here's the essence:

> I'm comin', I'm comin' but my head ain't bended low
> 'Cause this is a new Black Joe.

I think it brings out very definitely the way Negroes are feeling today.

ROSA PARKS: There were some resolutions submitted by the white people for ending our protest which were brought back to our meeting but they were turned down because they didn't meet the approval of the group.

MYLES HORTON: You mean the boycott was hurting business and they wanted to do something about it.

ROSA PARKS: Yes, they wanted to bring about an agreement.

MYLES HORTON: Well, why didn't they do something with the law enforcement officers there that brought all the suits?

ROSA PARKS: I don't know.

BEULAH JOHNSON: Well, then right after that, Rosa, you remember the resolution the whites adopted in their meeting pleading that both races try to break the tension and then went on to talk about the good relations which had existed? Rosa didn't tell you that you can to go Montgomery any day and find a parking space now. Not only are people not riding the buses but they are really not shopping. The people in Montgomery, particularly the Negroes, buy only what they have to have. . . .

Nonviolence and the Montgomery Boycott*

REV. MARTIN LUTHER KING, JR.

SINCE THE PHILOSOPHY of nonviolence played such a positive role in the Montgomery Movement, it may be wise to turn to a brief discussion of some basic aspects of this philosophy.

First, it must be emphasized that nonviolent resistance is not a method for cowards; it does resist. If one uses this method because he is afraid or merely because he lacks the instruments of violence, he is not truly nonviolent. This is why Gandhi often said that if cowardice is the only alternative to violence, it is better to fight. He made this statement conscious of the fact that there is always another alternative: no individual or group need submit to any wrong, nor need they use violence to right the wrong; there is the way of nonviolent resistance. This is ultimately the way of the strong man. It is not a method of stagnant passivity. The phrase "passive resistance" often gives the false impression that this is a sort of "do-nothing method" in which the resister quietly and passively accepts evil. But nothing is further from the truth. For while the nonviolent resister is passive in the sense that he is not physically aggressive toward his opponent, his mind and emotions are always active, constantly seeking to persuade his opponent that he is wrong. The method is passive physically, but strongly active spiritually. It is not passive nonresistance to evil, it is active nonviolent resistance to evil.

A second basic fact that characterizes nonviolence is that it does not seek to defeat or humiliate the opponent, but to win his friendship and understanding. The nonviolent resister must often express his protest through noncooperation or boycotts, but he realizes that these are not ends themselves; they are merely means to awaken a sense of moral shame in the opponent. The end is redemption and reconciliation. The aftermath of nonviolence is the creation of the beloved community, while the aftermath of violence is tragic bitterness.

A third characteristic of this method is that the attack is directed against forces of evil rather than against persons who

* Excerpts from pp. 83-85 from STRIDE TOWARD FREEDOM: *The Montgomery Story* by Martin Luther King, Jr. Copyright © by Martin Luther King, Jr., Harper & Brothers, Inc., Publishers. Reprinted with the permission of Harper & Row, Publishers, Inc., New York.

happen to be doing the evil. It is evil that the nonviolent resister seeks to defeat, not the persons victimized by evil. If he is opposing racial injustice, the nonviolent resister has the vision to see that the basic tension is not between races. As I like to say to the people in Montgomery: "The tension in this city is not between white people and Negro people. The tension is, at bottom, between justice and injustice, between the forces of light and the forces of darkness. And if there is a victory, it will be a victory not merely for fifty thousand Negroes, but a victory for justice and the forces of light. We are out to defeat injustice and not white persons who may be unjust."

A fourth point that characterizes nonviolent resistance is a willingness to accept suffering without retaliation, to accept blows from the opponent without striking back. "Rivers of blood may have to flow before we gain our freedom, but it must be our blood," Gandhi said to his countrymen. The nonviolent resister is willing to accept violence if necessary, but never to inflict it. He does not seek to dodge jail. If going to jail is necessary, he enters it "as a bridegroom enters the bride's chamber."

One may well ask: "What is the nonviolent resister's justification for this ordeal to which he invites men, for this mass political application of the ancient doctrine of turning the other cheek?" The answer is found in the realization that unearned suffering is redemptive. Suffering, the nonviolent resister realizes, has tremendous educational and transforming possibilities. "Things of fundamental importance to people are not secured by reason alone, but have to be purchased with their suffering," said Gandhi. He continues: "Suffering is infinitely more powerful than the law of the jungle for converting the opponent and opening his ears which are otherwise shut to the voice of reason."

A fifth point concerning nonviolent resistance is that it avoids not only external physical violence but also internal violence of spirit. The nonviolent resister not only refuses to shoot his opponent but he also refuses to hate him. At the center of nonviolence stands the principle of love. The nonviolent resister would contend that in the struggle for human dignity, the oppressed people of the world must not succumb to the temptation of becoming bitter or indulging in hate campaigns. To retaliate in kind would do nothing but intensify the existence of hate in the universe. Along the way of life, someone must have sense enough and morality enough to cut off the chain of hate. This can only be done by projecting the ethic of love to the center of our lives. . . .

INTEGRATED BUS SUGGESTIONS*

This is a historic week because segregation on buses has now been declared unconstitutional. Within a few days the Supreme Court Mandate will reach Montgomery and you will be re-boarding *integrated* buses. This places upon us all a tremendous responsibility of maintaining, in face of what could be some unpleasantness, a calm and loving dignity befitting good citizens and members of our race. If there is violence in word or deed it must not be our people who commit it.

For your help and convenience the following suggestions are made. Will you read, study and memorize them so that our non-violent determination may not be endangered.

First, some general suggestions:

1. Not all white people are opposed to integrated buses. Accept goodwill on the part of many.
2. The *whole* bus is now for the use of *all* people. Take a vacant seat.
3. Pray for guidance and commit yourself to complete non-violence in word and action as you enter the bus.
4. Demonstrate the calm dignity of our Montgomery people in your actions.
5. In all things observe ordinary rules of courtesy and good behavior.
6. Remember that this is not a victory for Negroes alone, but for all Montgomery and the South. Do not boast! Do not brag!
7. Be quiet but friendly; proud, but not arrogant; joyous, but not boisterous.
8. Be loving enough to absorb evil and understanding enough to turn an enemy into a friend.

Now for some specific suggestions:

1. The bus driver is in charge of the bus and has been instructed to obey the law. Assume that he will co-operate in helping you occupy any vacant seat.
2. Do not deliberately sit by a white person, unless there is no other seat.
3. In sitting down by a person, white or colored, say "May I" or "Pardon me" as you sit. This is a common courtesy.

* Leaflet distributed to bus protesters, reprinted in *Stride Toward Freedom*, pp. 144-45. The U. S. Supreme Court ordered desegregation of Montgomery buses in December, 1956.

4. If cursed, do not curse back. If pushed, do not push back. If struck, do not strike back, but evidence love and good-will at all times.

5. In case of an incident, talk as little as possible, and always in a quiet tone. Do not get up from your seat! Report all serious incidents to the bus driver.

6. For the first few days try to get on the bus with a friend in whose non-violence you have confidence. You can up-hold one another by a glance or a prayer.

7. If another person is being molested, do not arise to go to his defense, but pray for the oppressor and use moral and spiritual force to carry on the struggle for justice.

8. According to your own ability and personality, do not be afraid to experiment with new and creative techniques for achieving reconciliation and social change.

9. If you feel you cannot take it, walk for another week or two. We have confidence in our people. GOD BLESS YOU ALL. . . .

*People in Motion**
The Story of the Birmingham Movement

> *"We want a beginning now! We have already waited 100 years."*
> —*Alabama Christian Movement for Human Rights: the Statement of Principles*

IN MAY, 1956, Alabama politicians "stood on the beach of history and tried to hold back the tide." They outlawed the National Association for the Advancement of Colored People, in a desperate attempt to halt the movement for Negro equality. But their action had precisely the opposite effect. For almost immediately the Negroes of Birmingham came together to form a movement which during the last ten years has transformed life in Birmingham—which has shaken America.

"They could outlaw an organization, but they couldn't out-

* Published by the Alabama Christian Movement for Human Rights, in cooperation with the Southern Conference Educational Fund, Inc., 1966. Excerpted by permission of Rev. Fred L. Shuttlesworth, President, ACMHR.

law the movement of a people determined to be free," said the Rev. Fred L. Shuttlesworth, president of the new group. And at a mass meeting called by a committee of Negro ministers, the Alabama Christian Movement for Human Rights (ACMHR) was born. Many Negroes in "the Johannesburg of North America" were afraid to join. But many others echoed the sentiments of Mrs. Rosa Walker, one of the first members: "I was frightened, but I figured we needed help to get us more jobs and better education. And we had the man here to help us."

In its original statement of principles, the ACMHR stated:

As free and independent citizens of the United States of America, we express publicly our determination to press forward persistently for freedom and democracy, and the removal from our society of any forms of second-class citizenship . . . We Negroes shall never become enemies of the white people. But America was born in the struggle for Freedom from Tyranny and Oppression. We shall never bomb any homes or lynch any persons; but we must, because of history and the future, march to complete freedom with unbowed heads, praying hearts, and an unyielding determination.

The new organization's first efforts were directed toward getting the City of Birmingham to hire Negroes as policemen. When petitions and delegations failed, a suit was filed against the Personnel Board, demanding the right of Negroes to take examinations for all civil service jobs. But it was not to be until ten years later, after months of picketing and marching outside city hall and the county courthouse, that the first four Negro policemen were hired.

In its first year, the movement also filed suit in federal court on behalf of a Milwaukee couple arrested because they sat in the "white" waiting room in the city's railway station.

Both these actions followed the pattern of court action established by the NAACP, and indeed, suits have always been one of the ACMHR's most effective weapons. But in December, 1956, the movement entered a new phase, and took on the character it was to retain—of a movement of people putting their bodies into a challenge to the system.

It was in December, 1956, that the U.S. Supreme Court ruled that bus segregation in Montgomery was illegal. This was a climax to the historic year-long Montgomery bus protest.

Immediately, the ACMHR announced that a group of its members would test segregation laws in their city by attempting to integrate Birmingham buses. The protest was scheduled for December 26.

But Christmas night, the night before the protest, the home of Rev. Shuttlesworth was bombed. The bed in which he was sleeping was directly over the spot where the bomb went off. The bed was blown to bits, but he escaped unhurt. Members of the ACMHR say he was saved to lead the movement.

Shuttlesworth took a neighbor who was hurt in the explosion to the hospital. Then he took a bus home—and he rode in front. The bombing strengthened the determination of his followers in the same way.

"On the 25th day of December, that's when they blew up Rev. Shuttlesworth's house," says Mrs. Walker. "And when I went to the meeting the next morning Rev. Shuttlesworth was the first thing I saw. And I knowed as how their house was blowed up, and I couldn't figure out how he was there. And I said then, that I'm going into it. And I went into it on that day."

More than 250 others "went into it" with Mrs. Walker. Twenty-one of them were arrested that day, one the following day. They were convicted and fined, and they then filed suit in Federal Court, in January, 1957. . . .

The question of desegregating the buses wasn't over until late 1959. At that time, Federal Court rulings held the police were wrong in arresting Negroes who rode the buses integrated in 1958 and the Milwaukee couple who sat in the railroad station in 1959. But the segregation signs were still up, and by now ACMHR people knew that court rulings only come to life when people put their bodies on the line in a challenge to the old ways. . . .

The victories were important and gave people the knowledge that they do have strength, but as yet life in Birmingham had not really changed. Ever since the movement began leaders had received threats of death over the telephone and through the mail. Phones rang all night and strange cars circled the blocks where leaders of the movement lived. Every night after the first bombing in December, 1956, volunteer guards sat all night watching the Shuttlesworth house and church.

Police joined in the harassment. They tapped the telephones and searched and arrested guards at the Shuttlesworth home. Every non-white who came through his street was stopped and questioned. One man was arrested for distributing literature in alleged violation of Alabama's anti-boycott law. Each week city detectives attended the ACMHR mass meetings. They stopped and searched members leaving the meetings and charged them with blocking traffic. One man, the Rev. Charles Billups, was arrested on a charge of interfering with the entrance of a detective at a meeting; it was

said he "touched the officer's coat." Later he was tied to a
tree and beaten by the Ku Klux Klan. Other ACMHR members were threatened with loss of their jobs, and some were
actually fired. . . .

During 1960 and 1961 the ACMHR filed a variety of suits
—to desegregate the parks and schools, to open airport eating
facilities, and to stop the police from attending ACMHR
meetings. When the case against the police came to trial,
Shuttlesworth was the lawyer. He didn't win, but the trial
provided a dramatic moment as it brought face-to-face Birmingham's leading adversaries: Shuttlesworth and Police
Commissioner Eugene "Bull" Connor, notorious for his enforcement of segregation. Thus one of the South's leading in-
tegrationists was in the unusual position of firing the questions while one of the South's leading segregationists was
under oath on the witness stand. . . .

During the last three years Birmingham has been less in
the news than it once was. This does not mean that the movement has become any less active. Nor, unfortunately, does it
mean that the power structure has begun to meet most of its
demands. Masses of people have been demonstrating almost
constantly during that time.

In October, 1963, demonstrations were resumed because
city officials and business leaders had broken the agreements
which ended demonstrations the previous spring. They had
agreed to upgrade Negroes and to end segregation in places
such as the city hall rest rooms and eating places. Although
the signs came down, discrimination continued by subterfuge.
"Our officials appear to think that mere discussion by an advisory committee can take the place of positive action," Shuttlesworth said.

The new demonstrations lasted for more than a year,
through a winter so cold that pickets sometimes had to be relieved every fifteen minutes. Finally the 1964 Civil Rights
Bill was passed. Because the people of Birmingham were already in motion they were able to make this the first city in
the South to have mass tests of the new law.

Miss Notie B. Andrews described the first test:

After the Civil Rights Bill was passed, everybody knew we was
going to town that morning. All the newsfolks in town was there
—looked like everybody was there. We had a news conference
and then we hit the streets.
Around two o'clock we went to all the restaurants and theaters
downtown and stayed there all afternoon. Where I went, they
were real nice. The other people were staring at us to see how we
would react, but we acted just like they weren't there. We stayed
so long that when we got back we found Rev. Shuttlesworth was

wondering whether we was in jail, because the others were all back.

After that, every day for about two weeks we would send a different group of people, in order to let them know we really meant that we were going to come in.

It was in this period too, that each of the five major downtown stores finally hired at least one Negro clerk.

Also that summer, papers qualifying the NAACP to resume operations in Alabama were accepted and processed by state officials—eight years after the group had been banned, touching off the founding of the Alabama Christian Movement. Alabama officials removed the ban after the U. S. Supreme Court decided unanimously it was unconstitutional.

Now the movement turned its attention again to the police force. Renewing a campaign that had been started by Rev. Shuttlesworth ten years previously, even before the founding of the ACMHR, they demonstrated for the hiring of Negro policemen. Although the legal barriers to Negroes taking the civil service examinations had been dropped as the result of an ACMHR suit in 1958, no Negro policemen had ever been hired. From June until December, 1965, the movement staged mass marches to the courthouse and city hall, day and night. By the time they stopped, Negro clerks were employed at the city hall. And in March the first four Negro policemen were hired.

In December, 1965, SCLC workers entered Birmingham for the first time since the 1963 demonstrations, to help the ACMHR mount a massive campaign for voter registration. At the time, out of about 120,000 eligible Negro voters in metropolitan Birmingham only about 22,000 had registered to vote.

And again, as in every battle the Negroes of Birmingham have fought, they had to take to the streets to win.

In the winter of 1965–66, officials in Birmingham were still throwing up every possible roadblock to Negroes' registering to vote. So the ACMHR demanded federal registrars. They also demanded registration in the people's neighborhoods at night, instead of during hours inconvenient to working people. "We want the courthouse brought to the people," Shuttlesworth said.

They marched again in the streets—and they won these demands. By May it was estimated that as many as 50,000 new Negro voters had been registered.

The marchers were also demanding employment of Negroes in various civil service positions in the city and county governments. . . .

The Birmingham freedom movement today, in late 1966,

stands like the movement in many places at a crossroads.

When one considers the original demands of the Alabama Christian Movement for Human Rights when it formed in 1956, a remarkable number of them have been at least partially achieved. The buses are desegregated, and so are the parks with the shameful exception of the closed swimming pools. School segregation has been broken, even though integration is still token. Public eating places are integrated if one can afford to eat in them; Negro police have been hired, although in token numbers. At least a few Negroes are working in jobs never open to them before; the bars to Negro voter registration have been torn down.

And, all important, white police cannot with impunity terrorize and brutalize Negroes on the streets and in their homes as they once could and did in Birmingham.

But no one here feels that the struggle is over or that the perfect society has arrived. The integration that exists is still token, for the great masses of black people jobs are still nonexistent or at the lowest rungs of the economic ladder. And the old and dilapidated houses along the streets of Birmingham's inner city stand as a reminder that this city has slum ghettos as depressed as any in the South or the nation.

In short, the Birmingham movement stands before the problem that the movement faces everywhere: the fact that our society simply has not found the way to provide great numbers of its citizens with a chance for a decent life. . . .

2. FROM SIT-INS TO THE VOTE

*Student Nonviolent Coordinating Committee Statement of Purpose**

CARRYING OUT THE *mandate of the Raleigh Conference to write a statement of purpose for the movement, the Temporary Student Nonviolent Coordinating Committee submits for careful consideration the following draft. We urge all local,*

---

* Drafted by Rev. James Lawson for the Temporary Student Nonviolent Coordinating Committee, May 14, 1960. Rev. Lawson, a leading exponent of the philosophy of nonviolence, was active as a teacher of nonviolent techniques in the early sit-in movement. He was expelled from Vanderbilt University for participating in civil rights activities.

state or regional groups to examine it closely. Each member of our movement must work diligently to understand the depths of nonviolence.

We affirm the philosophical or religious ideal of nonviolence as the foundation of our purpose, the pre-supposition of our faith, and the manner of our action. Nonviolence as it grows from Judaic-Christian traditions seeks a social order of justice permeated by love. Integration of human endeavor represents the crucial first step towards such a society.

Through nonviolence, courage displaces fear; love transforms hate. Acceptance dissipates prejudice; hope ends despair. Peace dominates war; faith reconciles doubt. Mutual regard cancels enmity. Justice for all overthrows injustice. The redemptive community supersedes systems of gross social immorality.

Love is the central motif of nonviolence. Love is the force by which God binds man to himself and man to man. Such love goes to the extreme; it remains loving and forgiving even in the midst of hostility. It matches the capacity of evil to inflict suffering with an even more enduring capacity to absorb evil, all the while persisting in love.

By appealing to conscience and standing on the moral nature of human existence, nonviolence nurtures the atmosphere in which reconciliation and justice become actual possibilities.

The Fight for the Vote[*]
Fayette County, Tennessee

Q (Mr. Lawson) What is your name?

A John McFerren. I was born and raised in Fayette County, in the State of Tennessee.

Q What is the population there?

A The population of that county is 20,000 Negroes.

Q How many white people?

* Testimony of John McFerren, chairman of the Original Fayette County Voters' League, presented to the Volunteer Civil Rights Commission at hearings January 31, 1960, in Washington, D. C. The hearings were organized by Ella J. Baker of the Southern Christian Leadership Conference and Carl Braden of the Southern Conference Educational Fund, Inc., and fifteen local civil rights and civic organizations.

A I do not know the number of whites.

On August 1, 1959, the members and myself went up to the courthouse to vote. First we went to the fire station. I pulled out my registration card and handed it to the registration lady and she picked up the card and looked at it and said—she called one of the other men over and said—he asked her—he said, "What are you going to do with these people?" He said, "Where do you live, the country or in town?" She said, "You go to the courthouse and vote."

When I got to the courthouse, me and my four other companions, I pulled out my registration card and handed it to the lady. She looked at the card and called over the man. She said to the man, she said, "If we turn all of these people down, we will get in trouble with the federal government."

Then I immediately turned and went out and called our legal counsel and our legal counsel advised us later we would bring a federal suit against the county. During the federal suit, the F.B.I. came out in the field and investigated me. When they investigated me, he brought back the report and gave the report to the sheriff. That put me on the hot dog stand.

Johnson was the F.B.I. man. He gave the report to the sheriff and immediately after then, my life was threatened.

(At this point, the witness was unable to continue.)

Q We will give him a few minutes to relax and come back, if there is time.

(Witness temporarily excused.) . . .

Q Will you pick up where you left off?

A The F.B.I. notified the sheriff and the F.B.I. came out there while I was picking cotton. They told me to go to tell the sheriff everything I know, that that was the thing to do, and so that night, I received a threatening telephone call. From that day to this, my wife and family and myself were threatened. And this F.B.I. man who came out to investigate the rights to vote, he was a native of Fayette County. He knew my father and before him, my grandfather, and we went back and talked with our legal counsel and we wrote to Hoover here in Washington. They sent another investigator out. I was on the hot dog stand. That is where I was.

Now, the teachers in the county are scared to register. They are even scared to talk to me on the street. When they see me coming, they run the other way and many farmers are harmed, today, on account we want to come to be first class citizens. They are making a move by the hundreds. They took the crop from the farm; would not sell it. They made them move because they even tried to raise it. When we, go up to register, the landlord would walk up and down to see if any of his tenants were in line. When they go to register, the sheriff calls the names and calls the landlord, and the landlord would make him move that night.

Q Have you tried to make a loan? Do you know of any people who tried to make a loan down there and could not make it?

A No Negroes in the County of Fayette County have a G. I. loan for a farm. They are all local loans down there thrown on the Negro ten or fifteen years ago. You cannot get a local loan to buy a farm. Now there is a few local loans that charge 25 percent interest on the money, but where they put that interest on the money, they take it out before you get the money. If you borrow $200, he will take the interest out before you get the money and I have borrowed money in my lifetime. I know what he gives me.

Q Those 25 percent interest charges are from private lenders?

A They are from private lenders, but the banks, they charge us 12 percent interest. I had not borrowed no money from the bank in about two or three years, but I have some notes at home I can show you, that charge 12 percent interest. Here is the way they do that. If you go in there to borrow some money, he will take out the interest before you get your money. What have you got to show?

Q Does the note read 12 percent?

A They don't put no interest at all on the note.

MR. LAWSON: Any questions?

MR. CAMPONESCHI: What do they threaten to do?

THE WITNESS: They call my wife. I reported this to the F.B.I. headquarters. They call my wife over the telephone. They groan over the telephone like somebody died. And I have a two-and-a-half ton truck. I do public hauling on the side and they threatened my driver. They said they would push him off the road. And I, myself, was threatened in that way. "If you keep moving with that voting issue, you will come up with a necktie around your neck."

The teachers in our county are under a tremendous strain because they are between the other side and ourselves. Now, we have registered—I do not have the accurate number—but approximately between 1,000 and 1,300 registered, by standing at the door, counting. But this count is not accurate because I have no records of the books.

Q Have you ever voted?

A I never voted in my life.

Q Have you been trying to vote all these years, ever since you have been 21?

A I tried to vote this year—last year, pardon me. Last year.

Q Tell us precisely what happened last year. Very briefly, what happened when you tried to vote?

A Well, four of us went out there together to vote. When we went in to vote, to the fire station, when I pulled my card out the fire station lady, she called another man over, and said, the man said, "Where do you live. In the country or town?" I told him I lived in the country. He told me, "You have to go to the courthouse to vote." When I got to the courthouse, I pulled the card out and gave it to the registration lady and they called another gentleman over and asked him, "What are we going to do with these folks? There are too many of them coming here and trying to vote. We will get in trouble with the federal government." He said, "This is an all white, Democratic primary election." That is what he said.

MR. LAWSON: Thank you very much.

There is one final thing I think the audience would be interested in.

THE WITNESS: Now, you might know, because of this voting issue, my mother was run down with a two-and-a-half ton truck.

Q What happened? Has there been any investigation of that?

A In other words, my mother was up in the yard and this guy, this man, with the two-and-a-half ton truck, was riding eight or nine miles an hour. He hit me and went across to my mother's yard and ran over her. She has not come back, yet. She is going to get all right, yet.

Q She is in the hospital?

A She has been in there.*

(Witness excused.)

* Hundreds of Fayette County Negroes, evicted after voter registration attempts, lived in a "Tent City" until a federal suit brought agreement that local whites would stop economic reprisals.

Literacy and Liberation*

SEPTIMA P. CLARK

THE TEACHER WROTE "Citizen" on the blackboard. Then she wrote "Constitution" and "Amendment." Then she turned to her class of 30 adult students.

"What do these mean, students?" she asked. She received a variety of answers, and when the discussion died down, the teacher was able to make a generalization.

"This is the reason we know we are citizens: Because it's written in an amendment to the Constitution."

An elderly Negro minister from Arkansas took notes on a yellow legal pad. A machine operator from Atlanta raised his hand to ask another question.

This was an opening session in an unusual citizenship education program that is held once each month at Dorchester Center, McIntosh, Georgia for the purpose of helping adults help educate themselves.

In a five day course, those three words became the basis of a new education in citizenship for the Negroes and whites who attended the training session. Participants left with a burning desire to start their own Citizenship Education schools among their own communities.

The program now being sponsored by the Southern Christian Leadership Conference has resulted in the training of more than eight hundred persons in the best methods to stimulate voter registration back in their home towns. Their home towns comprising eleven southern states from eastern Texas to northern Virginia. The program was transferred to SCLC from The Highlander Folk School in Monteagle, Tennessee.

I learned of Highlander in 1952 but attended my first workshop in 1954. In 1955 I directed my first workshop and did door to door recruiting for the school. Unable to drive myself I found a driver for my car and made three trips from Johns Island, South Carolina to Monteagle, Tennessee. On

* Excerpts from Septima P. Clark, "Literacy and Liberation," *Freedomways*, 4 (First Quarter, 1964), pp. 113-124. Septima Clark is director, Teacher Training, Citizenship Education Program, Southern Christian Leadership Conference. Reprinted by permission of *Freedomways, A Quarterly Review of the Negro Freedom Movement*, 799 Broadway, New York City.

each trip six islanders attended and were motivated. They became literate and are still working for liberation.

In 1954 in the South, segregation was the main barrier in the way of the realization of democracy and brotherhood. Highlander was an important place because Negroes and whites met on an equal basis and discussed their problems together.

There was a series of workshops on Community Services and Segregation; Registration and Voting; and Community Development. Then it became evident that the South had a great number of functional illiterates who needed additional help to carry out their plans for coping with the problems confronting them. Problems such as the following: Six-year-old Negro boys and girls walking five miles on a muddy road in icy, wet weather to a dilapidated, cold, log cabin school house in most of the rural sections of the South. In cities like Charleston, South Carolina children of that same tender age had to leave home while it was yet dark, 7:00 A.M., to attend an early morning session and vacate that classroom by 12:30 p.m. for another group in that same age bracket which would leave 5:30 p.m. for home (night time during the winter months). These children would pass white schools that had regular school hours and fewer children enrolled. The Negro parents accepted this for many years. They did not know what to do about it. They had to be trained.

Highlander had always believed in people and the people trusted its judgment and accepted its leadership. It was accepted by Negroes and whites of all religious faiths because it had always accepted them and made them feel at home. The staff at Highlander knew that the great need of the South was to develop more people to take leadership and responsibility for the causes in which they believed. It set out on a program designed to bring out leadership qualities in people from all walks of life. . . .

Prior to the Supreme Court's decision of 1954 the Negro communities of the South would have been characterized as uncoordinated, made up of groups whose interests diverged or conflicted. Today one can say that the school integration issue has served to mobilize and unify the groups. The present psychological health of Negro leaders is good. Such a thing as an official ballot handed to Negro leaders in Alabama, on which is engraved a rooster crowing "white supremacy" will not weaken their determination nor courage to be free. They have amassed funds, sent men to the Justice Department and taken their gerrymandering cases to the courts. Today they are registering to vote. The registrars are not hiding in the bank vaults any more. Literacy means liberation. . . .

The lines of communication are open now in many south-
ern states. The Supreme Court decision on school integration
and the ferment among the Negroes are held responsible.
Communication in Atlanta, Savannah and Macon, Georgia;
Charleston, Greenville, Spartanburg and Columbia, South
Carolina; Charlotte, Durham, Greensboro, and Asheville,
North Carolina; Nashville, Chattanooga, Memphis and
Knoxville, Tennessee; Little Rock, Arkansas; and Miami,
Florida, is on the basis of mutual respect rather than on the
paternalistic basis of the past. Literacy means liberation!

Into one of our workshops a large number of people came
from the human relations councils. They were interested primarily in the promotion of law and order in connection with
integration in the public schools, in voter education, care for
the indigent sick, housing, merit employment and juvenile de-
linquency. They felt that professionals needed to be more involved in the civil rights struggle. So they had to prepare
themselves to speak out to the power structure which in most
cases was not the most learned but held the purse strings to
county treasurers and influenced the already biased attitudes
of the local officers. Mrs. Alice Spearman, executive secretary
of Human Relations Council in South Carolina, brought together biracial groups to discuss each issue mentioned above
and these groups appointed committees to present their findings to the proper source.

Other participants were mostly new volunteer leaders,
many with little formal education. They had been doing the
leg work to increase registration and voting and wanted to
find improved ways of combatting the apathy found in southern communities. They acquainted each other with the facts
of local restrictions, often unknown outside a small area, and
at the end declared their intention of going home to work for
increased registration. They would work to counteract
through education the deliberate confusion of issues by newspapers, to explain the use of voting machines and to make registration and voting more convenient and pleasant.

Still another group were former Highlander students. They
came to give reports of the work done in their communities:
developing leadership, working on literacy in adult schools
and on recreation and health. They wanted help on specific
problems, from other communities and from the staff at Highlander. One group told of a new community center. They built
it with volunteer help and donations. They wanted a place so
that their children could stay in the community at nights.
They were taken twenty miles every day to the nearest school.
Everyone discussed ways of getting maximum use out of such

buildings and also the techniques of passing on to other communities their knowledge and skills in organizing for action. Another group wanted to know how to encourage parents to send their children to newly integrated schools. It was suggested that parents who have already lived through this experience could best encourage other parents to do the same. We next planned a workshop for the two groups of parents. It was a great success. The next year more eligible parents in Nashville responded. Nashville was working on the grade-a-year plan. Others were interested in a credit union to combat the practices of loan sharks. Information was gotten from state and regional credit union representatives, then presented to a teachers' group in Charleston; when the banks refused to let teachers have money over the summer because of the 1956 law prohibiting teachers from being members of the NAACP, the credit union did. It flourished and expanded. Here was a case of people with degrees who had to become literate economically.

Legal and administrative barriers to voting have forced the Negroes, especially, to realize their lack of educational opportunities. Former Highlander students had started an adult school on Johns Island (S.C.), and many members of that community learned to read and write, thus being enabled to pass the reading and writing tests for voter registration. Then leaders from neighboring islands came to Highlander to learn how they could establish adult schools.

So it was with all the workshops. They came with many problems. They carried most of them back home but they became eager to work on them and had many new ideas, as well as the example and encouragement of others to help them.

The basic purpose of the citizenship schools is discovering and developing local community leaders. One of the unique practical features of the concept is the ability to adapt at once to specific situations and stay in the local picture only long enough to help in the development of local leaders. These are trained to carry on an ever growing program of community development. The secret stems from the emphasis and the reliance on local leadership. It is my belief that creative leadership is present in any community and only awaits discovery and development.

The Southeastern Georgia Crusade for Voters comprised of the First U.S. Congressional District (18 counties) of Georgia, was organized in April, 1960 and became an affiliate of SCLC in September, 1961. The objective was to coordinate the political abilities of the eighteen counties by organizing a Crusade for Voters League in each county.

The types of programs fostered by the respective Crusades for Voters were naturally determined by the needs and resources of the individual counties. In the past year the Southeastern Georgia Crusade for Voters has conducted the following:

Voter Education Programs in seven counties, including the surveying of more than 30,000 Negroes and the registration of 5,000.

Thirty Adult Citizenship Schools in seven counties.

Organized Crusade for Voters organizations in nine counties.

Developed political awareness programs in five counties.

Supported four Negroes for public office in two counties.

Negotiated the appointment of more than 20 Negroes to governmental boards, commissions, and committees in two counties.

Negotiated the up-grading of many Negroes in governmental positions in one county.

Negotiated the hiring of Negroes in positions previously held by white-only in one county.

Conducted a Direct-Action Program in one county. . . .

The Crusade for Voters conducted a major Direct Action Program against segregation this summer. This program was under the direct leadership of Hosea L. Williams, president of the Crusade for Voters, who was assisted by Benjamin Van Clark, director of the Crusaders' Youth Program. Activities of the Direct Action Program consisted of daily morning training workshops, noon downtown marches and speeches, nightly mass meetings, nightly mass marches (after nightly meetings), daily sit-in demonstrations and daily picketing of certain segregated establishments.

During the period of demonstrations many Negroes were beaten by police. At least four Negroes were shot by whites. Demonstrators were frequently gassed by the police department and Georgia state troopers. Demonstrators were housed in disbanded jails without beds or toilet facilities. In some cases juveniles were held in custody for more than 25 days. Many Negroes lost their jobs, cars, and in some few cases, their homes.

Although there are many demonstrators yet to come to trial (and it is feared they will not be able to be bonded out because the solicitor will accept only property bonds), integration of the hotels, motels, theaters and bowling alleys has taken place.

Literacy means liberation. There are many ways to communicate injustices to the American public. These dramatic confrontations were necessary to educate white people in Savannah, Georgia and to make Negroes free enough to vote wisely and speak out.

July 1, 1962—June 30, 1963 was a year showing maturity in South Carolina. Communication between the races opened up and barriers came down.

The voting strength of Negroes increased tremendously. The Negroes attended citizen schools, joined civic organizations, formed new Improvement Associations and listened to new leaders who mushroomed in communities (mostly young people). The white people, observing the courage, spirit and persistence of demonstrators plus the arduous work of citizenship school teachers, decided that the best thing to do was to adhere to law and order.

In July, 1962 there were 40 citizenship schools in South Carolina. Today there are 80. Seventeen new ones have started since the August, 1963 workshop. The Negro voting strength increased from 57,000 to 150,000. . . .

Letter to Northern Supporters

ROBERT MOSES[*]

THE FOOD DRIVE you organized and publicized with the help of Dick Gregory and others has resulted in and served as the immediate catalyst for opening new dimensions in the voter registration movement in Mississippi.

Wherever food has been sent it has given the opportunity, depending directly upon the amount of food, for:

1. Contact with hundreds or thousands of Negroes.
2. Development of a core of workers who come to help process the applications, packaging and distribution of the food, and stay to help on the voter registration drive.

[*] Robert Moses was Mississippi State Project Director for the Student Nonviolent Coordinating Committee and co-director of the Mississippi Summer Project with David Dennis of the Congress of Racial Equality. This letter was dated Feb. 27, 1963, Greenville, Miss. The food and clothing drive was a popular Northern support activity as were later book drives.

3. An image in the Negro community of providing direct aid, not just "agitation."

The food is identified in the minds of everyone as food for those who want to be free, and the minimum requirement for freedom is identified as registration to vote.

The voting drives I've experienced in Mississippi have proceeded by steppes instead of slopes and we have been on a deep plateau all winter, shaking off the effects of the violence of August and September and the eruption that was Meredith at Ole Miss.

We know this plateau by now; we have had to crawl over it in McComb city, Amite and Walthall Counties, Hattiesburg, Greenwood and Ruleville. You dig into yourself and the community to wage psychological warfare; you combat your own fears about beatings, shootings and possible mob violence; you stymy, by your mere physical presence, the anxious fear of the Negro community, seeded across town and blown from paneled pine and white sunken sink to windy kitchen floors and rusty old stoves, that maybe you *did* come only to boil and bubble and then burst, out of sight and sound; you organize, pound by pound, small bands of people who gradually focus in the eyes of Negro and whites as people "tied up in that mess"; you create a small striking force capable of moving out when the time comes, which it must, whether we help it or not.

When a thousand people stand in line for a few cans of food, then it is possible to tell a thousand people that they are poor, that they are trapped in poverty, that *they* must move if they are to escape. In Leflore County there are 14,400 nonwhite workers, 12,060 make less than $1,500 a year and 7,200 of these make less than $500 a year. After more than 600 lined up to receive food in Greenwood on Wednesday, 20 Feb., and Sam's subsequent arrest and weekend in prison on Thurs. 21, Feb., over 100 people overflowed city hall on Mon. 25 Feb. to protest at his trial, over 250 gathered at a mass meeting that same night and on Tues. by 10:30 A.M., I had counted over 50 people standing in silent line in the county courthouse; they say over 200 stood in line across the day.

This is a new dimension for a voting program in Mississippi; Negroes have been herded to the polls before by white people, but have never stood en masse in protest at the seat of power in the iceberg of Mississippi politics. Negroes who couldn't read and write stood in line to tell the registrar they still wanted to vote, that they didn't have a chance to go to school when they were small and anyway Mr. John Jones can't read and write either and *he* votes.

We don't know this plateau at all. We were relieved at the absence of immediate violence at the courthouse, but who knows what's to come next.

The weather breaks in mid-April and I hope you will be able to continue to send food until then.

Progress Report, Danville, Virginia

AVON W. ROLLINS*

I. City Government
 (a) Two social workers.
 (b) One Negro policeman (looking for more qualified applicants).
 (c) Fair Employment Law.
 (d) Chairs have been replaced in City library, which had been taken out previously in an attempt to keep the races separated.

II. Downtown and Surrounding Areas
 (a) Some twenty-five Negroes have been employed in sales positions.
 (b) There are some six lunch counters open to the public in the downtown area.
 (c) And six in the surrounding shopping centers.

III. Dan River Mills
 (a) Dan River Mills has dropped all physical signs of segregation.
 (b) The two previously segregated textile unions have merged.
 (c) The Negro who was previously president of local Negro textile union is now vice-president of the over-all union.
 (d) Dan River Mills night high school has opened to Negroes on the same basis as to whites.

* Avon Rollins was a field secretary of the Student Nonviolent Coordinating Committee and an organizer with the Danville Movement. This report was prepared in early 1964 after the turbulent summer of 1963 when massive nonviolent demonstrations and violent resistance took place.

    (e) Dan River Mills trade school has now opened to Negroes on an equal basis.

IV. Milk Dairies employed three Negroes in sales positions.

V. Coca-Cola Bottling Co. employed one Negro salesman.

VI. Token Integration of City Schools

    (a) Eleven Negro students enrolled in previously all-white schools.

VII. Up-Grading in the Tobacco Industry

    (a) Citizenship School.
    For adults to learn how to read and write, how to write checks, and how to apply to become registered voters.

    (b) Scholarships to local youth leaders working in the movement:
      1. Samuel Giler
      2. Howard Logan
      3. Thomas Holt

    (c) Help on home mortgages.

    (d) For those who lost jobs because of their involvement in demonstrations.

    (e) Help to those who lost checks coming from unemployment compensation because of their involvement in demonstrations.

VIII. The Reborn Negro in the Community

    (a) A new sense of dignity for himself and for his fellow man.

    (b) A new sense of civic responsibility.

    (c) The refusal to accept segregation in any form and pride that he is a black man.

IX. Voter Registration

    (a) We have registered some 1,500 Negroes.

We (S.N.C.C.) are grateful to the Negro community for their assiduous efforts in bringing about these token accomplishments.

Revolution in Mississippi*

TOM HAYDEN

We are smuggling this note from the drunk tank of the county jail in Magnolia, Mississippi. Twelve of us are here, sprawled out along the concrete bunker; Curtis Hayes, Hollis Watkins, Ike Lewis, and Robert Talbert, four veterans of the bunker, are sitting up talking—mostly about girls; Charles McDew ("Tell the story") is curled into the concrete and the wall; Harold Robinson, Stephen Ashley, James Wells, Lee Chester Vick, Leotus Eubanks, and Ivory Diggs lay cramped on the cold bunker; I'm sitting with smuggled pen and paper, thinking a little, writing a little; Myrtis Bennett and Janie Campbell are across the way wedded to a different icy cubicle.

Later on Hollis will lead out with a clear tenor into a freedom song; Talbert and Lewis will supply jokes; and McDew will discourse on the history of the black man and the Jew. McDew—a black by birth, a Jew by choice and a revolutionary by necessity—has taken on the deep hates and deep loves which America, and the world, reserves for those who dare to stand in a strong sun and cast a sharp shadow.

In the words of Judge Brumfield, who sentenced us, we are "cold calculators" who design to disrupt the racial harmony (harmonious since 1619) of McComb into racial strife and rioting; we, he said, are the leaders who are causing young children to be led like sheep to the pen to be slaughtered (in a legal manner). "Robert," he was addressing me, "haven't some of the people from your school been able to go down and register without violence here in Pike county?" I thought to myself that Southerners are most exposed when they boast.

It's mealtime now: we have rice and gravy in a flat pan, dry bread and a "big town cake"; we lack eating and drinking utensils. Water comes from a faucet and goes into a hole.

This is Mississippi, the middle of the iceberg. Hollis is leading off with his tenor, "Michael, row the boat ashore, Alleluia; Christian brothers don't be slow, Alleluia; Mississippi's next to go, Alleluia." This is a tremor in the middle of the iceberg—from a stone that the builders rejected.

Bob Moses

Nov. 1, 1961

SNCC, IN ITS attempt to ignite a mass non-violent movement, designated the formidable and sovereign state of Mis-

* Tom Hayden, *Revolution in Mississippi*. Students for a Democratic Society, 1962.

sissippi as the site of its pilot project. Moses moved to Mc-Comb, a city of 13,000. He found a number of local adults, high school students, and non-student youth eager to assist him. They provided contacts, housing, some transportation, and (particularly the students) began canvassing the surrounding area, determining the numbers of registered and unregistered voters, informing the citizens of the SNCC program and inviting them to participate. By the end of the first week, John Hardy, Nashville, and Reggie Robinson, Baltimore, had arrived as SNCC field representatives to help in the project.

On August 7, 1961, the SNCC Voter Registration School opened in Burglundtown in a combination cinder block-and-paintless wood frame two-story structure which houses a grocery below and a Masonic meeting hall above. A typical voter registration (or citizenship) class involved a study of the Mississippi State Constitution, filling out of sample application forms, description of the typical habits of the Southern registrar—whose discretionary powers are enormous—and primarily attempted the morale building, encouragement and consequent group identification which might inspire the exploited to attempt registration.

On the first day of the school, four persons went down to the registrar's office in nearby Magnolia, the county seat of Pike; three of them registered successfully. Three went down on August 9th; two were registered. Nine went down on August 10th; one was registered. By this time, articles in the local press, the (McComb) *Enterprise-Journal,* had increased awareness of the project, stirring a few Negroes from Walthall and Amite to come to the McComb classes. However, the thrust of the movement was somewhat blunted on the evening of August 10th when one of the Negroes who had attempted to register was shot at by a white. (It is now clear that the shooting had nothing to do with the attempted registration that day. However, in the minds of the Negro community, for whom the vote is intimately connected with intimidation and violence, the association was made between the two events.) Attendance at the Voter Registration School quickly diminished.

Moses and the others began to rebuild. People were talked to; nights were spent in the most remote areas; days were spent canvassing all around. Then on August 15th, the first of a still continuing series of "incidents" occurred. On that day, Moses drove to Liberty (yes, it is ironic), the county seat of Amite, with three Negroes (Ernest Isaac, Bertha Lee Hughes and Matilda Schoby) who wished to register. Moses was asked to leave the registrar's office while the three attempted to fill out the registration forms. The three claim that while they were so engaged the registrar assisted a white female in answering several of the questions. Upon completing the test, the applicants were told by the registrar that their attempts were inadequate. The registrar then placed the papers in his desk and asked the three not to return for at least six months, at which time presumably they might try further. (I have been told by a reliable federal source that the tests were not of a quality character.)

Leaving Liberty, driving toward McComb, the group was followed by a highway patrolman, Marshall Carwyle Bates of Liberty, who flagged them over to the side of the road. Bates asked the driver, Isaac, to step out of his car and get inside of the police car in the rear. Isaac complied. Then Moses left the car and walked back to the police car to inquire about the nature of the pull-over. Bates ordered Moses back to the car and shoved him. Thereupon, Moses began to write the Marshall's name on a pad of paper, and was shoved into the car. Moses, incidentally, was referred to as the "nigger who's come to tell the niggers how to register." Finally, the contingent of four Negroes was ordered to drive to the Justice of the Peace's office in McComb, where Moses was eventually charged with impeding an officer in the discharge of his duties, fined $50 and given a suspended sentence. Moses phoned the Justice Department, collect, from the station, which alerted the police to his significance. (The local paper called collect the next day, was refused by the Justice Department, and asked editorially why Moses was so privileged.) The fine was paid by the NAACP in order to appeal the case, and Moses did go to jail for a period of two days, during which he did not eat.

On the same day several other SNCC persons entered Pike County: Gwendolyn Green, Washington; Travis Britt, New York; William Mitchell, Atlanta; Ruby Doris Smith, Atlanta; James Travis, Jackson; and MacArthur Cotton, Jackson. Responsibilities were divided and the canvassing increased.

During this same time there had been requests from Negroes in Walthall county to set up a school there. A site for the school and living quarters were offered. John Hardy was selected to go to the area. Along with several others, he established the school on August 18th. About 30 persons attended the first session. Eighty percent of the Negroes in Walthall are farmers, and 60 percent own their own land. The heavy schedule imposed on the farmers at this time of year required that classes be scheduled so as not to conflict with the workday schedule. School was held at the Mt. Moriah Baptist Church and at private homes. Moses came into Amite several days later and remained for nearly a week, teaching and visiting "out the dirt roads." On August 22nd, four Negroes tried to register in Liberty; none succeeded; no incident occurred. By this time, however, dramatic events were occurring in Pike County.

On August 18th, Marion Barry from Nashville, a SNCC field representative particularly concerned with initiating direct action, arrived in McComb. Those students too young to vote, many of whom had canvassed regularly, were eager to participate actively. The Pike County Non-Violent Movement was formed; workshops in the theory and practice of nonviolence were held. On August 26th two of the youths, Elmer Hayes and Hollis Watkins (both 18), sat-in at the lunch counter of the local Woolworth's, the first direct action incident in the history of the county. The two were arrested and remained in jail 30 days. The charge: breach of peace. Their arrest set the stage for a mass meeting in McComb on August 29th. The Reverend James Bevel, of Jackson, spoke to a crowd of nearly 200. The paper of the following day carried the story lead, in large type, and the local columnists warned the citizens that the Negroes were not engaged in a mere passing fad, but were serious in intention.

On August 30th, a sit-in occurred at the lunch counter of the local bus station. Isaac Lewis, 20, Robert Talbert, 19, and Brenda Lewis, 16, were arrested on charges of breach of peace and failure to move on. They remained in jail for 28 days. By now, a current of protest had been generated throughout the counties. Subsequent events intensified the feeling. On August 29th, Bob Moses took two persons to the registrar's office in Liberty. They were met by Billy Jack Caston (cousin of the sheriff and son-in-law of State Representative Eugene Hurst) who was accompanied by another cousin and the son of the sheriff. (Should this seem peculiar, read Faulkner.) Caston smashed Moses across the head and dropped him to the street. The other Negroes were not harmed. Moses' cuts required eight stitches. Moses filed assault and battery charges against Caston, perhaps the first time in the history of Amite that a Negro has legally contested the right of a white man to mutilate him at fancy. Approximately 150 whites attended the trial on August 31st. Among other questions, Caston's attorney asked Moses if he had participated in the riots in San Francisco or Japan; Moses replied that he had not. Upon the suggestion of law officials, Moses left the trial, at which he was the plaintiff, before the "not guilty" verdict in order to escape mass assault.

Meanwhile in Walthall, the first attempt to register Negroes since the Justice Department suit of the Spring of 1961 was made. Five persons went to Tylertown, the county seat, with John Hardy. As all businesses close at noon on Thursdays, only two of the five had time to take the test. One was a teacher, the other a senior political science major at Jackson State College (Negro). Both failed. On the same day Hardy, in an interview with the editor of the *Tylertown Times,* made a remark which was interpreted as an endorsement of atheism. This was to "mark" Hardy, if he had not already been marked. (See pp. 308-311 below.) On the following evening a mass "encouragement" meeting was held in rural Tylertown; about 80 attended. Again, a mass meeting was held on September 4th to emphasize the significance of the vote and of citizenship. . . .

Chaos . . . during the previous day Martin Luther King sent an open telegram to President Kennedy protesting a "reign of terror" in McComb, and calling the Executive's attention to recent beatings. Several new SNCC people, returning from a successful national trip in quest of funds for bond for the sit-inners, had arrived in McComb on the morning of the 4th. Among those arriving was Robert Zellner, a white man from Alabama who, as a white, was even more susceptible to mob hostility than a Negro, though in no sense could the Negro SNCC representatives feel secure.

The students—remember, 100 under 18 years of age—spent the mid-day preparing signs, and at about 2:30 P.M., they started to march downtown. Never before in McComb —never before in an area so rural, so violent—never before *anywhere in the South* with students so very young. One of them, 13 years old, has been charged with "assault with intent to kill" because she ran over the foot of a white woman in a supermarket with a push-cart, and, subsequently, the two slapped each other. That is simply an example. The others, while a little older, suffer the same system and are moved by the same courage. And so they went downtown—with 119 in all, including 19 students over age 18, Bob Moses, Charles McDew and Robert Zellner. They walked through the Negro neighborhoods where families watched from the windows and steps and yards, through the downtown business district, down to the edge of McComb, and back up to City Hall. There the march halted. Elmer Hayes, one of the original McComb sit-inners, began to pray on the steps. Three times the police asked him to move on. He refused and was arrested. Then it was Lewis, Talbert, and 16-year-old Brenda, in order, all arrested, Brenda violating juvenile parole. Each individual in the march stood quietly, waiting to be arrested. Moments before, a white man had tried to run over them with his automobile; now there were whites on foot, yelling, cursing. And each of the 114 left was quietly standing. Too much time was being taken up, so the police blew their whistles and pronounced everyone under arrest.

The whole march started up the stairs, on its way to be booked. As they did, a local white citizen reached out for Zellner and began to beat him. Hurting Zellner with the first punch, the man then grabbed him around the neck and began choking him and gouging his eyes. Then Bob Moses and Charles McDew were there, one holding the white's wrists, one clasping Zellner in protection. Moses and McDew were struck and dragged into the station by police, who then pulled in Zellner. The first statement inside the Police Chief's office, according to Zellner, was, "Ought to leave you out there." Everyone was arrested and placed in jail. The nineteen over 18 years of age were arraigned on October 5th, after a night in Pike County Jail. Before Judge Robert W. Brumfield of McComb's Police Court, they pled innocent to charges of disturbing the peace; bond was $100 each. Nine also pled innocent to the charge of contributing to delinquency of minors; bond was $200 each. Trial was set for 9 A.M., October 23rd.

The Justice Department Acts
United States v. Wood*

THE UNITED STATES appeals from the denial of a temporary restraining order pending a hearing for a preliminary injunction.[1] The Government seeks to restrain the defendants

---

* The U.S. Fifth Circuit Court of Appeals upheld the government in 1961 in its suit to enjoin the prosecution of a civil rights worker charged with assault when he took a prospective voter to the registrar's office. The section of the court's opinion detailing the Justice Department's complaint is excerpted here (*U.S. v. Wood*, 295 F. 2nd 772).

[1] In the alternative, if the order is not appealable, the Government insists that this Court has jurisdiction of its petition for injunction under the all-writs statute, 28 U.S.C.A. § 1651.

from prosecuting one John Hardy, a Negro, before a Justice of the Peace in Walthall County, Mississippi. . . .

The facts as stated in the complaint and affidavits of the Government are as follows:

There are at the present time some 2,490 Negroes of voting age in Walthall County, Mississippi, none of whom are registered to vote. There are some 4,530 white persons of voting age in Walthall County, a substantial majority of whom are registered. In July 1961, John Hardy, a Negro citizen, resident of Nashville, Tennessee, having completed two years at the Tennessee Agricultural and Industrial State College, came to Mississippi as a member of the "Student Non-Violent Coordinating Committee" for the purpose of encouraging Negroes to register and vote. This organization is currently sponsoring a voter registration project in Walthall, Amite, and Pike Counties, Mississippi. In early August, John Hardy and several other Negro students came to Walthall County to set up a voting registration school to teach the qualified local Negroes how to register and to encourage them to make application to the Voting Registrar. From August 18 to September 9, they conducted classes for several hours a day. In these classes, Hardy and his helpers would issue facsimiles of the necessary registration forms and a copy of the Constitution of Mississippi. Those attending the classes would practice filling out the forms, copying sections of the Mississippi Constitution, and explaining their meaning. Attendance varied from 25 to 50 each evening.

The first attempt of participants in the school to register took place on August 30, when Hardy accompanied five Negroes to the Registrar's office, where at least two completed the registration forms. Outside the Registrar's office, Hardy encountered the Sheriff of Walthall County, Edd Craft (a defendant), in the company of the editor of the *Tylertown Times*. The Sheriff asked Hardy a number of questions about the registration school and whether he had a driver's license. The Sheriff soon left, but the editor of the *Tylertown Times* interviewed Hardy more extensively for an article which appeared on the front page of the *Tylertown Times* the next day. On September 5, 1961, three more Negroes went to register; on September 6, one Negro; on September 7, two Negroes. The incident giving rise to this action took place on September 7, and since then no Negroes have attempted to apply for registration in Walthall County.

On September 4, Mrs. Edith Simmons Peters, a Negro, aged 63, owner of an 80-acre farm in Walthall County, having had an eighth-grade education, attended her first registration class. On about the same day, Lucius Wilson, a Negro, aged 62, owner of a 70-acre farm in Walthall County, also started attendance. By September 6, they thought they were ready to apply and agreed to accompany Hardy to the Registrar's office the next morning. They arrived in Tylertown in Mrs. Peters' pickup truck at about 9:30 on the morning of September 7 and went to the Registrar's office in the courthouse. The Registrar, John Q. Wood, a defendant, was in an inner office; Mrs. Peters and Wilson went in and Hardy remained just outside the door. When Registrar Wood looked up, Mrs. Peters told him that they desired to register. Wood then replied that, "I am not registering anyone now. You all have got me in court and I refuse to register anyone else until this court is cleared up." John Hardy heard this from his position outside the door of the office some 5 or 6 feet away and came in. According to the affidavits of the Government, Hardy had given Wood only his name when Wood got up and said, "I want to see you John." He then brushed past Hardy into the main room and from the drawer of a desk took out a revolver. Holding the gun down by his right side he pointed to the door going outside and said, "Do you see that door, John?" Hardy replied, "Yes." Wood told him, "You get out of it." Hardy said OK, and turned to go. Wood followed him, and just as Hardy got to the door, Wood struck him on the back of the head, saying, "Get out of here you damn son-of-a-bitch and don't come back in here." Mrs. Peters and Wilson rushed on out, held Hardy up, and helped him out of the building. Hardy went first to the newspaper office, where he told the editor what had happened. The editor instructed him to get medical attention. Meanwhile, Wilson went to get the pickup truck, and Mrs. Peters helped Hardy eventually to a little cafe. Wilson returned and they headed out to the street. When asked what he was going to do, Hardy then told several people that he had better find the sheriff. Going up the street, they met the sheriff and, according to the affidavit of Mrs. Peters,

They met right where I was standing and the sheriff asked, "What happened to you, boy." John told the sheriff what had happened. The sheriff told him he didn't have no business in that courthouse. Wilson walked up at this time. The sheriff then said to John, "If that boy (pointing to Wilson) wants to register he know (sic) how to go down to that courthouse and he don't need you to escort him. You didn't have a bit of business in the world down there. You is from Tennessee, you was in Tennessee and you ought to have stayed there." The sheriff told him to "Come on." John asked him, "Are you arresting me?" The Sheriff said "Yes." John asked "On what charges" and the sheriff said for disturbing the peace and bringing an uprising among the people. John said, "Will you allow me to tell my side of the story." The sheriff said, "Don't give me none of your head boy, or I will beat you within an inch of your life." After the sheriff took John, I went home.

At the Tylertown jail, Hardy was interviewed twice during the day of the 7th—first, by the defendants Sheriff Edd Craft and City Attorney Breed Mounger, and later by the same two plus defendant Michael Carr, the local District Attorney for the State of Mississippi. That evening, because the feeling about the incident was evidently running high in the community, Hardy was transferred by the defendants to the jail in Magnolia, Mississippi. Hardy was released on bond the next morning and his trial for disturbing the peace was set for the 22nd of September.

Hardy claims in his affidavit that, about the time the formal charge was entered, the District Attorney took him into a room "and several white people whom I can't identify told me that I was in a lot of trouble and that I was asking for a lot of trouble to come down there; that they had good Negroes here and that they treated their darkies good but that I was causing a lot of trouble. The Justice of the Peace was present but the sheriff was out." There are no allegations that Hardy was otherwise mistreated in any way during his confinement.

The appellees move this Court to dismiss the appeal, and, at the very outset, this Court is faced with the question of its jurisdiction. The appeal is from the denial of a temporary restraining order. The Government admits that ordinarily the denial of a temporary restraining order is not an interlocutory order refusing an injunction within the meaning of 28 U.S.C.A. § 1292(a), and is not otherwise appealable. The Government claims that, under the special circumstances of this case, the denial of the temporary restraining order is in the nature of a final decision from which an appeal may be taken under 28 U.S.C.A. § 1291.

The substance of the Government's case under the "First Claim" of its complaint is that the prosecution of Hardy, regardless of outcome, will effectively intimidate Negroes in the exercise of their right to vote in violation of 42 U.S.C.A. § 1971. This, it insists, is a claim entitling it to injunctive relief.

The Limits of Nonviolence*

HOWARD ZINN

WHEN I WENT to Albany, Georgia, during the first wave of demonstrations and mass arrests in December of 1961, I had been in Atlanta for five years and thought I had learned some important things about the South, as observer and minor participant in the the civil rights struggle. I had written an optimistic article for *Harper's Magazine* about the possibility of changing the *behavior* (not immediately his *thinking*) of the white Southerner without violence, by playing upon his self-interest, whether through economic pressure or other means which would forcefully confront him with hard choices. And in Atlanta, I saw such changes come about, through the pressure of lawsuits, sit-ins, boycotts, and sometimes by just the threat of such actions. Nonviolence was not only hugely appealing as a concept. It worked.

And then I took a good look at Albany, and came back troubled. Eight months later, when the second crisis broke out in Albany, in the summer of 1962, I drove down again from Atlanta. The picture was the same. Again, mass demonstrations and mass arrests. Again, the federal government stood by impotent while the chief of police took control of the constitutional rights of citizens.

My optimism was shaken but still alive. To those people around me who said that Albany was a huge defeat, I replied that you could not measure victories and defeats only by tangible results in the desegregation of specific facilities, that a tremendous change had taken place in the thinking of Albany's Negroes, that expectations had been raised which could not be stilled until the city was transformed.

Today, over a year later, after studying events in Birmingham and Gadsden and Danville and Americus, after interviewing staff workers of the Student Nonviolent Coordinating Committee just out of jail in Greenwood, Mississippi, watch-

* Howard Zinn, "The Limits of Nonviolence," *Freedomways*, 4 (First Quarter, 1964), pp. 143-48. Reprinted by permission of *Freedomways, A Quarterly Review of The Negro Freedom Movement*, 799 Broadway, New York, N.Y. 10003. Howard Zinn was chairman of the History Department of Spellman College and now teaches history at Boston College.

ing state troopers in action in Selma, Alabama, and talking at length to voter registration workers in Greenville, Mississippi, I am rethinking some of my old views. Albany, it seems to me, was the first dramatic evidence of a phenomenon which now has been seen often enough to be believed: that there is a part of the South impermeable by the ordinary activities of nonviolent direct action, a monolithic South completely controlled by politicians, police, dogs, and prod sticks. And for this South, special tactics are required.

One portion of the South has already been removed from the old Confederacy. This part of the South, represented by places like Richmond, Memphis, Nashville, Louisville, and Atlanta, is still fundamentally segregationist—as is the rest of the nation, North and South—but the first cracks have appeared in a formerly solid social structure. In these places, there is fluidity and promise, room for maneuver and pressure and accommodation; there is an economic elite sophisticated enough to know how badly it can be hurt by outright resistance, and political leaders shrewd enough to take cognizance of a growing Negro electorate. There will be much conflict yet in Atlanta and in Memphis. But the tactics of nonviolent direct action can force ever greater gains there.

Then there is the South of Albany and Americus, Georgia; of Gadsden and Selma, Alabama; of Danville, Virginia; of Plaquemines, Louisiana; of Greenwood and Hattiesburg and Yazoo City, Mississippi—and a hundred other towns of the Black Belt. Here, where the smell of slavery still lingers, politicians are implacable, plantation owners relentless, policemen unchecked by the slightest fear of judgment. In these towns of the Black Belt, a solid stone wall separates black from white, and reason from fanaticism; nonviolent demonstrations smash themselves to bits against this wall, leaving pain, frustration, bewilderment, even though the basic resolve to win remains alive, and some kind of ingenuous optimism is left untouched by defeat after defeat.

I still believe that the Albany Movement, set back again and again by police power, has done a magnificent service to the Negroes of Albany—and ultimately, to the whites who live in that morally cramped town. I still believe that the three hundred Negroes who waited in line near the county courthouse in Selma, Alabama, from morning to evening in the shadow of clubs and guns to register to vote, without even entering the doors of that courthouse, accomplished something. But I no longer hold that a simple repetition of such nonviolent demonstrative action—which effectively broke through barriers in the other part of the South—will bring victory. I am now convinced that the stone wall which blocks expectant Negroes in every town and village of the hard-core South, a wall stained with the blood of children, as well as others, and with an infinite capacity to absorb the blood of more victims—will have to be crumbled by hammer blows.

This can be done, it seems to me, in one of two ways. The first is a Negro revolt, armed and unswerving, in Mississippi, Alabama and southwest Georgia, which would result in a terrible waste of human life. That may be hard to avoid unless the second alternative comes to pass: the forceful intervention of the national government, to smash, with speed and efficiency, every attempt by local policemen or politicians to deprive Negroes (or others) of the rights supposedly guaranteed by the Constitution.

Unaware of the distinction between the two Souths, not called upon for such action in places like Atlanta and Nashville, and uncommitted emotionally and ideologically to racial equality as a first-level value, the national government has played the role of a hesitant, timorous observer. It will have to move into bold action, or face trouble such as we have not seen yet in the civil rights crisis. This is my thesis here, and the story of Albany, Georgia may help illustrate it.

Federal law was violated again and again in Albany, yet the federal government did not act. In effect, over a thousand Negroes spent time in prison, and thousands more suffered and sacrificed, in ways that cannot be expressed adequately on paper, as a mass substitute for federal action.

Judicial decisions in this century have made it clear that the Fourteenth Amendment, besides barring officials from dispensing unequal treatment on the basis of race, also prohibits them from interfering with the First Amendment rights of free speech, petition, and assembly. Yet in Albany over one thousand Negroes were locked up in some of the most miserable jails in the country for peacefully attempting to petition the local government for a redress of grievances. *And the Justice Department did nothing.*

Section 242 of the U.S. Criminal Code, which comes from the Civil Rights Act of 1866 and the Enforcement Act of 1870, creates a legal basis for prosecution of: "Whoever, under color of any law . . . wilfully subjects . . . any inhabitant of any State . . . to the deprivation of any rights, privileges, or immunities secured or protected by the Constitution and laws of the United States. . . ." Three times in succession, in November and December 1961, the police of the city of Albany, by arresting Negroes and whites in connection with their use of the terminal facilities in that city, violated a right which has been made clear beyond a shadow of a doubt. Yet the federal government took no action.

Today, the wheels of the nonviolent movement are churning slowly, in frustration, through the mud of national indifference which surrounds the stone wall of police power in the city of Albany. As if to give a final blow to the Albany Movement, the Department of Justice is now prosecuting nine of its leaders and members, who face jail sentences up to ten years, in connection with the picketing of a white grocer who had served on a federal jury. One of the defendants is Dr. W. G. Anderson, former head of the Albany Movement. Another is Slater King, now heading the Movement. *It is the bitterest of ironies that Slater King, who pleaded in vain for federal action while he himself was jailed, while his wife was beaten by a deputy sheriff, while his brother was beaten, is now being vigorously prosecuted by the U.S. Department of Justice on a charge which can send him to jail for five years.*

The simple and harsh fact, made clear in Albany, and reinforced by events in Americus, Georgia, in Selma and Gadsden, Alabama, in Danville, Virginia, in every town in Mississippi, is that the federal government abdicated its responsibility in the Black Belt. The Negro citizens of that area were left to the local police. The United States Constitution was left in the hands of Neanderthal creatures who cannot read it, and whose only response to it has been to grunt and swing their clubs.

The responsibility is that of the President of the United States, and no one else. It is his job to enforce the law. And the law is clear. Previously the civil rights movement joined in thrusting the responsibility on Congress when the President himself, without any new legislation, had the constitutional power to enforce the Fourteenth Amendment in the Black Belt.

The immediate necessity is for a *permanent* federal presence in the Deep South. I am not talking of occupation by troops, except as an ultimate weapon. I am suggesting the creation of a special force of federal agents, stationed throughout the Deep South, and authorized to make immediate on-the-spot arrests of any local official who violates federal law. The action would be preventive, before a crisis has developed, and would snuff out incipient fires before they got going, by swift, efficient action. Such a force would have taken Colonel Al Lingo into custody as he was preparing to use his electric prod sticks on the Freedom Walkers crossing the border into Alabama. Such a force would have taken Governor Wallace to the nearest federal prison the very first time he blocked the entrance of a Negro student into the University of Alabama, and would have arrested Sheriff Jim Clark as he moved to drag those two SNCC youngsters off the steps of the federal building in Selma.

Many liberals are affronted by such a suggestion; they worry about civil war. My contention is that the white Southerner submits—as do most people—to a clear show of authority; note how Governors Wallace and Barnett gave in at the last moment rather than go to jail. Once Southern police officials realize that the club is in the other hand, that *they* will be behind bars, that *they* will have to go through all the legal folderal of getting bond and filing appeal, etc. which thousands of Negroes have had to endure these past few years—things will be different. The national government needs to drive a wedge, as it began to do in the First Reconstruction, between the officialdom and the ordinary white citizen of the South, who is not a rabid brute but a vacillating conformist.

Burke Marshall, head of the Civil Rights Division of the Department of Justice, has been much disturbed by this suggestion of "a national police force or some other such extreme alternative." If a national police force is extreme, then the United States is already "extremist," because the Federal Bureau of Investigation is just that. It is stationed throughout the country and has the power to arrest anyone who violates federal law. Thus, it arrests those who violate the federal statutes dealing with bank robberies, interstate auto thefts and interstate kidnapping. But it does *not* arrest those who violate the civil rights laws. I am suggesting an organization of special agents, who will arrest violators of civil rights laws the way the F.B.I. arrests bank robbers.

The continued dependence on nonviolence by the civil rights movement is now at stake. Nonviolent direct action can work in social situations where there are enough apertures through which economic and political and moral pressure can be applied. But it is ineffective in a totally closed society, in those Black Belt towns of the Deep South where Negroes are jailed and beaten and the power structure of the community stands intact.

The late President Kennedy's political style was one of working from crisis to crisis rather than undertaking fundamental solutions—like a man who settles one debt by contracting another. This can go on and on, until the day of reckoning. And that day may come, in the civil rights crisis, this summer just before the election.

There is a strong probability that this July and August will constitute another "summer of discontent." The expectations among Negroes in the Black Belt have risen to the point where they cannot be quieted. CORE (Congress of Racial Equality), SCLC (Southern Christian Leadership Conference) and the intrepid youngsters of the Student Nonviolent Coordinating Committee, are determined to move forward.

With the probability high of intensified activity in the Black Belt this summer, the President will have to decide what to do. He can stand by and watch Negro protests smashed by the local police, with mass jailings, beatings, and cruelties of various kinds. Or he can take the kind of firm action suggested above, which would simply establish clearly what the Civil War was fought for a hundred years ago, the supremacy of the U.S. Constitution over the entire nation. If he does not act, the Negro community may be pressed by desperation to move beyond the nonviolence which it has maintained so far with amazing self-discipline.

Thus, in a crucial sense, the future of nonviolence as a means for social change rests in the hands of the President of the United States. And the civil rights movement faces the problem of how to convince him of this, both by words and by action. For, if nonviolent direct action seems to batter itself to death against the police power of the Deep South, perhaps its most effective use is against the national government. The idea is to persuade the executive branch to use its far greater resources of nonviolent pressure to break down the walls of totalitarian rule in the Black Belt.

The latest victim of this terrible age of violence—which crushed the life from four Negro girls in a church basement in Birmingham, and in this century has taken the lives of over fifty million persons in war—is President John F. Kennedy, killed by an assassin's bullet. To President Johnson will fall the unfinished job of ending the violence and fear of violence which has been part of the everyday life of the Negro in the Deep South.

4. VIOLENT WHITE RESISTANCE

Freedom Riders in Montgomery*

STUART H. LOORY

MONTGOMERY, ALABAMA, MAY 20.—A wild mob of men and women, uncontrolled by police, pounced on newsmen and then on a group of nineteen Negro and white students who alighted today at the Greyhound bus terminal here after a ride from Birmingham to test segregated intrastate bus practices.

I trailed the bus from Birmingham to Montgomery in a car and was on the bus platform in the middle of the violence but escaped injury.

The small group of men and women was attacked by a mob of 100 at first. But the mob rapidly grew into the thousands.

"Get those niggers," one darkhaired woman, primly clad in a yellow dress, shouted.

The mob had first pummeled three National Broadcasting Co. newsmen and several other photographers, smashing their equipment. Then it turned to vent its unsatisfied fury on the band of students who stood quietly on the bus platform, apparently not knowing what to do after completing the ride from Birmingham.

Using metal pipes, baseball bats, sticks and fists, the mob surged on the small group of Freedom Riders, clubbing, punching, chasing and beating both whites and Negroes. When some of the bus riders began to run, the mob went after them, caught them and threw them to the ground. The attackers stomped on at least two of them. One of the mobsters carried an open knife but didn't use it.

In two hours it was over, after the police used tear gas.

* Stuart H. Loory, "Reporter Tails 'Freedom' Bus, Caught in Riot," *New York Herald Tribune*, May 21, 1961. (©) 1961, New York *Herald Tribune*. Reprinted by permission of the *World Journal Tribune*.

The Freedom Rides were a test of the Interstate Commerce Commission's order against segregation in interstate buses and terminals. The Rides were begun by the Congress of Racial Equality and later, after a bus was burned by a mob in Anniston, Alabama, and riders were beaten in Birmingham, the rides were continued by the Nashville Student Movement and CORE members. Over 50 Freedom Riders were jailed in Parchman penitentiary near Jackson, Miss.

The toll was twenty-two injured with five of them in the hospital. Of the injured, eight were white—four newsmen, two girls from the bus, a male student and John Seigenthaler, thirty-two, administrative assistant to United States Attorney General Robert F. Kennedy.

One woman was among the nine persons arrested—all of them white. Some were booked on charges of disorderly conduct and refusing to obey an officer. Two were held on drunk charges.

After the rioting came to an end in the terminal, two Negroes were attacked in front of the building. They were slapped, punched, knocked down and stomped on.

Then, in the intersection of Adams and Court Sts., a half block from the terminal, a mob of whites put upon a group of Negroes. A white threw a bottle at a Negro. The Negroes, all townspeople, retaliated with rocks. Then a white poured an inflammable liquid over a Negro and set his clothes on fire. The police and mounted sheriff's deputies broke the riot up with tear gas and the crowd dispersed for the day.

Gov. John Patterson in a statement said: "I have no sympathy for law violators whether they be agitators from outside Alabama or inside-the-state troublemakers."

An hour after the police broke up the mob, Gov. Patterson said:

"It is our duty to maintain the law and I will not allow any group to take the law into their hands. The good name of our state and our people is at stake, and I can state frankly that violence of any type will not be tolerated.

"The highways of Alabama are safe and state patrolmen will do all in their power to enforce law and order at all times. We have the men, the equipment and the will to keep the public peace, and we use no help—from the federal government, from 'interested citizens' or anyone else.

"While we will do our utmost to keep the public highways clear and to guard against all disorder, we cannot escort busloads or carloads of rabble-rousers about our state from city to city for the avowed purpose of disobeying our laws, flaunting (sic) our customs and traditions and creating racial incidents. Such unlawful acts serve only to further enrage our population. I have no use for these agitators or their kind."

From the time the split-level St. Petersburg Express pulled out of the Greyhound terminal in Birmingham at 8:30 a. m., Central Standard Time, until it arrived at the terminal here at 10:23 a. m., the ride went without incident. It was escorted by Birmingham motorcycle police, their sirens screaming, to the city limits and then picked up by the state highway patrol, which brought it almost to the city limits of Montgomery. One unmarked police car, carrying two plain-clothesmen, stayed behind the road cruiser constantly as it barreled down the highway at speeds up to eighty-seven miles an hour.

Overhead, a highway patrol airplane circled continuously, looking for potential danger on the seven-minute ride from the Montgomery city limits to the terminal. Two Montgomery detectives followed the bus in an unmarked car. Police cars were seen all along the route.

But when the bus pulled into the terminal, there was not a policeman in sight. The mob gathered quickly on the platform.

The students, somber and quiet, stepped off the bus. Newsmen, including the television men with cameras and microphones, approached them for an interview.

John Lewis, twenty-one, of Troy, Alabama, a student at the American Baptist Seminary in Nashville, Tennessee, acted as spokesman for the group. He was asked the purpose of the trip.

"We just got out of Birmingham. We got to Montgomery. . . ." he said and then his words trailed off as his gaze fixed over the shoulder of this reporter.

Mr. Lewis had spotted the mob approaching. The group of students and newsmen started to give way down the platform to the advancing crowd.

One of the mob hit Moe Levy of NBC across the face. That was the first blow. The mob surrounded the cameramen, grabbed their equipment and flung it against the pavement until microphone, recording equipment and cameras were broken shambles. Meanwhile, a *Life* magazine cameraman was attacked.

Then the mob turned to the students—sixteen Negroes, two white girls and a white man.

"Get those niggers!" the mob shouted.

The group was standing with their backs to a metal tube fence atop a ten-foot retaining wall. Below the wall was a post office parking lot and driveway. A white spectator was heard explaining what happened to a late coming friend this way:

"They just took those niggers and threw them over that fence. They didn't push them, they didn't shove them, they threw them over that rail."

His description was only a little exaggerated. Some of the students were indeed thrown, others jumped, some were pushed. All landed atop cars parked next to the wall. They scampered down from the cars and ran onto the post office loading platform. No asylum was granted.

Now it was five minutes after the outbreak started. There were still no police in sight. The fighting had spread to streets surrounding the terminal and the post office driveway.

The mob began hurling the baggage after the students. The suitcases landed on the cars and on the ground, spilling out their contents—here a black bow tie, there a religious picture postcard, somewhere else a purple nightgown and a Bible.

Then, ten minutes after the first slap, a squad of police arrived under the command of Public Safety Commissioner L. B. Sullivan.

"I really don't know what happened," Mr. Sullivan told this reporter. "When I got here all I saw were three men lying in the street. There was two niggers and a white man.

"We called an ambulance for the white man but it was broken down and couldn't come, so two policemen took him to the hospital. I don't know what happened to the niggers."

The one white man this reporter saw with severe head injuries—his face was covered with blood, his lips and eyes were swollen, his blond hair caked with matted blood and dirt—was identified by Mr. Lewis as James M. Zwerg, twenty-one, an exchange student from the University of Wisconsin attending Fisk University in Nashville this year.

Before the bus left Birmingham, Mr. Zwerg and two white girls had sat with the Negroes for eighteen hours waiting to board a bus to Montgomery. Two hours before the bus pulled out, they gathered on the platform and sang Negro spirituals and hymns. Mr. Zwerg sang a solo part in "Oh Lord, keep your eyes on the prize."

Now his beating was over. He stood between Mr. Lewis, who was also beaten, and William Barbee, nineteen, another Nashville Seminary student. All three were bleeding.

Police made no effort to render first aid.

"The niggers will have to get out of here in a nigger taxi. The white boy will have to go in a white taxi," one officer said.

Dazed, Mr. Zwerg was led to a green Chevrolet carrying the markings of Lane's Taxi at the terminal. He sat there. The taxi driver would not come near the car.

While policemen refused to interfere, two teen-agers from the mob poked their heads through the cab's open windows.

Mr. Zwerg's eyes were open but expressionless. He hardly moved. The bleeding had stopped.

Softly, one of his tormentors said:

"You're a rotten son of a bitch. Your mother is a dog. You are a dog. You know that? You ride the niggers."

Mr. Zwerg shook his head in agreement.

"Can't you do something to get him out of here," Mr. Lewis asked this reporter, who witnessed the exchange.

I turned to a detective and said, "Excuse me, I don't want to butt in, but can't you do something to get him out of here," pointing to Mr. Zwerg.

The detective, nattily dressed in brown suit, conservative tie and straw hat, a diamond Masonic sword in his lapel, said: "He's free to go."

"But can't you get the driver of this taxi to take him away?"

"We ain't arranging transportation for these people. We didn't arrange their transportation here and we ain't going to take them away."

I explained the situation to Mr. Zwerg.

"You can't get me out of here. I don't even know where I am or how I got here," Mr. Zwerg said.

An hour later, he was still sitting in the cab.

One eyewitness to Mr. Zwerg's beating said he was the first of the students struck. Dan O. Dowe, state editor of *The Alabama Journal*, said:

"Mr. Zwerg was hit with his own suitcase in the face. Then he was knocked down and a group pummeled him. Then one of the mob members picked him up and put his [Mr. Zwerg's] head between his [the mob member's] knees. Then the others took turns hitting him."

While all this was happening, I was standing next to a young father and his blonde, red-faced daughter who was about three.

"Daddy, what are they doing?"

The father didn't answer.

"Daddy, what's happening?"

"Well, they're really carrying on," the father said as he watched the mob.

A short-order cook joined the father. "Those niggers are getting what for today," he said, smiling. The father didn't smile.

"Daddy, what are they doing?"

I saw a reporter and photographer from *The Birmingham News* run for their car. The photographer had had his 35-mm. camera with expensive lens smashed by the crowd.

"Where are you going?" I asked.

"Take your tie off and get in this car. If anybody asks you, you're a Ku Kluxer, remember that."

I removed my tie. We drove around the block. I got out of the car and went back to the terminal.

Joe C. Morgan, president of Local 1314, Amalgamated

Street, Electric Railway and Motor Coach Employees of America, A. F. L.-C. I. O., along with J. T. Duncan, chief Greyhound dispatcher in Birmingham, had ridden with the students.

"We were told we would have protection all the way," Mr. Morgan said. "We had it right up to the terminal and then it disappeared."

"Would you have allowed the bus to come if you knew there would be no police here?" I asked.

"No sir," he answered.

The driver of the bus was Joe Caverno, a stocky, powerful man who had first refused to take the bus out. At 6:05 a. m., he came to the bus, waiting at the platform with the would-be passengers at the door.

He went to the bus and said:

"I'm supposed to drive this bus to Dothan, Alabama, through Montgomery, but I understand there is a big convoy down the road and I don't have but one life to give and I don't intend to give it to CORE or the N double A C P, and that's all I have to say."

Mr. Caverno disappeared back into a room marked "drivers only." Shortly before 8:30, he emerged after Birmingham Police Commissioner Eugene Connor arrived and apparently played a part in arranging the escort.

On Wednesday, Mr. Connor had escorted seven of the students to the Tennessee border, asking them to get out of the state to save themselves and Alabama "a lot of trouble."

The students returned with fourteen others yesterday. During the night they waited and tried, unsuccessfully, to board three buses for Montgomery. Intrastate bus transportation (but not local buses in Birmingham and Montgomery) is still segregated.

The students sat in the waiting room marked "white waiting room for intrastate passengers." They tested the men's room and the white ticket counters and were served. Mr. Zwerg was refused service at the lunch counter in the Negro waiting room and was removed by police.

Last night a crowd of 3,000 gathered and heaped abuse on the students, throwing soda pop in their faces and stepping on their feet as they sat.

Finally, Mr. Connor ordered barricades set up a block away from the terminal in each direction and the crowd thinned. Less than a hundred spectators and almost as many police saw the bus off.

Justice?*
A Committee of Inquiry, May, 1962

FIRST WITNESS RONNIE MOORE, *chairman of Baton Rouge, Louisiana, CORE, is twenty-one years old. A sophomore at Southern University majoring in sociology with the intention of becoming a minister, he was expelled last January for leading student civil rights action. Charged with criminal anarchy, he goes to trial in Baton Rouge in mid-September, 1962.*

He said that in November, 1961, he helped organize a CORE chapter at Southern University, the largest Negro university in the world, and that month tried to negotiate with merchants of twelve stores in nearby Baton Rouge toward desegregation of lunch counters and jobs. When merchants refused to see him CORE started a selective-buying program and, on December 7th and 8th, he directed a CORE workshop for about 170 students.

Q. What is a workshop, Mr. Moore?

A. Something like a school. We teach the rights of American citizenship, the right to picket, and we expose persons to the philosophy of non-violence.

Q. What was the outcome of the workshop?

A. The students went into the community, sat-in at the lunch counters.

Q. You were denied service, you were told to leave and you did leave?

A. Right.

Q. Then what happened?

A. On December 14th we decided to exercise our right to picket. We regarded that in America we had this right, and we still believe we have this right. Twenty-three students who picketed the stores for a minute and a half were arrested for obstructing the sidewalks.

Q. Were they obstructing the sidewalks?

---

* A Committee of Inquiry into the Administration of Justice in the Freedom Struggle was assembled by the Congress of Racial Equality in Washington, D.C., May, 1962, to hear testimony of civil rights workers on police and court action in the South. The committee was composed of: Mrs. Eleanor Roosevelt, chairman, and Roger Baldwin, Kenneth Clark, John Bolt Culbertson, Joseph L. Rauh, Jr., Boris Shishkin, Rev. Gardner Taylor, Telford Taylor, Norman Thomas. Excerpts from the testimony are reprinted here.

A.   They were picketing like the labor unions picket, in orderly manner, walking on the end of the sidewalk.

Q.   Then what happened?

A.   That evening I and a few others addressed a rally on campus. We discussed the unlawful arrest of the students, and decided we should go down to Baton Rouge the next day in non-violent fashion to redress our grievances with the parish officials.

Q.   How did you intend to do that?

A.   We intended to ride buses and catch cabs and go in automobiles down to Third Street and march two by two to the courthouse. We would sing and make a few statements in protest of the denial of the right to picket.

Q.   Did you do that?

A.   Well, as students moved off campus they were arrested, about fifty. Bus drivers were arrested.

Q.   For what?

A.   They claim the buses were overloaded and a lot of things, and ordered students back to the campus. As police pulled students off the buses, students continued to walk for seven miles to the courthouse.

Q.   How many students participated?

A.   Around 3,000 to 4,000.

Q.   You were not in the walk but were operating a sound truck, directing students?

A.   Right. I was arrested for illegal use of a sound truck. I created a nuisance by a protest of segregation in an all-Negro neighborhood.

Q.   In your opinion you were welcome?

A.   I think so.

Q.   Is a license required?

A.   A license is not required.

Q.   Are sound trucks used generally in that area?

A.   Politicians use them each and every year.

I was in jail about six hours, then my attorneys posted $1500 cash bond, and I came downstairs from the cell, and as I was going out of the door I was re-arrested, charged with conspiracy to commit criminal mischief, taken back to jail, and an additional $2000 bond.

Q.   Do you know what criminal mischief is?

A.   It was brought out that criminal mischief had something to do with the non-violent workshop.

Q.   The additional bond was posted?

A.   Twenty-one days later, when I was released.

Q.   Have you a comment about treatment in jail?

A.   Well, there were three incidents of police brutality. I made three requests to see a doctor. They were ignored, so I knocked on the door to go out. One officer reached through the bars and choked me and slapped me.

I spoke of the incident to students there and Dave Dennis, of CORE, approached the door to inquire about the beating. They opened the door to the Negro cell and reached in and grabbed Dennis. One officer pulled him up and slammed him against the iron bars and put him in solitary. Jerome Smith, of CORE, was beaten.

When we came out of jail we reported these incidents to the local FBI and they went to investigate with local police officers, and came out with "no violation of civil rights."

NORMAN THOMAS: That is civil rights as understood in Louisiana?

A. Apparently so.

On January 4th, Ronnie Moore and seventy-two other students returned to Southern University with the pledge of Dr. Felton G. Clark, its Negro president, that he would not expel them although the all-white State Board of Education demanded their dismissal. On the night of the 17th when it became known that Dr. Clark would expel seven CORE leaders, 1500 students gathered before his home to ask why. Dr. Clark refused to appear. The next morning he announced the closing of the university by five o'clock that afternoon and ordered all students off-campus by that hour. After attending court, Ronnie Moore returned to campus shortly before five, and after half an hour met his friend, Weldon Rougeau, at the gymnasium.

Q. Were you arrested?

A. Yes. It was raining so we went under the ramp of the gym and two officers came up and asked our names and said, "You are under arrest for criminal trespass and for disturbing the peace."

Q. Were there other students on campus?

A. Yes, over 500.

Q. Were any of them arrested?

A. No. The officers pointed out that all seven CORE leaders will be arrested. "You find the seven, you arrest them."

Q. Were you doing anything other than standing out of the rain?

A. I wasn't, no. We were talking.

Q. You were taken back to jail?

A. Yes, placed under $3000 cash bond.

Q. Bringing your collective bond to $6000?

A. Right.

Q. Do you know the maximum penalty for disturbing the peace?

A. Six months in jail and a $50 or $100 fine, something like that.

Well, we, (Moore and Rougeau) had to stay in jail in the same cell. It was a solitary confinement cell seven by seven feet. We stayed there fifty-eight days until bond could be raised.

Q. An additional charge was placed against you on February 12th?

A. Yes, the charge was criminal anarchy. It means I advocated in public and private opposition to the state of Louisiana by unlawful means.

Q. Bond?

A. $12,500.

Q. What is the penalty for criminal anarchy?

A. The count is ten years in the state penitentiary at hard labor. . . .

Robert Moses of SNCC, Harvard graduate, told of working on voter registration in southern Mississippi in the summer of 1961, and of the killing, on September 25th, of Herbert Lee.

Mr. Moses said that police rode around the area where voting schools were held, intimidating people; that some who attended meetings lost their jobs; that in Liberty a cousin of the sheriff attacked him in sight of officers, his head wound requiring eight stitches.

Q. Mr. Moses, did you know a person named Herbert Lee?

A. Yes, he was a Negro farmer who lived near Liberty.

Q. Would you tell the Committee what Mr. Lee was doing and what happened?

A. He was killed on September 25th. That morning I was in McComb. The Negro doctor came by the voter registration office to tell us he had just taken a bullet out of a Negro's head.

We went over to see who it was because I thought it was somebody in the voting program, and were able to identify the man as Mr. Herbert Lee, who had attended our classes and driven us around the voting area, visiting other farmers.

That night we went into the county to track down people who had seen the killing. Three Negroes told more or less the same story.

That they were at the cotton gin in Liberty and Mr. Lee drove up to gin, the cotton in his truck, followed by Mr.

Hurst in his car. He is representative to the Mississippi state legislature.

Q. Mr. Hurst is white?

A. Mr. Hurst is white. That he got out of his car and went over to the cab of Mr. Lee's truck. That they began talking. That Mr. Hurst was waving a gun. That Mr. Lee got out of his cab on the right side. That Mr. Hurst ran around the front and shot Mr. Lee one shot in his temple.

A Negro witness said a deputy sheriff asked him, "Did you see the tire tool?" The witness said he didn't see any tire tool in Mr. Lee's hand. The deputy replied, "Well, there was one."

The witness testified at the coroner's jury that there was a tire tool. When they had a grand jury, about a month later, the witness came to us to know whether he should testify that there was a tool, which he said there wasn't, though he had testified this at the coroner's jury.

We called Washington and Justice Department officials explained that they could not guarantee protection for individual witnesses. The man testified at the grand jury that there was a tire tool.

Q. The grand jury found no basis for an indictment against Rep. Hurst, is that correct?

A. Yes. . . .

Robert Zellner told the story of BRENDA TRAVIS, *seventeen-year-old high school student of McComb, Mississippi, under parole forbidding her to engage in civil rights action and hence unable to appear at the hearing.*

MR. ZELLNER: Brenda is a very dynamic person with great courage and determination. With two friends, she was arrested in the white section of the McComb bus station, on August 30, 1961. They had bought interstate tickets.

Sixteen then, she was convicted in adult court of disturbing the peace, sentenced to six months, fined $200, put on bond of $1000. She spent September in adult jail, awaiting bond.

October 4th she went back to her school. The principal said he'd sent her records off somewhere and she couldn't get back in.

About 115 students walked out of school in protest. Also the killing of Herbert Lee had fired them up. They determined to walk in orderly fashion to the county courthouse about eight miles away. I joined their march.

But it was late in the afternoon and it was decided to go into McComb. By the city hall there was a large mob. About twenty white men shoulder to shoulder across the sidewalk, with two police in front, stopped the march.

I was the only white person marching. About fifteen police

standing around allowed seven or eight men to attack me. Some students stood on the bottom step to pray and were arrested. Then we were all arrested.

Brenda was in jail three or four days. Then the prosecutor and the judge decided she should be treated as a juvenile. Two plainclothesmen took her out of her cell and told her they were taking her to a lawyer. They drove her eighty miles to the Oakley Training School. Brenda didn't know where she was. The men left and a lady told her she was in reform school.

She was there six months and three weeks. There was no class for her, she only went to one in home economics. She couldn't continue her education and this upset her. The food was very terrible with bugs. It was very degrading there.

Q. Tell about Brenda's release.

A. Professor Einsman, he had been an anti-Nazi in Germany and teaches German at Talledega College, was tremendously concerned when he heard Brenda's story. He said, "I'm going to Mississippi and talk to the judge."

(After several visits Dr. Einsman persuaded the judge to release Brenda in his custody.)

MR. ZELLNER: So they drew up papers for her release and Dr. Einsman took Brenda to Talledega College, where she is living with his family. . . .

Some Random Notes from the Leflore County Jail*

JAMES FORMAN

WE HAVE BEEN in jail one week today. Our morale is good, although there are serious undertones of a desire to be free among some members of the group. Now and then, the jokes of one or two turn to the outside. John Doar and the Justice

* These notes were written during a period in the movement when the tactic of "jail without bail" was being developed in an effort to dramatize the struggle for civil rights. Jail without bail was also an attempt to deal with the problem of soaring costs of the fight for justice —bail and other legal expenses. Forman and his co-prisoners had been attempting to help the Negroes of Greenwood, Miss. register to vote. During this campaign in 1963 police first used dogs against civil rights demonstrators. The selection is printed here for the first time with permission of James Forman, former executive secretary of the Student Nonviolent Coordinating Committee.

Department received some sharp, but still humorous comments from some of the fellows. They actually believed the Justice Department would have had them out by Monday. When we received news that the temporary injunction had been denied [we] were somewhat disappointed. Some of us tried to explain that we must prepare ourselves psychologically to spend six months in this jail.

The cell in which we are being held is not bad so far as American prisons go. (The entire penal system needs reforming.) We are eight in a cell with six bunks. We have two mattresses on the floor. There is an open shower, a sink, a stool. It took us two days to get a broom and five days to get some salt for our food. The inner cell in which we are "contained" is approximately 15' x 12'. Not much room, is there? . . .

People outside send us food. When we were in the city jail, we got food twice a day. Here we received a great deal Sunday, enough to last us till today. We are counting on someone to replenish our supply. However, [my doctor] has been to see me three times since I have been in the county jail. Each time she brings some food which I share with the fellows.

So far as my own diet is concerned, I have had sufficient eggs and bananas to sustain me. I must guard against giving these away since I don't want to become ill. They, the prison officials, have allowed me to take medicine and the doctor keeps me supplied. I am really not suffering due to my ulcers, although my sickness helps the group—through the visit of the doctor.

We are also improving our minds. We have been allowed to keep our books and we have sufficient cigarettes. I even have my pipe and some tobacco. Personally, I have tried to organize our lives. Do you expect anything else of me? We have occasional classes. Moses gave us an excellent math lecture the other day. I gave one lesson in writing and English. Guyot has delivered several in biology. We are always having discussions. Sometimes one of us will read a passage from a book and then we will discuss the meaning of it. We have had several stimulating conversations based on Thoreau's essay on civil disobedience and N'krumah's thoughts on positive action. . . .

Around eleven o'clock we usually turn out the one large light in the middle of the room. We do not have sheets or blankets. We sleep in our underclothes. I suppose if it got cold we would put on our clothes.

In the morning when we get up we have grits, biscuits, and a piece of salt pork for breakfast. Then we sweep the cell.

For the last two days Bob, Guyot and I have swept the cell and scrubbed it on our hands and knees. During the morning we usually have discussions, showers, play chess, talk and wait for beans or peas and cornbread which arrive around two o'clock. We do not have any more meals from the county until the next morning.

My personal opinions as to the significance of our staying in jail follow. I am convinced that all the people connected with SNCC are busily engaged in protesting our unjust imprisonment. This is as it should be. I am also convinced that others sympathetic to the cause of Freedom are also alarmed at this travesty of justice.

Perhaps more important is that only our bodies are confined to this cell. Our minds are free to think what we wish and we know our stay here will also pass away. Our imprisonment serves to dramatize to the nation and to the world that the black man does not even have the right to *try* to be an American citizen in some parts of our so-called democracy.

Our jail without bail may also serve to remind others in the movement of the need for some of us to stay in jail to dramatize the situation.

On a local and state level it is important that we stay in jail, for people are remembered more by what they do than by what they say. We have been telling Mississippians that we must prepare to die. We have encouraged them to accept our beliefs. Thus it follows that we must lead by example rather than by words.

Moreover, many acts of violence have been committed in Greenwood. The people are not afraid, but when, perhaps, they see our spirit and determination, they will have more courage. Then too, the government must assume its responsibility for our release. If the Civil Rights Act of 1960 is ever to mean anything, then those arrested in connection with voter registration activities must be released by the efforts of the U. S. Government.

When our people were arrested in Sunflower county for passing out leaflets announcing a voter registration meeting, it was really the government which should have sought their release. Instead of this, bond was posted and then the government moved slowly to get the cases dropped and some consent agreement from local officials about future arrests and interference with voter registration workers.

Perhaps more important than these social and political reasons is the personal significance that our imprisonment has for us. I have not yet asked each person for his personal reaction. As for myself, I am glad to make a witness for a cause in which I believe. I am glad for the chance to meditate, to think of many things, and to see the world continue as I sit here. . . .

All of us are determined that once we are out we will walk to the courthouse with some more people. We have been discussing the dogs which most Mississippi officials try to use to halt demonstrations. I personally feel that I must be bitten by one of these dogs for I don't believe we can continue to run from them. It must come to this, for the officials really believe and the record proves them correct, that Negro demonstrators or peaceful citizens are not willing for dogs to bite them. . . .

We sing of course. We are singing now. We love "We'll never turn back." We have added a new verse.

"We have served our time in jail with no money for to go our bail."

We place this as the second stanza.

Every night when the lights are out we sing this song. It is beautiful and it symbolizes our state—the entire song. Please tell Bertha [Gober, one of the Freedom Singers] to keep writing songs. She has a talent which should not be wasted. . . .

There is so much noise in the cell at times. We are trying to work out a schedule. Peacock suggested last night that our time might be better spent if we had a schedule. Concurrently with this idea Guyot was suggesting that if ever a dispute arose two people should take one side, two the other and the remaining four should decide. Consequently the question of a schedule was put before the floor. Surney and Smith objected to the schedule. Forman, McLaurin and Guyot favored it. All arguments were presented as if we were speaking before a court. James Jones just consented to act as judge. He resigned and Peacock accepted the judgeship.

Smith presented some reductio ad absurdum arguments which were easily shattered. Finally the judge ruled in favor of the schedule. By this time LaFayette was sleeping. The next incident around which there was disagreement was the light bulb. There is one light bulb in the middle of the room. Each night it seems that someone has objections to it being turned out. Usually a compromise is worked out.

Interestingly, people are quoting Thoreau—Government is best which governs least—and then applying it to the cell. There are many divergent wills operating in this cell; a few people seek to have their own way at all times and seldom, if ever, indicate a willingness to understand others and give a little.

From these random notes you will perhaps catch a glimpse of what life is like in the cell. It is this that I am trying to portray. . . .

We seem to have a morale problem. . . . [One person] wants to leave the cell and says if he is not out by Sunday he wants bail. We have to constantly remind him and a few others that one cannot depend upon the Justice Department. One must prepare himself psychologically to stay here six months. If the government gets us out, fine. If not, then we ought to be prepared to stay for the reasons I mentioned earlier.

I am hungry; I just asked Guyot for a biscuit. It is cold, not very appetizing. I can only eat a small piece and drink two cups of water. I now have a plastic cup from which to drink. Last night Annell Ponder sent Moses some tomato juice in a pitcher along with a plastic cup.

We have just had breakfast. . . . Rice, biscuits and a piece of oil sausage. I don't know if I am supposed to eat the sausage, but I did. I was very hungry. My supply of eggs is out. I have one left. I only have three small bananas. The next meal is at two o'clock. . . .

John Doar paid us a visit this morning and said that we would probably be taken to Greenville this afternoon or tomorrow morning. . . .

Doar . . . felt that their complaint was not sufficiently prepared to get the order Monday.

Also they [the Justice Department] did not have affidavits supporting the events of last Wednesday. He takes the position that people working on voter registration have the right to peaceful protest of incidents such as the last shooting. He also suggested that Judge Clayton was not going to let anyone take advantage of us but at the same time he was not going to allow anyone to be cute in his courtroom. Clayton is known to run a strict courtroom. We were also asked to be clean in the courtroom. Therefore we are sending for some more clothes, for we are in bad shape. . . .

12:30 p.m.: Sather of the Justice Department interviewed me about the events and while we were talking I heard some singing on the outside and our fellows yelling. Later we found out that 19 more people had been arrested. We sang and sang. There are five women in the cell next door. One old woman is now praying as the old folks pray in the South. Her voice has a musical quality as she appeals and prays to God, she is praying for freedom in Greenwood, she is praying for mercy on Greenwood, she is praying for forgiveness in Greenwood, please she cries, go into the hospital, hold the church of God, you told us to love one another, there does not seem to be any love in this, look this town over Jesus and do something about the condition. Whatsoever a man soweth, that also shall he reap, that we might have our equal rights. . . .

8:07 p.m. Wednesday, April 3, 1963.

We are now in the Washington County jail. We have been transferred so that we might testify in the injunction hearing tomorrow morning.

We were brought from Leflore County by Federal Marshals. When we came down from our cell we saw these Federal Marshals with handcuffs and chains. Each person had a chain placed around him and was handcuffed to the chain. Serious protests were made about this treatment. Such remarks as "the powerful Federal government" were uttered. It was somewhat ironic because upstairs we were all depending upon the Federal government. It was even more ironic because I am sure the local officials were against the government taking us to Greenville and interfering with their affairs. Perhaps it seemed strange to them that we were complaining about the same forces to which they were opposed. . . .

An interesting thing happened when the boys from the Justice Department were interviewing us this morning. Boll Weavill Styles locked them up also in the room. They were somewhat furious.

Well, when I was handcuffed, I asked the Deputy Marshal Hubert Jones to pick up my personal papers and my bag. He shoved the papers under my arms, put the tall shopping bag in my hands. I already had my suit hanging on my handcuffs. I had a hard time coming down the stairs trying to balance the bag. I asked Jones if he could help me with my bag. He simply gave me a slight shove on the back. . . .

The prisoners are now requesting that we sing songs.

Our plan has worked: We wanted to get them in the freedom mood. One wonders what the preachers are doing, today. They are not in the Mississippi struggle, nor do they visit the jails. These prisoners are not really prisoners; they are starving for companionship and some fresh insights to make a dull, routine life more pleasant. . . .

8:30 a.m.: Thursday, April 4, 1963. We have been up for two hours and a half.

8:45 a.m.: We are all dressed up in our best clothes, which is not to say very much, for most of them are borrowed clothes and hand-me-downs. Clothes in the movement are not very important. We often interchange from necessity. Most of the people working now complain that they have lost a few items in the movement. Peacock says he came into the movement with six pairs of shorts, now he has one. James Jones says that if Jessie Harris came up here now and demanded his clothes he would be naked. . . .

Let us discuss sanitation. Last night we were given large clean towels here and a blanket. In Greenwood, we had to beg for toilet paper and, imagine, they would never give us a towel. Frank Smith has a cold from the lack of a blanket in the Greenwood jail. There is something of a decent shower here—a shabby one in Greenwood. Even the cells, five to a block and a large playroom, makes for better sanitation.

11:45 a.m.: We are Free!

We sang this morning at the request of the prisoners. Many of them joined us. Each has the stories of many prisoners and I will get that from him. One of the things we have all discovered is that much prison reform is needed. There is absolutely no justification for the length of time people without bail must stay in jail waiting for their trial. I am reminded that I'm supposed to appear at some convention of criminologists in Louisville. I forget the date, but they are supposed to discuss some problems of race and jail procedure in the south. I imagine there are many whites who must stay in jail a long time waiting for their trial.

We had a good breakfast this morning. Rice, butter, jelly, light bread, eggs, gravy, coffee, and an orange. Compared to the diet of the Greenwood jail, it was a sumptuous meal. There is no justification for not feeding prisoners a balanced diet. Greenwood should be ashamed. We never had a cup of coffee during the entire week we spent there. I shall speak to the sheriff about this.

Three Lives for Mississippi*

WILLIAM BRADFORD HUIE

WHEN THE THREE were ordered or pulled from the station wagon, I think they must have been placed in handcuffs, though I was told that they were not. "They were still following orders," I was told, "and Schwerner and Goodman still didn't think they were going to be killed. They thought they were going to be whipped."

I was told that James Chaney recognized one of the men from Meridian, called him by name, and asked him for help.

The murder was done in the "cut" on Rock Cut Road, less than a mile from Highway 19, about four miles from where the three were taken from the station wagon. It was before midnight, and the moon was still high. Three cars were in the cut. I was told that the three victims said nothing, but that they were jeered by the murderers. Several of the murderers chanted in unison, as though they had practiced it:

"Ashes to ashes, Dust to dust, If you'd stayed where you belonged, You wouldn't be here with us."

Another said: "So you wanted to come to Mississippi? Well, now we're gonna let you stay here. We're not even gonna run you out. We're gonna let you stay here with us."

When Schwerner was pulled from the car and stood up to be shot, I was told that the man with the pistol asked him: "You still think a nigger's as good as I am?" No time was allowed for a reply. He was shot straight through the heart and fell to the ground.

Goodman was next, with nothing said. Apparently he stood as still as Schwerner did, facing his executioner, for the shot that killed him was the same precise shot. I was told that another man fired the shot, using the same pistol, but my opinion remains that one man fired both shots. I also still be-

* William Bradford Huie, *Three Lives for Mississippi* (New York: WCC Books, 1965), pp. 186-192, 240-45. Reprinted by permission of William Bradford Huie. *Three Lives for Mississippi* is the result of Huie's investigations of the murders of James Chaney, Andrew Goodman and Michael Schwerner, three civil rights workers in the Mississippi Summer Project, killed at the beginning of the summer of 1964. Training for the project and reactions of other workers to the deaths is described in the excerpt from *Freedom Summer* by Sally Belfrage on pp. 393-402.

lieve that both Schwerner and Goodman were in handcuffs, and that the cuffs were removed after they were dead.

Chaney was last, and the only difference was that he struggled while the others had not. He didn't stand still; he tried to pull and duck away from his executioner. So he wasn't shot with the same precision, and he was shot three times instead of once.

Because Chaney's wrist, shoulder, and skull were crushed, a reputable New York doctor who examined Chaney's body said that he had been beaten, perhaps with a chain. Certainly the murderers were capable of it: they were capable of anything. But I would guess that it didn't happen, though he certainly could have been badly hurt in the struggle. All three bodies were buried in darkness with a bulldozer. They were also uncovered, forty-four days later, with a bulldozer. The bulldozers could easily have done additional bone damage to Chaney.

The federal indictment concerned with these murders charges that the three were let out of jail about 10:30 P.M., and that they were murdered on June 21, 1964. This means that federal agents are convinced that the murder was done before midnight. So these murders were committed with dispatch. There was no horsing around, or "interrogation," or torture, as in the case of Edward Aaron. When white-supremacy terrorists are bent on murder they seldom pause to torture. And they usually hate "nigger-lovers" more than they hate "niggers." Which is why I think that—if they were going to single out a victim and beat him—Schwerner, not Chaney, would have been the preferred choice.

The three bodies were tossed into the station wagon and driven along dirt roads to a farm about six miles southwest of Philadelphia. A "cattle pond" was under construction on this farm. There are scores of such ponds in Neshoba County. A pond is created by erecting an earthen dam in a proper spot. To begin building a dam you generally dig a ditch maybe 30 feet wide and 5 feet deep and 100 or more feet long. Into this ditch you pack red clay; it hardens, and creates a base for the dam under which water will not seep. Onto this base you then pile dirt, sloping the sides, to whatever height is needed. You plant grass along the sides. A finished dam may be 30 feet wide at the base, 10 feet wide at the top, 20 feet high, and 100 feet long, all erected on the red-clay base.

Such a dam is a perfect place in which to hide bodies. On June 21 only the red-clay base had been built, and a bulldozer was parked at the scene. One of the conspirators operated the bulldozer. He was supposed to be waiting for the murderers, but he was late. They arrived before he did, and they had to wait almost two hours for him. The moon went down behind the trees. This wait must have been unpleasant, even for such patriots proud of their courage, and I was told that a gallon of corn whiskey was delivered to them to help them through their bloody wake. Many good stories must have been told, to cackling and thigh-slapping, during that two hours of drinking and waiting at a lonely construction site.

During the Second World War I remember seeing dead soldiers buried temporarily with bulldozers. We did this at Omaha Beach. Many Americans saw this done, and I suspect it was one such old veteran who thought of playing hide-and-seek with the agents of the United States by burying these bodies with a bulldozer.

When the bulldozer operator arrived, he dug a trench in the red clay along the length of the dam. The bodies, fully clothed, were tossed into this trench, face down, side by side. Goodman and Schwerner were head to head and feet to feet; Chaney, on the outside, was in the opposite position: his feet were at Schwerner's head. The two white men's arms were above their heads, indicating that they were dropped into the dirt by one man holding wrists and another holding ankles. Chaney's arms were at his sides, probably because his wrist was broken, so he would have been carried or dragged by his armpits. The bodies were then covered with two feet of dirt, and in subsequent weeks the dam was built to a height of eighteen feet. Heavy rains fell during July; so by August first the dam was massive and grassed over—a permanent tomb for three bodies if nobody ever talked.

After the burial the station wagon was driven to a point fifteen miles northeast of Philadelphia, to the edge of the Bogue Chitto swamp. There it was doused with diesel fuel and burned. The murderers thought this was clever, almost as clever as burying the bodies in the dam. They knew that only federal agents—no one else—would ever search for the bodies; so each move they made was part of a fascinating game they thought they were playing with the FBI.

Traditionally in race murders bodies have been thrown into rivers and swamps in Mississippi. So the murderers, by burning the station wagon on the edge of Bogue Chitto swamp, were leading the "federals" to begin by dragging the rivers and swamps. And the murderers thought this was funny because it was hot summertime and the swamps and rivers were teeming with snake, chiggers, and mosquitoes.

"It tickles the hell out of me," one of the murderers said, "just to think of old J. Edgar's boys sweatin' out there in that swamp, with all them chiggers, water moccasins and skee-ters."

Since the bodies were buried six miles *southwest* of Phila-delphia, and the station wagon was burned fifteen miles *north-east* of Philadelphia, this meant that the search would begin twenty-one miles from where the bodies were; and by the time all the rivers and swamps were searched, the dam would be completed and grassed over.

Shortly before the early dawn, the murderers had finished all their chores tidily, and the last group of them gathered on the courthouse square in Philadelphia to shake hands and congratulate one another. They all had been drinking though none could be called drunk. There they were met by an official of the state of Mississippi.

"Well, boys," he said, "you've done a good job. You've struck a blow for the White Man. Mississippi can be proud of you. You've let these agitatin' Outsiders know where this state stands. Go home now and forget it. But before you go, I'm looking each one of you in the eye and telling you this: the first man who talks is *dead!* If anybody who knows any-thing about this ever opens his mouth to any Outsider about it, then the rest of us are going to kill him just as dead as we killed those three sonsofbitches tonight.

"Does everybody understand what I'm saying? The man who talks is dead . . . dead . . . *dead!*" . . .

Momentarily, I comforted one of the murderers, then left him confused.

I said: "Well, you were correct on one point. You killed Schwerner because you said he was an 'agitating, trouble-making, nigger-loving, Communist, atheistic, Jew outsider.' It's true that he called himself an atheist."

"He did, huh? He didn't believe in *nothing?*"

"Oh, yes," I said, "he believed in something. He believed devoutly."

"What'd he believe in?"

"He believed in *you!*"

"In me! What the hell!"

"Yeah," I said. "He believed in you. He believed love could conquer hate. He believed love could change even you. He didn't think you were hopeless. That's what got him killed."

As I say, that left him somewhat confused.

5. NEGROES FIGHT BACK

Negroes with Guns*

ROBERT F. WILLIAMS

PROLOGUE

WHY DO I speak to you from exile?

Because a Negro community in the South took up guns in self-defense against racist violence and used them. I am held responsible for this action, that for the first time in history American Negroes have armed themselves as a group, to defend their homes, their wives, their children, in a situation where law and order had broken down, where the authorities could not, or rather would not, enforce their duty to protect Americans from a lawless mob. I accept this responsibility and am proud of it. I have asserted the right of Negroes to meet the violence of the Ku Klux Klan by armed self-defense —and have acted on it. It has always been an accepted right of Americans, as the history of our Western states proves, that where the law is unable, or unwilling, to enforce order, the citizens can, and must, act in self-defense against lawless violence. I believe this right holds for black Americans as well as whites.

Many people will remember that in the summer of 1957 the Ku Klux Klan made an armed raid on an Indian community in the South and were met with determined rifle fire from the Indians acting in self-defense. The nation approved of the action and there were widespread expressions of pleasure at the defeat of the Kluxers, who showed their courage by running away despite their armed superiority. What the nation doesn't know, because it has never been told, is that the Negro community in Monroe, North Carolina, had set the example two weeks before when we shot up an armed motorcade of the Ku Klux Klan, *including two police cars*, which had come to attack the home of Dr. Albert E. Perry,

* Robert F. Williams, *Negroes with Guns* (New York: Marzani & Munsell, Inc., 1962), pp. 39-41, 120-24. Reprinted by permission of Marzani & Munsell. Williams left the United States after his indictment on a charge of kidnaping a white couple during an outbreak of racial violence in Monroe, North Carolina in 1961. Williams fled to Cuba and later to China.

vice-president of the Monroe chapter of the National Association for the Advancement of Colored People. The stand taken by our chapter resulted in the official re-affirmation by the NAACP of the right of self-defense. The Preamble to the resolution of the 50th Convention of the NAACP, New York City, July 1959, states: ". . . we do not deny, but reaffirm, the right of an individual and collective self-defense against unlawful assaults."

Because there has been much distortion of my position, I wish to make it clear that I do not advocate violence for its own sake, or for the sake of reprisals against whites. Nor am I against the passive resistance advocated by the Reverend Martin Luther King and others. My only difference with Dr. King is that I believe in flexibility in the freedom struggle. This means that I believe in non-violent tactics where feasible and the mere fact that I have a Sit-In case pending before the U.S. Supreme Court bears this out. Massive civil disobedience is a powerful weapon under civilized conditions, where the law safeguards the citizens' right of peaceful demonstrations. In civilized society the law serves as a deterrent against lawless forces that would destroy the democratic process. But where there is a breakdown of the law, the individual citizen has a right to protect his person, his family, his home and his property. To me this is so simple and proper that it is self-evident.

When an oppressed people show a willingness to defend themselves, the enemy, who is a moral weakling and coward is more willing to grant concessions and work for a respectable compromise. Psychologically, moreover, racists consider themselves superior beings and they are not willing to exchange their superior lives for our inferior ones. They are most vicious and violent when they can practice violence with impunity. This we have shown in Monroe. Moreover, when because of our self-defense there is a danger that the blood of whites may be spilled, the local authorities in the South suddenly enforce law and order when previously they had been complaisant toward lawless, racist violence. This too we have proven in Monroe. It is remarkable how easily and quickly state and local police control and disperse lawless mobs when the Negro is ready to defend himself with arms.

Furthermore, because of the international situation, the Federal Government does not want racial incidents which draw the attention of the world to the situation in the South. Negro self-defense draws such attention, and the federal government will be more willing to enforce law and order if the local authorities don't. When our people become fighters, our leaders will be able to sit at the conference table as equals, not dependent on the whim and the generosity of the oppressors. It will be to the best interests of both sides to negotiate just, honorable and lasting settlements.

The majority of white people in the United States have literally no idea of the violence with which Negroes in the South are treated daily—nay, hourly. This violence is deliberate, conscious, condoned by the authorities. It has gone on for centuries and is going on today, every day, unceasing and unremitting. It is our way of life. Negro existence in the South has been one long travail, steeped in terror and blood —our blood. The incidents which took place in Monroe, which I witnessed and which I suffered, will give some idea of the conditions in the South, such conditions that can no longer be borne. That is why, one hundred years after the Civil War began, we Negroes in Monroe armed ourselves in self-defense and used our weapons. We showed that our policy worked. The lawful authorities of Monroe and North Carolina acted to enforce order *only after, and as a direct result of, our being armed*. Previously they had connived with the Ku Klux Klan in the racist violence against our people. Self-defense prevented bloodshed and forced the law to establish order. This is the meaning of Monroe and I believe it marks a historic change in the life of my people. This is the story of that change.

The tactics of non-violence will continue and should continue. We too believed in non-violent tactics in Monroe. We've used these tactics; we've used all tactics. But we also believe that any struggle for liberation should be a flexible struggle. We shouldn't take the attitude that one method alone is the way to liberation. This is to become dogmatic. This is to fall into the same sort of dogmatism practiced by some of the religious fanatics. We can't afford to develop this type of attitude.

We must use non-violence as a means as long as this is feasible, but the day will come when conditions become so pronounced that non-violence will be suicidal in itself. The day is surely coming when we will see more violence on the same American scene. The day is surely coming when some of the same Negroes who have denounced our using weapons for self-defense will be arming themselves. There are those who pretend to be horrified by the idea that a black veteran who shouldered arms for the United States would willingly take up weapons to defend his wife, his children, his home, and his life. These same people will one day be the loud advocates of self-defense. When violent racism and fascism

strike at their families and their homes, not in a token way
but in an all-out bloody campaign, then they will be among
the first to advocate self-defense. They will justify their position as a question of survival. When it is no longer some distant Negro who's no more than a statistic, no more than an
article in a newspaper; when it is no longer their neighbors,
but it means them and it becomes a matter of personal salvation, then will their attitude change.

As a tactic, we use and approve non-violent resistance. But
we also believe that a man cannot have human dignity if he
allows himself to be abused; to be kicked and beaten to the
ground, to allow his wife and children to be attacked, refusing to defend them and himself on the basis that he's so
pious, so self-righteous, that it would demean his personality
if he fought back.

We know that the average Afro-American is not a pacifist.
He's not a pacifist and he has never been a pacifist and he's
not made of the type of material that would make a good
pacifist. Those who doubt that the great majority of Negroes
are not pacifists, just let them slap one. Pick any Negro on
any street corner in the U.S.A. and they'll find out how much
he believes in turning the other cheek.

All those who dare to attack are going to learn the hard
way that the Afro-American is not a pacifist; that he cannot
forever be counted on not to defend himself. Those who attack him brutally and ruthlessly can no longer expect to attack him with impunity.

The Afro-American cannot forget that his enslavement in
this country did not pass because of pacifist moral force or
noble appeals to the Christian conscience of the slaveholders.

Henry David Thoreau is idealized as an apostle of non-violence, the writer who influenced Gandhi, and through Gandhi,
Martin Luther King, Jr. But Thoreau was not dogmatic; his
eyes were open and he saw clearly. I keep with me a copy of
Thoreau's *Plea For Captain John Brown*. There are truths
that are just as evident in 1962 as they were in 1859 when he
wrote:

. . . It was his [John Brown's] peculiar doctrine that a man
has a perfect right to interfere by force with the slaveholder, in
order to rescue the slave. I agree with him. They who are continually shocked by slavery have some right to be shocked by the
violent death of the slaveholder, but such will be more shocked
by his life than by his death. I shall not be forward to think him
mistaken in his method who quickest succeeds to liberate the
slave.

I speak for the slave when I say, that I prefer the philanthropy

of Captain Brown to that philanthropy which neither shoots me
nor liberates me. . . . I do not wish to kill nor to be killed, but I
can foresee circumstances in which both these things would be by
me unavoidable. We preserve the so-called peace of our community by deeds of petty violence every day. Look at the policeman's
billy and handcuffs! Look at the jail! . . . We are hoping only to
live safely on the outskirts of this provisional army. So we defend
ourselves and our hen-roosts, and maintain slavery. I know that
the mass of my countrymen think that the only righteous use that
can be made of Sharpe's rifles and revolvers is to fight duels with
them, when we are insulted by other nations, or to hunt Indians,
or shoot fugitive slaves with them or the like. I think that for
once the Sharpe's rifles and the revolvers were employed in a righteous cause. The tools were in the hands of one who could use
them.

The same indignation that is said to have cleared the temple
once will clear it again. The question is not about the weapon, but
the spirit in which you use it. No man has appeared in America,
as yet, who loved his fellowman so well, and treated him so ten-
derly. He [John Brown] lived for him. He took up his life and he
laid it down for him. What sort of violence is that which is encouraged, not by soldiers, but by peaceable citizens, not so much
by laymen as by ministers of the Gospel, not so much by the fighting sects as by the Quakers, and not so much by Quaker men as
by Quaker women?

This event advertises me that there is such a fact as death; the
possibility of a man's dying. It seems as if no man had ever died
in America before; for in order to die you must first have lived.

It is in the nature of the American Negro, the same as all
other men, to fight and try to destroy those things that block
his path to a greater happiness in life . . .

Birmingham Demonstration, 1963*

LEN HOLT

COMING FROM THE airport May 6, we drove past the post office and onto Fifth Ave. toward the A. G. Gaston Motel, integration headquarters. Then we saw why the downtown area
was "cop-less." On the roofs of the three and four story
buildings surrounding Kelly-Ingram Park were clusters of policemen with short-wave radios over their shoulders. At the

---

* Len Holt, "Eyewitness: The Police Terror at Birmingham," May
16, 1963, reprinted from *National Guardian* newsweekly, May 16, 1963,
by permission. Len Holt is a civil rights attorney and author of *The
Summer that Didn't End* and *Act of Conscience*.

four intersections surrounding the park were dozens of white-helmeted officers.

With the Birmingham police were reinforcements from such nearby cities as Bessemer, Fairfield, and Leeds. Also on hand were deputy sheriffs of Jefferson County and a sprinkling of State Troopers. The officers seemed fearful. This fear was expressed in marathon chatter and forced joviality as they waited for the ordeal that was to come: another massive demonstration.

Pressing on each cop were the eyes of 4,000 Negro spectators—women, men, boys, girls and mothers with babies. They were on the porches, lawns, cars and streets surrounding the park. They didn't talk much, just looked . . . and waited.

Frequently both the policemen and Negro spectators turned toward the 16th St. Baptist Church. From the more than 2,000 persons inside the church, and 300 pressing toward its doors on the outside—mostly grammar and high school students—came the loud songs of Freedom: "We Shall Overcome," "Ain't Gonna Let Nobody Turn Me Round."

The temperature hit 90 degrees. Everybody was sweating. "Freedom! Freedom!" A roar arose from the church. The cops almost as one, faced the church. Some unleashed clubs from their belts. The faces of those I could see had turned crimson. Jeremiah X, Muslim minister from Atlanta standing near me, commented: "At any moment those cops expect 300 years of hate to spew forth from that church."

"Y'all niggers go on back. We ain't letting no more get on those steps," a police captain ordered as I approached the church. I turned away. The time was 1:10 p.m. Four fire engines arrived at the intersections and set themselves up for "business." Each disgorged its high-pressure hoses, and nozzle mounts were set up in the street. I was to learn the reason for the mounts later, when I watched the powerful water stripping bark off trees and tearing bricks from the walls as the firemen knocked Negroes down.

Before I could get back to the motel the demonstrations began; 60 demonstrators were on their way, marching two abreast, each with a sign bearing an integration slogan. Dick Gregory, the nightclub comedian, was leading the group.

At a signal, 40 policemen converged, sticks in hand. Up drove yellow school buses.

"Do you have a permit to parade?" asked the police captain.

"No," replied Gregory.

"No what?" asked the captain in what seemed to be a reminder to Gregory that he had not used a "sir."

"No. No. A thousand times No," Gregory replied.

The captain said, "I hereby place you all under arrest for parading without a permit, disturbing the peace and violating the injunction of the Circuit Court of Jefferson County."

Bedlam broke loose. The young demonstrators began shouting a freedom song. They broke into a fast step that seemed to be a hybrid of the turkey-trot and the twist as they sang to the tune of "The Old Grey Mare":

> "I ain't scared of your jail
> cause I want my freedom!
> . . . want my freedom!"

And for the next two hours this scene was repeated over and over as group after group of students strutted out of the church to the cheers of the spectators, the freedom chants of those being carried away in buses and a continuous banging on the floors and sides of the buses—a cacophony of freedom.

That day, the dogs were kept out of sight. The Birmingham riot tank was on the side street. The fire hoses were kept shut. The police clubs did not flail. The thousands of spectators also kept calm. The police savagery of the preceeding week was contained.

Back at the Gaston Motel, there was a joyous air. Leaders in the organizational work, such as Dorothy Cotten, James Bevel and Bernard Lee of the Southern Christian Leadership Conference; Isaac Wright, CORE field secretary; and James Forman, William Porter, William Ricks, Eric Rainey and students of the Student Non-Violent Coordinating Committee, joined others in the motel parking lot in a parade and song fest.

Victory was suggested by the absence of the dogs, the lack of violence. Added to this was the news that a judge had continued the cases of 40 persons because "there was no room at the inn" for those sentenced. The threat of the Movement to fill the jails had been realized in Birmingham.

Rejoicing was short-lived. At 6 p.m. word got back to the motel that the 1,000 students arrested earlier had neither been housed nor fed. With Jim Forman of SNCC I drove to the jail. There were youths throwing candy bars over the fence to the students; spectators had passed the hat to purchase the candy. While we were there it began to rain. The students got soaked. The spectators, too, got wet. There was no shelter for the kids. The cops and their dog got into the squad car. They stayed dry.

Forman begged the cops to put the kids inside, in the halls, in the basement of the jail, anywhere. Nothing was done. A new day had not yet come to Birmingham.

That night the weather turned cool. We learned that the students were still in the jail yard, unsheltered and unfed. The same message got to the others in the Negro Community. An estimated 500 cars and 1,200 people drove to the jail with blankets and food. The police responded by bringing up dogs and fire hoses. The food and blankets were given to the kids. The crowd waited until all of the children were finally taken inside.

Later that night Forman and Dorothy Cotten of the Southern Christian Leadership Conference met with the student leaders. In the planning emphasis was placed on the need for speed and mobility. Heretofore the demonstrators seldom got downtown, or if they did, never in a large group. It was decided that instead of starting the demonstrations every day at 1 p.m., when the fire hoses were in place and the police were all on duty, an element of surprise would be introduced. The next demonstration would begin earlier. Picket signs would be taken downtown to prearranged spots in cars where the students could pick them up.

That night five of us slept in a motel room designed for two. We were crowded, but so were the 2,000 students crammed 75 or more in cells for eight in the city jail. Our room was hot that night, but not so hot as the unventilated sweat boxes in which Cynthia Cook, 15, and other girls were placed as punishment by the jail personnel when they refused to say "sir." Those on the outside were tired, but not so tired as the hundreds who had been forced to make marathon walks because they sang "We Shall Overcome" in jail. And there were beatings for many.

At 6 a.m. Tuesday SNCC and CORE fellows hurried to the schools to get out the students. Before 10—and before the police lines and firehoses were in place—600 students had been to the church and been given assignments downtown. Cars were dispatched with picket signs. The clock struck noon. The students struck. Almost simultaneously, eight department stores were picketed.

I was standing near a police motorcycle, and could hear the pandemonium at police headquarters. Police not due to report until after 12:30 were being called frantically. Policemen speeded, sirens screaming, from Kelly-Ingram Park to downtown. Inside the 16th St. Baptist Church the folk laughed and sang "We Shall Overcome."

Over the police radio I heard Bull Connor's voice. He was mad. He had been betrayed. Never before had the students demonstrated before 1 p.m. I suspect the merchants were mad. And the kids downtown, all 600 of them, sang "We Shall Overcome." And they did overcome. No arrests were made. When the police finally got to the area, they merely ripped up the signs and told the youngsters to go home. The jails were full.

For the students, "home" was back to the 16th St. Baptist Church. There they were reassigned to go to Woolworth's and six other department stores, sit on the floor, and not move unless arrested. Since the jails were full, the cops still weren't arresting. A policeman went to the church to tell somebody from the Movement to ask the students to leave. When the announcement was made in the church, 2,000 persons went downtown. These thousands were joined by 2,000 spectators and made a wild, hilarious parade through downtown Birmingham, singing "We Shall Overcome."

Then the nearly 4,000 persons returned to the church from the "victory march." And while the throngs joyously sang inside, preparations were being made outside. The cars with dogs drove up. About 300 police officers surrounded the church and park area. Fire hoses were set up.

For a few minutes I left the area of the church and went to a nearby office. When I emerged I saw 3,000 Negroes encircled in the Kelly-Ingram Park by policemen swinging clubs. The hoses were in action with the pressure wide open. On one side the students were confronted by clubs, on the other, by powerful streams of water. The firemen used the hoses to knock down the students. As the streams hit trees, the bark was ripped off. Bricks were torn loose from the walls.

The hoses were directed at everyone with a black skin, demonstrators and non-demonstrators. A stream of water slammed the Rev. Fred Shuttlesworth against the church wall, causing internal injuries. Mrs. Colia LaFayette, 25-year-old SNCC field secretary from Selma, Alabama, was knocked down and two hoses were brought to bear on her to wash her along the sidewalk. A youth ran toward the firemen screaming oaths to direct their attention from the sprawling woman.

Meanwhile, over the public address system inside the church, I could hear a speaker admonishing the people to be non-violent . . . "We want to redeem the souls of people like Bull Connor."

I wondered how long it would be before some Negro lost his restraint. It had almost happened Monday, the day before, when cops flung a Negro woman to the ground and two of them had put their knees in her breast and twisted her arm. This was done in the presence of the woman's 19-year-old son and thousands of Negro spectators. Four 200-pound Negro men barely managed to restrain the son.

The terrible Tuesday, May 7, ended finally. There was much talk about an impending "settlement." This news discouraged all but the most cursory plans for the next day. Everyone realized the influx of state troopers would make downtown demonstrations difficult.

A strange thing about the demonstrations up until Wednesday was that all of the brutality had been police brutality. Where were the thugs who with razor blades, a few years previously, had cut off the penis of a Negro? Where were the men who stabbed Mrs. Ruby Shuttlesworth when she attempted to enroll her child in the white high school? Where were the whites who repeatedly bombed Birmingham churches and synagogues?

On Wednesday, after almost five weeks of protesting, the non-uniformed racists had not spoken. On May 12th, Mother's Day, they spoke . . . and the cup of non-violence of Birmingham Negroes overflowed. America learned that the patience of 100 years is not inexhaustible. It is exhausted.

Harlem Riot, 1964*

FRED FERRETTI AND MARTIN G. BERCK

THE TAUT, UNEASY truce that had settled over Harlem late yesterday morning was broken last night as patrolling policemen were bombarded with bottles hurled from tenement roofs. Police reacted with a fusillade of warning shots.

The new outbreak of violence was not as severe as the first rioting. It came minutes before the start of funeral survices for James Powell, 15, the youth fatally shot by an off-duty

* Fred Ferretti and Martin G. Berck, "Outbursts Snap Uneasy Truce —City's Leaders Ask for Calm and Restraint," *New York Herald Tribune*, July 20, 1964. © 1964, *New York Herald Tribune*. Reprinted by permission of *World Journal Tribune*.

white police lieutenant last Thursday, and less than 24 hours after the start of the worst rioting in Harlem since 1943.

The new rioting, in which four Negroes were shot by police, followed a day of efforts by ministers, community leaders and city officials to stem the anger of the country's largest Negro community. During the day Acting Mayor Paul Screvane urged the city's residents to "help maintain calm."

Only three hours before last night's incidents began, shortly before 5 p.m., Harlem Rent Strike leader Jesse Gray had asked an audience—which roared its approval—for "100 dedicated men who are ready to die for Negro equality."

As 150 persons crowded into the Levy and Delaney Funeral Home, 2250 Seventh Ave. at 132nd St., police manned barricades outside. About 200 steel-helmeted police, walking the center mall of Seventh Ave. began to duck scores of whiskey and milk bottles flung upon them from rooftops.

Revolvers were drawn and a volley of shots were aimed at the rooftops. The bottle-throwing stopped. Minutes later, however, the bottle barrage again started. Again police fired warning shots. The pattern continued sporadically.

During the day, some 400 police patrolled the debris-strewn sidewalks of Lenox, Seventh and Eighth Avenues between 125th and 139th Streets, where, in yesterday's early morning darkness, scores of pitched and running battles raged between police and groups of Negroes.

The resumption of street battling that came with darkness last night subsided gradually, and by midnight a police spokesman said the tension had "eased visibly."

Fifteen persons were shot, one fatally, and 116 injured, including 12 policemen, in the 12 hours of violence that followed three street rallies protesting the shooting of young Powell by Lt. Thomas Gilligan.

All four of the victims of last night's shootings were hit while police were scattering gangs. . . .

Mr. Screvane, the Acting Mayor, will meet this morning at 9:30 at City Hall with Manhattan Borough President Edward R. Dudley, the City Commission on Human Rights and James Farmer, national director of the Congress of Racial Equality. . . . Mayor Wagner is in Europe. A spokesman said Mr. Wagner was in touch with the situation and did not plan to return home at this time.

One of the proposals presented last night which will be considered at the meeting today was one that Lt. Gilligan be suspended temporarily "with prejudice" pending a civilian-oriented inquiry into his action . . .

These were yesterday's developments:

In Harlem's churches, impassioned pleas were made for an end to strife. A statement by Police Commissioner Michael J. Murphy urging "calm, lawful action" was read.

Civil rights officials conferred throughout the day and urged Harlem residents to stay off the streets.

Policemen were kept overtime at the riot scene and beefed-up patrols began at dusk.

Harlem shopkeepers swept up shattered storefront glass and took inventory following looting.

Another rally was planned for today, the day James Powell is to be buried. Mr. Farmer, national director of CORE, demanded that Mayor Wagner return home from Spain. He also urged that Lt. Gilligan, who shot young Powell, be arrested "on suspicion of murder."

Bayard Rustin, who was jeered at the Jesse Gray rally, was hooted in the streets last night in front of the funeral home as he made repeated attempts to calm a crowd of angry Negro teenagers.

Mr. Rustin and Rev. Milton A. Galamison, both of whom engineered the first city school boycott, had attended the funeral services and listened to the Rev. Theodore Kerrison of St. Augustine Baptist Church, 469 W. 148th St., deliver a low-keyed eulogy to young Powell.

"Death has to come to us all sooner or later," said Rev. Kerrison. He read the 23rd Psalm and as he was saying ". . . though I walk through the valley of the shadow of death . . ." a volley of shots rang out, intermixed with the crash of breaking bottles.

Mrs. Annie Powell, the dead boy's mother, was near collapse and sobbed hysterically as she was led from the funeral parlor into a waiting auto.

As the family left, a sound truck drew up in front of the funeral parlor. Mr. Rustin entered the truck to speak to the restive crowd.

"I urge you to go home. We know there has been an injustice done. The thing we need to do most is respect this woman whose son was shot." The crowd shouted "Uncle Tom Tom Uncle Tom."

He looked calmly from the truck and said "I'm prepared to be a Tom, if it's the only way I can save women and children from being shot down in the street and if you're not willing to do the same, you're fools." He was showered with more boos.

Other speakers urged calmness and were greeted with "We want Malcolm X. We want Malcolm X." Mr. Rustin left the truck shortly afterward to take a young Negro, whose shirt was covered with blood, to the hospital.

Crowds of Negroes began gathering in the streets hours before the funeral service. Police ordered 57 blocks closed to traffic for the duration of the services. By 7 p.m. an estimated 1,000 persons lined both sides of Seventh Ave. between 132nd and 133rd Streets.

Occasional hoots from the sidelines followed the patrolling policemen as they roved the grassy mall of Seventh Ave. Then shortly before 8 p.m. the first barrage of bottles began to fall.

A policeman was hit on the arm with a pop bottle but he was not injured. A gang of Negro youths walked toward the funeral home with sticks and pieces of plank. A bottle was flung at a sergeant. He too, was hit but uninjured. Several shots were fired, and the gang fled.

At the sound of the shots, Seventh Ave. began to look like a town under siege. People raced in every direction, scurried into hallways, shouted, screamed. Police crouched against buildings and spread-eagled themselves on the mall grass.

Then they rose and waded into the crowds, nightsticks swinging.

This outbreak quickly subsided. But others followed. The Police Department's Tactical Patrol Force came roaring up in buses to various trouble spots. A volley of shots dispersed the crowds.

At 127th St. and Seventh Ave., Robert Daly, 45, of 643 E. 232nd St., a news cameraman for the Columbia Broadcasting System, was attacked by a band of Negro youths. He was beaten with clubs and fists, knocked to the ground and stepped on. His crew scattered. Mr. Daly was helped to an ambulance, unable to move his right arm.

In other sporadic attacks, the Tactical Police were showered with bottles as they moved off their bus at 130th St. and Seventh Ave. Police used clubs to break up angry crowds at 129th St. and at 130th along Seventh Ave.

At times, police picked up bricks, bottles and stones that had been thrown at them and threw them back at the rooftops. They also aimed fire directly at the roof lines.

A Molotov cocktail fell flaming into the middle of Seventh Avenue just off 128th St. and was greeted with a large cheer. There was evidence of more looting. A counterpoint to the shouting and shooting was the strident ringing of scores of burglar alarms, apparently tripped as doors were forced open and windows broken.

One reporter was told to go into a church doorway. "We don't shoot at churches," a policeman said.

Earlier in the day leaders of the full spectrum of civil rights activities in Harlem showed up at the Mount Morris Presbyterian Church, Mount Morris Ave. West, and W. 122nd St. to call for militancy at a stormy rally.

Mr. Gray, leader of the Harlem Rent Strike, said his "100 dedicated men" would be made captains in a revolutionary organization working towards equal rights for Negroes.

His face puffed from an alleged police beating during the night, Mr. Gray said to each of his 100 chosen men "We're going to make you a platoon captain and you're going to have to get another 100 that are loyal to you."

He said he would lead a demonstration at United Nations Plaza at 6 p.m. today to ask the UN to intervene in the "police terror in the United States."

He was wildly applauded and a young girl in blue dress rose and began shrieking "Let's bomb them. Let's get bombs and destroy them."

Following the rally, Mr. Gray said he had enlisted 85 volunteers.

James Farmer showed up at the rally, although he was not scheduled to be there. He came in for some boos and shouts that the "whites are not wanted" in the CORE membership. He said "that kid James Powell was my son and your son and the son of every black man . . ." and as he asked for the arrest of Lt. Gilligan scores of persons rose and shouted, "Let's go, what are we waiting for?"

Mr. Farmer stopped them with a raised hand:

"If you go out of here, one running one way, one running another, it will be slaughter." No one moved.

Following Mr. Farmer to the altar of the church was Mr. Rustin, the man who engineered the city's first school boycott.

He was booed loudly by the crowd, but he stared at them and said:

"There is nobody in this room who cares more than I do that a young boy was shot down like an animal. . . . There is nobody that has gone to jail more often than I have.

"I am not ready to die. I want no human being to die or be brutalized," he said. But to add to these "monstrous deeds is to make an animal of me as the police were animals."

He was booed off the altar, however, and as he left, a group of Negroes from the audience, apparently Black Nationalists, moved toward him threateningly. But another group formed a protective shield around him.

Mr. Rustin said later to the friendly group: "I want volunteers to man a command post at 125th St. and Eighth Ave. tonight where we can deploy young men to help disperse teenagers and give protection to women and children who are on the street."

Earlier in the rally Mr. Gray shouted to the singing, chanting crowd:

"We have one of the most corrupt, rotten police departments in this country. Murphy is nothing but a crumb-snatcher and a stoolie. Last night the police looked better [sic] than German Storm Troops."

"Nazis, Nazis. That's what they are," screamed the crowd.

Police stood around in groups of twos and threes with steel helmets in front of the church.

By the time Marshall England, president of Manhattan CORE, was introduced and began a rebuke of Negroes for failure to register and vote, the audience was beyond being criticized. He was booed off the rostrum.

The Saturday night, Sunday morning disorders, which police likened to the Harlem riots of 1943, grew out of a series of rallies at 125th St. and Seventh Ave. on Saturday evening. They had been called to protest young Powell's shooting in front of Robert F. Wagner Junior High School, where he had been a summer student.

In 1943, a hot summer's night exploded into a riot that left five Negroes dead, 543 injured, 484 arrested and hundreds of stores shattered and looted. It was touched off when a policeman shot a Negro soldier while attempting to make an arrest.

Mayor Fiorello H. LaGuardia sent 2,500 policemen into Harlem. Gov. Thomas E. Dewey put 8,000 National Guardsmen on alert. A curfew was imposed on Harlem then.

On Saturday, both the Congress of Racial Equality and the United African Movement rallied in front of the Theresa Hotel. At the CORE rally protest demonstrations at police precincts were urged. Following the United African Movement rally, a third impromptu rally was held. Demonstrators from the third rally eventually marched two blocks to the 28th Precinct at 123rd St. and Seventh Ave.

Police hastily erected barricades.

"Murphy the Murderer," shouted some of the demonstrators. "He must go." The wooden barricades fell before the press of the crowd. Bottles, bricks and rocks began flying down from rooftops. Policemen quickly donned steel helmets and cordoned off the station house.

Threatening advances by the crowds were stalled by police who fired warning shots into the air. Riot calls brought hundreds of police from various Manhattan precincts and divisions and from as far away as Queens to quell spontaneous outbursts that began not only in the precinct area but up and down Lenox Ave. between 125th and 130th Streets.

Refuse cans were set afire. More than a dozen false alarms were turned in, and to the confusion of screaming, shouting and physical collision were added the siren blasts of fire engines.

Lenox Ave. was closed to traffic. Along 125th St. near Seventh and Eighth Avenues, police closed intersections to all but residents who could prove they lived there. Patrol cars were sent by the station house to the amorphous riot scene at the rate of one a minute, according to police.

The salvos of warning shots did not dispel the rioters.

Groups of cop-taunters would race away when the shots were fired, then regroup and advance, only to retreat as other shots were fired. Other policemen directed their bullets to the rooftops where debris rained down on them, on passing pedestrians and motorists. One man, Jay Jenkins, about 35, of 2181 Eighth Ave., was shot dead through the forehead as he tossed bricks from a building at 174 W. 126th St. according to Commissioner Murphy. Jenkins, a Negro and an ex-convict with a record of 10 arrests, was yesterday's only fatality.

Crowds threatened police with cries of "killers, killers."

Several policemen who said they were helping a young Negro girl who was the apparent victim of a hit-and-run driver, were set upon, they said, by a crowd yelling "killers." Police said they fired warning shots.

Mr. Farmer said he spent the night on the streets in the midst of the violence. Yesterday he said, "I saw a bloodbath. I saw with my own eyes violence, a bloody orgy of police . . . a woman climbing into a taxi and indiscriminately shot in the groin . . . police charging into a grocery store and indiscriminately swinging clubs . . . police shooting into tenement windows and into the Theresa Hotel. I entered the hotel and saw bullet holes in the walls . . .

"I saw bloodshed as never before . . . people threw bottles and bricks. I'm not saying they were not partly to blame. But it is the duty of police to arrest, not indiscriminately shoot and beat."

Commissioner Murphy said at the 28th Precinct, where he arrived before daybreak after cruising the riot area in an unmarked car, "Some persons have used this unfortunate incident (the Powell shooting) as an excuse for looting and vicious, unprovoked attacks against police. In our estimation this is a crime problem and not a social problem." He repeated this analysis in his statement distributed to Harlem churches.

Deputy Commissioner Walter Arm attributed the rioting to "rowdies" whose purpose was looting, as in 1936 and 1943,** he said. Mr. Arm was a reporter for the New York *Herald Tribune* in 1936 and covered the riots then. He said "there were sporadic and unauthorized incidents sponsored by rowdies with the same excuse for riots in 1936 and 1943 . . . looting." He added "this is nothing compared to those . . . of 1936."

Harlem Hospital reported that 75 persons were treated for various bruises, cuts and stab wounds. The hospital said seven civilians were treated for gunshot wounds. Sydenham Hospital reported it treated about 30 people, seven with gunshot wounds. Knickerbocker Hospital said four people from the rioting were treated. . . .

At one point in the fighting, a bottle of flaming gasoline engulfed a patrol car. But it burned out and the policemen were unharmed.

Police said crowds shouted: "Don't kill our children. Don't kill our Negro babies."

"Save us from our protectors."

"Killer cops."

"Down with police brutality."

It was not until the early morning hours that the rioting began to subside, more of its own volition than by any effort of the police.

During the night police used thousands of rounds of ammunition.

Eventually a carload of cartridges had to be sent to Lenox Ave. from the department's depot in Rodman's Neck, the Bronx, to replenish the supply.

And even as Commissioner Murphy was talking to reporters yesterday morning, two riot calls came in, as the riot spurted one last time before ebbing away with daylight. . . .

**See James A. Jones and Linda Bailey, *A Report on Race Riots,* (New York: Haryou-Act, 1965).

Armed Defense*

CHARLES R. SIMS

Q. Mr. Sims, why do you feel there is need for the Deacons in the civil rights movement and in Bogalusa?

A. First of all, the reason why we had to organize the Deacons in the city of Bogalusa was the Negro people and civil rights workers didn't have no adequate police protection.

Q. Can you tell us what difference it may have made in Bogalusa to have the Deacons here?

A. Well, when the white power structure found out that they had mens, Negro mens that had made up their minds to stand up for their people and to give no ground, would not tolerate with no more police brutality, it had a tendency to keep the night-riders out of the neighborhood.

Q. You say the Deacons were formed because you were not given adequate police protection, does this mean that you consider the role of the Deacons to be a sort of separate police organ in behalf of the civil rights movement?

A. Well, I wouldn't say policemen, I would say a defense guard unit. We're not authorized to carry weapons.

Q. You say you're not authorized to carry weapons?

A. No we're not.

Q. Can you tell me how the Deacons view the use of weapons?

A. Self-protection.

Q. Do most Deacons, in their efforts to protect the civil rights movement, would they normally carry a gun or a pistol with them?

A. That's the only way you can protect anything, by having weapons for defense. If you carry weapons, you carry them at your own risk.

Q. Do the local authorities object to your carrying weapons?

A. Oh yeah, the local, the federal, the state, everybody object to us carrying weapons, they don't want us armed, but

* Interview with Charles R. Sims, President, Bogalusa chapter, Deacons for Defense and Justice, conducted by William A. Price, reporter for the *National Guardian* newsweekly, on August 20, 1965, in Bogalusa, Louisiana. Reprinted by permission of the *National Guardian.*

we had to arm ourselves because we got tired of the women, the children being harassed by the white night-riders.

Q. Have they done anything to try to get the weapons away from you?

A. Well, they threatened several times. The governor even said he was going to have all the weapons confiscated, all that the state troopers could find. But on the other hand, the governor forgot one thing—in an organization as large as the Deacons, we also have lawyers and we know about what the government can do. That would be unconstitutional for him just to walk up and start searching cars and taking people's stuff without cause.

Q. Has there been a court case to determine this?

A. No.

Q. The Second Amendment to the United States Constitution guarantees the right of the people to carry weapons, is that the way you feel about it, that the people have a right to carry weapons in their own self-defense?

A. I think a person should have the right to carry a weapon in self-defense, and I think the Louisiana state law says a man can carry a weapon in his car as long as it is not concealed. We found out in Bogalusa that that law meant for the white man, it didn't mean for the colored. Any time a colored man was caught with a weapon in his car, they jailed him for carrying a concealed weapon. So we carried them to court.

Q. It's your understanding then, that a person possessing a gun in his home, or carrying it in his car, that this is within your rights?

A. According to state law it is.

Q. When you confront a white man with a weapon as compared with confronting a white man without a weapon, could you tell us what the difference in the white man's reaction is; as to whether or not you are armed, or unarmed?

A. Well, I want to say when *I* confront a white man, I would be just as dangerous to the white man without a weapon as I would be with a weapon, if he didn't treat me right.

Q. But suppose he had a weapon, and you didn't?

A. Then he'd have the better hand.

Q. When the Deacons carry weapons, do they do this with any thought to use these in any way except in self-defense?

A. No man a member of the Deacons will attack anyone, he has to use his weapons in defense only.

Q. Have there been any examples of the actual use of weapons by the Deacons, have you ever had to use them?

A. I would rather not answer that.

Q. Can you tell me what difference it has made with the white community, the fact that there are the Deacons here in Bogalusa and that they are prepared to use arms even if they may not?

A. For one thing that made a difference, there were a lot of night-riders riding through the neighborhood; we stopped them. We put them out and gave them fair warning. A couple of incidents happened when people were fired on. So the white man right away found out that a brand new Negro was born. We definitely couldn't swim and we was as close to the river as we could get so there was but one way to go.

Q. So you think there has been a difference in the attitude of the white people towards the civil rights movement in Bogalusa because you have been here to protect it?

A. Yes, I do believe that. I believe that if the Deacons had been organized in 1964, the three civil rights workers that was murdered in Philadelphia, Mississippi, might have been living today because we'd have been around to stop it.

Q. Do the Deacons have any code or any instructions or any policy about the use of arms, about when they will use them?

A. Yes, we have our by-laws that each man must study to make sure that he understands them and must abide by them before he can become a Deacon.

Q. Is there anything you can say about the pledge that a Deacon takes, or the oath?

A. He pledges his life for the defense of justice, that's one thing he do, for the defense of the Negro people, and the civil rights workers in this area. When I say this area, that doesn't necessarily mean Bogalusa, that's anywhere we're needed in this vicinity.

Q. You mean in this parish?

A. That's right, and if necessary, out of this parish.

Q. What has been the response to the existence of the Deacons from the civil rights movement, from the Congress of Racial Equality, other civil rights organizations or from unaffiliated whites that come in like we might come in?

A. They're most glad we have the Deacons organized. See, right now it's rather quiet. Two months ago a white civil rights worker or even a colored civil rights worker, he couldn't come into Bogalusa unless we brought him in. The whites would be on the road trying to stop cars. We've taken on the job of transportation in and out of Bogalusa, bringing people backwards and forwards, making sure that they get here safe.

Q. Is this to protect against truckloads of whites, night-riders and that sort of thing?

A. Anybody that tries to get next to the civil right workers, anybody.

Q. Can you tell me what kind of weapons are preferred, is it a shotgun or a rifle or a pistol?

A. A shotgun is for close range stuff. I don't intend to let a man get close enough to me to hit me with a shotgun.

Q. So you prefer a rifle?

A. The best that they make.

Q. Do you have any recommendations for white people travelling in the South?

A. Yes, be careful. And if you're a civil rights worker, don't let nobody know it.

Q. Would you recommend that white persons interested in or working in the civil rights movement carry their own arms or guns when they travel in the South?

A. I will not recommend anyone to carry guns. I don't think that's my job to recommend people to carry weapons. When you carry a weapon, you have to have a made up mind to use it. I am president of the Deacons and not a legal advisor to everyone who passes through Bogalusa.

Q. Can you tell us anything about how you would operate in any particular kind of an emergency situation. Would you get a call by phone, or do you have a two-way radio set up? Suppose something was happening to somebody in an outlying district, how are you likely to know about it and how are you likely to respond to it?

A. The old saying that I've heard is that bad news travels fast. We have telephones, naturally, word of mouth, and we have some powerful walkie-talkies. We can receive a lot of different calls on the walkie-talkies that we can't transmit, but we can receive them. And that's what bugs the white man today, why was we able to be in so many places so quick. We was intercepting their calls.

Q. You were intercepting the calls of the white people?

A. Sure, the Ku Klux Klan, sometimes the police calls, all depends.

Q. You mean they have their own radios and you listen in to them?

A. Naturally.

Q. Could you give any kind of example of a situation like this?

A. There are so many of them, I don't know which one to pick out.

Q. Could you pick one where you got, say, a call from out of town and you had to go out there real quick?

A. Yes, we had a doctor coming into Bogalusa and they dropped him off in Covington. We received a call that peoples down there were asking him a lot of questions and we had to get to Covington quick, and get him out of there. That's about 28 miles. So about 16-17 minutes after I received a call, I pulled up at the gas station. When I pulled up at the gas station—well, I knew the doctor—and I had two carload of mens, maybe ten mens. And I walked up and picked up his bag and said "Let's go Doc," well two, three white boys started behind him. And I just turned around and said, "Partner, if you want to keep living you better go back, because if you come any closer to this car, I'm going to kill all three of you." I wasn't going to kill them; it was just a threat. So we had to bring Doc out and had to hurry up and get him out. So down the road we had two-three peoples tried to follow us, but we have some pretty fast automobiles. They're a little faster than the usual car.

Q. When you confronted the white people there at the service station, did you show a weapon at that point?

A. I didn't have to—they know me. I showed my face. That was weapons enough. And they know wherever they see me, my gun and the Deacons are close.

Q. The mere showing of a weapon, does that sometimes take care of a situation?

A. The showing of a weapon stops many things. Everybody want to live and nobody want to die. But here in Bogalusa, I'm one of the few peoples who is really known as a Deacon and anybody that I associate with, they just take for granted they are Deacons. I show up; then ten, twelve more mens show up, whether they Deacons or not, they branded, you know. That make the white man respect us even more, because nine out of ten he be right.

Q. There might be some people who feel that merely by your having weapons in your possession and being willing to use them, that this might create violence rather than stopping it . . .

A. Well some peoples ought to take one other thing into consideration. I owned three or four weapons long before the civil rights movement. I went to jail, I think about three times for carrying concealed weapons ten years before the movement start. So, I mean, having a weapon's nothing new. What bugged the people was something else—when they found out what was the program of the Deacons. I do have a police record.

Q. Do you want to talk about it?

A. It's no secret. Every time I went to jail it was for carrying a weapon or battery. I've never been to jail for drunks, stealing or nothing like that. But I used to fight all the time and when they discovered I was president of the Deacons, they looked up my record and checked how many times I whipped white boys on the biggest street they have in the city and I wasn't afraid of the law or nobody else they start thinking twice. It's good that they did because I meant business. I had made up my mind.

Q. If you say that the white man was not bugged until the Deacons were created, was it the organization of a group like the Deacons that made the difference rather than, say, you as an individual . . .

A. No, not me as an individual. See, the Southern white man is almost like Hitler in the South. He been dictating to the Negro people, "Boy, this," and "Uncle, that," and "Granma, go here," and people's been jumpin'. So he gets up one morning and discovers that "Boy," was a man, and that he can walk up and say something to "boy" and "boy" don't like what he say, he tell him to eat himself—you know? And then if he blow up, there's a good fight right there. So the man goes back home and sit down and try to figure out the Negro. Shortly after that we had several rallies. And I guess he received his answer—we told him a brand new Negro was born. The one he'd been pushin' around, he didn't exist anymore.

Q. Do you think people here in Bogalusa realize that now?

A. Oh, yes.

Q. Has it made a difference?

A. A great difference.

Q. Could you describe the difference?

A. First of all we don't have these people driving through this neighborhood throwing at people's houses, catching two or three fellows on the streets, jumping out their car, whipping them up 'cause these are Negroes and they are white. We don't be bothered because these paddies [whites] in the streets calling themselves collectors harassing the womens and going from door to door to see 'how that one is.' We don't have any of this. Because of the Deacons, we don't have any of this. We don't have much work to do now. But up until the middle of July we patrolled the streets 24 hours a day, ⌐ made sure we didn't have any of this. When we found ⌐ we hadded 'em up and if they give us any resistance, we, ⌐ w, shook 'em up.

⌐ t do you mean, "Shook 'em up?"

A. Well you know how to shake a man up, you know. Teach him that you mean business.

Q. Where we come from, that might be called "roughing him up."

A. Well, yes, a little Bogart, you know. Pop him up the side of his head, shake him up, take his weapon away from him and show him the way to get back to town.

Q. Has anyone ever been arrested for doing that?

A. No. One boy was arrested, he was accused of drawing a gun on a man, accused of it. It was two weapons against him and eight weapons for him. Now if a judge is trying you for something you done to me, even though you's guilty, if you have two mens in your defense and eight against you, who should the judge respect?

Q. I think *you* better answer that question.

A. The majority witnesses. And if he don't, we move it to a higher court until we find a court that respect the fact that eight people's word should be greater than two.

Q. Except for yourself, the names of the other Deacons are not known . . .

A. Only about four.

Q. Now outside of Bogalusa, when there is some news about a Negro carrying a gun or about some kind of violence, and people don't know who the Deacons are and who may not be Deacons, they may feel that this is the Deacons at work. Have there been instances like that where there has been violence and the Deacons were blamed for it?

A. Yes, a lot of cases. Any time a Negro and a white man have any kind of round up and the Negro decide he going to fight him back, he's a Deacon. We had one case here where a Negro and a white man had a round and a little shootin' was done. He was named a Deacon. Now I can truthfully say he was not a Deacon. But the papers, the government and everybody else say he was. So I laugh at the government to its face. I told them point blank; you do not know who Deacons is and quit gettin' on the air and telling peoples that people are Deacons just because they stood up to a white man.

Q. If no one knows who the Deacons are except you . . .

A. I didn't say except me, the secretary have to know—he keep the records.

Q. So the known Deacons are yourself and the secretary?

A. No, myself, the vice-president who is Roy N. Burris, weighs 116 pounds soaking wet but he's a man. Another man's name I will not give you because he's leaving. And Robert Hicks, he's public relations man for the Deacons.

Q. If the membership is not known, would you call it a secret society?

A. As far as the white man is concerned, yes.

Q. Could you say how many Deacons there are in Bogalusa and throughout the South?

A. No, but I'll tell you this, we have throughout the South at this time somewhere between 50 and 60 chapters.

Q. Roughly how many people in each chapter?

A. I won't tell you that.

Q. Could tell us what areas they cover?

A. Alabama, Mississippi, Arkansas, Louisiana, Texas.

Q. Georgia?

A. No. We have Georgia and North Carolina in mind. As a matter of fact I was supposed to go to North Carolina and organize the people there, and in Florida, but I don't have time right now to do it.

Q. Have you been making trips outside of Louisiana to see these other groups, to help them organize?

A. No, I send mens. And the headquarters in Jonesboro sends mens out.

Q. The headquarters is in Jonesboro, Louisiana.

A. Yes.

Q. Is Jonesboro near Bogalusa?

A. No, it's about 300 miles from here, way up North in Louisiana.

Q. Near the Arkansas border?

A. Shouldn't be too far.

Q. Could you tell us what views you might have on the civil rights tactic of non-violence?

A. The non-violent act is a good act—providing the policemens do their job. But in the Southern states, not just Louisiana, but in the Southern states, the police have never done their job when the white and the Negro are involved—unless the Negro's getting the best of the white man.

Q. How do you think the movement could best be advanced or get its aims the quickest if it didn't use non-violence?

A. I believe non-violence is the only way. Negotiations are going to be the main point in this fight.

Q. Would it be correct to put it this way, that you feel non-violence is the correct way to get political and economic things done . . .

A. Sure.

Q. But that behind that, behind the non-violence, the Deacons or organizations like the Deacons are necessary to protect the rights of this non-violent movement?

A. That's right.

Q. Do you find a noticeable change, not necessarily in the police here, but generally in the white people in this town that comes because they know there are people ready to defend the civil rights movement? Are they taking on some second thoughts?

A. Sure—who wouldn't? If you'd been walking down the streets doing anything you want and all at once you find out that you can't go down that street like you used to, wouldn't you make a change?

Q. Mr. Sims, just one last question, how long do you think the Deacons will be needed in the civil rights movement?

A. First of all, this is a long fight. In 1965 there will be a great change made. But after this change is made, the biggest fight is to keep it. My son, his son might have to fight this fight and that's one reason why we won't be able to disband the Deacons for a long time. How long, Heaven only knows. But it will be a long time.

PART VII

Political Action

INTRODUCTION

THE CURRENT MOVEMENT has attempted to involve the federal government actively in the quest for Negro rights. And increasingly these attempts have met with a measure of success. In recording the successes of the movement one should not underestimate the impact it has had on individual federal officials and on the government as a whole. There can be no doubt that the movement is responsible for the passage of the Civil Rights Acts of 1960 and 1963, and the Voting Rights Act of 1965, and the Interstate Commerce Commission order of 1961 to desegregate terminals in interstate transportation. Certainly influential individuals in government have seen the Negro in an entirely new light since the movement thrust black people into the national spotlight. Senators and Congressmen journeyed to Mississippi on several occasions to learn firsthand that Negroes were indeed murdered, tortured, intimidated with threats of violence or loss of job or credit, and to find that starvation does exist, and on a large scale, in this prosperous land.

During the years since 1960 more persons in government were in direct contact with more persons involved in the Negro struggle than at any other time in the history of the movement. A real effort has been made by many to understand the problems of the Negro in the United States. Unfortunately such understanding is difficult to acquire. Racism has developed stumbling blocks to understanding for the most reasonable white men of good will, and its effects have left Negroes with a viewpoint totally different from that of whites toward the condition and role of Negroes in American life.

Thus it could happen that in 1963 after a meeting of

Negro intellectuals with Robert Kennedy, then Attorney General, Negro psychologist Dr. Kenneth Clark would comment: "I didn't know whether to laugh or cry or both. We were unable to communicate clearly and skillfully that this was not a group of Negroes begging the white power structure to be nice to Negroes. We were trying to say that this was an emergency for our country, as Americans. This never got over."

And, again that same year in September after the Birmingham bombing in which four Negro children were killed and after state troopers had beaten and clubbed Negroes who were on the porches of their homes watching street riots, a group of 20 religious leaders leaving a meeting with the Attorney General said that they felt "a sense of despair" at the lack of urgency in Washington. Rabbi Richard Hirsch, director of the religious action center of the Union of American Hebrew Congregations, accused the President of "refusing to use his maximum powers" in support of the civil rights bill and refusing to fight for a fair employment practices provision because "he still fails to recognize the full extent of the rights revolution."

In addition to the intellectual and emotional gap between Negroes and government figures there was another important block to understanding and cooperation: politics itself. Journalist William V. Shannon pointed out in the *American Scholar* of Autumn, 1962 that on civil rights as on other questions the Administration had a "preoccupation with the political welfare of John F. Kennedy." This preoccupation got in the way. For example, in 1963, Shannon pointed out that the President kept hands off the fight to change Senate rules so that civil rights legislation would have a better chance through elimination of the possibility of death by filibuster. "Then last week he sent an eloquent, beautifully written message on civil rights legislation to Capitol Hill. The substantial recommendations in his message have no chance of passage because the liberal bloc lost the rules fight."

Negro leaders pointed to the deficiencies of each of the Civil Rights Acts and the weak fight put up for strong civil rights legislation. On the 1960 bill Roy Wilkins of the NAACP said: "Either party is welcome to claim credit for enactment of the wretched remnant of what was not very much at the outset." In 1963 the NAACP's Washington attorney, J. Francis Polhaus, said: "Because of the limited approach used by the President, it is necessary that civil rights supporters resist any effort to weaken or compromise his program. Not only should a fight be made against weakening amendments, but affirmative action should be taken to strengthen the pending bills." An NAACP memorandum urged that the Democratic Party platform plank of 1960 requiring all school districts to submit desegregation plans by a specific date be included in the 1960 civil rights bill.

Whitney M. Young Jr. of the Urban League said in May, 1964 that the Administration "is reacting and not acting" on Negro problems. He said that Washington's view is that good race relations is "not the presence of justice and true democracy, but how it [the Administration] can keep the people from revolting and thus embarrassing us."

Mrs. Victoria Gray testified on behalf of the Mississippi Freedom Democratic Party at hearings on the Voting Rights Bill of 1965. She endorsed provisions sought by other civil rights organizations, but in addition stressed the need for one provision requiring new elections within six months. She pointed out that though Negroes might be registered in large numbers under the bill which provided for federal registrars there would be no political participation for the new voters for several years. Mrs. Gray said: "In May or June of this year municipal elections will be held throughout the state. This will mean that mayors, local law enforcement officers, and other officials who have been the visible symbol of brutality and intimidation will be elected for four more years before Negro registration under this new law will be large enough to have any effect on these elections." She asked: "How effective will this bill be in Neshoba County, Mississippi, if local law enforcement remains in the hands of Sheriff Rainey and Deputy Sheriff Price [1] for four more years? How effective will it be in Selma if Negroes en route to the courthouse must pass by Sheriff Jim Clark and his posse?" [2]

The provision was not included in the bill. Nevertheless voter registration among Deep South Negroes increased substantially after the bill's passage. Perhaps more importantly, a drive was launched in one county to make sure that the new voters could cast votes that would count. In Sunflower County, Mississippi, the Mississippi Freedom Democratic Party (MFDP) instituted a suit to declare the 1966 elections invalid. The suit was won as to elections in the town of Sunflower, and new elections were held in April, 1967. The Negro slate lost by 30 votes because of intimidation by white election officials and white employers.

[1] Sheriff Lawrence Rainey and Deputy Sheriff Cecil Price were among those indicted on a charge of conspiracy to deprive persons of their civil rights in connection with the murder of three civil rights workers, James Chaney, Andrew Goodman and Michael Schwerner in June, 1964. Price and six others were convicted in October, 1967. Rainey and seven others were acquitted.

[2] Sheriff Jim Clark of Dallas County was in charge of a posse which tear gassed and beat demonstrators in 1963.

The attempt to obtain greater support for Negro rights reached a climax in the summer of 1964 in the Mississippi Summer Project and the Mississippi Freedom Democratic Party's challenge to the seating of the state's regular Democratic delegation at the national Democratic Party convention. The Summer Project, conducted by the Council of Federated Organizations (COFO), but staffed almost entirely by SNCC and CORE, was traumatic for the state and stirred the nation. Over 700 young people, mostly white, middle-class students, spent the summer in Mississippi teaching in Freedom Schools, doing voter registration canvassing, building community centers and helping the MFDP. The Summer Project was a conscious move to bring whites into the Deep South to focus the nation's attention on the plight of the Negro. COFO leaders knew that the young white volunteers would face dangers that they themselves had faced over the past months and years, and they felt that the involvement of volunteers might bring some federal protection at best, and at the least widespread public criticism of the Southern system. At the beginning of the summer what had been most feared happened: three young workers were brutally murdered. The deaths roused federal action. When the three young men disappeared, one a Negro from Meridian, Mississippi, one a white CORE staff member and one a white volunteer, federal forces, including the U.S. Navy, participated in the search In the efforts to locate the three rights workers one after another dismembered body of Negroes, who had long since disappeared, was dragged from Mississippi and Louisiana rivers.

Through other experiences of the summer the nation learned about the Mississippi way of life. At the beginning of the summer the Southern Regional Council reported that 64 known acts of violence in the state had been recorded between January, 1961, and March, 1963. During the summer of 1964, 33 churches were burned in the state, and there were hundreds of arrests and countless beatings and shootings in addition to the three deaths.

Other aspects of Mississippi life were revealed too. A convention of youngsters, who had attended Freedom Schools during the summer, adopted a series of resolutions which they sent to the Congress covering foreign affairs and voting rights and demanding minimum housing standards including a "full bathroom" per housing unit, widened school curricula to include vocational training and foreign languages, and paved streets. The students adopted a "Declaration of Independence" which concluded: "We, therefore, the Negroes of Mississippi assembled, appeal to the government of the state, that no man is free until all men are free. We do hereby declare independence from the unjust laws of Mississippi which conflict with the United States Constitution."

In the political sphere Mississippi Negroes were able to demonstrate conclusively that it was not apathy, but fear and deliberate exclusion by whites which had kept them from voting. The Mississippi Freedom Democratic Party had conducted a mock election in 1963 in which more than 80,000 Negroes cast "freedom votes" for MFDP candidates. Then in the summer of 1964 the party conducted a "freedom registration" and the people took an astounding political step. First they systematically followed the legal procedures for participation in the regular Democratic Party pre-convention meetings and were rebuffed. Then Negroes in a majority of Mississippi's 82 counties held precinct, district and county meetings, and attended a state-wide convention of their own to elect Freedom Democratic Party delegates to attend the national Democratic Party convention.

At the convention's Credentials Committee hearings MFDP delegates and supporters testified against the segregated regular delegation, and for the right of Mississippi Negroes to representation. Their claim was based on the fact that Negroes had been barred from regular party meetings in the state and on the regular party's opposition to the national party slate. Nationwide television viewers heard the emotional appeal of Mrs. Fannie Lou Hamer of Ruleville, Mississippi, an MFDP delegate who had been fired from a plantation, where she had worked for 18 years, the day she registered to vote.

Coalition politics received a death blow at the convention. The 60-odd members of the MFDP delegation, despite the entreaties of their liberal supporters from Vice-President-to-be Hubert Humphrey to Walter Reuther, refused to accept a compromise offered by the Party—the seating of two of their members-at-large, and a promise that the next convention would require a pledge of non-discrimination from regular delegations. The MFDP had made the country take notice and it had, in political terms, forced a serious confrontation. The old way of politics—placating the Southern Democrats to maintain national unity—had almost foundered on the rock of Negro determination. Answers by delegates on a questionnaire on rejection of the compromise reveal the sentiments of the Mississippi protest movement. They included: "This type of symbol is exactly what we were trying to fight in Mississippi." "Because it wasn't enough for all the work, all the fear and all the lives that have been lost." "We have always been promised a little and got less."

The MFDP delegation returned to Mississippi disillusioned with their liberal friends and wise in the workings of politics, and continued to organize around a legal challenge to the seating in Congress of the segregationist Mississippi delegation of five representatives. In freedom elections they had chosen their own Congressional delegation to represent them in the House of Representatives. Once again some liberals lined up in support, but the Democratic Study Group—the liberal caucus of the House—did not throw its full weight behind the challenge and the MFDP was defeated. But 115 members of the House did vote to unseat the Mississippi Congressmen.

Mississippi's systematic exclusion of Negroes from politics and government and the reluctance of Congress to depart from the path of political expediency had been demonstrated. Yet, after the passage of the Voting Rights Act of 1965 Negroes registered in large numbers. The Act suspended literacy and other similar voter qualification tests and provided for federal supervision of registration in states or counties where such tests were used Nov. 1, 1964, and in which less than 50 percent of voting age residents were registered. By the end of 1964, 43% of eligible Negroes were registered in counties where there were federal registrars, and only 13% in counties where no registrars were appointed.

In light of the MFDP experience with the Democratic Party many Negroes decided to go it alone. In Lowndes County, Alabama, where there were no Negroes registered in March, 1965, 2,000 registered after the Voting Act. Lowndes is 81% Negro. Negroes set up an independent party, the Lowndes County Freedom Organization, and ran a slate for local offices. Stokely Carmichael, former SNCC Chairman, who was an organizer in Lowndes, has written:

. . . [I] used to say to the black people there [Lowndes] that they should register to vote and then make their voices heard. They could assert their rights, take over the power structure. This was the prescription of the qualified. But these people said they didn't want to do that, they did not think they could, they did not even want to enter a machine headed by George Wallace. To them politics meant Wallace, Sheriff Jim Clark and Tom Coleman, who had been accused of the murder of Jonathan Daniels. To them the Democratic Party didn't mean LBJ, but a crew of racist bullies and killers. Entering politics meant, until last summer, confronting the tools of Wallace: the county registrars who had flunked Negroes consistently for years.

They asked if something different could not be created. They wanted to redefine politics, make up new rules, and play the game with some personal integrity. Out of a negative force, fear, grew the positive drive to think new.[3]

In the Nov. 8, 1966 election the Lowndes County Freedom Organization ran seven candidates who were defeated by whites by margins ranging from 273 votes to 677. There were 2,681 Negroes registered and 2,100 whites. The defeat was no doubt in part due to lack of experience in politics, but intimidation and the threat of economic reprisals also played a part. Of the seven LCFO candidates two were housewives and two were self-employed. The other three lost their jobs as did two LCFO poll watchers and the father of one of the candidates.

As the drive toward black independent political action has developed in the South, there has been a simultaneous attempt to mobilize Negro political strength in Northern ghettoes. There have been a few attempts by Negroes to organize third parties in the North, such as the Freedom Now Party in Detroit, but the independent action has mainly stressed the mobilization of a Negro bloc vote for selected Democratic candidates. In Cleveland, a Negro, Carl B. Stokes, running as an independent Democrat for mayor, polled over 85,000 votes, losing only by 2,458.[4] In Gary, Indiana, a Negro attorney ran first in a 9-man mayoralty race in the Democratic primary in the spring of 1967. He received 4.5 percent of the white vote and 70 percent of the Negro.

On the local level this political action has found expression primarily in the struggle for quality education, and in the fight for control of the "anti-poverty" boards of the Federal war on poverty program. The struggle over education progressed from school boycotts demanding a plan and timetable for total desegregation, conducted in 1963 and 1964 in Chicago and New York, to boycotts and sit-ins at the New York Board of Education for community control of school administration. A People's Board of Education was established in New York in 1967.[5]

The direction of the Northern struggle for Negro rights

[3] Stokely Carmichael, "Who is Qualified?", *The New Republic,* January 8, 1966, p. 22.

[4] In October, 1967, Stokes received 95% of the Negro vote and 10 to 14% of the white vote defeating the incumbent by 110,354 votes to 92,029.

[5] In the first New York school boycott on Feb. 3, 1964, 44.8% of the total pupils were absent: 92% in Central Harlem and 80.3% on the Lower East Side. This was the first mass action for civil rights conducted jointly by Negroes and Puerto Ricans.

has been dictated by the economic and political results of a population shift. As Negroes moved to the cities, whites moved away, first from areas of the city where Negroes lived, then outside the "center city" to outlying areas and suburbs. In eight cities with large Negro populations, Negroes live in areas of the cities which are over 95% Negro. The concentration of the Negro population in the "inner city" areas of large cities creates areas both of high unemployment and of potential political power.

As it had in the past the Negro movement once more turned its attention outward to the international scene. The significance of the new states in world politics increased after 1960 when large numbers of African states were admitted to the United Nations and the African caucus became a major force. By 1962 African states formed 26 percent of the General Assembly and the Afro-Asian bloc 47 percent. In 1964 Malcolm X, who had been suspended as a Muslim minister and then broke with Elijah Muhammad, the Muslim leader, to form his own organization, visited Mecca and attended the conference of the Organization of African Unity to urge African nations to bring the question of Negro rights to the United Nations. The student leaders of SNCC and James Farmer of CORE also visited Africa. The developing interest in the colored or "Third World" among movement participants led in large part to widespread criticism of U.S. involvement in the war in Vietnam. Some of the criticism stems from the fact that the young people in the movement are themselves subject to being drafted, but a more general concern arises from the contradiction which we have seen regarding other wars in which the United States was involved: the contradiction between the expressed goals of the wars—"fighting for freedom" abroad and the absence of freedom at home. Another basis is the diversion of funds from social welfare to warfare. On a political level, it has taken the form of opposition to imperialism. SNCC, CORE and SCLC have criticized the U.S. role in the Vietnam war for thwarting the struggle of colored peoples to become independent. On a philosophical plane some parts of the movement adhere to the principle of non-violence and condemn the war for pacifist reasons. Meantime, the struggle domestically more and more has turned again toward "wanting out"—a struggle for economic and political independence of the black ghettos.

1. APPEAL TO WASHINGTON

*March on Washington**

JOHN LEWIS

WE MARCH TODAY for jobs and freedom, but we have nothing to be proud of, for hundreds and thousands of our brothers are not here—for they have no money for their transportation, for they are receiving starvation wages . . . or no wages, at all.

In good conscience, we cannot support the Administration's civil rights bill, for it is too little, and too late. There's not one thing in the bill that will protect our people from police brutality.

The voting section of this bill will not help the thousands of citizens who want to vote; will not help the citizens of Mississippi, of Alabama, and Georgia who are qualified to vote, who are without a 6th grade education. "One Man, One Vote," is the African cry—it is ours, too.

People have been forced to move for they have exercised their right to register to vote. What is in the bill that will protect the homeless and starving people of this nation? What is there in this bill to insure the equality of a maid who earns $5.00 a week in the home of a family whose income is $100,000 a year?

This bill will not protect young children and old women from police dogs and fire hoses for engaging in peaceful demonstrations. This bill will not protect the citizens in Danville, Virginia, who must live in constant fear in a police state. This bill will not protect the hundreds of people who have been arrested on trumped-up charges, like those in Americus, Georgia, where four young men are in jail, facing a death penalty, for engaging in peaceful protest.

For the first time in 100 years this nation is being awak-

* Speech delivered at the March on Washington, Aug. 28, 1963. The talk was altered moments before delivery to tone down its criticism of the federal government to meet objections of some of the march's co-sponsors. For example, the second paragraph was delivered: "True, we support the Administration's civil rights bill but this bill will not protect young children and old women from police dogs and fire hoses . . ." John Lewis was then chairman of the Student Nonviolent Coordinating Committee.

ened to the fact that segregation is evil and it must be destroyed in all forms. Our presence today proves that we have been aroused to the point of action.

We are now involved in a serious revolution. This nation is still a place of cheap political leaders allying themselves with open forms of political, economic and social exploitation.

In some parts of the South we have worked in the fields from sun-up to sun-down for $12 a week. In Albany, Georgia, we have seen our people indicted by the Federal government for peaceful protest, while the Deputy Sheriff beat Attorney C. B. King and left him half-dead; while local police officials kicked and assaulted the pregnant wife of Slater King, and she lost her baby.

It seems to me that the Albany indictment is part of a conspiracy on the part of the federal government and local politicians for political expediency.

I want to know—which side is the federal government on?

The revolution is at hand, and we must free ourselves of the chains of political and economic slavery. The non-violent revolution is saying, "We will not wait for the courts to act, for we have been waiting hundreds of years. We will not wait for the President, nor the Justice Department, nor Congress, but we will take matters into our own hands, and create a great source of power, outside of any national structure that could and would assure us victory." For those who have said, "Be patient and wait!" we must say, "Patience is a dirty and nasty word." We cannot be patient, we do not want to be free gradually, we want our freedom, and we want it now. We can not depend on any political party, for both the Democrats and the Republicans have betrayed the basic principles of the Declaration of Independence.

We all recognize the fact that if any radical social, political and economic changes are to take place in our society, the people, the masses must bring them about. In the struggle we must seek more than mere civil rights; we must work for the community of love, peace, and true brotherhood. Our minds, souls, and hearts cannot rest until freedom and justice exist for *all the people*.

The revolution is a serious one. Mr. Kennedy is trying to take the revolution out of the streets and put it in the courts. Listen, Mr. Kennedy, listen, Mr. Congressman, listen, fellow citizens—the black masses are on the march for jobs and freedom, and we must say to the politicians that there won't be a "cooling-off period."

We won't stop now. All of the forces of Eastland, Barnett and Wallace won't stop this revolution. The next time we march, we won't march on Washington, but we will march through the South, through the Heart of Dixie, the way Sherman did. We will make the action of the past few months look petty. And I say to you, WAKE UP AMERICA!!

All of us must get in the revolution—get in and stay in the streets of every city, village and hamlet of this nation, until true freedom comes, until the revolution is complete. The black masses in the Delta of Mississippi, in Southwest Georgia, Alabama, Harlem, Chicago, Detroit, Philadelphia and all over this nation are on the march.

The New Jacobins and Full Emancipation*

JAMES FARMER

IT REMAINED FOR Birmingham and, before that, its dress rehearsal, Albany, Georgia, to learn from the Freedom Riders' mistakes, and launch massive demonstrations and jail-ins, wholly involving thousands, not hundreds, of Negroes—local citizens, not transients—and mobilizing the respective Negro communities *in toto*. A score of Birminghams followed the first. Birmingham thus set the stage for a full-scale revolt against segregation in this nation. Such a mass movement was possible because of the magic name of Martin Luther King, Jr. It was possible, in a more basic sense, because of an historical merger of two social forces.

What happened after World War II, or really after Montgomery, was a kind of wedding of two forces, both bred by the war: the means-oriented idealists of pacifistic turn of mind, for whom nonviolence was a total philosophy, a way of life, and the ends-oriented militants, the postwar angry young men who saw in direct action a weapon and viewed nonviolence as a tactic.

Without such a fusion, no revolutionary mass movement could have emerged. Without the young Turks, the movement never could have grown to mass proportions, and without the idealists it could not have developed revolutionary dimensions. The anger of one without the disciplined idealism of the other could have produced only nihilism. Without the

* Excerpt from James Farmer, "The New Jacobins and Full Emancipation," in Robert A. Goldwin, ed., *100 Years of Emancipation* (Chicago: Rand McNally & Co., 1964), pp. 95-102. Copyright © 1963, 1964 by the Public Affairs Conference Center, Kenyon College. Reprinted by permission.

indigenous anger of the Negro masses, the idealists, for all their zeal, would have remained largely irrelevant, socially speaking, and would have gone on talking to themselves and whispering through an occasional keyhole to another human heart.

As in any viable marriage, each party speaks much truth to the other. The idealists warn that the ends do not justify the means, and the militants assert with equal validity that means are worthless which do not achieve desired and verifiable ends. Each tempers the other, and out of the creative tension between the two has come a third position which, I believe, more accurately reflects the movement. Nonviolence is neither a mere tactic, which may be dropped on any occasion, nor an inviolable spiritual commitment. It is somewhere between the two—not a philosophy, not a tactic, but a strategy involving both philosophical and tactical elements, in a massive and widening direct action campaign to redeem the American promise of full freedom for the Negro.

This does not mean that all of the hundreds of thousands of Negroes involved in the street campaigns for equality accept nonviolence as strategy or tactic or anything else. It is only the leaders, members, and close associates of the nonviolent movement who accept it in any way as an integral part of the struggle. The masses who now join the determined folks on picket lines and sit-ins and protest marches share only a new-found willingness to become individually, physically involved and to risk suffering or jail for common goals. The masses have no commitment to nonviolence, or to any other specific response to abuse beyond that dictated by the natural desire to be accepted by, and to conform to the code of, the militants whom they join in action. Obviously, the urge to conformity is not enough, in and of itself, to maintain nonviolence through the stresses of a mass direct action movement. And that, precisely, is the chief tactical dilemma of today's Freedom Movement.

The nonviolent militants, seeking to mount a revolutionary force capable of toppling manifest racism, need those folk who are not yet wedded to nonviolence, who are wedded, indeed, only to their own fierce indignation. They need them from the pool halls and taverns as well as from the churches, from the unemployed and the alienated and the rootless. The entire Negro community wants now, more than ever before, to become directly involved in the "revolution." Either they will be involved or they will, by their separation from it, brand the movement as counterfeit and ultimately destroy it.

The problem, of course, is to see that they do not destroy it by their involvement. Small, disciplined groups are easy to control. Untrained masses are more difficult. Violence used against us by our opponents is a problem only in so far as it may provoke counterviolence from our ranks. Thus far, sporadic incidents of violence, where they have occurred in the movement, have been contained and have not become a contagion. We have been lucky, but we cannot afford any longer to leave such a vital matter to chance. Widespread violence by the freedom fighters would sever from the struggle all but a few of our allies. It would also provoke and, to many, justify, such repressive measures as would stymie the movement. More than that, many of our own nonviolent activists would be shorn away by disenchantment. None would profit from such developments except the defenders of segregation and perhaps the more bellicose of the black nationalist groups.

Recognition of the problem is half the solution. The other half lies not in stopping demonstrations, as is often counseled by those of faint heart or less than whole commitment. To give ear to such counsel would be, in a real sense, to betray the movement. Cessation of direct action is neither desirable nor possible.

What is possible, as well as desirable, is an expeditious and thorough program of discipline—both internal and external. Internally, the need is for rapid expansion of training for nonviolence in the ranks—classes, institutes, workshops—in every city where the struggle is in process or in preparation. The external requirement calls for a specially trained cadre of monitors for every mass demonstration, to spot trouble before it occurs and either resolve it or isolate it. With a sensitivity to any potential break in the ranks, the monitors must have specialized skills in dealing with the untrained who may join the ranks during action.

Herein, then, lies the answer to the danger of the movement's degeneration into mass violence: tighter discipline within the ranks and trained monitors to police the lines. Needless to say, these new demands upon the movement will be met with dispatch.

The second problem in the new militants' struggle for full emancipation is more functional than tactical. There has occurred in the past few years a proliferation, though not a splintering, of direct action organizations of a nonviolent character. In addition to CORE, there is the Southern Christian Leadership Conference of Dr. King, the Student Nonviolent Coordinating Committee, and various unaffiliated local groups, jealous of their autonomy. Such established organizations as the NAACP are also engaging increasingly in direct action. Church groups, too, and professional associations which previously had confined their action to pronouncements, are now "taking to the streets."

All of this strengthens the movement immeasurably. But it also poses a problem. What coordination exists between the groups is largely accidental rather than the product of systematic planning. Nor is there sufficient coordination of programs within each organization.

What we have, in essence, is a series of guerrilla strikes, generally unrelated to any totally conceived plan. An effective war cannot be waged in such a manner, nor can a revolution likely be won thus. Guerrilla warfare must have its place, but as part of an over-all plan.

An urgent need at this stage of the struggle, therefore, is for coordinated planning for full-scale nonviolent war against color caste. A revolution which, like Topsy, "just grew," must now submit itself to the rigors of systematization. Spontaneity, the trademark of the 1960 sit-ins, has served its purpose; a thrust in one sector must no longer be unrelated to a push in another. Comprehensive actions need to be fashioned now to fit an over-all conceptualization of the problem. And the only realistic concept of segregation is as a total unity, national rather than sectional, with all aspects being interrelated.

What we do in the South and in the North, for example, should be part of a whole, for though its dimensions and contours may vary from place to place, the institution of segregation has no separate existence anywhere. Without subsidies from both the federal government and northern capital, it could not persist in the South. And were the South not an open sore, pouring northward its stream of deprived human beings, the North could never rationalize and maintain its fool's defense—the *de facto* pattern on segregation. The tentacles of the beast are everywhere but none of them should be mistaken for the octopus itself.

This essential unity of the problem is beginning to take form in action with a growing clarity. If a lunch counter segregates in Atlanta or a retail store in Oklahoma City fails to hire Negroes in nontraditional jobs, while heretofore they were attacked in isolation, they are now coming to be dealt with in more realistic terms: as parts of chains if such they are. The economic boycott is a far more potent weapon when regional or national leverage can be used.

Action on any incident of discrimination should take its shape from the shape of the power structure or the machinery which controls, influences, or sustains the objectionable practice. Maximum effectiveness cannot be achieved otherwise. When, for instance, southern school bonds are floated to build and maintain segregated schools, they are marketed not in the South, but by brokers in New York, New Jersey, Massachusetts, Pennsylvania, Illinois, and California. Wittingly or unwittingly, northern investors thus provide the fuel to keep southern segregation going. Income from such investments is tax exempt. So, despite the Supreme Court's 1954 decision, the Federal government is providing in this manner a subsidy just as supportive of caste as are its outright grants to schools, hospitals, and services which are segregated. No campaign against segregation which fails to confront the source of funds can even approach adequacy. . . .

The Jacobins' activities are opening up jobs previously closed to Negroes. They are cracking barriers in northern housing in a neck and neck race against spreading residential segregation. The mask of hypocrisy has been ripped off northern school segregation, leaving exposed a largely semantic difference between *de facto* and *de jure*. Yet, the realization is growing among the new militants that even when the walls are down, and segregation is ended, the task of full emancipation will not be finished. Because of a hundred years of discrimination, the Negro is a built-in "low man on the totem pole." Even after job discrimination is gone, under normally accepted employment procedures the Negro will most often be starting at the bottom while others are already at the middle or the top. And, due to past educational inequities, even after school segregation is over, he cannot compete on an equal footing in this generation or the next.

The responsibility of accelerating the Negro's march to equality does not rest with the Negro alone. This cannot be a sheer bootstrap operation. When a society has crippled some of its people, it has an obligation to provide requisite crutches. Industry has an obligation not merely to employ the best qualified person who *happens* to apply, but to seek qualified Negroes for nontraditional jobs, and if none can be found, to help train them. If two or more applicants with substantially equal qualifications should present themselves, and one of them is a Negro, then he should be given a measure of preference to compensate for the discrimination of centuries.

Beyond that, a remedial education and training program of massive proportions needs to be launched. To accomplish more than a gesture, such a program will require billions of dollars—perhaps three billion a year for a five-year period. Anything less will be tokenism. The only source for funds in such amount is the Federal government.

Perhaps a portion of the money saved by virtue of the nuclear test ban should thus be used to reclaim a people and a nation. But whether or not the Federal government acts, the

New Jacobins will continue their revolutionary thrust. To paraphrase a beaten white Freedom Rider: "We'll take beating. We'll take kicking. We'll take even death. And we'll keep coming till we can ride, work, live, study, and play anywhere in this country—without anyone saying anything, but just as American citizens."

U.S. COMMISSION ON CIVIL RIGHTS

*Voting Rights**

RECOMMENDATIONS ON VOTING LEGISLATION AND SUMMARY OF RESULTING OR RELATED STATUTES

The U.S. Commission on Civil Rights was created by the Civil Rights Act of 1957. One of the Commission's duties has been to report and make recommendations to the President and Congress. Recommendations on voting were made in the Commission's 1959, 1961, and 1963 reports. These recommendations are set out in full below; each is followed by a summary of subsequent legislation following the outlines of the Commission recommendations or adopting alternative procedures to overcome the problem outlined.

1959 REPORT

Census
Recommendation No. 1.—The Commission found a general deficiency of information about nonvoting. It recommended that the "Bureau of the Census be authorized and directed to undertake, in connection with the census of 1960 or at the earliest possible time thereafter, a nationwide and territorial compilation of registration and voting statistics which shall include a count of individuals by race, color, and national origin who are registered, and a determination of the extent to which such individuals have voted since the prior decennial census."

This recommendation with certain alterations was enacted

* Summary of Commission's recommendations on Voting Rights 1959, 1961, 1963, submitted in hearings before Subcommittee No. 5 of the Committee on the Judiciary, House of Representatives, 89th Congress, 1st Session, on voting rights, March-April, 1965.

as Title VIII of the Civil Rights Act of 1964, 42 U.S.C. §
2000 (f).

Records

Recommendation No. 2.—The Commission found that the
absence of uniform provision for the preservation and inspection of public voting records impeded investigation of alleged
denials of the right to vote. It recommended that "Congress
require that all State and Territorial registration and voting records shall be public records and must be preserved for a period of 5 years, during which time they shall be subject to
public inspection, provided that all care be taken to preserve
the secrecy of the ballot."

A provision was enacted as part of the Civil Rights Act of
1960 requiring that all records relating to Federal elections including application and registration records be preserved for
22 months after any Federal election to which they pertain,
and be made available to the U.S. Attorney General upon his
written demand. 42 U.S.C. § 1974 *et seq.*

Inaction of State officials

Recommendation No. 3.—The Commission found that
State officials failed to register voters by refusing to meet as
required or by other inaction. It recommended that the Civil
Rights Act of 1957 (42 U.S.C. 1971) be amended by inser-
tion of the following paragraph:

"Nor shall any person or group of persons, under color of
State law, arbitrarily and without legal justification or cause,
act, or being under duty to act, fail to act, in such manner as
to deprive or threaten to deprive any individual or group of
individuals of the opportunity to register, vote and have that
vote counted for any candidate for the office of President,
Vice President, presidential elector, Member of the Senate, or
Member of the House of Representatives, Delegate or Commissioner for the Territories or possessions, at any general,
special, or primary election held solely or in part for the purpose of selecting or electing any such candidate."

A related provision was enacted in the Civil Rights Act of
1960, providing, at 42 U.S.C. 1971 (c), that where registration officials resigned without leaving successors, Department
of Justice litigation could be directed against the State.

Federal registrars

Recommendation No. 5.—The Commission found that substantial numbers of qualified citizens were being denied the
right to register by State officials. It made the following recommendation: "Upon receipt by the President of the United

States of sworn affidavits by nine or more individuals from any district, county, parish, or other political subdivision of a State, alleging that the affiants have unsuccessfully attempted to register with the duly constituted State registration office, and that the affiants believe themselves qualified under State law to be electors, but have been denied the right to register because of race, color, religion or national origin, the President shall refer such affidavits to the Commission on Civil Rights, if extended.

A. The Commission shall:

(1) Investigate the validity of the allegations.

(2) Dismiss such affidavits as prove, on investigation, to be unfounded.

(3) Certify any and all well-founded affidavits to the President and to such temporary registrar as he may designate.

B. The President upon such certification shall designate an existing Federal officer or employee in the area from which complaints are received, to act as a temporary registrar.

C. Such registrar-designate shall administer the State qualification laws and issue to all individuals found qualified, registration certificates which shall entitle them to vote for any candidate for the Federal offices of President, Vice President, presidential elector, Members of the Senate or Members of the House of Representatives, Delegates or Commissioners for the Territories or possessions, in any general, special, or primary election held solely or in part for the purpose of selecting or electing any such candidate.

D. The registrar-designate shall certify to the responsible State registration officials the names and fact of registration of all persons registered by him. Such certification shall permit all such registrants to participate in Federal elections previously enumerated.

E. Jurisdiction shall be retained until such time as the President determines that the presence of the appointed registrar is no longer necessary."

The Civil Rights Act of 1960 provided that if a court finds a pattern or practice of discrimination at the conclusion of a law suit, it may appoint a referee to register voters. 42 U.S.C. 1971 (c).

Voter qualifications

In 1959 three Commissioners recommended eliminating, by constitutional amendment, all State qualifications on the right to vote except requirements as to age, length of residence, and legal confinement.

No legislative action has yet been taken with respect to this proposal.

1961 REPORT

The Commission found that the application of voter qualification laws resulted in discriminatory denials of the right to vote. It made the following recommendations:

Voter qualifications

Recommendation No. 1.—"That Congress, acting under section 2 of the 15th amendment and sections 2 and 5 of the 14th amendment, (a) declare that voter qualifications other than age, residence, confinement, and conviction of a crime are susceptible of use, and have been used, to deny the right to vote on grounds of race and color; and (b) enact legislation providing that all citizens of the United States shall have a right to vote in Federal or State elections which shall not be denied or in any way abridged or interfered with by the United States or by any State for any cause except for inability to meet reasonable age or length-of-residence requirements uniformly applied to all persons within a State, legal confinement at the time of registration or election, or conviction of a felony; such right to vote to include the right to register or otherwise qualify to vote, and to have one's vote counted."

No legislative action has yet been taken upon this recommendation.

Literacy tests

Recommendation No. 2—"That Congress enact legislation providing that in all elections in which, under State law, a 'literacy' test, an 'understanding' or 'interpretation' test, or an 'educational' test is administered to determine the qualifications of electors, it shall be sufficient for qualification that the elector have completed at least six grades of formal education."

The Civil Rights Act of 1964 provided at 42 U.S.C. § 1971(c) that in a voting suit by the Attorney General there would be a rebuttable presumption of sufficient literacy to vote in Federal elections for any person who had completed the sixth grade.

Inaction of State officials

Recommendation No. 3.—"That Congress amend subsection (b) of 42 U.S.C. 1971 to prohibit any arbitrary action or (where there is a duty to act) arbitrary inaction, which deprives or threatens to deprive any person of the right to register, vote, and have that vote counted in any Federal election."

No general legislative provision of this nature has yet been enacted. Certain types of arbitrary action by State officials, such as refusal to register voters for immaterial errors on application forms, have been prohibited by the Civil Rights Act of 1964. 42 U.S.C. § a (2).

Reapportionment of voting districts

Recommendation No. 4.—The Commission found that malapportionment of voting districts dilutes the right to vote of many citizens. It made the following recommendation: "That Congress consider the advisability of enacting legislation (a) requiring that where voting districts are established within a State, for either Federal elections or State elections to any house of a State legislature which is elected on the basis of population, they shall be substantially equal in population; and (b) specifically granting the Federal courts jurisdiction of suits to enforce the requirements of the Constitution and of Federal law with regard to such electoral districts; but explicitly providing that such jurisdiction should not be deemed to preclude the jurisdiction of State courts to enforce rights provided under State law regarding such districts."

The House Judiciary Committee voted, on March 1, 1965, to report favorably on H.R. 5505 providing that all congressional districts be drawn so as to vary no more than 15 percent from the average.

Census

Recommendation No. 5.—"That Congress direct the Bureau of the Census promptly to initiate a nationwide compilation of registration and voting statistics, to include a count of persons of voting age in every State and territory by race, color, and national origin, who are registered to vote, and a determination of the extent to which such persons have voted since January 1, 1960; and requiring that the Bureau of the Census compile such information in each next succeeding decennial census, and at such other time or times as the Congress may direct."

This provision, which reaffirmed recommendation No. 1 of the 1959 report noted above was enacted with certain alterations as Title VIII of the Civil Rights Act of 1964. 42 U.S.C. § 2000 (f).

1963 REPORT

The Commission found that there was continuing discriminatory denial of the right to vote and that existing remedies for discrimination were ineffective. It made the following recommendations:

Voter qualifications

Recommendation No. 1.—"That Congress, acting under section 2 of the 15th Amendment and sections 2 and 5 of the 14th Amendment (a) declare that voter qualifications other than age, residence, confinement, and conviction of a crime are susceptible of use, and have been used, to deny the right to vote on grounds of race and color; and (b) enact legislation providing that all citizens of the United States shall have a right to vote in Federal or State elections which shall not be denied or in any way abridged or interfered with by the United States or by any State for any cause except for inability to meet reasonable age or length-of-residence requirements uniformly applied to all persons within a State, failure to complete six grades of formal education or its equivalent, legal confinement at the time of registration or election, judicially determined mental disability, or conviction of a felony; such right to vote to include the right to register or otherwise qualify to vote, and to have one's vote counted."

No legislative action has yet been taken with respect to this recommendation. (See also Recommendation 1, 1961.)

Registrars

Recommendation No. 2.—"That Congress enact legislation providing that upon receipt by the President of the United States of sworn affidavits by 10 or more individuals from any district, county, parish, or other political subdivision of a State, alleging that the affiants have unsuccessfully attempted to register with the duly constituted State registration office, and that the affiants believe themselves qualified under State law to be electors, but have been denied the right to register because of race, color, or national origin, the President shall refer such affidavits to such officer or agency of the United States as he shall designate.

A. Such officer or agency shall—

(1) Investigate the validity of the allegations.

(2) Dismiss such affidavits as proven, on investigation, to be unfounded.

(3) Certify any and all well-founded affidavits to the President and to such temporary registrar as he may designate.

B. The President upon such certification may designate an existing Federal officer or employee in the State from which complaints are received, to act as a temporary registrar.

C. Such registrar-designee shall administer the State qualification laws and issue to all individuals found qualified registration certificates which shall entitle them to vote in any Federal or State general, special, or primary election.

D. The registrar-designee shall certify to the responsible State registration officials the names and fact of registration of all persons registered by him. Such certification shall permit all such registrants to participate in the elections previously enumerated.

E. Jurisdiction shall be retained until such time as the President determines that the presence of the appointed registrar is no longer necessary."

No legislative action has yet been taken with respect to this recommendation. (See also Recommendation 5, 1959.)*

Enforcement of 14th amendment

Recommendation No. 3.—"That, if the steps previously recommended prove ineffective, Congress further act to assure the attainment of uniform suffrage qualifications as contemplated by section 2 of the 14th Amendment, through enactment of legislation proportionately reducing the representation in the House of Representatives in those cases in which voter qualifications continue to be used as a device for denying the franchise to citizens on the grounds of race, color, or national origin."

No legislative action has yet been taken with respect to this recommendation.

---

* In the Voting Rights Act of 1965, literacy tests were barred as qualification and provision was made for the appointment of federal registrars. See p. 372.

Voting Rights Act of 1965[*]

ROY WILKINS

MR. CHAIRMAN AND members of the Subcommittee. I am Roy Wilkins, executive director of the National Association for the Advancement of Colored People and chairman of the Leadership Conference on Civil Rights. The Leadership Conference is a cooperative group of 90 organizations united for freedom and justice in our country. Accompanying me is Mr. Joseph L. Rauh, Jr., who is counsel for the Leadership Conference.

We are here today because the best efforts of sincere men and women have not yet eradicated the blight of racial discrimination in voting. President Lyndon B. Johnson is in the forefront of those who recognize that this discrimination in voting still exists as was evidenced by his magnificent speech and pledge of March 15. Our organizations deeply appreciate the leadership of the President on this matter. Influential Republican spokesmen in both Houses and among the leaders of the party outside the Congress have likewise urged strong and sweeping legislation to correct this discrimination. Also several Republicans have introduced their own bills and a number of others have joined in bi-partisan sponsorship of the Administration bill.

The history of the struggle for the right to participate in Federal, state and local elections goes back to the period of Reconstruction. Some of the impediments imposed by state legislatures have been removed by court action on the part of the Federal Government and private organizations such as that which I have the honor to serve as Director. Examples are the grandfather clause, *Guinn* v. *U. S., 232 U. S. 347* (1915); the white primary, *Nixon* v. *Herndon, 273 U. S. 536* (1927); *Nixon* v. *Condon, 286 U. S. 73* (1932); *Smith* v. *Allwright, 321 U. S. 649* (1944); and the racially exclusive pre-primary party caucus *Terry* v. *Adams, 345 U. S. 461* (1953).

In 1957, the Congress passed a statute which gave the At-

* Statement of Roy Wilkins, Executive Director, NAACP and chairman of the Leadership Conference on Civil Rights before House Subcommittee No. 5 of the Committee of the Judiciary, House of Representatives, Washington, D.C., March 24, 1965. Voting Rights (Washington, D.C.: U.S. Government Printing Office, 1965), pp. 377–380.

torney General the power to institute civil actions on behalf of those who were deprived of the right to vote. At that time the men and women of good will assumed that the right to vote would be safe in the hands of the Federal judiciary. In some measure this was not a vain hope. Because of this statute, the courts struck down voting discrimination in Georgia, *U. S.* v. *Raines, 362 U. S. 17 Terrell Co., Georgia* (1960); Alabama, *U. S.* v. *Alabama, 192 Fed. Supp. 667, Macon Co., Alabama* (1961); and Tennessee, *U. S.* v. *Beaty, 288 Fed. 655, Fayette Co., Tennessee* (1961). On March 8, 1965, the Supreme Court in *U. S.* v. *Mississippi, 33 U. S. L. W. 4258* and *Louisiana* v. *U. S., 33 U. S. L. W. 4262*, made further inroads against voting discrimination in Louisiana and Mississippi. Yet, it is clear that the legal technicalities, the slow pace of court decisions and in some instances complete judicial hostility have combined to restrict the participation of voters in national, state and local elections.

In 1960 Congress strengthened the 1957 voting rights law. Only last year Congress tried again to make the 1957 law more effective. All three laws put together have not done the job of making the Fifteenth Amendment a living document. In too many areas of the Nation, Negroes are still being registered one by one and only after long litigation. We must transform this retail litigation method of registration into a wholesale administration procedure registering all who seek to exercise their democratic birthright. The time is long overdue to sweep the last vestiges of voting restrictions into the sea.

The nation has paid a great price for these restrictions. It has paid the price of getting into office public officials who are not responsive to the will of all the people. It has paid the price of mayhem, riots and murder because those who sought the right to vote were opposed by those who were willing to suppress rights with violence themselves or at least stand by while others perpetrated unspeakable crimes against American citizens. It is the hope of those who constitute the Leadership Conference that this time, by placing the executive branch of the Federal Government in a position to expedite registration and voting, we will have a formula for ending this long-standing evil.

The Administration bill introduced by the distinguished chairman of the Committee, Congressman Celler, is a good bill. It goes further than any other bill ever introduced on this subject and obviously it is an effort to correct disfranchisement on a wide scale. However, in our opinion, the bill is not enough. More is needed if it is to do the whole job. The Leadership Conference on Civil Rights strongly urges Congress to strengthen this bill in at least the following four respects:

1) The total elimination of the poll tax as a restriction on voting in state and local elections as well as in federal elections.

2) The elimination of the requirement in the bill that a prospective registrant must first go before the state official to attempt to register before going to the Federal registrar or examiner. The prospective registrant ought not to be put to the delays, the hardships, and the indignity of attempting to satisfy hostile state officials before he can come to the Federal registrar.

3) Extended coverage of the registrar or examiner provisions of the bill, so that persons who have been wrongfully denied the right to vote, regardless of their geographical location, will have the benefits of these provisions of the legislation.

4) Further and maximum protection of registrants and voters, both those who will be registered under the bill and those already registered, and prospective registrants, from all economic and physical intimidation and coercion. In extending such protection, the Federal Government should use the full range of its powers, criminal, civil and economic, to protect the citizens from the beginning of registration process until his vote has been cast and counted.

I would like to make special reference to the poll tax because this is complicated by developments in recent years. Our organization has traditionally insisted that the poll tax should be eliminated by statute. Others have argued that it should be ended by constitutional amendment. Those who favored the constitutional amendment approach prevailed. Although we did not favor this method we made a good faith attempt to see that the Twenty-fourth Amendment was ratified by the states of the union. It is a sad commentary on the vision of those who control the states that they have grudgingly acceded to the requirements of the constitutional amendment by continuing to charge a poll tax in state and local elections. Here we see the ultimate in absurdity. It is possible to vote for a Presidential candidate in Virginia without paying a poll tax, but, if one is to vote for a member of the state legislature or an alderman in a separate election, he must pay a poll tax.

The practice in Mississippi illustrates more strikingly how the poll tax payments can be manipulated to deter voting by Negro citizens and poor people generally. Dr. Aaron Henry, president of our Mississippi State Conference of branches who lives in Clarksdale, uses the following language to describe the process:

"The poll tax is a great deterrent to voting in Mississippi. It must be paid on or before the first day of February in the year that one intends to vote. A voter must pay the tax for two years before he can vote. You cannot pay back taxes. During the month of January we are at our peak in unemployment. This is the most likely time of the year not to have the $3 necessary to pay the poll tax in Coahoma County (in many counties the tax is $2 but in Coahoma County it is $3). Our experience here in Coahoma County is that one cannot pay taxes for another except in the immediate family. A man may pay the poll tax for his wife or she for him but not for one living in your household."

Historically, the poll tax is clearly a device used for attempting to prevent Negroes from voting. There are those who have Constitutional reservations and for this purpose, Mr. Joseph L. Rauh, Jr., who serves as counsel for the Leadership Conference on Civil Rights, is prepared to present views. We urge that the Congress approach this matter with the intention of doing the whole job at last.

The President has set an outstanding example by his appeal to the nation on March 15, but the legislation must match the boldness of the President if we are to come to grips with this problem.

We have reviewed quickly here the recent attempts at corrective legislative action. It is apparent to all that the 1957, 1960 laws and Title I of the 1964 Civil Rights Act, while good efforts, did not by any means reach the heart of the problem. We now know the extent of the evil and our experience at attempts to enforce legislation for the past seven years have made clear the ingenious evasions which must be rooted out. We, therefore, urge that the pending Administration bill be strengthened to such a degree that it will not be necessary in the next two years or four years or seven years to come back and add another patch in an effort to guarantee the basic American right to vote and to live under a government by consent of the governed. . . .

Freedom Summer[*]

SALLY BELFRAGE

THEN BOB MOSES, the Director of the Summer Project, came to the front of the floor. He didn't introduce himself, but somehow one knew who he was. Everyone had heard a little —that he was twenty-nine, began in Harlem, had a Master's degree in philosophy from Harvard, and that he had given up teaching in New York to go South after the first sit-ins. He had been in Mississippi for three years, and he wore its uniform: a T-shirt and denim overalls, in the bib of which he propped his hands. He began as though in the middle of a thought. "When Mrs. Hamer sang, 'If you miss me from the freedom fight, you can't find me nowhere; Come on over to the graveyard, I'll be buried over there . . .' that's true."

Moving up to the stage, he drew a map of Mississippi on a blackboard and patiently, from the beginning, outlined the state's areas and attitudes. The top left segment became the Delta; industry was cotton; power in the Citizens' Councils; and opposition to the movement systematic and calculated, aimed at the leadership (including Moses himself—in 1963, the SNCC worker beside him, Jimmy Travis, was shot in the neck and the shoulder as they rode together in a car outside Greenwood), and at decreasing the Negro population by the expedient of automating the cotton fields, thereby "getting it down to a livable ratio." The segment beneath the Delta was the hill country, mostly poor white farmers who had been organizing since the March on Washington. Amite County, McComb: Klan territory, where violence was indiscriminately aimed at "keeping the nigger in his place" and no one was safe. Five Negroes had been murdered there since December. No indictments.

Mississippi gained texture and dimension on the blackboard. Moses put down the chalk, paused, then looked out at us, his eyes reflective behind horn-rims. When he began again he seemed to be addressing each one separately, though talk-

* Excerpts from Sally Belfrage, *Freedom Summer* (New York: The Viking Press, Inc., 1965), pp. 15–19, 20–21, 26–29, 31–33. Copyright © 1965 by Sally Belfrage. All rights reserved. Reprinted by permission of The Viking Press, Inc. Sally Belfrage was librarian of the Greenwood, Miss. community center as a Summer Project 1964 volunteer. The selection describes an orientation session for Summer Project volunteers.

ing to no one at all, just thinking aloud. "When you come South, you bring with you the concern of the country—because the people of the country don't identify with Negroes. The guerrilla war in Mississippi is not much different from that in Vietnam. But when we tried to see President Johnson, his secretary said that Vietnam was popping up all over his calendar and he hadn't time to talk to us." Now, he said, because of the Summer Project, because whites were involved, a crack team of FBI men was going down to Mississippi to investigate. "We have been asking for them for three years. Now the federal government is concerned; there will be more protection for us, and hopefully for the Negroes who live there."

He stood looking at his feet. "Our goals are limited. If we can go and come back alive, then that is something. If you can go into Negro homes and just sit and talk, that will be a huge job. We're not thinking of integrating the lunch counters. The Negroes in Mississippi haven't the money to eat in those places anyway. They still don't dare go into the white half of the integrated bus terminals—they must weigh that against having their houses bombed or losing their jobs."

He stopped again, and everyone waited without a sound. "Mississippi has been called 'The Closed Society.' It is closed, locked. We think the key is in the vote. Any change, any possibility for dissidence and opposition, depends first on a political breakthrough." . . .

There was an interruption then at a side entrance: three or four staff members had come in and were whispering agitatedly. One of them walked over to the stage and sprang up to whisper to Moses, who bent on his knees to hear. In a moment he was alone again. Still crouched, he gazed at the floor at his feet, unconscious of us. Time passed. When he stood and spoke, he was somewhere else; it was simply that he was obliged to say something, but his voice was automatic. "Yesterday morning, three of our people left Meridian, Mississippi, to investigate a church-burning in Neshoba County They haven't come back, and we haven't had any word from them. We spoke to John Doar in the Justice Department. He promised to order the FBI to act, but the local FBI still says they have been given no authority."

He stood, while activity burst out around him. In the audience, people asked each other who the three were; volunteers who had been at the first week of orientation remembered them. Then a thin girl in shorts was talking to us from the stage: Rita Schwerner, the wife of one of the three.

She paced as she spoke, her eyes distraught and her face quite white, but in a voice that was even and disciplined. It was suddenly clear that she, Moses, and others on the staff had been up all the night before. The three men had been arrested for speeding. Deputy Sheriff Price of Neshoba claimed to have released them at 10 p.m. the same day. All the jails in the area had been checked, with no results. The Jackson FBI office kept saying they were not sure a federal statute had been violated.

Rita asked us to form in groups by home areas and wire our congressmen that the federal government, though begged to investigate, had refused to act, and that if the government did not act, none of us was safe. Someone in the audience asked her to spell the names. . . .

No one was willing to believe that the event involved more than a disappearance. It was hard to believe even that. Somehow it seemed only a climactic object lesson, part of the morning's lecture, an anecdote to give life to the words of Bob Moses. To think of it in other terms was to be forced to identify with the three, to be prepared, irrevocably, to give one's life.

The volunteers broke up into their specialized units—Freedom School, community center, voter registration—in the afternoons, and met again in the auditorium for general lectures in the mornings. Each day began with an announcement like Vincent Harding's on Tuesday: "There has been no word of the three people in Neshoba. The staff met all night. When we sing 'We are not afraid,' we mean we are afraid. We sing 'Ain't gonna let my fear turn me round,' because many of you might want to turn around now." . . .

A gaunt, fierce-eyed young man raised his hand and was recognized. When he began to speak it was in waves approaching hysteria. "It's hell in Mississippi!" he said, his voice breaking. "And you've got to realize that nobody *cares*. *We* care. We've got to change the *system*. It's hard. It's just like one person beating his head against this building to tear it down. It's impossible, but we have got to *do* it. They say that democracy exists in America. But it's an idea. It doesn't function. You have got to make it function in Mississippi, so that it can function in the rest of the country, and in the world."

There was a silence resembling fear in the room. "Who is it?" someone craned around and asked my row. "Jimmy Travis," another whispered. "The one who was shot. Didn't you see the scar on his neck?"

"The three people," Travis said. I think he was crying. "I don't know. I hurt. These people are lost. I don't know where they are. What can we do? The *system!* The system is the reason these people are missing. It's easier to know that someone is in jail, even that someone is dead, than to wait and wonder what happened."

He pointed to Chuck Morgan. "This cat is from Birmingham, Alabama. This cat knows what's going on. I'm black. You're white. If you're going down there, you're going to be treated worse than black. Because you are supposed to be free. But I say that no one is free until everyone is. And until we can show the people of Mississippi that we are willing to make the extreme sacrifice, we can't change the world.

"It's hard. So hard. But all we have is each other. When something happens to you, we care. We really *care*."

He slumped against the door behind him, then disappeared through it. There was a second's silence, then a splattering of applause which grew, wavered, died out. A girl stood in the uncomfortable quiet that followed, Morgan still at the podium, no one looking at anyone else. "You've got to understand Jimmy," she said. She was a Mississippi Negro. "He was nearly killed. It was something he had to say. You shouldn't applaud."

The lectures and classes continued, and there was no news from Neshoba. The tension clouded us in until it was all there was to breathe. In free time we composed letters and telegrams to anyone conceivably influential enough to get the government to act: to send federal marshals and outside FBI agents to Mississippi. Moses explained, "The inside agents, Mississippians, are psychologically incapable of carrying on the necessary investigations. We need the FBI before the fact. We have them now after the fact." It wasn't a question of military occupation, as Southerners were claiming: "We're not looking for generalized chaos in which troops can come and take over. We're looking for a framework in which people can do their work—for the summer, and then afterwards, a means of extending it to the Negroes of the state."

There was one television set on the campus, and the floor around it was jammed for news broadcasts. But when the next news arrived, it was during dinner on Tuesday night. Bob Moses came in quietly, turned on the microphone and said, "The car has been found outside Philadelphia. It's badly burned. There is no news of the three boys." . . .

Bayard Rustin, the next morning's speaker, had the crowd's respect before he began—not only for his organization of the March on Washington, but for his principled nonviolence based on a pacifism tested in many jails. "All mankind is my community," he said, and: "When I say I love Eastland, it sounds preposterous—a man who brutalizes people. But *you* love him or you wouldn't be here. You're going to Mississippi to create social change—and you love Eastland in your desire to create conditions which will redeem his children. Loving your enemy is manifest in putting your arms not around the man but around the social situation, to take power from those who misuse it—at which point they can become human too."

He suggested that our difficulties in connecting with white Mississippi might not be insurmountable. "One can evaluate others in the light of one's own experience, see them in one's self, understand how one can become that bestial." He smiled and bummed a cigarette off a volunteer in the first row. "Last week I was smoking and wondering why a white Southerner can't act on what he believes. Then I took another puff, I *know* cigarettes will give me lung cancer. Well, I can understand him. In this we are one. We are both intensely stupid."

The President sent two hundred sailors to search for the missing boys. Rita Schwerner and all the staff members who could be spared were in Meridian and Philadelphia. Nothing visible was being done by the authorities to prevent the same thing from happening to anyone else. We clung to the television set.

On Thursday there was a TV special: "The Search in Mississippi." Classes were scheduled for the same time, but everyone, thinking himself alone, was in the lounge—a couple of hundred in a space meant for a third that many, crammed in the room and out through the hall. On the screen appeared the faces of the enemy, the friend, the one who sat beside us now, the one who had gone ahead reporting how it was. The program contained interviews filmed the day before in the room where we sat.

The voice was SNCC Executive-Secretary James Forman's and he was speaking in the auditorium where we had spent half the week. The camera played around the audience, at the volunteers like us, some of them the same—staff and holdovers—and finally came to rest on a very young, dark, thin but tender face. Only when it was gone was it identified as Andrew Goodman's.

But then the face was Senator Eastland's—whose children we would redeem. "Around where I live it's seventy-five per cent colored," he was saying. "Many's the time I've slept at home with the doors unlocked. We don't have any racial fiction, uh, friction."

Aaron Henry, head of the Mississippi NAACP, and also of COFO: "Fifty-one per cent of the people in the Delta earn less than a thousand dollars a year. This is the fiftieth state economically. The reason we're fiftieth is because that's how many states there are. We used to be forty-eighth."

Senator Eastland: "There is no attempt to prevent Nigras registering. You go by what some agitator claims. They're perfectly free to go to the clerk's office to register to vote."

Mrs. Hamer: "I tried to register in 1962. I was fired the same day, after working on the plantation for eighteen years. My husband worked there thirty years. When my employer found out I'd been down to the courthouse, she said I'd have to withdraw or be fired. 'We are not ready for this in Mississippi,' she said. 'Well, I wasn't registering for you,' I told her. 'I was trying to register for myself.' "

Governor Johnson: "The hard core of this [COFO] group is your beatnik-type people. Nonconformists, hair down to their shoulder blades, some that you'd call weirdos. . . . They don't realize that they're following a group of professional agitators, many of them with criminal records, people who've been in trouble all their lives—you can see it in their face. We're not going to tolerate any group from the outside of Mississippi or from the inside of Mississippi to take the law in their own hands. We're going to see that the law is maintained, and maintained Mississippi style."

The audience in the lounge joined in the show, expressing some unequivocal opinions of the speakers. At the end, under the titles, we ourselves appeared, standing, singing "We Shall Overcome." We stood and joined our own voices:

> Black and white together now—
> Oh deep in my heart, I do believe,
> We shall overcome someday.

For a long time after the program had finished we remained there, while Mrs. Hamer led more stanzas, more songs.

There was one side still to be heard. John Doar of the Justice Department's Civil Rights Division came from Washington to speak, as he had the week before. I got to the auditorium early, after an 8 a.m. class, and found a seat near the front while volunteers drifted in. Near me a group began to sing in slow rhythm. "We need justice, Lord, come by here. Oh, Lord, come by here." An old Negro woman was weeping into her handkerchief. Behind her a white girl with high cheekbones and dark hair pulled severely back sang gravely while tears fell down her cheeks, oblivious of a movie camera on the stage poised on her face, just as it had been on Andrew Goodman's the week before.

Moses urged us to be polite to Doar, an effort at which the previous group had apparently failed. "A year ago this week Medgar Evers was buried. It was a near riot situation, and Doar was sent in to prevent worse. He has helped us." The camera buzzed behind his words. Doar arrived.

"This is a serious operation that you are involved in," he said straight off. "I wish the world were different; I don't like it any better than you do." He was tall, blue-eyed, narrow-shouldered, and his face wore a steady, concerned frown. He outlined the reasons why "there is no possible way that anyone can be completely protected from violence." Suggesting that there were many native white realists in the state, he asked us to "help them correct a problem that they must realize they want to get behind." On his own forces: "If we don't make good sound judgments and imaginative investigations, we should be criticized."

Perhaps some felt that this man and his government represented them, but in the past week many who had started out as ordinary college students with respect for all the ordinary institutions had learned about cynicism. Because of Moses' admonition, however, most of the muttering remained only that, and when Doar asked for questions just two hands were raised.

"How is it that the government can protect the Vietnamese from the Viet Cong and the same government will not accept the moral responsibility of protecting the people in Mississippi?"

"Maintaining law and order is a state responsibility," Doar said.

"But how is it"—the questioner persisted—"that the government can accept this responsibility in Vietnam?"

"I would rather confine myself to Mississippi."

Next was Staughton Lynd, a professor of history at Yale, who would run the statewide Freedom School program. "In 1890," he began, in his dry, quiet voice, "during the railroad strike, the government went into Illinois. Its right to do so was upheld by the Supreme Court. In a crisis, the President does have the established power to send a police force into a state, whether the state wants it or not. The question is, is the situation in Mississippi a crisis? What we are trying to communicate is that it *is*. . . . It's a moral question. If you have this power to act, and if you have the moral responsibility yet choose not to act, how in the world do all of you live with this responsibility?"

"I believe we are a government of law," Doar said. "I have taken a vow to uphold the law. I just try to do the best I can under law. I have no trouble living with myself. The people I know in the federal government and administration are fine people, and they have no trouble living with themselves either." . . .

Jim Forman had just arrived back from Mississippi. A large, rumpled, dark-brown man who needed a haircut, he had the good speaker's urgency, power over a mood. His volatility was the other side of Moses' pensive strength, but both earned an audience's total attention, total sympathy. He wanted to give us a little history and background. "I know Moses spoke on Monday, but he is a very shy person." Moses, crouched against the stage with his head down, smiled. It was the first time I had ever seen him smile.

Forman asked us to rise and sing "We'll Never Turn Back," with our arms around each other, and then he repeated some of the lines very carefully:

> We have hung our head and cried
> For those like Lee who died,
> Died for you and died for me,
> Died for the cause of equality,
> But we'll never turn back—

The song was written by a young SNCC worker in memory of Herbert Lee, shot to death in Amite County, Mississippi, by a member of the Mississippi State Legislature who was never indicted. Forman went over the details of the case, how the only witness to the crime, Louis Allen, was shotgunned dead in January 1964, on the night before he was to leave the state. He named these deaths as punctuations in the life of the Mississippi movement, as was Medgar Evers', and the five newest murders in as many months. Despite these events, he said, SNCC had developed from the first sit-ins to "Moses and His Boys, the Nonviolent Guerrillas," the Delta voter registration program, and, after the Civil Rights Bill, the Summer Project.

There was danger, and work to do. "You've got to get down to the nitty gritty. You've got to be willing to sweep the floors." He smiled and his voice took on a sarcastic tone. "Of course you're *teachers,* so you're more *sophis*ticated than the voter registration workers. In fact, some of you probably signed up because you think its safer work. But you can't start shouting, 'Hey, I'm a Freedom School teacher, I'm all right.' Because in Mississippi nobody has any rights.

"All of you should have nervousitis. If you have doubts, we'll admire you for dropping out. But I think the best thing to say is, you know, we'll be there with you, and . . . we'll never turn back."

It was Moses' turn. As he stood, he swayed slightly, then held the microphone. His head dropped, and the voice was so soft it seemed to stroke us. He wondered if any of us had read Tolkien's *The Fellowship of the Ring.* "There is a weariness . . . from constant attention to the things you are doing, the struggle of good against evil." I thought of what one of the volunteers had said that day of Moses: "He's like someone you only read about in novels. He has great currents of moral perplexity running through him."

Then Moses said, "The kids are dead."

He paused—quite without regard for dramatic effect. But long enough for it to hit us: this was the first time it had been spoken: they are dead. Up to now they had simply "disappeared." There had been no reason for us to believe anything else.

"When we heard the news at the beginning I knew they were dead. When we heard they had been arrested I knew there had been a frame-up. We didn't say this earlier because of Rita, because she was really holding out for every hope." Rita had gone to Meridian now.

"There may be more deaths." He waited, seeking the words he needed. "I justify myself because I'm taking risks myself, and I'm not asking people to do things I'm not willing to do. And the other thing is, people were being killed already, the Negroes of Mississippi, and I feel, anyway, responsible for their deaths. Herbert Lee killed, Louis Allen killed, five others killed this year. In some way you have to come to grips with that, know what it means. If you are going to do anything about it, other people are going to be killed. No privileged group in history has ever given up anything, without some kind of blood sacrifice, something."

He sank into his tiredness again and the volunteers just watched him. He wasn't looking at us, but at a space between him and the floor.

"There are people who left today, went home. I was worried yesterday because no one had left and that was bad, it was unreal.

"The way some people characterize this project is that it is an attempt to get some people killed so the federal government will move into Mississippi. And the way some of us feel about it is that in our country we have some real evil, and the attempt to do something about it involves enormous effort . . . and therefore tremendous risks. If for any reason you're hesitant about what you're getting into, it's better for you to leave. Because what has got to be done has to be done in a certain way, or otherwise it won't get done.

"You have to break off a little chunk of a problem and work on it, and try to see where it leads, and concentrate on it."

His voice had faded almost to a whisper, and it was as if he were speaking out of his sleep, out of his unconscious directly into ours.

"All I can say really is . . . be patient with the kids, and with Mississippi. Because there is a distinction between being slow and being stupid. And the kids in Mississippi are very, very . . . very slow."

He finished, stood there, then walked out the door. The silence which followed him was absolute. It lasted a minute, two; no one moved. They knew, now, what could not be applauded. Suddenly, a beautiful voice from the back of the room pierced the quiet.

> They say that freedom is a constant struggle.
> They say that freedom is a constant struggle.
> They say that freedom is a constant struggle,
> Oh, Lord, we've struggled so long,
> We must be free, we must be free.

It was a new song to me and to the others. But I knew it, and all the voices in the room joined in as though the song came from the deepest part of themselves, and they had always known it.

2. INDEPENDENT POLITICAL ACTION

The Lowndes County Freedom Party

JOHN HULETT*

. . . SOME TIME AGO, we organized a political group of our own known as the Lowndes County Freedom Organization, whose emblem is the Black Panther.

We were criticized, we were called communists, we were called everything else, black nationalists and what not, because we did this. Any group which starts at a time like this to speak out for what is right—they are going to be ridiculed. The people of Lowndes County realized this. Today we are moving further.

Too long Negroes have been begging, especially in the South, for things they should be working for. So the people in Lowndes County decided to organize themselves—to go out and work for the things we wanted in life—not only for the people in Lowndes County, but for every county in the state of Alabama, in the Southern states, and even in California.

* John Hulett, "How the Black Panther Party was Organized," in *The Black Panther Party* (New York: Merit Publishers, 1966), pp. 7–15. Hulett is chairman of the Lowndes County Freedom Party. Speech delivered in Los Angeles, May 22, 1966.

You cannot become free in California while there are slaves in Lowndes County. And no person can be free while other people are still slaves, nobody.

In Lowndes County, there is a committee in the Democratic Party. This committee not only controls the courthouse, it controls the entire county. When they found out that the Negroes were going to run candidates in the primary of the Democratic Party on May 3, they assembled themselves together and began to talk about what they were going to do. Knowing this is one of the poorest counties in the nation, what they decided to do was change the registration fees in the county.

Two years ago, if a person wanted to run for sheriff, tax collector or tax assessor, all he had to do was pay $50 and then he qualified to be the candidate. This year, the entrance fee is about $900. If a person wants to run, he has to pay $500 to run for office. In the primary, when they get through cheating and stealing, then the candidate is eliminated. So we decided that we wouldn't get into such a primary because we were tired of being tricked by the Southern whites. After forming our own political group today, we feel real strong. We feel that we are doing the right thing in Lowndes County.

We have listened to everybody who wanted to talk, we listened to them speak, but one thing we had to learn for ourselves. As a group of people, we must think for ourselves and act on our own accord. And this we have done.

Through the years, Negroes in the South have been going for the bones while whites have been going for the meat. The Negroes of Lowndes County today are tired of the bones—we are going to have some of the meat too.

At the present time, we have our own candidates who have been nominated by the Lowndes County Freedom Organization. And we fear that this might not be enough to avoid the tricks that are going to be used in Lowndes County against us.

In Lowndes County, the sheriff is the custodian of the courthouse. This is a liberal sheriff, too, who is "integrated," who walks around and pats you on the shoulder, who does not carry a gun. But at the same time, in the county where there are only 800 white men, there are 550 of them who walk around with a gun on them. They are deputies. This is true; it might sound like a fairy tale to most people, but this is true.

After talking to the sheriff about having the use of the courthouse lawn for our mass nominating meeting, not the courthouse but just the lawn, he refused to give the Negroes permission. We reminded him that last year in August, that one of the biggest Klan rallies that has ever been held in the state of Alabama was held on this lawn of this courthouse. And he gave them permission. A few weeks ago an individual who was campaigning for governor—he got permission to use it. He used all types of loud speakers and anything that he wanted.

But he would not permit Negroes to have the use of the courthouse. For one thing he realized that we would build a party—and if he could keep us from forming our own political group then we would always stand at the feet of the Southern whites and of the Democratic Party. So we told him that we were going to have this meeting, we were going to have it here, on the courthouse lawn. And we wouldn't let anybody scare us off. We told him, we won't expect you to protect us, and if you don't, Negroes will protect themselves.

Then we asked him a second time to be sure he understood what we were saying. We repeated it to him the second time. And then we said to him, Sheriff, if you come out against the people, then we are going to arrest you.

And he said, I will not give you permission to have this meeting here. I can't protect you from the community.

Then we reminded him that according to the law of the state of Alabama, that this mass meeting which was set up to nominate our candidates must be held in or around a voters' polling place. And if we decide to hold it a half a mile away from the courthouse, some individual would come up and protest our mass meeting. And our election would be thrown out.

So we wrote the Justice Department and told them what was going to happen in Lowndes County.

All of a sudden the Justice Department started coming in fast into the county. They said to me, John, what is going to happen next Tuesday at the courthouse?

I said, We are going to have our mass meeting. And he wanted to know where. And I said on the lawn of the courthouse.

He said, I thought the sheriff had told you you couldn't come there. And I said, Yes, but we are going to be there.

Then he wanted to know, if shooting takes place, what are we going to do. And I said, that we are going to stay out here and everybody die together.

And then he began to get worried, and I said, Don't worry. You're going to have to be here to see it out and there's no place to hide, so whatever happens, you can be a part of it.

And then he began to really panic. And he said, There's nothing I can do.

And I said, I'm not asking you to do anything. All I want you to know is we are going to have a mass meeting. If the sheriff cannot protect us, then we are going to protect ourselves. And I said to him, through the years in the South, Negroes have never had any protection, and today we aren't looking to anybody to protect us. We are going to protect ourselves.

That was on Saturday. On Sunday, at about 2 o'clock, we were having a meeting, and we decided among ourselves that we were going to start collecting petitions for our candidates to be sure that they got on the ballot. The state laws require at least 25 signatures of qualified electors and so we decided to get at least 100 for fear somebody might come up and find fault. And we decided to still have our mass meeting and nominate our candidates.

About 2:30, here comes the Justice Department again, and he was really worried. And he said he wasn't satisfied. He said to me, John, I've done all I can do, and I don't know what else I can do, and now it looks like you'll have to call this meeting off at the courthouse.

And I said, We're going to have it.

He stayed around for awhile and then got in his car and drove off, saying, I'll see you tomorrow, maybe. And we stayed at this meeting from 2:30 until about 11:30 that night. About 11:15, the Justice Department came walking up the aisle of the church and said to me, Listen. I've talked to the Attorney General of the state of Alabama, and he said that you can go ahead and have a mass meeting at the church and it will be legal.

Then we asked him, Do you have any papers that say that's true, that are signed by the Governor or the Attorney General? And he said no. And we said to him, Go back and get it legalized, and bring it back here to us and we will accept it.

And sure enough, on Monday at 3 o'clock, I went to the courthouse and there in the sheriff's office were the papers all legalized and fixed up, saying that we could go to the church to have our mass meeting.

To me, this showed strength. When people are together, they can do a lot of things, but when you are alone you cannot do anything.

There are 600 Negroes in the county who did not trust in themselves and who joined the Democratic Party. We warned the entire state of Alabama that running on the Democratic ticket could not do them any good, because this party is controlled by people like Wallace; and whoever won would have to do what these people said to do.

Now, to me, the Democratic Party primaries and the Democratic Party is something like an integrated gambler who carries a card around in his pocket and every now and then he has to let somebody win to keep the game going. To me, this is what the Democratic Party means to the people in Alabama. It's a gambling game. And somebody's got to win to keep the game going every now and then.

There is another guy who was running on the ticket calling himself a liberal, the Attorney General of the state of Alabama, Richmond Flowers. Most of you have heard about him. When he started campaigning to the people of Alabama, especially the Negro people, he assembled all their leaders and he made all kinds of promises to them—if you elect me for your governor, I'll do everything in the world for you.

And at the same time, he never made a decent campaign speech to the white people of this state. We kept warning our people in the state of Alabama that this was a trick and many Negroes listened to their so-called leaders, who profess to speak for the state of Alabama, and they got caught in the trap too.

I would like to say here, and this is one thing I am proud of, the people in Lowndes County stood together, and the 600 people who voted in the Democratic primary have realized one thing, that they were tricked by the Democratic Party. And now they too are ready to join us with the Lowndes County Freedom Organization whose emblem is the black panther.

We have seven people who are running for office this year in our county; namely, the coroner, three members of the board of education—and if we win those three, we will control the board of education—tax collector, tax assessor, and the individual who carries a gun at his side, the sheriff.

Let me say this—that a lot of persons tonight asked me, Do you really think if you win that you will be able to take it all over, and live?

I say to the people here tonight—yes, we're going to do it. If we have to do like the present sheriff, if we have to deputize every man in Lowndes County 21 and over, to protect people, we're going to do it.

There was something in Alabama a few months ago they called fear. Negroes were afraid to move on their own, they waited until the man, the people whose place they lived on, told them they could get registered. They told many people, don't you move until I tell you to move and when I give you an order, don't you go down and get registered.

Then all the people were being evicted at the same time and even today in Lowndes County, there are at least 75 families that have been evicted, some now are living in tents while some are living in one-room houses—with 8 or 9 in a family. Others have split their families up and are living together with their relatives or their friends. But they are determined to stay in Lowndes County, until justice rolls down like water.

Evicting the families wasn't all—there were other people who live on their own places who owe large debts, so they decided to foreclose on these debts to run Negroes off the place. People made threats—but we're going to stay there, we aren't going anywhere.

I would like to let the people here tonight know why we chose this black panther as our emblem. Many people have been asking this question for a long time. Our political group is open to whoever wants to come in, who would like to work with us. But we aren't begging anyone to come in. It's open, you come, at your own free will and accord.

But this black panther is a vicious animal, as you know. He never bothers anything, but when you start pushing him, he moves backwards, backwards, and backwards into his corner, and then he comes out to destroy everything that's before him.

Negroes in Lowndes County have been pushed back through the years. We have been deprived of our rights to speak, to move, and to do whatever we want to do at all times. And now we are going to start moving. On November 8 of this year, we plan to take over the courthouse in Hayneville. And whatever it takes to do it, we're going to do it.

We've decided to stop begging. We've decided to stop asking for integration. Once we control the courthouse, once we control the board of education, we can build our school system where our boys and girls can get an education in Lowndes County. There are 89 prominent families in this county who own 90 percent of the land. These people will be taxed. And we will collect these taxes. And if they don't pay them, we'll take their property and sell it to whoever wants to buy it. And we know there will be people who will buy land where at the present time they cannot buy it. This is what it's going to take.

We aren't asking any longer for protection—we won't need it—or for anyone to come from the outside to speak for us, because we're going to speak for ourselves now and from now on. And I think not only in Lowndes County, not only in the state of Alabama, not only in the South, but in the North—I hope they too will start thinking for themselves. And that they will move and join us in this fight for freedom.

Questions and Answers on New York's Schools*

CITY-WIDE COMMITTEE FOR INTEGRATED SCHOOLS

1. WHO ARE WE? We are all the major civil rights, parents, and church groups WORKING together to *end,* once and for all, the pattern of *inferior, segregated education* of our children. Segregated schools tend to produce *indifferent teaching* and *administrative attitudes,* watered-down *curriculum* and the *expectation* that our children *cannot* learn. Therefore, our children leave school—whether by graduating or dropping out—3 to 5 years below grade level. As a result, they are seriously handicapped in trying to go on to college or in trying to get a decent job. All they are prepared for are the lowest paying unskilled jobs.

Our American ideal is that all men are created equal and should have equal opportunity. If this is so, then *all are entitled to a complete and equal education.*

2. *What is our goal?* Our goal is to see that the 1954 supreme court decision is applied in New York to wipe out the last vestiges of 'de facto' segregated schools in order that our children no longer be disadvantaged by a system that is not only contrary to the law of the land but robs our children of the right to their place in tomorrow's world.

These inferior segregated schools in New York City are even acknowledged by Dr. Gross, Superintendent of New York City schools, to be inadequate in providing a good education.

3. *What are the demands of the City-Wide Committee to the Board of Education?* All that we are asking for is a PLAN for desegregation and a Timetable of steps to complete this integration plan.

* Leaflet on integration of New York City public schools circulated prior to a school boycott February 3, 1964. Reprinted by permission of Rev. Milton A. Galamison.

4. *What is a plan and timetable as demanded by the City-Wide Committee for Integrated Schools?* It is a City Wide school-to-school schedule showing each step that the Board of Education will take and the date that each step will be accomplished until the plan has been completely put into operation.

5. *Can segregated schools be made equal?* Throughout history segregated public schools have been separate but *never equal.* In the Harlems throughout the country, separate minority-group public schools have always resulted in inferior education. It is on this basis that the Supreme Court handed down its historic 1954 school decision.

6. *Should the Board of Education be concerned with school integration?* There are three basic reasons why the Board of Education must concern itself with integration:

> (1) The 1954 Supreme Court decision.
> (2) The announced and approved policy statement on integration by the Board of Education.
> (3) The fact that as educators they have no choice but to provide a *complete* education for *all* children and this will only be achieved through the integration of *all* our *schools.*

7. *What is the Board of Education's stated policy?* At the Board of Education's regular meeting, January 1955, the full board approved, without a dissenting vote, a strong, forward-looking policy statement on school integration.

8. *Has the Board acted on its stated policy?* To date, 10 years later, it remains mere 'stated' policy. For this reason the City-Wide Committee for Integrated Schools was formed to bring pressure to bear to translate that stated policy into immediate reality.

9. *Why integration now?* In today's rapidly changing world, *all* of our children must be trained to take their place as adults. The uneducated will have *NO* place, neither will those unprepared in basic attitudes to understand and respect the difference of others. Only a truly integrated education can properly prepare all children to function with dignity in that society.

10. *Does placing Negro and non-Negro children in the*

same school mean integration? No. The mere placing of a white child beside a Negro or Puerto Rican child is not, of itself, integration. It is only the necessary first step——DE-SEGREGATION. After this step, the Board of Education must be ready with schools, texts, attitudes and firm Board policy in order to create a meaningful integrated educational experience.

11. *What is the status of the neighborhood school?* Where the neighborhood school concept perpetuates segregation, it is legally and morally wrong. In spite of what some proponents of the neighborhood school concept imply, it is not guaranteed in either the constitution or state laws. This concept has developed over the years solely from restrictive housing patterns and is now used to maintain segregated schools.

12. *How can I, as a parent, help?* Exercise your constitutional and moral right by withholding your child from these inferior schools. BOYCOTT. Support further actions of the City-Wide Committee for INTEGRATED SCHOOLS in the fight for *quality integrated* education for *all* children.

13. *What will my child do out of school?* Send your child to the Freedom Schools that are organized in the churches.

14. *How long will the boycott last?* THE *FIRST BOY-COTT* WILL LAST ALL DAY, FEBRUARY 3, 1964, and a series of one-day boycotts thereafter.

15. *Can we win this fight?* YES. A united people with one goal must win——FREEDOM NOW!!!!!!!!!!

People's Board of Education, New York*

The People's Board has agreed to continue in existence with the clear understanding that it is not a body formed to hold power, but to encourage people in local communities to exercise power on their own behalf. The People's Board sees itself as a Symbol, created by concerned citizens, which will be at

* A memorandum of the People's Board of Education, January 3, 1967. Reprinted by permission of Rev. Milton A. Galamison, president.

the service of local communities to help them to take control of their public schools and to direct their children's education toward goals that they believe to be valuable and necessary.

The People's Board supports the following programs to help achieve local community control of the schools:

1. *Decentralization:* The school system must be decentralized to give local parents and community groups effective control over the education of their children.

2. *Accountability:* The school system must be made to answer to the people who entrust their children to them to be educated. There must be a continuing evaluation of the performance of teachers, supervisors, and all other school personnel. Salary is paid for an expected standard of performance. THE STANDARD FOR TEACHERS MUST BE STUDENT ACHIEVEMENT. The community must have a voice in determining the effective deployment of school personnel.

3. *Participation:* Parents and community groups must participate in the day-to-day operation of the school system at the local and city-wide levels. This participation, along with decentralization, will provide sufficient flexibility in the system to allow creative innovations developed at the local level.

4. *Non-professional Staff:* Provision must be made for the recruitment, training and creative employment of non-professional assistant teachers—indigenous personnel from the local communities who can add their own special knowledge and experience with the local children to the teachers' pedagogical expertise as part of an effective educational team. A regular career-development program must be created to allow local residents to acquire professional status.

Is This What You Want?

PHILADELPHIA FREEDOM ORGANIZATION[*]

PURPOSES AND AIMS

To unify the people

To aid in political education

To see that black people can participate freely in a true democracy

[*] This 1966 pamphlet, from Philadelphia, Pa., is typical of promotional literature of local independent political organizations in black communities.

To assure that the majority of Negroes in Philadelphia have candidates running in the general election that represent them

To assure that there will be Negro candidates on the ballot

To assure that the Negro community selects these candidates themselves

To organize and strengthen the black community

To register people and see that they get the candidate they want

VOTING

What is the vote?

Voting is when you can choose people to represent you locally, nationally, and internationally. When you vote you speak for yourself about things concerning your own welfare.

Why vote?

If you don't vote you let other people decide what is going to happen to you and your community and what is going to happen in the government and to your children. Your voice never gets heard if you don't vote.

How does voting work?

First of all, you have to register with the city and have your name placed on the city's registration book.

Can you vote?

Yes, if you are 21 years old, have lived in the state one year and in your election district two months since the last election, you can vote.

POLITICS

What Is Politics?

Politics is the coming together of people to make decisions about their lives. For example—who is going to be mayor, how people will be selected to the school board, who is going to be police commissioner and who is going to assess taxes. However, in the past, Negroes in Philadelphia have not been permitted to have real political power. A few people, most of them white, have controlled politics to benefit themselves, while holding us down.

How have we been allowed to vote but at the same time, been kept out of politics?

1. They told us that politics was "white people's" business
2. They told us voting did not matter anyway
3. They kept us out of the real decision making
4. They kept us poor so that they could buy our vote
5. They told us we were not "qualified" to practice politics

They say we are not "qualified" to run our own lives! The word "qualified" has been defined in such a manner as to mean "rich and well-educated." Everyone knows, if he would really think about it, that *each* and *every* grown man and woman is just as "qualified" as anyone else to decide what he wants his life to be like. There may be some information that some of us need to decide how to go about making our lives what we want them to be. They have controlled information which they have kept from us and lied to us. This information is information we can learn just as well as anyone else.

6. They told us that Negroes "just can't stick together."

Why Come Together?

When we come together we can determine who from our block and area can best represent us in getting the things we want done accomplished. If we don't come together, the people who have been running the show will put their own candidates up and vote for the programs that will benefit them only, and we will have no say at all.

What Can We Do When We Come Together?

We can form our own political organization.

How Can People Work Together in a Political Organization?

First of all, we have to "stick together." Then, we should decide, "What are our common needs?" We can decide this by asking ourselves, "Will the program and this candidate help us or people like us with problems common to ours?" Once you have a political organization you can go out and talk to your neighbors and friends and even to strangers, and find others who are willing to work with you.

Why Form a Political Organization?

When you form a political organization you can nominate for office candidates of your own choosing. And in a general election, you can vote to put your candidate into office.

How Does a Political Organization Become a Political Party?

In Philadelphia the law says that you must get signatures equal to one half of one percent of the largest vote cast for any candidate in state-wide elections during the last election. In city-wide or district elections you must get signatures of two percent of largest vote cast.

You must run a slate of candidates. The candidates must get at least two percent of the vote cast in at least ten counties. The group must get two percent of the largest vote cast for any candidate.

In Philadelphia you can stop police brutality. You can say who is going to be mayor or police commissioner. You can help run the government. There are at least 600,000 black people in Philadelphia. Negroes are over 30% of the population and growing. You should not just pay taxes, but run the government too.

No one is going to give you your rights! You will have to first come together and demand them—freedom now! One man—one vote! Negroes must come together and demand their political rights now! Tomorrow may be too late. Join the Freedom Organization.

Let's get together. Let's have a people's meeting. Let's get together and decide what we want our lives to be like.

If we get together we can nominate a slate of candidates and then we can work to get them elected. We will be working to get the power to change things.

Do you know someone who lives on your street who would make a good city councilman, a good state senator, a good congressman, a good mayor, or a good judge? Let us look for people who will represent us—someone who is honest and who will work for us. *Let us find men and women who believe that Negroes are "qualified."*

If we could elect people who are not ashamed of us or of being black or Negro, they would work for us. If we elected people who realize how powerful Negroes are going to be in Philadelphia they would work for our future and the future of our children.

Of the 274,000 city pupils enrolled in September, 1965, 57% of 153,500 were non-white—43% or 120,500 were white.

What Are The Duties of a Political Party?

1. To indicate to the government what the people want
2. To name the people who will run for office
3. To give the people direct control of politics and government

Now Is The Time!

If we in Philadelphia ever had a chance to come together to make political decisions about our lives—now is the time. If there was ever a time for Negroes to leave the white supremacy Democrat and Republican parties of Pennsylvania —now is the time!

If ever we had a chance to do something about the years of low pay, police brutality, slum housing, poor schools, bad education, high prices, humiliation, unemployment, public welfare, high taxes, poor hospital facilities, poor service and economic exploitation—now is the time!

Join the Philadelphia Freedom Organization now!
One man, one vote and self-determination for all people

3. CIVIL RIGHTS AND PEACE

*The War on Vietnam**

A McCOMB, MISSISSIPPI, PROTEST

HERE ARE FIVE reasons why Negroes should not be in any war fighting for America:

1. No Mississippi Negroes should be fighting in Vietnam for the White Man's freedom, until all the Negro People are free in Mississippi.

2. Negro boys should not honor the draft here in Mississippi. Mothers should encourage their sons not to go.

3. We will gain respect and dignity as a race only by forcing the U.S. Government and the Mississippi Government to come with guns, dogs and trucks to take our sons away to

* This was the first civil rights movement protest of the Vietnam war. It was circulated as a leaflet in McComb, Miss., and printed in the Mississippi Freedom Democratic Party newsletter of McComb on July 28, 1965. The statement was criticized by Southern Congressmen as an indication of the lack of patriotism of the MFDP. Lawrence Guyot, chairman of the MFDP executive committee and Rev. Ed King, a member of the executive committee, issued a statement on July 31 pointing out that the leaflet did not represent the position of the MFDP since policy was made only by the MFDP executive committee and not by local branches of the party. The statement said, however, that "it is very easy to understand why Negro citizens of McComb, themselves the victims of bombings, Klan-inspired terrorism, and harassment arrests, should resent the death of a citizen of McComb while fighting in Vietnam for 'freedom' not enjoyed by the Negro community of McComb." The leaflet had been circulated after the death of John D. Shaw, 23, of McComb, who had been a participant in civil rights demonstrations there in 1961.

fight and be killed protecting Mississippi, Alabama, Georgia, and Louisiana.

4. No one has a right to ask us to risk our lives and kill other Colored People in Santo Domingo and Vietnam, so that the White American can get richer. We will be looked upon as traitors by all the Colored People of the world if the Negro people continue to fight and die without a cause.

5. Last week a white soldier from New Jersey was discharged from the Army because he refused to fight in Vietnam; he went on a hunger strike. Negro boys can do the same thing. We can write and ask our sons if they know what they are fighting for. If he answers Freedom, tell him that's what we are fighting for here in Mississippi. And if he says Democracy, tell him the truth—we don't know anything about Communism, Socialism, and all that, but we do know that Negroes have caught hell right here under this American Democracy.

Statement on Vietnam, January 6, 1966*

STUDENT NONVIOLENT COORDINATING COMMITTEE

THE STUDENT NONVIOLENT Coordinating Committee assumes its right to dissent with the United States foreign policy on any issue, and states its opposition to United States involvement in the war in Vietnam on these grounds:

We believe the United States government has been deceptive in claims of concern for the freedom of the Vietnamese people, just as the government has been deceptive in claiming concern for the freedom of the colored people in such other countries as the Dominican Republic, the Congo, South Africa, Rhodesia and in the United States itself.

We of the Student Nonviolent Coordinating Committee have been involved in the black people's struggle for libera-

---

* This anti-Vietnam War statement was the first by a major civil rights organization. It received wide attention, especially after it was endorsed by SNCC's communications director, Julian Bond, who had just been elected to the Georgia House of Representatives. The House subsequently termed Bond disloyal and refused to seat him. He was seated after the Supreme Court ruled that the legislature's action was a denial of his freedom of speech. Sammy Younge, referred to in the text, was a SNCC worker who was shot after attempting to enter a "white" restroom at an Alabama gas station.

tion and self-determination in this country for the past five years. Our work, particularly in the South, taught us that the United States government has never guaranteed the freedom of oppressed citizens and is not yet truly determined to end the rule of terror and oppression within its own borders.

We ourselves have often been victims of violence and confinement executed by U. S. government officials. We recall the numerous persons who have been murdered in the South because of their efforts to secure their civil and human rights, and whose murderers have been allowed to escape penalty for their crimes. The murder of Samuel Younge in Tuskegee, Alabama is no different from the murder of people in Vietnam, for both Younge and the Vietnamese sought and are seeking to secure the rights guaranteed them by law. In each case, the U. S. government bears a great part of the responsibility for these deaths.

Samuel Younge was murdered because U. S. law is not being enforced. Vietnamese are being murdered because the United States is pursuing an aggressive policy in violation of international law. The U. S. is no respector of persons or law when such persons or laws run counter to its needs and desires. We recall the indifference, suspicion and outright hostility with which our reports of violence have been met in the past by government officials.

We know for the most part that elections in this country, in the North as well as the South, are not free. We have seen that the 1965 Voting Rights Act and the 1964 Civil Rights Act have not yet been implemented with full federal power and concern. We question then the ability and even the desire of the U. S. government to guarantee free elections abroad. We maintain that our country's cry of "Preserve freedom in the world" is a hypocritical mask behind which it squashed liberation movements which are not bound and refuse to be bound by the expediency of the U. S. cold war policy.

We are in sympathy with and support the men in this country who are unwilling to respond to the military draft which would compel them to contribute their lives to U. S. aggression in the name of the "freedom" we find so false in this country. We recoil with horror at the inconsistency of this supposedly free society where responsibility to freedom is equated with responsibility to lend oneself to military aggression. We take note of the fact that 16% of the draftees from this country are Negro, called on to stifle the liberation of Vietnam, to preserve a "democracy" which does not exist for them at home.

We ask: Where is the draft for the Freedom fight in the United States?

We therefore encourage those Americans who prefer to use their energy in building democratic forms within the country. We believe that work in the civil rights movement and other human relations organizations is a valid alternative to the draft. We urge all Americans to seek this alternative knowing full well that it may cost them their lives, as painfully as in Vietnam.

Beyond Vietnam*

REV. MARTIN LUTHER KING, JR.

. . . I COME TO this platform tonight to make a passionate plea to my beloved nation. This speech is not addressed to Hanoi or to the National Liberation Front. It is not addressed to China or to Russia.

Nor is it an attempt to overlook the ambiguity of the total situation and the need for a collective solution to the tragedy of Vietnam. Neither is it an attempt to make North Vietnam or the National Liberation Front paragons of virtue, nor to overlook the role they can play in a successful resolution of the problem. While they both may have justifiable reason to be suspicious of the good faith of the United States, life and history give eloquent testimony to the fact that conflicts are never resolved without trustful give and take on both sides.

Tonight, however, I wish not to speak with Hanoi and the NLF, but rather to my fellow Americans who, with me, bear the greatest responsibility in ending a conflict that has exacted a heavy price on both continents.

Since I am a preacher by trade, I suppose it is not surprising that I have several reasons for bringing Vietnam into the field of my moral vision. There is at the outset a very obvious and almost facile connection between the war in Vietnam and the struggle I, and others, have been waging in America. A few years ago there was a shining moment in that struggle. It seemed as if there was a real promise of hope for the poor—both black and white—through the Poverty Program. There were experiments, hopes, new beginnings. Then came the build-up in Vietnam and I watched the program broken and eviscerated as if it were some idle political plaything of a

* Excerpts from address given at Riverside Church Meeting, sponsored by Clergy and Laymen Concerned about Vietnam, New York, April 4, 1967. Reprinted by permission of Joan Daves. Copyright © 1967 by Martin Luther King, Jr.

society gone mad on war, and I knew that America would never invest the necessary funds or energies in rehabilitation of its poor so long as adventures like Vietnam continued to draw men and skills and money like some demoniacal destructive suction tube. So I was increasingly compelled to see the war as an enemy of the poor and to attack it as such.

Perhaps the more tragic recognition of reality took place when it became clear to me that the war was doing far more than devastating the hopes of the poor at home. It was sending their sons and their brothers and their husbands to fight and to die in extraordinarily high proportions relative to the rest of the population. We were taking the black young men who had been crippled by our society and sending them 8,-000 miles away to guarantee liberties in Southeast Asia which they had not found in Southwest Georgia and East Harlem. So we have been repeatedly faced with the cruel irony of watching Negro and white boys on TV screens as they kill and die together for a nation that has been unable to seat them together in the same schools. So we watch them in brutal solidarity burning the huts of a poor village but we realize that they would never live on the same block in Detroit. I could not be silent in the face of such cruel manipulation of the poor.

My third reason moves to an even deeper level of awareness, for it grows out of my experience in the ghettos of the North over the last three years—especially the last three summers. As I have walked among the desperate, rejected and angry young men I have told them that Molotov cocktails and rifles would not solve their problems. I have tried to offer them my deepest compassion while maintaining my conviction that social change comes most meaningfully through non-violent action. But they asked—and rightly so—what about Vietnam? They asked if our own nation wasn't using massive doses of violence to solve its problems, to bring about the changes it wanted. Their questions hit home, and I knew that I could never again raise my voice against the violence of the oppressed in the ghettos without having first spoken clearly to the greatest purveyor of violence in the world today—my own government. For the sake of those boys, for the sake of this government, for the sake of the hundreds of thousands trembling under our violence, I cannot be silent.

For those who ask the question, "Aren't you a Civil Rights leader?" and thereby mean to exclude me from the movement for peace, I have this further answer. In 1957 when a group of us formed the Southern Christian Leadership Conference, we chose as our motto: "To save the soul of America." We were convinced that we could not limit our vision to certain rights for black people, but instead affirmed the conviction that America would never be free or saved from itself unless the descendants of its slaves were loosed completely from the shackles they still wear. In a way we were agreeing with Langston Hughes, that black bard of Harlem, who had written earlier:

> O, yes,
> I say it plain,
> America never was America to me,
> And yet I swear this oath—
> America will be!

Now, it should be incandescently clear that no one who has any concern for the integrity and life of America today can ignore the present war. If America's soul becomes totally poisoned, part of the autopsy must read "Vietnam." It can never be saved so long as it destroys the deepest hopes of men the world over. So it is that those of us who are yet determined that America *will* be are led down the path of protest and dissent, working for the health of our land.

As if the weight of such a commitment to the life and health of America were not enough, another burden of responsibility was placed upon me in 1964; and I cannot forget that the Nobel Prize for Peace was also a commission—a commission to work harder than I had ever worked before for "the brotherhood of man." This is a calling that takes me beyond national allegiances, but even if it were not present I would yet have to live with the meaning of my commitment to the ministry of Jesus Christ. To me the relationship of this ministry to the making of peace is so obvious that I sometimes marvel at those who ask me why I am speaking against the war . . .

Finally, as I try to delineate for you and for myself the road that leads from Montgomery to this place I would have offered all that was most valid if I simply said that I must be true to my conviction that I share with all men the calling to be a son of the Living God . . .

And as I ponder the madness of Vietnam and search within myself for ways to understand and respond in compassion my mind goes constantly to the people of that peninsula. I speak now not of the soldiers of each side, not of the junta in Saigon, but simply of the people who have been living under the curse of war for almost three continuous decades now. I think of them too because it is clear to me that there will be no meaningful solution there until some attempt is made to know them and hear their broken cries.

They must see Americans as strange liberators. The Vietnamese people proclaimed their own independence in 1945 after a combined French and Japanese occupation, and before the Communist revolution in China. They were led by Ho Chi Minh. Even though they quoted the American Declaration of Independence in their own document of freedom, we refused to recognize them. Instead, we decided to support France in its re-conquest of her former colony. . . .

After the French were defeated it looked as if independence and land reform would come again through the Geneva agreements. But instead there came the United States, determined that Ho should not unify the temporarily divided nation, and the peasants watched again as we supported one of the most vicious modern dictators—our chosen man, Premier Diem. The peasants watched and cringed as Diem ruthlessly routed out all opposition, supported their extortionist landlords and refused even to discuss re-unification with the North. The peasants watched as all this was presided over by U.S. influence and then by increasing numbers of U.S. troops who came to help quell the insurgency that Diem's methods had aroused. When Diem was overthrown they may have been happy, but the long line of military dictatorships seemed to offer no real change—especially in terms of their need for land and peace.

The only change came from America as we increased our troop commitments in support of governments which were singularly corrupt, inept and without popular support. All the while the people read our leaflets and received regular promises of peace and democracy—and land reform. Now they languish under our bombs and consider us—not their fellow Vietnamese—the real enemy. They move sadly and apathetically as we herd them off the land of their fathers into concentration camps where minimal social needs are rarely met. They know they must move or be destroyed by our bombs. So they go—primarily women and children and the aged.

They watch as we poison their water, as we kill a million acres of their crops. They must weep as the bulldozers roar through their areas preparing to destroy the precious trees. They wander into the hospitals, with at least 20 casualties from American firepower for one Vietcong-inflicted injury. They wander into the towns and see thousands of the children, homeless, without clothes, running in packs on the streets like animals. They see the children degraded by our soldiers as they beg for food. They see the children selling their sisters to our soldiers, soliciting for their mothers. . . .

Perhaps the more difficult but no less necessary task is to speak for those who have been designated as our enemies.

What of the National Liberation Front—that strangely anonymous group we call VC or Communists? What must they think of us in America when they realize that we permitted the repression and cruelty of Diem which helped to bring them into being as a resistance group in the South? What do they think of our condoning the violence which led to their own taking up of arms? How can they believe in our integrity when now we speak of "aggression from the North" as if there were nothing more essential to the war? How can they trust us when now we charge them with violence after the murderous reign of Diem, and charge them with violence while we pour every new weapon of death into their land? Surely we must understand their feelings even if we do not condone their actions. Surely we must see that the men we supported pressed them to their violence. Surely we must see that our own computerized plans of destruction simply dwarf their greatest acts.

How do they judge us when our officials know that their membership is less than 25 per cent Communist and yet insist on giving them the blanket name? What must they be thinking when they know that we are aware of their control of major sections of Vietnam and yet we appear ready to allow national elections in which this highly organized political parallel government will have no part? They ask how we can speak of free elections when the Saigon press is censored and controlled by the military junta. And they are surely right to wonder what kind of new government we plan to help form without them—the only party in real touch with the peasants. They question our political goals and they deny the reality of a peace settlement from which they will be excluded. Their questions are frighteningly relevant. Is our nation planning to build on political myth again and then shore it up with the power of new violence?

Here is the true meaning and value of compassion and non-violence when it helps us to see the enemy's point of view, to hear his questions, to know his assessment of ourselves. For from his view we may indeed see the basic weaknesses of our own condition, and if we are mature, we may learn and grow and profit from the wisdom of the brothers who are called the opposition.

So, too, with Hanoi. In the North, where our bombs now pummel the land, and our mines endanger the waterways, we are met by a deep but understandable mistrust. To speak for them is to explain this lack of confidence in western words, and especially their distrust of American intentions now. In Hanoi are the men who led the nation to independence against the Japanese and the French, the men who sought membership in the French commonwealth and were betrayed by the weakness of Paris and the willfulness of the colonial armies. It was they who led a second struggle against French domination at tremendous costs, and then were persuaded to give up the land they controlled between the 13th and 17th parallel as a temporary measure at Geneva. After 1954 they watched us conspire with Diem to prevent elections which would have surely brought Ho Chi Minh to power over a united Vietnam, and they realized they had been betrayed again. . . .

At this point I should make it clear that while I have tried in these last few minutes to give a voice to the voiceless on Vietnam and to understand the arguments of those who are called enemy, I am as deeply concerned about our own troops there as anything else. For it occurs to me that what we are submitting them to in Vietnam is not simply the brutalizing process that goes on in any war where armies face each other and seek to destroy. We are adding cynicism to the process of death, for they must know after a short period there that none of the things we claim to be fighting for are really involved. Before long they must know that their government has sent them into a struggle among Vietnamese, and the more sophisticated surely realize that we are on the side of the wealthy and the secure while we create a hell for the poor.

Somehow this madness must cease. We must stop now. I speak as a child of God and brother to the suffering poor of Vietnam. I speak for those whose land is being laid waste, whose homes are being destroyed, whose culture is being subverted. I speak for the poor of America who are paying the double price of smashed hopes at home and death and corruption in Vietnam. I speak as a citizen of the world, for the world as it stands aghast at the path we have taken. I speak as an American to the leaders of my own nation. The great initiative in this war is ours. The initiative to stop it must be ours. . . .

If we continue there will be no doubt in my mind and in the mind of the world that we have no honorable intentions in Vietnam. It will become clear that our minimal expectation is to occupy it as an American colony and men will not refrain from thinking that our maximum hope is to goad China into a war so that we may bomb her nuclear installations. If we do not stop our war against the people in Vietnam immediately the world will be left with no other alternative than to see this as some horribly clumsy and deadly game we have decided to play.

The world now demands a maturity of America that we may not be able to achieve. It demands that we admit that we have been wrong from the beginning of our adventure in Vietnam, that we have been detrimental to the life of the Vietnamese people.

In order to atone for our sins and errors in Vietnam, we should take the initiative in bringing a halt to this tragic war. I would like to suggest five concrete things that our Government should do immediately to begin the long and difficult process of extricating ourselves from this nightmarish conflict:

1. End all bombing in North and South Vietnam.
2. Declare a unilateral cease-fire in the hope that such action will create the atmosphere for negotiation.
3. Take immediate steps to prevent other battlegrounds in Southeast Asia by curtailing our military build-up in Thailand and our interference in Laos.
4. Realistically accept the fact that the National Liberation Front has substantial support in South Vietnam and must thereby play a role in any meaningful negotiations and in any future Vietnam government.
5. Set a date that we will remove all foreign troops from Vietnam in accordance with the 1954 Geneva Agreement.

Part of our ongoing commitment might well express itself in an offer to grant asylum to any Vietnamese who fears for his life under a new regime which included the Liberation Front. Then we must make what reparations we can for the damage we have done. We must provide the medical aid that is badly needed, making it available in this country if necessary.

Meanwhile we in the churches and synagogues have a continuing task while we urge our Government to disengage itself from a disgraceful commitment. We must continue to raise our voices if our nation persists in its perverse ways in Vietnam. We must be prepared to match actions with words by seeking out every creative means of protest possible.

As we counsel young men concerning military service we must clarify for them our nation's role in Vietnam and challenge them with the alternative of conscientious objection. I am pleased to say that this is the path now being chosen by more than seventy students at my own Alma Mater, Morehouse College, and I recommend it to all who find the American course in Vietnam a dishonorable and unjust one. Moreover I would encourage all ministers of draft age to give up their ministerial exemptions and seek status as conscientious objectors. These are the times for real choices and not false ones. We are at the moment when our lives must be placed on the line if our nation is to survive its own folly. Every man of humane convictions must decide on the protest that best suits his convictions, but we must all protest. . . .

*Have You Ever Been One Day Late?**

One black boy from Tuskegee, Alabama came one day late to one white draft board's induction and one white clerk ordered him classified delinquent!

Today—right now—this very minute, this same black boy is serving 1,095 days in jail because he was one day late! Yes, that's right—one black boy came one day late and one white judge sentenced the boy to 1,095 days (26,280 hours) in a Federal penitentiary. He was sentenced to 26,280 HOURS away from his friends, family and loved ones.

Maybe you also have been late for an appointment.

Maybe you also have been late for an induction.

But, you should not expect a 1,095 day prison sentence for being one day late,

Unless you, like Simuel B. Schutz have tried to move black students to help black people in your own home town.

Unless you, like Schutz, have risked death in Mississippi in 1964 as you worked for your black people's right to free elections.

Unless you, like Schutz, have worked in 1965, 1966 in Lowndes and Macon County Alabama to help black people there get free elections.

Unless you, like Schutz, have been strangled, threatened and jailed for 60 days because you were opposed to the needless murder and abuse of Black G.I.'s in President Johnson's war on the Vietnamese people.

People have always been getting strangled, threatened, and jailed. You know that black men have always been catching hell from white judges, white juries and white draft boards.

Today, Schutz has to serve 1,095 days in prison unless he can raise $2,000 dollars to appeal this white judge's racist decision.

* Pamphlet of the Simuel Brent Schutz, Jr. Defense Committee, Atlanta, Ga., December, 1966.

PART VIII

Race and Economics

INTRODUCTION

THE CURRENT MOVEMENT which has more than once startled the nation with its actions and words dismayed its white allies with a new slogan in 1966—Black Power. The already frayed alliance with the liberals—almost severed by the disavowal of coalition politics as a valid method of gaining Negro rights, and the refusal of some sections of the movement to cooperate with the Government in such things as the White House Conference of 1966, "To Fulfill these Rights"—was shattered by the proclamation of the movement's goal as black power.

"Black power" as explained by its advocates has several connotations, many of them repetitions of themes of earlier struggles. It includes race pride, an interest in the history of the American Negro and his past in Africa, and a desire to educate the black American in the acceptance of black as something good, not bad; and beautiful, not something of which to be ashamed. Black power is part of the new drive of local people to control their local schools. This is a repudiation of the concept behind the decision in *Brown* v. *Board of Education* that separate schools of necessity must be unequal, and a substitution of a drive for quality education—an upgrading of separate schools where black children could learn skills *and* race pride.[1] Much of this, of course, had been put

---

[1] This idea had emotional appeal for ghetto parents, but it also is based on practical experience. In a highly successful experiment a St. Louis school district implemented a program to stimulate teachers to teach and parents to help learning. Dr. Kenneth Clark reports remarkable improvement in achievement levels and I.Q. scores and comments: "In spite of the fact that there had been no drastic change in curriculum, instructional technique, or the basic 'underprivileged' social situation, improvements were definitely evident. What had changed was the attitude and perspective of teachers which influenced the way in which the students were taught and learned." Kenneth B. Clark, *Dark Ghetto* (New York: Harper & Row, 1965), p. 144.

forth by Marcus Garvey in the twenties, by Elijah Muhammad in the fifties, and by Malcolm X in the sixties.

Black power also means independent black politics. The Lowndes County Freedom Organization's symbol—the "big, bad, bold, beautiful" black panther was expressive of a new, proud attitude which had developed. But it was more. Black power meant taking over control of the politics of the black ghettos in the North and the heavily or preponderantly black counties of the South. As a SNCC organizer, Ivanhoe Donaldson, put it, it meant treating these black areas as "colonies" to be liberated and controlled by black people. Such liberation would not only be political, but also economic. The youngsters of the movement had added economic power to the concepts of freedom and political action.

The enunciation of the slogan "black power" was not the first of the new movement's talk of or action around economic issues, by any means. One of the demands of the Montgomery, Alabama bus boycott in 1956 had been the employment of Negro bus drivers, and most of the mass demonstrations against discrimination in public accommodations had had jobs as one demand. But black power advocates began to talk of economic control of the ghetto—Negro ownership of ghetto businesses and housing.

SNCC, whose chairman, Stokely Carmichael, had been the first to use the slogan, became the leader of the black power movement. It went so far as to take away the right of white staff members to vote at staff meetings, thereby in effect driving them from the organization. The theory was that Negroes must organize Negroes to help bring about an increase in respect for blackness and that whites must organize in the white community to build a base for the future formation of a coalition of poor whites and poor blacks.

Over the years the idea that white people must organize whites has been prevalent in the South among those liberal organizations concerned with race relations which existed. In 1919 the Commission on Interracial Cooperation operated a moderate program of education against lynching and discrimination, but not segregation. Its successor was the Southern Regional Council, established in 1944. The SRC helps set up bi-racial human relations councils to establish dialogues between the Negro and white communities, and to help educate whites for better understanding. SRC also does excellent research studies of violence, education and voting and other civil rights subjects. The Southern Conference for Human Welfare was established in 1938 as an organization of Northern and Southern liberals to press for alleviation of the condition of both blacks and whites in the South. It was succeeded by the Southern Conference Educational Fund, an organization of Southern whites which has worked closely with predominantly Negro civil rights groups, but whose main aim is to organize in the white community, and whose consistent stand has been unequivocally for full Negro rights.

The black power advocates in the current movement have taken the position that in order for there to be a black-white alliance among the masses of people—the poor—whites must be organized. SNCC and CORE have stated that integration is a myth for American society, for what is called integration is in reality assimilation; absorption of individual Negroes into the mainstream of the white American middle-class culture. Floyd McKissick, chairman of CORE, has said: "We have made the slogan Black Power into a program destined to rescue Black people from destruction by the forces of a racist society which is bent upon denying them freedom, equality and dignity." McKissick outlined a six-point program: economic power, political power, improved self-image, militant Black leadership, enforcement of federal legislation and mobilization of Black consumer power.[2]

When it was founded in 1942 CORE was primarily a white and Northern organization. Its basic philosophy was based on pacifism, and it was the first civil rights group to conduct sit-ins for an end to discrimination in public accommodations. After the Southern sit-ins in 1960 CORE added more Negroes to its staff and board of directors and began to work in border areas and in the South, mainly in Louisiana. After "black power" was taken up as a slogan in ghettos across the country in 1966 and 1967, CORE moved its national headquarters to Harlem and voted at its 1967 convention to strike the word "multiracial" from its constitution, though it did not oust whites from the organization.

The Southern Christian Leadership Conference has had a predominantly black staff since its inception. The organization has been critical of the black power slogan. In an article called "Martin Luther King Defines 'Black Power'," King wrote:

When a people are mired in oppression, they realize deliverance only when they have accumulated the power to enforce change. . . .
The nettlesome task of Negroes today is to discover how to organize our strength into compelling power so that Government cannot elude our demands. We must develop, from strength, a sit-

[2] Floyd McKissick, address to the 24th national convention of CORE, "Black Power: A Blueprint for Survival," June 30-July 4, 1967, Oakland, California.

uation in which the Government finds it wise and prudent to collaborate with us.[3]

King said that with the heavy concentration of Negroes in the cities they should align themselves with white groups to elect candidates favorable to their program.

The older organizations, the NAACP and the Urban League, repudiated black power and retained integrated boards and staffs and their white support. Roy Wilkins of the NAACP does point out from time to time, however, that the organization's main financial support comes from black people in the form of membership dues.

The black-white alliance that participated in the huge March on Washington in 1963 no longer existed in 1967. There could be no such top-level group making civil rights policy as the "Big Ten" sponsors of that March who included a white labor leader, a Catholic bishop, a rabbi, the head of the Protestant National Council of Churches and leaders of the major national civil rights organizations. But white support continued to function in important ways: a committee to aid the Sunflower County electoral candidates; legal assistance organizations, and fund-raising groups. In addition, young white intellectuals continued to work on community organizing projects in Northern ghettos—sometimes among poor whites, but most often in the black ghettos. These projects sometimes involved running independent candidates for office as did the Newark Community Union Project in Newark, New Jersey. Most often the projects organize around a local issue (like a traffic light) and on economic concerns.

Negro leaders through the years have persistently pointed to the disparities between white and Negro employment, income, housing and education. But in the sixties discussion of the Negro's economic plight took on a tone of urgency. The economic gap between Negro and white was widening; [4] Negro unemployment was on the rise and what is worse, labor experts pointed to an even bleaker future, for the expansion of automation and a corresponding reduction of industry's need for unskilled labor (the largest market for Negro labor) foreshadowed even greater unemployment. One of the most alarming statistics was that of non-white youth unemployment. The teenage (14 to 19 years) unemployment rate in

[3] Martin Luther King, "Martin Luther King Defines 'Black Power'," *The New York Times Magazine*, June 11, 1967.

[4] The difference between non-white and white male average hourly earnings was $.90 in 1949 and had jumped to $1.45 in 1959. See Urban League study on pp. 476-80 below.

1964 was 13.3 percent white and 26.4 percent nonwhite. The Urban League states: "It is generally conceded that the real Negro teenage unemployment rate (not in school and not employed) may be nearer to 35-40 percent." [5]

In a 1962 article Herbert Hill, Labor Secretary of the NAACP, gave the following unemployment statistics: Chicago: 17.3 percent Negro unemployed and 5.7 total unemployment; New York: 10 percent Negro and 6.4 percent total; Columbus, Ohio: over 10 percent Negro and 5.6 percent total; Pittsburgh: 24 percent Negro and 11.6 total; St. Louis: 20 percent Negro and 8.4, total; Philadelphia: 28 percent Negro and 8.4, total; Gary, Indiana: 44 percent Negro and 6.3 total; Detroit: out of over 185,000 unemployed, 112,000 are Negro. [6]

As the civil rights movement noted that economic conditions were worsening they also pointed out that 1) civil rights gains were not keeping pace with Negro demands and 2) the victories were not benefiting the most oppressed, the masses of Negro people. Rev. Martin Luther King, Jr., wrote in *Life:*

After a decade of bitter struggle, multiple laws have been enacted proclaiming his [the Negro's] equality. He should feel exhilaration as his goal comes into sight . . . [But] Despite new laws, little has changed in his life in the ghettos. The Negro is still the poorest American—walled in by color and poverty. The law pronounces him equal, abstractly, but his conditions of life are still far from equal to those of other Americans. [7]

In the South Negro sharecroppers and maids formed the Mississippi Freedom Labor Union and struck for better wages, and Negro farmers ran for positions on Agriculture Stabilization and Conservation Service (ASCS) boards to gain some measure of control over crop allotments. In the North the NAACP and the Urban League continued their fight for equitable apprenticeship training programs and the NAACP, CORE and community organizations launched campaigns against job discrimination in the building trades and other industries.

In many young people, the revolt against conditions has been by striking out at "whitey" in any way; thus there has been a series of riots, rebellions, revolts, by Negro youth in

5 National Urban League, *Facts on the Many Faces of Poverty,* 1965.

6 Herbert Hill, "Racial Discrimination in the Nation's Apprenticeship Training Programs," *Phylon,* Vol. XXIII, Fall, 1962.

7 Martin Luther King, Jr., "Negroes Are *Not* Moving Too Fast," *Life,* Nov. 7, 1965.

the ghetto. The riots have been sparked by an incident, usually the shooting of a Negro by a policeman, but the direction the riots have taken—destruction of white-owned businesses, taunting of and attacks upon police—indicate the underlying causes. After the 1965 Watts rebellion in Los Angeles a federal investigating commission headed by John A. McCone recommended educational improvements, job training and placement and mass transit facilities for the area, but it discussed agitation over the conditions in the ghetto and civil disobedience as causes of the outbreak. More scholarly analyses of riots cite economic deprivation, resentment of white-owned businesses and police brutality as the primary causes. Almost two years after the Watts rebellion in which there were 34 deaths, 1,032 injuries and 3,952 arrests, a New York *Times* article said there were a number of small job-training programs, but little else had changed in Watts. Even the buildings which were burned down had not been rebuilt. The article was headlined "Black Nationalism Grows in Watts as Negroes Complain of Lack of Gains."[8]

Over the years the federal government had made some largely ineffective attempts to deal with the economic problems. In 1964, it appropriated $947,500,000 for a "war on poverty." Most of the militants in the Negro protest movement took the view that the extensive bureaucracy known nationally as the Office of Economic Opportunity, and with hundreds of subsidiary local orgnizations through which federal funds were channeled, was in reality an elaborate system for co-opting movement activists. Movement community organizers saw the effort as an attempt to neutralize militancy by giving high-paying jobs to the most qualified of local leaders, in effect buying them off. Many Negro leaders saw the government's approach, as epitomized in the Moynihan report on the Negro family,[9] as an attempt to deflect attention from the root causes of the Negro's condition to the effects. The reaction to the anti-poverty program was two-pronged. Many tried to continue their work independently of it; others sought to control it. The program was used as an organizing tool by many community organizers who waged long battles for representation of the poor on local anti-poverty boards.

Those outside the movement who opposed the program as another federal give-away fought against community control,

8 Earl Caldwell, *New York Times*, July 9, 1967.

9 *The Negro Family—the Case for National Action*, U.S. Labor Department, Office of Policy Planning and Research, Washington, D.C., March, 1965.

sought to cut appropriations and forced investigations of local programs on charges of financial irregularities.

Some of the problems of the anti-poverty program stemmed from its very nature. It was itself contradictory, for it fostered community action which developed into government-subsidized attacks upon the government. When funds were used by local agencies for the very purposes for which they had been allocated charges of mismanagement were made. In Mississippi, for example, the Child Development Group of Mississippi did hire the most militant organizers and local leaders who remained in the state after the upsurge of activity around the Summer Project of 1964. Mississippi's Senators instigated several investigations of CDGM mainly based on charges that the government was funding "agitators" and that the program was controlled by black power advocates.

Broadly speaking the criticisms had some validity, but were nonetheless not justified since the programs were functioning according to their mandate. CDGM gave poor Negroes a regular income, and more importantly gave both the teachers and the children a sense of their own worth. While it could not be true that the limited number of black power spokesmen could be in all of the places where their presence is decried, the concept of black power has been pervasive in Northern ghettos and in Southern Negro communities. Negroes do want to do it for themselves. Furthermore, since 1955-56 when Mrs. Rosa Parks walked her walk in Montgomery, Alabama, the number of black Americans willing to say that they, too, are fed up, has increased a thousandfold.

Today, the situation for the majority of Negroes has not changed, except in this all-important aspect: a major aim of the current movement, with all of its changes and floundering and periods of inactivity during which direction and goals seem to have been lost sight of, has been fulfilled. The masses of Negroes have been stirred, there is a widespread will to fight, a new-found ability to organize and a substantial decrease of fear.

1. BLACK AND WHITE

Farewell to Liberals*

LOREN MILLER

LIBERALS WHO WERE shocked or surprised at James Baldwin's recent statement that Negroes "twenty years younger than I don't believe in liberals at all" haven't been doing their homework. Discontent with the liberal position in the area of race relations has been building up for the past several years. Of course there are liberals and liberals, ranging from Left to Right; still, there does exist a set of beliefs and attitudes, not easily defined but readily identified, constituting the liberal outlook on the race question. Simply stated, it contemplates the ultimate elimination of all racial distinctions in every phase of American life through an orderly, step-by-step process adjusted to resistance and aimed at overcoming such resistance. In the field of constitutional law, the classic liberal position, exemplified in the Supreme Court's "all deliberate speed" formula of the school-segregation cases, requires and rationalizes Negro accommodation to, and acquiescence in, disabilities imposed because of race and in violation of the fundamental law.

On his part, the Negro has to put up with such practices, but he cannot admit that they have constitutional sanction; to do so would be to give away his case and knuckle under to the revisionist theory that the Civil War Amendments conferred less than complete equality under the law. The liberal sees "both sides" of the issue: the force of the Negro's constitutional argument and the existence of customs, sometimes jelled into law, that justify the gradualist approach. He is impatient with "extremists on both sides."

The Negro is outraged at being called an extremist. Since he takes the position that the Constitution confers complete equality on all citizens, he must rest his case on the proposition that there is only one side: his side, the constitutional side. That his attitude in that respect is firming up is evidenced by the fact that Negro spokesmen who once won ap-

* Excerpts from Loren Miller, "Farewell to Liberals: A Negro View," *The Nation,* 195 (October 20, 1962), pp. 235-38. Reprinted by permission of *The Nation.*

plause by claiming that their activities made for progress in race relations are being elbowed aside by others whose catchword is Freedom Now. "We want our Freedom Here; we want it Now, not tomorrow; we want it All, not just a part of it," Martin Luther King tells receptive audiences. Whoever opposes, or even doubts, that doctrine is cast in the role of a foe, whether he calls himself conservative or liberal. The middle ground on which the traditional liberal has taken his stand is being cut from beneath him.

Every civil rights victory adds to the Negro's intransigence; he becomes ever more impatient and demanding. To the extent that this attitude tends to precipitate radical conflict, a substantial number of liberals shy away. . . .

The liberal dilemma does not spring solely from doubts as to the advisability of direct action or the disobedience doctrine. The hard core of the difficulty lies in the circumstance that in the eighty years since the failure of Reconstruction, racial discrimination has become deeply rooted and thoroughly institutionalized in governmental agencies (local, state and federal), in the civil service and in churches, labor unions, political parties, professional organizations, schools, trade associations, service groups and in that vast array of voluntary organizations which play such a vital role in our society. Racial discrimination can't be uprooted unless government agencies are administered with that purpose in mind and unless voluntary organizations exert constant and consistent pressure to that end on local, state and federal governments, and at the same time accord Negroes all of the privileges and benefits that accrue from membership in such organizations. Those requirements aren't being met. Negroes are dismayed as they observe that liberals, even when they are in apparent control, not only do not rally their organizations for an effective role in the fight against discrimination, but even tolerate a measure of racial discrimination in their own jurisdictions.

Again, the liberal is restrained by his historical choice of seeing "both sides" of the issue. He understands the justice of the Negro's claim, but he argues that as a responsible administrator, he must reckon with deep-seated resistance to quick change and with the breakdown that might follow precipitate disruption of institutionalized practices. He may vacillate, as the President has done in the case of the Executive housing order, in an attempt to coax a consensus favorable to a change in policy. In any event, he is not, he says, as free as the Negro thinks; he must gauge the situation and settle for progress in the face of Negro clamor for immediate action. . . .

Civil service is a trap for unwary Negroes who enter it and

find themselves frozen in its lower reaches. The United States Civil Rights Commission has found that, just as in private industry, there are "Negro" jobs and "white" jobs with Negroes at the bottom of the civil service heap. The liberal who comes to head a civil service-staffed department of government is caught in a web of rules and regulations deliberately designed, in some instances, to institutionalize racial discrimination, or having that effect. Again there may be token appointments and token promotions, but the establishment yields slowly. The Negro looks for results and what he sees often makes him take the cynical position that the liberal differs no whit from his conservative predecessor.

Or take the situation in the AFL-CIO, where discrimination is rife in craft unions. The federation professes an inability to compel constituent unions to abandon time-honored racial practices. That is bad enough. What is worse is the stance of liberal-led industrial unions. The Steelworkers maintain Jim Crow locals in the South, where union halls double in brass as meeting places for White Citizens Councils. It is an open secret that Negroes have next to nothing to say in the policy-making bodies of unions, craft or industrial, on local, state or national levels. When the Pullman Porters' A. Philip Randolph, the only Negro member of the AFL-CIO Executive Board, urged reforms in federation, George Meany, described in labor circles as a liberal, shouted at him, "Who the hell gave you the right to speak for Negroes?" and accused him of attacking the labor movement. The Executive Board, at Meany's urging, then censured Randolph for antiunion activities—without a dissent from such liberals as Walter Reuther or David Dubinsky. Randolph's answer was the formation of a *Negro* labor council; he was denounced again by labor leaders of all shades of opinion on the ground that he was fathering "Jim Crow in reverse." Yet for many years, the AFL-CIO has thrown its official weight behind state and federal fair housing, fair employment and other civil rights legislation and has assisted in tests of segregatory laws.

An examination of the practices of other voluntary organizations, including churches, would produce a similar yield of institutionalized discriminatory practices. In almost every case in which the leadership of such organizations is classified as liberal, there has been announced public support of civil rights objectives. Everybody seems to want everybody else to practice what he preaches and nobody seems to be able, or willing, to practice what everybody else preaches.

It is very easy to charge hypocrisy in the situation, but what is really at play here is a cleavage between the burgeoning Freedom Now thinking of the Negro and the old progress concept to which liberals still cling. That conflict flares into the open when liberals exercise the prerogative, long held by them, of speaking *for* the Negro, and of espousing views which the Negro is abandoning. The liberal custom of speaking for the Negro is rooted in history; there was a time when the Negro needed spokesmen. Inevitably, a measure of paternalism and a father-knows-best attitude developed. But as the Negro becomes more articulate and discerning, he insists on voicing his own aspirations, particularly in the light of what he regards as the shortcomings of liberal leadership.

When the Negro insists on speaking for himself, the rebuffed liberal may shout at Meany did at Randolph that the dissenters are agitators or trouble makers (another replication, in a liberal context, of a familiar Southern cliché). Others take the tack popularized by John Fischer in *Harper's* and, transforming themselves into spokesmen for all whites, issue stern warnings that discrimination will prevail until all Negroes conform to middle-class standards of morality—a cozy variant of the theme that all Negroes are chargeable with the sins of every Negro. Negroes aren't dismayed at the opposition to their taking matters into their own hands. Detroit Negroes, led by unionists, revolted against the UAW's mayoralty endorsement in that city and turned the tide against the union's choice; the NAACP and the AFL-CIO are increasingly at odds over the treatment of Negroes in the labor movement; Roy Wilkins defended bloc voting by Negroes in his Atlanta keynote speech. Muslims are drawing substantial urban support by proposing to have done with all "white devils."

There is a growing cynicism about the current stress being laid on absolute fairness in public and private employment and in political appointments—beginning as of today. The Negro wants a little more than that. One hundred years of racial discrimination have produced a wide gap between him and white Americans. The Negro wants that gap closed in political appointments, in civil service, in schools and in private industry. He sees no way to close it unless he gets preferential treatment. Logic favors his position, but such a proposal runs into opposition from those who argue, correctly, that preferential treatment cannot be extended to a Negro without impinging on the personal rights of the white person over whom he will be preferred.

In truth, the impasse between liberals and Negroes is the end-product of a long historical process in which Americans of African, or partially African, descent have been treated as Negroes rather than as individuals, in legal lore as well as in popular concept. But constitutional protections run to persons —individuals—rather than to groups; American idealism exalts the individual and insists that group identification is an irrelevance. The liberal's historic concern is with individual rights and he seeks to apply that formula in the area of race relations. The Negro, whose ultimate ideal is the attainment of the right to be treated as an individual without reference to his racial identification, sees his immediate problem as that of raising the status of the group to which he has been consigned by popular attitude and action and by laws which permit racial classification. The liberal sees progress in the admission of a few select Negro children to a hitherto white school; the Negro wants all Negro children admitted and spurns the concession as mere tokenism. . . .

It is against this background, and to some extent because of it, that the young Negro militants "don't believe in liberals at all." Profoundly influenced by the overthrow of white colonialism in Asia and Africa, they not only want Freedom Now, but insist on substituting a grand strategy for the liberal tactics of fighting one civil rights battle at a time. They are determined to plot the strategy and dictate the tactics of the campaign. The details of the grand strategy haven't been blueprinted as yet, but in bold outline it calls for direct action by way of sit-ins, stand-ins, kneel-ins, boycotts, freedom rides, civil disobedience and as-yet-unheard-of techniques as the occasion demands, with resort to legal action when expedient—all under Negro leadership, all calculated to produce immediate results. Heavy stress is being laid on voter registration in the Deep South and it is significant that student leaders make no bones about the fact that *Negro* voting is seen as a device to elect *Negroes* to public office. The very choice of weapons, incidentally, requires action by Negroes. Only Negroes can desegregate a cafe or a hotel or an airport by a sit-in, or a beach by a wade-in, or a church by a kneel-in, or withdraw Negro patronage through a boycott.

It would not be accurate to say that the direct actionists speak for all Negroes under all circumstances. It is fair to say that their philosophy is ascendant, that their influence is becoming pervasive and that their voices are heard with increasing respect and diminishing dissent in Negro communities. Those voices are harsh and strident, and jarring to the liberal ear. Their message is plain: To liberals a fond farewell, with thanks for services rendered, until you are ready to re-enlist as foot soldiers and subordinates in a Negro-led, Negro-officered army under the banner of Freedom Now.

Crisis in Black and White*

CHARLES E. SILBERMAN

NEGROES' DETERMINATION TO speak and act on their own behalf has produced the greatest strain where it was least expected: in the alliance that bound Negro organizations, civil rights
and civil liberties groups, interfaith organizations, church
groups, and trade unions together in a great liberal coalition.
Quite suddenly in 1962 and 1963—or so it seemed to the
white liberals—they found themselves under bitter attack and
heard themselves denounced in terms usually reserved for the
most rabid southern racists.

The reasons lie deep in the history of the civil rights movement—particularly in the fact that the movement has been
dominated by whites until fairly recently. . . . There was a
vacuum of Negro leadership and Negro support that could be
filled only by whites. Thus, the NAACP was founded by
whites because the Niagara Movement was falling apart, and
whites provided much of the leadership and financial support
until recent years.[1] Whites still provide most of the funds
raised by Martin Luther King's Southern Christian Leadership Conference; for all his charismatic appeal, he has been
unable to raise more than a fraction of the funds he needs
from the Negro community. Equally important, the civil
rights organizations depended on political support from white
liberals—trade unions, civil liberties organizations, interfaith
organizations, church groups, and the like. Negroes depended
on the liberal coalition because their own strength was too
slight to offer any chance of victory. . . .

But Negroes always resented the relationship; their dependence on their white allies created an underlying animus that
was no less real for being carefully suppressed. Besides re-
senting their dependency, Negroes have never really trusted

* From CRISIS IN BLACK AND WHITE, by Charles E. Silberman.
© Copyright 1964 by Random House, Inc. Reprinted by permission.

[1] The NAACP proper now draws most of its revenues from Negroes;
income comes largely from membership dues, and the membership is
predominantly Negro. The separate NAACP Legal Defense and Education Fund, however, whose budget is about as large as that of the
NAACP proper, still draws most of its revenue from white contribu-
tors.

their white allies; they have always had a nagging suspicion that the whites were holding them back, that they could gain more, and faster, if they were only free to act on their own. "They are betraying us again, these white friends of ours," one of the Negro participants shouted during the meeting at which the NAACP was founded; and other Negroes have echoed this cry ever since. In the lengthy monograph on Negro organizations and leadership which he prepared for Gunnar Myrdal in 1942, for example, Ralph Bunche delivered a stinging attack on the NAACP's interracial composition:

The interracial make-up of the NAACP is an undoubted source of organizational weakness. There can be no doubt that the Negro leaders in the organization have always kept a weather eye on the reactions of their prominent and influential white sponsors . . . These white sympathizers are, in the main, either cautious liberals or mawkish, missionary-minded sentimentalists on the race question. Their interest in the Negro problem is motivated either by a sense of "fair play" and a desire to see the ideals of the Constitution lived up to, or an "I love your people" attitude. Both attitudes are far from touching the realities of the problem.[2] But the evident concern for the opinions of the white supporters of the organization, especially on the part of the National Office, has been a powerful factor in keeping the Association thoroughly "respectable," and has certainly been an influence in the very evident desire of the Association to keep its skirts free of the grimy bitterness and strife encountered in the economic area . . . The liberal . . . recognizes and revolts against injustices, but seeks to correct them with palliatives rather than solutions; for the solutions are harsh and forbidding, and are not conducive to optimism and spiritual uplift.

The point is not whether this animus against white supporters was justified. In large measure it was not; at the time Bunche wrote, the NAACP depended on white support because it could not get support from Negroes. Indeed, the apathy and disinterest of the Negro community was revealed dramatically in 1948, when the NAACP raised its minimum dues from $1 to $2—and lost half its membership as a result; membership did not return to the old level until the early 1960s. What is crucial is that Negroes *did* resent and distrust their white allies long before they felt secure enough to express it. And their resentment, while not particularly admirable, certainly is understandable; people who are permanently on the receiving end come to hate their benefactors, as the

---

[2] Ironically enough, when Adam Clayton Powell attacked the NAACP in similar terms in 1963, Dr. Bunche denounced him as a racist as dangerous as the Southern white racists.

United States is discovering with its foreign aid program. "The politics of life do not provide for equality when one is always in the high position of the magnanimous giver and the other in the low position of the grateful receiver," Saul Alinsky has written. "This kind of relationship is devoid of that dignity essential to equality."

If Negroes are to gain a sense of potency and dignity, it is essential, therefore, that they take the initiative in action on their own behalf. For the moment, at least, it is far more important that things be done *by* Negroes than that they be done *for* them, even if they are not done as well. Whites will have to learn that most difficult lesson of parenthood: to allow one's children to become adults. Whites, that is to say, will have to abandon their tradition of command and their habit of speaking for, and acting for, the Negroes. Their role must be limited: to stimulate indigenous leadership and activity, and then to retire to the sidelines—to retire to the sidelines even if the black neophytes are making mistakes. To the suggestion that Negroes are too inexperienced to get things done properly, some Negroes are likely to retort with the remark of Jomo Kenyatta: "If there is going to be a mess, let it be a black mess." Given the historical pattern of dependency, in short, there seems to be no way of avoiding a certain amount of race chauvinism; it is ironic but nonetheless necessary that, for a time at least, organizations working on behalf of Negroes be led and manned largely by Negroes. This does not mean that Negroes do not want help from white liberals. They expect it—but on their own terms. . . .

There is another source of strain between Negroes and white liberals that is likely to take on more importance as the years go by: the fact that when the struggle for Negro rights moves into the streets, the majority of liberals are reluctant to move along with it. They are all for the Negroes' *objectives,* they say, but they cannot go along with the *means.* Rightly or wrongly, Negroes receive this sort of statement with a good deal of cynicism; as Bismarck once remarked, "When you say that you agree to a thing in principle, you mean that you have not the slightest intention of carrying it out in practice."

The problem is a real one. There is a fundamental difference in the situation of Negroes and of whites that leads almost inevitably to conflict over tactics and strategy: Negroes are outside the main stream of middle-class American life, whereas their liberal allies are on the inside. Hence the latter have a deep interest in preserving the status quo, in the sense of maintaining peace and harmony. The trade union movement, for example, is no more racist than any other group, and probably less so; yet to the Negro, labor acts as a conservative establishment primarily concerned with maintaining the job monopolies of its members.

Other liberals want only to maintain the peace and comfort of the lives they now enjoy; they want racial change, all right, but without trouble or turmoil, and without upsetting the existing organizations and institutional arrangements. Indeed, the whole profession of "inter-group relations" is dedicated to the goal of preventing or minimizing tension and conflict, with persuasion the favored technique; the approach inherently assumes gradualism, since it takes some time to rid people of prejudice or to change their minds. But the Negro, as David Danzig has written in *Commentary*, is "no longer addressing himself to the white man's attitude of prejudice toward color, with the gradualism that this approach compels; he now confronts the white community on the issue of Negro rights and opportunities as a matter of politics, economic power, and justice." And so "whites whose ultimate perspective on race relations envisaged the gradual absorption of deserving Negroes one by one into white society are suddenly hard-pressed to come to terms with a demanding Negro community."

The point is that changes of the sort Negroes now demand, at the speed they insist upon, cannot be provided without considerable conflict: too many Americans will have to give up some privilege or advantage they now enjoy or surrender the comforting sense of their own superiority. There is nothing in American history, past or present, to suggest that Negroes can gain their rightful place in American society without direct confrontation. In Frederick Douglass' words, "If there is no struggle, there is no progress. Those who profess to favor freedom, and yet deprecate agitation, are men who want crops without plowing up the ground. They want rain without thunder and lightning. They want the ocean without the awful roar of its waters." . . .

The Black Revolution and the White Backlash*

JOHN O. KILLENS, JAMES WECHSLER, LORRAINE HANSBERRY

MR. JOHN O. KILLENS: . . . How many white liberals are prepared to go all the way? How many will fall on the side, fall on the wayside at the first turn of the road? How many will be like Gideon's army? You know, Gideon was testing his army out, I believe. He asked for all—he put them through quite a few tests and when he got ready to fight, he only had about three hundred.

How many are the winter soldiers of white America? How many are the sunshine patriots? How many cold war liberals will desert our ranks when we assert the right of self-defense? [Applause] Because we must assert this right. We must affirm this right. This is one of the most fundamental rights recognized by all men everywhere, because we must dispel this new myth. You know, Negroes have always been trapped in so many myths. Now there's a myth that the Negro is nonviolent. [Laughter]

. . . will the liberals of white America desert our ranks when we say that we will not love our enemies? That's a pretty sick bit, anyhow. [Laughter and applause] Unrequited love.

For example, what if Harlem organized a vigilante group? Would the newspapers and the police be so tolerant? To defend themselves. [Applause]

And another big test is where will the cold war liberals be when we place our case before the United Nations, [applause] which we must do in due time since it is a case of a denial of human rights? [Applause] I believe there is a Human Rights Commission. When we assert our rights to political power, when we assert our rights to speak for ourselves and for the nation in all the halls of the legislatures throughout the land, how many white liberals care about the nation enough to criticize us fundamentally? Because I got a feeling

---

* Excerpts from a transcript of a forum sponsored by the Association of Artists for Freedom at Town Hall, New York, June 15, 1964. Panel members were: Ossie Davis, Ruby Dee, Lorraine Hansberry, Leroi Jones, John Killens, Paule Marshall, Charles E. Silberman, James Wechsler, and David Susskind, moderator.

the white liberals that—you know, America is sick, America is sick and is in need of basic surgery while the Madison Avenue fellows with more sense than anybody sitting here try to cure the world with plastic surgery, with a face uplifting job when she needs basic surgery.

There are a few myths we must be willing to relinquish. The one that I mentioned before, that there is no revolution yet; another one, that we have let the establishment get by a long time on, is telling us that we are second-class citizens. Who in the hell ever heard of a second-class citizen until they were invented in the United States? [Applause] A person is either a citizen or he is not a citizen. You are either free or you are a slave. Thank you. [Laughter and applause] It's like being a woman that is half pregnant. [Laughter]

The backlash is a counterrevolution before the revolution has gotten underway.

Another myth—and we've kept ourselves in this trap too —is to imagine that we are all one big happy family. We're not even all one big unhappy family. [Laughter] You know, if we're all one big happy family, this means, of course, that the Negro must not think of embarrassing big daddy before the world, you see.

The United Nations—with this big family approach, the United Nations and a lot of other avenues of protest are ruled out. It's like a woman whose husband beats her and she doesn't cry out loud because she doesn't want the neighbors to know. Well, if we play that role, we deserve to be beaten. [Applause]

So many liberals in the freedom movement are long on advice and short on action. [Applause] . . . too many are willing to lead us down the freedom road but not to follow black leadership. But in the final analysis, that is how it must be, that is how it will be. American black folk will with white assistance great or small change America if it can be changed and that's what it's all about, to change the country fundamentally and lead her out of the muck and mire of obsolescence of nineteenth-century racialism into the new world of the freedom century which is already magnificently here all over the world. You know, I really marvel at the patience and fortitude displayed by many liberal Americans in the face of other people's degradation. . . .

Fortunately or unfortunately, depending on your point of view, the black move generally speaking is one of great impatience to emancipate the country. Thank you. [Applause]

MR. JAMES WECHSLER: I would not contribute anything to the spirit of this evening nor would I honor those who have spoken before me if I were simply to say that I agree with some of the things that have been said, or even to cite them. I assume that we are here for an authentic dialogue and not for a resignation of—[applause].

Perhaps I should first begin by disagreeing with Mr. Silberman's suggestion that the white has the role of water boy in the freedom movement and that he'd better damned well accept it. I find myself increasingly, as I grow older, feeling that old fashioned American liberalism had some great, deep strains. One of them was the sense that separatism was disastrous to any human cause. . . .

I find it hard to participate in some of the conversation here tonight because it is my own conviction that the issue we're discussing is essentially in many areas, in its most profound senses, a social—a status conflict. We talked, I think, in some of the discussions of what this meeting was about that who spoke for whom. I should like to venture the opinion that all of us on this platform don't speak for a hell of a lot of people. [Applause] I should like to venture to remind those who have spoken here tonight with great militancy on certain aspects of this situation that the latest opinion polls show that among Negroes as well as among whites, Lyndon Johnson is the most popular American. Now, you may not like that. You may not like it and it may disturb your own preconceptions about life. It just happens to be the facts of life.

And let me add further that I found myself—and I noticed some of you laughing as if to suggest that this is an implausibility. Well, I suggest that you read the poll.

Now, let me go beyond that to a more serious point. There were many moments this evening when I felt that the discussion here did not involve white liberals. It involved the question of whether Jim Farmer was Jim Crow. Now, I submit that this suggestion that the Negro leadership has somehow betrayed the cause of civil rights, that we need some great new organization under some undesignated auspices, is to me again no contribution to the very difficult and dangerous and dramatic times in which we live. [Applause]

And I do not believe that those who say these things do speak for any substantial portion of the American community.

. . . I think the underlying difficulty in our discussion really is that we have somehow passed from a question of complexity of the problems that we face into a series of assaults on the—I was going to say responsible Negro leadership, but now the word responsible, it's assumed, has become a very bad word. Now when we went to school, the opposite of responsible was irresponsible and I find it very hard to regard this as a terrible word. I don't happen to be in favor of the word moderation, but I do not believe that it is an essential characteristic and qualification for leadership to demonstrate one's irresponsibility.

And so, let me in two final remarks perhaps dramatize my point. It is easy to say that in revolutions we blow up the bridge. The truth of the matter is, however, that one of the greatest revolutions in our time was conducted by a man named Gandhi. The truth of the matter is that he didn't blow up any bridges. And those of you who murmur at this I assume are going to suggest that the people of India were really having a pretty mellow time until Gandhi took over. Well, I think this is a matter of difference.

I find it embarrassing and weird that I am here tonight pleading with some of you to recognize that the message of Martin Luther King still has some meaning and that perhaps those of you on this platform [applause] who have repudiated it are indulging yourselves without serving what I regard as a common cause.

And finally, let me say in the same spirit that just as I believe that one ought to speak with damned free candor in this discussion if it's to mean anything, I have found as the editor of a newspaper in this town and as a writer of editorials that there are those who regard criticism of Adam Clayton Powell as tantamount to a form of treason; I would take the view that the tragedy—one of the tragedies of our time is that A. Philip Randolph is not a member of the United States Senate and I am perfectly prepared to argue this point with anybody in the audience. As for Mr. Powell, I do wish that he'd spend a little more time working for his constituency and less time delivering orations. [Applause]

And I do have to add a final word which is I don't know what the phrase "cold war liberal" means. It does not seem to me that I must not care about the fate of Djilas in a Yugoslav prison in order to care about the freedom struggle in America. It does not seem to me that I must be tolerant of oppression and tyranny and enslavement in fascist and communist countries in order to be a participant in the freedom movement in America. . . . It seems to me that if there is any meaning to our struggle in this country, it is the obvious point that freedom and liberation are indivisible, and that goes from Africa to Hungary to Mississippi to Manhattan. [Applause]

MISS LORRAINE HANSBERRY: Was it ever so apparent we need this dialogue? [Applause]

How do you talk about three hundred years in four minutes? I wrote a letter to the *New York Times* recently which didn't get printed which is getting to be my rapport with the *New York Times*. They said that it was too personal. What it concerned itself with was, I was in a bit of a stew over the stall-in, because when the stall-in was first announced, I said, Oh, My God, everybody's gone crazy, you know, tying up traffic. What's the matter with them? You know. Who needs it? And then I noticed the reaction, starting in Washington and coming on up to New York among what we are all here calling the white liberal circles which was something like, you know, you Negroes act right or you're to ruin everything we're trying to do. [Laughter] And that got me to thinking more seriously about the strategy and the tactic that the stall-in intended to accomplish.

And so I sat down and wrote a letter to the *New York Times* about the fact that I am of a generation of Negroes that comes after a whole lot of other generations and my father, for instance, who was, you know, real American type American, successful businessman, very civic-minded and so forth, was the sort of American who put a great deal of money, a great deal of his really extraordinary talents and a great deal of passion into everything that we say is the American way of going after goals. That is to say that he moved his family into a restricted area where no Negroes were supposed to live and then proceeded to fight the case in the courts all the way to the Supreme Court of the United States. And this cost a great deal of money. It involved the assistance of the NAACP attorneys and so on and this is the way of struggling that everyone says is the proper way to do and it eventually resulted in a decision against restrictive covenants which is very famous, *Hansberry versus Lee*. And that was very much applauded.

But the problem is that Negroes are just as segregated in the city of Chicago now as they were then and my father died a disillusioned exile in another country. That is the reality that I'm faced with when I get up and I read that some Negroes my own age and younger say that we must now lie down in the streets, tie up traffic, stop ambulances, do whatever we can, take to the hills if necessary with some guns and fight back, you see. This is the difference.

And I wrote to the *Times* and said, "You know, can't you understand that this is the perspective from which we are now speaking. It isn't as if we got up today and say, you know, what can we do to irritate America, you know. It's because that since 1619, Negroes have tried every method of communication, of transformation of their situation from petition to the vote, everything. We've tried it all. There isn't anything that hasn't been exhausted. [It's] rather remarkable that we can talk about a people who were publishing newspapers while they were still in slavery in 1827, you see. We've been doing everything, writing editorials, Mr. Wechsler, for a long time, you know. [Applause]

And now the charge of impatience is simply unbearable. I would like to submit that the problem is that, yes, there is a problem about white liberals. I think there's something horrible that Norman Podhoretz, for instance, can sit down and write the kind of trash that he did at this hour.[1] [Applause] That is to say that a distinguished American thinker can literally say that he is more disturbed at the sight of a mixed couple or that anti-Semitism from Negroes and anti-Semitism from anybody is horrible and disgusting and I don't care where it comes from, but anti-Semitism, somehow, from a Negro apparently upsets him more than it would from a German fascist, you see. This was the implication of what really gets to him. Well, you have to understand that when we are confronted with that, we wonder who we are talking to and how far we are going to go.

The problem is we have to find some way with these dialogues to show and to encourage the white liberal to stop being a liberal and become an American radical. [Applause]

I think that then it wouldn't—will not become as true, some of the really eloquent things that were said before about the basic fabric of our society, which after all, is the thing which must be changed, you know, [applause] to really solve the problem, you know. The basic organization of American society is the thing that has Negroes in the situation that they are in and never let us lose sight of it.

When we then talk with that understanding, it won't be so difficult for people like Mr. Wechsler, whose sincerity I wouldn't dream of challenging, when I say to him—his sincerity is one thing; I don't have to agree with his position. But it wouldn't be so difficult for me to say, well, now, when someone uses the term "cold war liberal" that it is entirely different, you see, the way that you would assess the Vietnamese war and the way that I would because I can't believe

[1] The article, "My Negro Problem and Ours" by Norman Podhoretz, in the February 1963 *Commentary*, which presented miscegenation as the solution to *the* Negro problem. The reference here is to the following passage: "How, then, do I know that this hatred has never entirely disappeared? I know it from the insane rage that can stir in me at the thought of Negro anti-Semitism; I know it from the disgusting prurience that can stir in me at the sight of a mixed couple; and I know it from the violence that can stir in me whenever I encounter that special brand of paranoid touchiness to which many Negroes are prone."

[applause]—I can't believe that anyone who is given what an American Negro is given—you know, our viewpoint, can believe that a government which has at its disposal a Federal Bureau of Investigation which cannot ever find the murderers of Negroes and by that method [applause]—and shows that it cares really very little about American citizens who are black, really are over somewhere fighting a war for a bunch of other colored people, you know, [laughter] several thousand miles—you just have a different viewpoint. This is why we want the dialogue, to explain that to you, you see. It isn't a question of patriotism and loyalty. My brother fought for this country, my grandfather before that and so on and that's all a lot of nonsense when we criticize. The point is that we have a different viewpoint because, you know, we've been kicked in the face so often and the vantage point of Negroes is entirely different and these are some of the things we're trying to say. I don't want to go past my time. Thank you. [Applause]

2. BLACK POWER

*Malcolm X at the Audubon**

WHEN YOU GO back over the period of struggle, I think it would be agreed that we've gone through different patterns of struggle, that we've struggled in different ways. Each way that we tried never produced what we were looking for. If it had been productive, we would have continued along that same way. We've tried probably more different methods than any people. But at the same time, I think we've tried more wrong methods than any other people, because most others have gotten more freedom than we have. Everywhere you look, people get their freedom faster than we do. They get more respect and recognition faster than we do. We get promises, but we never get the real thing. And primarily because we have yet to learn the proper tactic or strategy or method to bring freedom into existence.

I think that one of the things that has caused our people in this country to try so many methods is that times have changed so rapidly. What would be proper ten years ago

* Malcolm X, *Malcolm X Speaks* (New York: Merit Publishers, 1965), excerpts from pp. 115-136.

would not have been proper seven years ago, or five years ago, or three years ago. . . .

Several persons have asked me recently, since I've been back, "What is your program?" I purposely, to this day, have not in any way mentioned what our program is, because there will come a time when we will unveil it so that everybody will understand it. Policies change, and programs change, according to time. But objective never changes. You might change your method of achieving the objective, but the objective never changes. Our objective is complete freedom, complete justice, complete equality, by any means necessary. That never changes. Complete and immediate recognition and respect as human beings, that doesn't change, that's what all of us want. I don't care what you belong to—you still want that, recognition and respect as a human being. But you have changed your methods from time to time on how you go about getting it. The reason you change your method is that you have to change your method according to time and conditions that prevail. And one of the conditions that prevails on this earth right now, that we know too little about, is our relationship with the freedom struggle of people all over the world. . . .

I, for one, believe that if you give people a thorough understanding of what it is that confronts them, and the basic causes that produce it, they'll create their own program; and when the people create a program, you get action. When these "leaders" create programs, you get no action. The only time you see them is when the people are exploding. Then the leaders are shot into the situation and told to control things. You can't show me a leader that has set off an explosion. No, they come and contain the explosion. They say, "Don't get rough, you know, do the smart thing." This is their role—they're there just to restrain you and me, to restrain the struggle, to keep it in a certain groove, and not let it get out of control. Whereas you and I don't want anybody to keep us from getting out of control. We want to get out of control. We want to smash anything that gets in our way that doesn't belong there. . . .

So, brothers and sisters, the thing that you and I must have an understanding of is the role that's being played in world affairs today, number one, by the continent of Africa; number two, by the people on that continent; number three, by those of us who are related to the people on that continent, but who, by some quirk in our own history, find ourselves today here in the Western hemisphere. Always bear that in mind that our being in the Western hemisphere differs from anyone else, because everyone else here came voluntarily.

Everyone that you see in this part of the world got on a boat and came here voluntarily; whether they were immigrants or what have you, they came here voluntarily. So they don't have any real squawk, because they got what they were looking for. But you and I can squawk because we didn't come here voluntarily. We didn't ask to be brought here. We were brought here forcibly, against our will, and in chains. And at no time since we have been here, have they even acted like they wanted us here. At no time. At no time have they even tried to pretend that we were brought here to be citizens. Why, they don't even *pretend*. So why should we pretend? . . .

This is the richest country on earth and there's poverty, there's bad housing, there's slums, there's inferior education. And this is the richest country on earth. Now, you know, if those countries that are poor can come up with a solution to their problems so that there's no unemployment, then instead of you running downtown picketing city hall, you should stop and find out what they do over there to solve their problems. This is why the man doesn't want you and me to look beyond Harlem or beyond the shores of America. As long as you don't know what's happening on the outside, you'll be all messed up dealing with this man on the inside. I mean what they use to solve the problem is not capitalism. What they are using to solve their problem in Africa and Asia is not capitalism. So what you and I should do is find out what they are using to get rid of poverty and all the other negative characteristics of a rundown society.

Africa is strategically located, geographically between East and West; it's the most valuable piece of property involved in the struggle between East and West. You can't get to the East without going past it, and can't get from the East to West without going past it. It sits right there between all of them. It sits snuggled into a nest between Asia and Europe; it can reach either one. None of the natural resources that are needed in Europe that they get from Asia can get to Europe without coming either around Africa, over Africa, or in between the Suez Canal which is sitting at the tip of Africa. She can cut off Europe's bread. She can put Europe to sleep overnight, just like that. Because she's in a position to; the African continent is in a position to do this. But they want you and me to think Africa is a jungle, of no value, of no consequence. Because they also know that if you knew how valuable it was, you'd realize why they're over there killing our people. And you'd realize that it's not for some kind of humanitarian purpose or reason. . . .

Another reason the continent is so important is because of

its gold. It has some of the largest deposits of gold on earth, and diamonds. Not only the diamonds you put on your finger and in your ear, but industrial diamonds, diamonds that are needed to make machines—machines that can't function or can't run unless they have these diamonds. These industrial diamonds play a major role in the entire industrialization of the European nations, and without these diamonds their industry would fall. . . .

Not only diamonds, but also cobalt. Cobalt is one of the most valuable minerals on this earth today, and I think Africa is one of the only places where it is found. They use it in cancer treatment, plus they use it in this nuclear field that you've heard so much about. Cobalt and uranium—the largest deposits are right there on the African continent. And this is what the man is after. The man is after keeping you over here worrying about a cup of coffee, while he's over there in your motherland taking control over minerals that have so much value they make the world go around. While you and I are still walking around over here, yes, trying to drink some coffee—with a cracker.

It's one of the largest sources of iron and bauxite and lumber and even oil, and Western industry needs all of these minerals in order to survive. All of these natural minerals are needed by the Western industrialists in order for their industry to keep running at the clip that it's been used to. . . .

I say this because it is necessary for you and me to understand what is at stake. You can't understand what is going on in Mississippi if you don't understand what is going on in the Congo. And you can't really be interested in what's going on in Mississippi if you're not also interested in what's going on in the Congo. They're both the same. The same interests are at stake. The same sides are drawn up, the same schemes are at work in the Congo that are at work in Mississippi. The same stake—no difference whatsoever. . . .

These people are beginning to see that. The Africans see it, the Latin Americans see it, the Asians see it. So when you hear them talking about freedom, they're not talking about a cup of coffee with a cracker. No, they're talking about getting in a position to feed themselves and clothe themselves and make these other things that, when you have them, make life worth living. So this is the way you and I have to understand the world revolution that's taking place right now.

When you understand the motive behind the world revolution, the drive behind the African and the drive behind the Asian, then you get some of that drive yourself. You'll be driving for real. The man downtown knows the difference between when you're driving for real and when you're driving not for real. As long as you keep asking about coffee, he doesn't have to worry about you; he can send you to Brazil. So these dams being set up over there in different parts of the continent are putting African nations in a position to have more power, to become more industrial and also to be self-sustained and self-sufficient. . . .

Politically, Africa as a continent, and the African people as a people, have the largest representation of any continent in the United Nations. Politically, the Africans are in a more strategic position and in a stronger position whenever a conference is taking place at the international level. Today, power is international, real power is international; today, real power is not local. The only kind of power that can help you and me is international power, not local power. . . .

. If your power base is only here, you can forget it. You can't build a power base here. You have to have a power base among brothers and sisters. . . .

When you see that the African nations at the international level comprise the largest representative body and the largest force of any continent, why, you and I would be out of our minds not to identify with that power bloc. . . .

*A Position Paper on Race**

MEMBERS OF THE ATLANTA PROJECT

IN ATTEMPTING TO analyze where the movement is going, certain questions have arisen as to the future roles played by white personnel. In order to make this issue clearer, we have written a few paragraphs, stemming from our observations and experiences, which serve as a preview to a broader study on the subject.

The answers to these questions lead us to believe that the form of white participation, as practiced in the past, is now obsolete. Some of the reasons are as follows:

The inability of whites to relate to the cultural aspects of Black society; attitudes that whites, consciously or unconsciously, bring to Black communities about themselves (western superiority) and about Black people (paternalism); inability to shatter white-sponsored community myths of Black inferiority and self-negation; inability to combat the views of

* Excerpts from a discussion paper by members of the Atlanta Project of the Student Nonviolent Coordinating Committee, presented to SNCC in 1966. The project has since been disbanded.

the Black community that white organizers, being "white,"
control Black organizers as puppets; insensitivity of both
Black and white workers towards the hostility of the Black
community on the issue of interracial "relationships" (sex);
the unwillingness of whites to deal with the *roots* of racism
which lie within the white community; whites though individually "liberal" are symbols of oppression to the Black community—due to the *collective* power that whites have over
Black lives.

Because of these reasons, which force us to view America
through the eyes of victims, we advocate a conscious change
in the role of whites, which will be in tune with the developing self-consciousness and self-assertion of the Afro-American people.

In concluding, we state that our position does not stem
from "hatred" or "racism" against white people, but from a
conscientious effort to develop the best methods of solving
our national *problem*. . . .

Negroes in this country have never been allowed to organize themselves because of white interference. As a result of
this the stereotype has been reinforced that Blacks cannot
organize themselves. The white psychology that Blacks have
to be watched also reinforces this stereotype. Blacks, in fact,
feel intimidated by the presence of whites, because of their
knowledge of the power that whites have over their lives.
One white person can come into a meeting of Black people
and change the complexion of that meeting, whereas one
Black person would not change the complexion of that meeting unless he was an obvious Uncle Tom. People would
immediately start talking about "brotherhood," "love," etc.;
race would not be discussed.

If people must express themselves freely, there has to be a
climate in which they can do this. If Blacks feel intimidated
by whites, then they are not liable to vent the rage that they
feel about whites in the presence of whites—especially not
the Black people whom we are trying to organize, i.e., the
broad masses of Black people. A climate has to be created
whereby Blacks can express themselves. The reason that
whites must be excluded is not that one is anti-white, but because the efforts that one is trying to achieve cannot succeed
because whites have an intimidating effect. Oft-times the intimidating effect is in direct proportion to the amount of degradation that Black people have suffered at the hands of
white people.

It must be offered that white people who desire change in
this country should go where that problem (of racism) is

most manifest. That problem is not in the Black community. The white people should go into white communities where the whites have created power for the express purpose of denying Blacks human dignity and self-determination. Whites who come into the Black community with ideas of change seem to want to absolve the power structure of its responsibility of what it is doing, and saying that change can only come through Black unity which is only the worst kind of paternalism. This is not to say that whites have not had an important role in the Movement. In the case of Mississippi, their role was the very key in that they helped give Blacks the right to organize, but that role is now over, and it should be. People now have the right to picket, the right to give out leaflets, the right to vote, the right to demonstrate, the right to print. . . .

If we are to proceed towards true liberation, we must cut ourselves off from white people . . . We must form our own institutions, credit unions, co-ops, political parties, write our own histories. One illustrating example is the SNCC "Freedom Primer." Blacks cannot relate to that book psychologically because white people wrote it and therefore it presents a white viewpoint. . . .

In an analysis of our history in this country we have been forced to come to the conclusion that 400 years of oppression and slavery suffered in this country by our Black forebears parallels in a very graphic way the oppression and colonization suffered by the African people. The questions can be rightfully asked, what part did the white colonizers play in the liberation of independent African Nations? who were the agitators for African independence? Answers to those questions compel us to believe that our struggle for liberation and self-determination can only be carried out effectively by Black people.

The necessity of dealing with the question of identity is of prime importance in our own struggle. The systematic destruction of our links to Africa, the cultural cut-off of Blacks in this country from Blacks in Africa are not situations that conscious Black people in this country are willing to accept. Nor are conscious Black people in this country willing to accept an educational system that teaches all aspects of western civilization and dismisses our Afro-American contribution with one week of inadequate information (Negro History Week) and deals with Africa not at all. Black people are not willing to align themselves with a western culture that daily emasculates our beauty, our pride and our manhood. It follows that white people being part of western civilization in a

way that Black people could never be are totally inadequate
to deal with Black identity which is the key to our struggle
for self-determination.

When it comes to the question of organizing Black people
we must insist that the people who come in contact with the
Black masses are not white people who, no matter what their
liberal leanings are, are not equipped to dispel the myths of
western superiority. White people only serve to perpetuate
these myths; rather, organizing must be done by Black people
who are able to see the beauty of themselves, are able to see
the important cultural contributions of Afro-Americans, are
able to see that this country was built upon the blood and
backs of our Black ancestors.

In an attempt to find a solution to our dilemma . . . we
propose that our organization (SNCC) should be Black-
staffed, Black-controlled and Black-financed. We do not want
to fall into a similar dilemma that other Civil Rights organizations have fallen. If we continue to rely upon white financial support we will find ourselves entwined in the tentacles
of the white power complex that controls this country. It is
also important that a Black organization (devoid of cultism)
be projected to our people so that it can be demonstrated that
such organizations are viable.

More and more we see Black people in this country being
used as a tool of the white liberal establishment. Liberal
whites have not begun to address themselves to the real problems of Black people in this country; witness their bewilderment, fear and anxiety when Nationalism is mentioned concerning Black people. An analysis of their (white liberal)
reaction to the word alone (Nationalism) reveals a very
meaningful attitude of whites of any ideological persuasion
towards Blacks in this country. It means that previous solutions to Black problems in this country have been made in
the interests of those whites dealing with these problems and
not in the best interests of the Black people in this country.
Whites can only subvert our true search and struggle for
self-determination, self-identification, and liberation in this
country. Re-evaluation of the white and Black roles must
now take place so that whites no longer designate roles that
Black people play but rather Black people define white people's roles.

Too long have we allowed white people to interpret the importance and meaning of the cultural aspects of our society.
We have allowed them to tell us what was good about our
Afro-American music, art and literature. How many Black
critics do we have on the "jazz" scene? How can a white per-

son who is not a part of the Black psyche (except in the oppressors role) interpret the meaning of the Blues to us who are manifestations of the songs themselves?

It must also be pointed out that on whatever level of contact that Blacks and whites come together, that meeting or confrontation is not on the level of the Blacks but always on the level of whites. This only means that our everyday contact with whites is a reinforcement of the myth of white supremacy. Whites are the ones who must try to raise themselves to our humanistic level. We are not, after all, the ones who are responsible for a genocidal war in Vietnam; we are not the ones who are responsible for Neo-Colonialism in Africa and Latin America; we are not the ones who held a people in animalistic bondage over 400 years.

We reject the American Dream as defined by white people and must work to construct an American reality defined by Afro-Americans. . . .

It is a very grave error to mistake Black self-assertion for racism or Black supremacy. Black people in this country more so than the colonial peoples of the world know what it means to be victims of racism, bigotry, and slavery. Realizing our predicament from these inhuman attitudes it would be ridiculous for us to turn around and perpetuate the same reactionary outlook on other people. We more than anyone else realize the importance of achieving the type of society, the type of world whereby people can be viewed as human beings. The means of reaching these goals must be, however, from the point of view of respecting the differences between peoples and cultures and not pretending that everyone is the same; the refusal to respect differences is one of the reasons that the world is exploding today. Also, expanding upon the differences among peoples and the respect [these differences] should be accorded: if one looks at "integration" as progress then one is really perpetuating the myth of white supremacy. One is saying that Blacks have nothing to contribute, and should be willing to assimilate into the mainstream of the great white civilization i.e., the West.

A thorough re-examination must be made by Black people concerning the contributions that we have made in shaping this country. If this re-examination and re-evaluation is not made, and Black people are not given their proper and due respect, then the antagonisms and contradictions are going to become more and more glaring, more and more intense until a national explosion may result. . . .

Malcolm Was a Man*

OSSIE DAVIS

Mr. Davis wrote the following in response to a magazine editor's question: Why did you eulogize Malcolm X?

YOU ARE NOT the only person curious to know why I would eulogize a man like Malcolm X. Many who know and respect me have written letters. Of these letters I am proudest of those from a sixth-grade class of young white boys and girls who asked me to explain. I appreciate your giving me this chance to do so.

You may anticipate my defense somewhat by considering the following fact: no Negro has yet asked me that question. (My pastor in Grace Baptist Church where I teach Sunday school preached a sermon about Malcolm in which he called him a "giant in a sick world.") Every one of the many letters I got from my own people lauded Malcolm as a man, and commended me for having spoken at his funeral.

At the same time—and this is important—most all of them took special pains to disagree with much or all of what Malcolm said and what he stood for. That is, with one singing exception, they all, every last, black, glory-hugging one of them, knew that Malcolm—whatever else he was or was not —*Malcolm was a man!*

White folks do not need anybody to remind them that they are men. We do! This was his one incontrovertible benefit to his people.

Protocol and common sense require that Negroes stand back and let the white man speak up for us, defend us, and lead us from behind the scene in our fight. This is the essence of Negro politics. But Malcolm said to hell with that! Get up off your knees and fight your own battles. That's the way to win back your self-respect. That's the way to make the white man respect you. And if he won't let you live like a man, he certainly can't keep you from dying like one!

Malcolm, as you can see, was refreshing excitement; he scared hell out of the rest of us, bred as we are to caution, to

* Ossie Davis in *The Autobiography of Malcolm X*, Malcolm X (New York: Grove Press, Inc., 1964), pp. 453-55. Reprinted by permission of Grove Press, Inc. Copyright © 1964 by Alex Haley and Malcolm X, © 1965 by Alex Haley and Betty Shabazz; and by permission of Ossie Davis. Mr. Davis was one of the speakers at the funeral of Malcolm X.

hypocrisy in the presence of white folks, to the smile that never fades. Malcolm knew that every white man in America profits directly or indirectly from his position vis-à-vis Negroes, profits from racism even though he does not practice it or believe in it.

He also knew that every Negro who did not challenge on the spot every instance of racism, overt or covert, committed against him and his people, who chose instead to swallow his spit and go on smiling, was an Uncle Tom and a traitor, without balls or guts, or any other commonly accepted aspects of manhood!

Now, we knew all these things as well as Malcolm did, but we also knew what happened to people who stick their necks out and say them. And if all the lies we tell ourselves by way of extenuation were put into print, it would constitute one of the great chapters in the history of man's justifiable cowardice in the face of other men.

But Malcolm kept snatching our lies away. He kept shouting the painful truth we whites and blacks did not want to hear from all the housetops. And he wouldn't stop for love nor money.

You can imagine what a howling, shocking nuisance this man was to both Negroes and whites. Once Malcolm fastened on you, you could not escape. He was one of the most fascinating and charming men I have ever met, and never hesitated to take his attractiveness and beat you to death with it. Yet his irritation, though painful to us, was most salutary. He would make you angry as hell, but he would also make you proud. It was impossible to remain defensive and apologetic about being a Negro in his presence. He wouldn't let you. And you always left his presence with the sneaky suspicion that maybe, after all, you *were* a man!

But in explaining Malcolm, let me take care not to explain him away. He had been a criminal, an addict, a pimp, and a prisoner; a racist, and a hater, he had really believed the white man was a devil. But all this had changed. Two days before his death, in commenting to Gordon Parks about his past life he said: "That was a mad scene. The sickness and madness of those days! I'm glad to be free of them."

And Malcolm was free. No one who knew him before and after his trip to Mecca could doubt that he had completely abandoned racism, separatism, and hatred. But he had not abandoned his shock-effect statements, his bristling agitation for immediate freedom in this country not only for blacks, but for everybody.

And most of all, in the area of race relations, he still delighted in twisting the white man's tail, and in making Uncle

Toms, compromisers, and accommodatio̶n̶
include myself—thoroughly ashamed of the
ing hypocrisy we practice merely to exist in a
values we both envy and despise.

But even had Malcolm not changed, he would
been a relevant figure on the American scene, standin̶
lation as he does, to the "responsible" civil rights leaders̶
about where John Brown stood in relation to the "respo̶r̶
ble" abolitionist in the fight against slavery. Almost all disa̶
greed with Brown's mad and fanatical tactics which led him
foolishly to attack a Federal arsenal at Harpers Ferry, to lose
two sons there, and later to be hanged for treason.

Yet, today the world, and especially the Negro people, proclaim Brown not a traitor, but a hero and a martyr in a noble
cause. So in future, I will not be surprised if men come to see
that Malcolm X was, within his own limitations, and in his
own inimitable style, also a martyr in that cause.

But there is much controversy still about this most controversial American, and I am content to wait for history to
make the final decision.

But in personal judgment, there is no appeal from instinct.
I knew the man personally, and however much I disagreed
with him, I never doubted that Malcolm X, even when he
was wrong, was always that rarest thing in the world among
us Negroes: a true man.

And if, to protect my relations with the many good white
folks who make it possible for me to earn a fairly good living
in the entertainment industry, I was too chicken, too cautious, to admit that fact when he was alive, I thought at least
that now, when all the white folks are safe from him at last, I
could be honest with myself enough to lift my hat for one
final salute to that brave, black, ironic gallantry, which was
his style and hallmark, that shocking *zing* of fire-and-be-
damned-to-you, so absolutely absent in every other Negro
man I know, which brought him, too soon, to his death.

Black Power*

STOKELY CARMICHAEL

. . . It seems to me that the institutions that function in
this country are clearly racist, and that they're built upon rac-

* "Black Power," speech by Stokely Carmichael, former chairman of
the Student Nonviolent Coordinating Committee, University of California, Berkeley, November 19, 1966. Transcribed from taped remarks.

...is, how can black people inside
...how can white people, who say
...institutions, begin to move, and
...clear away the obstacles that we
...keep us from living like human
...o build institutions that will allow
...ther as human beings? This coun-
...Especially around the concept of

...been upset because we've said
...nt when initiated by blacks and
...fuge, an insidious subterfuge for
the maintenance of white supremacy. We maintain that in the
past six years or so this country has been feeding us a thalid-
omide drug of integration, and that some Negroes have been
walking down a dream street talking about sitting next to
white people, and that that does not begin to solve the problem. When we went to Mississippi, we did not go to sit next
to Ross Barnett; we did not go to sit next to Jim Clark; we
went to get them out of our way, and people ought to understand that. We were never fighting for the right to integrate,
we were fighting against white supremacy. . . .

Now we are engaged in a psychological struggle in this
country and that struggle is whether or not black people have
the right to use the words they want to use without white
people giving their sanction to it. We maintain, whether they
like it or not, we gon' use the word "black power" and let
them address themselves to that. We are not gonna wait for
white people to sanction black power. We're tired of waiting.
Every time black people move in this country, they're forced
to defend their position before they move. It's time that the
people who're supposed to be defending their position do
that. That's white people. They ought to start defending
themselves, as to why they have oppressed and exploited us.

It is clear that when this country started to move in terms
of slavery, the reason for a man being picked as a slave was
one reason: because of the color of his skin. If one was
black, one was automatically inferior, inhuman, and therefore
fit for slavery. So that the question of whether or not we are
individually suppressed is nonsensical and is a downright lie.
We are oppressed as a group because we are black, not because we are lazy, not because we're apathetic, not because
we're stupid, not because we smell, not because we eat wa-
termelon and have good rhythm. We are oppressed because
we are black, and in order to get out of that oppression, one
must feel the group power that one has. Not the individual

power which this country then sets the criteria under which a man may come into it. That is what is called in this country as integration. You do what I tell you to do, and then we'll let you sit at the table with us. And then we are saying that we have to be opposed to that. We must now set a criteria, and that if there's going to be any integration it's going to be a two-way thing. If you believe in integration, you can come live in Watts. You can send your children to the ghetto schools. Let's talk about that. If you believe in integration, then we're going to start adopting us some white people to live in our neighborhood. So it is clear that the question is not one of integration or segregation. Integration is a man's ability to want to move in there by himself. If someone wants to live in a white neighborhood and he is black, that is his choice. It should be his right. It is not because white people will allow him. So vice-versa, if a black man wants to live in the slums, that should be his right. Black people will let him, that is the difference.

It is this difference which points up the logical mistakes this country makes when it begins to criticize the program articulated by SNCC. We maintain that we cannot afford to be concerned about 6 percent of the children in this country. I mean the black children who you allow to come into white schools. We have 94 percent who still live in shacks. We are going to be concerned about those 94 percent. You ought to be concerned about them, too. The question is, are we willing to be concerned about those 94 percent. Are we willing to be concerned about the black people who will never get to Berkeley, who will never get to Harvard and cannot get an education, so you'll never get a chance to rub shoulders with them and say, "Well he's almost as good as we are; he's not like the others." The question is, how can white society begin to move to see black people as human beings? I am black, therefore I am. Not that I am black and I must go to college to prove myself. I am black, therefore I am. And don't surprise me with anything and say to me that you must go to college before you gain access to X, Y, and Z. It is only a rationalization for one's oppression.

The political parties in this country do not meet the needs of the people on a day-to-day basis. The question is, how can we build new political institutions that will become the political expressions of people on a day-to-day basis. The question is, how can you build political institutions that will begin to meet the needs of Oakland, California; and the needs of Oakland, California is not 1,000 policemen with submachine guns. They don't need that. They need that least of all. The question is, how can we build institutions where those people can begin to function on a day-to-day basis, where they can get decent jobs, where they can get decent housing, and where they can begin to participate in the policy and major decisions that affect their lives. That's what they need. Not Gestapo troops. Because this is not 1942. And if you play like Nazis, we're playing back with you this time around. Get hip to that.

The question then is, how can white people move to start making the major institutions that they have in this country function the way they are supposed to function? That is the real question. And can white people move inside their own community and start tearing down racism where, in fact, it does exist? It is you who live in Cicero and stop us from living there. It is white people who stop us from moving into Grenada. It is white people who make sure that we live in the ghettos of this country. It is white institutions that do that. They must change. In order for America to really live on a basic principle of human relationships, a new society must be born. Racism must die, and the economic exploitation of this country, of non-white people around the world, must also die.

There are several programs that we have in the South among some poor white communities. We're trying to organize poor whites on a base where they can begin to move around the question of economic exploitation and political disenfranchisement. We know we've heard the theory several times, but few people are willing to go into this. The question is, can the white activist not try to be a Pepsi generation who comes alive in the black community, but that he be a man who's willing to move into the white community and start organizing where the organization is needed? . . .

We've been saying that we cannot have white people working in the black community and we've based it on psychological grounds. The fact is that all black people often question whether or not they are equal to whites because everytime they start to do something white people are around showing them how to do it. If we are going to eliminate that for the generations that come after us, then black people must be seen in positions of power doing and articulating for themselves. . . .

Now then, the question is, how can we move to begin to change what's going on in this country? I maintain, as we have in SNCC, that the war in Vietnam is an illegal and immoral war. And the question is, what can we do to stop that war. What can we do to stop the people who, in the name of our country, are killing babies, women and children. What

can we do to stop that? And I maintain that we do not have
the power in our hands to change that institution, to begin to
recreate it so that they learn to leave the Vietnamese people
alone, and that the only power we have is the power to say
"Hell, no!" to the draft. . . . There isn't one organization
that has begun to meet our stand on the war in Vietnam. Because we not only say we are against the war in Vietnam; *we
are against the draft.* We are against the draft. No man has
the right to take a man for two years and train him to be a
killer. . . .

It is impossible for white and black people to talk about
building a relationship based on humanity when the country
is the way it is, when the institutions are clearly against us.
We have taken all the myths of this country and we've found
them to be nothing but downright lies. This country told us
that if we worked hard we would succeed, and if that were
true we would own this country lock, stock and barrel. It is
we who have picked the cotton for nothing; it is we who are
the maids in the kitchens of liberal white people; it is we who
are the janitors, the porters, the elevator men; it is we who
sweep up your college floors; yes, it is we who are the
hardest working and the lowest paid. And that it is nonsensical for people to start talking about human relationships until
they're willing to build new institutions. Black people are economically insecure. White liberals are economically secure.
Can you begin an economic coalition? Are the liberals willing
to share their salaries with the economically insecure black
people who they so much love? Then if you're not, are you
willing to start building new institutions that will provide economic security for black people? That's the question we want
to deal with. . . .

We have to raise questions about whether or not we need
new types of political institutions in this country and we in
SNCC maintain that we need them now. We need new political institutions in this country. And any time Lyndon Baines
Johnson can head a party which has in it Bobby Kennedy,
Wayne Morse, Eastland, Wallace and all those other supposedly liberal cats, there's something wrong with that party.
They're moving politically, not morally. And if that party refuses to seat black people from Mississippi and goes ahead
and seats racists like Eastland and his clique, then it is clear to
me that they're moving politically and that one cannot begin
to talk morality to people like that. We must begin to think
politically and see if we can have the power to impose and
keep the moral values that we hold high. We must question
the values of this society. And I maintain that black people
are the best people to do that because we have been excluded

from that society and the question is, we ought to think whether or not we want to become a part of that society. That's what we want. And that is precisely what, it seems to me, the Student Nonviolent Coordinating Committee is doing. We are raising questions about this country. I do not want to be a part of the American pride. The American pride means raping South Africa, beating Vietnam, beating South America, raping the Philippines, raping every country you've been in. I don't want any of your blood money. I don't want it . . . don't want to be part of that system. And the question is, how do we raise those questions. . . . How do we raise them as activists?

We have grown up and we are the generation that has found this country to be a world power, that has found this country to be the wealthiest country in the world. We must question how she got her wealth. That's what we're questioning. And whether or not we want this country to continue being the wealthiest country in the world at the price of raping everybody across the world. That's what we must begin to question. And because black people are saying we do not now want to become a part of you, we are called reverse racists. Ain't that a gas?

How do we raise the questions of poverty? The assumptions of this country is that if someone is poor, they're poor because of their own individual blight, or they weren't born on the right side of town. They had too many children; they went in the Army too early; their father was a drunk; they didn't care about school; they made a mistake. That's a lot of nonsense. *Poverty is well calculated in this country.* It is well calculated. And the reason why the poverty program won't work is because the calculators of poverty are administering it. That's why it won't work.

So how can we, as the youth in the country, move to start tearing those things down? We must move into the white community. We are in the black community. We have developed a movement in the black community that challenges the white activist who has failed miserably to develop the movement inside of his community. The question is, can we find white people who are going to have the courage to go into white communities and start organizing them? Can we find them? Are they here? And are they willing to do that? Those are the questions that we must raise for white activists.

We are never going to get caught up with questions about power. This country knows what power is and knows it very well. And knows what black power is because it's deprived black people of it for 400 years. So it knows what black power is. But the question is, why do white people in this country associate black power with violence? Because of their own inability to deal with blackness. If we had said Negro power, nobody would get scared. Everybody would support it. And if we said power for colored people, everybody would be for that. But it is the word 'black,' it is the word 'black' that bothers people in this country, and that's their problem, not mine. . . .

So that in conclusion, we want to say that first, it is clear to me that we have to wage a psychological battle on the right for black people to define their own terms, define themselves as they see fit and organize themselves as they see fit. Now, the question is, how is the white community going to begin to allow for that organizing, because once they start to do that, they will also allow for the organizing that they want to do inside their communities. It doesn't make any difference. Because we're going to organize our way anyway. We're going to do it. The question is, how we're going to facilitate those matters. Whether it's going to be done with a thousand policemen with sub-machine guns or whether or not it's going to be done in the context where it's allowed to be done by white people warding off those policemen. That is the question.

And the question is, how will white people who call themselves activists get ready to start moving into the white communities on two counts? On building new political institutions, to destroy the old ones that we have, and to move around the concept of white youth refusing to go into the army. So that we can start then to build a new world.

It is ironic to talk about civilization in this country. This country is uncivilized. It needs to be civilized. We must begin to raise those questions of civilization. What it is, and we'll do it. And so we must urge you to fight now to be the leaders of today, not tomorrow. We've got to be the leaders of today. This country is a nation of thieves. It stands on the brink of becoming a nation of murderers. We must stop it. *We* must stop it.

And then, in a larger sense, there is the question of black people. We are on the move for our liberation. We have been tired of trying to prove things to white people. We are tired of trying to explain to white people that we're not going to hurt them. We are concerned with getting the things we want, the things that we have to have to be able to function. The question is, can white people allow for that in this country? The question is, will white people overcome their racism and allow for that to happen in this country? If that does not happen, brothers and sisters, we have no choice, but to say very clearly, move on over, or we're going to move on over you.

'Black Power' and Coalition Politics*

BAYARD RUSTIN

THERE ARE TWO Americas—black and white—and nothing has more clearly revealed the divisions between them than the debate currently raging around the slogan of "black power." Despite—or perhaps because of—the fact that this slogan lacks any clear definition, it has succeeded in galvanizing emotions on all sides, with many whites seeing it as the expression of a new racism and many Negroes taking it as a warning to white people that Negroes will no longer tolerate brutality and violence. But even within the Negro community itself, "black power" has touched off a major debate—the most bitter the community has experienced since the days of Booker T. Washington and W. E. B. Du Bois, and one which threatens to ravage the entire civil-rights movement. Indeed, a serious split has already developed between advocates of "black power" like Floyd McKissick of CORE and Stokely Carmichael of SNCC on the one hand, and Dr. Martin Luther King of SCLC, Roy Wilkins** of the NAACP, and Whitney Young of the Urban League on the other.

There is no question, then, that great passions are involved in the debate over the idea of "black power"; nor, as we shall see, is there any question that these passions have their roots in the psychological and political frustrations of the Negro community. Nevertheless, I would contend that "black power" not only lacks any real value for the civil-rights movement, but that its propagation is positively harmful. It diverts the movement from a meaningful debate over strategy and tactics, it isolates the Negro community, and it encourages the growth of anti-Negro forces.

In its simplest and most innocent guise, "black power" merely means the effort to elect Negroes to office in proportion to Negro strength within the population. There is, of course, nothing wrong with such an objective in itself, and nothing inherently radical in the idea of pursuing it. But in Stokely Carmichael's extravagant rhetoric about "taking over" in districts of the South where

* Bayard Rustin, " 'Black Power' and Coalition Politics," *Commentary*, 42 (September, 1966), pp. 35-40. Bayard Rustin is executive director of the A. Philip Randolph Institute. Reprinted by permission.
** We were unable to obtain from Roy Wilkins of the NAACP permission to include in this anthology his speech, "Where We Stand," which presents the NAACP position on black power and the current movement.

Negroes are in the majority, it is important to recognize that Southern Negroes are only in a position to win a maximum of two congressional seats and control of eighty local counties.*** (Carmichael, incidentally, is in the paradoxical position of screaming at liberals—wanting only to "get whitey off my back" —and simultaneously needing their support: after all, he can talk about Negroes taking over Lowndes County only because there is a fairly liberal federal government to protect him should Governor Wallace decide to eliminate this pocket of black power.) Now there might be a certain value in having two Negro congressmen from the South, but obviously they could do nothing by themselves to reconstruct the face of America. Eighty sheriffs, eighty tax assessors, and eighty school-board members might ease the tension for a while in their communities, but they alone could not create jobs and build low-cost housing; they alone could not supply quality integrated education.

The relevant question, moreover, is not whether a politician is black or white, but what forces he represents. Manhattan has had a succession of Negro borough presidents, and yet the schools are increasingly segregated. Adam Clayton Powell and William Dawson have both been in Congress for many years; the former is responsible for a rider on school integration that never gets passed, and the latter is responsible for keeping the Negroes of Chicago tied to a mayor who had to see riots and death before he would put eight-dollar sprinklers on water hydrants in the summer. I am not for one minute arguing that Powell, Dawson, and Mrs. Motley should be impeached. What I am saying is that if a politician is elected because he is black and is deemed to be entitled to a "slice of the pie," he will behave in one way; if he is elected by a constituency pressing for social reform, he will, whether he is white or black, behave in another way.

SOUTHERN Negroes, despite exhortations from SNCC to organize themselves into a Black Panther party, are going to stay in the Democratic party—to them it is the party of progress, the New Deal, the New Frontier, and the Great Society—and they are right to stay. For SNCC's Black Panther perspective is simultaneously utopian and reactionary—the former for the by now obvious reason that one-tenth of the population cannot accomplish much by itself, the latter because such a party would remove Negroes from the main area of political struggle in this country (particularly in the one-party South, where the decisiv⟨e⟩ battles are fought out in Democratic primaries), and would ⟨give pr⟩iority to the issue of race precisely at a time when the f⟨undamental⟩ questions facing the Negro and American society ⟨are econo⟩mic and social. . . .

The winning of the right of Negroes to ⟨vote⟩ ⟨as⟩sures the eventual transformation of the ⟨⟩ controlled primarily by Northern mach⟨ines and South⟩ern Dixiecrats. The Negro vote will ⟨⟩ the party and from Congress, whic⟨h⟩ tion facing us today is who will ⟨⟩ civil-rights leaders (in such t⟨⟩

*** See "The Negroes E⟨⟩
Dissent, July-August 1966.

mingham, Alabama; and even to a certain extent Atlanta) can organize grass-roots clubs whose members will have a genuine political voice, the Dixiecrats might well be succeeded by black moderates and black Southern-style machine politicians, who would do little to push for needed legislation in Congress and little to improve local conditions in the South. While I myself would prefer Negro machines to a situation in which Negroes have no power at all, it seems to me that there is a better alternative today —a liberal-labor-civil rights coalition which would work to make the Democratic party truly responsive to the aspirations of the poor, and which would develop support for programs (specifically those outlined in A. Philip Randolph's $100 billion Freedom Budget) aimed at the reconstruction of American society in the interests of greater social justice. The advocates of "black power" have no such programs in mind; what they are in fact arguing for (perhaps unconsciously) is the creation of a *new black establishment.*

Nor, it might be added, are they leading the Negro people along the same road which they imagine immigrant groups traveled so successfully in the past. Proponents of "black power"—accepting a historical myth perpetrated by moderates—like to say that the Irish and the Jews and the Italians, by sticking together and demanding their share, finally won enough power to overcome their initial disabilities. But the truth is that it was through alliances with other groups (in political machines or as part of the trade-union movement) that the Irish and the Jews and the Italians acquired the power to win their rightful place in American society. They did not "pull themselves up by their own bootstraps"—no group in American society has ever done so; and they most certainly did not make isolation their primary tactic. . . .

"Black power" is, of course, a somewhat nationalistic slogan and its sudden rise to popularity among Negroes signifies a concomitant rise in nationalist sentiment (Malcolm X's autobiography is quoted nowadays in Grenada, Mississippi as well as in Harlem). We have seen such nationalistic turns and withdrawals back into the ghetto before, and when we look at the conditions which brought them about, we find that they have much in common with the conditions of Negro life at the present moment: conditions which lead to despair over the goal of integration and to the belief that the ghetto will last forever.

It may, in the light of the many juridical and legislative victories which have been achieved in the past few years, seem strange that despair should be so widespread among Negroes today. But anyone to whom it seems strange should reflect on the fact that despite these victories *Negroes today are in worse economic shape, live in worse slums, and attend more highly segregated schools than in 1954.* Thus—to recite the appalling, and appallingly familiar, statistical litany once again—more Negroes are unemployed today than in 1954; the gap between the wages of the ⬛⬛ worker and the white worker is wider; while the unemploy⬛⬛ among white youths is decreasing, the rate among ⬛⬛⬛ has increased to *32 per cent* (and among Negro ⬛⬛ more startling). Even the one gain which has ⬛⬛⬛ase in the unemployment rate among ⬛⬛ it represents men who have been called back to work after a period of being laid off. In any event, unemployment among Negro men is still twice that of whites, and no new jobs have been created.

So too with housing, which is deteriorating in the North (and yet the housing provisions of the 1966 civil-rights bill are weaker than the anti-discrimination laws in several states which contain the worst ghettos even with these laws on their books). And so too with schools: according to figures issued recently by the Department of Health, Education and Welfare, 65 per cent of first-grade Negro students in this country attend schools that are from 90 to 100 per cent black. (If in 1954, when the Supreme Court handed down the desegregation decision, you had been the Negro parent of a first-grade child, the chances are that this past June you would have attended that child's graduation from a segregated high school).

To put all this in the simplest and most concrete terms: the day-to-day lot of the ghetto Negro has not been improved by the various judicial and legislative measures of the past decade. . . .

Then there is the war in Vietnam, which poses many ironies for the Negro community. On the one hand, Negroes are bitterly aware of the fact that more and more money is being spent on the war, while the anti-poverty program is being cut, on the other hand, Negro youths are enlisting in great numbers, as though to say that it is worth the risk of being killed to learn a trade, to leave a dead-end situation, and to join the only institution in this society which seems really to be integrated. . . .

The Vietnam war is also partly responsible for the growing disillusion with non-violence among Negroes. The ghetto Negro does not in general ask whether the United States is right or wrong to be in Southeast Asia. He does, however, wonder why he is exhorted to non-violence when the United States has been waging a fantastically brutal war, and it puzzles him to be told that he must turn the other cheek in our own South while we must fight for freedom in South Vietnam.

Thus, as in roughly similar circumstances in the past—circumstances, I repeat, which in the aggregate foster the belief that the ghetto is destined to last forever—Negroes are once again turning to nationalistic slogans, with "black power" affording the same emotional release as "Back to Africa" and "Buy Black" did in earlier periods of frustration and hopelessness. This is not only the case with the ordinary Negro in the ghetto; it is also the case with leaders like McKissick and Carmichael, neither of whom began as a nationalist or was at first cynical about the possibilities of integration. It took countless beatings and 24 jailings—that, and the absence of strong and continual support from the liberal community—to persuade Carmichael that his earlier faith in coalition politics was mistaken, that nothing was to be gained from working with whites, and that an alliance with the black nationalists was desirable. In the areas of the South where SNCC has been working so nobly, implementation of the Civil Rights Acts of 1964 and 1965 has been slow and ineffective. Negroes in many rural areas cannot walk into the courthouse and register to vote. Despite the voting-rights bill, they must file complaints and the Justice Department must be called to send federal registrars. Nor do children attend integrafed schools as a matter of course. There, too, complaints must be filed and the Department of Health, Education and Welfare must be notified. Neither department has been doing an effective job of enforcing the bills. The feeling of isolation increases among SNCC workers as each legislative victory turns out to be only a token victory—significant on the national level, but not affecting the day-to-day lives of Negroes. Carmichael and his colleagues are wrong in refusing to support the 1966 bill, but one can understand why they feel as they do.

It is, in short, the growing conviction that the Negroes cannot win—a conviction with much grounding in experience—which accounts for the new popularity of "black power." So far as the ghetto Negro is concerned, this conviction expresses itself in hostility first toward the people closest to him who have held out the most promise and failed to deliver (Martin Luther King, Roy Wilkins, etc.), then toward those who have proclaimed themselves his friends (the liberals and the labor movement), and finally toward the only oppressors he can see (the local storekeeper and the policeman on the corner). On the leadership level, the conviction that the Negroes cannot win takes other forms, principally the adoption of what I have called a "no-win" policy. Why bother with programs when their enactment results only in "sham"? Why concern ourselves with the image of the movement when nothing significant has been gained for all the sacrifices made by SNCC and CORE? Why compromise with reluctant white allies when nothing of consequence can be achieved anyway? Why indeed have anything to do with whites at all?

On this last point, it is extremely important for white liberals to understanding—as, one gathers from their references to "racism in reverse," the President and the Vice President of the United States do not—that there is all the difference in the world between saying, "If you don't want me, I don't want you" (which is what some proponents of "black power" have in effect been saying) and the statement, "Whatever you do, I don't want you" (which is what racism declares). It is, in other words, both absurd and immoral to equate the despairing response of the victim with the contemptuous assertion of the oppressor. It would, moreover, be tragic if white liberals allowed verbal hostility on the part of Negroes to drive them out of the movement or to curtail their support for civil rights. The issue was injustice before "black power" became popular, and the issue is still injustice.

In any event, even if "black power" had not emerged as a slogan, problems would have arisen in the relation between whites and Negroes in the civil-rights movement. In the North, it was inevitable that Negroes would eventually wish to run their own movement and would rebel against the presence of whites in positions of leadership as yet another sign of white supremacy. In the South, the well-intentioned white volunteer had the cards stacked against him from the beginning. Not only could he leave the struggle any time he chose to do so, but a higher value was set on his safety by the press and the government—apparent in the differing degrees of excitement generated by the imprisonment or murder of whites and Negroes. The white person's importance to the movement in the South was thus an ironic outgrowth of racism and was therefore bound to create resentment. . . .

Nevertheless, pride, confidence, and a new identity cannot be won by glorifying blackness or attacking whites; they can only come from meaningful action, from good jobs, and from real victories such as were achieved on the streets of Montgomery, Birmingham, and Selma. When SNCC and CORE went into the South, they awakened the country, but now they emerge isolated and demoralized, shouting a slogan that may afford a momentary satisfaction but that is calculated to destroy them and their movement. Already their frustrated call is being answered with counter-demands for law and order and with opposition to police-review boards. Already they have diverted the entire civil-rights movement from the hard task of developing strategies to realign the major parties of this country, and embroiled it in a debate that can only lead more and more to politics by frustration.

On the other side, however—the more important side, let it be said—it is the business of those who reject the negative aspects of "black power" not to preach but to act. Some weeks ago President Johnson, speaking at Fort Campbell, Kentucky, asserted that riots impeded reform, created fear, and antagonized the Negro's traditional friends. Mr. Johnson, according to the New York *Times*, expressed sympathy for the plight of the poor, the jobless, and the ill-housed. The government, he noted, has been working to relieve their circumstances, but "all this takes time."

One cannot argue with the President's position that riots are destructive or that they frighten away allies. Nor can one find fault with his sympathy for the plight of the poor; surely the poor need sympathy. But one can question whether the government has been working seriously enough to eliminate the conditions which lead to frustration-politics and riots. The President's very words, "all this takes time," will be understood by the poor for precisely what they are—an excuse instead of a real program, a cover-up for the failure to establish real priorities, and an indication that the administration has no real commitment to create new jobs, better housing, and integrated schools.

For the truth is that it need only take ten years to eliminate poverty—ten years and the $100 billion Freedom Budget recently proposed by A. Philip Randolph. . . .

Mr. Randolph's Freedom Budget not only rests on the Employment Act of 1946, but on a precedent set by Harry Truman when he believed freedom was threatened in Europe. In 1947, the Marshall Plan was put into effect and 3 per cent of the gross national product was spent in foreign aid. If we were to allocate a similar proportion of our GNP to destroy the economic and social consequences of racism and poverty at home today, it might mean spending more than 20 billion dollars a year, although I think it quite possible that we can fulfill these goals with a much smaller sum. It would be intolerable, however, if our plan for domestic social reform were less audacious and less far-reaching than our international programs of a generation ago.

We must see, therefore, in the current debate over "black power," a fantastic challenge to American society to live up to its proclaimed principles in the area of race by transforming itself so that all men may live equally and under justice. We must see to it that in rejecting "black power," we do not also reject the principle of Negro equality. Those people who would use the current debate and/or the riots to abandon the civil-rights movement leave us no choice but to question their original motivation. . . .

3. THE ECONOMIC THRUST

The Economy of Ruleville, Mississippi*

CHARLES COBB AND CHARLES MCLAURIN

THE COTTON PICKING season in the Mississippi Delta lasts from the middle of August until the middle of December. At the end of the season, all of the debts incurred by the Negro sharecropper during the year are totaled up by the plantation owner and deducted from the money that the sharecropper has made during the cotton picking season. The sharecropper plays no part in the totaling up of debts which include: cost of raising cotton crop, rent, food, and miscellaneous bills such as doctor's bills, cost of buying a car, etc.

The agreement between sharecropper and plantation owner is that the sharecropper will raise a crop of cotton, and split it 50-50 with the plantation owner. But the cost of raising the cotton crop is paid entirely by the sharecropper. All of the cotton is sold by the plantation owner, who in turn tells the sharecropper how much the cotton was sold for. The fact that all finance is handled by the plantation owner makes the sharecropper subject to all sorts of financial chicanery from the plantation owner. In fact, several sharecroppers and day workers have reported that they have had to pay out Social Security even though they have no Social Security number. Mrs. Irene Johnson of Ruleville, who is active in the voter registration drive there, reports that even her ten-year-old son has had Social Security taken from him.

Mrs. Willie Mae Robbinson, who sharecrops on a plantation near Ruleville, picked twenty (20) bales of cotton this

* Charles Cobb and Charles McLaurin, *"MEMORANDUM* Re: Preliminary survey on the condition of the Negro farmers in Ruleville, Mississippi, at the close of the cotton season. This report is based on a few hours spent talking with people in Ruleville. November 19, 1962." McLaurin and Cobb were field secretaries of the Student Nonviolent Coordinating Committee.

season; yet she only cleared three dollars ($3.00) for the entire year. (There are approximately 550 lbs. in a bale of cotton; and the current selling price per pound of picked cotton is $.34. Simple arithmetic shows that before deductions, Mrs. Robbinson should have made $3,740.00.) It is true that she had to split her gross with the plantation owner, and pay for her yearly expenses, but as one man told us in reference to the plight of this lady, "I know that she hasn't eaten what would have come out of ten bales."

We cannot report in much detail on settlements, because most won't be made until after Christmas.

The average amount of money made by sharecroppers for the year is between $300–400. The average amount of money made by day laborers for the year is between $150–160.

The general opinion among the Negro community in Ruleville is that they "won't make anything much" and will need commodities.

Commodities are surplus government foods given out to people on welfare and farming people in need of them. The commodities are usually meal, rice, flour and dry milk. Last year it was announced in Ruleville's paper that butter, peanut butter, and canned meat would be given out; but several people have told us that they never get any.

Before this year, all one had to do in order to receive commodities was to go to City Hall, and sign up. This year, however, there is a registration form to be filled out before anyone becomes eligible. This form has to be signed by the applicant and countersigned by his boss, or a responsible person (which usually means a white person). Due to the voter registration drive that has been and is being carried on in Ruleville, the "responsible people" are not particularly inclined to favors for the Negro.

Mrs. Mary Burris of Ruleville went to City Hall to sign up to receive commodities. As she approached City Hall, she met several Negro citizens coming out. They told her that all persons with their own homes now had to go to the Welfare Department in Indianola (county seat) to sign up for commodities. When she got there, the lady in charge asked her why she hadn't signed up in Ruleville. Mrs. Burris explained that she was told to come to Indianola. She was then told to take a seat. After about two hours, another lady came out and told Mrs. Burris that her papers (registration for commodities) were not filled out properly. Mrs. Burris was told that she would have to go to every person she had picked for, and bring back something showing how much she had earned from each of them. She was given until 9 a.m. the next morning to do this. Mrs. Burris has been receiving commodities for the past three years, and she says that this is the first time this has happened. She said that this is also the first time that she has had to fill out papers to get food.

Mrs. Gertrude Rogers of Ruleville went to City Hall to sign up to receive commodities. She was given a card. She heard the Mayor of Ruleville, C. M. Dorrough, say "most of them with cards ain't going to get any food." Mrs. Rogers reports that the Mayor also said that those who went down to register were not going to get anything, "that he was going to mess up all of them."

At this point, I would like to bring to your attention something Mayor Dorrough said a month or two ago in reference to Negro participation in the voter registration drive in Ruleville: "We gonna see how tight we can make it—gonna make it just as tight as we can—gonna be rougher, rougher than you think it is."

When Mrs. Leona McClendon, a day laborer, went to sign up to receive commodities, she was told that she could not get the food because she had a job, and had earned $15.00 per week. Mrs. McClendon says, "I did not earn $15.00 the whole year."

Mrs. Bessie Lee Greene was told the same thing as Mrs. Mary Burris. In addition, Mrs. Greene was told she would have to bring in what her son-in-law had earned. Both Mrs. Greene and Mrs. Burris have stated that they do not believe that the various bosses they worked for kept records of that sort.

Mrs. Lucy Sadies, a day worker, went to the Ruleville City Hall to apply for receipt of commodities. She was told that she received a check and was not eligible to get the food. When Mrs. Sadies told him that she did not receive a check, she was told to go and talk with the Social Security agent, and that he would apply for her.

Grocers in Ruleville have always objected to commodities being issued there.

Commodities are the only way many Negroes make it from cotton season to cotton season. If this is taken from them, they have nothing at all; and the success of our voter registration program depends on the protection we can offer the individual while he is waiting for his one small vote to become a part of a strong Negro vote. It doesn't take much to tide over the rural Mississippi Negro, but the commodities are *vital*.

The mechanical cotton picker is still imperfect; but it is

being used more and more. Essentially what makes the mechanical picker disliked by the plantation owner is that it chops the cotton as it picks, giving a shorter fiber, and thereby lowering the value of the cotton.

Still, Negroes tell us that the machines were used with increasing frequency this year: "cotton picking machines used all the way this year." Where cotton grew in greatest quantity this year, the machines were used. More cotton was picked by machine than by hand.

Mrs. Anderson runs a small grocery store, and is full of ideas and gossip. She had something to say on where Ruleville stands economically. "People haven't made anything this year . . . Folks don't have any money now."

Mrs. Anderson told of how the "soda pop man" came to her store, and told her that the reason he was there so early was because he had been driving all over town, and hadn't sold a single soda . . . to either Negro or white store owners.

Mrs. Anderson said that the children hadn't been buying their nickel cookies like they used to. "And when the kids aren't buying their cookies, you know things are bad."

The Many Faces of Poverty*

NATIONAL URBAN LEAGUE

THE DIRECT AND self-perpetuating relationships between poverty, unemployment, low income, lack of education, infant deaths, dilapidated and overcrowded housing, crime and various other important demoralizing socio-economic conditions are only too well known. The data contained in this fact book, primarily from government sources, are graphic evidence of this. Poverty tends to perpetuate itself in ever widening areas of disability. Its costs, human and financial, thereby become ever greater.

According to the mandate of our country and our President, all poor Americans are to be helped to help themselves. The Negro American poor in our nation continue to suffer the added jeopardy of color. To overcome poverty, they must first struggle to obtain the equal opportunity that our national

* National Urban League, *Facts on the Many Faces of Poverty* (National Urban League, Inc., 1965), pp. 1-4. Reprinted with permission of the National Urban League, Inc.

laws and courts have repeatedly declared to be the right of all Americans. Equalizing the life chances of this important segment of our society, the nonwhite American, has rightly become a national task. The urgent nature and increasing extent of this task is indicated by the information in this booklet.

It should be noted that for many areas, averages used greatly understate the problems. For example, the 1961 infant mortality for the whole United States was 25.3, but the rate for all whites was a lower 22.3; for nonwhites, it was an almost double 40.7 deaths. Whether viewing New York City (total city rate of 25.7, 21.4 for whites and 40.0 for nonwhites) or St. Louis, Missouri (total rate 31.4, with 24.5 for whites and 42.1 for nonwhites), without exception the ten major cities of the U.S. (located in the North, South, West and Midwest) had much higher rates for nonwhites. And one-fourth of all U.S. Negroes live in these ten cities.

EQUALIZING LIFE CHANCES

"The notable advances in Negro civil rights, education, occupational distribution, housing and earnings have led to a widespread assumption that the economic gap between them and the white population of the country is consistently narrowing. Such an assumption ignores the economic progress of the white population which has been even more rapid than that of the Negro in the past decade. As a result, the differences between the two racial groups have not only failed to narrow but have actually widened in such major areas as housing, income, and employment. Only in education is the gap narrowing, and the full rewards of this development have yet to be reaped."

Manpower Report to the President
March 1964 - U.S. Dept. of Labor

INCOME AND EMPLOYMENT

Income and Education:
The Persistence of Economic Discrimination

Plagued by discrimination, the Negro worker continues to be lower paid, more underemployed and unemployed than his white counterpart. The highly regarded Research Center of the University of Michigan found last year that "even when educational levels were comparable, smaller proportions of nonwhite than white respondents reported having worked as much as they desired."

The figures below bear witness to this discrimination. The Negro worker, male and female, has been improving his education much faster than the white worker so that today he is catching up with the white. Despite this, the nonwhite worker is earning no more relatively; in fact, he is earning less. Instead of catching up, the average hourly earnings of the nonwhite is falling farther behind that of the white worker. The 90¢ an hour *difference* between the white and nonwhite male worker jumped in a decade to a difference of $1.45 per hour.

Average Hourly Earnings - Male

	White	Nonwhite	White/Nonwhite Difference
1949	$1.90	$1.00	$0.90
1959	$3.20	$1.75	$1.45

Commenting in July 1964 that the earnings average of the nonwhite worker is about half that of white workers, Secretary of Labor W. Willard Wirtz said: "There is a continuing lag, and it is getting worse." This is evident in the table below which indicates that the nonwhite income in relation to the white declined from 56% in 1954 to exactly half (50%) in 1959 and little more than half (53%) in 1963.

PROFILE IN BLACK AND WHITE
(U.S. Averages)

INCOME AND EMPLOYMENT	White	Nonwhite
Family Income—Total U. S.	$5,893	$3,161
Family Income–Female Head	$3,538	$1,734
Female Heads of Families	9%	23%
Urban Family Income	$7,000	$4,100
Annual Income:		
Male 14 years & over	$4,337	$2,254
Female 14 years & over	$1,510	$ 905
Hourly Male Income	$3.20	$1.90
Estimated Lifetime Earnings—		
Experienced Male	$241,000	$122,000
With 4 yrs. College	$395,000	$185,000
Families in Poverty ($3,000 or under)	19%	48%
1 or more Earners—Male Head	69%	85%
1 or more Earners—Female Head	58%	68%
Families Earning under $4,000	30%	61%
Married Women in Labor Force	30%	41%
Average Persons per Family	3.6	4.4
Unemployment Rate	4.6	9.8

	White	Nonwhite
Teenage Unemployment Rate........	13.3	26.4
Professional, Managerial, Sales, Skilled Workers—Male	53.9%	18.8%*
White Collar Workers–All..........	46.5%	18.4%

EDUCATION

	White	Nonwhite
Gain in School Years 1940-59, Male 25-29 years..............	2.0	4.4
Gain in School Years, 1952-64, Female 18 yrs. & over........	0.2	2.7
Years of School Completed.........	12.2	10.1
Increase in Enrollment in College and Professional Schools, 1953-61...	55.5%	82%
High School Dropouts..............	25%	60%

HEALTH AND WELFARE

	White	Nonwhite
Physicians per 100,000 Population....	157	27
Life Expectancy (years)—Male......	67.55	61.48
—Female....	74.19	66.47
Infant Deaths per 1,000............	22.4	40.7
Maternal Deaths per 10,000 Live Births	2.6	9.8
Failed Pre-induction Exams for Armed Forces **	15%	56%

HOUSING

	White	Nonwhite
Lacking Facilities, Deteriorating or Dilapidated.................	20%	56%
More than 1 person per Room......	10%	28%
Home Ownership	64%	38%
Population Living in Cities..........	70%	73%
In Central Cities***...........	47%	78%
In Suburbs***.................	52%	22%

Average Wage or Salary Income of Primary Families and Individuals

	1954	1955	1956	1957	1958	1959	1960	1961	1962	1963
White	$4,201	$4,150	$4,331	$4,685	$4,831	$4,882	$5,252	$5,424	$5,570	$5,808
Nonwhite	2,357	2,333	2,418	2,429	2,536	2,437	2,672	3,058	2,908	3,088
Ratio Nonwhite to White	.56	.56	.56	.52	.52	.50	.51	.56	.52	.53

The relatively nonwhite income is evident in many ways. The nonwhite's share of all the money income in the U.S. in the last decade has varied between 5.5% and 6.2% (6.0% in 1963) even though nonwhites have accounted for about 11%

* Mostly Negro teachers, clergy, social workers, lawyers, doctors, and dentists.

** Due to poor health and/or education.

*** 212 standard metropolitan statistical areas (SMSA's).

of U.S. population and labor force. The effect of discrimination is evident in all sections of the country, whether measured by individual or family income.

Average Income—1959
Individuals 14 years and over

Region	All Families	White	Nonwhite
Northeast	$3,249	$3,332	$2,487
North-Central	$3,033	$3,099	$2,334
South	$2,120	$2,529	$ 992
West	$3,246	$3,322	$2,437

Average Family Income—1959

Region	All Families	White	Nonwhite
U.S.	$5,660	$5,893	$3,161
Northeast	$6,191	$6,318	$4,371
North-Central	$5,892	$5,994	$4,320
South	$4,465	$5,009	$2,322
West	$6,348	$6,444	$4,937

The U.S. Department of Labor estimated that the family of four cost of living on a "modest but adequate" budget for 20 large U. S. cities in 1959 ranged from $4,622 to $5,607. Not one of the four regions' average for nonwhite families attained this level of income, but all the regions' white average exceeded this by a large margin despite the fact that more nonwhite married women than white married women work (41% nonwhite vs. 30% white).

Labor Unions and the Negro*

HERBERT HILL

THE REMOVAL OF the sanction of law from racial segregation has sharply posed the issue of the Negro's status in virtually every area of American life. As much as the public schools,

* Excerpts from Herbert Hill, "Labor Unions and the Negro," *Commentary*, 28 (Dec., 1959), 479-488. Copyright ©1959 by the American Jewish Committee. By permission. For other pertinent works by Mr. Hill see the bibliography, page 506.

religious organizations, and business firms, the labor movement is on trial today. For labor's democratic ideals are in serious conflict with a tradition of racial discrimination in the unions that is currently very much alive. . . .

The Negro worker's historical experience with organized labor has not been a happy one. In the South, unions frequently acted to force Negroes out of jobs that had formerly been considered theirs. Before the Civil War, Negroes had been carpenters, bricklayers, painters, blacksmiths, harnessmakers, tailors, and shoemakers. However, in urban centers like New Orleans, the historian Charles B. Rousseve observed in *The Negro in Louisiana*, "the Negro who in ante-bellum days performed all types of labor, skilled and unskilled, found himself gradually almost eliminated from the various trades." Unionization in the South often led to the redesignating of "Negro jobs" as "white man's work," and even to excluding Negroes from entire industries.

In the North, unions were stronger at an earlier period, especially among the craft occupations. But, as Gunnar Myrdal stated in *An American Dilemma*, "most of the time they effectively kept Negroes out of skilled work." The fact, Myrdal continued, "that the American Federation of Labor as such is officially against racial discrimination does not mean much. The Federation has never done anything to check racial discrimination exercised by its member organizations."

The AFL's failure to organize the Negro worker and to accord him full brotherhood within the union ranks was not a policy born of necessity. The old Knights of Labor, the International Workers of the World, and (much later) industrial unions in the Congress of Industrial Organizations were able to organize Negro and white workers together, in the North and in the South; whereas the early AFL attacked the organizing activities of the Knights of Labor among unskilled and Negro workers.

To be sure, the AFL executive council stated, shortly after the organization's founding, that a union that draws the color line "cannot be admitted into affiliation to this body." But soon afterward, in 1895, the AFL admitted the International Association of Machinists, then a rigid "lily-white" organization. And the traditional hostility of the AFL leaders to immigration—particularly Asian immigration—fostered a veritable racist ideology. . . .

In the early years of this century, the hostile feeling toward Negroes in American trade unions often led to racial and ethnic violence. In the tragic East St. Louis race riots of July 1917, trade union provocation was a major factor.

When workers at the Aluminum Ore Company went on

strike, the firm brought up a small number of Negroes from the Deep South to be used as strikebreakers. In response, the local AFL leaders provoked a veritable hysteria of race hatred. Finally, raging fires on July 2, 1917 engulfed the entire Negro residential district of East St. Louis, destroying $7,000,000 worth of property, driving 10,000 colored persons from their homes, and ending in the death of more than two hundred Negroes and eight whites.

About a month before the riots, Edward F. Mason, secretary of the East St. Louis AFL Central Trades & Labor Union, called on union members to march to City Hall on May 28, 1917, to demand a halt to "the importation" of Negroes. "The immigration of the Southern Negro into our city," Mason stated, "for the past eight months has reached a point where drastic action must be taken. . . . On next Monday evening the entire body of delegates to the Central Trades and Labor Union will call upon the Mayor and the City Council and demand that they take some action to retard this growing menace and . . . get rid of a certain portion of those who are already here." . . .

Special investigators for the National Association for the Advancement of Colored People later reported that "by all accounts of eye-witnesses, both white and black, the East St. Louis outrage was deliberately planned and executed." As for the excuse offered by the unions, William English Walling, a highly respected liberal journalist and reformer, noted in a telegram to President Wilson: "The pretext of labor from the South is invalid."

AFL President Gompers, however, attempted to defend the rioters, in response to a sharp attack on them by former President Theodore Roosevelt. At a meeting held at Carnegie Hall in New York City, welcoming envoys from the new Russian Provisional government, Roosevelt (according to the New York *Herald*) heatedly condemned the riot, "for which, so far as we can see, there was no justification and no provocation, and which was waged with such appalling fatality as to leave an indelible stigma upon the American name." Gompers rose to excuse the rioters, on the grounds that the capitalists of East St. Louis had been "luring colored men into that city to supplant white labor." Roosevelt would not be put off. "Justice with me is not a mere form of words," he shouted. "In the past I have had to listen too often to the same kind of apologies for the murders committed against the Armenians and the Jews. . . . I say to you, sir, that there can be no justification, no apology for such gross atrocities. . . ."

Few union officials today would dare speak out as bluntly as Gompers did half a century ago. The new era of public relations in the AFL began in the 1920's under the leadership of benign William Green, who occasionally spoke against racism but did nothing to curb it in the AFL. The Negro had established his first beachheads in industry during World War I, but most AFL unions still practiced a rigorous exclusionist policy throughout the 1920's. In some instances still, Negroes were able to enter industry only when employers hired them as strikebreakers.[1] In other industries, predominantly those employing mass production methods, the Negro was able to gain a modest foothold because the craft-proud AFL would not organize them. But the limited gains of the Negroes in the 20's were destroyed during the Depression, largely because the AFL had not extended union protection to the Negro in the earlier period. As late as 1933, the Brotherhood of Sleeping Car Porters, with 35,000 members, had almost half the total number of Negro members in the AFL.

As a result of pressure by the National Association for the Advancement of Colored People, the AFL's 1934 convention passed a resolution authorizing a "Committee of Five to Investigate the Conditions of Negro Workers." Green called a meeting of the committee in Washington in 1935, at which the NAACP was represented by its Chief Counsel, Charles H. Houston. The latter reported that signed statements of specific acts of racial discrimination by AFL affiliates were being collected by NAACP branches throughout the country for presentation at subsequent hearings. But Green soon afterward notified the NAACP that no more hearings would be held, since the first Washington hearing had gathered "sufficient information."

John Brophy, of the Mine Workers Union, who was secretary of the Committee of Five, resigned in protest. "The maneuvering," said Brophy, "on the part of the Executive Council plainly indicated that you wanted the 'Committee of Five to Investigate Conditions of Negro Workers' to be merely a face-saving device for the AFL rather than an honest attempt to find a solution to the Negro problem in the American labor movement." . . .

In 1941, the Federation rejected resolutions, introduced by A. Philip Randolph and Milton P. Webster of the Brother-

---

[1] According to the Inter-Church Commission of Inquiry into the 1919 Steel Strike: "It is evident that the great numbers of Negroes who flowed into the Chicago and Pittsburgh plants were conscious of strikebreaking. For this attitude, the steel strikers rightly blamed American organized labor. . . . Through many an experience Negroes came to believe that the only way they could break into a unionized industry was through strikebreaking." This was also a factor in the terrible Chicago race riots of 1919 and in other racial disturbances of that period.

hood of Sleeping Car Porters, condemning auxiliary "Jim Crow" locals, exclusion of Negroes, and other discriminatory practices of AFL affiliates. At the 1944 convention, when twenty-two international unions still barred Negroes from membership by constitutional provision, John P. Frey, secretary of the Resolutions committee, defended the AFL's policies in these terms: "I am familiar with the South. I spent many years there as an organizer and otherwise, and I know that in some of the denominations the whites go to their church and the colored go to their church buildings, of the same denominations. They get along as Christians should. In fact, the colored members prefer to have the privilege of employing and discharging their own pastors."

This basic AFL attitude continued after the end of the Second World War. The 1946 AFL convention defeated resolutions aimed at ending the system of "Jim Crow" auxiliary locals. In 1949, a resolution endorsing federal Fair Employment Practices legislation passed only after delegates deleted the words "and labor unions" from a motion, calling for the "elimination of discrimination in industry and labor unions based upon race, color, religion, national origin or ancestry. . . ."

Discrimination has traditionally been most severe in the AFL building trades unions and the powerful railroad brotherhoods. The result of this today is that when the colored worker is forced out of the railroad industry, where employment is diminishing, he is prevented from finding employment in the construction industry, where the job market has been rapidly expanding. . . .

But the American Federation of Labor and the railroad brotherhoods were never able to hold the fate of America's working people, white or colored, in their unchallenged control. The phenomenal success of union organization in major manufacturing centers across the country in 1937 and 1938 was not limited to white industrial workers. In the early Congress of Industrial Organizations, for the first time in American labor history, tens of thousands of American Negroes became union members.

In the great sit-down strikes involving entire industries, Negroes were placed on organizing committees, appointed as picket captains, and participated in the local union leadership. Even in the South, though organizers were kidnapped, clubbed, tarred and feathered, and a few lost their lives, the CIO was able to organize important numbers of white and Negro workers in the same unions.

The CIO record in race relations toward the end of its years as a separate organization did not always fulfill the bright promise of its early days. In some Southern plants, rigid patterns of job discrimination were established based on separate racial lines of advancement, limiting all Negroes, however well qualified, to menial job classifications, and denying them equal seniority rights. Nevertheless, the rise of the CIO was a great step forward for tens of thousands of colored and white workers alike.

At the merger convention of AFL and CIO in 1955, a constitutional provision was adopted declaring that "all workers without regard to race, creed, color, national origin or ancestry shall share equally in the full benefits of union organization." In both North and South, however, racial discrimination and segregation have continued in the merged labor movement. . . .

The record seems clear: in the four years since the merger of the AFL and the CIO, the national labor organization has failed to eliminate even the most obvious instances of racism within affiliated unions. As for the Federation's Civil Rights Department, its performance would seem to indicate that its major function is to create a "liberal" public relations image.

The AFL-CIO convention in San Francisco this past September differed little from the pattern of AFL conventions under Gompers and Green. Even as the delegates were meeting, the local Fair Employment Practices Commission was investigating the complaint of Ray Bass, a Negro who for over a year has been denied membership in the Bartenders Union solely because of his color and therefore denied employment. Meanwhile, the convention again rejected proposals to compel the railroad brotherhoods and other unions to end discrimination in the near future. It also prepared to readmit (provisionally) the International Longshoremens Association to the Federation, despite Randolph's charge that the ILA discriminated against Negro and Puerto Rican workers.[2] (Since the merger, the AFL-CIO had also admitted the Railroad Trainmen, and the Locomotive Firemen and Enginemen —both with racial-exclusion clauses in their constitutions. In November 1958, the Locomotive Firemen and Enginemen

[2] AFL-CIO President George Meany claimed ignorance of such discrimination. He said: "Now, in regard to Phil Randolph . . . I never knew of discrimination in the ILA . . . and to come at this late date where he has an audience, a convention of the AFL-CIO, and come up with this material, I just don't think is playing the game." However, the Urban League had a week before the convention, sent a lengthy report on waterfront discrimination to Meany, members of the AFL-CIO Executive Council, and members of its special subcommittee on the ILA. Several of these members—including Meany—had formally acknowledged receipt of the report.

successfully defended these clauses in the Federal Court of Appeals in Cincinnati, Ohio; and the continued silence of the national AFL-CIO in this case is instructive, indeed.)

Negro wage earners, perhaps more than any other group among American workers, need the protection and benefits that derive from full membership in a trade union. And international unions can, if they are prepared to invoke authority, eliminate discriminatory employment practices. In 1958, for example, the United Automobile Workers eliminated the traditional discriminatory seniority provisions which limited Negro seniority and promotion at the General Motors Fisher Body plant in St. Louis. At the large Magnolia Oil Refinery in Beaumont, Texas, thirty-two Negro workers were recently promoted for the first time into the hitherto all-white "process mechanical division," and several other Negroes were employed in production departments previously barred to them. The Oil, Chemical and Atomic Workers International Union helped, rather than resisted, their efforts. A new union policy formally prohibited separate lines of promotion in collective bargaining agreements; and the union called on its members to eliminate discriminatory practices and segregated locals. The International Association of Machinists, which until a decade ago had an all-white clause in its constitution, has also cautiously begun to curb discrimination within its ranks. In too many trades and crafts, however, union power today remains a major obstacle to securing equal employment opportunities for the Negro.

This is not the only obstacle the Negro worker faces, of course. Because there is a disproportionate concentration of Negro workers in the ranks of the unskilled and semi-skilled, there has already been a high rate of Negro displacement and unemployment as the result of automation and other technological innovations. Periodic recessions, too, have had a devastating effect on the Negro community; during several months in 1958, non-white unemployment was more than two-and-a-half times as great as unemployment among white workers. Inevitably, then, in the face of these developments, and the continued inability of the AFL-CIO to curb discrimination in its ranks, the Negro worker has turned to government agencies, and to the courts, for protection.

In several cases, discriminatory unions have invoked the legal doctrine of "voluntary association" to justify their exclusion of Negroes. In the Wisconsin Supreme Court, for example, the Bricklayers Union in 1956 challenged the Wisconsin Industrial Commission's recommendation that it admit two Negroes to membership. The Court upheld the union; it declared that "membership in a voluntary association is a privilege which may be accorded or withheld, and not a right which can be gained and then enforced. The courts cannot compel the admission of an individual into such an association, and if his application is refused, he is entirely without legal remedy, no matter how arbitrary or unjust may be his exclusion. . . ."

Nevertheless, the body of law that has been evolving over the last two decades has tended to forge new protections for the Negro worker. In these cases,[3] the principle of "voluntary association" has been no defense to the charge of racial discrimination. . . .

Negro workers have placed so many of their hopes in the courts, and in state and local Fair Employment Practices Commissions, because organized labor seems incapable of overcoming its habitual discriminatory practices. On the level of the small shop and local union, the traditions of discrimination have often been institutionalized. A form of caste psychology impels many workers to regard their own positions as "white men's jobs," to which no Negro should aspire. These workers and, often, their union leaders regard jobs in their industries as a kind of private privilege, to be accorded and denied by them as they see fit. Often, Negroes are not alone in being barred from such unions, which attempt to maintain an artificial labor shortage. This is expecially true in the building and printing trades, which have much of the character of the medieval guild. On the local level, the inertia which sustains discrimination is to be found among skilled workers in big industry as well as among craftsmen, and in the North almost as commonly as in the South.

The national labor leadership, for its part, indignantly explains that it is besieged at this time by too many enemies to risk internal conflict over discrimination. The presence of a Republican in the White House since 1953, the Congressional exposures of union corruption, industry's more aggressive attitude in the last two years *—all of these have caused labor's leadership to adopt a defensive posture. Within the large unions, automation and technological progress have stimulated new tensions between skilled and unskilled workers; the

---

[3] Among them: *Joseph James* v. *Marinship Corporation and International Brotherhood of Boilermakers, Tunstall* v. *Brotherhood of Locomotive Firemen & Enginemen, Steele* v. *Louisville & Nashville Railroad Company,* and *Betts* v. *Easely* and *Syres* v. *Oil Workers International Union.*

* See "Labor's Time of Troubles," by A. H. Raskin in our August issue.—[*Commentary*] ED.

struggles between unions in various jurisdictions, and in various parts of the country, continue unabated. Because of these pressures, the very AFL-CIO leaders who oppose bias in other institutions have been reluctant to combat it within the labor movement. "We don't want to be torn apart," is their argument. They fear that any militant decision to ban discrimination, no matter how gradually it was applied, would split the AFL-CIO wide open, and thus weaken the liberal cause.

However, for the Negro seeking employment, union discrimination is a cruel fact which these other considerations can hardly be expected to make easier. Given union control of the hiring process and of apprenticeship programs in the building trades, the printing trades, on the waterfront, on the railways, and in so many other industries, labor bias is no longer the private matter of a "voluntary association"—or of a "quasi-sovereignty," as Robert M. Hutchins describes American labor today. Such discrimination is a fundamental social barrier to the Negro, hardly less serious than segregation in the public schools. The intervention of the larger community may, it seems, be necessary to remove that barrier.

The Struggle for the Liberation of the Black Laboring Masses*

A. PHILIP RANDOLPH

IN THIS MID-TWENTIETH century black labor is one hundred years behind white labor. Black labor is behind white labor in the skilled crafts. They are behind in trade union organization. They are behind in workers' education. They are behind in employment opportunities.

Why? The answer is not because white labor is racially superior to black labor. Not because white labor is more productive than black labor.

In the race between black and white labor in American industry, black labor never had a chance. How could it be oth-

* Excerpts from A. Philip Randolph, "The Struggle for the Liberation of the Black Laboring Masses in this Age of a Revolution of Human Rights," Keynote Address by A. Philip Randolph, National President, Negro American Labor Council, at NALC Second Annual Convention, Hamilton Hotel, Chicago, Illinois, November 10-12, 1961. Reprinted by permission of A. Philip Randolph.

erwise when Negro workers began as slaves while white workers began as free men, or virtually as free men?

In addition to a quarter of a thousand years of captivity in the labor system of chattel slavery, black labor, even after emancipation, has been a prisoner for a hundred years of a moneyless system of peonage, sharecropper-plantation-farm laborism, and a helpless and hopeless city-slum proletariat. . . .

No greater tragedy has befallen the working class anywhere in the modern world than that which plagues the working class in the South. Both white and black workers turned against their own class and gave aid to their enemy, the feudalistic-capitalist class, to subject them to sharper and sharper exploitation and oppression.

Verily, black and white workers did not fight each other because they hated each other, but they hated each other because they fought each other. They fought each other because they did not know each other. They did not know each other because they had no contact or communication with each other. They had no contact or communication with each other because they were afraid of each other. They were afraid of each other because each was propagandized into believing that each was seeking to take the jobs of the other.

By poisonous preachments by the press, pulpit and politician, the wages of both black and white workers were kept low and working conditions bad, since trade union organization was practically non-existent. And, even today, the South is virtually a "no man's land" for union labor.

There is no remedy for this plight of the South's labor forces except the unity of the black and white working class.

It is a matter of common knowledge that union organization campaigns, whether under the auspices of the old American Federation of Labor, or the younger Congress of Industrial Organizations, or the AFL-CIO, have wound up as miserable failures.

The reason is not only because the southern working class is divided upon a basis of race, but also because the AFL, the CIO, and the AFL-CIO never took cognizance of this fact. They never built their organization drives upon the principle of the solidarity of the working class. On the contrary, they accepted and proceeded to perpetuate this racial-labor more, the purpose of which was, and is, the perpetuation of segregation—the antithesis of trade union organization.

Thus, they sowed the winds of the division of the workers upon the basis of race, and now they are reaping the whirlwinds.

The leadership of the organized labor movement has at no time ever seriously challenged Jim Crow unionism in the South. White leaders of labor organizations, like white leaders of the Church, business, government, schools, and the press, marched together, under the banner of white supremacy, in the Ku Klux Klan, to put down and keep down by law or lawlessness, the Negro. . . .

While, before Emancipation, the Negro only had job security as a slave because he toiled for nothing, so, following Black Reconstruction, black freedmen labored within the framework of a peonage-sharecrop, labor-barter commissary system for, perhaps, a little more than nothing.

And, despite the Thirteenth, Fourteenth, Fifteenth Amendments, clear commitments to the protection of the freedmen, the Negro laboring masses have never fully broken through the barrier of the ethnic-labor mores of the South, which were hardened into a racially segregated order by the celebrated *Plessy v Ferguson* decision of the U.S. Supreme Court of 1896. Moreover, like the proverbial locusts, the doctrine of least ethnic-labor costs, or a racial sub-wage differential, spread in every area of American industry.

Thus, Negro workers are not yet fully free in the South. By the same token, white workers in the South are not yet fully free, because no white worker can ever become fully free as long as a black worker is in southern Bourbon bondage. And as long as white and black workers in the South are not fully free, the entire working class, North, East, South and West, is not and will not become fully free. There is no principle more obvious and universal than the indivisibility of the freedom of the workers regardless of race, color, religion, national origin or ancestry, being based, as it were, upon the principle of least labor costs in a free market economy.

This is why the racial policies of the American Federation of Labor and Congress of Industrial Organizations have so devastatingly weakened, morally, organizationally, and politically, the American labor movement before the Congress, the public, and the world.

One has only to note that while trade unions, such as the Amalgamated Clothing Workers, Ladies' Garment Workers, and United Textile Workers, are building up decent wage rates and sound rules governing working conditions in New York, Massachusetts, Pennsylvania and Illinois, corporate capital, highly sensitive to the least threat to high rates of profits and interest upon investments, promptly takes flight into the land of non-union, low wage, low tax, race bias, mob law, and poor schools, namely, Dixie. Southern mayors, governors, and legislatures make special appeals in the northern press to industries to come South for non-union, cheap labor.

But this anti-trade union condition in the South is labor's fault. It is the direct result of the fact that neither the old AFL, nor the CIO, nor the AFL-CIO ever came to grips with the racial-labor problem in the South. Instead of meeting the racial-labor issue head on, organized labor has always adopted a policy of appeasement, compromise and defeatism. The evidence exists in the fact that it has recognized and accepted:

(a) The Jim Crow union

(b) The color bar in union constitutions, rituals, or exclusionary racial policies by tacit consent

(c) Racially segregated seniority rosters and lines of job progression

(d) Racial sub-wage differential

(e) Indifferent recognition, if not acceptance of the concept and practice of a "white man's job" and a "black man's job"

(f) Racial barriers against Negro participation in apprenticeship training programs

(g) Failure to demand Negro workers' participation in union democracy

(h) Racially segregated State conventions of the AFL-CIO in southern cities

(i) Racially segregated city central labor bodies of the AFL-CIO

Is there anyone so naive or cynical as to believe that these forms of race bias are not organizationally and economically disadvantageous to the black laboring masses? Not only has the long system of color caste condition in American industry thrust the Negro workers to the lowest rungs of the occupational hierarchy, but it tends to reinforce the accepted inferiority hereditary position of black labor, which drastically limits their economic mobility and viability.

Although not unaware of the fact that racial discrimination in trade unions affiliated to the AFL-CIO has existed for almost a century, no profound concern is now manifest by the leadership about this dreadful evil.

Instead of becoming aroused and disturbed about the existence of race bias in unions that affect employment opportunities and the economic status of the Negro worker, AFL-CIO leadership waves aside criticism of the movement's racial policies, as pure exaggeration unworthy of dispassionate examination.

Such was the reaction to a memorandum on race bias in

trade unions, together with corrective proposals, I submitted to George Meany and the Executive Council at Unity House, Pennsylvania, June 1961.

Instead of giving the memorandum a painstaking, rational analysis to determine if it contained any meritorious suggestions, it became the occasion of voluminous rebuttal and attack upon, and censure of, myself.

The rebuttal was not only innocuous, barren and sterile of a single new, vital, creative and constructive idea with which to grapple with the menace of race segregation and discrimination, but was a distressingly vain effort to justify a "do little" civil rights record in the House of Labor. . . .

Just a word now about the objective effects and results of race bias in trade unions and industry in two major cities that are generally considered to be relatively liberal, New York and Detroit.

In New York City, as well as throughout the State, non-white persons make up a very large part of those who live in poverty; a poverty that is frequently related to discriminatory racial practices that force Negroes into a marginal position in the economy, even though opportunities may increase for other groups within the community.

The two major industries in New York City are garment manufacturing and printing and publishing. The printing and publishing industry alone employs more than 160 thousand workers, or about nine percent of the manufacturing labor force. In both garment manufacturing and printing, however, we find that Negroes and Puerto Ricans are concentrated in the low paid, unskilled job classifications.

The Graduate School of Public Administration of Harvard University recently conducted a series of case studies in New York metropolitan manufacturing and concluded that in the New York garment industry Negroes and Puerto Ricans "were largely to be found in the less skilled, low-paid crafts and in shops making the lower priced lines, and in this industry their advancement to higher skills is not proceeding very rapidly. In the higher skilled coat and suit industry the new ethnic groups have hardly made an appearance."

The New York metropolitan region has twenty percent of the nation's employment in printing and publishing. In a survey made by the NAACP of Negro employment on the seven major New York City newspapers we find that, with the exclusion of building service and maintenance, less than one percent of those employed on the seven major newspapers are Negroes. Virtually all of the Negroes that are employed on these newspapers are within the white collar jurisdiction of the New York Newspaper Guild.

We estimate that less than one-half of one percent of those currently employed in the newspaper crafts outside of the Guild's jurisdiction are Negroes. This includes printing pressmen, compositors, photoengravers, stereotypers, paper handlers, mailers and delivery drivers.

In the past decade very little progress has been made in eliminating the traditional pattern of Negro exclusion and discrimination in the Plumbers and Pipe Fitters Union; the Iron and Structural Steel Workers; the Plasterers and Lathers; the Sheet Metal Workers; the Boiler Makers; the Carpenters, as well as the Bricklayers, Masons and Plasterers Union, and others.

In New York City, Negro waiters and bellboys are more noted by their absence than presence in the hotels and restaurants except, perhaps, in a token form at some banquets. However, Negroes are members of the Hotel and Restaurant Employees Union. One will need the proverbial microscope to discover a Negro bartender anywhere in the city except in a Negro community.

Negro motion picture operators have no job mobility. They are chiefly confined to the second-class motion picture theatres in Negro communities where they receive a sub-wage differential paid operators in this class of theatre.

At present there is a broad exclusion of Negro youth from major apprenticeship programs jointly conducted by industrial management and labor unions in the City of New York. For many occupations the only way a worker can be recognized as qualified for employment is to complete the apprenticeship training program. This is true for the printing trades, among machinists and metal workers, the construction industry, and others.

The role of the labor union in these occupations is decisive because the trade union usually determines who is admitted into the training program and, therefore, who is admitted into the union. This is especially true when the union controls access to employment.

In the New York metropolitan area there are many apprenticeship training programs in the building trades. Apprenticeship programs provide essential training for a wide variety of skills in their important area of the region's economy. These include apprenticeship programs for asbestos workers, electrical workers, glaziers, ironworkers, latherers, painters, plumbers and sheetmetal workers.

A recent study by the NAACP clearly indicates that less

than one percent of the apprentices in the construction industry throughout the nation are Negroes. Unfortunately, the number of Negroes in apprenticeship training programs in the New York construction industry differs little from the national pattern.

The lack of apprentice-trained Negro craftsmen directly affects the economic standing of Negroes as a whole. Data indicates that craftsmen command substantially higher incomes than unskilled workers. If, then, Negroes are not employed in such occupations in large numbers, a potential source of high income is removed from this group. When this is coupled with other income limitations it becomes apparent why Negroes constitute a permanently depressed segment of American society. . . .

The Problem Is Poverty*

DONALD A. JELINEK

The problem, as you can see, is poverty. It is poverty that keeps the Negro in his place—poverty that keeps him from registering, poverty that keeps his children in segregated schools, poverty that keeps him from enjoying the comforts and privileges of white society. This poverty is enabling the white Southerner to enter upon a new post-Reconstruction period, when once again federal legislation is nullified and past gains are repealed. As things now stand in Alabama there are only two ways in which Negroes can be sure of equal opportunities. They can get themselves arrested and go to jail —where by recent court order, all phases of life must be integrated. Or they can join the Army and go off to Vietnam, where they can die alongside a white man.

The federal government can cure the problem of poverty. I'm not talking about a guaranteed annual income, or even an increased expenditure on the part of the federal government. I'm talking about providing the Southern Negro with millions of dollars—in cash, rights, and services—that are

* Speech delivered at National Lawyers Guild convention, New York City, February 12, 1967. Jelinek was an attorney for the Lawyers' Constitutional Defense Committee working in Mississippi. Published for the first time here, by permission of Donald Jelinek.

rightfully his, but are taken away by Southern-born, Southern-bred, and federally-salaried employees.

These human obstacles are usually known as county agents for federal programs in the South. Would you believe me if I told you that Negroes in any rural Southern county would rather have a sympathetic county agent than a sympathetic governor?—for these county agents can exercise the power of life or death over the day-to-day economic life of the Negro farmer. These agents have one or two other things in common. They all dispense federal funds, and most are paid with federal funds. Yet all too often, they work to frustrate the expressed purposes of their government.

Of course, these agents aren't the only ones keeping the Negro down. The economic pressures on Negro farmers begin with the plantation owner, who not only provides what meager employment there is, but runs the company store and keeps his employees wrapped in a continuous line of credit. High city and county officials are usually the attorneys for the plantation owner, and mayors and judges are his cronies. There is little enough we can do about this part of the economic structure. We can attempt to stop the landlord from evicting tenants who register to vote or participate in civil rights activities—but few of these cases have been successful. (Morty Stavis is looking into a case in Lowndes County where the plantation owner required his tenants to say they were illiterate, so they would have to take an Alabama election official into the voting booth with them.) The plantation owners and their allies in the local government can dilute civil rights gains in all sorts of ways.

But the county agent, more often than not, is in league with these people. He is one of them, and *they* command his loyalty—not the federal government, and certainly not the Negro farmers he is supposed to serve. Usually, the agent's office is in the county courthouse. For all practical purposes, he is a county official, not a federal representative. There is no question that the federal government has the power and the ability to control these agents. But does it control them? Rarely.

Some of the agencies I'm talking about are the Agricultural Stabilization and Conservation Service (ASCS), the Farmers Home Administration (FHA), the Soil Conservation Service (SCS), the Federal Extension Service (FES) and the low-income housing projects supported by the Department of Housing and Urban Development (HUD).

The ASCS, which we'll discuss in greater detail later, doles out $43 million annually in Alabama alone, subsidizing cotton farmers and others against the decreasing world market.

The ASCS in each county tells farmers how much they can plant. For example, a white man may have 25 acres and a Negro may have 25 acres. But in a given case, a white man is given all 25 acres for cotton while the Negro is given only 5 acres. The result is that the Negro must work for the white man to support his farm, because at this time other crops are not feasible without co-oping.

The ASCS also measures the land. There are indications that another acre or two of that decreasing allotment is being taken away by a loaded measurement. Needless to say, the Negro farmer has neither the money to hire a professional nor the expertise himself to challenge the measurement. In addition, the ASCS controls its own elections to determine who shall dispense the funds. More about this later.

Next in importance is probably the Federal Extension Service (FES). This agency's job is to provide technical aid in all areas of farming, including livestock mortality problems, pasture problems, corn storage, livestock fertility problems, dairy farming, home management, veterinary medicine, and services to youth. FES, which spent $2½ million in Alabama last year, denies this technical assistance to Negro farmers, preventing them from properly using the land not allotted for cotton. For example, I have in my hand a proposal for an OEO grant of $218,000 for an Alabama Negro farmers cooperative association. Almost every penny of the grant would go to supply experts who are already on the FES payroll but are not available to Negro farmers. If OEO grants the $218,000, the 800 farmers involved estimate that their long-range gains would be substantial. In any agency such as FES, it is the denial of advice that hurts the Negro farmer, not the denial of money.

When it comes to capital expenditures to improve the land, increase the size of the farm or acquire additional livestock or equipment, the Negro farmer looks to the Farmers Home Administration (FHA), but usually in vain. This agency, which doles out $25 million in Alabama, grants loans to Negroes for operating expenses which further increase his debt, but is loathe to provide money for the acquisition of land. I think of one farmer, Mr. Rogers, who was afraid even to let the FHA agent know that he was buying land lest the agent spread the word, which would eventually intimidate the white landowner involved from selling the land to a Negro.

And when it comes to improving the land through sound conservation treatment and avoidance of soil exhaustion, the Negro farmer is supposed to turn to the Soil Conservation Service (SCS). This agency's expenditure of $4 million nually does not noticeably aid the Negro farmer, eith

There are over a quarter of a million Negro farmers in the South. This is the hard-core poverty belt. These are the Negroes who will be forced into the ghettos of Northern cities if their farms peter out. Federal money could give them a chance to work the land, more allotments of cotton to produce, improvement in farming and soil conditions and all the needed expertise to make a profit and employ more labor to work the land.

This is the briefest outline of a few of the federal regulatory agencies.

Now let me give you an illustration of what can happen when you take on one of these agencies. It is a story about the lawsuit we brought last summer against the United States Department of Agriculture and its ASCS, and the strange, even dramatic, ramifications of that suit.

Forgive me if I bore you with a few details about the ASCS, so you can understand what was at stake. The ASCS dispensed more than $15,000,000 in Alabama alone in 1966. It operates the cotton program in the South, and is responsible for allotting the acreage to be planted. I think it is fair to say that no cotton farmer—no matter how large or small—can survive by selling on the world market without government subsidies. But the farmer must limit his acreage if he wants to stay in the program.

So the national ASCS sets a national quota, the state ASCS the state quota and the county ASCS sets quotas for the individual farmers. The County tells you how much you can plant. The men who make these important decisions, and who appoint the county agent and other employees, are chosen in annual elections. In these elections—theoretically at least—all farmers, from sharecropper to plantation owner, have an equal vote. Nominations may be made by the people themselves, and by the incumbent county committee. The system may sound good, but there are many ways to frustrate it, and in Alabama they have tried them all.

Before 1964, virtually no Negroes participated in the yearly elections. In the 1964 elections, when the movement made its first effort to give Negro farmers a voice, the result was violence and large-scale intimidation. The federal government then tightened its regulations, but in 1965, the outcome of the elections was the same. No Negroes were elected to a county committee anywhere in Alabama—even in counties 80 percent Negro.

ce was the successful tactic in 1964, but in 1965 the key. For example, in Lowndes County—which cent Negro—the incumbent county committee ballot with more than 70 names of Negroes, using fathers, brothers, and so on, to confuse and divide the Negro voters. The real Negro candidates were lost in the confusion, and the result, once again, was an all-white county committee. (This particular election was set aside by the U.S. Department of Agriculture.)

In 1966, the movement was geared for a massive push. But the ASCS, on 35 days' notice, set elections for August 15, instead of the usual October-November date. This broke the back of any effort to organize the electorate. It was at this point that LCDC was approached, and after a few futile phone calls to Washington, we began suit to delay the elections and at the same time reform the regulations. . . . Before the hearing, the judge urged a meeting with Department of Agriculture officials. This meeting was held in a massive conference room, with some 18 officials representing Agriculture and with myself and two D. C. local counsels representing the farmers. I produced affidavits of Negro residents and civil rights workers testifying to the abuses of county officials, failure to supply election information, and so on. After four hours, I learned that there was a "delicate balance" between federal and state officials, that "great changes" had been accomplished, and that although no Negro had ever been elected, all would come to those who sat and waited, as opposed to those like us, who can never have enough. In the next days, preliminary conferences with the judge produced statements from the various officials that under no circumstances would the United States Department of Agriculture overrule a decision of the Alabama ASCS, and they doubted the court could order it to do so.

With those hopeful signs, the hearing began. While the negotiations were going on, 40 to 50 Negro farmers managed to drive to Washington in their old cars—along with Stokely Carmichael, whose presence provided the press. So we began to get front-page stories in the Washington *Post*.

Our first witness, Peter Agee of Marengo County, testified that he was threatened with death if he dared to take the stand in this case. The second witness told of bribes of increased allotments and livestock, conditional on his refusing to testify. That was followed by the introduction of a secret report, prepared by the Negro who headed the Agriculture Department's civil rights office, which began "If you wish to transmit this report to the White House, you may wish to omit the sections entitled 'Evaluation'."

The next day, the government's lawyers quoted Secretary Freeman to the effect that the "delicate balance" could stand a 30-day extension of the election deadline. The farmers voted to accept this.

Subsequently, Peter Agee was shot at in his home, and forced to flee Marengo County. Eight other families who took part in the case were threatened with eviction (law suits are pending). Another district judge, Holtzoff, dismissed our suit, charging [that] Administrative discrimination does not state a cause of action—this decision is presently on appeal. And the elections were lost anyhow—30 days weren't enough. . . .

Without going into great detail on other federal agencies, be assured that each one—to a greater or lesser degree—restricts the economic life of the Southern Negro. Nothing is being done to attack this situation. I know of no legal or civil rights group that is planning to undertake the work that is required. The work is dull, the work is tedious, and the work is difficult. But it must be done.

Mississippi Freedom Labor Union
1965 Origins*

EVERYBODY SHOULD BE on strike because you are not getting anything for your work. Why work and be hungry when you can gain the union some support? All the people that have children really should be on strike. Why make your child work for low wages when you all of your life have been working for nothing? Why buy the white man steak when you can't hardly eat neckbones? As cheap as chicken is you can't eat it but once a week on Sunday. Wake up and think. We as Negroes should want to be equal and get high wages. For over two hundred years we have been working for nothing. Please join the union because if you are not in a union you just aren't anywhere.

Here's how we got started.

The union started in January. A group of people at a freedom school discussion got together and decided that they weren't getting anything for their work. They formed a union

* An MFLU mimeographed report, 1965. The Mississippi Freedom Labor Union was organized in 1965, when sharecroppers in the Mississippi Delta organized a strike for higher wages. Many Delta families were evicted from plantations for union activities and subsequently lived for many months in a tent city near Tribbett, Mississippi. To press the federal government for aid 70 persons occupied a barracks at the Greenville air force base. A report of this action is given on pp. 501-05.

and started paying dues. They went to other counties in Mississippi spreading the ideal.

In March the people in Shaw, Mississippi, about 90 people, canvassed trying to get people to strike for higher wages. At that time the union didn't have a name and they didn't have papers for people to sign to go in the union. But now the union have improved a lot since this. They didn't have any way of knowing how they were going to get support then.

In April we found a name for the union and drew up the rules and they were decided on at the state workshop. Some of the people all over the Mississippi Delta are on strike.

Shaw is the headquarter since it started in Shaw. Every month we have a state meeting. Some of the things we do at this meeting are people from every precinct give us a report on what they have been doing in their county. We have officers. We have 1325 members in the union and 350 people on strike. The way we got these many people is talking to them and showing them the point of how important it is to form a union. We talk to people in the homes and on plantations at store, churches and town.

City workshop

The city workshop was held in Shaw by the chairman with local people to discuss what we would talk about at the statewide workshop. We also elected committees to issue. And we selected the rules for the union.

Statewide workshop

In the statewide workshop we had people from the following places—Glenallen, Winstonville, Louise, Greenville, Batesville, Rosedale, Carroll County, Vicksburg, Thorn, and Marks, Mississippi.

Out of these places we have 100 people on strike in Rosedale, 68 in Glenallen and 135 in Shaw.

What we talked about

We talked about the support of the union and we adopted the same rules for the state that we had in Shaw.

We also discussed ways of getting funds for the union strikers. We decided to write letters to people everywhere and ask for help. We also talked about why it was important for people to join the union.

Offering houses

The people in the union stated they would let people live in their homes if they get thrown off the plantation. So far none have been thrown off.

The union handed out $50.00 from dues

We gave $50.00 to three union members who need it very badly. One member needed it because they were threatened to be thrown out of their house and it was being used as a center. The second was threatened by the man she owed. And the third member and family was starving or living poverty. So that is how we use our dues to help the members.

On April 14th and 15th people from 8 counties picketed the Motor Inn Hotel in Greenville. They were having a U.S. Department of Labor meeting. We were trying to get them to let us in and meet our demands. The second day they let us come in and listen to speeches. Mr. Hawkins a Shaw union member asked a question about wages for farm work. Mrs. Hamer spoke inside the meeting the first day and she read the union forms her and 6 more people sent in.

The people are on strike in other places like Greenville, Winterville, Laymont, Rosedale, Batesville, Tribbett, and Anguilla.

The most strikers we have are cotton workers that mostly what about 100% of the Negroes in Mississippi depend on.

Two maids quit jobs to join the strikers and one tractor driver which was very good.

One plantation 37 people in Issaquena county went on strike for $.50 an hour and they were successful on Monday they will strike for $1.00 an hour. They only work 9 hours a day.

There are 9 tractor drivers on strike on a plantation in Glenallen. On a place in Shaw they struck for more money. Friday they found out they got a raise from $6.00 to $7.50 tractor drivers. They are planning to strike again as soon as it dries up.

The strikers started with the people who chop and pick cotton and tractor drivers and now the people on various plantations are striking.

Each town is organizing their strike and officers. The chairman in Shaw is George Shelton, Jr., Shaw.

We need help raising money so the people on strike can pay their house rent and bills.

The way we got land to raise gardens the landowner gave us a few acres to plant gardens on. The union started because the colored people weren't getting anything for their work. We will help the Negro farmers that gave us land to raise the gardens.

The money we raise we give it to the people to pay their house rent and bills. We would like for everyone to help support the strikers.

The food we are trying to get for people are just regular food like milk, canned meat, pinto beans, butter bean, lard, white corned meal.

We Have No Government[*]

Mr. Foster: The people are going to set up a tent city out at Tribbett and work on getting poor peoples to come and build a new city. Because of the fact that we was refused by the Federal Government and evicted, it's important that we start planning our own government.

Mrs. Blackwell: I feel that the federal government have proven that it don't care about poor people. Everything that we have asked for through these years has been handed down on paper. It's never been a reality. We the poor people of Mississippi is tired. We're tired of it so we're going to build for ourselves, because we don't have a government that represents us.

Mrs. Lawrence: See, you can only accept poor people by being poor and really knowing what being poor is like. And all this stuff about poverty programs and federal funds, that's out for poor peoples. We were looked upon as just a civil rights demonstration. But really we were there demanding and waiting and asking that these things be brought there to fill some desperate needs. And we was asking that the poor peoples be accepted as they stood. And instead of getting what we was asking, we got the whole air force troopers in on us. To me, that's our government.

Mr. Foster: Was.

Mrs. Lawrence: Yeah, was. Now, we're our own government—government by poor people. Where do we go from here? To brighter days on our own. And we know we'll reach that goal. But in their world, that's something that doesn't exist.

Reporter: About the poor people's government. Would this be an idea for a lot of people to come and live around Tribbett or somewhere in particular? Would this be a larger tent city?

* This is an edited transcription of a press conference held in the Greenville office of the Delta Ministry, Tuesday evening, February 1 1966. The participants included the three spokesmen for the over 70 poor Negroes who occupied the barracks of the Greenville Air Force Base. They were Mr. Isaac Foster of Tribbett, a leader in last spring's strike of plantation workers; Mrs. Unita Blackwell of Mayersville, a member of the Freedom Democratic Party executive committee; Mrs. Ida Mae Lawrence of Rosedale, chairman of her Mississippi Freedom Labor Union local; and Rev. Arthur Thomas of Greenville, director of the Delta Ministry of the National Council of Churches.

Mr. Foster: I know and you know that the tents are not going to stand forever. But I wouldn't be surprised it it wouldn't start that way.

Reporter: Does this mean that you would not consider yourselves bound by the restraints, the actions of county, state or federal law enforcement officers?

Mr. Foster: From nothing we must start building a new country, with our own laws, our own enforcement. No part of the system has any authority or control over us. Our goal is leading away from depending on the system for anything. And I would like to say that every poor person that will come is welcome.

Mrs. Blackwell: Not only from Mississippi but from all over the United States. And elsewhere, if they want to join. We will be sending telegrams to other nations, including African nations, for support.

Reporter: Does this mean that you won't sit down and talk to the Attorney General or other government representatives about your grievances?

Mr. Foster: If they would like to talk, we'll be willing to talk. But they didn't want to talk. They sent some Mississippian—chief or sergeant or something. He said give me the names of people who need relocation and I'll see what can be done about it. How can we leave the base when peoples don't have a house to stay in?

Mrs. Lawrence: The base is more thought of than the poor peoples was. The buildings weren't doing anything but just sitting there. The building was more respectable than poor hungry peoples with nothing and nowhere to go. If the peoples was satisfied and willing to sit there to find ways for themselves, the government should have let them stay there. The building was more important than poor folks.

Mr. Foster: The only reason that Colonel Jones could give for eviction was that the building that we was in didn't have running water and didn't have any type of fire protection. And see I know that the federal government can't tell me that was the reason we was put out, because all over Mississippi houses don't have running water or fire protection.

Rev. Thomas: It was cruel and inhuman of Orville Freeman and Nicholas Katzenbach to send the kind of message to us at the air base they sent today. They said nothing to us that hasn't been said for months and years. We were tired of waiting around for these people to live up to their words.

Reporter: Mr. Thomas, could you go into Operation Help?

Rev. Thomas: Over a year ago the Delta Ministry, in cooperation with the National Students Association, pointed out the need for a commodity program for Mississippi poor people. And we gave as an example of what local people could do, what was happening in Forrest County, where the people had set up their own distribution systems for contributed food and clothing. It works very well.

We offered to make Forrest County a trial case for food distribution if the Department would release the commodities to us.

Instead, the Department of Agriculture notified the State Department of Welfare that volunteer groups were willing and able to distribute commodities in Forrest County. In the face of that kind of possibility the county Board of Supervisors voted for the first time in years and years to participate in a commodity program. Immediately, the Department of Agriculture found it necessary to send an investigator in there to investigate charges of discrimination in that program.

We then made the same offer in regard to Madison County. Again Washington called the state welfare people, who notified the county Board of Supervisors. They came up with a Food Stamp program. Of course poor people can't afford to be in a food stamp program because it costs money and they don't have any income.

We then offered to set up distribution in any county that didn't have a program. In the face of this possibility the state Welfare Department came up with the proposal called Operation HELP—and keep in mind this was in August. All over the state people had gone without food through the winter while the Welfare Department and the Agriculture Department played politics with each other.

Under this plan, the Welfare Department will get 24 million dollars' worth of surplus commodites from the Department of Agriculture and 1.6 million dollars from the Office of Economic Opportunity to distribute the food to 500,000 people for six months.

In view of the criticisms of the program—which is based on the untenable assumption that welfare agencies and county boards of supervisors will act in a nondiscriminatory manner—OEO put certain conditions on the grant: one, that a bi-racial committee supervise the program, and two, that hiring and distribution be done on a non-discriminatory basis.

Our information has it that no such committee has been set up, although the proposal was submitted in August and granted in November. Dr. Aaron Henry, head of the state NAACP, was asked to nominate the Negroes for the committee. Why weren't poor people asked to nominate people?

In regard to the second condition, the food was supposed

to be ready for distribution by January 23. When that day came we could not find one poor person employed in the program and no food being given out. And now it's February.

Mrs. Lawrence: I'd like to add [to] that. To live, we got to go out and chop cotton for $3 a day, maybe two or three days a week. At the end of cotton picking, we gets the same for picking the scrap the machines leave. Then in November when they start qualifying you for the commodities, they say you got to find out how many people you worked for and get them to sign for you as being poor. If they don't feel like signing, like maybe they don't like you for civil rights activities, you don't get commodities. But you still poor, whether the white boss says so or not.

Mrs. Blackwell: See, if you belong to any civil rights group or participate, they tell you you can't get a job with the poverty program, because that's political and you know you can't have that. And that what's happening with the poverty program: it's political—that's the reason it's not doing anything for the poor.

Reporter: Mr. Thomas, why do you think the federal government is afraid to let poor Negroes go ahead and run the program?

Rev. Thomas: I could try to avoid that question and say that it is their problem. These people have the problem of not being dead. I will not avoid it and say nobody is unaware of the power of Congressman Whitten in the House Subcommittee on Agriculture. Nobody is unaware of the critical power of John Stennis in the Senate and its Finance Appropriations Committee. And these are the kinds of people who are supposed to represent the poor people in Congress.

Reporter: Are you saying that the people who run the poverty programs are kowtowing to the white power structure from here?

Rev. Thomas: That's what I'm saying. The poverty program and the Department of Agriculture.

I'd like to add one footnote. OEO says it's introducing an experimental program for food distribution. Well, I don't think these people ought to be experimented on. They're hungry now. They need food now. And there's no reason why food could not have been airlifted to those people.

Also, poor people in this state last year organized themselves into a Headstart program through the Child Development Group of Mississippi. Shriver and others said it was one of the best Headstarts anywhere in the country. In September they were told they would be funded in October; in October, the money was coming in November, in November, the money was coming in December, and so on and so on each month. Over 1000 local Mississippi poor people who have been promised money have been cheated by OEO.

Mrs. Lawrence: You know, we ain't dumb, even if we are poor. We need jobs. We need food. We need houses. But even with the poverty program we ain't got nothin but needs. That's why we was pulled off that building that wasn't being used for anything. We is ignored by the government. The thing about property upset them, but the things about poor people don't. So there's no way out but to begin your own beginning, whatever way you can. So far as I'm concerned, that's all I got to say about the past. We're beginning a new future.

PART IX

PREFACE TO THE 1974 EDITION

"Now, there is simply no possibility of a real change in the Negro's situation without the most radical and far-reaching changes in the American political and social structure. And it is clear that white Americans are not simply unwilling to effect these changes; they are, in the main, so slothful have they become, unable even to envision them. It must be added that the Negro himself no longer believes in the good faith of white Americans—if indeed, he ever could have."

James Baldwin, *The Fire Next Time*

EARLY ON THE civil rights movement of the '60s had spoken of the need for radical change in the structure of American society, but it was rhetoric without much substance. It was not until the late '60s, when the national alliance of large civil rights organizations had broken up and after the assassination of the Rev. Martin Luther King, Jr., that the necessity of "radical and far-reaching changes" in the political and social structure was fully recognized. Sixties activitists had talked of changing the system, but not until the '70s did many cite socialism as the goal. The Panthers were one of the earliest to define their ideology as "the historical experiences of Black people in America translated through Marxism-Leninism."[1]

By 1967, when the national alliance broke up, it had become clear that the gains represented only a small chipping away at the results of racism, and that barely a dent had been made in racism itself. The majority of blacks had not been much affected by the movement or its success, though large numbers had gained a measure of hope and a will to fight, and there was widespread anger. During the summer of 1967 there had been black rebellions in many major U.S. cities—all very similar. Black people attacked the nearest symbols of oppression—white-owned stores and the police. The summer's rebellions had been preceded by a significant one in Harlem in

[1] *The Black Panther*, Nov. 8, 1969.

1964 and by the Watts rebellion in Los Angeles in 1965—an historic one because it seemed to be so carefully planned: in block after block lone black-owned stores were left standing amidst the rubble of burned-out, white-owned establishments.

Then after King's assassination there were riots in 100 cities with 48 persons killed and about 200,000 arrested.

The movement did not stop when the national coalition of civil rights organizations dissolved.[2] The National Association for the Advancement of Colored People continued as it had before the nation turned its attention to Negro rights in the '60s though it became much more of a social service organization emphasizing such community-aid programs as the establishing of day-care centers, the building of housing projects, re-integration of ex-prisoners into the community.

Many local people who had been active in the days of mass marches, sit-ins and jail-ins formed community organizations which encouraged voter registration and ran election campaigns, helped build cooperatives to stem the decline of black landowners, organized unions and fought for better working conditions, established day-care centers. The major national organization which developed in this period was the National Welfare Rights Organization, a grass-roots organization of people which fought for the dignity and rights of welfare recipients.

Hundreds of small, militant groups were organized primarily around local issues in the late '60s and early '70s. Such groups sometimes joined in regional or national conferences, but there was no national coordination. The need for the development of a national movement was clear, but activists felt that a new mass movement must be built slowly and could not burgeon as the massive outpouring of the early 60's had.

While many upward striving blacks continued to believe in the vaunted virtues of the American Way and the Puritan ethic and pursued happiness through hard work, higher education and a house in the suburbs, most still felt the pinch of last-hired, first-fired and knew that they were the ones who suffered most from higher prices and lack of jobs, and that this would always be so unless some equity were forced by a change in the system.

[2] CORE, the Congress of Racial Equality, became a smaller, nationalist oriented organization; SNCC, the Student Nonviolent Coordinating Committee, withered away; SCLC, the Southern Christian Leadership Conference, lost much of its influence after Dr. King's death; liberal, white support diminished with the advent of black power.

These, the majority, knew that they continued .
prived, despite the new equality which did indeed exis.
Woolworth counters, at the polls, on the buses. It be
clear that the gains that had been made had benefited ь.
black middle class and had helped the masses only to the extent that the black middle class could represent the poor, could make their lives a little less harsh. To the black activists it also had become clear that there was no way that they could make America work for all without a change in the power relationships. Fifteen black members of Congress in no way changed the balance of power. And black people in the '70s came to recognize this.

Just as a more realistic view of power relationships came to the Mississippi farmer who participated in the MFDP, so a deeper understanding came from the fact of more blacks in so-called positions of power, nationally and locally. As one militant put it: if the elected leaders don't produce, people may rise against them as they did in destroying their own communities in the rebellions of the '60s. Another pointed out that people are continually learning: we are setting up our own schools, he said, because the whites aren't going to give up these schools until they are so decrepit that they don't want them anymore. This is a lesson that blacks have been learning and which has turned them more and more toward affiliations with other poor peoples and more and more to international relationships with the deprived, depressed, colonized, colored masses.

Black Liberation

INTRODUCTION

Several new trends emerged in the black struggle in the 1970s, among them a deeper involvement in the electoral politics, an increased concern about economic issues, and a renewed emphasis on the need for drastic change in the nation's economic and social system. These trends grew out of the civil rights movement of the 1960s and indeed had roots further back in history. They were a continuation of the historical dual nature of the black movement. Black people have always wanted in and wanted out of American life. Gaining more political power through the ballot and a larger share of America's riches are ways of seeking to gain entrance to the mainstream. Fighting for fundamental change in the system or opting out altogether through cultural black nationalism are ways of expressing black people's disillusionment with the American way.

The black liberation movement of the 1970s abandoned the goals of the civil rights movement of the '60s: integration, equal rights, and justice. That movement had lost momentum primarily because of its successes. Lunch counters, drinking fountains, and buses had been desegregated, and blacks were visible in jobs as bank tellers and department-store clerks. The battle for equal access to public accommodations had been won and the struggle had brought to the black masses new strength, dignity and hope, a will to fight and pride in blackness. What is more, black people had made substantial advances toward winning the right to vote. Black registration rose from 28% of those eligible in 1960 to 66% in 1968, though abridgements of the right to vote continued to abound.

Rather than outright intimidation, harassment, and violence, these took the form of gerrymandering, complicated registration procedures, and political machinations, such as exclusion of blacks from precinct meetings and disqualification of black ballots.[3] Many changes had taken place, but, as in the past, the gains tended to increase the recognition and resentment of the inequities which remained.

The civil rights movement of the '60s, for a short period before it faded, had thought of itself as a human rights movement and did in fact become more international in outlook. Civil rights leaders took a stand against the Vietnam war and more and more the movement concerned itself with the plight of Third World peoples. The national civil rights coalition broke up—the only two national organizations with the same leadership and policies still functioning in 1970 were the National Association for the Advancement of Colored People and the National Urban League—but the movement left a legacy to the liberation movement of the '70s. The international outlook was among the benefits. Many people in the later movement looked at the problems of the American black as part of a worldwide problem of exploitation of colored peoples and the movement for the first time took on a class and anti-imperialist perspective. Another legacy of the '60s was a drive for black power, both within the context of the social and economic system and outside it. After 1966 when it was first articulated, the concept of black power led to the drives for black political and economic power. By 1973 there were 2,621 black elected officials in the nation. Ninety percent of these were local officials. There were 82 mayors (in such large cities as Los Angeles, Washington, D.C., Detroit, Gary, Indiana; Atlanta and Newark) and 43 vice mayors, and, what is perhaps more important to the quality of life, in the Southern states there were 198 elected law enforcement officers. Although the total number of black elected officials represented an increase of 121% over 1969 and compared to 62 black elected officials in the U.S. in 1962, the number of elective offices held by blacks represented only a small proportion of all elective offices—five-tenths of one percent. It should also be noted that while the increase was great, black interest in electoral politics was low, with only 52.1% of those eligible turning out to vote in the 1972 elections.

[3] See *Abridging the Right to Vote, A Study of State Restrictions and Black Political Participation,* National Urban League, Inc., 1972.

There were, by 1973, 15 black members of the House of Representatives and one black Senator. The House members had formed the Congressional Black Caucus in 1969 to press for more legislative attention to black concerns. In 1970 its then nine members sought a meeting with President Nixon, but indicating a change in the government's interest in black problems, the CBC was ignored for a year. Then, after its members boycotted his State of the Union message, the President met with them to hear their 60 pages of recommendations. This was consistent with the policy of "benign neglect" proposed by Daniel P. Moynihan, counselor to the President. The Moynihan proposal said: "The time may have come when the issue of race could benefit from a period of 'benign neglect.' The subject has been too much talked about." It proposed a consultation on the subject within the administration, crime studies, more emphasis on Mexican Americans, Indians, and Puerto Ricans and more recognition of the "silent black majority."[4]

The CBC attempted to spotlight some black issues by holding hearings around the country on the Chicago deaths of Black Panther leaders Fred Hampton and Mark Clark, on prison conditions, on the rights of black servicemen. Then in 1971 the CBC sponsored a meeting out of which came the call for a national black political convention. In the end, though the CBC did not endorse the convention held in March, 1973, in Gary, Indiana, several of its members took part in the historic meeting. Convention participation ranged over most of the spectrum of black political opinion (though the far left seemed to have been excluded) and adopted a National Black Agenda. [see page 521 for excerpts]. Several continuations bodies carried on aspects of the Agenda's recommendations for action, e.g., participation in the defense of black political prisoners, a boycott of oil companies dealing with Portugal, support for the Democratic Party's struggle to retain the liberal convention rules adopted for its 1972 convention, plans for unified electoral action.

The black power thrust not only led to increased participation in the electoral system but also to an intensification of the separatist trend always present in American Negro history. Two national Black Power Conferences were held from which plans developed for the Gary convention representing,

---

[4] For text see *The New York Times*, March 1, 1970.

as Imamu Baraka, a co-convenor, termed it, a "broad-based operational unity" and the more "specifically ideological" cultural nationalist organization, the Congress of African Peoples.

The period saw the rise in several communities around the country of small nationalist groups based on separation from the white community and economic cooperation within their own group. Many of these taught Swahili and some set up private, independent schools covering nursery age through high school.

One of the most widely known political groups which grew out of the black power concept was the Black Panther Party. Part of its reputation was based on the fear it produced in whites because of its stress on armed defense. The Panthers startled the nation in 1967 when a group of Party members entered the California State Legislature armed with automatic weapons to protest a gun control bill. Panthers had also adopted the tactic of placing armed guards around street-corner rallies, of providing legal advice and protection to persons arrested on the street, and of patrolling the streets of the black community armed. An offshoot of the Panther Party, the Black Liberation Army, in the '70s extended the concept of armed defense to one of offense—attacks on the police.

By 1974 the Panther Party had little influence, having been greatly weakened by internal splits and by government efforts to suppress it. Many Panthers were killed in gun battles with police,[5] and scores were involved in long legal battles on various charges, including murder. Significantly, the government was unable to obtain convictions in most Panther trials as well as in other political trials of blacks in the early '70s. Partly this was because more blacks were serving on juries, and partly because jurors seemed to hold the view that many political trials had come about through the activities of *agents provocateurs* and police spies. Many dissenting jurors simply avowed that they did not believe government witnesses. With the revelations of governmental clandestine activity against "enemies" and political dissenters in the Watergate investi-

---

[5] Charles Garry, Panther attorney, claimed that 28 party members had been murdered by the police. The claim was widely publicized and garnered support for the Panthers though it was disputed in a highly controversial article by Edward Jay Epstein, "The Panthers and the ━ A Pattern of Genocide?", which appeared in *The New York* 1971.

gation, skepticism of governmental denials of persecution of such groups as the Panthers increased. Charges of attempts by the government to disrupt radical political groups (black and white) were substantiated. A memo from J. Edgar Hoover, late Director of the Federal Bureau of Investigation, dated May 10, 1968, said the purpose of its counterintelligence program "is to expose, disrupt, and otherwise neutralize the activities of the various New Left organizations, their leadership, and adherents."[6] In a 1970 memo, the Director ordered FBI Special Agents to watch all Black Student Unions and similar groups "which are targets for influence and control by violence-prone Black Panther Party (BPP) and other extremists."[7] The surveillance was so thorough that it included the "monitoring" of the bank account of the National Black Economic Development Conference.[8]

Though they emphasized the need to fight police repression and to emphasize blackness, the Panthers did not shrink from alliances with whites. In 1968 they were aligned with the interracial Peace and Freedom Party and by 1973 they had entered electoral politics on their own, and were appealing to white and black voters when Panther Chairman Bobby Seale ran for Mayor of Oakland.

At the same time that many black groups were turning to electoral politics, black people were also concerning themselves with a worsening economic situation. Despite political gains, the relative income gap between black and white families widened after 1970.[9] Black family income was 61% that of white in 1969, representing a steady closing of the gap, but it fell to 59% in 1970. A National Urban League study pointed out: "Although blacks made steady progress during the 1960's, their economic status has deteriorated since 1969. Between 1969 and 1972, the unemployment rates among blacks jumped from 6.4 percent to 10.0 percent. . . . And the unemployment rates among black teenagers skyrocketed from

[6] "Counterintelligence Program, Internal Security, Disruption of the New Left," Memo from Director, Federal Bureau of Investigation, to all Special Agents in Charge, May 10, 1968.
[7] *State Secrets Police Surveillance in America*, Paul Cowan, Nick Egleson and Nat Hentoff; Holt, Rinehart and Winston, New York, 1974, pp. 195–6.
[8] There is no reason to believe that such surveillance was limited to the Philadelphia area, though the particular organization cited here was the Philadelphia chapter of the BEDC.
[9] *Benign Neglect Revisited: The Illusion of Black Progress*, Robert B. Hill, National Urban League Research Department, Washington, D.C., '73.

about one out of four in 1969 to about one out of three in 1972."

In 1968, 44.9% of blacks had incomes below the poverty level. Among the actions black people took was the Poor Peoples' Campaign in which blacks, Chicanos, Puerto Ricans, and Native Americans joined together under the initial sponsorship of the Southern Christian Leadership Conference to present economic demands in Washington. Over 50,000 persons took part in a "Solidarity Day" demonstration and 3,000 camped on the Mall in Resurrection City. On the last day of the protest, 115 persons who had elected to remain in Resurrection City were arrested.

In 1969, in the first large-scale claim that black people were due reparations for 300 years of deprivation, the Black Economic Development Conference adopted the Black Manifesto which demanded of white churches and synagogues $500 million to be used to help develop communications skills, establish a labor strike and defense fund, a Southern land bank, and a United Black Appeal to set up cooperative businesses. The churches were shocked when James Forman (prominent in the national civil rights coalition of the '60s as executive secretary of SNCC) interrupted the church service at Riverside Church, New York, to read the Manifesto to the congregation. But the churches responded. While the goal of the Manifesto was not reached, churches gave millions of dollars to black community organizations around the country and to the Black Economic Development Conference itself. Church action was also sparked by black caucuses formed within denominations though the Manifesto was the most powerful impetus to church funding of the black struggle. The Interreligious Foundation for Community Organization was a prime spark of religious involvement for it planned and convened the Black Economic Development Conference and provided about $300,000 yearly to nearly 50 minority organizations.

Inter-religious Foundation for Community Organization and similar groups tended toward a cooperative rather than an individualistic approach to economic improvement. The movement in the ghetto for "economic empowerment" of black people led also to an interest in "black capitalism"—individual operation of stores and other businesses for private profit, but the most progressive forces leaned toward community enterprises. In urban areas one of the forms this took was the Community Development Corporation, which grew out of a recognition of the drive for black control and community involvement. The CDC idea was also an outgrowth of the urban rebellions of the late '60s which saw the destruction of millions of dollars of ghetto property. In rural areas, particularly of the South, the form "economic empowerment" took was the rural cooperative—credit unions, marketing cooperatives, consumer and producer cooperatives.

A major aim of the cooperative movement was to help stem the decline in land ownership by blacks. By 1972 the cooperatives had shown some success. There were about 75 co-ops with between 200 and 300 members each. Individual farmer income had increased and one or two co-ops had shown some profit. However, both the rural cooperatives and the CDC's suffered from the fact that the bulk of their financing had originally been white and would of necessity remain white. Further, it appeared that, despite church support, with government retrenchment both programs would become more and more dependent on national, white foundations.[10]

Another cooperative Southern program was Southern Rural Action, Inc., with a self-help program for economic development. In its first seven years SRA provided technical assistance to over one hundred communities. SRA also established 19 factories and built over 400 homes.

One section of society in which militant action was renewed in the '70s was the black working class. Black caucuses existed in most unions where there was black membership and across the country blacks were organizing workers into unions or forming black workers organizations outside their union locals as bases from which to fight both unions and management. Some of these groups such as the League of Revolutionary Black Workers were Marxist.

In many cases blacks played leadership roles even when both black and white workers were involved. In most labor union activity of this period, nonwhites were the militants— the hospital workers in New York, the farmworkers in the Western and Southern states. This was partly because blacks, Puerto Ricans, and Chicanos had been on the lowest rung of the ladder and were fighting to climb upwards. The prepon-

[10] For an evaluation of CDC's, see "Special Issue: Community Development Corporations," *The Review of Black Political Economy*, Vol. 3, No. 3, Spring, 1973.

derance of nonwhite activism had resulted from the substantial increase in the number of black and other nonwhite workers in heavy industry. Herbert Hill, labor director of the NAACP, pointed out that the percentage of black workers in the major automotive plants had risen by 1968 to 65% in some to 75% in others. Much of this increase occurred because whites were leaving for jobs in other fields such as electronics. Wilbur Haddock of the United Black Workers, an organization of black auto workers, pointed to a high degree of racial tension in plants. Many nonwhites in the new job force were veterans of the Vietnam war, or they were immigrants, veterans of revolutionary struggle in Haiti or the Dominican Republic, who were not prepared to "take it" as the older generation had. Blacks agitated in the plants for better conditions and in unions for more black union leadership and more militance. They also went to court fighting for such things as compensation for lost seniority rights, for preferential hiring, and against discrimination in hiring halls.

In the South an astonishing development took place. Some of the union organizing was interracial with former Ku Klux Klan members joining blacks in a fight against low pay and bad working conditions in hospitals, the pulpwood and poultry industries.

Blacks were also using traditional middle-class methods to gain a foothold. PUSH, People United to Save Humanity, Jesse Jackson's Chicago-based organization, negotiated agreements with major national corporations for the hiring of blacks and use of black banks, black contractors, and other black-owned enterprises.

Perhaps the overwhelming trend of the period was the emphasis on the necessity of having black people lead the struggle. This held true for the assimilationists, the separatists, and the Marxists. The second most important trend was the alliance of blacks and Third World creased interest in internationali again on the rise. This interest h '60s when large numbers of Afri dence, but in the '70s the focus can blacks to the African hom marily spiritual, but much of t the '70s stressed political ties. Tl land or as part of a black l America's cultural past remain

" Lerone Bennett;
*Black Panther Pa
by permission.

part of a struggle of Third World colonized peoples against imperialist control became more widely held. Black people were acutely aware that, as writer Lerone Bennett, Jr., put it, "Above all else, there is a confusion of the interests of white people, a tiny minority of the world's population, and the interests of the world."[11] Many militants had come to the conclusion that while a black movement might continue to fight in the United States without a free, united, and independent Africa, such a movement could not win its fight. Many black people felt that the Third World peoples were interdependent and saw the struggle in the United States as bound up in the worldwide struggle against the political and economic control of the Western, industralized nations.

1. POLITICS

*Black Panther Party Platform**

1. WE WANT FREEDOM. *We want power to determine the destiny of our Black Community*.

We believe that black people will not be free until we are able to determine our destiny.

2. We want full employment for our people.

We believe that the federal government is responsible and ~~ted~~ to give every man employment or a guaranteed in- ~~We~~ believe that if the white American businessmen will ~~full~~ employment, then the means of production

Jr., *Ebony*, August, 1970.
~~ty~~ Platform and Program, October, 1966. Reprinted

should be taken from the businessmen and placed in the community so that the people of the community can organize and employ all of its people and give a high standard of living.

3. We want an end to the robbery by the white man of our Black Community.

We believe that this racist government has robbed us and now we are demanding the overdue debt of forty acres and two mules. Forty acres and two mules was promised 100 years ago as restitution for slave labor and mass murder of black people. We will accept the payment in currency which will be distributed to our many communities. The Germans are now aiding the Jews in Israel for the genocide of the Jewish people. The Germans murdered six million Jews. The American racist has taken part in the slaughter of over fifty million black people; therefore, we feel that this is a modest demand that we make.

4. We want decent housing, fit for shelter of human beings.

We believe that if the white landlords will not give decent housing to our black community, then the housing and the land should be made into cooperatives so that our community, with government aid, can build and make decent housing for its people.

5. We want education for our people that exposes the true nature of this decadent American society. We want education that teaches us our true history and our role in the present-day society.

We believe in an educational system that will give to our people a knowledge of self. If a man does not have knowledge of himself and his position in society and the world, then he has little chance to relate to anything else.

6. We want all black men to be exempt from military service.

We believe that black people should not be forced to fight in the military service to defend a racist government that does not protect us. We will not fight and kill other people of color in the world who, like the black people, are being victimized by the white racist government of America. We will protect ourselves from the force and violence of the racist police and the racist military, by whatever means necessary.

7. We want an immediate end to POLICE BRUTALITY and MURDER of black people.

We believe we can end police brutality in our black community by organizing black self-defense groups that are dedicated to defending our black community from racist police oppression and brutality. The second Amendment to the Constitution of the United States gives us a right to bear arms. We therefore believe that all black people should arm themselves for self-defense.

8. *We want freedom for all black men held in federal, state, county and city prisons and jails.*

We believe that all black people should be released from the many jails and prisons because they have not received a fair and impartial trial.

9. *We want all black people when brought to trial to be tried in court by a jury of their peer group or people from their black communities, as defined by the Constitution of the United States.*

We believe that the courts should follow the United States Constitution so that black people will receive fair trials. The 14th Amendment of the U.S. Constitution gives a man a right to be tried by his peer group. A peer is a person from a similar economic, social, religious, geographical, environmental, historical and racial background. To do this the court will be forced to select a jury from the black community from which the black defendant came. We have been, and are being tried by all-white juries that have no understanding of the "average reasoning man" of the black community.

10. *We want land, bread, housing, education, clothing, justice and peace. And as our major political objective, a United Nations-supervised plebiscite to be held throughout the black colony in which only black colonial subjects will be allowed to participate, for the purpose of determining the will of black people as to their national destiny.*

When, in the course of human events, it becomes necessary for one people to dissolve the political bands which have connected them with another, and to assume, among the powers of the earth, the separate and equal station to which the laws of nature and nature's God entitle them, a decent respect to the opinions of mankind requires that they should declare the causes which impel them to the separation.

We hold these truths to be self-evident, that all men are created equal; that they are endowed by their Creator with certain unalienable rights; that among these are life, liberty, and the pursuit of happiness. *That, to secure these rights, governments are instituted among men, deriving their just powers from the consent of the governed; that, whenever any form of government becomes destructive of these ends, it is the right of the people to alter or to abolish it, and to institute a new government, laying its foundation on such principles, and organizing its powers in such form, as to them shall seem most likely to effect their safety and happiness.* Prudence, indeed, will dictate that governments long established should not be changed for light and transient causes; and, accordingly, all experience hath shown, that mankind are more disposed to suffer, while evils are sufferable, than to right themselves by abolishing the forms to which they are accustomed. *But, when a long train of abuses and usurpations pursuing invariably the same object, evinces a design to reduce them under absolute despotism, it is their right, it is their duty, to throw off such government, and to provide new guards for their future security.*

*National Black Political Agenda**

INTRODUCTION

THE BLACK AGENDA is addressed primarily to Black people in America. It rises naturally out of the bloody decades and centuries of our people's struggle on these shores. It flows from the most recent surgings of our own cultural and political consciousness. It is our attempt to define some of the essential changes which must take place in this land as we and our children move to self-determination and true independence.

The Black Agenda assumes that no truly basic change for our benefit takes place in Black or white America unless we Black people organize to initiate that change. It assumes that

*Adopted at National Black Political Convention, Gary, Indiana; March, 1972. Reprinted by permission.

we must have some essential agreement on overall goals, even though we may differ on many specific strategies.

Therefore, this is an initial statement of goals and directions for our own generation, some first definitions of crucial issues around which Black people must organize and move in 1972 and beyond. Anyone who claims to be serious about the survival and liberation of Black people must be serious about the implementation of the Black Agenda.

We come to Gary in an hour of great crisis and tremendous promise for Black America. While the white nation hovers on the brink of chaos, while its politicians offer no hope of real change, we stand on the edge of history and are faced with an amazing and frightening choice: We may choose in 1972 to slip back into the decadent white politics of American life, or we may press forward, moving relentlessly from Gary to the creation of our own Black life. The choice is large, but the time is very short . . .

A Black political convention, indeed all truly Black politics must begin from this truth: *The American system does not work for the masses of our people, and it cannot be made to work without radical fundamental change.* (Indeed, this system does not really work in favor of the humanity of anyone in America.) . . .

Here at Gary, let us never forget that while the times and the names and the parties have continually changed, one truth has faced us insistently, never changing: Both parties have betrayed us whenever their interests conflicted with ours (which was most of the time), and whenever our forces were unorganized and dependent, quiescent and compliant. Nor should this be surprising, for by now we must know that the American political system, like all other white institutions in America, was designed to operate for the benefit of the white race: It was never meant to do anything else . . .

So we come to Gary confronted with a choice. But it is not the old convention question of which candidate shall we support, the pointless question of who is to preside over a decaying and unsalvageable system. No, if we come to Gary out of the realities of the Black communities of this land, then the only real choice for us is whether or not we will live by the truth we know, whether we will move to organize independently, move to struggle for fundamental transformation, for the creation of new directions, towards a concern for the life and the meaning of Man. Social transformation or social destruction, those are our only real choices.

If we have come to Gary on behalf of our people in America, in the rest of this hemisphere, and in the Homeland—if we have come for our own best ambitions—then a new Black Politics must come to birth. If we are serious, the Black Politics of Gary must accept major responsibility for creating both the atmosphere and the program for fundamental, far-ranging change in America. Such responsibility is ours because it is our people who are most deeply hurt and ravaged by the present systems of society. That responsibility for leading the change is ours because we live in a society where few other men really believe in the responsibility of a truly humane society for anyone anywhere.

The challenge is thrown to us here in Gary. It is the challenge to consolidate and organize our own Black role as the vanguard in the struggle for a new society. To accept that challenge is to move independent Black politics. There can be no equivocation on that issue. History leaves us no other choice. White politics has not and cannot bring the changes we need . . .

So when we turn to a Black Agenda for the seventies, we move in the truth of history, in the reality of the moment. We move recognizing that no one else is going to represent our interests but ourselves. *The society we seek cannot come unless Black people organize to advance its coming.* We lift up a Black Agenda recognizing that white America moves towards the abyss created by its own racist arrogance, misplaced priorities, rampant materialism, and ethical bankruptcy. Therefore, we are certain that the Agenda we now press for in Gary is not only for the future of Black humanity, but is probably the only way the rest of America can save itself from the harvest of its criminal past.

We begin here and now in Gary. We begin with an independent Black political movement, an independent Black Political Agenda, an independent Black spirit. Nothing less will do. We must build for our people. We must build for our world. We stand on the edge of history. We cannot turn back.

ACTION AGENDA

POLITICAL EMPOWERMENT: The bondage of Black people in America has been sanctioned and perpetuated by the American political system—for the American political system is one of politics dedicated to the preservation of white power.

It was white politics that enslaved Black people and disfranchised them without a second thought.

At this moment in history then, Black people must decide whose side they are on. Are they for or against this system? This is the question of our future and of America's which Blacks must honestly face with all its implications and with all its meanings.

The Black politics we need goes far beyond electoral politics and far beyond 1972. WE NEED PERMANENT POLITICAL MOVEMENT THAT ADDRESSES ITSELF TO THE BASIC CONTROL AND RESHAPING OF AMERICAN INSTITUTIONS THAT CURRENTLY EXPLOIT BLACK AMERICA AND THREATEN THE WHOLE SOCIETY. The unifying objective of this political movement must be the empowerment of the Black community, not simply its representatives. It must offer basic alternatives to all the existing American political, economic and cultural systems.

The National Black Assembly should pledge itself to organize and mobilize such a community-based movement towards amassing the needed resources and power to achieve full Black empowerment.

The National Black Assembly should create a Black Commission to study reapportionment and redistricting and develop and implement strategies for striking down gerrymandering by whites designed to destroy Black power.

The National Black Assembly should initiate a national voter education and registration drive among Black voters. . . .

There must be two-way Black political accountability in which the Black community gives financial support to Black candidates and they, in turn, when elected, promise faithfully to represent the Black community. Black delegates and candidates must account for themselves and their policies to functioning and duly authorized structures of the national, state or local Black Political Convention structures. . . .

There should be support of the right of the Government of the Republic of New Africa to hold plebiscites in the predominately Black counties of the Deep South, to determine whether the inhabitants of these areas wish their counties and themselves to be part of an independent New African Nation

(Republic of New Africa) or wish to remain under the captive sovereignty of the United States.

The National Black Assembly has the right and responsibility to have observers present at the time and place of all aforementioned independence and self-determination plebiscites in order to insure that they are justly and peacefully administered. . . .

ECONOMIC EMPOWERMENT: . . . an incalculable social indebtedness has been generated, a debt which is owed to Black people by the general American society. So, while the moral horrors of slavery and the human indignities visited upon our people by racial discrimination can never really be compensated for—we must not rest until American society has recognized our valid, historic right to reparations, to a massive claim on the financial assets of the American economy. At the same time, it is necessary that Black people realize that full economic development for us cannot take place without radical transformation of the economic system which has so clearly exploited us these many years. . . .

Establish a national Black commission (chosen by the National Black Assembly) to determine a procedure for calculating a reparations schedule in terms of land, capital and cash, and to explore the ways in which the Black community prefers to have this payment implemented.

Establish a Black United Fund with regional and representative Black leadership. All Black persons will be solicited to contribute toward this fund in proportion to their annual income, with the proceeds to be used for Black charitable and development purposes.

Encourage Black consumers to spend as much of their purchasing power as possible in Black-owned and operated stores, and to avoid firms having negative impact on the Black community. Form a national Black consumer protective committee. . . .

Establish, where racial discrimination exists in labor unions, Black parallel unions which are automatically afforded the same privileges as those enjoyed by the discriminatory unions.

Encourage exploration of alternative forms of economic organization and development of an economic system that promotes self-reliance, cooperative economics, and people ownership and control of means of production and distribution of goods.

Initiate Black community-based efforts to pressure churches, educational institutions and corporations to make more meaningful investments in Black-controlled community development projects.

Initiate Black community-based efforts against specific churches and educational institutions which are involved in the exploitation of Black people here and abroad.

HUMAN DEVELOPMENT: . . . Act to develop mechanisms for Black control of the schools where Black children are educated, moving beyond the sterile issue of "busing" to the basic issue of the redistribution of educational wealth and control . . .

Establish drug information programs geared toward Black youth and controlled by the Black community. . . .

Act to constitute investigative teams of Black citizens to systematically review the treatment and legal status of Black people within mental institutions and prisons (civilian and military) to ensure that basic human rights are not infringed, and that treatment is fair and equitable. . . .

Oppose the present plans for a National 1976 Bicentennial and all other anti-human events celebrated by white American society. The millions of dollars now available and being directed toward this "Giant Birthday Party" should be directed toward the provision of adequate housing, jobs, quality education and sufficient food and jobs for Black people.

INTERNATIONAL POLICY AND BLACK PEOPLE: Because the history and culture of Black people is fundamentally related to our African birthright, we are concerned about the movement of colonized African countries from subjugation to independence and from neo-colonized states to fully independent ones. In the southern African areas of Azania (South Africa), Zimbabwe (Rhodesia), Namibia (South West Africa), Angola, Mozambique and Guinea Bissau, African people are dominated, exploited and brutalized by Europeans, and particularly the NATO powers—headed by the United States. This situation manifests itself not only in Africa but also in Vietnam, the Middle East, the Caribbean and other places in the Third and Pan-African World. It is world-wide military imperialism.

This situation of global white oppression arises because the European countries, supported by the United States, need to expand their control of sources of cheap labor and raw materials into Africa and the Third World in order to continue to reap profits. These white countries seek to protect their domination and exploitation by the establishment of treaties which provide for military bases and communication facilities used to suppress Africa and Third World revolutions and maintain the racist *status quo.*

Therefore: Black people will no longer abdicate their international responsibilities but will support an international policy agenda designed to:

1. Further the progress of provisional governments and the revolutionary movements in Africa, especially in Azania, Namibia, Mozambique, Angola, Zimbabwe and Guinea Bissau, and to assist other African countries in their movement toward meaningful political independence.

2. Promote African economic independence and help these countries achieve self-sufficiency, thus ending their role as the suppliers of labor and raw materials for European, American and other imperialists.

3. Effect the world-wide disintegration of the economic and political control and racist exploitation of African and Third World peoples by Europeans and Americans . . .

Recognize the importance of the models provided by Tanzania and the Peoples Republic of China for fundamental political and economic transformation of African and Third World states.

Support the complete self-determination of Puerto Rico and the Virgin Islands and the elimination of overt and covert intervention by the United States into the domestic affairs of the Caribbean countries.

Organize Black action groups to demand that the United States end economic and political sanctions against Cuba and ends its occupation of Guantanamo Bay.

Organize Black action groups to demand economic sanctions against the products of specific companies, national and international, which are involved in the exploitation of Black people here and abroad.

Denounce and withhold Black participation in wars which suppress revolutionary struggles in Africa and the non-white Third World . . .

Support the positions of the Organization of African Unity and the U.N. Commission on Human Rights in opposing the Israeli government's expansionist policy.

a. Whereas, as an African People we fully support the struggle of oppressed peoples against their oppressors, and Whereas, we recognize that there is a crisis in the Middle East involving the oppressed people of North Africa, and Whereas, we support the O.A.U. as the representative body which speaks for our brothers on the continent, and recognize that the positions of the O.A.U. and the U.N. Commission on Human Rights are valid and fair; Therefore, be it resolved that the Convention go on record as being in agreement with the O.A.U. positions that call for:

1. The Israeli Government to be condemned for her expansionist policy and forceful occupation of the sovereign territory of another state.
2. Measures to be taken to alleviate the suffering and improve the position of Palestinian people in Israel.

b. The National Black Political Convention resolves to support the struggle of Palestine for self-determination.
c. The National Black Political Convention concurs also with the U.N. position that Israel rescind and desist from all practice affecting the demographic structure or physical character of occupied Arab territories and the rights of their inhabitants.

Support International African Liberation Day and join with African people in Canada, the Caribbean, and throughout the world in a display of solidarity and support for oppressed African people of Southern Africa on May 27, 1972 and annually thereafter.

COMMUNICATIONS: . . . Move to control television and radio outlets. . . . Form media watchdog committees to document unfair media practices in hiring, news coverage, entertainment and advertising. . . . Move to transfer certain local and national radio and television properties (including cable TV) to Black community control. . . .

RURAL DEVELOPMENT: . . . Act to provide financial and political support for the further development by Blacks of new communities in rural areas.

Act to establish Land Banks to assure continual Black ownership and control of land to be used for cooperative crop production, soil fertilization research and animal husbandry.

The National Black Assembly to create a Council on Rural Development to lend technical assistance to Black farm owners, to create cooperative marketing ventures, to develop ways of creating food processing plants in the South, to conduct research into modern farming methods, and to plan a national design for rural development.

Encourage young Blacks through scholarships and other aids to pursue careers and training in food technology, parasitology, bio-medical research, and agricultural management to provide the technicians for the Council on Rural Development.

Mount a major organizational effort to develop cooperative farms across the country in conjunction with Black groups and organizations functioning in rural areas.

[In addition, there were proposed programs for environmental protection, self-determination for the District of Columbia and an action agenda for political officeholders and seekers. *Ed.*]

*To Past and Present Gang Members**

IT ALL STARTED in late 1957 or 1958. I'm jiving on Decatur St. between Hopkinson Ave. and Broadway, a Brooklyn Black Colony. I'm around 12 or 13 years old. For the next five years I will be known as a jitterbug, a be-bop, a skitter Hop, a Club Member or a plain old gang member. Through this traumatic experience my rewards and hardships have been many. I received my first baptism of fire and dug a lot of Brothers offed by other Brothers. While we were getting down on Hopkinson and Rockaway Aves against the Corsair Lords, (so was Che and Fidel from the mountains of Cuba against fascist Batista). While our tactics were the same, the enemy was not clearly defined as in the case of Che and Fidel. While we were on the corners of the Colonies Jungle, singing and dancing to the Spaniel's "Stormy Weather" and Bobby Days Rocking Robin, Che and Fidel were in the mountains of Cuba dancing to the sound of gunfire, music to make revolution by. While it has been stated that history is best to reward all information, I would add also to learn by other's mistakes, because one does not live long enough to make them all him-

*Reprinted by permission

self. All we have to do, is to look at the state of affairs we are faced with today. Once you do study and investigate, I think most of you will stop dealing in that reactionary era of history, and come together to form that focal point in the People's Liberation Army, that Comrade George Jackson spoke of while those of us who were in that past era of clubs or gangs, may have had the excuse that the political level of America was not then what it is today. That surely does not hold true for you today in 1972. And once one thinks about it, there really was no excuse for us.

Although this is '72 and the enemy has clearly been defined; Stompers, Chaplins, Corsairs, Nits, Bishops, El Quinto's, Ellery Bops, John Quills, Black Diamonds, Stone Killers, Buccaneers, Viceroys, Sportsman, Enchanters, Frenchman, etc; etc; some of the most notorious niggers that ever stepped out of history—where are you niggers? We must not let this part of history keep on repeating itself. I remember some words of a song that the Stomper Debs used to sing in 58 on Stuyvesant and Greene Aves, in B'klyn. "Down on the corner of Stuyvesant and Greene, beat three cops and it wasn't no dream." Whatever happened to that part of the era? And they were not dreaming, it was a reality; it went down. We must define the real enemy, using against them the tactics which you now use against your Brothers and Sisters. These tactics must be perfected into a science. In a way that was pointed out to me rather beautifully recently, Lumpen plus science equals a pat hand on the dialectical side, and we go for that. Now who is the real enemy, if not the Brothers and Sisters you are rolling on? He is the one that is keeping you in those slum dwellings where it's so cold in the winter time that ice cicles wear overcoats, that causes babies to die of pneumonia, rat bites, because they think it's a pet and you can't afford a pet, or they are not allowed. Because the slumlords have a pet, *you*. The ones who spread that TRAGIC MAGIC into the colony and your turf, that causes Brothers and Sisters to kill for it, or be killed by it, along with our babies.

You get an extra thrill when Marvin Gaye sings the words "save the babies," but you are not making that a reality. The "running dogs" who have created the hard hats in living color unions, that you are kept out of, who have created the underemployed or unemployed, where People are faced with welfare that's made to seem that they are giving you something, when it's designed to keep you passive.

It's not working, thanks to the Welfare Rights Organization.

A country where two percent out of the 250 millions own the means of production. A country that is invading, or trying to invade all freedom-loving countries of the world, to set up capitalist and reactionary leaders to suck the blood out of freedom loving People. Those who have set up courts and laws of injustice, designed to railroad or dispose (kill) those who stand up and say we ain't going for this shit.

A country that has more concentration camps (prisons) than all other countries put together. A ruling class that finds it more to their benefit to stockpile arms in the pig departments, than to feed the hungry. Those who word indictments wrong, the state versus you when it's the other way around. Those who have betwitched a People and created Mr and Mrs Amerikkkan Negro. Those who have centralized technology and kept it for themselves, creating a wretched condition for those it is kept from.

The ones who keep you warring against one another through rumors and absurd bullshit, because he doesn't want you to realize your real strength and view him as the enemy that he is. Those who take the position that what we have said here is extreme, we view their diagnosis as a healthy sign. Because we would be very sick not to be extreme when faced with an extreme situation. Those who are responsible for the People of the world being pushed down into the level of shit that's going on. To put it even more clearly the enemy is the same old motherfucker, that's responsible for us being held captive here in the St. Louis pig-pen. Identification of the enemy held can clearly be made by us opening our eyes. At the same time we must keep our best eye on the snake in the grass, the bourgeoisie capitalist, the petty-bourgeoise Niggers, Fake Liberal Crackers and the reactionaries who come in various colors and class backgrounds. In view of this situation we are faced with, the call goes out to all get-down Brothers and Sisters to past and present gang members. Let's prepare to roll and get down, the shit has already been called on, in the morning there surely will be war, D.T.K.L.M.F.

To Sandra Pratt, Ronald Carter, Harold Russell, Harold Webb, we are still slipping into darkness.

Perfect Disorder
"Blood"

Black Elected Officials in the United States

As of April, 1973

	TOTAL	FEDERAL SENATOR	FEDERAL REPRESENTATIVES	STATE EXECUTIVES	STATE SENATORS	STATE REPRESENTATIVES
Alabama	149					2
Alaska	5					2
Arizona	4					2
Arkansas	141				1	3
California	130		3	1	1	6
Colorado	8				1	3
Connecticut	48				1	5
Delaware	12				1	2
District of Columbia	8		1			
Florida	58					3
Georgia	104		1		2	14
Illinois	137		1		5	14
Indiana	57				1	6
Iowa	8					1
Kansas	22				1	4
Kentucky	55				1	2
Louisiana	130					8
Maine	3					1
Maryland	55		1		4	14
Massachusetts	20	1				5
Michigan	179		2	1	3	12
Minnesota	7				1	1
Mississippi	152					1
Missouri	85		1		2	13
Nebraska	3				1	
Nevada	6				1	2
New Hampshire	1					
New Jersey	134				1	6
New Mexico	4					1
New York	164		2		4	11
North Carolina	112					3
Ohio	111		1		2	9
Oklahoma	67				1	3
Oregon	6					1
Pennsylvania	65		1		2	10
Rhode Island	7					1
South Carolina	99					4
Tennessee	71				2	7
Texas	101		1			8
Vermont	2					
Virginia	62				1	2
Washington	13				1	1
West Virginia	5				1	1
Wisconsin	9				1	2
Wyoming	2					
TOTALS	2621	1	15	2	42	196

	COUNTY		MUNICIPAL				LAW ENFORCEMENT				EDUCATION		
COMMISSIONERS, SUPERVISORS, COUNCILMEN	OTHER COUNTY OFFICIALS	MAYORS	VICE MAYORS, MAYORS PRO TEM	COUNCILMEN, ALDERMAN, COMMISSIONERS	OTHER LOCAL OFFICIALS	JUDGES, JUSTICES, MAGISTRATES	CHIEFS OF POLICE, CONSTABLES, MARSHALS, SHERIFFS	JUSTICES OF THE PEACE	OTHER LAW ENFORCEMENT OFFICIALS	STATE AND COLLEGE BOARDS	LOCAL SCHOOL BOARDS	OTHER EDUCATION OFFICIALS
9	11	8	1	46	.	1	55	.	.	.	16	.
.	.	.	.	1	.	.	.	.	.	.	2	.
.	.	.	.	.	.	.	1	.	.	.	1	.
.	1	8	1	47	11	.	.	19	.	.	50	.
.	.	4	3	33	5	14	.	.	.	4	56	.
.	.	.	.	3	.	1	.	.	.	.	.	.
.	.	.	.	20	6	.	4	.	.	.	12	.
.	.	.	.	8	.	.	.	.	.	.	1	.
.	.	.	.	.	.	.	.	.	.	.	7	.
.	.	3	5	42	1	1	.	.	.	.	3	.
8	1	.	3	39	1	1	.	5	1	.	27	1
2	.	7	.	49	7	13	.	.	.	1	38	.
1	1	1	.	23	6	3	4	.	.	.	11	.
.	.	.	.	2	.	1	.	.	.	.	4	.
1	.	2	.	6	.	1	.	.	.	.	7	.
3	.	1	1	33	.	2	4	.	.	1	7	.
29	.	3	1	24	.	2	13	11	.	.	39	.
.	.	.	.	.	1	.	.	.	.	.	1	.
.	.	3	.	22	.	5	.	.	2	.	4	.
.	.	.	.	5	4	.	.	.	.	.	5	.
27	4	5	4	33	13	20	2	.	.	8	45	.
.	.	.	.	1	.	1	.	.	.	.	3	.
8	19	4	1	39	7	.	22	19	1	.	31	.
3	2	2	.	27	5	8	1	.	.	2	19	.
.	.	.	.	1	.	.	.	.	.	.	1	.
1	.	.	.	.	.	.	1	1	.	.	1	.
3	.	5	2	38	2	.	2	.	.	1	74	.
.	.	.	.	3	.	.	.	.	.	.	.	.
6	.	.	1	11	3	25	.	.	.	.	101	.
7	.	4	9	57	.	2	.	.	.	.	30	.
2	1	8	.	46	5	14	1	.	.	2	20	.
.	.	6	.	27	10	1	.	.	.	.	18	1
.	.	.	.	1	.	1	.	.	.	.	3	.
.	1	.	.	13	.	19	3	.	.	.	16	.
.	.	.	.	2	.	.	.	.	.	.	4	.
14	.	5	.	39	.	12	.	.	.	.	24	.
25	.	.	2	19	.	2	1	.	.	.	13	.
.	.	3	1	38	.	1	1	.	.	2	46	.
.	.	.	.	1	.	.	.	.	.	.	1	.
16	2	.	7	28	.	.	.	6	.	.	2	.
.	.	.	.	5	1	3	.	.	.	.	.	.
.	.	.	1	3	.	.	.	.	.	.	.	.
2	.	.	.	4	.	.	.	.	.	.	1	.
.	.	.	.	1	.	.	.	.	.	.	.	.
167	44	82	43	840	88	154	115	61	4	21	744	2

Unemployment Rates: 1954 to 1972*

(ANNUAL AVERAGES)

Year	Black	White	Ratio: Black to white
1954	9.9	5.0	2.0
1955	8.7	3.9	2.2
1956	8.3	3.6	2.3
1957	7.9	3.8	2.1
1958	12.6	6.1	2.1
1959	10.7	4.8	2.2
1960	10.2	4.9	2.1
1961	12.4	6.0	2.1
1962	10.9	4.9	2.2
1963	10.8	5.0	2.2
1964	9.6	4.6	2.1
1965	8.1	4.1	2.0
1966	7.3	3.3	2.2
1967	7.4	3.4	2.2
1968	6.7	3.2	2.1
1969	6.4	3.1	2.1
1970	8.2	4.5	1.8
1971	9.9	5.4	1.8
1972	10.0	5.0	2.0

Note: The unemployment rate is the percent unemployed in civilian labor force.

*Black includes other nonwhites. Prepared by the National Urban League Research Department from data in U.S. Department of Labor *Manpower Report of the President—March 1972,* Table A-14 and the Bureau of Labor Statistics, *The Employment Situation:* December 1972. Reprinted by permission.

Distribution of Family Income in 1972 Above and Below BLS Standard Budget Levels by Race†

(PERCENT DISTRIBUTION)

BLS Standard Budgets*	White Families			Black Families		
	Total	Above	Below	Total	Above	Below
Higher Level ($16,558)	100%	28	72	100%	13	87
Intermediate Level ($11,446) **	100%	56	44	100%	26	74
Lower Level ($7,386)	100%	75	25	100%	46	54

*These Bureau of Labor Statistics standard family budgets are designed for an urban family of four and are illustrative of three different levels of living. For methodology, see U.S. Bureau of Labor Statistics, *Three Standards of Living for an Urban Family of Four Persons*, BLS Bulletin No. 1570-5, (Spring 1967), Government Printing Office, Washington, D.C.

**According to NUL definition, "middle-class" families apply only to those with incomes *above* the intermediate BLS budget level.

†Prepared by the National Urban League Research Department from data in U.S. Bureau of Labor Statistics, "Autumn 1972 Urban Family Budgets and Geographical Comparative Indexes," Department of Labor, Office of Information, June 15, 1973 and U.S. Bureau of the Census, "Money Income in 1972 of Families and Persons in the United States," Advance data from March 1973 *Current Population Survey*, Series P-60. Reprinted by permission.

Black Labor in White America*

HERBERT HILL

AT THE BEGINNING of the decade of the 1970s, according to the last census, Black family income for the nation was sixty-one percent of white family income. This is an increase from fifty-seven percent in 1945 at the end of World War II, and it means that Black families gained four percentage points in twenty-five years. At this rate of increase, equality with whites may be achieved by the year 2275, a period of over three centuries. This is very dubious "progress" and is totally unacceptable.

But even this statistic provides a misleading picture of the comparative economic status of the Black family. First, it must be noted that nonwhite families on the average tend to be substantially larger than white families.

Secondly, and of the greatest importance, is the fact that in a majority of Black families, two or more persons work to bring in the same dollar that one wage-earner brings into the white family.

Thirdly, the rate of increase—four percentage points over twenty-five years—is a fluctuating figure. According to the most recent census data, the earnings of Black workers remain significantly below the earnings of whites in every educational category. Black educational levels have been steadily rising for the past two decades and by 1970, median Black education was within six months of white education. Nevertheless, the disparity in dollar income between Blacks and whites has increased: in constant dollars, the difference in 1947 between Black and white family income was $2,303; by 1967, the disparity had risen to $3,133. Dr. Vivian Henderson, one of the nation's leading economists and the president of Clark College stated, "People spend and save dollars. It is this dollar difference that counts. Pronouncements regarding economic progress which are confined to acceleration concepts and per-

*Herbert Hill is National Labor Director of the National Association for the Advancement of Colored People and author of *Black Labor and the American Legal System.* This essay is excerpted from an address delivered by Mr. Hill to the annual convention of the NAACP, July 5, 1973, Indianapolis, Indiana. Reprinted by permission.

centage change obscure the real predicament—Negroes are losing ground rapidly in gaining dollar parity with whites."

The first comprehensive statistical survey ever made of minority employment patterns was the analysis released by the Equal Employment Opportunity Commission based on a nationwide reporting system. The data on the occupational status of nonwhite workers reveals that:

Four out of five Negroes are employed in semiskilled blue collar jobs; for the population as a whole, the proportion is about two out of five.

While 28 percent of Negro women are employed in white collar jobs, the proportion is only 7 percent for Negro men. By contrast, for the population as a whole, 57 percent of women workers and 37 percent of men workers hold white collar jobs.

For every 40 white collar jobs, one is held by a Negro; obviously, the number of Negro white collar workers could double—and Negroes would still be outnumbered by 20 to 1. If the number tripled, Negroes would hold 7.5 percent of white collar jobs—a figure which would be fairly close to the 8 percent which Negroes should be expected to hold on the basis of their representation in the overall workforce.

As far as Negro men are concerned, discrimination is apparently strongest in the skilled trades; for Negro women, in the clerical category.

Only one out of 14 Negroes was classed as a skilled craftsman compared to a ratio of one out of seven for all workers.

The trend in America is clear. A changing industrial structure is producing a persistent movement toward inequality, inequality in the distribution of income among skilled and unskilled. And between whites and Blacks, racial discrimination is the main cause of income inequality.

This was most recently confirmed again by an analysis of 1972 census data which revealed that despite a decrease in the total number of persons living in poverty, as defined by the government, the number of poor black persons actually increased during the last year. During a year in which the majority of whites were moving in the opposite direction, 500,000 more Black people moved into poverty.

A more accurate description of the status of Blacks in the American economy is derived from the Government's 1970 Census Study, which reported that "While Negroes were slightly more than one-tenth of the population they comprised approximately three-tenths of all persons below the low-income level in 1969. Of all low-income family heads, about twenty-seven percent were Negro; however, forty percent of all children of low-income families were Negroes."

In 1972, over a third of the Black population was living in officially defined poverty and over forty percent of Black children under eighteen years of age were growing up in poverty.

The most critical aspect of the economic status of the Black population is the plight of ghetto youth. The 1970 census forecasts a fifteen-million-member increase in the labor force by 1980. The number of Black youth entering the working-age group will increase at a rate five times greater than the rate of increase for young white workers. But what is their future? While there has been some relative improvement for a narrow stratum within the Black middle class, future prospects for youth trapped in the ghetto are bleak. Official reports indicate that the unemployment rate for Black ghetto youth will be in excess of fifty percent by the end of the summer.

The fact that the overwhelming majority of Blacks and members of other minority groups working in the building trades are excluded from the high-paying craft unions was confirmed by the Equal Employment Opportunity Commission, which revealed statistics based upon reports from referral unions. The last EEOC report states that, "Almost three of every four Negroes in the building trades were members of the Laborers Union." Furthermore, the data for the entire nation reveals a general pattern of racial discrimination against Black workers—ranging from total exclusion in some crafts to mere tokenism in others.

Information from the Bureau of Labor Statistics covering all building trades jobs, skilled and unskilled, shows that the percentage of all minorities working in the construction industry actually decreased between 1969 and 1972 from 9.6 percent to 9.2 percent.

Furthermore, an analysis of the data from specific cities where there has been a significant increase in the nonwhite population reveals that the status of Black workers in the craft unions has actually deteriorated. For example, in 1960, Blacks were 14.7 percent of the population of New York City and constituted 1.5 percent of the total journeymen membership of the craft unions in the building trades. By 1970, twenty-three percent of New York's population was Black; and Black workers constituted two percent of the total journeymen membership of the craft unions in the city. In Local 28 of the Sheet Metal Workers Union in New York City, to cite one instance, after more than a decade of litigation there are exactly twenty Afro-Americans with journeyman status and they are there only because of court orders. But, this hardly represents progress given the sixty percent increase of the Black population in New York City.

The same pattern is repeated in many other urban centers throughout the country. In Philadelphia, where the Black population is now almost forty percent, the proportion of Blacks employed in skilled construction jobs, relative to their total percentage in the population, is actually smaller now than it was in 1900.

The rapidly changing population characteristics of the Black community provide the only meaningful context in which to measure the rate of progress in organized labor and in all other institutions. In relation to the very significant increase in the Black urban labor force, the percentage of Black journeymen members of craft unions in the construction industry has deteriorated during the past two decades.

It is now nineteen years since the NAACP's victory in the school segregation cases known as *Brown* v. *Board of Education*, and it is nine years since Congress enacted the historic Civil Rights Act of 1964. But, instead of realizing the full potential of these great possibilities, our country is experiencing not merely a "backlash," but is in the grip of a dangerous counter-revolution against the cause of racial integration.

It is within this context that one must understand the significance of the attack upon job quotas. The antiquota movement has become a complacent cover for retreat in the civil rights battle and the attack upon job quotas has become a major rallying cry in the counter-revolution against the struggle for civil rights.

The issue of preferential hiring is now a major national controversy. . . . Judging by the vast outcry, it might be assumed that job quotas in employment had become as widespread and destructive as racial discrimination itself. As with the much distorted subject of busing, the defenders of the racial *status quo* have once again succeeded in confusing the remedy with the original evil. The word "quota" like "busing" and "open housing," has become another code word for resistance to Black demands for the elimination of widespread patterns of racial discrimination.

Much of the current controversy involves federal civil rights enforcement efforts in the construction industry and in educational institutions which do billions of dollars worth of research and provide other services for government agencies.

Common to most attacks upon preferential hiring systems is the assumption that such approaches are both a "new form of discrimination" and that the quality of performance and work standards will be severely diminished as a result of the employment of nonwhites and women. The *a priori* assumption that no "qualified" Blacks or women exist is implicit in the argument. Also implicit is the assumption that if Blacks and women were to be employed, the alleged current high standards would be diminished. In reality, the so-called merit system in education operates to give preference to mediocre or incompetent whites at the expense of highly-talented Blacks, as well as at the expense of mediocre and incompetent Blacks.

To argue that there is a merit system in the building trades, as spokesmen for organized labor frequently do, is to depart from all reason and reality. As has been demonstrated in many lawsuits throughout the country, the worst forms of nepotism and favoritism prevail.

It should be evident that what is really involved in the debate over hiring quotas is not that Blacks and other minorities will be given preference over whites, but, rather, that a substantial body of law now requires that discriminatory systems which operate to favor whites at the expense of Blacks must be eliminated.

During the past quarter-of-a-century, the federal courts have increasingly recognized the validity of numerical quotas to eliminate traditional forms of discrimination. The courts had used quotas as a remedy to eliminate systematic discrimination in the selection of juries, in legislative reapportionment litigation, and in school segregation cases.

Although the courts have repeatedly spoken on this issue, the extensive public discussion of preferential hiring has ignored the major legal interpretations of the validity of quotas in civil rights enforcement efforts.

In the past decade, there has emerged a new judicial perception of racial discrimination in employment. There now exists an extensive body of case law in which federal courts recognize that racial discrimination in employment does not occur as individual random acts of bigotry; but, rather, it is the result of systemic patterns which keep Black workers as a class in a permanent state of economic and social depression.

The most important consequence of the new judicial perception of employment discrimination is to be found in the nature of the sweeping relief and remedies ordered by the federal courts. In practical terms, this has taken two specific forms. First, the awarding of large sums of money as back pay to an entire effected class of minority workers who have been found to be the victims of discriminatory practices. These substantial back pay awards are certain to have an important deterrent effect upon the discriminatory practices of both employers and labor unions. Secondly, there are many decisions where the courts have required new preferential hiring remedies.

Because "voluntary compliance" and "good faith efforts" do not work in eliminating job discrimination, and because years of experience have demonstrated that the piling of pledge upon pledge not to discriminate by employers and labor unions changes nothing, it is now necessary for government agencies charged with enforcement of the legal prohibitions against job discrimination to operate with new standards. The new standards must be based upon the manning-table concept; that is, tangible numerical goals and assigned quotas for the employment of Black workers and members of other minority groups in specific job classifications within a stated time period.

The record of thirty years of fair employment practice law makes it absolutely clear that the concept of passive nondiscrimination is totally inadequate and obsolete. A ritualistic policy of "nondiscrimination," or of "equal opportunity," in practice usually means perpetuation of the traditional discriminatory patterns or, at best, tokenism.

The law now requires the broad application of preferential hiring systems to eliminate, at long last, the pervasive effects of racial discrimination in virtually every part of the American economy. The use of quotas is not an end in itself but, rather, an effective means to achieve a necessary end, the elimination of racial discrimination.

3. LIBERATION

Black Manifesto*

JAMES FORMAN

TOTAL CONTROL AS THE ONLY SOLUTION TO THE ECONOMIC PROBLEMS OF BLACK PEOPLE

BROTHERS AND SISTERS:

We have come from all over the country, burning with anger and despair not only with the miserable economic plight of our people, but fully aware that the racism on which the Western World was built dominates our lives. There can be no separation of the problems of racism from the problems of our economic, political, and cultural degradation. To any black man, this is clear.

But there are still some of our people who are clinging to the rhetoric of the Negro and we must separate ourselves from those Negroes who go around the country promoting all types of schemes for Black Capitalism.

Ironically, some of the most militant Black nationalists, as they call themselves, have been the first to jump on the band-wagon of black capitalism. They are pimps: Black Power Pimps and fraudulent leaders and the people must be educated to understand that any black man or Negro who is advocating a perpetuation of capitalism inside the United States is in fact seeking not only his ultimate destruction and death, but is con-tributing to the continuous exploitation of black people all around the world. For it is the power of the United States

*Presentation by James Forman, delivered and adopted by the National Black Economic Development Conference in Detroit, Michigan, on April 26, 1969. Reprinted with the permission of James Forman.

542

Government, this racist, imperialist government that is choking the life of all people around the world.

We are an African people. We sit back and watch the Jews in this country make Israel a powerful conservative state in the Middle East, but we are not concerned actively about the plight of our brothers in Africa. We are the most advanced technological group of black people in the world, and there are many skills that could be offered to Africa. At the same time, it must be publicly stated that many African leaders are in disarray themselves, having been duped into following the lines as laid out by the Western Imperialist governments . . .

In Africa today, there is a great suspicion of black people in this country. This is a correct suspicion since most of the Negroes who have left the States for work in Africa usually work for the Central Intelligence Agency (CIA) or the State Department. But the respect for us as a people continues to mount and the day will come when we can return to our homeland as brothers and sisters. But we should not think of going back to Africa today, for we are located in a strategic position. We live inside the U.S. which is the most barbaric country in the world and we have a chance to help bring this government down.

Time is short and we do not have much time and it is time we stop mincing words. Caution is fine, but no oppressed people ever gained their liberation until they were ready to fight, to use whatever means necessary, including the use of force and power of the gun to bring down the colonizer.

We have heard the rhetoric, but we have not heard the rhetoric which says that black people in this country must understand that we are the Vanguard Force. We shall liberate all the people in the U.S. and we will be instrumental in the liberation of colored people the world around. We must understand this point very clearly so that we are not trapped into diversionary and reactionary movements. Any class analysis of the U.S. shows very clearly that black people are the most oppressed group of people inside the United States. We have suffered the most from racism and exploitation, cultural degradation and lack of political power. It follows from the laws of revolution that the most oppressed will make the revolution, but we are not talking about just making the revolution. All the parties on the left who consider themselves revolutionary will say that blacks are the Vanguard, but we are saying that not only are we the Vanguard, but we must assume leadership, total control and we must exercise the humanity which is inherent in us. We are the most humane people within the U.S. We have suffered and we understand suffering. Our hearts go out to the Vietnamese for we know what it is to suffer under the domination of racist America. Our hearts, our souls and all the compassion we can mount goes out to our brothers in Africa, Santo Domingo, Latin America and Asia who are being tricked by the power structure of the U.S. which is dominating the world today. These ruthless, barbaric men have systematically tried to kill all people and organizations opposed to its imperialism. We no longer can just get by with the use of the word capitalism to describe the U.S., for it is an imperial power, sending money, missionaries and the army throughout the world to protect this government and the few rich whites who control it. General Motors and all the major auto industries are operating in South Africa, yet the white dominated leadership of the United Auto Workers sees no relationship to the exploitation of black people in South Africa and the exploitation of black people in the U.S. If they understand it, they certainly do not put it into practice which is the actual test. We as black people must be concerned with the total conditions of all black people in the world.

But while we talk of revolution, which will be an armed confrontation and long years of sustained guerrilla warfare inside this country, we must also talk of the type of world we want to live in. We must commit ourselves to a society where the total means of production are taken from the rich people and placed into the hands of the state for the welfare of all the people. This is what we mean when we say total control. And we mean that black people who have suffered the most from exploitation and racism must move to protect their black interest by assuming leadership inside of the United States of everything that exists. The time has passed when we are second in command and the white boy stands on top. This is especially true of the Welfare Agencies in this country, but it is not enough to say that a black man is on top. He must be committed to building the new society, to taking the wealth away from the rich people such as General Motors, Ford, Chrysler, the Du Ponts, the Rockefellers, the Mellons, and all the other rich white exploiters and racists who run this world . . .

Racism in the U.S. is so pervasive in the mentality of whites that only an armed, well-disciplined, black-controlled government can insure the stamping out of racism in this country. And that is why we plead with black people not to be talking about a few crumbs, a few thousand dollars for this cooperative, or a thousand dollars which splits black people into fighting over the dollar. That is the intention of the government. We say. . . . think in terms of total control of the U.S. Prepare ourselves to seize state power. Do not hedge, for time is short and all around the world, the forces of liberation are directing their attacks against the U.S. It is a powerful country, but that power is not greater than that of black people. We work the chief industries in this country and we could cripple the economy while the brothers fought guerrilla warfare in the streets. This will take some long range planning, but whether it happens in a thousand years is of no consequence. It cannot happen unless we start. . . .

THE MANIFESTO

We the black people assembled in Detroit, Michigan for the National Black Economic Development Conference are fully aware that we have been forced to come together because racist white America has exploited our resources, our minds, our bodies, our labor. For centuries we have been forced to live as colonized people inside the United States, victimized by the most vicious, racist system in the world. We have helped to build the most industrial country in the world.

We are therefore demanding of the white Christian churches and Jewish synagogues which are part and parcel of the system of capitalism, that they begin to pay reparations to black people in this country. We are demanding $500,000,000 from the Christian white churches and the Jewish synagogues. This total comes to 15 dollars per nigger. This is a low estimate for we maintain there are probably more than 30,000,000 black people in this country. $15 a nigger is not a large sum of money and we know that the churches and synagogues have a tremendous wealth and its membership, white America, has profited and still exploits black people. We are also not unaware that the exploitation of colored peoples around the world is aided and abetted by the white Christian churches and synagogues. This demand for $500,000,000 is not an idle resolution or empty words. Fifteen dollars for every black brother and sister in the United States is only a beginning of the reparations due us as people who have been exploited and degraded, brutalized, killed and persecuted. Underneath all of this exploitation, the racism of this country has produced a psychological effect upon us that we're beginning to shake off. We are no longer afraid to demand our full rights as a people in this decadent society.

We are demanding $500,000,000 to be spent in the following way:

(1) We call for the establishment of a Southern land bank to help our brothers and sisters who have to leave their land because of racist pressure for people who want to establish cooperative farms, but who have no funds. [We have seen too many farmers evicted from their homes because they have dared to defy the white racism of this country. We need money for land.] We must fight for massive sums of money for this Southern Land Bank. We call for $200,000,000 to implement this program.

(2) We call for the establishment of four major publishing and printing industries in the United States to be funded with ten million dollars each. [These publishing houses are to be located in Detroit, Atlanta, Los Angeles and New York.] They will help *to generate* capital for further cooperative investments in the black community, provide jobs and an alternative to the white-dominated and controlled printing field.

(3) We call for the establishment of four of the most advanced scientific and futuristic audio-visual networks to be located in Detroit, Chicago, Cleveland and Washington, D.C. These TV networks will provide an alternative to the racist propaganda that fill the current television networks. Each of these TV networks will be funded by ten million dollars each.

(4) We call for a research skills center which will provide research on the problems of black people. This center must be funded with no less than 30 million dollars.

(5) We call for the establishment of a training center for the teaching of skills in community organization, photography, movie making, television making and repair, radio building and repair and all other skills needed in communication. This training center shall be funded with no less than ten million dollars.

(6) We recognize the role of the National Welfare Rights Organization and we intend to work with it. We call for ten million dollars to assist in the organization of welfare recipients. [We want to organize the welfare workers in this country so that they may demand more money from the government and better administration of the welfare system of this country.]

(7) We call for $20,000,000 to establish a National Black

Labor Strike and Defense Fund. This is necessary for the protection of black workers and their families who are fighting racist working conditions in this country.

[1](8) We call for the establishment of the United Black Appeal. (UBA) This United Black Appeal will be funded with no less than $20,000,000. The UBA is charged with producing more capital for the establishment of cooperative businesses in the United States and in Africa, our Motherland. The United Black Appeal is one of the most important demands that we are making for we know that it can generate and raise funds throughout the United States and help our African brothers. The UBA is charged with three functions and shall be headed by James Forman:

(a) Raising money for the program of the National Black Economic Development Conference.

(b) The development of cooperatives in African countries and support of African Liberation movements.

(c) Establishment of a Black Anti-Defamanation League which will protect our African image.

(9) We call for the establishment of a Black University to be funded with $130,000,000 to be located in the South. Negotiations are presently under way with a Southern University.

(10) We demand that IFCO allocate all unused funds in the planning budget to implement the demands of this conference.

In order to win our demands we are aware that we will have to have massive support, therefore:

(1) We call upon all black people throughout the United States to consider themselves as members of the National Black Economic Development Conference and to act in unity to help force the racist white Christian churches and Jewish synagogues to implement these demands.

(2) We call upon all the concerned black people across the country to contact black workers, black women, black students and the black unemployed, community groups, welfare organizations, teachers organizations, church leaders and organizations explaining how these demands are vital to the black community of the U.S. Pressure by whatever means necessary should be applied to the white power structure of the racist white Christian churches and Jewish synagogues. All black people should act boldly in confronting our white

[1](Revised and approved by Steering Committee).

oppressors and demanding this modest reparation of $15 per black man.

(3) Delegates and members of the National Black Economic Development Conference are urged to call press conferences in the cities and to attempt to get as many black organizations as possible to support the demands of the conference. The quick use of the press in the local areas will heighten the tension and these demands must be attempted to be won in a short period of time, although we are prepared for protracted and long range struggle.

(4) We call for the total disruption of selected church sponsored agencies operating anywhere in the U.S. and the world. Black workers, black women, black students and the black unemployed are encouraged to seize the offices, telephones, and printing apparatus of all church sponsored agencies and to hold these in trusteeship until our demands are met.

(5) We call upon all delegates and members of the National Black Economic Development Conference to stage sit-in demonstrations at selected black and white churches. This is not to be interpreted as a continuation of the sit-in movement of the early sixties but we know that active confrontation inside white churches is possible and will strengthen the possibility of meeting our demands. Such confrontation can take the form of reading the Black Manifesto instead of a sermon or passing it out to church members. The principles of self-defense should be applied if attacked.

(6) On May 4, 1969, or a date thereafter, depending upon local conditions, we call upon black people to commence the disruption of the racist churches and synagogues throughout the United States.

(7) We call upon IFCO to serve as a central staff to coordinate the mandate of the conference and to reproduce and distribute en masse literature, leaflets, news items, press releases and other material.

(8) We call upon all delegates to find within the white community those forces which will work under the leadership of blacks to implement these demands by whatever means necessary. By taking such action, white Americans will demonstrate concretely that they are willing to fight the white skin privilege and the white supremacy and racism which has forced us as black people to make these demands.

(9) We call upon all white Christians and Jews to practice patience, tolerance and understanding and nonviolence as

they have encouraged, advised and demanded that we as
black people should do throughout our entire enforced slavery
in the United States. The true test of their faith and belief in
the Cross and the words of the prophets will certainly be put
to a test as we seek legitimate and extremely modest reparations for our role in developing the industrial base of the
Western world through our slave labor. But we are no longer
slaves, we are men and women, proud of our African heritage, demanding to have our dignity.

(10) We are so proud of our African heritage and realize
concretely that our struggle is not only to make revolution in
the United States, but to protect our brothers and sisters in
Africa and to help them rid themselves of racism, capitalism,
and imperialism by whatever means necessary, including armed
struggle. We are and must be willing to fight the defamation
of our African image wherever it rears its ugly head. We are
therefore charging the Steering Committee to create a Black
Anti-Defamation League to be funded by money raised from
the United Black Appeal.

(11) We fully recognize that revolution in the United
States and Africa, our Motherland, is more than a one dimen-
sional operation. It will require the total integration of the political, economic, and military components and therefore, we
call upon all our brothers and sisters who have acquired training and expertise in the fields of engineering, electronics, research, community organization, physics, biology, chemistry,
mathematics, medicine, military science and warfare to assist
the National Black Economic Development Conference in the
implementation of its program.

(12) To implement these demands we must have a fearless
leadership. We must have a leadership which is willing to battle the church establishment to implement these demands. To
win our demands we will have to declare war on the white
Christian churches and synagogues and this means we may
have to fight the total government structure of this country.
Let no one here think that these demands will be met by our
mere stating them. For the sake of the churches and synagogues, we hope that they have the wisdom to understand that
these demands are modest and reasonable. but if the white
Christians and Jews are not willing to meet our demands
through peace and good will, then we declare war and we are
prepared to fight by whatever means necessary. . . .

Brothers and sisters, we no longer are shuffling our feet and
scratching our heads. We are tall, black and proud.

And we say to the white Christian churches and Jewish synagogues, to the government of this country and to all the white racist imperialists who compose it, there is only one thing left that you can do to further degrade black people and that is to kill us. But we have been dying too long for this country. We have died in every war. We are dying in Vietnam today fighting the wrong enemy.

The new black man wants to live and to live means that we must not become static or merely believe in self-defense. We must boldly go out and attack the white Western world at its power centers. The white Christian churches are another form of government in this country and they are used by the government of this country to exploit the people of Latin America, Asia and Africa, but the day is soon coming to an end. Therefore, brothers and sisters, the demands we make upon the white Christian churches and the Jewish synagogues are small demands. They represent 15 dollars per black person in these United States. We can legitimately demand this from the church power structure. We must demand more from the United States Government.

But to win our demands from the church which is linked up with the United States Government, we must not forget that it will ultimately be by force and power that we will win.

We are not threatening the churches. We are saying that we know the churches came with the military might of the colonizers and have been sustained by the military might of the colonizers. Hence, if the churches in colonial territories were established by military might, we know deep within our hearts that we must be prepared to use force to get our demands. We are not saying that this is the road we want to take. It is not, but let us be very clear that we are not opposed to force and we are not opposed to violence. We were captured in Africa by violence. We were kept in bondage and political servitude and forced to work as slaves by the military machinery and the Christian church working hand in hand.

We recognize that in issuing this manifesto we must prepare for a long range educational campaign in all communities of this country, but we know that the Christian churches have contributed to our oppression in white America. We do not intend to abuse our black brothers and sisters in black churches who have uncritically accepted Christianity. We want them to understand how the racist white Christian Church with its hypocritical declarations and doctrines of brotherhood has abused our trust and faith. An attack on the religious beliefs of black people is not our major objective, even though we know that we were not Christians when we were brought to this country, but that Christianity was used to help enslave us. Our objective in issuing this Manifesto is to force the racist white Christian Church to begin the payment of reparations which are due to all black people, not only by the Church but also by private business and the U.S. government. We see this focus on the Christian Church as an effort around which all black people can unite.

Our demands are negotiable, but they cannot be minimized, they can only be increased and the Church is asked to come up with larger sums of money than we are asking. Our slogans are:

ALL ROADS MUST LEAD TO REVOLUTION

UNITE WITH WHOMEVER YOU CAN UNITE

NEUTRALIZE WHEREVER POSSIBLE

FIGHT OUR ENEMIES RELENTLESSLY

VICTORY TO THE PEOPLE

LIFE AND GOOD HEALTH TO MANKIND

RESISTANCE TO DOMINATION
BY THE WHITE CHRISTIAN CHURCHES
AND THE JEWISH SYNAGOGUES

REVOLUTION BLACK POWER

WE SHALL WIN WITHOUT A DOUBT

*What We Are Fighting For**

UNITED BLACK WORKERS

WE HEREBY STATE that as oppressed workers here at the Mahwah Plantation (Ford Plant) we are not bound by any constitution, contracts, agreements, known or unknown, by-laws or company policies agreed upon by management and the

*Reprinted by permission United Black Workers.

U.A.W. that are racist or tend to deprive Black, Third World and all oppressed workers of their basic constitutional and moral rights. These rights being human dignity, health and safety, better working conditions, and equal job opportunities.

We further state it is our right as workers to demand that both labor and management make use of large portions of the monies gained from our labors to improve the living, educational and health conditions in our communities with no strings attached.

To obtain these rights the U.B.W. are committed to organize, agitate, expose, inform and use all means at our disposal, not settling for anything short of victory.

We further state that we are not bound to respect, obey or follow the leadership of any plant manager, supervisor, union official or any other underlings who negate any claim they might have for these rights when they place personal ambition self interest, profit and property rights over the human rights of workers.

The factories belong to the people and we workers are the people.

1. End of Ford Motor Company paying union officials' salaries.

2. End of racism, exploitation and oppression of all workers.

3. Transportation provided for workers who must travel long distances back and forth to work. Many cannot afford to buy a car and must depend upon car pools.

4. Waiver of 90 day eligibility for Viet Nam veterans. Make them eligible as of the first day on the job.

5. A complete revision of grievance procedures.

6. Mandatory medical check up every three months for all workers who paint, spray, grind lead or metal, welders, drivers and all workers who are exposed to the deadly pollution which fills the air throughout this plant.

7. End of compulsory overtime.

8. End of line speed-up.

9. End of white skin privilege.

10. Mandatory printing in Spanish and Creole of all bulletins, pamphlets and job applications put out by Ford Motor Company and the U.A.W.

11. To get more Black and Third World workers into skilled trades; many already qualify but racism is keeping them out. A strong and effective apprenticeship program to

prepare young Black and Third World workers for skilled trades.

12. Mandatory English classes in plant for non-English speaking or reading workers.

13. Ford Motor Company to announce a policy of complete disengagement from South Africa since all Amerikans doing business in South Africa reinforce that racist system and its government.

Statement of Principles*

AFRICAN LIBERATION SUPPORT COMMITTEE

WORLD VIEW

"If there is no struggle, there can be no progress. . . . ."

Black people throughout the world are realizing that our freedom will only be won through a protracted struggle against two forces—racism and imperialism. The world imperialist system festers in Africa and Asia and engulfs the Western Hemisphere as well. In the United States we know it as monopoly capitalism, in Africa it is imperialism in its colonial or neo-colonial form. Wherever it appears, its cornerstone is the white ruling class of the United States of America.

Imperialism is neither invincible nor invulnerable. As the blows against it increase, the crisis of imperialism heightens and leads to new levels of exploitation of Black People in the Western Hemisphere, Africa and the rest of the world.

AFRICA

In Africa, the remains of classical European colonialism is held together by Portugal (in Guinea-Bissau, Angola, and Mozambique). The United States government has been a constant supporter and ally of Portuguese oppression through direct aid (such as the $430 million Azores agreement) and gifts of planes, arms, and military training (at Fort Bragg, North Carolina) through NATO. White settler rule is based in police state South Africa, and extends to Namibia (South-West Africa) and Zimbabwe (Rhodesia) as well. There is

*Reprinted by permission.

hardly a single major U.S. or multinational Corporation, or bank that does not have investments in Southern Africa. Chase Manhattan Bank, Firestone Rubber and tires, Gulf Oil, Holiday Inn, General Motors and some 300 other firms have investments totalling over 1 billion dollars. Several major problems face the people of Southern Africa and Guinea-Bissau as a result of the present crisis:

1. Resettlement schemes to absorb unemployed European workers as new colonists in Africa; They will be expected to fight against liberation forces. An example is the Cabora Bassa Dam project in the Tete province of Mozambique, where over 1,000,000 European workers are expected to settle.

2. Increased levels of exploitation caused by the relocation of factories from advanced capitalist countries—"run'away shops." The conditions that generally accompany this new investment are no-strike laws, forced labor, slave-wages, no right-to-organize laws, and neo-facist policies of political repression against all dissent.

3. Militaristic and aggressive expansionist policies of South Africa and Israel to recolonize "independent" Africa using capital invested by multinational corporations based in the U.S., Europe and Japan.

WESTERN HEMISPHERE (U.S., Canada and the Caribbean)

Black people in the Western Hemisphere equally caught in the racist imperialist net, also face major problems in the present state of our struggle:

1. Problems on the job-unemployment, low wages, job insecurity, racism by management and union leadership discrimination in hiring and promotions (especially in skilled crafts), and super-exploitation in the shops (speed-up, compulsory overtime, etc.)

2. Continued neglect, and indeed cutbacks in the area of social services; public welfare, transportation, housing, sanitation, health facilities, and education, etc.

3. Political-police-military repression with facist-type hit squads (like the STRESS squad was in Detroit), increased use of electronic surveillance and informers, a rising rate of Black Youth in prisons, and systematic introduction of heroin (or heroin substitutes) into the Black Communities.

4. Continued onslaughts on efforts to preserve and develop revolutionary culture among Black people, including the use of distorted fragments of Black history and the accomplish-

ments of "distinguished Black Americans." These onslaughts are in fact cultural aggression. Cultural aggression, like all other forms of racism, seeks to impose the way of life, values and institutions of one culture on another culture. Culture here defined as a way of life, values, and those institutions set up to maintain and develop that way of life and its values.

FINALLY GOT THE NEWS

Black people throughout the world have finally got the news—the news that racism and imperialism, the two-headed monster—are our enemies. The major historical trends of the moment in Southern Africa can be summed up as:

1. The heightened struggle and increasing success of the liberation movements, which win new victories every day. Their struggle has been aided by the support of the Socialist countries, and by other anti-imperialist forces, especially the increasing support of progressive Black people in the United States.

2. The increasing support for the liberation movements by independent African countries, even conservative ones, through the OAU Liberation Committee and by direct aid.

3. The rising desperation of the Portuguese governments in the face of liberation groups marching towards total victories in the "colonies". This desperation is reflected by the cowardly assassination of Amilcar Cabral, Secretary-General of the PAIGC, on the streets of Conakry by Portuguese agents.

4. Increased co-operation between colonial and imperialist governments especially Rhodesia, South Africa, Portugal, Israel, and the United States in these areas; first, collective military arrangements; second, the wooing of governments of certain African countries in an attempt to seduce them into "dialogue" with South Africa or otherwise breach the anti-colonial unity of Africa; third, the development of schemes to hand the Portuguese colonies over [to] the phoney "independent" Black governments—in reality puppets for the Portuguese.

5. The increasing awareness of Black workers in Southern Africa who are mounting demonstrations and strikes to prove that the system of internal oppression under which they suffer can be overthrown.

The major historical trends at the present time in the United States may be summed up as follows:

1. The international crisis of capitalism has produced effects—rising market price of gold, falling value of the dollar

—that have put the U.S. economy on very shaky ground; unemployment, high food prices, run away shops are a few indications of the instability of the domestic market.

2. The increasing manifestations of frustrations and anger of people in the U.S. especially Black people—battered back and forth by forces which they do not understand.

3. The exposure of corruption in government from Nixon and Haldeman to Mayors Daley and Addonizio, down to the cop on the corner. People increasingly realize that this corruption is linked to control of government by large corporations and the rich in their own interests.

4. The increasing attempts by the white ruling class of the USA and their apologists, to blame many social problems on Black People: (high taxes, welfare, unemployment for white workers; inflation).

We can clearly see that the imperialist monster has two heads—in the Western Hemisphere and elsewhere in the world. We here have the same duty as all progressive Black people—to fight imperialism in all its manifestations. To do this we must build an anti-racist, anti-imperialist United Front among Black people.

TOWARDS A UNITED FRONT

"If we do not formulate plans for unity and take active steps to form political union, we will soon be fighting and warring among ourselves with imperialists and colonialists standing behind the screen and pulling vicious wires, to make us cut each others throats for the sake of their diabolical purposes. . . . ."

Kwame Nkrumah

Black people throughout the world face a future of struggle to put together a movement with the theoretical and organizational tools and the practical experience necessary to defeat enemies and build a new world.

Theory

We must learn from the experience of other movements and other struggles experience which teaches that "there can be no revolutionary movement without revolutionary theory." We have learned rich lessons from struggles with no theory at all. Those lessons teach us two important things about unity and theory:

1. We cannot be dogmatic. Once we have rooted ourselves in certain principles, we must direct our struggle according to the concrete, changing conditions around us.

2. *Real* unity will come about *not* by ignoring differences but by airing those differences and struggling to resolve them. It is through the interplay of ideas and the testing of those ideas in practice that a correct position will be hammered out.

Organization

We must struggle to improve our organization work. Building unity means finding ways of utilizing the abilities and skills of everyone who is serious about struggling.

Practice

The real test of our united front work is, of course, in practice. We must engage in principled work both inside and outside of the anti-imperialist front; in addition we must develop our ability to carry the fight against racism and imperialism to different groups of people around different issues, yet maintain our course.

The principal task of our movement at this time has two aspects. We must merge the Black liberation struggles in the U.S. with the National liberation struggles in Africa, because a victory anywhere in the fight against U.S. imperialism is a victory everywhere. We must coordinate the Black Liberation struggles in the Western Hemisphere with the overall struggle of People of Color to change the fundamental nature of this society, because we have a responsibility to the world to fight exploitation and oppression in this very stronghold.

The time is ripe to develop a United Black people's struggle, a struggle to merge the Black liberation movement with the process of World Revolution. The question is: HOW?

Summation

In summary we have presented three major points:

1. The new unity of the Black Liberation struggle must be anti-racist, anti-imperialist and anti-capitalist in character.

2. The struggle to unify Black anti-racist, anti-imperialist forces is our source of strength in building an ideologically advanced movement.

3. Our unity must involve all Black social groups and class formations and we propose that *Black workers take the lead*.

Basic Program for African Liberation Support Committee

1. Raise money for liberation groups in Southern Africa and Guinea-Bissau through the United African Appeal.

2. Conduct educational seminars and programs on racism, feudalism, imperialism colonialism and neo-colonialism and its effect on the continent of Africa, especially South Africa and Guinea-Bissau.

3. Develop and distribute literature, films, and other educational materials on racism, feudalism, imperialism, colonialism and neo-colonialism and its effect on the continent of Africa, especially South Africa and Guinea-Bissau.

4. Participate in and aid Black community and Black workers in the struggles against oppression in the U.S., Canada, and the Caribbean.

5. Engage in efforts to influence and transform U.S. policy as regards to its imperialist role in the world.

6. Engage in mass actions against governments, products, and companies that are involved in or are supportive of racist, illegitimate regimes in Southern Africa and Guinea-Bissau.

7. Support and spearhead annual ALD demonstrations in conjunction with the International African Solidarity Day.

Bibliography

"The A.F. of L. and the Negro," *Opportunity*, VII (November, 1929), pp. 335-36.

American Anti-Slavery Society. *American Slavery As It Is.* Compiled and with an introduction by Theodore Weld, New York: American Anti-Slavery Society, 1839.

Aptheker, Herbert. *American Negro Slave Revolts.* New York: Columbia University Press, 1943.

────── *A Documentary History of the Negro in the United States.* New York: Citadel Press, 1951.

────── "Militant Abolitionism," *Journal of Negro History,* XXVI (October, 1941), pp. 438-84.

────── "South Carolina poll tax, 1737-1895," *Journal of Negro History,* XXXI (April, 1946), pp. 131-9.

Association of Artists for Freedom. *Forum at Town Hall.* June 15, 1964.

Bacote, Clarence Albert. *The Negro in Georgia Politics, 1880-1908.* Chicago: Ph.D. Dissertation, University of Chicago, 1955.

Baldwin, James. *The Fire Next Time.* New York: Dial Press, Inc., 1963.

Bates, Daisy. *The Long Shadow of Little Rock.* New York: David McKay Company, Inc., 1962.

Barnes, Gilbert. *The Anti-Slavery Impulse, 1830-1844.* New York: Harcourt, Brace & World, Inc., 1964.

Bauer, R. A. and Bauer, A. H. "Day to Day Resistance to Slavery," *Journal of Negro History,* XXVII (October 1942), pp. 388-419.

Bell, Howard H. "Negro Nationalism: A Factor in Emigration Projects, 1858-1861," *Journal of Negro History,* XLVII (January, 1962), pp. 42-53.

────── "A Survey of the Negro Convention Movement 1830-1861." Unpublished dissertation, Northwestern University, 1953.

Bittker, Boris L., *The Case for Black Reparations.* New York: Random House, 1973.

Blackburn, Sara, ed. *White Justice, Black Experience Today in America's Courtrooms.* New York: Harper & Row, 1971.

Broderick, Francis L. and August Meier. *Negro Protest*

Thought in the Twentieth Century. New York: Bobbs-Merrill Co. Inc., 1965.

Brown, John. Old South Leaflets, IV (Doc. 84).

Calista, Donald J. "Booker T. Washington: Another Look," Journal of Negro History, XLIX (October, 1964), pp. 240-50.

Carmichael, Stokley. "Toward Black Liberation," The Massachusetts Review, VII (Autumn, 1966), pp. 639-51.

––––– "Who Is Qualified?" The New Republic, 154 (January 8, 1966), pp. 20-22.

Channing, William Ellery. Slavery. 4th ed. revised. Boston: James Monroe & Co., 1836.

Clark, Kenneth B. Dark Ghetto; Dilemmas of Social Power. New York: Harper & Row, Publishers, 1965.

Clark, Septima P. "Literacy and Liberation," Freedomways, 4 (First Quarter, 1964), pp. 113-24.

––––– Echo in My Soul. New York: E. P. Dutton & Co., 1962.

Coffin, Joshua. An Account of Some of the Principal Slave Insurrections. New York: American Anti-Slavery Society, 1860.

Cornish, Dudley Taylor. The Sable Arm: Negro Troops in the Union Army, 1861-1865. New York: W. W. Norton & Co., 1966.

Danzig, David. "In Defense of 'Black Power,'" Commentary, 42 (September, 1966), pp. 41-46.

Dennett, John Richard. "1865: The South As It Is," The Nation, I (September 7, 1865), pp. 298-300.

Douglass, Frederick. Life and Times of Frederick Douglass, Written by Himself. Boston: De Wolfe & Co., 1895.

––––– "Reconstruction," Atlantic Monthly, XVIII (December, 1866), pp. 761-65.

Douglass, William. Annals of the First African Church in the United States of America now styled the African Episcopal Church of St. Thomas, Philadelphia. Philadelphia: King & Baird, Printers, 1862.

Drake, St. Clair, and Cayton, Horace. Black Metropolis: A Study of Negro Life in a Northern City. Vol. I, Revised and enlarged edition. New York: Harper Torchbooks, Harper & Row, Publishers, 1962.

Drake, Thomas E. Quakers and Slavery in America. New Haven: Yale University Press, 1950.

Du Bois, W. E. Burghardt. Black Folk: Then and Now. New York: Henry Holt, 1939.

––––– Black Reconstruction in America 1860-1880. New York: S. A. Russell, 1935.

——— *Dusk of Dawn: An Essay Toward an Autobiography of a Race Concept.* New York: Harcourt, Brace & Co., Inc., 1940.

——— *The Souls of Black Folk.* Fawcett Publications, Inc., 1961.

——— *The Suppression of the African Slave-Trade to the United States of America, 1638-1870.* New York: Longmans, Green & Co., 1896.

Dumond, Dwight L. "Emancipation: History's Fantastic Reverie," *Journal of Negro History,* XLIX (January, 1964), pp. 1-12.

——— *Antislavery: The Crusade for Freedom in America.* New York: W. W. Norton & Co., Inc., 1961.

Edelstein, Tilden G. "John Brown and His Friends," in Hugh Hawkins, ed., *The Abolitionists, Immediatism and the Question of Means.* Boston: D. C. Heath & Co., 1964.

Elkins, Stanley M. *Slavery: A Problem in American Institutional and Intellectual Life.* New York: The Universal Library, Grosset & Dunlap, 1959.

Essien-Udom, E. U. *Black Nationalism: A Search for an Identity in America.* Chicago: University of Chicago Press, 1962.

Farmer, James. *Freedom—When?* New York: Random House, Inc., 1965.

Filler, Louis. *Wendell Phillips on Civil Rights and Freedom.* New York: Hill & Wang, 1965.

Fleming, Walter L. *Documentary History of Reconstruction.* New York: McGraw-Hill Book Co., 1966. Originally published by Arthur H. Clark, Cleveland, 1906-1907.

Foner, Philip S. *The Black Panthers Speak.* Philadelphia: J. B. Lippincott Co., 1970.

——— *Frederick Douglass.* New York: Citadel Press, Inc., 1964.

Franklin, John Hope. *The Emancipation Proclamation.* New York: Doubleday & Co., 1963.

——— *From Slavery to Freedom.* Second ed., revised and enlarged. New York: Alfred A. Knopf, Inc., 1967.

——— *Reconstruction After the Civil War.* New York: Oxford University Press, 1967.

Frazier, Edward Franklin. *The Negro Family in the U.S.* New York: The Dryden Press, 1948.

Genovese, Eugene D. "The Legacy of Slavery and the Roots of Black Nationalism," *Studies on the Left,* 6 (November-December, 1966), pp. 3-24.

Granger, Lester B. "The Negro—Friend or Foe of Organized Labor?", *Opportunity*, XII (May, 1935), pp. 142-44.

―――― "Barriers to Negro War Employment," *The Annals of the American Academy of Political and Social Science*, 223 (September, 1942), pp. 72-80.

Grimké, Angelina E. *Appeal to the Christian Women of the South*. New York: American Anti-Slavery Society, 1836.

Harlan, Louise R. "Booker T. Washington and the White Man's Burden," *American Historical Review*, 71 (January, 1966), pp. 441-67.

Harrison, Hubert H. *When Africa Wakes*. New York: The Porro Press, 1920.

Hayden, Tom. *Revolutionary in Mississippi*. Students for a Democratic Society, 1962.

Hill, Herbert. "Labor Unions and the Negro," *Commentary*, 28 (December, 1959), pp. 479-88.

―――― The Racial Practices of Organized Labor 10 Years After the Merger: The Contemporary Record, in *The Negro and the American Labor Movement*, ed. by Jacobson. New York: Doubleday Anchor Books, 1968.

―――― The Racial Practices of Organized Labor—The Age of Gompers and After, in *Employment, Race and Poverty*, ed. by Ross and Hill, New York: Harcourt, Brace & World, 1967.

―――― Racial Inequality in Employment: The Patterns of Discrimination. *The Annals of the American Academy of Political and Social Science* (January, 1965).

―――― Racism within Organized Labor: A Report of 5 Years of the AFL-CIO, 1955-1960. *The Journal of Negro Education* (Spring, 1961).

―――― Twenty Years of State Fair Employment Practice Commissions: A Critical Analysis with Recommendations, in *Negroes and Jobs*, ed. by Ferman, Kornbluh and Miller. Ann Arbor: University of Michigan Press, 1968.

Holmes, John Haynes. *The Disfranchisement of Negroes*. New York: Publication of the National Association for the Advancement of Colored People, 1910 (?).

Holt, Len. *Act of Conscience*. Boston: Beacon Press, 1965.

Hughes, Langston. *Fight for Freedom, the story of the NAACP*. New York: W. W. Norton & Co., Inc., 1962.

Huie, William Bradford. *Three Lives for Mississippi*. New York: WCC Books, 1965.

Jackson, Luther B. "Race and Suffrage in the South Since 1940," *New South*, 3 (June-July, 1948).

Jefferson, Thomas. *Notes on the State of Virginia.* Boston: David Carlisle, 1801.

Johnson, James W. *Along this Way: the Autobiography of James Weldon Johnson.* New York: The Viking Press, 1933.

Johnson, Charles S. *The Economic Status of Negroes.* Nashville: Fisk University Press, 1933.

—— "The Negro and the Present Crisis," *Journal of Negro Education,* X (July, 1941), pp. 585-95.

Johnson, Lyndon B. "To Fulfill These Rights," (June 4, 1965), *Public Papers, LBJ,* 1965, II, pp. 653-640.

Kahn, Tom. *The Economics of Equality.* New York: League of Industrial Democracy, 1964.

Kellogg, Charles Flint. *NAACP: A History of the National Association for the Advancement of Colored People.* Vol. I, 1909-1920. Baltimore: Johns Hopkins Press, 1967.

Kennedy, Stetson. *Southern Exposure.* Garden City, New York: Doubleday & Co., Inc., 1946.

King, Jr., Martin Luther. *Stride Toward Freedom.* New York: Harper & Row, Publishers, 1958.

—— "Martin Luther King Defines 'Black Power,' " *The New York Times Magazine,* June 11, 1967.

—— "Negroes Are *Not* Moving Too Fast," *Life,* November 7, 1965.

Lay, Benjamin. *All Slave-Keepers, That Keep the Innocent in Bondage, Apostates* ... Philadelphia: Printed for the author [By B. Franklin], 1737.

Lester, Julius. "The Angry Children of Malcolm X," *Sing Out,* Oct.-Nov. 1966. Vol. 16, No. 5.

Lewis, Anthony, and the New York Times. *Portrait of a Decade: the Second American Revolution.* New York: Random House, Inc., 1964.

Lewinson, Paul. *Race, Class and Party.* New York: Oxford University Press, 1962.

Lincoln, C. Eric. "The Black Muslims in America," in Earl Raab, ed., *American Race Relations Today.* New York: Anchor Books, 1962.

Litwack, Leon. *North of Slavery.* Chicago: Phoenix Books, The University of Chicago Press, 1960.

Locke, Alain. *The Negro in America.* Chicago: The American Library Association, 1933.

—— *The New Negro.* New York: A. & C. Boni, 1925.

Lynd, Staughton. *Reconstruction.* New York: Harper & Row, Publishers, 1967.

McWilliams, Carey. "How the Negro Fared in the War," *Negro Digest*. IV (May, 1946), pp. 67-74.

McPherson, James M. *The Negro's Civil War: How American Negroes Felt and Acted During the War for the Union.* New York: Pantheon Books, Division of Random House, Inc., 1965.

Mannix, Daniel P. and Cowley, Malcolm. *Black Cargoes: A History of the Atlantic Slave Trade.* New York: The Viking Press, 1962.

Mays, Benjamin E. and Nicholson, Joseph W. *The Negro's Church.* New York: Institute of Social and Religious Research, 1933.

Miller, Kelly. "An Appeal to Reason on the Race Problem: An Open Letter to John Temple Graves Suggested by the Atlanta Riot," in *Race Adjustment.* New York: The Neale Publishing Company, 1908.

Miller, Loren. "Farewell to Liberals: a Negro View," *The Nation,* 195 (October 20, 1962), pp. 235-38.

Moon, Henry Lee. *Balance of Power: The Negro Vote.* Garden City, New York: Doubleday & Co., 1948.

Myrdal, Gunnar, with the assistance of Richard Sterner and Arnold Rose. *An American Dilemma: The Negro Problem and Modern Democracy.* Vol. I and II. New York: Harper & Row, 1944.

National Committee of Negro Churchmen. "Black Power," advertisement in *The New York Times,* July 31, 1966.

National Urban League. *Facts on the Many Faces of Poverty.* New York: National Urban League, Inc., 1965.

Nelson, Truman. *Documents of Upheaval.* New York: Hill and Wang, 1966.

Olmstead, Frederick Law. *The Slave States.* Edited by Harvey Wish. New York: G. P. Putnam, 1959.

Osofsky, Gilbert. *Harlem: The Making of a Ghetto.* New York: Harper & Row, Publishers, 1965.

Otis, James. *The Rights of the British Colonies . . .* Boston: Printed and sold by Edes and Gill, 1764.

Patrick, Rembert W. *The Reconstruction of the Nation.* New York: Oxford University Press, 1967.

Peck, James. *Freedom Ride.* New York: Simon and Schuster, 1962.

Pennypacker, Samuel W. "The Settlement of Germantown, and the Causes which led to it." *The Pennsylvania Magazine of History and Biography.* IV (January, 1880), pp. 1-42.

Poussaint, Alvin F. "The Negro-American: His Self-Image

and Integration," *Journal of the National Medical Association*. 58 (November, 1966), pp. 419-23.

Price, Hugh Douglas. *The Negro and Southern Politics: a Chapter of Florida History*. New York: New York University Press, 1961.

Quarles, Benjamin. *The Negro in the American Revolution*. Durham, North Carolina: University of North Carolina Press, 1961.

Raab, Earl. *American Race Relations Today*. New York: Doubleday & Co., 1962.

Redpath, James. *The Roving Editor or, Talks with Slaves in the Southern States*. New York: A. B. Burdick, 1859.

Ruchames, Louis, ed. *The Abolitionists: A Collection of Their Writings*. New York: Capricorn Books, 1963.

―――― *Race, Jobs and Politics*. New York: Columbia University Press, 1953.

Russ, Jr., William A. "The Negro and White Disfranchisement During Radical Reconstruction," *Journal of Negro History*. XIX (April, 1934), pp. 171-92.

Rustin, Bayard. "Black Power and Coalition Politics," *Commentary*, 42 (September, 1966), pp. 35-40.

―――― "From Protest to Politics," *Commentary*, 39 (February, 1965), pp. 25-31.

Scott, Emmett J. "Letters of Negro Migrants, 1917-1918," *Journal of Negro History*, IV (July, 1919), pp. 290-340.

Sherwin, Oscar. "Sons of Otis and Hancock," *The New England Quarterly*, XIX (June, 1946), pp. 212-23.

Shoemaker, Don, ed., *With All Deliberate Speed*. New York: Harper & Row, Publishers, 1957.

Shriver, Sargent. "How Goes the War on Poverty?", *Look*, 29 (July 27, 1965), pp. 30-34.

Silberman, Charles E. *Crisis in Black and White*. New York: Vintage Books, Random House, Inc., 1964.

Stanford, Max. "Revolutionary Nationalism and the Afro-American Student," *Liberator*, V (January, 1965), pp. 13-15.

Stowe, Harriet Beecher. *Men of Our Times*. Hartford, Conn.: Hartford Publishing Company, 1868.

Sumner, Charles. "Argument before the Supreme Court of Massachusetts, in the Case of Sarah C. Roberts *v.* The City of Boston, December 4, 1849," in *The Works of Charles Sumner*. Vol. II. Boston: Lee and Shepard, 1870.

Sutherland, Elizabeth, ed. *Letters from Mississippi*. New York: McGraw-Hill Book Co., 1965.

ten Broeck, Jacobus. *Equal under Law.* New York: Collier Books, 1965.

Truth, Sojourner. *Narrative and Book of Life.* Boston, 1875.

U.S. The Mississippi Advisory Committee to the United States. Commission on Civil Rights, *Administration of Justice in Mississippi.*

U.S. The National Emergency Council. Report on Economic Conditions of the South. [1938]

U.S. Labor Department. *The Negro Family: The Case for National Action.* Office of Policy Planning and Research, Washington, D. C. March, 1965.

U.S. *Senate Report on Labor and Capital,* testimony, iv., p. 382. [883]

Volte, Charles G. and Harris, Louis. *Our Negro Veterans.* Public Affairs Pamphlet No. 128, 1947.

Wade, Richard C. *Slavery in the Cities: The South, 1820-1860.* New York: Oxford University Press, 1964.

Walker, David. *An Appeal, to the Coloured Citizens of the World.* Boston: 1829.

Washington, Booker T. *Up From Slavery, An Autobiography.* New York: Doubleday, Page & Co., 1901.

Watson, Thomas E. "The Negro in the South," *Arena,* IV (October, 1892), pp. 540-50.

Webb, A. B. W. *A History of Negro Voting in Louisiana, 1872-1906.* Baton Rouge, La.: Thesis, Louisiana State University, 1962.

Weisberger, Bernard A. "The Dark and Bloody Ground of Reconstruction Historiography," *Journal of Southern History,* XXV (November, 1959), pp. 427-47.

Wesley, Charles H. "The Civil War and the Negro American," *Journal of Negro History.* XLVII (April, 1962), pp. 86-93.

White, Walter. *Rope & Faggot: A Biography of Judge Lynch.* New York: Alfred A. Knopf, 1929.

_____ "What the Negro Thinks of the Army," *The Annals of the American Academy of Political and Social Science,* 223 (September, 1942), pp. 67-71.

Williams, Robert F. *Negroes with Guns.* New York: Marzani & Munsell, Inc., 1962.

Wish, Harvey. "American Slave Insurrections before 1861," *Journal of Negro History.* XXII (July, 1937), pp. 299-320.

_____ *The Negro Since Emancipation.* Englewood Cliffs, New Jersey: Prentice-Hall, Inc., 1964.

———— *Slavery in the South*. New York: Noonday Press, 1964.

Woodward, C. Vann. *The Burden of Southern History*. New York: Vintage Books, Random House, Inc., 1960.

———— *Origins of the New South 1877-1913*. Vol. IX, *A History of the South*. Baton Rouge, La.: Louisiana State University Press and the Littlefield Fund for Southern History of the University of Texas, 1951.

———— *The Strange Career of Jim Crow*. New York: Oxford University Press, 1957.

Work, Monroe N. *Negro Year Book*. Tuskegee Institute, Ala.: Negro Yearbook Publishing Company, 1937-38.

X, Malcolm, with the assistance of Alex Haley. *The Autobiography of Malcolm X*. New York: Grove Press, Inc., 1964.

Zinn, Howard. *Albany, a Study in National Responsibility*. Atlanta, Ga.: Southern Regional Council, 1962.

———— "The Limits of Nonviolence," *Freedomways*, 4 (First Quarter, 1964), pp. 143-48.

———— *SNCC, the New Abolitionists*. Boston: Beacon Press.

Index